Lana Turner

Hearts & Diamonds Take All

Twelve Years and Forty Titles of Award-Winning Entertainment
About How America Interprets
Its Spinmeisters, Its Celebrities, and Its Politicians

www.BloodMoonProductions.com

Lana Turner

Hearts & Diamonds
Take All

Darwin Porter & Danforth Prince

Lana Turner
Hearts & Diamonds Take All

Darwin Porter and Danforth Prince

Copyright 2017, Blood Moon Productions, Ltd.
All Rights Reserved

www.BloodMoonProductions.com

Manufactured in the United States of America

ISBN 978-1-936003-53-2

Cover Designs by Danforth Prince
Distributed worldwide through National Book Network
(www.NBNBooks.com)

Howard Hughes, Hell's Angel

Steve McQueen, King of Cool, Tales of a Lurid Life

Paul Newman, The Man Behind the Baby Blues

Merv Griffin, A Life in the Closet

Brando Unzipped

Katharine the Great, Hepburn, Secrets of a Lifetime Revealed

Jacko, His Rise and Fall, The Social and Sexual History of Michael Jackson

Damn You, Scarlett O'Hara, The Private Lives of Vivien Leigh and Laurence Olivier (co-authored with Roy Moseley)

FILM CRITICISM
Blood Moon's 2005 Guide to the Glitter Awards
Blood Moon's 2006 Guide to Film
Blood Moon's 2007 Guide to Film, and
50 Years of Queer Cinema, 500 of the Best GLBTQ Films Ever Made

NON-FICTION
Hollywood Babylon, It's Back! and **Hollywood Babylon Strikes Again!**

NOVELS
Blood Moon,
Hollywood's Silent Closet,
Rhinestone Country,
Razzle Dazzle
Midnight in Savannah

OTHER PUBLICATIONS BY DARWIN PORTER
NOT DIRECTLY ASSOCIATED WITH BLOOD MOON

NOVELS

The Delinquent Heart
The Taste of Steak Tartare
Butterflies in Heat
Marika (*a roman à clef based on the life of Marlene Dietrich*)
Venus (*a roman à clef based on the life of Anaïs Nin*)
Bitter Orange
Sister Rose

TRAVEL GUIDES

Many Editions and Many Variations of *The Frommer Guides*,
The American Express Guides, *and/or TWA Guides, et alia* to:

Andalusia, Andorra, Anguilla, Aruba, Atlanta, Austria, the Azores, The Bahamas, Barbados, the Bavarian Alps, Berlin, Bermuda, Bonaire and Curaçao, Boston, the British Virgin Islands, Budapest, Bulgaria, California, the Canary Islands, the Caribbean and its "Ports of Call," the Cayman Islands, Ceuta, the Channel Islands (UK), Charleston (SC), Corsica, Costa del Sol (Spain), Denmark, Dominica, the Dominican Republic, Edinburgh, England, Estonia, Europe, "Europe by Rail," the Faroe Islands, Finland, Florence, France, Frankfurt, the French Riviera, Geneva, Georgia (USA), Germany, Gibraltar, Glasgow, Granada (Spain), Great Britain, Greenland, Grenada (West Indies), Haiti, Hungary, Iceland, Ireland, Isle of Man, Italy, Jamaica, Key West & the Florida Keys, Las Vegas, Liechtenstein, Lisbon, London, Los Angeles, Madrid, Maine, Malta, Martinique & Guadeloupe, Massachusetts, Melilla, Morocco, Munich, New England, New Orleans, North Carolina, Norway, Paris, Poland, Portugal, Provence, Puerto Rico, Romania, Rome, Salzburg, San Diego, San Francisco, San Marino, Sardinia, Savannah, Scandinavia, Scotland, Seville, the Shetland Islands, Sicily, St. Martin & Sint Maarten, St. Vincent & the Grenadines, South Carolina, Spain, St. Kitts & Nevis, Sweden, Switzerland, the Turks & Caicos, the U.S.A., the U.S. Virgin Islands, Venice, Vienna and the Danube, Wales, and Zurich.

BIOGRAPHIES

From Diaghilev to Balanchine, The Saga of Ballerina Tamara Geva

Lucille Lortel, The Queen of Off-Broadway

Greta Keller, Germany's Other Lili Marlene

Sophie Tucker, The Last of the Red Hot Mamas

Anne Bancroft, Where Have You Gone, Mrs. Robinson?
(co-authored with Stanley Mills Haggart)

Veronica Lake, The Peek-a-Boo Girl

Running Wild in Babylon, Confessions of a Hollywood Press Agent

HISTORIES

Thurlow Weed, Whig Kingpin

Chester A. Arthur, Gilded Age Coxcomb in the White House

Discover Old America, What's Left of It

CUISINE

Food For Love, Hussar Recipes from the Austro-Hungarian Empire,
with collaboration from the cabaret chanteuse, Greta Keller

AND COMING SOON, FROM BLOOD MOON

Rock Hudson, Erotic Fire
Carrie Fisher & Debbie Reynolds: Princess Leia & Unsinkable Tammy in Hell
Rita Hayworth, Love Goddess of the World
Hefner, Guccione, and Flynt: Empires of Skin

This Book is Dedicated to

Virginia Grey

(1917-2004)

Superstar Lana Turner (left) with her friend and confidante, actress Virginia Grey,
source of some of the information contained within this biography.

WITH RESPECT AND ADMIRATION, REST IN PEACE, and
THANKS FOR THE MEMORIES.

What is Blood Moon Productions?

"Blood Moon, in case you don't know, is a small publishing house on Staten Island that cranks out Hollywood gossip books, about two or three a year, usually of five-, six-, or 700-page length, chocked with stories and pictures about people who used to consume the imaginations of the American public, back when we actually had a public imagination. That is, when people were really interested in each other, rather than in Apple 'devices.' In other words, back when we had vices, not devices."

—The Huffington Post

Contents

iday. James Stewart becomes Lana's on-screen and off-screen boyfriend. Lana sails to Hawaii with Desi Arnaz occupying her cabin ("a taste of Cuban sausage). An abortion that goes wrong. Lana and singer toney Martin become Hollywood's new glamour couple. Victor Mature provides "Lana's biggest thrill."

Musicians and Hipsters Gene Krupa, Tommy Dorsey, Buddy Rich, Benny Goodman, *et al.* make music with Lana. Lana enjoys a fling with the best-looking gangster in America. She competes with Hedy Lamarr for George Montgomery. Sexual chemistry explodes between Clark Gable and Lana in *Honky Tonk.*

Lana succumbs to Robert Taylor in *Johnny Eager* and in her dressing room, arousing the ire of his wife, Barbara Stanwyck. A former boxer turned actor, John Payne scores a knock-out punch with Lana. The Aviator, Howard Hughes, wings into her life. Touring the country, Lana sells war bonds and her kisses. She discovers Guy Madison at the Hollywood Canteen and samples a French delight, Jean-Pierre Aumont.

Lana and Clark Gable sizzle on the screen once again in *Somewhere I'll Find You.* Their affair may have caused Carole Lombard to take a doomed flight back to Hollywood to save her marriage. Lana meets a stranger (Stephen Crane) across a crowded room and marries him. Then she learns that Sugar Hill, Bugsy Siegel's mistress, is "keeping" (financially supporting) her new husband. Crane is exposed as a bigamist. She and her infant daughter almost die in a hospital. Lana shacks up with Errol Flynn & Victor Mature in New Orleans.

Tennessee Williams tries to fashion a "Celluloid Brassiere" for Lana. She dates "The Body Beautiful" (John Derek), and finds that her new beau, Peter Lawford, likes to travel down the oral road. She discovers the macho charm of Robert Mitchum, and spends more than a *Week-End at the Waldorf* with her co-stars, James Craig and John Hodiak. She gets a special boudoir welcome from Conrad Hilton and his young son, Nicky. Turhan Bey takes off the turban and pantaloons for Lana. Moving in on Susan Hayward's husband. The blonde goddess gets involved with raven-haired Rory Calhoun. Lana has a fling with Ava Gardner's young "trick" (Burt Lancaster). She learns why Steve Cochran is called "The *Schvantz.*" Peter Shaw slides between her satin sheets before marrying Angela Lansbury.

Tyrone Power becomes the love of Lana's life. A brief fling with "Sexy Rexy" (Rex Harrison). A young Navy lieutenant, John F. Kennedy, gives Lana a lot of loving. John Garfield: Murder on the screen, love-making off the screen. Robert Hutton dances into Lana's life. FrankSinatra threatens breaking with his wife, Nancy, over Lana. Evita Perón develops a "crush" on Lana.

THE MAN WHO GOT AWAY
Lana weds a tin-plate heir whose figure is less than Greek. Tyrone Power dumps Lana for an international starlet. The fire of September burns on low flame in *Homecoming* for Clark Gable and Lana. An interlude with Howard Keel. Lana as Lady de Winter has murder on her mind. Scandal with Billy Daniels.Stealing Joan Crawford's husband.

ANOTHER DIVORCE: LANA EMERGES AS THE MERRY WIDOW
Lana becomes *The Bad and the Beautiful.* She detests opera star Ezio Pinza, her co-star in *Mr. Imperium.* Disenchanted with life, she attempts suicide. The Argentine Heartthrob, Fernando Lamas, waltzes into Lana's life. A brief interlude with James Dean. Ava Gardner, Lana Turner, and Frank Sinatra churn out drama in a scandalous Love Triangle.

TARZAN, THE APEMAN, SWINGS INTO THE LIFE OF LANA TURNER
The loincloth hides his "Biggest, Deepest, & Darkest Secret." Ricardo Montalban becomes another of Lana's on-screen *Latin Lovers.* In Italy, she has a fling with Carlos Thompson, her lover from Argentina. In *Betrayed,* Lana has a reunion with yesterday's lovers: Clark Gable and Victor Mature. *The Prodigal* casts Lana as a pagan sex goddess in a camp classic. Her love for John Wayne in *The Sea Chase* was strictly on the screen. "Lana was addicted to my Welsh Dick." Or so said Richard Burton in their co-starring vehicle, *The Rains of Ranchipur.*

TARZAN REVEALED AS A CHILD RAPIST
Lex Barker has a cheating heart. So does Lana when Gregory Peck rents house. In *The Lady Takes a Flyer,* Lana is romanced by Jeff Chandler.Off screen,she's in for a shocker. She dumps Tarzan and has a fling with Chuck Connors. ("What a man!"). Rising star Steve McQueen enters Lana's life on the same night JFK "had his fun." Lana's film career is saved when she agrees to play a mother role in *Peyton Place.*

WHO KILLED JOHNNY STOMPANATO?
Lana learns the secret behind the new mystery man in her life, a studly enigma calling himself "John Steele. Mickey Cohen's henchman, Johnny Stompanato, becomes Lana's latest lover, a disastrous affair. She flies to England for the filming of *Another Time, Another Place,* and falls into the arms of Sean Connery.

Stompanato threatens to kill the future James Bond. Stompanato is stabbed to death in Lana's home. The debate still goes on: Did Lana really murder the gangster and let her daughter, Cheryl, take the fall? Years later, Lana admits that she was the one who stabbed her hustler lover.

Acknowledgments

Tracing the incredible story of the blonde cult goddess, Lana Turner (1921-1995), was a daunting task whose compilation extended over decades.

The research of her remarkable life was finally completed in 2015, in honor of the 20th anniversary of her death.

The research actually began in 1937 when Lana stormed Hollywood as a starlet for Warner Brothers. She had hooked up with another rising star, Ronald Reagan.

Soon after that, she met Stanley Mills Haggart (1910-1980), who worked part-time as a "leg man" for Hedda Hopper. As such,he prowled the clubs of Greater Los Angeles at night, picking up indiscreet stories and gossip about the stars, would-be stars, and wannabes whose stars flickered out early.

Hedda didn't print much of the data Stanley collected—"It's too scandalous"—but she wanted to know everything that was going on after dark, especially who was sleeping with whom.

On his nightly rounds, Stanley was joined by William Hopper, Hedda's only son.

Each of them, had they wanted, could have written a detailed account of Lana's life, with special emphasis on her heyday years from the late 1930s till the end of the 1950s. I will always be grateful to both men for supplying such rich and detailed notes about early Lana, wartime Lana, and post-war Lana.

Other than those two night owls, no one was more helpful than the beautiful and charming actress, Virginia Grey, the longtime lover of Clark Gable. She met Lana on the set of *Rich Man, Poor Girl* in 1938. They became close friends and confidantes, with Virginia serving as a sounding board for Lana's consternation about her many love affairs—some of them satisfying, others disastrous.

In the late 1950s, I began my life-long fascination with the blonde film icon, gathering my own material. Boxes and boxes of data later, I finally got to meet the still-beautiful Love Goddess.That happened in the 1970s, when I was working in Los Angeles, a city I documented in a travel guide for Simon & Schuster.

Sometimes Lana liked to talk about her illustrious, even scandalous, past, including "the good stuff" (her words) that she chose not to record in her official memoirs.

But, of course, I didn't rely on just her revelations alone. Over the years, with every chance I got, I spoke about Lana to producers, directors, makeup men, hairdressers, fashion designers, talent agents such as Henry Willson, and especially the actors and actresses who worked with Lana on each of her pictures.

She certainly made lasting impressions. Everyone who had come into contact with her, including her many lovers, had an opinion about her. Many times, they were loving and understanding about what had driven Lana and her passions to do what she did. In other instances, the images that were remembered were not favorable.

To list all the people over the years who contributed to this biography would fill twenty-five pages of print. But to all of them, living and dead, I express my gratitude for helping me complete the mysterious puzzle that was Lana Turner.

Often, when I could not contact people directly, I relied on the hundreds of interviews these people gave to newspapers and magazines. Sometimes, I got only a paragraph, but it was revelatory.

On one point, her friends and foes agreed: Lana Turner truly deserved an unvarnished memoir that would present her attributes, including her flaws; a bio that would eulogize her beauty, praise her too often underrated talent, and show her as a living and imperfect woman whose major flaw involved searching for love in all the wrong places.

Darwin Porter
February, 2017
New York City

A Word About Phraseologies:

Since we at Blood Moon weren't privy to long-ago conversations as they were unfolding, we have relied on the memories of our sources for the conversational tone and phraseologies of what we've recorded within the pages of this book.

This writing technique, as it applies to modern biography, has been defined as "conversational storytelling" by *The New York Times,* which labeled it as an acceptable literary device for "engaging reading."

Blood Moon is not alone in replicating, "as remembered" dialogues from dead sources. Truman Capote and Norman Mailer were pioneers of direct quotes, and today, they appear in countless other memoirs, ranging from those of Eddie Fisher to those of the long-time mistress (Verita Thompson) of Humphrey Bogart.

Some people have expressed displeasure in the fact that direct quotes and "as remembered" dialogue have become a standard—some would say "mandatory"—fixture in pop culture biographies today.

If that is the case with anyone who's reading this now, they should perhaps turn to other, more traditional and self-consciously "scholastic" works instead.

Best wishes to all of you, with thanks for your interest in our work.

Danforth Prince
President and Founder
Blood Moon Productions

Prologue

In the little mining town of Wallace, Idaho, it had rained all night before the dawn of February 8, 1921. That date would have faded into oblivion, were it not for the birth of a beautiful baby girl—Julia Jean Turner. She would be called "Judy" until she went to work in Hollywood.

From this modest beginning, the newly dubbed Lana Turner became America's "Sweater Girl," a pinup of World War II, and ultimately, the movie star goddess of the Silver Screen, a *femme fatale* linked to scandal and sex.

No role she ever played, from *The Postman Always Rings Twice* to *The Bad and the Beautiful* and *Peyton Place*, ever matched the soap opera of her real life.

In satins and white fox furs, she carved a trail through the boudoirs of Hollywood, collecting diamond rings from seven husbands, including Lex Barker, the screen version of Tarzan.

She seduced two future U.S. Presidents (Ronald Reagan and John F. Kennedy), and a host of Hollywood hunks, often her leading men: Clark Gable, Robert Taylor, Gary Cooper, James Stewart, Spencer Tracy, John Garfield, Richard Burton, Victor Mature, Fernando Lamas, Sean Connery, and Frank Sinatra. Her great love was Tyrone Power, "Hollywood's handsomest matinee idol."

She was labeled Hollywood's party girl, and her boss, Louis B. Mayer, excoriated her as amoral. "If she saw a stagehand with tight pants and a muscular build, she'd invite him to her dressing room."

Her most notorious episode included the fatal stabbing of her gangster lover, Johnny Stompanato. Cheryl Crane, her teenage daughter, took the blame, but Hollywood insiders suspected it was Lana herself who was the murderess.

She not only enchanted men, but was the object of adoration from other beautiful women, notably such bisexuals as Ava Gardner. Evita Perón, the dictator of Argentina, was obsessed with Lana, as was Eva Braun, the mistress of Adolf Hitler.

Robert Taylor said, "Lana Turner virtually invented the Hollywood blonde bombshell, and was the inspiration for Marilyn Monroe."

How did Lana view her own incredible life?

"I did what other women only fantasized about doing, but lacked the courage. I actually lived out my wildest dreams. Yes, even those!"

She expressed her sentiment about Tinseltown as she was dying in the 1990s: "Once upon a time, there really was a Hollywood. It was called the Dream Factory. It's gone today, but let it be known that for one moment long ago, I was its dream girl."

Glamorous Lana, clad in ermine at at the peak of her beauty and popularity during the deprivations of post-Depression America, greeting her adoring fans in 1941.

Hollywood's Future Blonde Venus

"Getta Load of That Kid! Whatta Pair of Tits!"

According to a long-enduring legend, Lana Turner was discovered sipping a soda at Schwab's Drugstore. The soda-sipping part was true, but the drugstore wasn't Schwab's.

The legend was reinforced when she was depicted in a grisly thriller as an innocent sixteen-year-old, enjoying her last moments alive before she dies in a "sex murder."

"I've never known what it is I was supposed to have had. Something, obviously, otherwise I wouldn't have had so many fans. I wouldn't have survived so long on the screen. All I do know is that sex appeal is not make-believe. It is not the way you look or the way you walk or the way you smile. It's the way you are!"

—Lana Turner

As suggested by her porcelain skin, young Lana was of Irish, English, and Scottish descent on her mother's side; Dutch on her father's side. Born in 1896 in Montgomery, Alabama, into a family with eleven other brothers and sisters, John Virgil Turner spoke with a very thick Southern accent. Once, he'd entered an *Amos 'n' Andy* sound-alike contest. [*At the time, they were the two most famous African-American entertainers of their day, starring in a popular radio show.*]

At the age of twenty-four, Virgil had returned from World War I, where he had served as an infantry platoon sergeant.

Ruggedly handsome, he had a muscular build, blonde hair, and sparkling blue eyes. He also possessed slim hips and broad shoulders.

"From the picture or two I have of my father, I looked like him and also had his temperament," Lana recalled years later. "He had a sense of humor and a devil-may-care attitude."

Back home in Alabama, he tried his luck as an insurance salesman, but sold no policies, so he told his family goodbye and headed west, perhaps to Dallas.

However, he ended up in the little town of Picher, Oklahoma. It was a Saturday night, and he was directed to Picher's Roof Garden Restaurant, which hired a dance band once a week. Tonight was the night, and he was looking for a good time. He liked, in this order, sex, gambling, and dancing. He was a skilled dancer and had a good singing voice. It was rumored that he had once appeared in vaudeville in Birmingham, Alabama, before he went off to war.

It was to this very restaurant that Mildred Frances Cowan was headed with her father, a mining engineer. Born in Lamar, Arkansas, in 1904, she had accompanied her father to Picher on a mining inspection tour. Her mother had died during childbirth, owing to complications from the Rh blood factor, a problem that would

Who could have predicted that this little eight-year-old, raggle-taggle schoolgirl, walking the streets of San Francisco, would in a few short years morph into "The Love Goddess of Hollywood?"

also plague Lana for most of her life.

Mildred had just turned sixteen, and Virgil found her the prettiest girl in the room. He went over and asked her to dance. Her stern father, Henry Cowan, didn't want his young daughter taking up with this older man, whom he didn't trust.

He would later warn her to stay away from Virgil, but she was a strong-willed teenager. After he'd held her close on the dance floor, she had just "folded into his arms."

She'd later tell her daughter, "For both of us, it was love at first sight."

In Picher, despite her father's objections, she slipped away and saw Virgil while her father toured the mines. Within five days, he'd asked her to run away with him and get married. She knew very little about him, but she wanted to be his bride.

[Picher, Oklahoma, now a ghost town, is among a small number of communities, worldwide, to be evacuated and declared uninhabitable because of environmental and health damage caused by the mines the town once serviced.

Once a thriving community in Ottawa County, Oklahoma, Picher—in addition to its role as the venue for the romance that eventually sired Lana Turner—was once a major center for the mining of lead and zinc. Generations of unrestricted subsurface excavations dangerously undermined most of the

Mildred Turner and her only daughter, then known as Julia Jean, posed for their first photograph in 1924.

Humble origins: Picher, Oklahoma, circa 1917, a few years before 16-year-old Mildred would elope with Virgil to eventually produce Lana Turner. Thriving as a mining center, Picher was later evaluated by the EPA as an environmental disaster and eventually abandoned, forcibly, as a region prone to birth defects and cancer.

township's buildings and left enormous mounds of toxic debris piled in fields and vacant lots.]

With Virgil, years before anyone ever knew about the toxic after effects of its mines there, Mildred fled north from Picher in a pickup truck. He'd met someone in Wallace, Idaho, who had offered him a job running a little dry cleaning store there, and he'd accepted.

Mildred recalled in horror her wedding night. She was a virgin. He caused her great pain because of the size of his endowment, and she had bled a lot. She had locked herself in the bathroom at the motor court where they were staying. When she emerged that morning, he was waiting for her, and he raped her again. "He would never take 'no' for an answer," she told Lana. "He could never get enough—sometimes four times a day. I thought all husbands demanded that. Boy, did I find out differently. I came to dread sex and avoided it whenever I could."

"As time went by, I was relieved when he started sneaking off with other women."

Before reaching Wallace, the couple ran out of money. Mildred said that her new husband had the tightest pair of pants she'd ever seen on any man. "At least two sizes too small. They practically showed everything he had."

En route to Idaho, they stopped off at a little town where he took her to a honky tonk with live music and hamburgers. She recalled that when Virgil had three beers and had to go to the men's room, two men from the bar rose from their seats and followed him. Then she saw him disappearing into the back alley with the two men. He seemed gone for a long time. Eventually, he returned about forty minutes later with $15 in his pocket, which paid for the motor court and gas.

"I was very innocent in those days," Mildred said. "I'd heard of men paying whores for sex, women whores. But I didn't find out until months later that homosexuals would pay certain virile men for sex, too. Whenever Virgil had to get money for us, he knew what to do."

Shortly after their arrival in Wallace, the dry-cleaning establishment that had embraced Virgil into its fold went out of business. Not too many locals needed any of their clothes dry-cleaned.

Out of a job and with a family to support, Virgil went to work in the local mine.

Straddling the rugged terrain of Idaho's northern panhandle, Wallace had been nicknamed "The Silver Capital of the World." It was the largest and busiest of the half-dozen towns within the Coeur D'Alene silver-mining district, which produced more silver than any other mining district in America.

[The townspeople there still cite Lana Turner (1921-1995) as its most famous former resident.]

Depicted above In a rare photograph, Lana's father, handsome, studly, blonde-haired Virgil Turner, used his "best asset" to make money for his family during lean times.

Lana remembered Virgil coming home all grimy from working in the mines. After a bath, he often put a record on their old phonograph and danced with Mildred. A young Lana tried to join in. Her father's favorite song was "You're the Cream in My Coffee." Sometimes, he would win at poker, and Lana remembered that he always kept his money in his left sock. "That was his bank. But as soon as he got some dough, he wanted to spend it."

"Money is to be spent, not hoarded," he'd always say.

It was in Wallace that Lana made her first public appearance. She was only four years old. An attractive woman, Mildred had been asked to model some furs at a local fashion show.

Lana went backstage and watched from the wings as her mother modeled. Wanting to imitate her, she picked up one of the fur garments (in this case, something made from fox), wrapped it around her body, and tottered out onto the stage. The women in the audience burst into wild applause. "From that day forth," she later half-jokingly recalled, "I knew I was going to be a star."

***

In Wallace, Virgil ran up $500 in gambling debts without the money to pay for them. Most of his debts were owed to a native of Boulder, Colorado, a 40-year-old, 300-pound bully named Sam Waters. The gambling kingpin of Wallace, he was known for his violence, his main goal involved separating miners from their paychecks. If a gambler didn't pay up within a certain deadline, he'd often find himself badly beaten up in a back alley with a broken bone or two.

Adding to Virgil's problems was the fact that he had also been arrested for bootlegging liquor down from Canada. Within three days, he was scheduled for a confrontation with a judge who was likely to put him in jail.

Using the popular expression of the day, he told Mildred, "It's time to get out of Dodge," meaning that the time had come to flee. A month before, he'd purchased, secondhand, a battered old Star.

[The Star, aka the Star Car, was a brand of low-priced automobile assembled between 1922 and 1928 by the Durant Mo-

Mother and daughter (Mildred and Lana) would in the 1940s become "fashion plates" in Hollywood, but not when this picture was taken in 1924.

tors Company as a usually less expensive competitor of the Ford Model T.]

Discreetly, and in the middle of the night, he packed up the family's meager belongings and headed west toward the promises of San Francisco. The year was 1927.

Their trip over mountainous terrain was rough, and the scorching hot weather was mitigated only with torrential downpours. At one point, the road ahead had been washed away, forcing them, for a period of ten boring days, to camp beside the highway, sustaining themselves with hot dogs cooked over an open fire. Back on the road again, Virgil gave in to Lana's demand to sit on his lap as he drove so that she could handle the steering wheel.

Lana and her parents fled from Virgil's gambling debts in Wallace to wide open new terrains in the undeciphered West in a car like this—a Star Car, manufactured by the Durant Motor Company as an alternative to Henry Ford's Model T.

At around three o'clock one hot afternoon, with Lana sitting on his lap and behind the wheel, and with Mildred asleep in the back seat, he dozed off. For about ten miles, the seven-year-old (presumably with no control of the accelerator or brakes) steered the Star herself until Virgil was suddenly awakened by a bump in the road.

Later in life, Lana told boyfriends that she had been driving a car since the age of seven.

As part of some mysterious trip, Virgil had previously visited San Francisco, and he told Lana about the glories of that city by the Bay. She was enthralled when he spoke of the Golden Gate Bridge, thinking it was real gold. At the approach to the city, she was bitterly disappointed to learn that the bridge was not made of actual gold.

The heart of San Francisco also turned out to be a disappointment, too, because they could find no place to live within their meager budget.

He drove the Star to a little suburb, Daly City, where they rented a dreary room in a rundown motor court for $3 a night. Accessible from the hallways were cubicles with toilets and segregated showers for men and women. It turned out that the roadside dive was used mostly by married men who took hookers there for "hot bed" sessions before driving back into the city.

There was a hotplate in the room, where Mildred cooked skimpy meals for her family for a week.

Finally, Virgil got a job as a stevedore working on the docks of the Pacific Steamship Company. With his first paycheck, he filled two paper bags with groceries and brought them home, along with a $2 red-and-white polka dot dress for "my little girl." Lana was thrilled with it and also glad to eat a pork chop for supper. "There's a time limit on how long a growing girl can hold out on soda crackers and milk," she recalled, years later.

With his next paycheck, Virgil rented a little apartment in Stockton with what

Mildred called "hot and cold running rats." After one trip down into the building's cellar, she never went there again.

In the meantime, he installed a still and invited Lana (that is, Judy) down into the cellar to show off his strange contraption: a large copper vat with rubber tubes.

He told her it was a still from which he would make moonshine to sell in Mason canning jars, swearing her to secrecy.

He was always running short of money because of his addiction to gambling. Whenever he was in trouble, he put on those too-tight pants and headed to San Francisco to pick up extra cash.

One afternoon, Lana was playing with three girls who lived in the modest homes nearby. Each was bragging about how successful their fathers were. Not wanting to be outshone, Lana said, "My daddy has all your daddies beat. He has a still and makes and sells his own liquor."

Apparently, one of the girls told her parents that night, and the next morning, two policemen arrived on the doorstep to destroy the still and pour out the moonshine. Virgil was locked up for three nights and had to pay a $100 fine.

He didn't always go into San Francisco to earn money. Sometimes, a strange man, perhaps two or three men, would arrive in a car and drive off with him for five or six hours. He told Mildred he was trying to make a business deal with some men from San Francisco.

After three months, Lana arrived home from school one afternoon to learn that Virgil had deserted them. He'd gone to live with a 73-year-old insurance executive on Nob Hill. Virgil promised to send them money every week. On most weeks, he kept his promise, sometimes giving them as much as fifty dollars. On other weeks, he seemed to forget about them.

To supplement the family's income, Mildred went to work in a beauty parlor in San Francisco, where she washed hair and swept the floor, occasionally bringing coffee or tea to the patrons from a little café across the street.

She also learned to style women's hair. Through some connection, she was offered a better paying job in Sacramento. She took Lana out of school and enrolled her in a Catholic school run by Dominican sisters in Sacramento, even though Lana wasn't Catholic, and had been baptized a Methodist.

The sisters were kind to her and, after the first month, urged her to grow up to become a nun and "the bride of Jesus."

She seemed swayed by the idea until she learned that the nuns had to cut off all their hair. She thought she had beautiful hair and would never do that.

That hair proved to be a problem. She became aware that "little bugs" had infested her head and went home crying to her mother. Mildred examined her head and discovered that she had picked up lice in school. She rushed to the drugstore and purchased a bottle of Black Mange Cure. Returning home, she lathered Lana's head. For three days, she kept a towel wrapped around her head (perhaps a precursor of the turbans in which she'd be famously photographed later), repeating the treatments until all the lice were gone, and she was sanitary once again.

Mildred worked mostly for tips, and some weeks there was almost nothing left to buy food after she'd paid the rent. Lana remembered she and her mother survived for one week on three bottles of milk and a box of soda crackers.

One day, Mildred was abruptly fired and told Lana that she'd been dismissed after being accused of stealing money from the cash register. She denied having taken the money, but had an unexpected $75 in her purse, money she used to put Lana and herself on a bus heading back to San Francisco.

Once there, Mildred moved in with two other beauticians who immediately objected to living in the cramped apartment with a growing little girl.

One of the women knew a family in Modesto, where Lana could stay, and Mildred drove her there. She met the Hislops, who had a daughter, Beverly, who was two years older than Lana. She was to room with the older girl in her bedroom.

Every Sunday, she attended Catholic services with the Hislops. Eventually, she was christened. Her original name had been Julia Jean, and she chose to be christened "Julia Jean Mildred Frances Turner," borrowing two of the names from her mother.

For two years, she lived with the Hislops, which she later characterized "as the most miserable years of my life."

"Beverly was very mean to me, and Mrs. Hislop treated me like a scullery maid. I had to do most of the work around the house. I did the wash on Saturday, the ironing on Sunday. I did all the housekeeping. One time, while doing the wash, I got my hand caught in the wringer of this old Maytag and my fingers were nearly crushed."

"I was just a cheap Cinderella with no hope of a pumpkin," she said.

Mildred visited her once or twice a month, and sometimes brought her a new dress or some underwear. Virgil almost never showed up. When he did, he often had candy for her. He never spoke of his new life, but he appeared well dressed, so she assumed that he had a very good job. She was surprised by his choice of clothing, as he tried to dress like a much younger man. He'd dyed his golden blonde hair platinum, telling her, "It makes me look younger."

One afternoon, he asked her what he could bring her on his next visit. "I want a bike, Daddy. *Pretty please!*"

"Okay, I'll get you one," he promised. "A nice shiny red one."

That was the last time she ever saw him.

Her mother arrived at the Hislops unexpectedly and told the family she had to take her daughter back into San Francisco. The date was December 15, 1930, in the midst of the Depression.

As Lana remembered: "At first, I thought she was going to tell me she was pregnant, because I had learned that she was dating a lot of different men."

In the city, Mildred told her the bad news. Virgil had been murdered the previous evening. It turned out that he'd had a winning streak in a poker game in the basement of *The San Francisco Chronicle*. As he left the game, he'd told the other players that he was going to buy a bicycle "for my little girl" with his winnings. The next morning, his badly beaten body was found at the corner of Minnesota and Mariposa Streets. He'd been bludgeoned with a blackjack. His shoes were found near his body, but his left foot was bare—his sock had been removed. Both Mildred and Lana knew that he kept his money in his left sock.

Lana screamed when she realized the importance of that news. "I killed him!" she shouted at her mother. "If I hadn't asked for that bike, he'd be alive today."

That same day, Mildred escorted Lana to a funeral home, where she lifted her up to stare into the coffin holding her dead father. She remembered his face as looking like a wax dummy. Mildred asked if she wanted to kiss her dead father, but the thought of kissing a corpse horrified her. She begged to be taken away.

The next afternoon, mother and daughter attended Virgil's funeral at Presidia, where five uniformed soldiers fired their rifles into the air in a final salute paying homage to Virgil's heroic war efforts in 1918.

Mildred later summed up her feelings at the time to both Lana and her friends: "My life has been wayward," she said, "moving from place to place like a vagabond. I was always searching for something, but never found it. Whatever joy I felt with Virgil was just temporary. It would soon disappear as disappointment and disillusionment set in. Because of the rough life I've endured, I think I should be forgiven for any mistakes in my future, including my failure as a mother."

After the funeral, Mildred drove Lana back to the Hislops in Modesta, a place that Lana loathed. But she'd be forced to live there for nearly another year. One day, what Lana later called "my months as a slave" came to an end. It was a Sunday, and Lana, while ironing, burned Mrs. Hislop's favorite dress. When the woman found out, she'd exploded into a rage and beat Lana so severely, she had to go to the hospital.

Mildred heard about this and rushed to the bed of her daughter, who shared the room with two other patients. She inspected her daughter's black-and-blue body, and the doctor told her that Lana had also been hit on the head, suffering a concussion.

Upon her release, Lana thought that she was going to be allowed to live with Mildred again. But her mother said no. Lana suspected that Mildred was living with some boyfriend who didn't want her to move in.

Instead, through some connection, she found lodgings for Lana with a large Sicilian family in Lodi, outside San Francisco

Unlike the Hislops, the Sicilians became almost foster parents to Lana. The house was small but big enough to sleep mama, papa, and three of their sons and two daughters, one of whom was Lana's age. Her name was Pier, and she shared a bedroom with the newcomer. In exchange for housing and feeding her daughter, Mildred gave the family $20 a week.

Once again, she was enrolled in a Catholic school, which she attended five days a week with Pier. She enjoyed the family meals—pasta every night—and learned to drink wine, which was always weakened with water. "Italians don't believe in making children wait until they're eighteen before tasting *vino*," Lana recalled.

She also remembered that if she had any complaints at all, it was from papa, insisting she sit on his lap for long periods of time. "He was just a little too friendly, if you get my drift," Lana later said.

On Sunday nights, the family gathered around the piano for sing-alongs, mostly Sicilian favorites. Lana learned some of the songs so she could join in. The family liked her voice so much, they urged her to audition for *The Major Bowes Amateur Hour*, a popular radio show broadcast from San Francisco at the time.

"I performed a number 'The Basin Street Blues,' but I was no Lena Horne," she recalled. "I not only lost, but some of the real singers made fun of me. I decided then and there that stardom was out of the question for me. I was not a performer. I might begin to dream of becoming a dress designer, not only designing and making my own clothes, but for other stylish women as well."

Finally, Mildred came for her daughter and moved her out of the Sicilian family house and in with Chila Meadows, with whom they shared an apartment in San Francisco's Richmond district. A kindly woman, Chila had a son, George, and a daughter, Hazel.

"They became the brother and sister to me that I never had," Lana recalled.

She was enrolled into Presidio Junior High School, and it was here that Lana captured her first male heart. A tall, slim, blonde-haired boy, William Gerst, developed a passionate crush on her, falling madly in love, or in "puppy love" with her.

For Valentine's Day, she was the only girl in her class who received a heart-shaped red box filled with creamy chocolates. For years, Lana kept that empty red box as a remembrance of her first love.

Her greatest thrill at the time was not boys, but the handsome young men on the movie screen. She and her mother tried to see every romantic feature playing at the local Bijou. Mildred admired Kay Francis, especially her fabulous wardrobe. She even styled her hair like Francis did.

But for Lana, it was always a Clark Gable or Robert Taylor movie which thrilled her. She saw Gable in *Manhattan Melodrama, Forsaking All Others, The Call of the Wild,* and *Mutiny on the Bounty.* She tried never to miss a Robert Taylor movie, including *Society Doctor, Small Town Girl,* and *Magnificent Obsession.*

"I saved the nickels that mother gave me for lunch until they added up to a quarter. Then I would rush off to the movies to see those beautiful men on the screen."

"When I saw Tyrone Power in *Lloyd's of London,* I could not believe that any man could be that gorgeous. The first time he appeared on the screen, I swooned. Never in my wildest dreams did I realize that in a few short years, I would not only be making love to both Robert and Clark on and off the screen, but in time, I would meet Tyrone, the love of my life."

When Lana entered Washington High School, she became a cheerleader. "She wore a white skirt and sweater with our school colors of red and gray," said Willie Edmonds. "All the boys were crazy about her, when she jumped up and down and showed off her gams. She was really hot, but the word was that she didn't put out, unlike some of the other girls. I guess she was saving it for some guy."

On the home front, Mildred was finding it harder and harder to make a living during the Depression. She was a widow with a single child to support. She missed many days of work at the beauty parlor because she was prone to respiratory ailments. She came down with what is known as "the San Joaquin Valley Fungus," a lung ailment, which meant she coughed a lot. A lot of the patrons didn't want her to work on their hair because they told her boss that they feared she was infected with something contagious.

In a doctor's office, she was told that the frequent fogs of San Francisco were bad for her lungs. He advised her to move to a drier climate, like Los Angeles.

"Mother had a friend in Los Angeles, Gladys Heath," Lana recalled. "She phoned Gladys, whom she called 'Gladdy.' She had a spare room and could accommodate us in her apartment."

"Come on down," Gladdy said.

The next day, Mildred packed all their possessions and agreed to split the gas bill with a fellow beautician, Stella Tiffin, who was driving to Los Angeles to attend to her ailing mother.

There wasn't much room in the car for all their possessions, so Mildred tied their suitcases to the top of the car with a rope. Lana remembered that Stella was a chatterbox with a fondness for stepping on the brake all the time. She was a nervous driver with a tendency to panic whenever another car approached. One afternoon, as they neared the town of Paso Robles, the rain began to pour down heavily. Approaching a truck, Stella slammed on the brakes. The road was slippery, and, as she braked, she lost control of the car. It skidded off the highway and into a large drainage ditch, where it flipped over.

Stella escaped with minor injuries, but Mildred suffered two cracked ribs and had to go to the emergency room of the nearby hospital. Lana ended up with a bump on her forehead, the size of a large egg, and a severe cut on her right arm from a shard of shattered window glass.

That night, they found lodgings in a rundown motor court. "It reminded me of the place where Claudette Colbert and Clark Gable landed in *It Happened One Night*," Lana said.

The car was pulled from the ditch and, although it was caked with mud, it was still in running order.

All bandaged, Mildred sat in the front seat, Lana in the back, as Stella headed south to Los Angeles once again. "Her car shook, rattled, and rolled all the way there," Lana later said. "We looked like one motley crew."

Stella wanted to be rid of Lana and Mildred and dumped them at the intersection of Highland Avenue and Sunset Boulevard. Mildred put through a call to Gladdy, who drove over to pick them up. "We must have looked like the saddest mother-and-daughter refugees in L.A.," Lana said.

Gladdy had a little Andalusian-style house on Glencoe Way. Mildred and Gladdy occupied the two bedrooms, and Lana was assigned a cot in the utility room, where the ironing was done.

The next week, Mildred found work at the Lois Williams Beauty Salon, which was only an eight-block walk from their little house. The beauticians made it known to their patrons that they'd be capable of crafting, on demand, replicas of the hairdos of their favorite movie stars—Jean Harlow, Kay Francis, Greta Garbo, Joan Crawford, whomever.

School had already begun when Lana enrolled at Hollywood High School.

Within a month, her life would change for all time.

***

In September of 1936, Lana Turner (then known as Judy) headed for Hollywood High School, near the corner of West Sunset Boulevard and North Highland Avenue. Founded in 1903, it had begun as a two-room schoolhouse. In time, it be-

13

came the most famous high school in America because of all the movie stars who were enrolled there, none more legendary than Lana Turner and Judy Garland.

Lana never pretended to be a good student, and simply could not comprehend mathematics at all. Her mother urged her to take a class in typing, thinking that she might find a job as a secretary. "I'd rather be a dress designer," Lana countered.

One day in late October, Lana decided to skip out on the typing class since at the last session, she'd broken a fingernail. She headed across the street to the Top High Malt Café, where she had a nickel to spend on a Coca-Cola.

She had become well aware of her looks. A classmate, Nanette Fabray, remembered her. "I had never seen a more beautiful girl, and Hollywood High was filled with beauties, most of whom, or so it seemed, wanted to become a movie star. When Judy strolled down the hall, the other girls just stopped and stared at her, mostly with envy. The boys often whistled. I know this sounds like a contradiction, but her face was innocent yet reflected a know-it-all look. Even her teachers predicted stardom for her."

There was a problem: Lana couldn't act. She tried out for a school play, but was rejected. The drama teacher gave her lines to read, and she was asked to play a scene that was charged with emotion. But during her performance, "her face was carved in stone," according to the teacher. "She read her lines like reciting a recipe in a cookbook."

There was another problem, too. She couldn't sing or dance, except a few steps Virgil had taught her.

In vivid contrast, her classrooms were filled with talented boys and girls, often the children of movie stars. Fabray herself had performed in vaudeville as a child and would later enjoy a big career as an actress, singer, and dancer in the musical theater of the 1940s and 50s.

At Top Hat, Lana sipped her coke, acutely aware that some middle-aged man at the end of the counter was staring at her. "I felt he was undressing me with his eyes. I wore this white sweater, and he kept looking down at my breasts."

At the time, she was worthy of attention. Her measurements were 35-24 ½-34 ½. At the age of fifteen, she stood 5'3", with perfectly formed breasts. Large blue-gray eyes were set in a beautiful face crowned by silky auburn hair. She had a peach-colored complexion that was free of any imperfection, and her skin was so porcelain smooth she could have advertised a skin-care product.

[Indeed, by the early 1940s, she would appear in ads in magazines across the country, promoting the glories of Lux Toilet Soap. The ads cited her as having "the world's most beautiful complexion."]

The soda jerk at the Top Hat came over to Lana. "That gentleman over there would like to meet you. It's not a come-on. He comes in here every day for lunch and works down the street as a newsman. Can he introduce himself?"

She looked at him squarely for the first time, finding that he wore a dark business suit, had a pencil-thin mustache, and his head was crowned with brilliantined black hair graying at the temples.

She signaled to him that it would be all right if he approached her.

"Hello, young lady," he said to her. "I'm Billy Wilkerson, the publisher of *The Hollywood Reporter*. Forgive me for using what usually is a pick-up line, but I think

14

you should be in pictures."

"I don't know about that," she answered. "I've been told I can't act."

"I should clarify my remark. I said you should be in pictures. You could be a movie star. With your looks, you wouldn't have to act." Then he handed her his business card.

"I'd have to talk it over with my mother," she said. "She makes the big decisions for me."

"I want your mother to call me, and both of you to visit me at my office down the street. I think I can hook you up with the right people."

"Well, maybe," she said, sounding both thrilled but strangely hesitant.

"Goodbye," he said. "I hope to hear from your mother in the morning. By the way, what is your name?"

"Judy Turner."

***

[That drugstore encounter on that October afternoon became one of the most enduring legends in the history of Hollywood. But the facts got distorted over the years.

The first article about Lana's discovery was more or less accurate, appearing in the December 23, 1940 edition of Life *magazine. It correctly identified the venue as the Top Hat Café.*

However, by the mid-40s, when Lana was reigning as the Queen of MGM, the venue of her inaugural meeting with Wilkerson had morphed into Schwab's Pharmacy at the corner of Sunset Boulevard and Laurel, two miles from Hollywood High.

Opened by the Schwab brothers in 1932, the drugstore in time became the hangout of young actors, male and female, dreaming of stardom. Its most famous client was the popular columnist Sidney Skolsky, who used Schwab's as his unofficial office, conducting his interviews there and even picking up his mail there.

In his memoir, Don't Get Me Wrong—I Love Hollywood, *he wrote that almost daily, he encountered some young wannabee actress who asked him which stool was it that Lana Turner sat on when she was discovered by a talent agent.*

"I'd direct her to this one stool where the poor girl would sit there in vain all day waiting to become the next Lana."]

Many of the girls at Hollywood High were jealous of the future Lana Turner—not only for her looks, but because all the boys were in pursuit of her. Nearly every reasonably attractive girl in school wanted to be a movie star, if not Carole Lombard, then perhaps Barbara Stanwyck.

Back home that evening, Lana showed Mildred and Gladdy the business card that Billy Wilkerson had given her. Her mother dismissed it as some come-on by an aging Hollywood wolf lusting after a young girl, but Gladdy wasn't so sure. She had heard of Wilkerson, who was quite famous in Hollywood because of his newspaper and nightclubs.

Finally, Lana persuaded Mildred to accompany her to the office of *The Hollywood Reporter* after a call was put through to Wilkerson.

He turned out to be legitimate and was a friend of the Hollywood elite, including Louis B. Mayer and Nicholas Schenck, with whom he often played poker. He was also a nightclub impresario, having founded the Café Trocadero in 1934. In a few short years, Lana herself would be a regular at his other celebrated clubs, including Ciro's in 1940 and LaRue of Hollywood in 1943.

Billy Wilkerson, founder of *The Hollywood Reporter* and "discoverer" of young Lana Turner, in 1939.

[*William R. Wilkerson would also become a controversial figure in Hollywood history—and not just for having discovered Lana Turner. In 1946, the year after World War II ended, he began to publish a series of columns in* The Hollywood Reporter *called "Billy's List," in which he printed the names of alleged Communist sympathizers.*

In time, and with a lot of help from the FBI's J. Edgar Hoover, "Billy's List" became the infamous Hollywood Blacklist, which destroyed the careers of directors, producers, and screenwriters such as Dalton Trumbo.]

Wilkerson was frank that he himself could not advance Lana's career, but he could introduce her to a man who might. He agreed to set up an appointment with his friend, Zeppo Marx, who ran a successful theatrical agency, which in time specialized in handling the careers of married couples, including Clark Gable and Carole Lombard and Robert Taylor and Barbara Stanwyck.

[*Born in 1901, Zeppo (aka Herbert) Marx was the youngest of the five Marx Brothers. From 1929 to 1933, he appeared with his brothers in their films. They included* Duck Soup *and* Monkey Business. *Eventually, he distanced himself from their filmmaking agendas to become a theatrical agent and an engineer, the latter pursuit of which made him a multimillionaire. In the late 1930s, he invented a type of fastener, a "Marman ring," a heavy-duty band clamp that allows the butt ends of tubes or pipes to be interconnected and subsequently "fast-disconnected" whenever necessary. An adaptation of his invention was used to hold "Fat Man," an atomic bomb inside the B-29 bomber that flew over and subsequently demolished Hiroshima.*]

An appointment was arranged with Zeppo, who asked Lana, in front of her mother, "Raise your dress. I wanna see your legs."

Lana looked over at her mother, who nodded her approval. "I'm not putting the make on you. This is standard in the business. You've got a beautiful face, but you can't become a show girl with ugly legs."

She raised the hem of her dress and Zeppo approved. "You've got the body of a nineteen- or twenty-year-old." He was very frank, telling her that he had time only for his A-list clients.

He'd assign her to his assistant, Henry Willson. "He's great at developing hot young males, his specialty. But occasionally, he devotes some time to a gal. I'll call him and set up a time. And don't worry, Mildred, your daughter's virginity will be safe with Henry Willson."

Zeppo's parting remark to Lana was "From now on, kid, you're eighteen years old. Got that? Eighteen. Not a day younger."

***

Talent agent Henry Willson always boasted, "Regardless of what you read, I was the fucker who really discovered Lana Turner and made her a star."

A day after meeting Zeppo Marx, Mildred, accompanied by Lana, found herself sitting across from the cluttered desk of Willson, an ugly man with a fatty figure who—although he occasionally took on a female client—specialized mainly in booking actors with perfect physiques.

Years later, he recalled, "Only twice in my life did I ask an aspirant actor or actress to read a page or two of dialogue for me. Both of them gave a disastrous reading. I mean, really awful. They had no talent at all. Minus zero. But they had something else, and that was this intangible thing called sex appeal. That young man and young woman who read for me were renamed Rock Hudson and Lana Turner."

When Willson met Lana, she was still known as Judy Turner. "Her mother, Mildred, brought this underage girl in to see me. Zeppo had sensed something about her and turned her over to me, the future starmaker. Mildred had dressed her like a jailbait hooker—a cheap fur stole—rather ratty, paste jewelry, hair piled on top of her head, and enough makeup to cover eight chorus cuties. I cut our meeting short and asked her to come back the next morning with no makeup and dressed like a schoolgirl at Hollywood High."

Over coffee with Lana the next morning, Willson confirmed that Billy Wilkerson had not put the make on her, as he had so often with his other "discoveries."

"I don't know how you escaped. When he's not losing money gambling, he sleeps with every gal not named Mrs. Billy Wilkerson."

He liked Lana's schoolgirl look and the fact that she combined innocence with sex appeal. "Men go home to fuck their wives out of duty, but what the bastards really want is to bed a gal who looks like you."

In the next two months, Willson and Judy, as she was still being called, would see a lot of each other. He took her from MGM to Paramount, from Columbia to RKO, but to no avail. Some casting directors

Henry Willson, depicted here with an effigy of Uncle Sam, used the infamous Hollywood casting couch, but with a male-dominated twist. In the case of this talent agent, only handsome, well-built men were sent to the sofa for a workout.

had a certain appeal, and some commented on her beauty, but he heard the line repeated endlessly: "Henry, you of all people, know that Hollywood is flooded with beautiful girls, or, in your case, pretty boys."

One director at 20th Century Fox had a role for her but on one condition: "She's got to let me fuck her—or else it's no way, José!"

Willson, as a go-between, asked Lana if she'd be willing to cooperate, but she rejected the offer.

It's not going to happen," Willson told the director. "But if you're horny, I'm good for a quickie."

"*Get the fuck out of here, faggot!*" the director responded.

Gradually, Lana began to find out who Willson really was, not so much from him, but from gossipy members of the entertainment industry.

A native New Yorker, born in 1911, he drifted to Hollywood, where his first major job was that of a talent scout for producer David O. Selznick. "Most of my job involved getting beautiful gals for his casting couch," Willson recalled.

While doing that, Willson as a talent agent maintained a casting couch of his own. Only well-built men need apply. It was said that in time, he practically invented the word "beefcake," as opposed to the girly, then-more-widely accepted term, "cheesecake."

"I was a connoisseur of male flesh," he admitted. "Talent didn't matter so much if these guys looked great without their shirts."

In time, he would become known as "The Man Who Created Rock Hudson." He also gave his discoveries catchy names that went over well in the 1950s, including "Tab" and "Rock." In his stable were such well-built, good-looking guys as Guy Madison, Rory Calhoun, Tab Hunter, Robert Wagner, John Derek, Troy Donahue, Clint Walker, John Saxon, and so many others. None of them, however, attained the top box office appeal of Hudson.

"Willson's hands-on lechery gave new meaning to the proverbial casting couch," Selznick said. "His couch was even more active than that of Harry Cohn over at Columbia. It was rare, but Willson did help launch the careers of a few women, including Lana Turner, Natalie Wood, and Rhonda Fleming, that Queen of Technicolor."

"Most fans thought Lana was an overnight sensation," Willson said. "That was far from the truth. She was turned down again and again. She needed money when she wasn't making the rounds of the studios with me. She went to school and worked at this lingerie shop on Hollywood Boulevard for $12.50 a week."

Lana had told Willson that she knew how to dance, although he never put her through the test. He arranged for RKO to test her for a possible role in *The New Faces of 1937*, at first known as *Young People*. She arrived at the studio with a familiar face, Mickey Rooney, who, it was understood, would accompany her on the piano. Perhaps he'd taught her some dance steps, as he was an expert dancer.

But the casting director abruptly canceled, without explanation, her audition, and she left the studio frustrated and disappointed.

When the film was released, Lana went to see it. "I would have been outclassed," she admitted. "There were dozens of talented young dancers in that film. Hell, the lead number, 'New Faces,' was danced by none other than Ann Miller.

Who could compete with her? Perhaps Eleanor Powell—and that was about it."

***

True to his promise, Willson managed to get her a job in a movie produced by his associate, David O. Selznick. It was *A Star Is Born*. Released in 1937 it starred Janet Gaynor and Fredric March, two leading stars of the 1930s. Each of them would eventually be nominated for a Best Actor and Best Actress Oscar for their respective performances.

Its plot focused on an aspiring Hollywood actress whose star is about to ascend. She marries an egocentric actor whose Hollywood stardom (and life in general) is fading and falling apart. Its plot was said to have been (discreetly) based on Barbara Stanwyck's disastrous marriage to the closeted Frank Fay.

[Seventeen years later, in 1954, A Star Is Born *was remade into what is arguably Judy Garland's most dramatically successful movie. Much of Hollywood asserted that she should have won the Oscar for Best Actress in 1954 after it was awarded instead to Grace Kelly for her role in* The Country Girl.

In 1976, Barbra Streisand made a stab at the by-now-overworked theme of A Star Is Born, *an remake that was relatively unsuccessful.]*

Ironically, although Lana was already being hailed for her beautiful face, only the back of her head, wearing a silly cap, appeared in the 1937 version of the film's final cut. She appeared in a crowd scene at the Santa Ana racetrack. In that scene, the characters portrayed by Fredric March and Lionel Stander had a fight, attracting a crowd, a member of which was the (anonymous) character played by Lana.

Also making her debut in a very small role was blonde-haired Carole Landis, who would in time become Lana's rival for screen roles and World War II pinup popularity. "She was also the girl who chased after some of my boyfriends," Lana said, referring to Tony Martin, Victor Mature, and Ronald Reagan.

The two aspirant actresses, Lana and Landis, had hamburgers for lunch in the commissary. Lana was surprised at how candid Landis, a native of Wisconsin, was. She admitted to having been a call girl in San Francisco, and claimed that she planned to sleep her way to the top through "performances" on one casting couch after another. She

Lana, as she looked in her first role in a movie. She was hired as an extra in the 1937 *A Star Is Born*, starring Janet Gaynor and Fredric March. "Everybody told me how beautiful I was, but the bastards only showed my back."

19

named some of her latest conquests—Charlie Chaplin, Hal Roach, Jr., and Darryl F. Zanuck.

Lana differed, telling Landis, and so many others, "I plan to get ahead on my looks—not by sleeping with studio bosses."

***

Girls at Hollywood High tended to shun Lana, perhaps out of jealousy. There was one exception: Born in British Columbia, Alexis Smith had migrated south to grow up in Los Angeles. Unlike Lana, she had been trained as a dancer, and made her debut as a ballerina at the Hollywood Bowl when she was only thirteen.

She soon deserted The Dance and dreamed instead of becoming a movie star. She wasn't discovered by a Warner Brothers talent agent until 1940, when she was in college.

Her first featured film role was *Dive Bomber* (1941), in which she'd starred opposite Errol Flynn. In time, she'd make other movies with Flynn and also appeared opposite such leading men as Clark Gable, Humphrey Bogart, Charles Boyer, Ronald Reagan, Bing Crosby, and Burt Lancaster.

One Saturday, Alexis invited Lana to a matinee to see *Sylvia Scarlett* (1935), starring Katharine Hepburn and Cary Grant. Alexis insisted that they sit in a remote section of the balcony, an area of the theater that was virtually empty at 2PM.

Twenty minutes into the movie, Lana felt Alexis' hand on her knee. At first, she dismissed it as just a friendly gesture. But soon, that hand began a northward trek. At the time, a shocked Lana knew very little about lesbianism. She rose abruptly from the seat, and, in tears, made her way toward the exit. She wasn't really certain about what women did to satisfy each other sexually.

Her budding friendship with Alexis ended abruptly in the movie palace that afternoon, although the two actresses would meet socially on other occasions. No mention was ever made of that long-ago encounter at a matinée.

However, Alexis did make a comment about Lana to an editor at a movie magazine: "She had a glorious look about her in high school, a really beautiful girl, a face made for the Silver Screen. She could have had anybody she wanted. And from what I've heard, she has."

That last line was censored, and never appeared in the magazine's "final cut."

While still in high school, Lana received her first lesbian advance from another young actress, the bisexual Alexis Smith, who was dreaming of becoming a ballet dancer. She and Lana were the same age. Here, she appears in *The Constant Nymph* (1943).

***

20

What teenaged Lana wanted was a boyfriend, and one afternoon she found him. He was in the hallway of Hollywood High, putting his books and a duffel bag into his locker. She recognized him at once: He was a movie star.

Jackie Cooper, a year younger than she was, had been a child star, and had been the youngest performer at that time to be nominated for an Academy Award as Best Actor for his role in the 1931 movie, *Skippy*.

Jackie Cooper, child star and Young Rascal, in *School's Out* (1930)

He had appeared in his first film in 1929 at the dawn of the Talkies, and had starred in the *Our Gang* comedies produced by Hal Roach, Sr.

Cooper had also been in movies with crusty old Wallace Beery, including *The Champ* (1931). Lana later learned that the two actors, a perfect match on the screen, detested each other.

When Lana encountered Cooper, it seemed an instant attraction. Before her English class began, he'd asked her out on a date, and she accepted, giving him her phone number.

She had met him at a critical point in his life. Facing a dilemma encountered by most child actors, even the most successful, he was having trouble getting cast into parts that portrayed adolescents on the brink of manhood.

Since he was not yet old enough to drive, he asked his mother to hire a chauffeur to drive them around throughout the course of their evening together. He made an impressive entrance at Gladdy's home and was introduced to Mildred,

Jackie Cooper (center), a decade and a carload of sexual experience later, in 1940, with budding (and competing) *ingénues* who included, left to right, Judy Garland, Bonita Granville, his girlfriend (Lana Turner), and Robert Stack, Lana's future lover.

who complimented him on his screen performances.

He and Lana were driven to a movie palace, where they sat in orchestra seats, unlike her experience with Alexis Smith, who had sought out a remote balcony perch.

They'd come in late for the movie, but when the lights went on, many fans in the theater asked Cooper for his autograph, an experience that Lana herself in a few short years would experience, and would continue to experience throughout the rest of her life.

Later, they were driven to a hamburger joint serving greasy food. As she nibbled on French fries, she discussed dreams for her future. Mostly, however, he wanted to talk about himself. She was soon to find out that talking about one's self was the favorite conversational pursuit of most Hollywood actors.

Cooper was a young man who kissed and told. He boasted of his experience as a lover, having been seduced by Kathryn, a twenty-year-old chorus girl who lived across the street from him in Ocean Beach. At the time, he was only thirteen.

His friend, Bill Smith, who once caught Cooper in bed with an older vaudeville actress, said, "Coop was one smart little son of a bitch. He could always get the broads."

Lana was fascinated by Judy Garland, and had read that she and Cooper had dated. She was eager for details, and he seemed flattered that she was viewing him as a young man of the world. He told her he'd met Judy, who was nine months older than him, when they appeared on a radio show hosted by Wallace Beery.

"Our romance began with a walk on the beach one night," he said. "A kiss, another kiss, and the inevitable happened."

In many ways, Lana envied Garland who, as a young girl, seemed to be having experiences usually associated with women far older than she was.

"Judy is very fickle," Cooper said. "After three months, she dumped me for another actor, Billy Halop."

On their third date, the young actor asked their driver to divert his rear-view mirror. He made a play for Lana, trying to feel her up. But she wasn't yet ready to relinquish her virginity. She later admitted, however, that she gave in for some "heavy petting."

He unbuttoned his trousers to present her with an erect penis. She'd never seen a man with an erection before.

Some wag later joked, "After Jackie Cooper, Lana Turner never saw a man without an erection."

Like Garland, Lana dated Cooper for only about three months before she took up with another actor about her same age. And although Cooper's glory days as an actor seemed to be receding, her new boyfriend was on the dawn of a spectacular career, and about to become the biggest box office attraction in Hollywood.

He was Mickey Rooney.

Subsequently, she broke off her romance with Cooper, with the promise, "Let's be friends."

***

Christmas of 1937 was rapidly approaching, and Lana was busy. She wasn't emoting before the camera, but selling lingerie at a fast pace in the shop where she worked on Hollywood Boulevard.

Except for that day's work on *A Star is Born* (1937), no other job had surfaced, although a photographer had approached her about posing for some nudes. She turned him down, although the blonde who would later "replace" her, Marilyn Monroe, would eventually say "yes" to an equivalent request.

One day, during one of those chance encounters that often happens in Hollywood, Solly Baiano, a former tennis champion representing California in competitions, came into the dress shop to purchase lingerie for his girlfriend.

At the time, he was working for Henry Willson, and he recognized Lana from the 8" x 10" glossies that Willson kept of his mostly shirtless male clients.

He introduced himself to Lana, and was struck by her beauty. "If only she would take off fifteen pounds."

Baiano, in his capacity as a talent scout, often "hustled the flesh" of unknown newcomers to casting directors at various studios. For the most part, the orders transmitted by the studio bosses, through him, were usually the same. "Walk for me, turn around, lift your skirt."

With Willson, Lana had made many calls on various studios. So far, every casting director had told Willson, "Don't call us, we'll get back to you." Of course, they never did.

Seeing Lana in the flesh gave Baiano an idea. His best friend was Barron Polan, an assistant to director Mervyn LeRoy. He'd heard that LeRoy had been unsuccessful in casting "the right girl" to open his latest drama, *Murder in the Deep South*. He thought Lana might be just what LeRoy was seeking.

That evening, he phoned Polan, who agreed to set up an appointment with the director at Warner Brothers the next day. Lana agreed to call in sick for work at the lingerie shop that day, even though it was the Christmas rush, and the store was mobbed.

In the meantime, Lana spent her night learning, "Who in the hell is Mervyn LeRoy? Never heard of him."

She may not have heard of LeRoy, but ninety percent of Hollywood had. Although he would go on to greater glory as a director, Mervyn LeRoy was known at Warner Brothers for making mostly taut, punchy, and socially critical films such as *Little Caesar* (1930), starring Edward G. Robinson and *I Am a Fugitive from a Chain Gang* (1932) starring Paul Muni. His latest film was based on Ward Greene's novel, *Death in the Deep South*, a social melodrama about prejudice and corruption at the trial and subsequent lynching of an innocent man.

One of the most astute and talented directors at Warners, LeRoy had helped launch the careers of a young Ginger Rogers (with whom he had an affair) and Loretta Young.

LeRoy wanted Gable for the role of Massara in *Little Caesar* (1930), but Jack Warner laughed at the screen test. "Look at the ears on that jerk. You wasted $500 on testing him. Give the role to Douglas Fairbanks, Jr."

LeRoy had launched his career as an actor himself, but later switched to producing and directing. In time, he would make 75 movies over a period of four decades, boasting, "I never repeated myself, and I never made a flop."

Among his greatest future successes were *"Madame Curie* (1943); *Thirty Seconds Over Tokyo* (1944); and the religious epic *Quo Vadis?* (1951). He also produced *The Wizard of Oz* (1939), starring Judy Garland.

Before he met Lana, LeRoy estimated that he had interviewed at least thirty young women, finding none of them suitable for the role of Mary Clay. "I wanted a girl who was very sexy, but very clean and wholesome. None of the girls I saw were right for the part until Judy Turner walked in. I knew from the first minute that she was right. Fortunately, she was wearing a high school sweater. The role called for the girl to be a knock-out in a sweater. Judy (later, Lana) sure had the right equipment."

"I was shuffling through papers on my desk when she walked in. At

Director Mervyn LeRoy always took the credit for putting that schoolgirl sweater onto the newly emerging Lana Turner.

She would become known as America's "Sweater Girl," increasing sales of that garment across the nation. "I wanted her to have a 'flesh impact,'" as he called it. "As inexperienced as she was, she pulled it off like a pro."

first, I didn't look up, expecting another disappointment. When I did look up, I saw this girl with dark hair standing in the doorway, her nervous hands shaking. She had on a blue cotton dress. Her hair was impossible looking, as if she'd never run a comb through it. She wasn't wearing any makeup, and she was so shy, she could hardly look me in the face. Yet there was something about her I knew was right. She had tremendous appeal. An audience would respond to that."

When LeRoy stood up from behind her desk, she found him almost as short as she was. Out of the corner of his mouth extended a large stogie. "You're quite pretty. Tell me what experience you've had?"

"Not a thing," she said. "No acting class. No elocution lessons."

"I see," he answered. "Wait outside, if you don't mind."

She sat in his outer office for at least a half-hour while he conferred with Baiano, whom he had summoned

Then LeRoy emerged from his inner office, walking toward Lana and reaching for her hand. "The role is yours. It's a small part: Off camera, you get raped and murdered at the beginning of the flick. The part pays fifty bucks. Are you ready to sign a contract?"

"I'll have to ask my mother," she answered.

That night, Mildred agreed and on February 12, 1937, Lana signed her first movie contract, the debut of many more to come. It wasn't a contract with Warner Brothers, but a personal contract with LeRoy.

It called for her to begin at the starting salary of $50 a week, twice what Mildred earned at the beauty parlor.

LeRoy met with her two days later in his office. "I don't like the name Judy Turner. It's not special."

"My full name is Julia Jean," she answered.

"That's even worse. Turner's okay, very American. But we need a first name, something glamorous."

They went down through the alphabet from Anne to Betty and on to Irene and Joan before halting at the Ls. "Perhaps Leonore. Loretta has already been taken. Lurlene, no. Lulu is too much."

Suddenly, Lana, or so she recalled later, asked "What about Lana? Pronounced *Lah-nuh.*"

LeRoy thought for a minute. "Sounds sexy to me. Lana Turner it is!"

Years later, the actress recalled, "At the time, I didn't know that Lana in Spanish meant wool."

LeRoy later disputed her claim, saying that he named her Lana after one of his old girlfriends.

The next day, she appeared in the wardrobe department for a fitting of her one outfit, a skirt, a blue sweater, high-heeled pumps, and a saucy beret.

Contrary to legend, she did wear a brassiere beneath her sweater. Lined with silk, and with no uplift, it allowed her breasts to bounce freely up and down.

Over the years, it was assumed that her walk along a street was her only scene in the movie. But actually, there was another scene at a soda fountain, where she orders a malt. She tells the soda jerk, "Drop an egg in it as fresh as you are."

She later recalled, "That may explain the legend of my being discovered drinking a malt at Schwab's."

In addition to that, an opening scene in a classroom shows her seductively asking her flustered male teacher (Edward Norris) to help her with a school assignment.

After exiting from the drugstore, she is seen walking down the sidewalk, a scene that would become one of the most iconic in movie history until Marilyn Monroe did "that walk" in the 1950 film, *Niagara.*

"Lana's debut didn't require great screen acting," LeRoy said. "All she had to do was walk, and, boy, did she know how to do that. I had the music scored to match the up-and-down movements of tits and ass."

In a long, 75-foot tracking shot, the camera followed her, not just her breasts bouncing, but her "rotating buttocks" too. Throughout the scene, she held her shoulders back and her head high.

Lana had about eighteen lines of dialogue, but never was the word "rape" uttered, since it was forbidden by the censors of that era. In fact, her rape and murder are suggested—but never depicted—on the screen.

By the end of the shoot, Lana was informed by LeRoy that he'd changed the title of the picture to *They Won't Forget.*

Lana had no scenes with the other actors in the movie. However, after the shoot was finished, she hung around the set for the next few days, wanting to see how movies were made. The star of the film was the venerable actor Claude Rains, who had been born in London and had vast stage experience. She had seen him in *The Invisible Man* (1933). He had been cast as an ambitious and immoral Southern lawyer in *They Won't Forget*.

The only other actor of note was Otto Kruger, who played the lawyer for the accused. His character of Gleason is skilled enough to save his client from the electric chair, but not from a lynching.

Once a leading matinee idol on the stage, Kruger had made such films as *Chained* (1934), with Joan Crawford and Clark Gable.

Another newcomer like Lana, Gloria Dickson (as Sybil Hale) was widely heralded in movie magazines before the picture was released. She was written up as "New Star of the Year," but when *They Won't Forget* was shown, Lana got all the media attention.

Edward Morris played the doomed teacher, Robert Hale, who is falsely accused of the murder. He'd married Ann Sheridan that year and brought her to the set. Sheridan complained to Lana about how much she detested being billed as "The Oomph Girl."

Soon, Lana would be labeled "The Sweater Girl."

In a few short months, both Sheridan and Lana would be considered for the role of Scarlett O'Hara in *Gone With the Wind*.

Lana and Sheridan would have another bizarre link because of a so-called scientific survey by Dr. Joseph Catton, a Stanford University psychiatrist. Based on his survey, he rated the three sexiest actresses in Hollywood, giving Marlene Dietrich 90%, Lana 86%, and Ann 85%.

***

LeRoy didn't let Lana and Mildred see the rushes, but they attended a preview at the Warner Brothers Hollywood Theater. The moment Lana did "the walk" on screen, a man in the back yelled out, "Get a load of that kid! Whatta pair of tits!"

His remark was met with hoots and whistles.

Lana later said, "Mother and I scrooched down in our seats, covering our faces. This Thing with the bouncing bosom came on the screen. Not only that, but her ass was undulating. I was beyond embarrassment."

In tears, Lana fled from the theater and hailed a taxi with Mildred. They rode to Gladdy's home in silence. "I was so self-conscious, I tried not to bounce in the back seat of the taxi."

The next morning, she phoned her agent, Henry Willson. "Oh, Henry," she cried out. "I almost died watching myself. Men were screaming obscenities about my breasts. I hope I don't look like that girl up there on the screen.

"Fortunately, you do!" Willson said.

Billy Wilkerson of *The Hollywood Reporter* wrote the film's first review. "Short on playing time is the role of the murdered schoolgirl played by Lana Turner. It is worthy of more than passing note. This young lady has vivid beauty, personality, and charm."

The *National Board of Review* named *They Won't Forget* one of the best dramas of the year in its depiction of prejudice and corruption. *Life* magazine put it on its list of American film classics. Writing in *The New York Herald Tribune,* Howard Barnes pronounced it "a vivid work of art."

Frank S. Nugent in *The New York Times* labeled the movie "a brilliant sociological drama and a trenchant film editorial against intolerance and hatred."

In 1987, the same story was dramatized in a four-hour TV miniseries called *The Murder of Mary Phagan,* written by Larry McMurtry and starring Jack Lemmon and Kevin Spacey.

As soon as the film was released, Warners was swamped with fan mail. "Tell us more about that girl in the sweater." Within the month, Lana had become America's "Sweater Girl."

She hated the label. "It took years of hard work to get rid of it," she said.

Henry Willson went with a handsome young actor to see *They Won't Forget.*

When he left the movie palace, he told his lover, "Tonight there's another star that has risen in the firmament. She's Lana Turner."

Few movie fans at the time of *ingénue* Lana's propulsion into fame as the shy and relatively awkward "Sweater Girl" could have imagined the cinematic heights she'd eventually climb.

When Lana began "The Walk," in a tight skirt and dangerously high heels, she could have no idea that she was walking into screen immortality, shooting one of the most famous scenes in Hollywood history as the innocent Mary Clay.

With her breasts bouncing up and down, "She was a flower waiting to be deflowered," in the words of one critic. Another wrote, "A girl as tempting as Lana Turner would definitely bring out the rapist beast in men that lurks deep within their dark desires."

Chapter Two

So Many Men, So Little Time

Lana Dates a Future President

When Lana Turner and Ronald Reagan were both struggling contract players at Warner Brothers, they posed for publicity pictures, which led to their dating. The picture above, with the young stars in riding outfits, was taken at a ranch.

"He taught me how to ride a horse before getting in the saddle himself. Did I say that diplomatically?"

He told his close friend, Dick Powell, "Lana was one of my greatest conquests, a flamboyant feather in my cap."

Later, she denied having an affair with him, perhaps because of her burgeoning friendship with MGM starlet Nancy Davis. "She guarded him like Fort Knox," Lana claimed.

After signing her first contract—partly for fun and partly as a career-building device—Lana set out to become the "Queen of the Night." She was seen dancing at all the hot spots of Los Angeles: Ciro's, the Trocadero, Palladium, Mocambo, the Clover Club, and invariably, Cocoanut Grove. She was attired in form-fitting designer gowns borrowed from wardrobe at Warner Brothers.

Thus began a series of dizzying romantic encounters with some of Tinseltown's handsomest actors. She was later said to have invented the tagline, "So many men, so little time."

Depending on the night and their schedule, she was spotted with, among others, handsome, blonde, and beefy Wayne Morris ("my first big crush"), or Ronald Reagan ("he showered before and after our encounters").

She also dated western star Don ("Red") Barry ("only two inches taller than me but he made up for those inches elsewhere"), and George Montgomery ("before Dinah Shore snared him").

Some young studs had a more lasting impact: Victor Mature ("my biggest thrill), attorney Greg Bautzer ("he took my virginity"), or singer Tony Martin ("he always hit the high note—never failed").

Along the way she also found time to allow herself to be wooed by some of the biggest marquee names on the Silver Screen—Errol Flynn, Gary Cooper, James Stewart, and Mickey Rooney ("he knocked me up").

Between pictures, Warners didn't know quite what to do with its still-undefined starlet. Early publicity photographs reveal that she was searching for a screen identity. She was depicted in a sweater with those protruding breasts from *They Won't Forget,* or else in a clinging satin gown that might have been alluring on Marlene Dietrich.

At other times, "Hayseed Lana" appeared in a barnyard with a straw sticking out of her succulent mouth. She could be photographed with a come hither gaze or else in a lace collar looking like a refugee from Louisa May Alcott's *Little Women.*

Some photos show her smouldering and sophisticated. Others made her look like a wild and crazy girl with the wind blowing through her hair. As late as 1930, Lana, as a red-haired beauty with scarlet lips, looked like the girl next door—that is, if you lived next door to the winner of the *Miss California* beauty pageant.

During her nightly prowls, whenever she made an entrance into a chic club, she was always a show-stopper. Since she was still young enough to look beautiful, she could party all night and still emerge from makeup the next morning at 5AM looking fresh, young, and glamorous.

After *They Won't Forget* (1937) until as late as 1941, she had no more particularly memorable movie roles. But she was learning her trade, building up a name in Hollywood, and studying how to be a movie star.

Frances Wyndham, in *The London Times,* summed up her status at this time: "Wearing sweater and skirt, insolently hunched over an ice cream soda, Lana Turner exuded a homespun glamour in the late 1930s that was particularly American. Both frail and tough, she appealed to the masculine protective instinct at the same time she promised danger."

At the age of sixteen, she truly discovered men, diversions which would become her life-long passion. Her legend was birthing.

Years later, she recalled, "I dated them young, perhaps too young, and even older, maybe too much older."

"She was both warm and beautiful," said Mickey Rooney. "I should know."

Billy Wilkerson of *The Hollywood Reporter* continued to grind out publicity, as did the fan magazines and the newspaper gossip columnists.

"Lana's phone number was passed around a lot in the late 1930s, 1940s, 1950s, 1960s, and even beyond," said gossip maven Louella Parsons. "How did she find time to work in all those husbands?"

"I know one Sunday, she had a luncheon date that turned into love in the afternoon beside his pool. That morphed into a supper club date and dancing with another man ending in a sneak-away midnight romp in a bachelor pad, with a third lover. And she still made that make-up call at 5AM."

That was the voice of Louella's rival, Hedda Hopper, speaking off the record.

***

For some bizarre reason known only to himself, her agent, Henry Willson, hooked Lana up with George Raft for a date. Raft had been born in 1895 in New York's Hell's Kitchen, that poverty and crime-infested stretch of "Midtown West" in Manhattan. [*Hell's Kitchen, which has since then been gentrified, is traditionally considered to stretch north-south between 34th and 59th Streets, and east-west between Eighth Avenue and the Hudson River.*]

In time, he became a "taxi dancer" at Churchill's Tea Room, along with his roommate, Rudolph Valentino. They danced with older women and often accepted invitations for sex-for-pay later at their apartments. Marlene Dietrich once said, "When I sang, 'Just a Gigolo,' I thought of George."

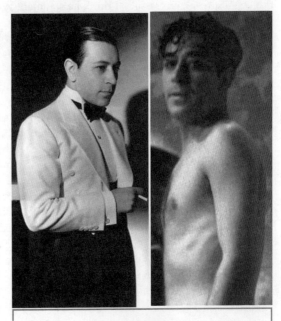

In the 1930s at Warner Brothers, Raft had evolved into a movie gangster icon, along with Edward G. Robinson, James Cagney, and Humphrey Bogart. He was also known as a "ladies' man," with a string of seductions that included not only Dietrich, but Mae West, Lucille Ball, Norma Shearer, and hundreds of hookers and showgirls."

A frequent movie goer, Lana had seen only two of his films, *Night After Night* (1932) with Mae West ("She stole the picture from me"), and *Scarface* (also 1932) with Paul Muni. [*In Scarface, Raft had played coin-tossing Rinaldo, bumped off by a vicious killer, Tony Camonte (Paul*

Movie actor and part-time gangster, George Raft devoted his other waking hous to seductions. "Screwing was his only game," said Mack Grey, his closest friend. "He could devote a whole day to doing just that." But Lana never got to sample "Black Snake."

31

Muni).]

Lana didn't know what to expect when Raft showed up on her doorstep. He was the best dressed man she'd ever seen, with a tight-fitting tailored black suit, black shirt, and white tie. She'd never seen a man dressed in a black shirt before. He'd slicked back his hair with Vaseline, and he wore a pearl gray Fedora pulled down over one eye, which he did not remove. His pointy shoes were so shiny she could almost see her reflection in them. He was sleek, solemn faced, and imbued with a sexual menace.

He arrived in a black Packard with a driver to take her to the Cocoanut Grove. "Don't worry," he said. "It's bulletproof."

"Of all the men I ever danced with, and we're talking dozens upon dozens, Raft had the best movement. He'd been a professional dancer in New York, known for his erotic movements such as rubbing parts of his body as he performed."

"He was a smooth talker and had a real big ego," she recalled.

On their third date, he invited her to his lavishly decorated home. Although she fully realized that he wanted to seduce her, she had reached that point in her young life where the most she allowed was for men to indulge in "heavy petting."

For Raft, that meant fondling her breasts while he masturbated "Black Snake."

His nearly nine-inch penis had been nicknamed "Black Snake" by Mae West, since it was many shades darker than the rest of his body's skin tone.

Lana later talked to Betty Grable about their joint involvements with Raft. She delivered a frank appraisal. "I think he's a latent homosexual. He and Valentino were lovers when they lived together. He never touched me except to beat me up."

Willson was at the Trocadero to witness Lana's final date with Raft—the one that gossips claimed ended their romance. Lana was table hopping, going around introducing herself to established stars, producers, and directors, and pointedly not including Raft in any of her hob-nobbing.

He sat alone looking depressed. He never drank liquor. "When I came up to him, it was obvious he'd soured on Lana," Willson said.

"She's still wearing the god damn chastity belt," he said. "I even gave her a fur coat, and she still is holding off. I wanted to teach her the facts of life, but some other guys will have to do that. I've moved on to Ann Sheridan and Betty Grable."

Within days, Raft was back to hosting his nude pool parties. On his patio, clad in a silk robe, overlooking the pool and its terrace, he seemed to be deciding which woman, or women, would "get lucky" that night.

Months after he stopped dating Lana, she agreed to star with him in the radio dramatization of his 1941 film, *They Drive by Night*. The film had starred truck-driving brothers, Raft and Humphrey Bogart, with the women's roles played by Ida Lupino and Ann Sheridan. Since they were not available for the radio broadcast, Lucille Ball and Lana assumed their roles.

***

Additional roles, albeit small, weren't long in coming, yet Lana was disappointed when she read the script that outlined the small part she'd been offered in what evolved into her second movie, *The Great Garrick* (1937), a Warner Brothers

32

film. Its director was James Whale, and its stars included Olivia de Havilland and the English actor, Brian Aherne.

Set in the 18th Century, the plot was a fictionalized episode in the life of David Garrick (1717-1779), acclaimed as one of the greatest of all English actors.

In the drama, he travels to France to appear at *La Comédie française* during the most dissipated days of the *ancien régime*. In a farewell speech at the Theatre Royal on Drury Lane in London, he announces that he is going to Paris to teach Frenchmen how to act.

Apprised of his arrogance, the French actors decide to play a dirty trick on him They take over an inn in the French countryside where Garrick is scheduled to spend the night *en route* to Paris. Maliciously, the French actors assume the role of landlord and servants, and try to scare Garrick out of his wits.

The exception to that is the lovely, demure Olivia, cast as Germaine Dupont, a countess who falls in love with the dashing English actor.

As for Lana, she was cast as a scullery maid. "It was type casting," she said. "After all, I was a virtual scullery maid when I lived with that horrid family in Modesto."

Her fellow chambermaids included Linda Perry, whose film career was to go virtually nowhere, and Marie Wilson, who would go on to stardom as a radio, TV, and film actress, scoring great success in *My Friend Irma* (1949), and its spin-offs.

***

Lana was directed by James Whale, who had "frightened the daylights out of me when I went to see his classic horror film, *Frankenstein* (1932). He was very dear and kind to me. I was mildly surprised that he was quite open about his homosexuality."

Throughout her life, Lana easily related to the many homosexuals who paraded through her films. She had none of the usual prejudice of the day, and gay men became her most enduring fans.

One day, Whale invited her to lunch, predicting big stardom for her. "I don't know what it is, but you have something that's just bursting into bloom. I predict you'll become the *femme fatale* of the 1940s."

He was fascinating to talk to, telling her at one point that he had been captured in Flanders in August of 1917 and had become a prisoner of war. "I staged amateur theatricals for my fellow English soldiers in camp. It was the only amusement they had. Some of them showed their gratitude to me by slip-

"My role in *The Great Garrick* called for me to squeal, giggle, and curtsy in several scenes, all in Restoration costume," Lana said. "I tried to provide a certain lustiness, but I fear I didn't succeed."

ping into my bunk late at night."

Whale's fellow Englishman, Brian Aherne, the star of the film, was elegant with a certain charm and style. He gave Lana little attention, having preferred the romantic company of such illustrious women as Marlene Dietrich and tobacco heiress Doris Duke.

The actor in *The Great Garrick* who caught Lana's roving eye was handsome Craig Reynolds, a rising star of the 1930s. At the time, he had a small fan club and was getting letters from young girls who found him sexier than Errol Flynn.

"I slipped around and dated him three or four times—that is, when Jane Wyman didn't have her claws in him. Like a fool, I was still holding onto my virginity. I later regretted not surrendering it to Craig."

Sixteen-year-old Lana Turner, cast as a bawdy Restoration wench, flirts with studly Craig Reynolds. But was he really sexier than Errol Flynn?

***

Despite countless offers, some of which were most persuasive, from some of the handsomest men in Hollywood, Lana was still "sweet sixteen" and had never lost her cherry. *[That fruity reference derived from the appraisal of her casual friend, Ann Sheridan.]*

Lana expressed an almost daily confessional of details associated with her heavy dating schedule to two of her best friends, both of them actresses. One was Ann Rutherford, who would soon be cast as Scarlett O'Hara's sister in *Gone With the Wind* (1939). The other was Bonita Granville, the sharp-nosed, brazen child star, two years younger than Lana, who had just scored a big hit in the 1936 *These Three*. She played a monstrous brat who, by spreading vicious gossip, ruins the lives of Miriam Hopkins, Joel McCrea, and Merle Oberon.

"Lana was just itching to get deflowered, but holding back," Granville said.

"Lana faced a dilemma," Rutherford said. "She wondered if it would hurt or feel good."

"It must feel good or else gals wouldn't chase after guys so much," Lana told her friends.

One night at the Café Vendome, in Los Angeles, in early February of 1939, her life was about to change. She was on the dance floor twirling around with actor Alan Curtis when attorney Greg Bautzer cut in.

She'd read about him in the gossip columns, as he was called "Hollywood's Bachelor Number One."

34

He was also known as "The Don Juan of the Hollywood Boudoir." In time, he'd seduce some of the most glamorous movie queens of the 20th Century, not only Lana, but Joan Crawford, Ava Gardner, Rita Hayworth, Jane Wyman, singer Peggy Lee, Ginger Rogers, Dorothy Lamour, Merle Oberon, and Ingrid Bergman. His reputation as a "swordsman" had already been well-established by the time he danced into Lana's life.

As an attorney, he was known for his high-profile clients, none more notable than Howard Hughes, the billionaire aviator and film mogul.

As Bautzer would later inform Lana, "Most of my job with Hughes involves writing checks to his harem of kept women."

The first time Bautzer and Lana were mentioned as an item in gossip columns was on February 13, 1938, in the "Beau Peep Whispers" section of the *Los Angeles Times*. As a couple, they were spotted by *tout* Hollywood at the Riviera Club in the Pacific Palisades. The writeup stated that Bautzer—"that man about town with the roving eye"—had been seen with a "new Titian-haired beauty decorating his arm." The reference was to teenaged Lana on the arm of a man a decade older than she was.

"He was tall and husky, with soulful dark eyes, a tanned complexion, and a flashing smile that showed a lot of white teeth," she wrote. "He was so smooth, so self-assured, that all the other boys I knew seemed like children."

He phoned Lana the following night, and the two of them began to see one another at a rate estimated by Lana at around three evenings a week. On nights when he wasn't seeing her, he falsely told her that he was involved with business clients. On the party and nightclub circuit, "Lana & Greg" became an item, often closing down Ciro's or the Mocambo.

As she accurately stated, "Greg was far too sophisticated to wrestle me in the front seat of a car or steal a kiss at the front door. On the dance floor, he rubbed himself against me until he produced an erection. I knew he was going to seduce me, but when?"

He was taking his time, not rushing her into bed. That came one rainy Saturday night when he pulled up at his house and invited her inside, telling her that his mother was away playing cards with her women friends.

"That later turned out not to be true, as we heard

"There was no way, with my heavy dating schedule, that I was to remain a virgin until I got married," Lana said. "I decided the man to do the honors was Greg Bautzer, an experienced lover to judge by his conquests of the most beautiful women in Hollywood. I was seventeen when I lost it. Greg was my first love, my first heartbreak."

her going down the stairs to the kitchen," Lana said.

She would remember the experience for the rest of her life. Greg Bautzer became the first of dozens of men who would seduce her in her future.

"He was loving and patient with me, even though I was awkward," she wrote. "I had no idea how to move or what to do. The act itself hurt like hell, and I must confess I didn't enjoy it. I didn't even know what an orgasm was. But I loved being close to Greg and holding him, and the feeling that now, at least, I was giving myself to him."

The next day over lunch, she confided to Rutherford and Granville, "Last night Greg Bautzer made a woman out of me. And I'm still sore."

In gossipy Hollywood, Lana soon learned that those other four nights a week, when he wasn't with her, he was not entertaining business clients. He was out with other beauties, especially Joan Crawford, with whom he seemed to be having the most serious engagement.

Lana was furious and cried one night, but woke up determined to take a different course of action. She complained to Granville, "I'm very, very jealous, but I'm going to get back at him. Now that Greg has broken me in, I'm going to let other guys get what they want. Serves him right!"

***

Lana was thrilled when she heard the news that Samuel Goldwyn had borrowed her for his next big epic, *The Adventures of Marco Polo* (1938), starring Gary Cooper. She looked upon him as the handsomest and sexiest actor in films, even more so than Clark Gable and Robert Taylor.

She had to go to the library to look up who Marco Polo (1254-1324) was. He was, of course, the great Venetian explorer who traveled to China to establish trade with the Far East. While there, he met Kublai Khan and was introduced to his fabulous court.

The script by Robert Sherman was rather tongue-in-cheek and by today's standards, even a bit campy. Originally, Goldwyn had selected John Cromwell to direct, but within five days, after some bitter disputes about presentation and content, he was replaced.

Archie Mayo, who had worked in silent films since 1917, was brought in at the last minute to take over.

One of the most elaborate and costly

The picture, *The Adventures of Marco Polo*, bombed at the box office, but Lana was enthralled to meet her screen idol, Gary Cooper, cast as the handsome explorer popular with the ladies of Venice's back canals. When Lana met him, the horse-hung "Montana Mule" had already seduced *tout* Hollywood, from Mae West to Cary Grant. He told Lana, "Grow up real soon and come back around."

films Goldwyn ever made, *Marco Polo* had a strong supporting cast. The villain, Ahmed, was played by Basil Rathbone, the devious, crooked adviser to Kublai Khan (George Barbier).

Lana had a small role, cast as the maid to Nazama (Binnie Barnes). "Another maid part," she lamented. A Londoner, Barnes had been working in films since 1923, her most memorable role that of Katherine Howard, the monarch's fifth wife, in *The Private Life of Henry VIII* (1933).

"She was rather rude to me, insisting, for example, that I bring her fresh coffee," Lana said. "That was not part of the script."

In the film, Lana is also pawed over by a Chinese warlord, the improbably cast Alan Hale, Sr. "I was supposed to be this Oriental sex object," she said. "Nothing more, nothing less. Alan helped me in the role."

In an attempt to add a sweeping kind of grandeur to the clunky script, Goldwyn had signed a cast of 5,000 extras, and Lana felt lost among the hordes. On her first day on the set, she was introduced to him.

He shocked Lana when he informed her that he had instructed the makeup department to pluck her natural eyebrows and to apply fake ones, glued on each morning and yanked off at the end of every day of filming.

Each morning, any new growth of her eyebrows was stripped away, a rather painful process. She also had to wear a Chinese-inspired black wig that had to be glued around her face with spirit gum. Regrettably, after weeks of punishment, her real eyebrows never grew back, and throughout the remaining years of her life, she had to pencil them in.

As dictated by the script, Marco Polo falls madly in love with the Princess Kukachiun, who is betrothed to the King of Persia. Goldwyn had cast Sigrid Gurie as the Princess, and was giving her a massive publicity buildup as "Norway's Answer to Greta Garbo," and as "The Siren of the Fjords."

Lana never got to meet her screen idol, Gary Cooper, who played Marco Polo in the film until the end of the shoot. She introduced herself to him while he was having lunch in the commissary, and was surprised that this entire meal consisted of Sauerkraut. "It keeps you regular," he told her. He was leaving that afternoon for a vacation in Idaho.

"Mr. Cooper," she said. "I'm your greatest fan. I think you are the most beautiful man in pictures. No one can top you. I even dream about you."

"I think you're a right pretty girl," he

"Samuel Goldwyn in *The Adventures of Marco Polo* miscast me as an Oriental siren," Lana said. "Instead of vamping Gary Cooper, I ended up with an unappetizing Chinese war lord (Alan Hale). Not only that, but makeup plucked my eyebrows to make me look Chinese. They never grew back."

said. "But jailbait. Just how old are you?"

"I'm about seventeen," she answered.

"I'll make a deal with you," he said. "Call me on your eighteenth birthday, and I'll give you the thrill of your life."

"That's a promise I'm going to hold you to," she said. "You are more of a dreamboat offscreen than on, and you're pretty special on screen, too. What a man!"

"Grow up soon and get back to me, girl," he told her. "I can't wait."

The Adventures of Marco Polo bombed at the box office. A critic for *The New York Sun* wrote: "In spite of the elaborate settings and the presence of Gary Cooper, it never quite lives up to its promise."

John Mosher of *The New Yorker* called the film "a big disappointment, the dialogue having the swing of a bad libretto."

The movie lost $700,000 at the box office, a monstrous sum in 1938.

When the film was re-released in 1945, Lana was at the peak of her career. The Goldwyn picture was advertised as "starring Gary Cooper with Lana Turner."

***

Lana Turner's days at Warner Brothers were numbered, as were Mervyn LeRoy's. Under personal contract to the director, Lana was said to view him as a father figure, although she denied that. "He was more of a mentor," she said. "I turned to him for guidance in my career. He taught me how to act, even how to dress."

In his first appraisal of her outfits, he had compared her to a hooker, especially in her choice of imitation jewelry, a component of which included a large glass ring with rhinestones. "Don't wear all that flashy fake jewelry that only Barbara Hutton could afford if it were real. You're going to be a genuine movie star, the real thing, not some imitation. When you're making the big bucks, you can afford genuine stones."

"I took his advice," she said. "When I became Queen of MGM, I bought my own diamonds, or else had my beaus—or husbands, as the case may be—buy diamonds for me, which is preferable, of course."

During her brief stint at Warners, she met the studio mogul, Jack Warner, only once. He was used to working with such icons as Bette Davis, Errol Flynn, Olivia de Havilland, Humphrey Bogart, James Cagney, and George Raft. Abrupt, staccato, and ruthless, the film tycoon was not impressed with Lana, and predicted no future for her in movies.

In league with his brothers, Jack had been working in film production since 1910, and he had a cocky attitude when he came to judging future stars. "Gals like the Turner dame are a dime a dozen in Hollywood," he told LeRoy.

When LeRoy informed Warner that he was going to shift over to better working conditions at Metro-Goldwyn-Mayer, Warner responded, "Since Turner is under contract to you, take her along—and good riddance. All she's got is a pair of bouncing boobs—no talent whatsoever."

***

On the night Greg Bautzer was bedding some other movie star, Lana dated a number of beaus. She referred to them as "mere flings while I wait for the right man to give my heart to."

Don Barry, who was about her same height, came into her life. He would soon be widely known as "Red" Barry after appearing in the highly successful 1940 film, *Adventures of Red Ryder*. A Texan from Houston, Barry had red hair to match his nickname.

"Mildred liked him because in some ways, he reminded her of Virgil," Lana said. "She encouraged me to date him."

Their first major public outing was at the 1937 premiere of *The Life of Émile Zola* at Graumann's Chinese Theater on Hollywood Boulevard. Wearing a satin gown and a fur borrowed from wardrobe, Lana made a stunning appearance. Broadcasting from the lobby, George Jessel hailed her as "the beautiful Lana Turner, a rising young Hollywood star."

During Barry's dating of Lana, "he got lucky just one night," she told Ann Rutherford. But during their brief romance, he gave her two bottles of expensive French perfume and a jeweled vanity case. Two weeks after she broke up with him, she got the bills for those two items.

Joan Crawford also dated Barry, and had a similar experience with him, although he presented her with more expensive presents—a white mink coat and a diamond necklace. Later, the merchants came to reclaim the items because Barry had not paid for them.

***

Another cowboy star, Tim Holt, briefly flitted in and out of Lana's life during this period of intense (some said "promiscuous") dating. Although he'd been born in Beverly Hills, he seemed completely at home on the range. The son of actor Jack Holt, Tim had dreamed of becoming a star of movie westerns ever since he was a boy.

At the time Lana met Tim, he was under contract to producer Walter Wanger. Against type, Orson Welles later cast Holt in his 1942 *The Magnificent Ambersons*.

"Try me on for size," Don Barry said when introduced to Lana. He was the shortest man she ever dated, vying for him with Joan Crawford. "He wasn't my type, but a lot of fun...for a while. Actually, he preferred orgies."

***

Many suitors, some of whom were on the Hollywood A-list, pursued Lana, but not all of them were successful. A case in point was William Powell, born in 1892, the star with the sensually drooping eyelids. Dapper, suave, and ever so self-assured, he had a pencil mustache and slicked-back hair like George Raft. A true gentleman, he evoked a member of a turn-of-the-century barbershop quartet.

Lana had a brief fling with the cowboy star Tim Holt, pictured above. "Holt came and went from my life like a tumbling tumbleweed," she said. "After he made love to me, he'd walk up and down the hall stark naked, practicing drawing his six-shooter. No, not that one!"

A major star at MGM, he would in time make fourteen *Thin Man* movies with Myrna Loy, based on the Nick and Nora Charles characters created by Dashiell Hamett. They were sophisticated sleuths always ready with a smart ass line as well as a bucket of ice for their dry martinis.

When Lana met Powell, he'd already been nominated for two Best Actor Oscars, one for *The Thin Man* (1934) and another for *My Man Godfrey* (1936), in which he had co-starred with his former wife, Carole Lombard.

Lana was introduced to him at the home of Mervyn LeRoy.

Well past his prime, he was in a rather shaky condition. In 1935, he had co-starred with Jean Harlow in *Reckless* and had fallen in love with her. They had planned to be married. But at the age of 26, the platinum blonde goddess had died from uremia at the peak of her career.

He became morbidly depressed after learning of her death. To compound his misfortune, he'd undergone surgery, an experimental radium treatment for cancer which had greatly slowed him down.

He met Lana on the first night he'd ventured into the world again. He seemed enchanted with her, and she was awed by what a great star he was. Ironically, within a few short months, with her hair dyed blonde, she would be billed as "the new Jean Harlow."

Powell called her for a date the following morning, and she accepted. He did most of the talking, even sharing his concept of what formed the perfect union between a man and a woman. "The man should be older, and the couple should be diametrically opposite each other."

"Are you talking about any couple we know?" she asked, provocatively.

Powell was a charming suitor with impeccable manners. But the following day, she told her girlfriends, "Bill lacks sex appeal, at least for me."

He sensed that, and on a subsequent date, he touted his other qualities, promising to guide her in her career and to help her fine-tune her acting.

He urged her to drop Henry Willson as her agent and to sign instead with

Myron Selznick, the brother of producer David O. Selznick. "Myron is the best agent in the business and can do wonders for your career."

On their third date, he took her to the home of his closest friends, Ronald Colman and Richard Barthelmess. As a trio, the men seemed to have bonded into something of a cultural clique, and she, a high school drop-out, often didn't understand what they were talking about.

On their fifth date, he tried to seduce her, but, as she later told her girlfriends, "It didn't work out. I had these painful menstrual cramps."

As their dating proceeded, he was getting serious, calling her two or three times a day. She was drifting away. Although she admired his mind, sex was too important to her, and that's why she turned once again to younger, more virile men.

As a gift, he sent her a lovely glass cabinet about five feet tall with mirrored shelves. In a note, he told her that the shelves were suitable only for holding the most expensive French perfumes.

"The Thin Man," suave and dapper William Powell was well suited to any Art Deco café society of the 1920s or 1930s. "But I refused to become a replacement for Jean Harlow in his life," Lana said.

She composed her thank-you note to him as a "kiss-off."

"My dearest Bill, what a beautiful gift and how very thoughtful. But I fear those shelves will hold perfume purchased for me by other suitors. I'm so sorry. But I wish you all the best and thank you for the good times. Love, Lana."

***

As Lana admitted in her highly unreliable memoirs, Greg Bautzer finally taught her what the female orgasm was. Her first with him would become one of thousands she'd experience in her romantic liaisons to come. "I did feel passion for him, and eventually, I did achieve orgasm," she wrote. "But what I really wanted was to have Greg hold me, keep me safe in his arms."

After Lana and Bautzer returned from a romantic holiday in Palm Springs, they learned that Bautzer's mother had died.

Her death transpired on February 13, 1938. Blanche Bautzer Smith was fifty-four at the hour of her unexpected death. Lana attended the funeral of her lover's mother at the Little Church of the Flowers at the Glendale Forest Lawn Mortuary.

In tears, Bautzer, twenty-seven years old at the time, told her, "No other woman will ever replace what my mother meant to me. No one!"

***

When he recovered a bit from his mother's death, Bautzer started dating and seducing her again. A favorite nightclub of theirs was La Conga, where both of them, after some lessons from a teacher, became the best rumba dancers among the patrons.

To publicize both himself and Lana, Bautzer fed items to Hedda Hopper about his dating of Lana, which she published in her column in the *Los Angeles Times*. Bautzer ignored her rival, Louella Parsons.

Of course, in exchange all this free publicity, Hopper expected a series of expensive gifts above and beyond the fresh flowers that arrived at her doorstep from the attorney every morning.

At one point in their relationship, Bautzer and Lana made a pact. Should either of them tire of each other, one or the other were to send a box of red roses to the other's home as a signal that their affair was over.

Bautzer had to fly to Chicago for two weeks to defend a client in a lawsuit. Before rushing to catch his plane, he called his florist and asked him to send Lana a dozen of the most beautiful white roses he had in stock. When the box arrived, Bautzer was airborne. She opened the box and burst into hysterical tears when she saw a dozen red roses.

During his time in Chicago, Bautzer was very busy. When he did try to phone her, he could not get through.

Two weeks went by, during which she regretted his loss. Then one afternoon, he phoned after his return to his home.

When Lana came to the phone, Bautzer spoke to her in his most seductive voice, "My darling, I've missed you so. Dreamed of you every night."

"You mean, we're on again?" she asked.

"We were never off," he protested.

"Your damn florist sent me a box of red roses. I've been devastated ever since."

"That fucker! I'll fire him! I ordered WHITE roses as a token of my love."

That night, as Lana later confessed to Ann Rutherford, "Greg gave me the greatest sex of my life. Three orgasms before the rooster crowed."

***

"Every time I get involved with an actor at Warner Brothers, I find that Jane Wyman got to the guy before me," complained Lana over lunch one day with actor Alan Hale, who had co-starred with her in *The Adventures of Marco Polo*. Such was the case with Wayne Morris, on whom she had had a really big crush.

Ever since she saw Wayne play this boxer in *Kid Galahad* (1937), she had wanted to date him. That was the film that made him a leading man. He played a former bellhop turned boxer in a Warner Brothers picture that also starred Edward G. Robinson, Bette Davis, and Humphrey Bogart.

The first time she was ever alone with Morris was when she maneuvered to get him to invite her to lunch in the commissary. Naturally, they talked about movies, especially those at Warner Brothers.

"Before I got into the business I wasn't much into films," he said. "I liked going to movie palaces, however—not so much to see what was showing. The upper balcony was a good place where me and a girl could make out."

He had high hopes for his career, telling her he'd heard from director Michael Curtiz that Jack Warner had thoughts of grooming him to become the next Errol Flynn. "That hellraiser might go too far, and I'll be ready to step into parts slated for him."

"Flynn is just getting started," she said. "Isn't it a bit early to be grooming the next Errol Flynn?"

"That's how it goes in this town."

"Don't tell me that the next Lana Turner is being groomed while I'm still at the starting gate."

Speaking with a slow drawl, Morris, unlike most stars, had actually been born in Los Angeles. Growing up to become a handsome, tall, muscular blonde, he had played football at Los Angeles Junior College before getting a job as a forest ranger.

He studied acting at the Pasadena Playhouse where a Warners talent scout had spotted him, That led to a contract in 1937. It wasn't a very good contract. In *Kid Galahad*, he was paid only $66 a week, as opposed to Robinson who got $50,000 for the picture.

"When we made the movie, Davis kept inviting me into her dressing room, and I kept rejecting her come-on. I asked Bogie how to get this hot-to-trot mama off my back. I told him 'I'm not into mothers this year.'"

[At the time, Morris said this, he was 23 years old, Davis only 29.]

"Bogie suggested I throw her a mercy fuck, but I still refused, earning her undying animosity. I like 'em young. Sweet sixteen like you, Lana baby."

"Davis wanted me so bad, she even went to Michael Curtiz, the director, and urged him to have the screen writers insert a passionate love scene between us. But Curtiz, thank god, refused."

During the course of Lana's brief fling with him, Morris invited her to spend the weekend with him at a rented villa in Palm Springs. "I didn't know what I was getting into," she confessed to LeRoy. "I was carried away with the magic of Palm Springs. It conjured up images for me of those silent screen stars like Valentino and Theda Bara, who came here for 'off-the-record' weekends. I liked the desert atmosphere of palm trees and sipping cocktails around a swimming pool."

But, as she admitted, it didn't work out that way. Once they settled in, Morris stripped off all his clothes. "He was justifiably proud of

"Wayne Morris was blonde and I hadn't become one yet," Lana said. "When I started dating this handsome stud, Jane Wyman vied for him. She praised his 'football player physique and virility,' but I was more awed by 'jumbo.'"

43

this dangling thing he called 'Jumbo,' and really showed it off."

He didn't bother to get dressed, even when his guests arrived. She was expecting he might know some movie stars, but his friends were on the fringe of the industry—grips, technicians, cameramen.

Within the hour, all the guests, male and female, had their clothes off, frolicking in the pool. Lana refused to strip down and retreated to one of the villa's bedrooms.

Three hours later, Morris joined her. "His idea of seducing a woman is to jump on her and pound for dear life, asserting his masculinity. His technique is to overpower with brute strength."

"Needless to say, my big crush on him ended that weekend," she said.

Wayne was a genuine exhibitionist.

He told Lana that, "In Hollywood, it pays to advertise your assets, like you did with those bouncing boobs in *They Won't Forget.*"

"Word about me spread to producers and directors," Morris continued, "especially the homos. I'll get roles through stints on the casting couch. A lot of actors—not just female starlets—put out from a prone position on that casting couch. Ask your agent, Henry Willson. He knows all about that, and so does his brigade of young, handsome studs."

"Doesn't that make you feel like a whore?" she asked.

"I don't think about that," he said. "When I first hit town, a director told me that in Hollywood, a pretty boy doesn't have to go hungry. I followed his advice."

***

Although at first he'd resisted, Jack Warner no longer opposed his publicity department's policy of posing Ronald Reagan with the most beautiful women on the Warners lot for cheesecake photographs. At that time in Reagan's film career, Warner felt that it enhanced the sex appeal of the clean-cut Midwesterner, and he ordered that the focus on Reagan as beefcake vs. cheesecake continue..

It was around this time that Warner began promoting the sexual allure of the future President, defining him as "a better swordsman on the Warners lot than Errol Flynn."

He specifically ordered Reagan to regularly escort Warners starlets to movie premieres, events where they'd be widely photographed. When Susan Hayward, who was enamored with him at the time, heard that he'd be escorting other women on studio-arranged "dates," she warned him: "Make sure you escort them and nothing else."

Ironically, she, too, was ordered to participate in photo ops with rising young male stars, so she came to realize it was strictly business.

Soon, the publicity department instructed Reagan to configure himself as Lana Turner's date at the next Warners gala—in this case, the world premiere of *Jezebel* (1938), a Deep South plantation saga co-starring Bette Davis and Henry Fonda.

Wearing a dinner jacket borrowed from the studio's wardrobe department, Reagan, with his hair slicked back, took a taxi to retrieve the starlet Lana at her home. The date was March 7, 1938.

In pursuit of his date (Lana) for *Jezebel's* premiere, Reagan arrived at a modest little apartment on Highland Avenue, above Hollywood Boulevard. It was a neighborhood filled with low-rent apartments, catering mostly to transients who had flocked to Hollywood to break into the movie business.

When he knocked on Lana's door, it was opened by Mervyn LeRoy.

Reagan congratulated LeRoy on his casting of Turner in *They Won't Forget.*

"Lana signed a contract just four days after she turned sixteen," LeRoy claimed.

For some reason, perhaps because he was overstocked at the time with beautiful young women, Reagan had been somewhat reluctant to date Lana. He asked a publicist at Warners, "Do I have to go to the premiere of *Jezebel*?"

"No, but you'll be hanging out a lot longer at Warners if you do," the publicist had responded.

From the bedroom of her apartment, Lana emerged looking dazzling in a white gown borrowed from the wardrobe department. Reagan looked stunned when introduced. He finally said, "You're the most beautiful gal I've ever seen."

"You're not bad yourself, buster," she replied.

After she kissed LeRoy goodbye, she headed out the door with Reagan.

Years later, in the Polo Lounge of the Beverly Hills Hotel, Lana recalled her first date with Reagan to author Darwin Porter. "He said I was the most beautiful girl he'd ever seen, but he was not the best looking man I'd ever seen. I mean, he was handsome but not a beauty contest winner. I found him very appealing, with the most wonderful manners, and he knew how to treat a lady. He made me feel grown up even though I was only a teenager."

He complimented her on *They Won't Forget.*

"Oh, please," she said. "Don't bring that up. I'm still embarrassed. My mother, Mildred Turner, told me I move with coltish grace, sinuously, undulating. But all I saw on that screen was those jiggling jugs of mine."

Reagan had hailed a taxi to take her to the theater, because he felt that his own car was too battered to show up at a premiere with such a glamorous star.

"I hear that *Jezebel* is an unashamed rip-off of *Gone With the Wind*, even though Selznick's movie hasn't yet been

In his early days at Warner Brothers, Ronald Reagan was always willing to pose for what is now known as "beefcake photos," as opposed to cheesecake.

His lean, thin chest would not be considered developed by the "gym rat" standards of today, but he was flattered when a female reporter gushed, "the beautiful long legs of Ronald Reagan make him the male equivalent of the celebrated legs of Betty Grable."

released," he said.

"Like everyone else, I read *Gone With the Wind*, but I know I could never play Scarlett," she said to him. "It isn't right for me."

Before arriving at the premiere, she turned to Reagan and gripped his hand. "I'm afraid! All eyes will be on us. Deep down, I'm still a frightened little girl. But when that car door opens, I'll try to camouflage my insecurities by throwing my head up high in the air and walking along the red carpet like I own Tinseltown."

At the theater, a pedestrian walkway had been built above the roaring traffic of the boulevard in front. A reporter for *The New York Times* later wrote that "Lana Turner on the arm of Ronald Reagan made a dazzling appearance crossing the bridge of stars, even though they aren't stars yet. Klieg lights brightened the night sky over Hollywood, as hundreds of fans showed up."

After the premiere, where the night and most of its credits belonged to Bette Davis, Reagan invited Lana to dinner. He was happily surprised that she enjoyed the same type of food that he did: Hot dogs, macaroni and cheese, barbecued ribs, and spaghetti with meatballs.

When their food was served, she removed a bottle of chili peppers from her purse. She sprinkled it over the ribs, telling him that she was convinced that it removed toxins from one's body.

What happened after dinner has grown hazy in Hollywood lore, with various versions repeated, most of them inaccurate.

On the golf course the following Sunday, Reagan confided to Dick Powell that, "Lana is just as oversexed as I am. I spent the night with her after seeing *Jezebel*, and I hope it'll be the beginning of many more nights to come. I've got to slip around, though, because I don't want Susan Hayward to find out."

Edmund Morris, Reagan's official biographer, noted, "Dutch was not yet a one-girl guy. He was soon seen squiring dishy Lana Turner around town, joking that he 'wasn't acting' in her company."

His pursuit of Lana was made easier when Warners publicity department asked them to pose for pictures together for distribution nationwide.

"Lana and I did whatever the studio wanted us to do," Reagan later said. "Put on our clothes, take off our clothes. Susan would kill me if she ever heard me say this, but Lana looks hotter in a bathing suit than she does."

Late one morning, Reagan, in his battered car, drove Lana to the Warners ranch outside Los Angeles, where they would be photographed together in riding costumes. An expert horseman, he taught her how to ride.

That night, back at her apartment, she cooked a meal for him, filet mignon coated with cracked peppercorns, lots of salt, and mustard. He was no longer surprised when she sprinkled hot sauce over it. "Too much sauce gives me the runs," he said. "You must have a cast-iron stomach." He also noted that she was "the world's slowest eater, chomping down on a piece of steak for at least fifteen minutes before swallowing it."

News of the Reagan/Turner affair eventually reached Wayne Morris at Warners. One afternoon, he confronted Reagan in the commissary. "What is this shit about you moving in on Lana? Before you, I was taking advantage of the big crush she had on me."

"Isn't Priscilla Lane enough for you?" Reagan said.

"Isn't Susan Hayward enough for you?" Morris asked.

"*Touché*," Reagan answered.

In her memoirs, *Lana—The Lady, The Legend, The Truth*, she was discreet. She did recall posing for pictures with Reagan, defining him as "a nice young man," but provided no other insights.

In his memoirs, Reagan didn't even mention her.

***

A friendly young reporter from Des Moines visited Reagan at Warners. He had seen pictures of him posing with Lana, and he asked what it was like for a local boy to find himself dating glamour queens.

"Miss Turner is an actress of natural beauty that gets worked over by the studio makeup department that creates a make-believe character for her. She is very down to earth, kind and considerate. Young girls across America, so I'm told, are trying to imitate her. Of course, Hollywood publicists like to rewrite her story. If a girl gets a high school diploma, it suddenly appears in print that she's got a doctorate. If she spends all Saturday afternoon in the beauty parlor, that isn't talked about. Magazines and newspapers print that she spends all her spare time helping homeless refugees from Europe."

Reagan would have more or less agreed with Patrick Agan's conclusion in *The Decline and Fall of the Love Goddesses*. "To millions, the Love Goddesses were surrogate mistresses, ladies of incredible beauty who afford at least a visual satisfaction that men were able to indulge in even in the company of their wives. The Love Goddesses were an inspiration, Everests of glamour for both men and women."

In the 1980s, after Reagan had been elected to the Oval Office, author Darwin Porter met with Lana in the Polo Lounge of the Beverly Hills Hotel. "Now that Ronnie is President, the press is always asking me about my former relationship with him," she said. "Somebody wrote that I didn't even remember dating him— that is pure crap! Of course, I remembered him. I've even been asked to describe what kind of lover he is. I'll never tell, but I'll give you a hint. He's a man who likes to take his time, unlike another future President of the United States I used to know."

"I liked Ronnie right from the beginning, and we became friends. Later, I got to know Nancy Davis when she was a starlet at MGM. After she married Ronnie, I visited their home on many occasions."

"I recall one very formal party I attended with Ronnie in the mid-50s," she said. "I was still trying to hold onto my beauty, but for the first time, I realized that he'd lost his looks. His face had aged a lot. That Midwestern farm boy appeal of his had faded with my romance with Artie Shaw. He still had that beautiful head of hair, perhaps dyed, but he had begun to look the way he did when he was governor of California."

"I liked Nancy, but detested Jane Wyman," Lana continued. "I first met her when we were both starlets at Warners. Later, for the 1982-83 season, I appeared with her on TV in *Falcon Crest*. After an initial introduction and a chat, she didn't even speak to me. She always resented my beauty. Not only that, but she learned that I had dated Reagan before she did. She was one icy cold bitch."

***

Lana's biggest disappointment was the loss of a role in the 1939 MGM comedy-drama, *Idiot's Delight,* starring Clark Gable and Norma Shearer, the reigning King and Queen at Metro. The film was released the same year that Gable portrayed Rhett Butler in *Gone With the Wind* (1939).

Even though she was no great dancer, Lana was to play one of the girls traveling with Harry Van's *Les Blondes Troupe of Dancers.* Gable was cast as Harry Van, and he even dances himself in one of the scenes.

Three days before she was to report for filming, Lana collapsed at her home, complaining of excruciating pain. Mildred immediately called an ambulance, which rushed her to the nearest hospital. After extensive examinations, doctors determined that she needed surgery for the removal of scar tissue from her ovaries and colon. The scars had resulted from a botched appendectomy she had endured when she was fourteen.

A rumor was spread that Carole Lombard had been the force behind getting Lana fired from *Idiot's Delight* because she'd come on seductively to Gable.

She was surprised when a studio delivery boy arrived with a note from Gable himself. "Too bad, kid. A bad break. But chin up. I've got this gut feeling that one day, sooner than later, you are going to be my leading lady."

The King of Hollywood turned out to be a prophet.

***

Olivia de Havilland introduced Lana to Errol Flynn right before lunch in the Warner commissary. A romantic adventurer both on and off the screen, he was known in Hollywood as a "swordsman," the ultimate sexual athlete and the seducer of countless women. He was a handsome, devilish, demi-god, a survivor of bar room brawls, exotic drugs, sex orgies, and scandal.

He invited her to his dressing room after rather gallantly kissing her hand. Once inside, he kissed more than her hand.

"Suddenly, I had two feet of tongue down my throat, and something like steel pressing hard against me," she later confided to Carole Landis.

"Been there, done that,"

Flynn had urgently wanted to continue, but there was a knock on the door. It was Michael Curtiz, who demanded an emergency conference with Flynn. He broke away from Lana, but only after she'd accepted an invitation to go swimming that Saturday afternoon in his pool.

Right before she left, he took her arm. "Just how old are you?" he asked.

"Fifteen."

Actually, she was sixteen, but she'd been told that Flynn liked to seduce fifteen-year-old girls.

She would recall that afternoon, not only to Ann Rutherford and Bonita

48

Granville, but to other girlfriends of the future, including Ava Gardner.

"I had changed into this peach-colored, one-piece bathing suit," she said. "My feet were dangling in the water. But I didn't want to go in and get my hair all messed up. I thought he'd gone to change into his suit, but when he came onto the patio, he was completely nude. I didn't at that time have much basis of comparison, but his manhood looked impressive to me."

"Before I knew it, he pushed me in the water and was kissing me and feeling north, south, east, and west. He could really arouse passion, even in the water. Before long, we were out of the pool, and I was getting seduced by the world's expert. Before the night ended, he'd made love to me three times. Hell with Greg Bautzer!"

On their second date, he invited her to go to Mexico for a long weekend. He spoke of the bullfights, the endless rounds of tequila in the cantinas, the fishing, the boating, the swimming, the love-making. She turned him down, but agreed to go away with him the following weekend, sailing to the island of Catalina when she heard that other men and women would be on board.

On her next visit to his dressing room, on the set of *Four's a Crowd*, he offered her some bourbon for lunch, but she said no. "You're just like Ronald Reagan," he said. "He was in here yesterday. He accepted some bourbon from me, but dumped it in my cuspidor when I went to take a piss."

He gently touched her arm. "At the feel of a girl's arm, I get all fired up, old girl. I know I have to go as far as she'll let me. Please let me. I don't want to have to force you, since I'm so much bigger than you are."

"That you are," she said. "I might as well say yes, because you'd overpower me if I didn't."

"How right you are, old girl!" he answered.

"And you can dispense with the old girl thing," she chastised him.

As she later told Landis, "As you know, Errol is a demon in bed. I'd never had oral sex performed on me until he came along. He also told me that he hated being a phallic symbol for the world. Most men I've dated want to feel my breasts. Not Errol. He's different. He told me he's a leg man. He said, 'How can you make love to a breast?'"

"Hell with that!" Landis said. "Men can make lots of love to a woman's breasts. Do a lot of things."

Errol Flynn and Lana Turner never got to make a movie together, although all their friends said that as a pair, they would "sizzle" on the screen. However, in 1942, CBS hired them for the radio dramatization of *Mr. and Mrs. Smith* for the Screen Guild Players.

***

The sail to Catalina aboard Errol Flynn's luxurious yacht, *Sirocco,* marked Lana's introduction at a tender age into the world of Hollywood decadence.

For the cruise, he'd gathered together several members of his private club, the *Olympiads,* a society of heavy drinkers who included his co-star and sometimes lover, Patric Knowles, along with actor William Lundigan (another sometimes lover), Bruce Cabot, and Alan Hale, who had appeared with Lana in *The Adventures of Marco Polo.*

The group was anti-Semitic, and had turned down a membership bid from Edward G. Robinson. On rare occasions, Errol's close friend, John Barrymore, was a member of the Olympiads; also Alan Mowbray and W.C. Fields.

Other founding members included Grant Mitchell and the author, Gene Fowler, who would later write *Good Night, Sweet Prince,* the biography of Barrymore.

Aboard the *Sirocco,* there were six other young aspirant actresses in addition to Lana. Each of the female guests shared a large communal cabin filled with bunk beds, with the understanding that they'd be housed there until they were summoned to the various cabins of the male passengers.

There was a seemingly endless supply of cocaine and booze. In her dialogues with the other young women, Lana surmised that each of them knew what was expected of them. As captain, Errol had first choice, but for this trip, he seduced only Lana among the girls, and only Knowles and Lundigan among the men.

On one moonlit night, Flynn opened up to Lana about his adventures as a young man, referring to the months he lived in New Guineau, where he'd cut an imposing figure in a pith helmet and walking cane. "I had so many adventures. Of course, there were poisoned arrows to deal with, along with malaria, leeches, and cannibals. Inevitably, my buddies and I got gonorrhea. Those bordellos were wretched hellholes."

He also spoke about the years he'd spent in England, where he became interested in acting. "It was tough going. I arrived with two shillings in my pocket. I was on the stage in Northampton, where the boots are made. In *Jack and the Beanstalk,* I played the wicked prince."

"One thing led to another, and a talent scout from Warners discovered me. I sailed to New York in November of 1934 aboard the *SS*

Errol Flynn, looking macho and virile in *The Charge of the Light Brigade* (1936) and, below, in *The Perfect Specimen* (1937). "He was a devil-may-care ladykiller both on and off the screen," Lana claimed.

50

Paris."

"In New York, I asked this Warners' publicity agent to take me to Harlem. I wanted to see Harlem more than any other place. In this seedy dance club, I met this exotic beauty, a real African princess—or so I thought. I quickly slipped away with her to a darkened part of the balcony, looking forward to some really hot action. But within minutes, I discovered that 'she' was a 'he,' but I was too far gone then to protest. Surely, she had the most talented throat in all of Harlem."

After the cruise, back in Hollywood, Lana supplied very few details about what actually happened during that long weekend in Catalina. "It was total debauchery, with nothing off limits, not my scene at all. I was too well bred as a young lady for some of the stuff going on. People, I learned, go crazy snorting cocaine."

"At times, when he was sober, I realized that Errol was not only attractive and charming but well read. He was far more intelligent than the rest of the crew and could even talk about Shakespeare, stuff like that. He had read everything Rudyard Kipling had ever written."

"Unlike nearly all actors I would meet in the future, he was not ambition-crazed. He believed that a man should live for the moment and let tomorrow take care of itself."

"His drinking, or so I feared, would lead to his self-destruction, but he brushed aside my concerns. I told him he should lay of the booze at least until sunset."

He answered, "Look at it this way. By starting to drink early in the morning, I'll have a head up over the other blokes. For me, I will be ready for party time all day long and into the night. I don't want to be a sucker who goes to his grave without ever having lived."

***

The call came in right before midnight on a Tuesday. It was from Mervyn LeRoy with big news.

"I've just returned from the home of Louis B. Mayer. He made me an offer I can't refuse. Six thousand dollars a week. A salary like that is almost unheard of."

"Wow!" she said. "That sounds great. Can I go with you?"

"As my discovery, you're part of the deal. Mayer knows about you and, unlike Jack Warner, he thinks you have potential star power."

"That's terrific," she said. "MGM has my favorite male stars, Clark Gable and Robert Taylor."

"I got a salary increase for you. A hundred big ones a week."

"That's a lot of money."

"There may be problems," he said. "Mayer will want you to give him a blow-job, and your first picture will be with that runt, Mickey Rooney, and you'll have to fight that midget off."

"Don't worry," she said. "After Greg Bautzer and Errol Flynn, I sure know how to handle men."

51

Starlet Lana Turner arrived on the lot of Metro-Goldwyn-Mayer, little knowing that within months, she would reign as its queen.

Damn You, Scarlett O'Hara

Mickey Rooney (aka Andy Hardy) Knocks Up Lana Turner

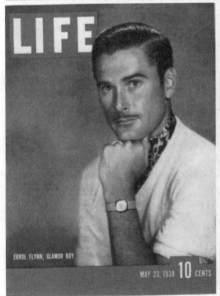

It seemed inevitable that the actor hailed as "Hollywood's most glamorous male star" and Lana Turner, heralded as its "most glamorous female star" would come together (no pun intended).

Later in his short life (1909-1959), Errol Flynn claimed he'd seduced from 12,000 to 14,000 "people." He racked up that number by having sex with four or five at once, often in his dressing room while filming.

Lana never made siuch a claim for herself, perhaps settling for 150 conquests.

Hardened to some degree after her inaugural stint at Warner Brothers, Lana Turner arrived, upbeat and enthusiastic, at the gates of Metro-Goldwyn-Mayer, the "Tiffany of Movie Studios." It was home to such superstars as Clark Gable, Greta

Garbo, Joan Crawford, Norma Shearer, Spencer Tracy, John and Lionel Barrymore, Hedy Lamarr, and that nightingale, Jeanette MacDonald. In time, it would develop, nurture, and promote such future stars as Grace Kelly, Elizabeth Taylor, Judy Garland, Ava Gardner, and Esther Williams.

It would be at MGM that Lana set out on the road to worldwide fame and glory. It would be from a base within MGM that she'd become a benchmark for Hollywood glamor during the war years when American GIs made her one of their most desired pin-up girls.

Although in years to come, snobby film critics would deride her acting, her presence on the screen was electrifying.

As she emerged as a rising star at MGM, young women across America were already padding their bras in imitation of her "Sweater Girl" look from *They Won't Forget.*

Twelve days after turning seventeen on February 20, 1938, she signed with MGM. On her first day at the studio, Mervyn LeRoy told her that her debut picture would be *Love Finds Andy Hardy*, in which she would co-star with two future legends, Mickey Rooney and Judy Garland, the two most talented young performers in Hollywood.

Enabled by her new $100-a-week paycheck, Lana and Mildred moved into a rented house on Kirkwood Drive, high up Laurel Canyon. Built on the side of a mountain the house was reached after a climb of seventeen steps. Each of the women had a bedroom of her own, and there was also a separate bedroom for guests, and a working, marble-framed fireplace in the living room.

Lana wanted all the furnishings and walls to be in white. Sprawled before the fireplace was a white bearskin rug still attached to the animal's skull, still with its ferocious teeth, the furry face of the bear trapped in its death agony.

With her new riches, she put a down payment on a fire-engine red roadster. "The car attracts attention from guys," she said. "Then they take in who's behind the wheel. I'll even give a good-looking guy a lift from time to time, so to speak."

As her time became increasingly monopolized by MGM, Lana dropped out of Hollywood High and enrolled in the studio's Little Red Schoolhouse, where she would eventually earn her high school diploma. Under the supervision of a state-approved teacher, Mary MacDonald, she often did her homework right on the set of whatever movie was being filmed at the time.

In the classroom, she sat next to Mickey Rooney, the star of her next movie. As he wrote, "I assumed full gazing rights. The teacher often caught me in fervent contemplation of Lana's bosom and other parts, enough so that I was often called out."

"Lana's body said it all," Rooney continued, "and I got the message loud and clear. Her auburn hair, her deep green eyes, her long lashes, the tip of her nose, her pouty lips, her graceful throat, the curve of her shoulders, her tiny waist, and, yes, the nicest knockers I'd ever seen."

Her fellow pupils included Jackie Cooper, whom she'd previously dated, and Ann Rutherford, one of her best friends and confidantes, especially when it came to gossiping about boys.

Of all the students, London-born Freddie Bartholomew was the most polite and sensitive, the ultimate *Little Lord Fauntleroy*, the title of his hit movie. Three years younger than Lana, he shocked her when he asked her out on a date. He assured her that he would not seduce her, and that he had something else in mind.

"I want to suck your toes, give tender loving care to them from the big toe to the little toe. I can suck toes for hours."

Ever so politely, she turned him down.

She was always asking MacDonald if she could be excused to go to the bathroom. "The teachers must have thought I had weak kidneys. Exactly what I was doing was having a quick smoke outside the courtyard. From my teenage years and on, I was almost a chain smoker."

During her first week as an MGM starlet, she met the studio's greatest star, Greta Garbo, at an afternoon tea hosted at the home of Mervyn LeRoy. She was astonished to find the great Garbo sitting alone in a corner of the living room.

"I was too intimidated to go over and speak to her, but I kept staring at her," Lana said. "I was wearing a white sweater that showed off my tits, and my bosom was repeatedly noticed by Miss Garbo. I felt she was undressing me with her eyes. In spite of her affair with John Gilbert, MGM buzzed with rumors that she was a lesbian. With that penetrating Garbo gaze, I believed she was."

Back at the schoolhouse, she finally decided to accept Rooney's barrage of invitations for a hot date. "He wasn't really my type. But since he was becoming the biggest box office attraction at MGM, and was the star of my next picture, I finally gave in to him, even though I prefer men at least six feet tall. I just hoped he wasn't small all over."

When Lana first met the young British actor, Freddie Bartholomew, she found him "polite and sensitive, almost like a character in a Charles Dickens novel." That is, until she got to know him. "I learned his favorite form of sex was toe-sucking. He said that while George Cukor directed him in *David Copperfield* (1935), "I made him suck my toes for about an hour before I'd let him suck anything else."

In the photo above, Bartholomew appears as the 12-year-old juvenile lead in *Little Lord Fauntleroy* (1936).

In his memoirs, Rooney wrote, "I soon found out that Lana was as oversexed as I was, warm, passionate, soft, and moist in interesting places."

He claimed that together, in the front seats of his convertible, parked high on Mulholland Drive, he could make her breathless.

Thus began a series of seductions that would have dire consequences.

As Lana was soon to find out, the real Mickey Rooney was very different from his on-screen portrayals of the relatively innocent All-American Andy Hardy. As authors Richard Lertzman and William Birnes described the star in their biography, *The Life and Times of Mickey Rooney,* he could be abrasive and vulgar.

"He would brag to anyone within earshot about his masculine prowess and the girls with whom he'd had sexual relations. He was on a tear, and the people he boasted to were shocked by the crude way he spoke. His close friends, however, were amused by his frankness and brand of *braggadocio* too soon a man in the body of a child, now boozing, chasing women with fervor, and cursing like a stagehand in burlesque, as his hormones and lack of impulse took over."

It didn't take long before both Lana and Rooney became Party Girl #1 and Party Boy #1 in Hollywood, where the competition was stiff.

During her first weeks at MGM, Lana began affairs with Rooney, and with many other men, too.

She also evolved into the leader of a separate clique of young, soon-to-be stars. Chief among them was Robert Stack, with whom she would begin an on-again, off-again affair that stretched over many a year. Jackie Cooper, whom she'd once dated, was part of her circle of friends, as were three beautiful starlets: Gene Tierney, Ann Rutherford, and Linda Darnell.

Their favorite restaurant was the Beverly Hills Tropics. After Lana appeared on the cover of *Life* magazine, management even named a lethal drink after her. It was called "Lana Untamed."

Choreographer Jack Cole, who knew Lana during her early days at MGM, gave a blunt assessment. "She really liked men a lot. She just liked to fuck a lot."

With an exception here and there, she preferred good-looking men with exceptional endowments. "I liked the boys, and they liked me. The gal who denies that men are exciting is either a lady with no corpuscles or a statue," she said. "It's the physical that attracts at first. If you get to know a man's heart and soul, call it icing on the cake."

Pint-sized Mickey Rooney stumbles into *Love Finds Andy Hardy* (1938) when he was cast opposite two rising stars, Lana Turner and Judy Garland. More than 200 starlets were interviewed for the role of the erratic, feather-brained vamp of Carvel High.

Lana won out. On screen, Rooney didn't seduce her. Off-screen was a different matter. "To my regret, I found out that Mickey didn't practice safe sex."

All this gossip and press attention about both Lana, Rooney, and their wild escapades were bound to come to the attention of MGM mogul, Louis B. Mayer. One afternoon, when they weren't needed on the set, he ordered both of his young stars into his office.

Mayer had recently learned

that in addition to Lana and countless other conquests, Rooney, age sixteen, was having an affair with Norma Shearer, the 36-year-old former Queen of MGM, and the widow of Irving Thalberg, Mayer's former right-hand man.

"You're Andy Hardy!" Mayer shouted at Rooney. "You're the United States! You're the Stars and Stripes! Behave yourself! You're a symbol!"

"As for you, Lana, you seem interested in only one thing," He stood up from his desk and grabbed his crotch. "That's what you seem to want from any man you meet. You're getting a bad reputation. At the rate you're going, you'll soon be pregnant. If both of you continue as you're doing, your days at MGM may be numbered."

Mayer desperately wanted Rooney's Andy Hardy pictures to represent a wholesome (fantasy-based) interpretation of the American family, "even though I've got three young whores in the lead roles." He was, of course, referring to Lana, Rooney, and Judy Garland.

"I want Judge Hardy, the patriarch of the family, to be a paragon of wisdom and fatherly virtue," said Mayer. "I want Andy to be not too serious, but filled with energy, a wholesome boy who is charming and engaging and always willing to turn to Judge Stone for advice when he gets into a jam. Andy Hardy movies should stand for God, Motherhood, Respect for one's father, and apple pie."

The young stars were directed in the series by George B. Seitz, a Boston-bred playwright, screenwriter, and film actor born in 1888. He'd helmed his first movie, *Perils of Pauline*, back in 1914. At this point in his career, he was deeply familiar with Rooney's antics.

When Lana met him, she was surprised by his odd style of dress. He wore a blue suit with yellow accessories that included his tie, shirt, and gloves. His head was crowned with a wide-brimmed Panama hat, and he also wore purple socks and yellow shoes with chartreuse shoelaces.

"I know this is supposed to be wholesome fare," Lana said to him. "But how sexy am I to be?"

"Just be yourself. You couldn't look anything but sexy."

At home, Mildred joined in attempts to get Lana to cut back on her heavy partying, but to no avail. All that Lana had to do was to curtly inform her mother that she was now the breadwinner of the family for the

During the filming of the Andy Hardy movie, Lana's private life became the subject of gossip, even in the press. Louella Parsons "scolded" her in her column. "If Lana Turner will behave herself and not go completely berserk, she is headed to a top spot in motion pictures."

pressure to stop.

Feeling that he needed reinforcement, Mayer also summoned Mildred to his office. "Your daughter comes on like a romantic teenager and then turns into a feverish, passionate tiger who can't get enough. She's only seventeen, and reporters are calling her the Queen of the Night. This is hardly the clean, all-American image that we promote at MGM in our pictures. We abide by the rules that society dictates. If some jailbait like Lana gets knocked up, she might be shown the door. Do you understand me?"

***

Cast as Cynthia Parker, the small town flirt in *Love Finds Andy Hardy*, Lana plays the *ingénue* who tempts and tangles with Andy. She wants to kiss him, but he already has a girlfriend, Polly Benedict, as portrayed by Ann Rutherford.

Andy's attempt to resist Cecilia causes him to question his own masculinity. He turns to his father, Judge Hardy (Lewis Stone). "D'ya think there's anything wrong with a guy that don't want a girl to kiss him all the time?" Andy asks.

A very young Judy Garland plays Betsy Booth, the helpful (and romantically available) girl next door. Befriending Andy, she sympathizes with his problems. At the prom, as the film's musical climax, she's persuaded to sing three jazzy numbers, winning the hearts, once again, of Judy fans on and off the screen.

Rooney later claimed that Judy was terribly jealous of Lana's beauty.

Lana felt at ease in the role of "that red-headed vampire. "I was a juvenile *femme fatale*. I'd rather kiss than *kibbutz*."

One writer observed that during the course of the film [Love Finds Andy Hardy *was selected for preservation in the United States National Film Registry by the Library of Congress as being "culturally, historically, or aesthetically significant"*] "Garland sang, Rooney mugged, and Stone pontificated, while Lana was whining, pouting, dimpling, and winking."

By now, Lana was skilled at evaluating camera angles, making her almost as adept as Joan Crawford. "I taught her what I knew about acting, and she was a fast learner," Rooney said to Busby Berkeley. "Privately, I taught her how to make love to a man's balls." She'd never done that before. And, as the Mexicans say, I've got a big pair of *cojones* in spite of my small size."

The kissing scenes between Rooney and Lana, as innocuous as they might be, encountered some minor trouble from movie censors. Rooney denounced "These blue noses. Lana and I were like a couple of aging virgins. The scenes were left in the final cut and appear harmless today."

At the end of the film, Lana suggested a title change. "Call it *Andy Hardy With a Hard-On*."

***

Lana's long friendship with Judy Garland, which over the years would wax and wane both hot and cold, began on the set of *Love Finds Andy Hardy*.

The friendship had hardly begun when both of them embarked on the pursuit of Artie Shaw, each of the young starlets wanting to marry the dashing bandleader.

When Garland and Lana first bonded, Judy said, "You and I have something in common. From what I hear, each of us lost our virginity at age fifteen. Word gets around."

The same could be said of Rooney. "We were just teenagers, but Lana, Judy and I were doing what comes naturally."

Gossip was also spread that Garland and Rooney were having an affair. "At least that's what the gossip columns of that day reported. They keep saying that about Mickey and me," Garland said. "They must have me mixed up with Lana. The gossip upsets me, it really does, because there's not a bit of truth in it. Mickey and I are swell friends, and he's full of fun. I enjoy working with him and playing with him. Outside the studio, we rarely see each other. We're pals—that's all!"

***

One day, Lana abruptly ended her affair with Rooney. "It's been great," she told him. "You're a lot of fun. But it's time to move on."

He later revealed, "At the time, I thought she'd outgrown me and wanted other guys like Greg Bautzer. But months later, at a fund raiser, I ran into her, and she told me the truth."

"Do you know you put me in a family way?" she asked, referring in modest terms to her pregnancy.

"I was stunned," Rooney said. "She never told me at the time. Had she done so, I might have insisted she have our kid. Of course, aborting the child made sense. It protected our careers and, besides, we were just children ourselves."

He later learned that Eddie Mannix, known as "The Fixer" at MGM, had arranged for Lana's abortion through the studio doctor, Edward Jones. Previously, Mannix had warned Mayer that Rooney was "a loaded gun ready to go off."

"Eddie worked in publicity for the studio," Mervyn LeRoy said. "Most of his job involved suppressing scandal. He even covered up crimes such as murder. He kept the secrets of the stars, even protecting our beloved but pregnant Lana."

Howard Strickling, one of the directors of MGM's Publicity Department, said, "Our job was to publicize our new stars. But both Lana and Mickey were their own self-generating publicity machine. As time went by, our main job with them was to keep their names out of the gossip columns."

In 1991, when Rooney published his autobiography, *Life Is Too Short,* he revealed for the first time that Lana had aborted their child many decades before. She was furious, and at one point called her lawyer to suggest a lawsuit for libel. He wisely advised her not to sue.

When Rooney heard of her denial, he said, "Of course, she denied it. Why not? I would expect no less of her. But I stand by my story."

"All I can say is that if it didn't happen, it was the most beautiful, the most realistic, dream I ever had. MGM gals in those days were taught to deny any scandals."

***

One night, Errol Flynn phoned Lana, finding her at home for a change and not out night-clubbing. He told her he'd been cast in the most exciting role of his career, and that his new film included "the greatest role for a young woman I've ever read."

"I can just see us on the marquee, "Errol Flynn as Rhett Butler and Lana Turner as Scarlett O'Hara in *Gone With the Wind.*"

The characters were the creation of the genteel Southern novelist Margaret Mitchell, who had written *Gone With the Wind*. Published in 1936, and set in Georgia during the American Civil War and its Reconstruction Era, it became a million copy bestseller.

Confronted with that kind of temptation, Lana quickly acquiesced. After climbing into her red roadster, she drove to Flynn's home on a mountainside to read two or three scenes with him that he'd selected from the novel.

During the first hour, Flynn carried through with his promise, reading scenes with her from the book. He told her that not only would Rhett Butler be his greatest role, but that if she got cast as Scarlett, it might be the apex of her career, with perhaps a Best Actress Oscar looming in her future. "The role could immortalize you and make you one of the biggest stars in Hollywood."

It was long past midnight when he launched into a pivotal scene in which Rhett Butler takes Scarlett in his arms and carries her to the bedroom, perhaps to rape her if she refuses his advances. Whereas, based on the censorship standards of that era, the actual seduction scene could not be filmed, Scarlett would be depicted the next morning waking up fully relaxed and with a satisfied smile.

"Let's go for it," she said, perhaps surprising him with her directness.

Consequently, he hauled her off to a large bed, suitable for an orgy with six or seven participants, the scene of at least a thousand prior conquests.

As Lana later described to Linda Darnell, Flynn, living up to his reputation, turned out to be a talented, virile lover. He'd seduced her before, beside his swimming pool and on Catalina. The difference this time was that he rubbed cocaine on the tip of his penis.

According to Lana, as filtered later through Darnell, "If I had any complaint at all, it was that

Of the many photographs snapped of Errol Flynn, dressed or undressed, this snapshot was his favorite. He had only one complaint: "It doesn't show my most celebrated asset.

Lana found out what that was when they had "rehearsals" together for the rape scene depicted in *Gone With the Wind*

Errol, in the heat of passion, likes to exchange a lot of saliva."

Evoking the heroine in Mitchell's novel, Lana woke up the next morning, alone in Flynn's bed, with a smile on her face. He had truly satisfied her.

Donning one of his terrycloth bathrobes, she wandered down to his pool where she found him swimming nude. Dropping the robe, she dived in with him. "We made love underwater," she later informed Joan Blondell.

Nearly two years would pass before Lana learned that while Errol was making love to her, their interchanges were observed by his two "fuck buddies," David Niven and Bruce Cabot. In his bedroom, he had installed a two-way mirror, and they were silently positioned within the darkened space on the other side.

***

The next day, Lana began to read Margaret Mitchell's saga. "As I read and read, I had a hard time seeing myself as a drapery-wearing, Yankee soldier killer, and 'fiddle-dee-dee' type of bitchy Southern heroine."

She was even more put off when she read *Time* magazine's assessment of what kind of actress was needed to play Scarlett. "She has to be tempestuous, intense, scheming, and case hardened, with diamond dust in her voice, bug eyes lit with cold blue glitter, and as wide a dramatic range as any cinema-actress in the business."

"That might be Bette Davis, but not me," Lana said.

That afternoon, Lana read in Louella Parsons' column that Jack Warner wanted Davis and Errol Flynn for the roles. "That devil tricked me," she told Blondell, who had made *The Perfect Specimen* (1937) with Flynn. "He knew I wasn't even being considered."

"But if he'd called you over without that temptation of a role, you would have gone anyway, right?"

"I hate to admit it, but it's true," Lana said. "Day or night, rain or shine, when Errol calls, Lana will come running."

In the weeks ahead, she followed news associated with *Gone With the Wind*. Jack Warner had allowed his option to lapse, and subsequently, producer David O. Selznick had picked up the film rights from Mitchell for only $50,000.

Gable was hauling in 2,400 fan letters a week, and most of his women fans demanded that Selznick cast him as Rhett Butler. Louis B. Mayer, Selznick's father-in-law, at least for the moment, had rejected any immediate and direct involvement with *Gone With the Wind*. "I don't think the public will flock to see a picture about the Civil War." But with the book's massive sales, he changed his mind.

Warner seemed upset that he'd let his option lapse. In an attempt to at least benefit in some way from the growing buzz about the film, he offered Selznick a package of two of his biggest stars, Davis and Flynn. As pre-released buzz increased, Mayer reminded Selznick that the public was demanding Gable for the role. "I'll give you Gable if you'll give me distribution rights."

Selznick already had a deal with United Artists to distribute his films, so, after rejecting Mayer's distribution proposal, he contacted Samuel Goldwyn and asked him if he could spare Gary Cooper for the role of Rhett Butler.

Although every actor or actress under the age of 40 in Hollywood seemed desperate for the lead roles, Cooper wasn't impressed. He didn't want to play Rhett Butler. Subsequently, he sent a memo to Selznick. "I think *Gone With the Wind* will be the biggest flop in the history of Hollywood. I'm just glad it'll be Clark Gable who's falling flat on his face—and not Gary Cooper."

Eventually, Selznick got Gable to sign on the dotted line, only to learn that his lover, Carole Lombard, had her heart set on playing Scarlett.

The producer decided to launch the greatest talent search in the history of Hollywood for the perfect newcomer who could play Mitchell's heroine.

The nationwide search to play Scarlett led to some 1,400 wannabee actresses, most of them Southern, to be interviewed. He found none of them suitable, but enjoyed the national publicity his stunt provided.

After searching for young

As the world knows, Gable as Rhett Butler and Lana as Scarlett O'Hara never got to co-star in *Gone With the Wind.*

This photo, taken on the set of their 1941 movie, *Honky Tonk*, showed what they might have looked like as Rhett and Scarlett.

women across the country to play Scarlett, he turned to established actresses. He was receiving dozens of letters demanding that he award the role to Tallulah Bankhead, a true Southern belle from Alabama.

George Cukor, named as the director of the picture, was a friend of Tallulah's. He made three tests of her as Scarlett, the first two in black and white, the latter in Technicolor. "In color, Tallulah looked a fright," he said.

The choices narrowed. Among the finalists was Paulette Goddard. Selznick considered her ideal in many ways, but he didn't want any scandal connected to his multi-million dollar picture. Goddard was living with Charlie Chaplin at the time and claiming to be his wife. Selznick demanded that she produce a marriage license, and she failed to do so. Consequently, he did not award her with the part.

Almost as an afterthought, Lana was ordered by MGM to make a screen test, with the understanding that it would be directed by Cukor, who had been named director of *Gone With the Wind.* He would later be fired.

Lana had already portrayed a Southern girl in her debut movie, *They Won't Forget,* but that hardly meant that she would be suitable for the role of Scarlett. Nevertheless, she bravely moved forward with the test.

She met Melvyn Douglas, who had agreed to a screen test in which he'd portray Ashley Wilkes, a part he coveted. With Lana, he wanted to show Cukor that he would be the ideal Ashley, knowing that the British actor, Leslie Howard, was also under consideration, although he didn't seem to want the role.

"Lana had none of the fire and intensity of Scarlett," Cukor said, after directing Douglas and her. "This cute blonde from Idaho had a horribly fake Southern accent, and there was absolutely no chemistry between Douglas and her."

Selznick viewed Lana's test and agreed with Cukor. As later stated in one of his many memos: "Miss Turner has absolutely no conception of who Scarlett O'Hara is."

***

In this rare photograph, Lana is seen trying to perform as Scarlett O'Hara opposite veteran actor Melvyn Douglas. George Cukor tested her for the role, with Douglas hoping to co-star as Ashley Wilkes.

"The test was dismal," Cukor said. "Lana was no Scarlett, and she knew it."

"Lana, dear," came the screen-familiar voice of Joan Crawford. "I'm extending a sudden invitation for a *tête-á-tête* for you and me at my home in Brentwood. Would you drive over to see me? I have something very important to discuss with you. It's very personal."

Lana agreed and after transforming her face with makeup and slipping on her most expensive and stylish day dress, she got into her roadster and drove to Crawford's immaculate house, a building as well-groomed as its occupant.

Like herself, Crawford preferred an all-white living room. "Please take off your shoes, darling," she told Lana. "The carpet is snow white, and shoes are just too dirty."

Then she fussed over Lana, making sure she was totally comfortable before bringing her a cup of tea and just one small cookie on a pink napkin embroidered with the initials "JC."

"Now let's get down to business," Crawford said after they'd sipped their tea. "You know I'm just a tiny bit older than you."

[At the time, Crawford was thirty-three, Lana still a teenager.]

"I've been around long enough to learn a few lessons you might not have, so I can advise," Crawford said. "After all, when it comes to men, this is not my first time at the rodeo."

"What kind of lessons?" Lana asked.

"Well, dear, when you're young, you see things in a certain way, perhaps not as they are in the real world. The young often live in a fantasy world. As you get older, you realize how relationships—and life itself—can get god damn complicated."

"Miss Crawford, exactly what is it you want me to know?" Lana asked.

"Greg Bautzer doesn't love you," Crawford said bluntly. "He hasn't for a long

time, if he ever did. I can't let you go on believing that he does. What Greg and I have is
real. It's me he truly loves. He just hasn't figured out how to get rid of you. So why don't
you be a good little girl and let him know that
it's over between the two of you? Make it easy
on yourself."

"Get rid of me?" Lana asked in astonishment, as she was highly insulted. "That
sounds like something you do with trash
headed for the garbage can. Or maybe it's
some disease you cure yourself from."

"I know your heart must be breaking,
but I felt it was my duty to tell you," Crawford said. "You must be realistic to save yourself from more heartbreak. Dear heart, I
know how painful I must be for you to hear
these words from me. But they are true."

Flashing anger, Lana said, "You're a liar.
I don't believe a word out of your mouth."

"I would not lie to you, darling girl. I'm
trying to get you to face the truth so you
won't be devastated suddenly when he
drops you. I know you have a date with him
tonight. He's probably about to tell you the
bad news unless you get a jump on him and
cancel your date tonight...and every other night."

One of the reigning goddesses of
MGM, Joan Crawford summoned
Lana to her house to tell her that
Greg Bautzer was off limits.

Lana had long been dazzled by
Crawford's iconic beauty and her
onscreen toughness. She answered the summons, but didn't
respond to Crawford's lesbian advance.

Lana rose to her feet. "I'm getting out of here."

Crawford, too, rose to her feet. On the screen, she always looked much taller.

"I could comfort you in your grief. I suggest you come upstairs. I have this
beautiful new designer gift Adrian did for me. However, I think it would look stunning on you. I'll give it to you. Why not come to my bedroom and try it on?"

"I'm not sure..." Lana seemed hesitant.

Before she could finish her sentence, Crawford embraced her tightly, planting
a deep kiss on her lips while fondling a breast with one hand. Pulling back from
her, Lana slapped her face really hard. Then she rushed out of the living room and
into the vestibule, rescuing her shoes before heading out of the house and into the
safety of her roadster.

She had to escape.

The next few hours were painful. She couldn't get Bautzer on the phone. He
had agreed to come by her house at 8PM. Almost on the dot, he arrived. She immediately confronted him with what Crawford had told her.

"That old bitch!" he said, reaching to take her in his arms. "It's you I want."
Then he kissed her deeply, as she folded into his protective arms.

That night, after drinking the bottle of champagne he'd brought, he made love
to her in front of her marble fireplace. Fortunately, Mildred was gone for the night.

Before 3AM, when he made love to her for the third time, he asked, "Do I seem like a man who's about to dump you?"

When he left the next morning at 7AM, he'd convinced her that he was madly in love with her, and was considering marriage. He didn't exactly ask for her hand in marriage, but he put a diamond ring on her finger anyway.

***

Lana had dreamed a lot about Gary Cooper ever since working on his movie, *The Adventures of Marco Polo*. When she came of legal age, she placed a call to him on the set of his latest movie, *The Cowboy and the Lady*.

She was drawn to his lanky, hollow-cheeked male beauty, his unflappable strength, and a certain stumbling sincerity and wholesome gallantry.

"Hi," she said when he came on the phone. "I'm Lana Turner. You said to call you when I'm no longer jailbait. I'm old enough now. You can make love to me without facing life imprisonment."

"Sounds good to me," he said.

"I hope you don't think I'm forward with all my dates like this."

"That's not something I need to worry about," he answered. "You're one very attractive gal, but I've got to be discreet."

"Gary Cooper was everything that John Wayne, my future co-star, pretended to be but wasn't," Lana claimed. "He was all male...and how! I couldn't believe he'd turned down the role of Rhett Butler."

His reputation had preceded him. His director, Stuart Heisler, once said, "Coop was probably the greatest cocksman who ever lived."

That made Lana wonder, "How did he know that?"

She knew why. In 1933, he'd married the socialite-actress Veronica Balfe, whose friends called her "Rocky."

And discreet he was, taking her to a rustic beachfront dive in Laguna Beach, where they were seated at a table in an alcove in the kitchen, with table service provided by his friend, Bugsy Barbato, the restaurant's owner and chef. *[Cooper avoided the tables in the dining room, as he did not want to be recognized by his fans.]*

Lana later discussed her romance with Cooper with Ruth Hussey, when both actresses appeared in *Rich Man, Poor Girl* (1938).

"He has eyes the blue of the sky," Lana said. "When he looks at a gal, she thinks she's the only woman in the universe. And he has another endearing quality, too. He takes your hands and presses them against his cheeks. Isn't that the most adorable thing you've ever heard of?"

Later that night in Laguna, he drove her to a remote villa set high in the hills, but with a view of the ocean. He never told her who owned the house.

Both of them sat outside on a terrace, enjoying the stars and moonlight. "A walk through the forest when leaves are turning," he said. "The rain, the wind, a sunrise. Those things are real. What's not real is Tinseltown. Hollywood is nothing if not superficial. All of us movie stars are applesauce. We deceive the public, and we get paid very well for it. Since I get paid extra special, I deceive the public extra good."

She admitted to Hussey that she was a bit intimidated before going to bed with him. After all, he'd been seduced by world-class sirens like Tallulah Bankhead, Clara Bow, Claudette Colbert, Carole Lombard, Marlene Dietrich, and Mae West.

"We'd had a few drinks by the time we moved on to the bedroom," Lana confessed to Hussey. "He took off my blouse and brassiere. He borrowed a tube of lipstick from my purse and painted a face around my breast, making my nipple a nose. Then he made love to that breast. I later learned he'd picked up that trick from Lupe Velez, the Mexican Spitfire."

"Gary was more man than boy," Lana told Hussey. "What a guy! Now I know why he's called the Montana Mule."

Rumors about his sexual prowess had preceded him.

Clara Bow had claimed "he's hung like a horse and can go all night." Ava Gardner would later express the same sentiment. Carole Lombard told friends, "After hitting town, Coop learned he could do two things well: Ride a horse and fuck."

Lana later learned that men were attracted to him as frequently as women. He'd sustained an enduring affair with Anderson Lawler, the tobacco heir, and also with Cary Grant, Randolph Scott, and Howard Hughes. When Edmund Goulding had directed Cooper in *Paramount on Parade* in 1930, the director was said to have "worshipped" him twice a day.

During his fling with Lana, Gary proposed getaways where the two of them might escape from Hollywood. He wanted to take her to Sun Valley, Idaho, perhaps inviting his friends, Barbara Stanwyck and Robert Taylor. But on only one occasion did he introduce her to one of his friends or associates.

That was the night they dined with Charlie Chaplin, a sincere devotee of Cooper's "natural" style of acting.

Chaplin had acquired the film rights to a story about a young millionaire who goes on a cruise to China, where, in a dance hall, he falls in love with a lovely White Russian. The Little Tramp wanted the movie to showcase his girlfriend (or wife), Paulette Goddard, with whom Lana would soon be co-starring in a film. "It's a comedy with social implications," Chaplin told them.

After deciphering the plot, Lana told Chaplin, "If Paulette doesn't do it, I'm always available. I'd be great playing a White Russian."

The movie was never made. After reading the script, Cooper turned it down.

Far away from the nightclub scene, Lana came to enjoy the precious few nights she spent alone with Cooper. Except for that time they dined with Chaplin, their dates invariably included just the two of them.

"One night, I asked Mildred to vacate the building and go out with the girls. In her place, I invited Gary for a home-cooked meal," Lana told Hussey.

"I'm not the world's best cook, but I tried. He arrived with these very ripe avocados, from which he made the world's best guacamole. Lupe Velez had taught him how. I cooked veal chops, mashed potatoes, and a salad, which was fine with him. For dessert, we retired to bed."

"He wore these expertly crafted Indian boots, which he asked me to remove." Lana said. "When I'd taken them off and removed his socks, I was confronted with the longest, most awful feet I'd ever seen on a man. He wanted me to massage his feet, which led to a request for toe-sucking. I had never done that before, and I just know I'll never do it again. But for Gary, anything."

"Everybody has some annoying little habit," she said. "For Gary, it's his love of licorice. I detest it. It makes your teeth black."

There was no goodbye, no final farewell. "We had a fabulous dinner, great love-making, and I fell asleep in his arms. In the morning, when I woke up, he was gone. He never phoned for another date. I guess he went home to Rocky."

In 1943, she heard rumors that Cooper was involved in a torrid love affair with Bergman on the set of *For Whom the Bell Tolls*.

"It was tolling for Ingrid—not me," Lana said. "In later years, I would encounter Gary at various functions. He was always gracious, always the gentleman, never a mention made of our previous affair."

***

Henry Willson, Lana's agent, received an angry, early-morning call from her. She demanded that he use all his influence to get her a meatier role than that "extra bit I did in *The Chaser* (1938) with Dennis O'Keefe. I want to be a movie star—not a god damn $10-a-day extra!"

He promised he would "empty oceans and topple mountains" to get her a better part. Through it had not resulted from his intervention as her agent, he learned that MGM had cast her as one of the four leads in *Rich Man, Poor Girl*, where she received fourth billing to Robert Young, Lew Ayres, and Ruth Hussey. Of course, when Willson called her with the news, he took all the credit for getting her the role. Shooting was to begin at once, as the 72-minute film had been scheduled for distribution in August of 1938.

In the meantime, Willson asked her to go out on a series of widely publicized dates with whatever star he was specifically promoting at the time—namely, Jon Hall and Alan Curtis. "They're both gorgeous guys, with great bodies, and, most important, each is well hung. I know that's a requirement for you, Lana. We both

During her heavy period of "studio dating," a photographer captured Lana with MGM contract player Alan Curtis.

Hedda Hopper was in the room that night and said "I can't decide which one is the more gorgeous."

have the same expectations in men."

"And how do you know how well-hung they are?" she asked provocatively.

"Never mind how I know," he answered. "Henry knows."

Both of the young actors, Lana was soon to discover, lived up to Willson's advance billing.

The popular New York columnist, Walter Winchell, often flew to Hollywood for interviews with the stars he later wrote about. He later recalled a time in the late 1930s. When he'd attended a glittering star-studded night at the Trocadero, he had spotted Lana enter the club on the arm of Alan Curtis.

Although he didn't print it, he told the manager that, "The Curtis kid is one good-looking hunk of male flesh, and Lana is a picture that could be used for masturbatory fantasies."

During their dates together, Curtis and Lana seemed ideal for each other, except for one problem: In 1937, he'd married actress Priscilla Lane, a marriage that would end in a divorce court in 1940.

Lane, a native of Indiana, seven years older than Lana, was known for her role as Princess Aura in the original *Flash Gordon* serial (1936). Curtis married her after she became Miss Miami Beach. She was later to lose a leg when she served in the Women's Army Corps during World War II.

Born in Chicago, Curtis was twelve years older than Lana, but didn't look it. Willson had orchestrated a change in his name to Alan Curtis, since his real name, Harry Ueberroth, wouldn't look good on a marquee.

Lana learned that he'd worked as a model before becoming an actor. "In Chicago, I posed for figure studies," he told her. "Word got around. Soon the class was filled only with young men concentrating on only one part of my anatomy."

He admitted that to get launched in Hollywood, he'd had to participate at the rate of about two dalliances a week on Willson's notorious casting couch.

"He's so repulsive physically," Lana asked. "How can you manage?"

"I just close my eyes and imagine it's Alice Faye doing the dirty deed down below."

When she'd first met him, he was interpreting a secondary role in a Technicolor picture, *Hollywood Cavalcade* (1939), starring the blonde-haired Faye and Don Ameche.

As Lana later told Willson, "As you, of all people know, Alan is a dreamboat, and the sex is just great. But I think he's more interested in free publicity than in dating me."

In spite of that assessment, Lana developed a friendship with Curtis that lasted for years.

She was pleased to learn that his big break would come in 1941, when director Raoul Walsh gave him the third lead in a *film noir* heist movie, *High Sierra*, starring Humphrey Bogart and Ida Lupino. Curtis played "Babe Kozak," a hardened criminal who arrives at a fortified mountain hideaway with a dance hall girl (Lupino).

In 1941, Lana was surprised when she read that Curtis had married Ilona Massey, the Hungarian film, stage, and radio performer hailed as "The New Dietrich." One night three months later, he came over to Lana's and wanted to spend the night. He'd been kicked out of the house by this temperamental singing star.

They divorced the following year.

When Lana encountered him again, he'd replaced John Garfield in *Flesh and Fantasy* 1943), playing a ruthless killer opposite Gloria Jean.

It represented the biggest break so far in his career. An A-list picture starring Edward G. Robinson, Charles Boyer, and Barbara Stanwyck, it consisted of four free-standing segments that combined into an "anthology," inspired by Oscar Wilde's short story, *Lord Arthur Savile's Crime*, originally published in 1891. Curtis appeared in the first of the four segments, interpreting the role of an escaped killer. Regrettably (for him), that segment was yanked from the "anthology" and never released.

In an attempt to salvage some of its footage, the studio expanded it into a full-length *film noir* entitled *Destiny* (1944). In it, a fugitive (Curtis) finds refuge with a blind girl (played by Gloria Jean) in a secluded farmhouse.

On rare occasions, Lana would sometimes go out with Curtis—who by then had become type-cast in hard-bitten roles—when they weren't involved with other lovers or spouses.

Curtis died in 1953 after a botched, but supposedly routine, kidney operation in New York City. "How sad for poor Alan," she said. His career didn't pan out the way he wanted. Or his life, either, for that matter. The Hollywood Hills are filled with stars, male and female, who never achieved their dream. I live in fear every day of becoming a has-been. I'm determined that it won't happen to me."

***

The movie star, Jon Hall, born Charles Locher in Fresno, California, had been reared in Tahiti by his Swiss-born father, Felix Locher. Jon was a nephew of writer James Norman Hall, the author of the novel, *Mutiny on the Bounty*.

In 1934, he'd married the singer, Frances Langford, but neither of them was faithful.

Although the virile but rather bland star had appeared on the screen under two names, Charles Locher and, later, Lloyd Crane, he achieved fame as Jon Hall when he starred in *Hurricane* with Dorothy Lamour, both of them wearing sarongs. Willson had taken Lana to see it.

Lana's fling with Jon Hall was brief. To her dismay, she learned that he was an exhibitionist. "I knew he went around his house naked. But I didn't realize he gave public performances." She'd learned that Hall liked to strip down at parties, the guests forming a ring around him to watch him masturbate.

"I can't understand," Lana said. "He's got me and he prefers self-satisfaction."

"He needs the admiration of a room full of people," Henry Willson said.

"Jon has quite a following," she said to Willson. "You should know. The men seemed to go after him more than the women."

"It's because they, like you, want to know what's inside the sarong."

"Does Jon, like Curtis, lie with you on your couch?"

"It's mandatory," he answered.

She abruptly stopped dating him. He went on to make movies with bombshell Maria Montez, the "Cobra Woman" from the Dominican Republic.

Lana was an avid reader of gossip columns, especially those by Hedda Hopper and Louella Parsons, and she always followed news about her lovers long after they'd separated.

It saddened her when she read that so many of them ended their life much too young and tragically. Hall, a star of silly adventure movies, was actually an inventor and highly skilled aviator.

But shortly before Christmas in 1979, after his doctor told him he had incurable bladder cancer, he went home, took out his gun, and committed suicide.

***

Reporting for work at MGM, Lana appeared on the set of *Rich Man, Poor Girl*, her next picture.

The first person she met was the German Jewish director, Reinhold Schünzel, who called over Lew Ayres, the co-star of the picture, to introduce them.

She would always remember the occasion and the romance that followed. He held her hand tenderly and kissed her on both cheeks. Their first encounter ended abruptly when Ayres was called to the phone.

After he'd left, she turned to Schünzel. "Mark my words, that good-looking devil is the guy I'm going to marry."

"Perhaps," the director answered. "After all, this is Hollywood, where marriage is but an afterthought. There is one problem. You'll have to get rid of his wife. Ginger Rogers is bigtime competition. She dances better than you, but, then again, you're more gorgeous."

Chapter Four

Stardom at Last
For that "Ball of Fire," Lana Turner

Her Ongoing Affair with Lew Ayres, Ginger Rogers' Husband

Romping in the swimming pool, and later in bed, "bathing beauties" Robert Stack and Lana Turner had a lot of fun.

"In her heart, Lana is a total romantic," he said. "Even when she claims she does, she doesn't really want to settle down and raise a brood of kids. She thinks marriage should be like a romantic scene in a movie, a constant flurry of fun and courtship, not the day-to-day reality of a man and wife."

"Even though she denies it, sex is of paramount importance to her. I don't want to call her a nympho, but she confided to me, 'I don't get enough sex. I don't know why Mother Nature designed men to give up after only one of two explosions. She played a trick on men, and women are the ultimate losers."

Rich Man, Poor Girl (1938) was based on a 1925 Broadway play, *White Collars,* a satire on socialism. In 1929, it was turned into a Pre-Code comedy by MGM, *The Idle Rich,* starring Conrad Nagel and Bessie Love. The film was the first directorial effort of William C. de Mille, a former screenwriter of silent movies and the older brother of Cecil B. DeMille, who slightly altered the spelling of their last name.

The 1938 remake was directed by Reinhold Schünzel, a Jewish refugee from Nazi Germany, who had been one of the better-known film stars in Berlin after World War I. In spite of his Jewish heritage, Josef Goebbels and Adolf Hitler had allowed him to work in films after they came to power.

But because of their constant interference in his scripts, Schünzel decided to escape from Germany anyway. Years later, he told Lana, "Hitler had the worst possible dramatic taste."

In Hollywood, Schünzel continued to both direct and act. His most memorable film appearance was in the 1946 Alfred Hitchcock film, *Notorious,* co-starring Cary Grant and Ingrid Bergman.

On the second day of the shoot, Clark Gable, a star Lana idolized, showed up for a working luncheon with Schünzel. Lana just happened to be standing next to the director when Gable approached.

"I was horrified," she said. "For my role in the movie, wardrobe had given me the worst dress in the history of fashion. In a three-button suit, Gable had never looked handsomer, with a lock of hair falling over his forehead, very sexy. A pho-tographer snapped a picture of the three of us. I was caught gazing up at him with stardust in my eyes, but he doesn't seem to know I exist. All the pretty gals were after him. In my wildest dreams, I never knew I'd be co-starring with him in the months ahead."

In a nutshell, *Rich Man, Poor Girl* was the story of a wealthy businessman (Robert Young) who falls in love with his secretary Joan Thayer (Ruth Hussey), who comes from a poor and eccentric family. Joan does not immediately accept his proposal because of the difference in their backgrounds. As a means of testing their compatibility, she proposes that he come to live for a while with her family. At their home, he meets her radical cousin Henry (Lew Ayres) and her starry-eyed sister Helen (Lana herself), plus the rest of the crazy clan.

At first, Lana had been told she'd be working with Franchot Tone. She planned to chase after him, since he'd been married to

On the set of *Rich Man, Poor Girl,* Lana met her screen idol, Clark Gable, for the first time. He had come to call on his friend, the film's director, Reinhold Schünzel.

"Unfortunately, I was drably dressed for my role in the picture," Lana said. "I looked like some waitress behind a soda fountain."

Joan Crawford, and she wanted to get even with Crawford, based on her flare-up over Lana's dating of Greg Bautzer. But it was soon announced that Tone was out, and the lead role went instead to Robert Young.

"As a leading man, Young did absolutely nothing for me," Lana told Rita Johnson, one of the stars of the movie. "He's one of those solid family men types who marries one gal and stays married to her until the cows come home."

[Lana was right about that. Young married Betty Henderson in 1933, the union lasting until her death in 1994.]

As Hussey's "jitterbug sister," Lana had one scene where she got to do the rumba, and another where she shows off her body in a scanty petticoat. She utters such lines as, "Love is wonderful but it can't survive seven people *[competing]* for one bathtub."

As part of their buildup to the release of the film, MGM billed Lana as "The Kissing Bug of Andy Hardy." Around the same time, *Variety* would deliver faint praise, defining her as a "promising youngster."

The first actor Lana dated was a Texan, Don Castle, who at the time was interpreting one of the film's minor roles. She didn't agree, but the press often mentioned his resemblance to Clark Gable. Many of her outings with Castle were configured, with aggressive input from the studio, as double dates with her girlfriend, Bonita Granville and her beau of the moment.

[In less than a decade, Castle would become the TV producer for Jack Wrather's Lassie *series. Wrather was married to Granville at the time.*

"Like so many of my early boyfriends, Don was to have a short life," Lana lamented. "He was a great guy, but died in 1966 at the age of 48. After a traffic accident, he was given a medication overdose."

The plot of *Rich Man, Poor Girl* called for Lana's character to dream of living the plush life married to some rich man, and she tangles with her onscreen cousin, Ayres' socialist character, who loudly defends the glories of the working class.

In the film, she defines the Thayer home as "a dump," long before Bette Davis delivered her famous and equivalent line in *Beyond the Forest* (1949).

"I play the jackass cousin with his lunatic left philosophy," Ayres told Lana.

She bonded with her other female co-stars, Hussey, Rita Johnson and Virginia Grey. Collectively, they often lunched together during the filming. She and Grey would remain friends for decades, in spite of their shared competition for certain roles and one man (Clark Gable) in particular.

Johnson defined her origins as derived from a working class background in New England. As a teenager, she had served hot dogs from her mother's roadside diner to drivers along the Boston/Worcester turnpike.

One day, she told Lana that MGM had tested her suitability for stepping into the Jean Harlow role in *Saratoga* (1937) after the unexpected death of its platinum blonde star.

"After I made a screen test with Clark Gable, I was rejected. The director told me that my mouth was too big."

Gable said, 'Tough break, kid. They once told me my ears were too big for the movies."

Hussey, a native of Rhode Island, told Lana, "I don't have your beauty, but I'm always quick with a wisecrack. I guess that means that my destiny will be that of a second stringer for the rest of my life."

That was to some degree true, but fortunately for Hussey, in 1940, she earned a "Best Supporting Actress" Oscar nomination, based on her performance as the cynical photographer lusting for James Stewart in *The Philadelphia Story,* co-starring Cary Grant and Katharine Hepburn.

Grey had spent her childhood in Hollywood and always bragged that, "My claim to fame was that Gloria Swanson was my first babysitter, changing my diapers." She had been born the youngest daughter of director Ray Grey, a friend of Swanson's.

Grey had made her film debut at the age of ten, playing Little Eva in the silent version of *Uncle Tom's Cabin (1927).*

Ironically, when Lana had to drop out of Gable's *Idiot's Delight* (1939), Grey was assigned to take over her role of one of his dancing chorus girls. Later, she confessed that Gable had seduced her during the filming of the movie. Thus began and on-again, off-again affair that would survive well into the 1940s.

MGM signed Grey to a contract in 1936 which laid out the terms of the role she'd play as the love interest in Bruce Cabot's "B" movie, *Bad Guy (1937).* Cabot, a close friend of Errol Flynn, had an affair with Grey. She was the one who warned Lana that Flynn had installed a two-way mirror in his bedroom

Lana's glamorous cohort, confidante, and friend, Virginia Grey, retained a friendship with Lana for decades after their appearance together as budding starlettes on the make in *Rich Man, Poor Girl.*

so his "fuck buddies" could oversee his conquests, or he theirs. Lana was furious when she heard she'd sexually "performed" for unseen voyeurs who had included, thanks to their concealment behind the two-way mirror, both Cabot and David Niven.

"Lana talked to me a lot about her boyfriends," Hussey said, "and talked a lot about her affair with Lew Ayres. I'm named Hussey, but Lana—although I just adored her—was the real hussy."

Many of Lana's fans cite *Rich Man, Poor Girl* as the movie in which she showed off her natural beauty before it was garnished and accessorized with the studio's barrage of makeup and glamor.

As one reviewer noted, "Without a doubt, the person who made the biggest splash in this film is Lana Turner in her nascent phase. She's sweet, still a brunette, and full of the dewy youth and kittenish sexuality she exuded in the early phase of her career."

Another critic wrote, "Lana Turner makes every single one of today's screen beauties fade into mediocrity by comparison."

Bosley Crowther of *The New York Times* wrote: "*Rich Man, Poor Girl* is a genial and heartwarming little comedy which crackles and pops so pleasantly that you can hardly hear its joint creaks."

***

According to Ruth Hussey, "Lana fell in love with Lew Ayres during the making of *Rich Man, Poor Girl*. Virginia Grey and Rita Johnson, along with yours truly, were witnesses to this ongoing affair. Who wouldn't adore Lew? He was a delight. Even his wife, Ginger Rogers, thought so…at least until she divorced him *[in 1940]* two years later."

When Lana worked with Ayres, he was best known for his interpretation of the German soldier in Paul Bäumer's film classic, *All Quiet on the Western Front* (1930), based on the haunting German-language novel of World War I by Erich Maria Remarque.

"I think I was mature for my age," Lana told Grey. "I mean, I had the hots for boys when I was a child. After seeing Lew on the screen as a German soldier, I really daydreamed about him. Even though he was fighting for the Germans, all my sympathy was for him. I left the movie house in a daze. Someday, of my days to come, I just knew I would meet this handsome guy. I just knew he'd fall for me when that day came."

She had also seen him in an earlier film. As a child, her mother, Mildred, had taken her to see his performance opposite Greta Garbo in the silent film, *The Kiss* (1929). "Both Mildred and I swooned over him," Lana said. "Call it a little girl's first crush."

[Most movie audiences of the late 1930s and early 40s would remember Ayres for his

In *Rich Man, Poor Girl*, Lana interacts with Lew Ayres. This was one of her most playful roles before she became super glamorous.

"He was a wonderful lover, taking me on picnics and drives up the coast. In some ways, it was like a schoolgirl romance. He was idealistic, a conscientious objector, devouring books on religion and philosophy. I listened politely, waiting until he got around to fucking me."

starring role in nine Dr. Kildare *films, including one that he filmed with Lana. Another famous role had been his interpretation of Ned in* Holiday *(1938), in which he'd starred with Katharine Hepburn and Cary Grant.]*

On the set, she learned from the director that, though still married to Rogers, he was not actually living with her. Consequently, she felt more comfortable making herself available to him for a date.

"Lana was definitely hot to trot," Hussey observed. "Even on days when she wasn't needed on the set, she showed up. She brought Lew coffee and invited herself to his dressing room one afternoon, in theory, at least, for some acting tips. Yeah, right!"

On their first date, he drove up the Pacific coast in his Packard to an out-of-the-way beachfront dive not usually frequented by other movie stars or photographers.

"My heart was beating like a tom-tom the night he came to pick me up," she told Grey. "I'd spent all afternoon making myself glamorous, only to find out that he preferred the natural look in a girl."

"After dinner, we took off our shoes and went for a hand-in-hand walk along the moonlit beach. It couldn't have been more romantic. He could make a girl forget that Greg Bautzer—that two-timing bastard—ever existed. The sound of the waves. My bare feet in the sands."

He told her he couldn't take her out dancing "because I'm lousy at dancing. Fortunately, Ginger gets enough dancing on the screen with Fred Astaire."

"And then it happened," Lana confessed. "He stopped, gently pulled me into his arms, and gave me the kiss of a lifetime. Wow! He was great."

Apparently, Lana did not exaggerate. In Ginger Rogers memoirs, *My Story*, Rogers later described her first kiss from Ayres: "I've never been rocked by a kiss before. He planted a super kiss on my lips. At that very instant, the ground under our feet moved again, as if by command."

As Lana related to Grey, "Lew delivers the most gentlemanly fuck a gal can ever have—no rough stuff, but passionate, thorough. Fortunately, he brought a rubber along. I guess he knew I'd give in, since I'd been throwing myself at him. I find him *yummy-yummy*, good enough to eat!"

On subsequent dates, Lana discreetly inquired about Rogers, since she loved gossip. "Lew hates Hollywood gossip, I soon learned. He prefers to put his arm around me in his living room. We listen to classical music. He prefers the three B's—Beethoven, Bach, and Brahms. He played the piano for me, even the banjo and guitar. In 1927, he'd appeared with Henry Halstead's Orchestra. I mean, he's really good, and he studies arranging and composing."

After her third date with Ayres, Lana appeared on the set and called Grey aside to tell her the news. Later, according to Grey, "She was bubbling over with excitement and could hardly contain herself. In an almost breathless voice, she told me that Lew was going to divorce Ginger Rogers and marry her."

***

As the weeks passed, Lana dated Greg Bautzer less and less, and the frequency of his "sleepovers" dwindled to once a week, if that. Sometimes, he'd bring her home before 11PM—no more closing down of night clubs—and he'd give her a kiss on her doorstep before bidding her good night and driving off into the night, presumably for a late-night rendezvous with someone else.

At first, she suspected that Joan Crawford had commandeered most of his nights, but she was soon to learn differently.

"Our romance is cooling," Lana told Grey. "He's obviously getting it somewhere else."

Nonetheless, even on days he didn't see her, he faithfully sent a bouquet of white roses. They still maintained an agreement that the arrival at her door of a box of red roses would signal the end of their love affair.

On the nights he did take her out, she still preferred La Conga, where they were generally acknowledged as the best rumba dancers on the floor. There was an occasional weekend at the desert resort of Palm Springs. They were seen at the Racquet Club, and once, they were photographed at the Assistance League Benefit at the Roller Bowl.

It was one night in the desert, at the edge of a swimming pool, that she confided in him that her real desire was not to be a movie star, but a married woman with children. He couldn't believe that. He'd dated dozens of actresses, and invariably, each of them had wanted to become movie stars.

"You truly mean you'd like to be a dreary little housewife, changing shitty diapers, cooking dinner for a hubbie when, or if, he comes home for dinner?"

"I want what most girls want," she said. "Is that so strange?"

Somehow, he managed to change the subject.

***

When Lana wasn't spending the night with Ayres, she—on that rare occasion—found Bautzer in her bed. But, as she told her girlfriends, "Greg is the biggest escape artist in Hollywood when it comes to marriage."

One morning, she read in a gossip column that Crawford and Bautzer had concluded a public fight at Mocambo's, and that she had stormed out of the club, roaring off into the night in a taxi, alone.

This did not surprise Lana at all, since she, along with Louella Parsons and Hedda Hopper, were familiar with the ongoing feuds and reconciliations of the infamous couple.

However, even after his breakup with Crawford, he continued his pattern of infrequent rendezvous with Lana. "What's he up to now?" she asked anyone who might know. Then one morning, she read in the newspaper that Bautzer was dating the French actress, Simone Simon.

That afternoon, a box of red roses arrived from him. She knew that was the end of their affair.

Simon was a name that was vaguely familiar to her. She had read two or three items about her in *Variety*—and that was it. She'd never seen one of her American movies. In the fading afternoon, she called Billy Wilkerson at *The Hollywood Reporter*, the publisher who had discovered her. "Just who in hell is this Simone

Simon?"

He invited her over to read his file on her in the newspaper's morgue.

After scanning the file, she soon learned details about her competitor. To her delight, she found out that the actress was twelve years older than she was—in fact, she was slightly older than Bautzer himself.

Simon had been born in Marseille, the daughter of Henri Louis Firmin Champmoynat, a French-Jewish engineer and airplane pilot. During World War II, he had been captured by the Nazis and later died in a concentration camp.

Simon had lived in Madagascar, Budapest, Turin, and Berlin before settling into Paris with an ambition to become a fashion designer like Chanel. Spotted by a talent agent, she was offered a film contract, making her debut in 1931 in *The Unknown Singer*.

She had become one of the best-known actresses in France before Darryl F. Zanuck of 20th Century Fox brought her to Hollywood in August of 1935.

At Fox, she was known for her temper tantrums, which would ultimately lead to her dismissal. Zanuck might have put up with her had her American films made any money, but they had flopped. During the 1937 remake of the silent film classic, *Seventh Heaven* (1927), she was cast in the Janet Gaynor role. The movie bombed, even though its star was James Stewart.

Lana learned that Bautzer's affair with Simon was over when she returned to Paris to resume her film career there, even though war clouds loomed over Europe.

Two weeks later, a box of white roses arrived on Lana's doorstep with a note from Bautzer. "Lana, I love you passionately. I want to come over right now and make love to you all day, but I will have to force myself to wait until I come by for you at eight. Cancel any date you've made. You belong to me…and me only."

***

VIRGINIA GREY. ANN RUTHERFORD.

Friends, Nymphs, and Frenemies: Virginia Grey and Ann Rutherford, two of Lana's friends, confidantes, and sometimes competitors, in a press and publicity postcard of their heydays. Along with Lana, they were cast in what they each remembered years later as a major break, secondary roles in a movie with lots of good-looking young women, *Dramatic School*.

Since bringing Lana to Metro-Goldwyn-Mayer, she had not heard from Mervyn LeRoy for several weeks until he phoned her. He had decided to cast her in *Dramatic School* (1938), a romantic drama about a troupe of young aspiring actresses hoping to become the next Duse or Bernhardt. The film was to be directed by Robert B. Sinclair, with an all-star cast headed by Luise Rainer, Paulette Goddard, and Alan Marshal.

Dramatic School was to have marked the American film debut of the British actress, Greer Garson, but she hurt her back and had to be replaced by Rainer.

Although Lana did not voice her complaints to LeRoy, she was disappointed with her small role in this low budget version of the movie, *Stage Door* (1937), set in a theatrical boardinghouse and starring Katharine Hepburn and Ginger Rogers.

In spite of her meager role as "Mado," Lana was given fourth billing. "I was such a bitch in the film," she later said. "Audiences must have hated me, especially when I deliberately spilled a glass of champagne on Rainer's beautiful gown designed by Adrian. Stacked up against the others, I was just a kid, a teenager really, although I looked older."

Professor Jeanine Basinger, an author and film historian, summed up Lana's role: "At this stage, she is all dimples, curly hair, and a high school charm, more of a cheerleader than Cleopatra. The idea of her as a serious dramatic student is a bit far-fetched. She is exceptionally pretty, but not yet glamorous—the kind of girl every boy in school might want to take to the senior prom, provided it wouldn't worry his mother too much."

The supporting roles had been cast with a remarkable troupe of talented actors, and Lana set out to meet all of them, since she was eager to learn about how to make movies.

LeRoy introduced her to the Viennese actress, Luise Rainer, who had become famous for winning back-to-back Oscars—the first for *The Great Ziegfeld* (1936), the second for *The Good Earth* (1937).

Lana joined others in referring to Rainer as "the Viennese teardrop," because of her long phone scene in *The Great Ziegfeld* when she hears the news that the man she loves is going to marry another woman.

When Lana met her, Rainer looked at

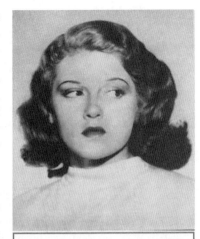

Lana in *Dramatic School:* As she recalled (with a touch of envy) about that film's female lead, "Paulette (Goddard) had her heart set on playing Scarlett O'Hara in *Gone With the Wind.*"

"I didn't dare tell her that at the time, I, too, was being tested for the role. She claimed that even though it hadn't yet been announced, David O. Selznick had, more or less, already given her the part."

Lana boasted, "I got the Argentine singer, Dick Haymes, before that other goddess, Rita Hayworth. He could melt you knees with a smile and cause your heart to flutter with a touch."

79

Lana with a certain kind of disdain and did not extend her hand. Behind Lana's back, Rainer referred to her as "LeRoy's little piece of fluff."

Lana was delighted to be cast with two of her favorite friends, Ann Rutherford and Virginia Grey. During the shooting of *Dramatic School,* her friendship with Grey strengthened.

As the days went by, it became obvious to LeRoy and others that for Lana's interpretation of her role, she was inspired by Ginger Rogers in films such as Warner musicals *42nd Street* and *Gold Diggers of 1933.*

Goddard cattily remarked to Sinclair, "Since Lana is also stealing Ginger's husband (a reference to Lew Ayres), why not her screen persona, too?"

Lana found the Los Angeles native, John Shelton, "very handsome in a bland sort of way. He wanted to join the ranks of Tyrone Power, Robert Taylor, and Clark Gable, but lacked the charisma of super-stardom," she said.

"I liked John, and the sex wasn't as vanilla as I thought it might be," Lana confided to Grey. "He has passion that rises to the surface."

On the set, the most sparks were generated between Lana and Dick Haymes, the singer from Buenos Aires. She would get to know him far more intimately when she became involved with such singers and musicians as bandleader Tommy Dorsey and Frank Sinatra. Haymes had married Edith Harper,

"In many ways, Lana wanted to be me," claimed Paulette Goddard. "She also envied the chest of jewelry—lots and lots of it—I had accumulated over the years and the millions of dollars."

When Lana last encountered Goddard, Lana was (disastrously) married to Ronald Dante, a nightclub hypnotist.

At the time, in glaring contrast, Goddard was married to the wealthy, charismatic and dashingly handsome novelist, Erich Maria Remarque.

Lana's somewhat bitter final words to Goddard were, "Some girls have all the luck."

but their marriage was being annulled. "I'm free as a bird," he told Lana. "We don't have to sneak around."

As Lana confided to Grey, "Dick is good in bed, very satisfying. He whispers dirty stuff in your ear as he makes love to you. I find him irresistible."

Lana and Paulette Goddard *[eventually the wife, or mistress of Charlie Chaplin],* one of her co-stars in *Dramatic School,* maintained a superficial friendship for many decades. They would occasionally encounter each other at parties or at special events such as Oscar night. When they would come together, they would air kiss and exchange compliments, which always included an assessment of each other's looks, "You look absolutely stunning, darling."

***

80

In 1937, Paramount had released *Internes Can't Take Money* starring Joel McCrae in the role of Dr. Kildare. The movie was a financial success at the box office. Later, MGM picked up the option for a series of low-budget melodramas, the *Dr. Kildare* series, each of which highlighted the struggles and travails of a heroic, highly principled doctor.

MGM cast Lew Ayres as Dr. Kildare in many of them, the first of which was *Young Dr. Kildare* (1938). Ayres would go on to churn out nine more of them until his pacifist stance during World War II made him unpopular. The studio eventually replaced him with actor Philip Dorn.

Bad girl Lana, playing a shameless adventuress, taking advantage of Lew Ayres as the very eligible Dr. Kildare. Only eighteen, she plans to seduce him.

A Londoner, Harold S. Bucquet, would direct many of the *Dr. Kildare* movies. For the second such movie with Ayres *[Calling Dr. Kildare]*, he cast Lana in the "sexy role"; Lionel Barrymore as the wise old Dr. Gillespie, his mentor; and Laraine Day as the second female lead, a nurse, Mary Lamont.

Lana had continued her affair with Ayres, but they had to be discreet, since he was still married to Ginger Rogers. Lana, enamored with him at the time, was delighted to be working with him again.

On the set, during the first day of shooting, she told Bucquet, "I can't imagine that little Miss Lana Turner of Wallace, Idaho, would one day be working with one of the great Barrymores." Although she didn't specifically mention how delighted she also was to be working with Ayres, Bucquet and the rest of his staff eventually became aware of their affair, based on her frequent visits to his dressing room.

Lana became extremely nervous whenever she filmed scenes with Barrymore, a longtime and widely acclaimed star. Despite her lack of experience, she managed to pull them off.

Her scene with Barrymore called for her to shed tears, and to come apart before his eyes. She knows she's been a bad girl, but vows to reform and make a fresh start, "if I'm going to amount to something."

On camera, Barrymore assures her, "Well, you're young," holding out a hopeful promise for her future.

According to the script, Dr. Kildare and his mentor, Dr. Gillespie, have had one too many arguments, and his mentor dismisses him from his duties at Blair General Hospital. Gillespie, however, remains interested in his younger *protégé,* and as a means of keeping tabs on him, he assigns Nurse Lamont (Day) as a secret spy. Soon, she reports that the young doctor is emotionally entangled with this sexy blonde, Rosalie (Lana), and that the younger doctor (because of his involvement with Rosalie) is also implicated in the cover-up of a murder.

Barrymore gives Ayres some fatherly advice of the type Jude Lewis Stone provided for Andy Hardy. "Rosalie (Lana) is a bad little girl, and you should have known that. Books could be written about her."

Playing the sultry *femme fatale,* Lana had just turned eighteen when shooting began.

One reviewer defined her as "a baby doll." As Rosalie, she was asked to deliver such lines as "I'm city people. I like great big shiny limousines and orchids in a vase. I love the cold wind whipping around a skyscraper—and a sable coat to keep it out."

As Bucquet quipped, "That girl could probably raise a hard-on from cantankerous old Lionel." Years later, Lana could hardly remember Barrymore except to claim that, "Every time I encountered him, he was in his cups" (i.e., drunk).

One day on the set, she was introduced to an actor about eleven years older than herself, Phillip Terry. Born to German Americans in San Francisco, he was known as a Hollywood Romeo, a legend he'd been developing since his bit part in *Mannequin* (1938), starring Joan Crawford. During the shooting of that movie, he'd made frequent visits to her dressing room. He would later become her wartime husband.

Together, they would adopt their first child, Christina, a decision that Crawford would later bitterly regret. Fortunately, Crawford died before the publication of her daughter's notorious memoir, *Mommie Dearest,* a vengeful rant that was later adapted into a film starring Faye Dunaway impersonating Crawford.

Terry had built up an impressive set of muscles, in part because of his back-

Lana viewed her seduction of Phillip Terry, Joan Crawford's wartime husband, as a triumph over her nemesis. Crawford and Lana often competed for the same men.

Crawford referred to sex with the studly actor as "going to heaven."

Lana countered, "Phillip and I only made it to the clouds in the sky."

In this publicity still for *Young Dr. Kildare,* Laraine Day (left) looks on in a disapproving rage at the growing bond between bad Lana and the impressionable, morally upright Dr. Kildare (Lew Ayres).

This is not just acting on Day's part: She thoroughly loathed Lana, who detested her as well.

ground as a football player and roustabout in the oil fields of Texas and Oklahoma.

For a while, he had studied acting at the Royal Academy of Dramatic Arts in London.

Lana began to date him during the making of *Dr. Kildare*. As she told Ann Rutherford, "Terry must have put a smile on Crawford's face. He might have been a roustabout in the oil fields, but he has culture, too, and seems well read. He pronounces certain words with a British accent, no doubt from his studies in London."

As a sex object, he was eagerly pursued by both men and women, but it would be years later that Lana would learn that he was bisexual. It turned out that both Terry and Lana were dating the same man at the same time, the matinee idol, Robert Taylor, another bisexual married to a bisexual, Barbara Stanwyck.

Socialite Elsa Maxwell wrote, "Joan Crawford weeps openly when the violinist at L'Aiglon plays her favorite classical piece. Lana Turner likes torch songs; Rita Hayworth prefers gypsy music, and Hedy Lamarr likes waltzes."

What she didn't print but knew: "All of these ladies desired Phillip Terry, as do Robert Taylor, Errol Flynn, Tyrone Power, and Cary Grant."

MGM aggressively promoted *Calling Dr. Kildare*, suggesting that viewers "watch these exciting new beauties—Laraine Day and Lana Turner." But it was probably Lana who aroused the most intense sexual interest among men in the audience. The film was the first of seven in which Day would appear as a player in the *Dr. Kildare* series. As nurse Mary Lamont—in distinct contrast to Lana, who was interpreted as a "siren"—she was frequently cited for her wholesomeness.

In the publicity department's build-up, they distorted her background, claiming that "Lana Turner was educated in San Francisco and was a model and designer before her discovery by Mervyn LeRoy."

Bucquet said that Laraine didn't like Lana, and that Lana didn't like Laraine. "When those two came together, an Arctic wind blew in. I think Lana also resented Laraine getting billing over her, because she considered her own role flashier and more important."

"At first, Lana feared Laraine, but by the time they made *Keep Your Powder Dry* (1945), it was Lana who was the Queen of MGM, Laraine a second-stringer.

Day eventually gained a distinct new fame of her own when, in 1947, she married Leo Durocher, the manager of the New York Giants baseball team.

After working with her, Lana later wrote: "Many people found her a cold and rigid woman."

Reviews for Lana were good, *Variety* claiming that she was "a fine type as the gal who nearly leads Dr. Kildare astray."

Eventually, in reference to *Calling Dr. Kildare*, Billy Wilkerson of *The Hollywood Reporter* wrote, "Lana Turner was a bit uncertain in early scenes, but she warms to her work and registers with excellent effect in later chapters." Even *Family Circle* wrote, "Lana goes glamorous on us, and she needn't take a back seat to any of the other glamor girls."

***

At long last stardom—or at least a minor version of it—came for Lana as a result of her casting as the female lead in *These Glamour Girls* (1939) by its director, S. Sylvan Simon and its producer Sam Zimbalist. She would appear in it with her sometimes lover, Lew Ayres.

Simon had wanted to work with her before, and now was his chance to direct her. During the second week of the shoot, he told the press, "I venture to predict that in another year, Lana Turner will be one of the biggest stars on the screen."

And how right he was.

Once again, she was teamed with Ann Rutherford, with whom she continued to confide details of her romances. After surveying the attractive men in the cast, Lana told Rutherford, who that year was appearing as Scarlett O'Hara's sister, "I could go for Tom Brown, Richard Carlson, or Peter Lind Hayes, at least when Lew isn't around. As for Don Castle, I've already made two films with him—and know him quite well, if you get my drift." She was referring to her involvements the year before in *Love Finds Andy Hardy* (1938) and *Rich Man, Poor Girl* (also 1938).

When Lana showed up for work, she found that even though she'd been designated as the film's female lead, she had nonetheless been assigned to a communal dressing room. She quickly surmised that in marked contrast, the film's other (male) stars had each been assigned private dressing rooms.

The next morning, as part of a campaign to change all that, she showed up with a maid and a small dog on a leash, announcing "I am a star!"

Word quickly spread around the studio. That afternoon, she called Louis B. Mayer, demanding her own dressing room. He did not protest. When she arrived the next morning, she was, indeed, shown to a room that had been hastily designated as hers, the first of many others to come.

It was not as luxurious as she'd wanted, but at least she'd have some degree of privacy and a spot to "audition" in quarters that she controlled.

"The dressing room was one thing," she claimed. "But I didn't know I was a real star until the commissary named a salad after me. It was the 'Lanallure' Salad, and I ordered it every day for lunch."

The writer, Anita Loos *[not to be confused with Anita Louise, an actress who also appeared in These Glamour Girls]*, compared Lana's role of the dime-a-dance girl, Jane Thomas, to that of a young Clara Bow, the silent screen vamp. The writer found that Lana had some of the quintessential flapper quality of Bow, who was known for her cupid bow lips, her bobbed hair, and devil-may-care *joie de vivre.*

About a decade before, Bow had been publicized as "The It Girl," and MGM heralded Lana for bringing "It" back to the screen.

Originally, it had been Jane Hall who devised the plot, formatted as a story for *Cosmopolitan* magazine, of social snobbishness at an East Coast college.

One drunken evening, a rich college boy, Philip S. Griswold (as played by Lew Ayres), meets a taxi dancer (Lana) and invites her as his weekend date for a heavily scheduled round of loosely chaperoned fraternity parties.

[Taxi Dancing was a social phenomenon that reached its peak during the 1930s. Taxi dancers were (in theory at least) young women who were paid to dance with male patrons, who would typically buy dance tickets for ten cents each, and then maneuver their partners of the moment around the floor with varying degrees of lechery, sometimes as a prelude to

prostitution.]

The character played by Lana accepts his invitation, even though when she arrives on campus, he's forgotten all about her.

Ayres was obviously too old to play a college boy, and although Lana—who was still a redhead at the time—was the right age to be a college girl, she was too young to have been realistically cast as a taxi dancer in a seedy dive. Makeup made her appear older than her years.

In the film, when Ayres wants to get rid of her, knowing she would not fit in and realizing that the other upper-class girls would probably snub her, she refuses to leave the campus. And predictably, when the young women learn that her profession was that of a low-end taxi dancer, they alternately mock and snub her.

Nonetheless, her character remains steadfast at the Kingsford Prep School (where the unwritten norm is "champagne for breakfast, two-timing for lunch) for the duration of the weekend. Amid these steamy inequities, love affairs go awry, but somehow, Lana's ill-conceived coupling gets rectified before the end of the final reel.

Lana's character eventually gets some pithy advice from her taxi driver, who tells her, "There's only one way to get a college boy to look up to you—climb a ladder."

On the dance floor, Lana looks stunning in a black satin gown as she pretends to emulate the dance skills of Ginger Rogers. Within minutes, young college men flock around her, adoringly, as snobby, brittle debs look on with jealousy and dismay.

One of the most dramatic visual episodes in the film occurs in a funhouse with distorted mirror images. Did Orson Welles steal that idea for his film, *The Lady from Shanghai* (1948), starring Rita Hayworth?

In the end, Lana, as the vindicated taxi dancer, triumphs over the other less attractive debs and walks off into the sunset with Ayres, the most sought-after young man on campus.

Off screen, he and Lana argued when he told her that as a pacifist, he would not participate in military service.

She objected, saying that if American men or women didn't fight if attacked, "the Japs and Nazis might invade the United States, capture us, and turn us into slaves. We'd no longer be free."

"You're just a teenager," he said, dismissing her concerns. "There are larger issues."

***

MGM had been billing itself as "having more stars than there are in heaven," and many of its budding starlets and starlettes, both male and female, were showcased in *These Glamour Girls*.

Lana met an aspiring young actor, Robert Walker, and she dated him, but only briefly. He would appear with her in her next film, *Dancing Co-Ed*, during the filming of which they became better acquainted. Their friendship, which sometimes involved sex, stretched over many years, even during his subsequent affairs with her future best friend, Ava Gardner, and the MGM starlet Nancy Davis (who later changed her name to Nancy Reagan).

When he first met Lana, Walker wasn't looking for love outside the marriage bed. He had recently married another aspiring actress, Phylis Isley, in Tulsa, Oklahoma, on January 2, 1939.

[In a few years, Phylis would become world famous as the actress Jennifer Jones.]

The other desirable male in the cast included Richard Carlson. The son of a lawyer, this former school teacher had just moved to California and had been cast in a secondary role in the David O. Selznick comedy, *The Young in Heart* (1938). "He was handsome enough, and quite charming, but he'd married Mona Carlson that year and she had him pretty much bound and gagged." Lana said.

In one sequence of *These Glamour Girls*, Lana, the out-of-place taxi dancer, twirls around the floor with Peter Lind Hayes in a "clear-the-floor" sequence.

A bevy of beautiful young women was cast in the film as the snobby debs. They included Lana's friend, Ann Rutherford, playing the bubble-brained Mary Rose Wilston.

Mary Beth Hughes was cast as the dizzy blueblood, Ann Van Richton. The Illinois beauty was significant in Lana's life in that one afternoon, she introduced her to her agent, Johnny Hyde. He would soon become Lana's agent, too. Hyde, of course, later became famous for the pivotal role he played in the career and tragic life of Marilyn Monroe.

The Hollywood-born actress, Jane Bryan, was cast as a poor socialite whose family had lost its money. She was hoping to marry a rich man.

One day, Ronald Reagan, with whom Lana had "flamed briefly," appeared on the set. At first, Lana thought that he had come to see her, but instead, he smiled and shook her hand before inviting Bryan for lunch in the commissary.

The New York Times wrote, "We like everything about *These Glamorous Girls,* and we like Lana Turner. The film is the best social commentary of the year."

***

In her coffee table book, *Lana Turner: The Memories, the Myths, the Movies,* Lana's daughter, Cheryl Crane, accurately stated that Peter Lawford and Robert Stack were her mother's "dancing partners who might be called fill-ins between more serious relationships."

An exceedingly handsome man, Stack had been born into a rich family in Los Angeles two years before Lana. He would meet her when she was seventeen. He joined her crowd, whose

While filming *These Glamour Girls,* Lana posed for a publicity picture, part of MGM's campaign to segué its *ingenue* into a full fledged vamp.

Boxoffice wrote "Young blades especially may be expected to do nipups over a ball of fire named Lana Turner."

86

other members loosely included Linda Darnell, Bonita Granville, Ann Rutherford, Jackie Cooper, and "that adorable nut," Mickey Rooney. Frequently, Stack functioned as Lana's date whenever her crowd went on a fun trip, perhaps to a beach picnic at Malibu.

Stack had grown up in Europe and been reared by his mother, Mary Elizabeth, who had long been a member of the Hollywood elite. *[She had attended Rudolph Valentino's wedding party.]* Stack's father, James Langford Stack, was a wealthy advertising executive who created the slogan, "The Beer That Made Milwaukee Famous."

His parents separated when their son was a year old.

When Lana first met Stack, he was an athlete, a polo player and "the world's best skeet shooter," winning two global records.

Back in Hollywood after his long adolescent sojourn in Europe, he decided to give acting a try. Through a connection, he was cast as the co-star of Deanna Durbin, that teenaged box office sensation who became the favorite singer of, among many others, both Winston Churchill and Josef Stalin. In *First Love* (1939)—a cinematic reprise of the Cinderella myth—Stack gave Durbin her first (and widely ballyhooed) onscreen kiss.

At the time, Jack Warner said, in reference to Stack, "I could make this kid a star, but he doesn't need me—he's not hungry enough."

Briefly, at least, Lana thought she might be falling in love with Stack, but she soon realized how hopeless that would be. He was enjoying his "swinging bachelor" days, which would last until 1956, when he married Rosemarie Bowe and settled down.

He admitted to Lana that he'd lost his virginity when he was sixteen to "a petite redhead with big smiles and boobs to match."

While dating Lana on and off, he managed to have affairs with such leading ladies as Diana Barrymore, Yvonne De Carlo, Judy Garland, Betty Grable, and even, in time, a too-young Elizabeth Taylor.

In 1940, his roommate was none other than a young John F. Kennedy, the son of Ambassador Joseph P. Kennedy, during one of JFK's visits to Hollywood. When he was introduced to Stack, libidinous JFK and Stack moved together into a cramped apartment, where they enjoyed a steady stream of starlets and even on occasion

Lana was known for retaining friendships with former dates and colleagues. Here, in 1944, years after their inaugural contacts, Robert Stack, to some degree as part of their morale-building efforts during wartime, teaches Lana how to salute.

big name actresses.

Stack said, "Most of the great male stars in Hollywood passed through my life, including Clark Gable. Gable was a man's man, but liked a lot of different women on the side. But he was nothing compared to Jack."

"Jack was the only man in Tinseltown better looking than me, and all the hot *tamales* on the West Coast took notice. He really needed a date book. I've known him to have sex in the afternoon, sex at cocktail time, sex after dinner, and even a sleepover after midnight—each with a different woman."

Lana wanted to meet him, but, although he kept promising an introduction, that didn't happen until JFK returned from the battlefields of World War II in 1946.

Years later, Stack recalled one of his outings with Lana. In this case, it involved their joint involvement at the Ernest Belcher School of Dance in Los Angeles, where they were each pursuing a course in tap dancing, as mandated by the studio.

Stack's original memoirs, entitled *Straight Shooting* and issued in 1980, included extensive sections on his interchanges with Lana. In advance of its publication, he gave her the privilege of reading it before publication. She phoned and politely requested that he remove the pages that addressed their long-ago romantic involvement. After her edits, he was left with only a paragraph or so, in which was revealed that during the heat of their early affair, he gave her his first skeet trophy as a "love bauble."

Privately, however, Stack admitted that he never fell in love with Lana, although he did, for a while, idolize both Betty Grable and Carole Lombard, Gable's wife at the time. "Betty made sex look like an American hobby everybody should enjoy, and about as illicit as apple pie."

On dates with Stack, or at parties at his home, Lana met the cream of Hollywood royalty, some of whom she would know intimately, including Howard Hughes, Errol Flynn, and Robert Taylor. In passing, she was also introduced to Edward G. Robinson, Nelson Eddy, Will Rogers, Ernst Lubitsch, and Joe Pasternak.

After knowing Stack for several months, he invited her to a screening of his latest movie, *The Mortal Storm* (1940), co-starring Margaret Sullavan and James Stewart. In it, he played a young man who joins the Nazi Party. After the screening, she praised his performance, although admitting, "You are such an All-American boy. You'd be the last man I'd ever cast as a Nazi."

She later recalled, "Robert never used rose-colored glasses when he looked at Hollywood."

He told her, "Seldom does Hollywood shake off its self-satisfied superiority and remember its beginnings as a nondescript village of Nickelodeon salesmen. The surest road to distaste in Tinseltown is to know, or to be brash enough to remember, the humblest origins of our great leaders."

Stack provided more insight about Lana to friends (Gable, Judy Garland, and others) than he revealed in his memoirs.

"There are two Lana Turners," Stack said. "One Is a sex kitten with a pouty mouth, a kind of Baby Doll to cuddle. Another is a panther-like woman with an appetite that is almost insatiable. I'll fuck her but I'll never marry her. In fact, I don't plan to marry for a long, long time. Right now, my phone rings off the wall. Even June Allyson called one night. No sooner had I come back to Hollywood than Joan

Crawford was on the phone. She always wants to be the first to seduce the newest stud in town."

***

Lana had been in films for just two years when her favorite director (at the time), S. Sylvan Simon, phoned her. He'd received Louis B. Mayer's permission to give her top billing for her next picture, *Dancing Co-Ed.*

She was pleased that she'd be working with her close friend, Ann Rutherford, again. And indeed, it was Rutherford ("Scarlett O'Hara's sister") who evolved into the best source for what really happened during the shooting of *Dancing Co-Ed.*

The film was conceived as part of a series of college-themed "programmers" in vogue at the time. Sometimes, at a different studio, a variation of this theme would focus on Betty Grable as the featured coed. Ironically, neither Grable nor Lana had ever been enrolled in any college or university.

Lana was informed that her leading man and love interest would be Richard Carlson, with whom she'd just finished her last movie, *These Glamour Girls. Dancing Co-Ed's* third lead, she was told, would be the bandleader, Artie Shaw, who had sustained a smash hit with "Begin the Beguine," earning him the title of the "King of Swing," toppling Benny Goodman from his throne. On the fourth day of the shoot, Lana met the bandleader himself.

Richard Lamparski, in his memoir, *Hollywood Diary,* recorded how that footnote in Hollywood history transpired:

Ann Rutherford was one of Lana's most enduring friends and confidantes. Here she is, as she appeared as Scarlett O'Hara's sister in *Gone With the Wind* (1939).

> *"Lana Turner entered and walked toward the bandstand. Shaw was facing his music makers and couldn't see her, but within seconds, he was aware that someone of great interest was approaching behind him from the eyes of the musicians he was leading 'The Sweater Girl' on this day was wearing tight white shorts and two bandanas tied into a halter.*

> *"The leader came down from the podium, and there was a brief exchange that concluded when Lana stood on her tip toes, tilted her head upward, and closed her eyes. Shaw bent down slightly and kissed her. As he did so, he ran his left hand appreciatively, slowly, over her ass. Then she turned and walked away and sashayed across the vast floor and out. The only sounds were of her sandals flapping. With the thump of the quilted door, Lana Turner and her ass were gone."*

After her exit, the boys in the band responded with a series of hoots, hollers, and wolf whistles.

Conditions changed by the third day on the set. Rutherford and Lana skipped lunch in the commissary and had sandwiches and cokes delivered to them on the set. They were sitting on a bench in back of the bandstand, where they could hear Shaw gossiping with Simon and two members of his band.

The talk was about "hot chicks."

"Even though I detest Hollywood, I feel like a sultan in his harem here," Shaw said. "The pussies out here come at you like gangbusters. To use another image, I feel like a kid who's been given free run of a candy store."

"So far, the most beautiful girl I've found is Betty Grable," Shaw claimed. "She's got the most incredible body, especially those legs of hers. She wraps them around a man and doesn't let him go until he's satisfied her. There's not much going on upstairs. She's a total Hollywood creation. If movies did not exist, she'd be a waitress in some hamburger joint working for dime tips and getting offered five dollars for a quickie later that night."

"She told me she soured on Jackie Coogan and got tired of him coming in at three in the morning and pissing in her bed," Shaw said. "She also sold all their wedding gifts for ready cash."

"What about Lana Turner?" Simon asked.

"From what little I've seen in talking to her, she's more empty-headed than Betty," Shaw said. "A bubblehead, but good for a quick fuck—nothing else. Nice ass, though. I think the first time I plow her, it'll be through the back door."

Enraged, Lana dropped her sandwich and stood up, taking Rutherford's hand. "Let's get the hell out of here," she whispered. "What an arrogant prick that Shaw is! I'd never let that conceited bastard touch me if he were the last man on earth."

The arrogance of youth and beauty:

Then-*ingenue* Lana Turner, from the late 1930s, on the verge of becoming a major-league *femme fatale*, seductress, and vamp .

Chapter Five

Lana's Marriage to a Clarinet Player Warbles Off Key

America's "Blonde Spitfire" Proves Too Hot to Handle

Call it "Scenes from a Marriage": The four-month marital union of Artie Shaw with Lana Turner was not a match made in heaven. Instead, it's best described as a union crafted somewhere in the darker regions of hell. From the beginning, she realized she'd made a horrible mistake in marrying him, but for a while, she was determined to stick it out.

A great deal of their conflict arose from his frequent charge that she was uneducated. He assumed the role of Pygmalion to her Galatea, loading her down with books to improve her mind. She never read any of them.

"We began a sort of love-hate relationship," she said to listeners who included both her mother Mildred and Johnny Hyde.

A Metro-Goldwyn release, *Dancing Co-Ed,* Lana's first starring film, was shot during the hot summer of 1939 as the world was about to go to war. It was a historic year in Hollywood, when studios were turning out some of their greatest and most enduring films. Contenders that year included not just *Gone With the Wind,* but Judy Garland's *The Wizard of Oz,* Laurence Olivier's *Wuthering Heights,* John Wayne's *Stagecoach,* Greta Garbo's *Ninotschka,* James Stewart's *Mr. Smith Goes to Washington,* Bette Davis' *Dark Victory,* and Robert Donat's *Goodbye, Mr. Chips.*

At the time she joined the cast of *Dancing Co-Eds,* Lana was in the "white heat' weeks of her torrid affair with attorney Greg Bautzer. She had forgiven him for having dumped her for Simone Simon, whom he defined as "my brief fling with a French Fifi."

The film's director, S. Sylvan Simon, had assembled a cast of longtime pros in the business, along with a series of rising stars. Richard Carlson had the romantic lead, with bandleader Artie Shaw billed in third position. Two of the film's uncredited players, Veronica Lake and Robert Walker, were each on the verge of stardom, and Lee Bowman, a credited player with a small part, would shoot to stardom during the war years.

It was only after shooting began that Lana learned she had been the second choice for the role of Patty Marlow. Her role in the *Dancing Co-Ed* had originally been offered to Eleanor Powell, who was not available.

Lana was aware that she'd have to rehearse and rehearse to succeed at the intricate dance steps demanded by the choreographer. It became immediately obvious, however, that she'd never be able to replicate the exhausting spins and rapid-fire clicking of heels that Powell had adopted as her trademark.

In the movie, Lana plays a professional dancer who enrolls in a Midwestern college as a pretense for garnering publicity for her involvement in a (rigged) college dance contest, part of a stunt dreamed up by a press agent, as portrayed by Roscoe Karns. Viewers were apprised that the movie's dance contest wasn't a fair fight. It had been determined in advance that the character portrayed by Lana would walk off with the venue's first prize, and, consequently, get billed as the award-winning dance partner of Freddy Toman (as portrayed by Bowman).

The then A-list actor, Richard Carlson, was cast as the college's newspaper editor, "Pug" Braddock, who uncovers the scam. Things get complicated for him after he falls in love with the character played by Lana.

Motivated by their embarrassing introduction, Lana tried to avoid Artie Shaw throughout the remainder of the shoot. She'd overheard the vulgar remarks that the bandleader had made about her.

"I remember that she sat at the opposite end of the sound stage from me," Shaw recalled. "At our first meeting, I'd been able to kiss her. No more. She looked gorgeous, but she didn't talk very much. I tried to break through to her by telling her that I was going to fuck up her music. I just was kidding, but she looked horrified, since this was her first chance in the number one spot in billing."

She poured out her distaste for Shaw to Simon. "I heard he calls me the blonde savage, even though I'm a redhead. He thinks he's so smart, and he says I'm untutored. God, I hate that son of a bitch. He's all ego. I noticed he hogs the camera, and I hear he spends more time with his hairdresser and makeup man than Marlene Dietrich does. Frankly I don't think he's at all good looking. Hollywood is full of much handsomer guys."

Before the end of filming, Shaw emerged as thoroughly disliked not just by Lana, but by most of the rest of the cast and crew, too. She agreed with her co-workers that the bandleader was "an intellectual snob."

Shaw clearly demonstrated that appearing in a silly college drama was beneath him. He complained all the time and had arguments with Simon and his fellow performers. The crew came to detest him to the degree that they plotted to drop an arc light on his head. "He could have been killed," Simon said. "Thank God it was just a threat."

Shaw later told *The Hollywood Reporter,* "*Dancing Co-Ed* reeks of pig heaven. Everybody was against me, including its so-called star, Lana Turner. I don't care. I was supposed to play myself. Simon had promised me he'd let me write my own lines. But he doublecrossed me and went back on his word. The screenwriter, Albert Mannheimer, gave me stupid lines like 'Hi-ho, lads and lassies!' That was pure Rudy Vallee crap."

During Lana's second meeting with Robert Walker, who had been assigned an uncredited role as a student in *Dancing Co-Ed,* she interpreted him as a sensitive, troubled man. Dysfunctionally married at the time to the actress who would later change her name to Jennifer Jones, he seemed severely tormented. During one of their rare encounters, Lana noticed that he was drinking from a flask, later realizing that at the time he was beginning his

Artie Shaw with Lana Turner: "Call it 'Young Man with a Horn,'" he said. "She got my horn...time and time again. Once I'd broken her in, she couldn't get it enough."

93

long descent into acute alcoholism.

"I got married thinking that it would fulfill this desperate need I have to be loved," Walker had told her, "but that hasn't happened. I don't feel fulfilled. As a child, I wanted to escape from life, finding it too painful. I love my wife, maybe too much, but I find her self-enchanted."

The petite actress with the "peek-a-boo" hair style, Veronica Lake, also made a (very brief) appearance in *Dancing Co-Ed.* Years later, in Miami, she told this book's author, Darwin Porter, "I was introduced to Lana Turner, but I don't think the stuck-up bitch even remembered meeting me. When I met her, she didn't even pay attention, and snubbed me. But I've always been an intuitive person, and I knew that she represented tomorrow's competition."

Reviews of *Dancing Co-Ed* were generally favorable, *The New York Times* declaring, "Miss Turner wears abbreviated dancing togs with what seems almost like originality."

Billy Wilkerson, in *The Hollywood Reporter,* called her, "A new MGM star, one destined to reach as far in selling tickets as any this great company has ever produced. *Dancing Co-Ed* definitely *makes* Lana Turner. This little lady has been launched."

Lana became acutely aware of Veronica Lake during World War II, when Lake developed an enthusiastic fan base of her own, and competed with Lana and Betty Grable as the most-desired "Pinup Girl of World War II."

One reason Lana might not have remembered Lake was that she was being billed at the time as Constance Keane.

Years later, when Lana was asked "Whatever Became of Veronica Lake," she answered, "I heard she was working as a barmaid in a Manhattan cocktail lounge."

***

Director S. Sylvan Simon must have contracted a case of Lana Turner fever. He cast the budding star as the lead of his third picture, *Two Girls on Broadway* (1940), billing her ahead of two more experienced show business veterans, Joan Blondell and George Murphy.

Although she was delighted with her billing, she had hoped for fresh and original material. To her chagrin, she learned that the script, based on an original story by Edmund Goulding, had been recycled. MGM had released its first talkie, *Broadway Melody of 1929,* starring Bessie Love. In spite of its flaws, it had won an Oscar as Best Picture of the Year.

In the film, Blondell and Lana played two stage-struck sisters, Molly and Pat Mahoney, newly arrived on Broadway from the hinterlands Both of them fall in love with a song-and-dance man, Eddie Kerns (Murphy).

With two blondes and only one man, something's got to give. Sacrificing her personal dreams in favor of those of her sister, Lana decides to accept a marriage proposal from a dissipated playboy, as portrayed by Kent Taylor, despite the fact that he's been married four times previously, and even though she doesn't love him.

In *Two Girls on Broadway*, Lana's true love, Eddie, as played by Murphy, rushes frantically to City Hall, objecting loudly to her marriage ceremony to the dissipated playboy she doesn't love, as portrayed by Kent Taylor.

At the conclusion of the film, the character played by Blondell ends up as the sacrific-

When two sisters, Lana Turner (left) and Joan Blondell, each fall in love with the same man, hoofer George Murphy, something's got to give.

ing sister. She relinquishes Murphy to Lana after they emerge on Broadway as a successful dance team. Blondell, known as the wisecracking but vulnerable blonde with the heart of gold, is subsequently degraded to status as a cigarette girl in the nightclub where her sister (Lana) reigns as a dance star and a woman in love.

Lana had seen several of Blondell's films, especially *The Public Enemy* (1931), a movie she'd made at Warner Brothers long before she ever met Lana.

Hailing from New York, Blondell usually played brassy, sassy, wisecracking blondes. In 1927, she'd made her Broadway debut in *The Trial of Mary Dugan*.

She and Lana became quite close during the filming, and Lana turned to her like an older sister. Blondell was too generous of heart to be jealous of Lana. During their filming of *Two Girls on Broadway*, Blondell was married to crooner Dick Powell.

MGM's publicity department hyped *Two Girls on Broadway* as "The Girl They're All Talking About...Lovely Lana Turner, America's Blonde Spitfire, in Her Hottest, Most Daring Film."

Despite whatever other distractions emerged from her private life, on set of

Two Girls on Broadway, at least, Lana was a genuine professional, devoting tireless hours to her dance routines. At first, she'd been intimidated for having been teamed with such a seasoned hoofer like Murphy, but when the cameras were rolling, at least, they danced together in harmony.

In his memoirs, *Say…Didn't You Use to Be George Murphy?*, the star wrote, "Everyone at Metro was talking about this fascinating new blonde who danced so beautifully with me. You could hardly get on the set, so many people had come to see the lovely newcomer in the flesh. And that's how Lana Turner got her big boost to stardom."

During its filming, Lana became popular with both cast and crew. They threw a party for her to celebrate her nineteenth birthday. A dedication read, "To the Sweater Girl from the gang who made the yarn."

Once again, the ever-faithful *Hollywood Reporter* came through for her, writing that "Lana Turner's latest film seems to be a fairly entertaining bit of fluff. It proves that she is the gal Fred Astaire should be dancing with if MGM wants to duplicate

George Murphy's dance routine with Luscious Lana in *Two Girls on Broadway*: "George Murphy may not have been dynamite as an actor, but that guy could sure dance," Lana said.

One critic wrote, "George Murphy had his dedication and inoffensiveness to pull him through, not being any great threat to those more talented in the dramatic, comedic, and dancing departments."

the Astaire-Rogers sizzle."

***

Although Lana's relationship with Artie Shaw had started with a kiss on the set of *Dancing Co-Ed*, it soon degenerated into a wall of hostility because, as he admitted himself, "I'm a difficult man to work with."

But on Monday, February 12, 1939, the pair took a detour that surprised Hollywood and, on Shaw's part, broke the hearts of an impressionable Judy Garland and a more hardened Betty Grable.

Comedian Phil Silvers had signed a contract with MGM, a studio that liked his frantic, jabbering *schtick*, thinking his idiotic behavior might work if he played the role of best pal to a leading man in certain lightweight films.

Silvers phoned one of "my best pals" (Shaw himself), and invited him to MGM one afternoon. Silvers remembered that Shaw, based on their first meeting on the set of *Dancing Co-Ed*, had loudly and repeatedly referred to Lana as being "hot as a firecracker," so he decided to bring them together again. He later explained, "Artie was in a black funk, and needed cheering up. I thought Miss Turner might turn the trick."

Silvers and Shaw arrived at the same time on the set of *Two Girls on Broadway*, the picture Lana had been shooting at the time with George Murphy and Joan Blondell. They watched as she performed a dance routine with Murphy.

Surprisingly, when Lana spotted Shaw on the set, she went over to him and welcomed him, seemingly having forgotten—or else forgiven—him for the previous vulgar comments he had made about her. As Silvers later asserted, "Lana took to Artie like a bee to honey."

"I'm sure Lana never looked lovelier—or sexier—than she did that afternoon," Silvers said. "She was a real knockout in a green satin gown that looked like it had been sewn onto her curvy body. It outlined everything, even her nipples. What a sight! Even I felt a stirring down below."

As Shaw remembered the historic moment: "Lana had been hostile to me ever since she heard me putting her down to some of the boys. But when I saw her again, she was open and friendly, a sweet, charming, sexy baby doll. I invited her to dinner and she told me, 'Give me a raincheck.'"

During their conversation, which ended when the director called Lana back to the set, she seductively told Shaw, "I'm not free tonight. But who knows? Give me a call some long, lonely night. We'll see." Then she kissed him lightly on the cheek and departed.

A notorious womanizer, Shaw managed to get Lana's phone number before he left. As they were leaving MGM, he told Silvers, "I'm determined to fuck that little hottie."

The following week, he called on two more occasions, and each time, Lana turned him down. She didn't tell him, but for each of the venues proposed by Shaw, she'd already arranged a date with Bautzer. She was, in fact, wearing an engagement ring he'd given her, although all of her friends had warned her, "Greg is not the marrying kind."

97

Bautzer was invited to all the most prestigious parties in Hollywood. On one of their dates, he introduced Lana to Noël Coward, who at the time was visiting from London. "Lana, my dear, you're 'The Sweater Girl,' right? I see that Greg has already discovered you. You're lucky. I would have snared him for myself, but the dear chap simply has too many teeth."

***

Lana arrived early at her home one afternoon to dress up and make herself look particularly glamorous for her date with Bautzer.

Since her birthday and Mildred's were four days apart, he had invited both of them for a celebratory dinner. However, he called at 6:30PM, claiming he had a stomach ache. "I had some bad oysters at lunch."

Horribly disappointed, she decided to stay in for the evening, despite Mildred's urging to go out to dinner with her as a mother-daughter twosome. Lana, however, prevailed, based to some degree on her status as the family's breadwinner, Ultimately, despite her mother's objections, she stayed home.

[Months later, Lana learned that on the night that Bautzer had broken their date, he was actually entertaining the English actress, Wendy Burrie, with whom he enjoyed a romantic evening at his home.

Bautzer was treading on dangerous ground, since Barrie was the girlfriend of the gangster and mobster, Bugsy Siegel.

After Lana learned about Greg's affair with Barrie, she hooked up with the gangster and, perhaps as payback, inaugurated a brief affair with him herself.

"I always believe in the revenge fuck," she told several of her girlfriends, including Ann Rutherford and Rita Johnson.]

Shaw had planned an evening with band singer Helen Forrest, with whom he'd been having an on-again, off-again affair. But Helen had gotten a last-minute singing gig and had to cancel. Scrambling to recoup what was left of his evening, Shaw remembered Lana's allure on the set of *Two Girls on Broadway*.

Spontaneously, at 7PM, he telephoned Lana. Thinking it was Bautzer phoning to apologize, she answered the ring herself. Impulsively, perhaps with the intention of stabbing back at Bautzer, she accepted Shaw's last-minute dinner invitation.

Later that evening, after retrieving her at her home, Shaw drove her to Victor Hugo's, a chic restaurant in Beverly Hills, where she was surprised to learn that Phil Silvers would be joining them at table. She later said, "I didn't know why Artie had invited that comic. Didn't Phil know that three's a crowd?"

As Silvers wandered off, she danced with Shaw. He pressed his hard body close to hers as they moved in rhythm to the music of Guy Lombardo and his Royal Canadians.

As Silvers was "chasing after some dame" across the room, Lana and Shaw ditched him and went for a ride along Mulholland Drive.

At a secluded spot, they sat and talked. "No fast moves," she recalled. "No feeling me up."

In her memoirs, Lana does not mention Silvers having dined with them that night. She asserted, instead, that she and Shaw drove along Sunset Boulevard, heading toward the ocean.

Years later, Shaw's account differed from Lana's. He recalled driving up into the Hollywood Hills, where they found a secluded spot that looked out over the lights of Los Angeles.

He discussed his dreams for the future. They included his hope that his jazz would be taken more seriously, and his plans to compose music and write books. He even quoted from Nietzsche and Schopenhauer, two philosophers whose work at the time was unknown to her. Shaw also revealed that there was much he disliked about being a celebrity, especially all those jitterbugging girls who pestered him for autographs and tried to rip off his clothing as souvenirs.

Both of them, or so they claimed, shared the same dream: to live in a rose-covered cottage surrounded by picket fences. He said that he wanted a faithful wife who would bear and nurture his children.

"That's what I want, too," she said. "I want to be married and to have babies. I just love children. I don't like acting. It means getting up at some horrendous hour every morning and driving to the studio to sit through long makeup sessions. Then it's on to the set to be directed by some ego or perhaps called into Mayer's office for a lecture on who I can love...or not. I'd give up my career to become a wife and mother."

Even though she claimed not to have been physically attracted to Shaw, and certainly not in love with him in the way she was with Bautzer, she seemed to have been colluding with him in some shared romantic dream. Later, she'd be dismissive of the events of that night, asserting that her intentions involved "just a desire to get even with Greg."

After their intimate conversation in the parked car on Mulholland Drive, Shaw tossed out a dare: "Let me charter a plane tonight and fly us to Vegas to get married. Will you go with me and become my bride?"

She didn't hesitate before impulsively answering, "I'm your girl. Consider me airborne from this moment on."

It was a spur-of-the-moment decision she'd later regret.

***

Although in any stereotypical Lana Turner movie, this would be the point at which the protagonists would kiss, Lana claimed that there, on Mulholland Drive, that didn't happen. Instead, Shaw took her hand and held it for a while before starting the motor and driving her to his nearby home.

At his house, Shaw made a late night call to Paul Mantz, Hollywood's most famous pilot after aviator Howard Hughes. Mantz was known as "the Honeymoon Pilot," since he often flew couples to Las Vegas, many of whom, like Lana and Shaw, were in the emotional throes of impulsive wedding ceremonies.

Mantz was very discreet, having been involved, as he had been multiple times, in the transportation of lovers to secluded rendezvous and off-the-record trysts.

Airborne and looking down over the flickering lights of Los Angeles from a high-altitude perspective, Shaw was said to have kissed Lana shyly, evoking the gentle kiss he'd delivered on the day they first met on the set of *Dancing Co-Ed.*

In Vegas at 4AM, Shaw persuaded Justice of the Peace, George E. Marshall, to hustle himself out of bed to perform the ceremony. He wore red-and-white polka dot pajamas and a tattered robe, and his wife, Bertha, still in pin curlers, was a witness.

Lana later wrote, "The first time I ever kissed Artie was when we were pronounced man and wife." [*Actually, she'd kissed him the first day she'd met him, and again (several times) during the plane ride to Vegas from Los Angeles.*]

When asked by the Justice of the Peace for a wedding ring, Shaw removed a blue star sapphire set in platinum from his own finger. Of course, it didn't fit. He'd later buy her a gold wedding band to replace it.

Before Mantz transported the newlyweds back to Burbank, they celebrated their honeymoon dinner at an all-night hamburger shack—"no onions, please."

Just before they boarded the plane, Lana sent a cryptic telegram to Mildred. "GOT MARRIED IN LAS VEGAS. CALL YOU LATER. LOVE, LANA."

When it arrived, Mildred assumed that Lana had finally married Bautzer. She was at first delighted with the idea of this up-and-coming lawyer as a son-in-law. Then, uncertain and searching for details, she phoned Bautzer and was shocked to find him at home. Actually, as it turned out, he was in bed at the time with Wendy Barrie.

When he learned about Lana's marriage, he told Mildred, "I think I know who the lucky guy is. I'll get back to you."

Within the hour, he phoned a nervous and impatient Mildred. "She married Artie Shaw."

"I don't believe it," she answered. "She hates that son-of-a-bitch. She told me so herself." Then, with a shaky voice, she said, "I've lost her."

"So have I," he said.

***

When Mr. and Mrs. Artie Shaw flew back to Los Angeles, he drove her to his home on Summit Ridge. Instantly, he flew into a rage after seeing that his house was surrounded by photographers, reporters, fans, and the idle curious. Somehow, probably through Bautzer, word of his *blitzkrieg* marriage to Lana had reached the press, and his house was under siege.

He cursed the reporters, surprising Lana with his venom. She'd never seen such temper in him before. He used vulgar, foul language, even threatening to kill a photographer. Enraged, he grabbed her arm and shoved her inside the house.

Then he slammed around the house, locking all the windows and bolting the doors. Fifteen minutes later, she heard the sound of breaking glass coming from the back door. After that, genuinely frightened, she phoned the Head of Publicity at MGM, Howard Strickling, who promised to send three of his staff members to deal with the swarm of reporters and photographers.

Eventually, although most of the crowd dispersed, others vowed to remain onsite till dawn. Shaw phoned his friend, Edgar Selwyn, the producer of *Dancing Co-Ed,* who offered them his guest bedroom for the night. Escaping hastily through the crowd assembled in front of his house, Shaw hustled Lana into his car and fled.

By now, Lana wanted a bath and a change of clothing, since she'd been wearing the same navy blue dress for twenty-four hours.

When they reached their destination, Selwyn kissed her good night and then departed, and Shaw ushered her into the bedroom.

That night, in bed with him for the first time, she realized "I've married a stranger. I really didn't know this man at all." She suggested to him that since both of them were totally exhausted and needed sleep, any possible love-making could be postponed.

Defiantly, however, he pulled off his clothes and for the first time, his erection was exposed to her. He wanted her and was determined to have her.

She later wrote about the seduction, calling him "clumsy and fumbling. It was horrible, meaningless. When we finally got into position...well, it was just horrible, over in a minute. He just went limp. As for me, I experienced nothing but a question—what am I doing under this man? There had been no kissing and no cuddling, either before or afterward. He turned over and fell immediately asleep."

The morning after her so-called "honeymoon night," when she heard her new husband in the shower, she put through a call to her mother, Mildred, telling her, "I showed Greg Bautzer that he can't break a date with me."

About an hour later, after Shaw left the house, she drove over to see Mildred. Mother and daughter had moved into a large, Spanish-style home on Beverly Glen Boulevard. Mildred's first words to her were, "Why did you do it?"

"I'm very happy, mother," she answered, which was not true.

That day, she packed only a small percentage of her wardrobe and returned for a rendezvous with her new husband, dressing provocatively to greet him when he returned home.

"You look camera ready, too much makeup, and you're overdressed," he told her. Then he ordered her to change into a skirt and a blouse and shoes with flat heels. "And for god's sake, remove that god damn lipstick."

She would later ask her new agent, Johnny Hyde, "Why did he marry one of the most glamorous women in the world if he wanted a drab, dreary, and dowdy housewife?"

She didn't even know how old Shaw was until the next day when she read it in the newspapers. She figured he was somewhere between twenty-five and thirty-five. It turned out that he was twenty-eight.

***

Her quickie marriage made frontpage news around the country. Gossips surmised, "There's a baby in the oven."

Bautzer pretended to be heartbroken when he spoke to the press. "My God, I'm shocked. She was wearing my engagement ring. I can't put into words how much I care for my baby."

George Murphy described what happened when he reported to work that day to dance with Lana on the set of *Two Girls on Broadway*. "All hell had broken loose," he said. "No one knew where Lana was. She just didn't show up for work. All of us were really surprised when we heard she'd eloped. Things happened quickly in Hollywood in those days."

In her column, Louella Parsons wrote, "Both Artie Shaw and Lana Turner are trusting and lovable, and they use their hearts instead of their heads. Lana, of course, has never been in any scandal, but she always acts hastily and is guided by her own ideas rather than by any advice the studio gives her."

***

Betty Grable was in Manhattan when she read about Shaw's elopement with Lana. Later that day, she confronted the press. She issued only a brief statement. "This love of Artie's must have come on very suddenly."

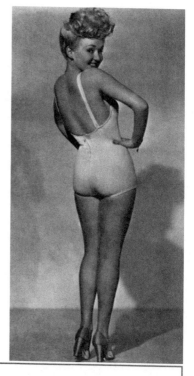

Inside, she was grieving, as she confessed to her fellow cast members when she showed up for work on Broadway. At the time, she was playing the second female lead in *DuBarry Was a Lady,* starring Ethel Merman and Bert Lahr.

Three days before he'd eloped with Lana, Shaw had written--not phoned—Grable in Manhattan, asking her to marry him. For some reason, she chose not to call him, but sent him a "snail mail" letter instead: "Darling, this is what I've been waiting for. I've just handed in my notice to the show. Let's get married tomorrow. Fly to New York!"

Disappointed and enraged, Grable phoned Phil Silvers in Hollywood. "Married to that little blonde slut, is he?" she shouted, referring to Shaw's marriage to Lana. "Just who in hell does he think he is?"

"Betty, I'm so sorry," Silvers said. "I took

When Betty Grable posed for the most famous pinup picture of World War II, the photographer asked her to pose for a rear view since she was secretly pregnant at the time.

Before that, she and her husband, actor Jackie Coogan, often went nightclubbing with Artie Shaw. He claimed that, "Betty kept rubbing her knee against mine under the table at restaurants and clubs."

One night, a drunken Coogan came home and urinated all over Grable as she slept. In a rage, and in tears, she fled into the night and arrived at Artie Shaw's home. Their affair began, Grable hoping that it would lead to marriage.

That was before Lana impulsively decided that Shaw was "husband material."

your letter out of his mailbox and put it on his desk. He's probably not even read it yet."

"Go fuck yourself!" she yelled, slamming down the receiver.

What Grable didn't tell Silvers, and what she had not confided to Shaw, was that she was pregnant with his baby.

That night, before going onstage, she asked Merman, "You know everything on Broadway. Surely you must know who's the best abortion doctor in town."

"Leave it to me, child," Merman said. "I'll phone my friend, J. Edgar Hoover. He can set you up with the best abortion doctor in the country—and not some quack."

[Betty Grable and Lana Turner were destined to be rivals. And because they didn't work for the same studios, they didn't have to compete with each other for roles. They did vie, however, more or less ferociously, for the title of "Pinup Girl of World War II."]

***

Betty Grable wasn't the only star in Hollywood whose heart had been broken (or was eventually broken) by Shaw. Judy Garland's mother, Ethel Gumm Gilmore, woke up her daughter to show her the morning's headline—ARTIE SHAW ELOPES WITH LANA TURNER.

Judy screamed before bursting into tears. "But Artie's in love with ME! He was with me only two nights before. He told me then that he loved me—and only me! The son of a bitch has betrayed me!"

Two days later, when an enraged Ethel finally succeeded in getting Shaw on the phone, the bandleader denied that he'd ever had sex with a teenaged Garland. Because of Garland's age, he had a good reason to deny that their relationship had turned sexual.

But to her friends, including Mickey Rooney, Garland admitted that she and Shaw were having sex.

While making *The Wizard of Oz*, Judy Garland fell in love with Artie Shaw. When he collapsed on stage at the Palomar on February 10, 1939, he was rushed to the hospital. He was suffering from a rare blood disease, granulocytosis, comparable to leukemia. He fell into a coma.

His first memory when he woke up was of Judy hovering over him. "That absolutely marvelous little face, with freckles, the brown eyes, the reddish hair, looking at me with consummate tenderness—myth-like, dreamlike, not real."

"You're going to be all right, Artie," she assured him.

"I couldn't help it that she'd fallen in love with me."

"First, me, then Lana. I think our clarinet player likes teenage gals," she said.

Shaw and Garland indulged in long talks together. She remembered that one day he had told her, "You're little Francis Gumm of Grand Rapids, and I'm little Arthur Arshawsky from Manhattan's Lower East Side. Just look at where we are now!"

One afternoon, in her despair, Garland indiscreetly phoned columnist Hedda Hopper. "After Artie left me, I felt at times I couldn't make it through another day. I'd have my driver circle around MGM because I felt I didn't have the stamina to go inside and perform, much less dancing down that Yellow Brick Road in ruby-red slippers. I'm a wreck, and I fear I'm taking too many prescription drugs."

Fortunately, one of Shaw's best friends, the musician, David Rose, came along just in time to heal Garland's broken heart. She soon fell in love with him, and married him. "It all began one day when he brought me a piece of chocolate cake baked by his mother," she said, years later.

***

Three days after their hasty wedding in Las Vegas, from their now-shared home in Los Angeles, Shaw demanded that Lana accompany him on the 20th Century Limited for a honeymoon in New York City, where he had to meet and make deals with some of his fellow musicians.

Acquiescing to this sudden demand, and fearful of its implications at the studio, Lana phoned a furious Louis B. Mayer, who was already angered at her elopement and the ways in which it had delayed production on *Two Girls on Broadway*. He demanded that she report to work at once—or else face suspension. But after pleading with him, he relented. "Three days…that's it. Or else." Then the studio boss slammed down the phone.

Arriving at Grand Central in Manhattan, the couple was mobbed by fans, photographers, and reporters. Shaw fought to clear a pathway for them, herding her into a taxi and ordering the driver to take them to the exclusive Sherry-Netherland Hotel, where he'd booked a suite for them on the 21st floor.

Dinner that night was at Reubens, where they sat at table with the popular gossip columnist Leonard Lyons and his wife, Sylvia. As Lana and Shaw left the restaurant, more fans awaited them, both his and hers, beseeching them for their autographs. As flashbulbs popped, he cleared a way for her and pushed her into a taxi. "Hell, we'll be here all night," he was heard shouting at her.

The next day, he told her that he had some business with a recording studio, but gave her no further details, not even an idea of when he'd be coming back.

She already knew that he was estranged from his mother, Sarah Arshawsky. Anxious to meet her, Lana searched for her telephone number in his address book and, without his permission or approval, called her.

A woman with a thick Jewish accent picked up the phone and seemed delighted to be speaking to her new daughter-in-law. She told Lana, "I've seen two of your movies. You're a beautiful girl. So young."

Sarah seemed very disappointed that her son hadn't phoned her himself, but she was glad to receive Lana. Dressing herself chicly and applying perhaps too much makeup, Lana got into a chauffeur-driven limousine and headed for her mother-in-law's modest apartment.

Inside, Sarah welcomed Lana warmly and served her tea. Then, she wanted to know if she could invite some of her women friends over "to get a look at how beautiful you are." Lana declined.

Since she knew so very little about the man she'd impulsively married, she pumped Sarah for information. Her son had been born in the Bronx, but grew up in New Haven. Coming from a Russian Jewish background, he faced anti-Semitism. His (deceased) father Harry Arshawsky, had been a dressmaker and photographer.

Shaw's relationship with his mother had been stressful and difficult almost from birth. She told Lana that one day, she'd threatened to jump out the window to her death. "You know what my boy did? He ran down the stairs and stood on the sidewalk to watch me jump."

As if that weren't shocking enough, it was followed by yet another revelation: Lana was the third Mrs. Shaw. In 1932, he'd married a very young girl, Jane Cairns, but her family had had the marriage annulled because of her age. Then, from 1934 to 1937, he'd been married to Margaret Allen.

While married to her, and while at the woodpile, he had almost chopped off his left forefinger. A nurse, she had been able to sew it back together.

"Artie told me he feared he might not play the clarinet ever again," Sarah said.

Overwhelmed with all this new and in some ways unwelcome information, Lana had heard enough. As she prepared to leave, Sarah begged her "to bring Artie to dinner."

Lana kissed the woman on her cheeks and left, never to see her again.

Years later, looking back at her first marriage, and with the added perspective of six subsequent (and also ill-fated) unions, Lana said, "That was not the way I planned my life. I wanted to have one husband and seven babies. It worked out just the opposite."

***

Before leaving New York, Shaw introduced her to many of his musician friends, some of whom were performing on the nights they met. Together, Shaw and Lana hung out at lots of late-night jazz clubs. Following her divorce from Shaw, Lana would continue the pattern she'd previously established of late-night club-going. Her daughter, Cheryl Crane, called the post-Artie Shaw period as "Lana's Boys in the Band" era.

"Mother was a bit infatuated with all of the incredible musicians whose talent thrilled her," Cheryl said. "She loved being in on their late-night jam sessions, and they loved having her present. There were a number of big band names whom she dated...all young and talented. Whatever was in town and not on the road might become number one in her date book."

She met, and would later date, Tommy Dorsey, one of the most famous band-leaders of the Big Band era. She also met Buddy Rich and Gene Krupa. In her immediate future would appear such figures as Desi Arnaz, Tony Martin, and Frank Sinatra, each of whom would be a future lover.

105

"While I was married to Artie, I had to put these boys on hold, at least for the moment," she told Joan Blondell when she returned to complete *Two Girls on Broadway*. "Every one of them flirted with me, I mean a little more than flirted, and I liked them all. But I had to bide my time."

***

Back at MGM, Lana met with her mentor, Mervyn LeRoy, who advised her that she needed a new agent. "That Henry Willson spends all his time seducing his male clients, and doesn't pay enough attention to you and your career. I'd recommend that you sign with Johnny Hyde, a VP at the William Morris Agency."

She followed his advice and arranged a meeting with Hyde, whom she found grotesquely ugly but possibly effective as an agent, since he represented some of the biggest names in the business. She later told LeRoy, "I call him The Dwarf, and he seemed to have the hots for me."

Born in Russia in 1895, he'd moved with his parents to America when he was only five.

He took her to dinner at Ciro's. Later, in her description of the evening to LeRoy, she said, "He drooled over me, but made good points about my career."

"You've served your time in 'B' pictures," he told her. "Now it's time to move up to the classy ones, as soon as you get your present crapper out of the way."

No doubt, he was referring to the 1940 melodrama, *We Who Are Young*, that she was shooting at the time.

"To capture the throne as Queen of MGM, you've got to appear with really big male stars," Hyde told her.

"I'm dreaming of Clark Gable, Robert Taylor, Errol Flynn, and Tyrone Power," she said.

"Forget Ty and Errol," he answered. "Those faggots belong to either Fox or Jack Warner. Stick to MGM stars."

From the beginning, Hyde earned her respect, renegotiating her contract with MGM, increasing her pay to $250 a week, with yearly escalations.

"That was a huge sum in those days," she later wrote. I could buy clothes I'd always dreamed of wearing. I also bought a new Chrysler *coupé*."

Two months after she signed with Hyde, he called with good news. "In your next two pictures, you're going to appear with two of the biggest male stars at Metro."

Young Marilyn Monroe with her adoring agent, Johnny Hyde.

First, he had been Lana's agent.

"You mean, Clark Gable and Robert Taylor?" she asked.

"No, later for those guys. Right now, I'm talking about James Stewart and Spencer Tracy. Not bad, huh? You'll owe me."

After screening two pictures she'd recently made, he took her to Ciro's to show her off. She'd dressed in up-to-the-minute designer clothes.

"On film, you come off as a beautiful mannequin," he told her. "To be a star, you've got to have more expression on your face. I want you to watch some silent films. Those stars, like a young Garbo in the late 1920s or Chaplin, had great expressions on their faces, and they also acted with their bodies, too. To be a big star, you've got to do that. Being beautiful is one thing, being an actress is another. Your face has got to express what you're feeling inside."

"I will do that because I want to succeed," she said. "Before I married Artie, I thought I wanted to be a wife and mother. But when I see how awful marriage can be, I think I prefer stardom to being a *hausfrau.*"

During the next few weeks, she learned that she was slated to co-star in two big MGM pictures, *Ziegfeld Girl* (1941), with James Stewart, Judy Garland, and Hedy Lamarr; and *Dr. Jekyll and Mr. Hyde* (also 1941) with the seasoned actor, Spencer Tracy, and with the new discovery from Sweden, Ingrid Bergman.

Also in the coming weeks, Hyde would come to her rescue on a personal level when she faced crisis after crisis, beginning with a divorce and subsequently, an abortion.

***

When Tommy Dorsey dropped in to visit Shaw during one of his trips to Hollywood, Shaw complained to him, "Lana doesn't know Nietzsche from Schopenhauer."

"Neither do I," Dorsey answered. "But Lana has other assets. Oh, what a lucky guy you are. You're complaining?"

Her new agent often functioned as the recipient of her complaints about her marriage to Shaw. "I never

Lana with John Shelton in *We Who Are Young.* Off screen, Shelton struck out.

107

mastered the art of cooking, house cleaning, and washing dishes. But that's the kind of wife he wants, even though he can afford a maid, since he makes a big salary."

He demanded that she be home every evening before 6PM, which was the hour he usually returned from work. When she was held up, he accused her of sleeping around—"Maybe with a studio grip."

"I don't know what his IQ was, but he was very smart," Lana said. "One night, I asked how such and intelligent man would marry a dumb gal like me. He had an answer for that:"

"You've got great knockers. My intellect isn't linked to my pelvis."

"My husband likes to dominate, and he's always putting me down, especially in front of his friends," she said.

***

Mildred called every morning, beseeching her daughter to leave Shaw and suggesting that Greg Bautzer might know how to get the marriage annulled. "He doesn't love you. He loves the idea of screwing Lana Turner—that's all your marriage is about, nothing else. I predict it'll be over in ten minutes, if that."

Mildred and her son-in-law barely concealed their contempt for each other. Privately, he referred to her as "a hard-assed man-eater."

He decided to cure her of her annoying habit of dropping in at any time of the day or evening, always unannounced, and usually at an inappropriate time. One morning, he decided to do something about that.

After Lana had left for the studio at 5AM, he sat in their kitchen, wearing only a silk robe, reading his newspaper and drinking a cup of coffee. Then he heard Mildred's car pull into the driveway. "I'd recognize that bad muffler anywhere."

He walked to the door. Before opening it, he pulled off his robe and fluffed himself as a means of inducing an erection. Then he threw open the door. "Sorry," he said to his mother-in-law. "I was expecting Judy Garland."

Mildred let out a scream and raced back to her car.

In spite of the horror stories Lana spread about their marriage, there were moments of tenderness. He told her that she had been the inspiration for one of his signature compositions, "Summit Ridge Drive," a reference to their hilltop home.

Occasionally, as a couple, she and Shaw entertained friends and acquaintances at home, usually visiting with musicians or with boys in his band, all of whom seemed to dote on Lana. Other women visitors were rare, with the noteworthy exception of Judy Garland.

Partly because she had become romantically involved with one of his best friends, David Rose, Garland had forgiven Shaw for running off and marrying Lana. Their relationship was a bit stiff for a while, but Garland seemed to possess a warm and forgiving heart.

One night, when Garland and Lana were chatting in the kitchen, the singer told Lana, "I'm glad you took Artie off my hands. If I'd married him, it would rank as one of my bigger mistakes—and I've made a few. I see how he treats you—that's not for me."

108

One Sunday night, Garland had been most affectionate, kissing and hugging both Shaw and Lana. When she left, Shaw turned to Lana. "I know Judy very well. You may not know this, but she's a bisexual, and she probably wants to have a three-way with us."

"I don't believe you—not Judy!" Lana said. "You're making this up. What a terrible thing to say about a sweet girl like Judy!"

During a talk with Hyde the next day, he suggested that her husband was the one who wanted a three-way. Since he was hip to the latest Hollywood gossip, she asked if he'd heard that Garland was bisexual.

"Everybody knows that, including Louis B. Mayer," Hyde answered. "Howard Strickling, keeper of the secrets, wants that to stay under wraps. Imagine if the public ever found out that Dorothy from Kansas was a lesbian."

Another night, when Garland was a guest, Shaw told Lana to go to their bedroom and fetch his slippers. At the top of the stairs, slippers in hand, Lana heard Garland and Shaw talking about her.

"Why don't you come around more?" he asked. "I miss you a lot."

"I miss you, too," she said. "Lana's nice, but, you know, talking to her is like talking to a beautiful vase filled with red roses."

***

During the miserable course of her marriage to Shaw, Lana continued to report for work at MGM. There, on one or another of its soundstages, she would make her last B movie before evolving into a major movie star.

For reasons known only to himself, Harold S. Bucquet, who had directed Lana in *Calling Dr. Kildare*, cast "America's Number One Dreamgirl" as a drab housewife in a soapy melodramatic programmer, *We Who Are Young* (1940). It was the story of a struggling young couple trying to make enough money to feed themselves, pay the rent, and negotiate with debt collectors and loan sharks about repossession of their furnishings.

Amazingly, this minor soap opera had been written by Dalton Trumbo, one of Hollywood's finest (and most politically persecuted) writers. One of the story readers at MGM had sent a memo: "Much of the world is now at war, and the United States may be sucked into it soon. Along comes Trumbo with a tired old Depression era story that might have been written by a Hollywood hack back in 1933. REJECT!"

Obviously, no one heeded the reader's suggestion. Lana was cast as the struggling housewife, Margy Brooks. Her natural beauty was still evident and was indeed highlighted by the photographer, Karl Freund, one of the best in the business. It would be her last movie for some time in which she would appear as a brunette.

Gene Lockhart was cast as C. B. Bemais, their insensitive boss, who morphs into their benefactor. In the final reel, Lana's husband, William (John Shelton), has to steal a car to rush his wife to the hospital, where she gives birth to twins. As Lana later said, "It was my first mother role."

On the first day of the shoot, Lana was reintroduced to the handsome but rather bland Shelton, who had been given a co-starring role. During the making of

Dramatic School, the two of them had had a brief fling, and he seemed to want to reignite the flame. But for Lana, it had flickered out.

She invited Shaw to a sneak preview of the movie in Pasadena. He didn't like it, although he admired the way she was dressed as an unglamorous housewife. "This is the way I prefer you."

Shaw vehemently objected to one scene in particular—the sexiest in the movie—in which she was fetchingly depicted in a satin *négligée.*

He recalled, "That scene had a tremendous impact on the audience, especially horny college boys who wolf-whistled at the screen. I didn't like my wife showing herself off like that, driving the guys wild. I didn't want to be married to some striptease artist."

As for *We Are Too Young,* MGM ditched its former ad campaign and promoted Lana in the scene wearing the satin nightgown. The ad read: "*MODERN YOUTH IN SEARCH OF ALL THE ANSWERS—LANA TURNER, THE BLAZING BLONDE IN HER MOST DARING ROLE!*"

Reviewers were kind for the most part, at least to Lana, although critics agreed with the sarcastic assessment of the original MGM script reader. Based on its premises, at least, the film belonged somewhere in the Depression-soaked mid-1930s.

Time magazine wrote, "Lana Turner turns into a dramatic actress of some talent, hiding her much-publicized charms behind a simple gingham house dress."

The New York Daily News claimed, "Lana Turner, who has not been much more than a glorified sweater model on the screen up to now, is turning out to be a surprise at the Criterion Theatre. MGM decided to de-glamourize their young star and prove that she could get along without that sweater. They assigned her to a role that required natural acting ability. *Lo and behold!* She turns in a fine performance."

Her reputation as "The Sweater Girl" still lingered, as sales of the garment across the country rose by 22%, even attracting the ire of the Breen Office (formerly known as the Hayes Office). In a memo to producers and directors, the censors issued a warning that declared that it would be forbidden "for an actress to be shown on the screen wearing a sweater in which breasts were clearly outlined."

***

Shaw's close friend, comedian Phil Silvers, came to dinner one night to discuss an appearance of the three of them at Earl Carroll's, a nightclub on Sunset Boulevard, which was gaining in popularity. He'd devised a routine where Shaw played the clarinet, Silvers did his jabbering comedy routine, and Lana danced one of her numbers from *Two Girls on Broadway.* The act played to a packed house.

Lana was not charmed by Silvers' second visit to their apartment, when he brought with him a stash of marijuana for an evening of "reefer magic." At the time, marijuana was not unfamiliar to her, as many musicians, including members of Shaw's band, made use of it regularly. As she declared in her memoirs, she had never smoked it before, and refused to do so that night.

She later told Hyde, "I've never seen Artie enjoy himself so much. The whole room was going up in a cloud of smoke. I left the boys to enjoy themselves and went to bed early. The next morning, I found they had opened practically every can of food in the pantry in an attempt to make a stew. Most of the food seemed to have made it to the floor."

It was a very different night when Gene Krupa and Desi Arnaz showed up, as she found both young men charming, seductive, and handsome. Shaw told her that Krupa, born in Chicago, was the best drummer in America, and a high-energy entertainer known for his flamboyant showmanship. He'd made his first recording in 1927.

Born in Cuba, Arnaz had fled to Miami following the 1933 revolution in his country. He'd been cast in his first Broadway musical, *Too Many Girls* (1940), and later figured he might try Hollywood. RKO had bought the film rights and planned to configure him as its star.

Desi Arnaz later boasted, "Long before there was Lucille Ball in my life, there was Lana!"

Lana was assigned the job of cooking dinner, and, since she'd worked at the studio all day, she thought spaghetti might be the safest bet. But when she served it, Shaw took only one bite before he yelled at her, "What crap!" Then he tossed the pasta platter out into the dining room and onto the floor. Then he announced to Krupa and Arnaz that he'd take them out to dinner—"Maybe line up some broads for you horndogs, too."

Humiliated, Lana attempted to clean it up, but Krupa intervened, volunteering to deal with the mess. After Shaw had retreated upstairs to change his clothes, he put his arm around her and gently but seductively kissed her as Arnaz looked on.

"Gentleman Gene" Krupa comes to Lana's rescue after another domestic brawl with Shaw.

Timed as it was in the immediate aftermath of her husband's brutal rejection, Lana was thrilled at Krupa's kiss. "Artie can be a bit much at times," he whispered in her ear. "Some night you're going to need me, and I'll come running at your call."

As Krupa scooped the mess up from off the floor, she retreated from the dining room back into the kitchen. Arnaz followed her.

"You're the most beautiful gal in the world," he told her. "I can't take my eyes off you."

Then he flashed a smile at her. As she turned to face him, he took her possessively into his arms. "Within minutes, I felt a foot of Cuban tongue," she'd later tell Hyde. "It was the wettest and most delicious I'd ever tasted. He was rubbing up against me with such passion, I think he almost shot off. He was totally uninhibited. What a lover I thought he'd make. He took my hand and pressed it against his crotch. "I can really take care of a woman, and I want that woman to be you. Unlike my friend, Artie, I'll treat you nice."

At that point, she heard Shaw coming down the steps from their bedroom above. Within full view of his increasingly estranged wife, he then invited Krupa and Arnaz out to a restaurant for a continuation of their aborted dinner, but pointedly did not include her.

The next day she told Hyde, "My days with Artie are numbered. But I've entered both Desi Arnaz and Gene Krupa into my datebook for sometime in the future. I can't wait!"

Lana Turner in her early days at MGM wasn't always photographed in ermine, diamonds, and satin gowns. She posed for this postcard dressed in high boots and wearing a leopard-skin bathing suit

Chapter Six

Lana's Rise to Super-Stardom

The World's Most Beautiful Blonde Competes With the World's Most Gorgeous Brunette

In *Ziegfeld Girl,* Lana was never more gorgeous, enveloped in pink tulle with sequins, spangles, and silvery stars.

"I gave the film my heart and soul. I played an elevator operator from Flatbush in Brooklyn, who was discovered by Ziegfeld himself. Joan Crawford was originally to take my role, but she was far too old, I mean, really ancient."

As the 1940s began, Lana Turner—shortly before she hit major stardom during World War II—had already become one of America's leading sex symbols. Hundreds of letters from fans arrived weekly at MGM, mostly from men. Some of them included semi-nude or nude pictures of themselves.

"The whole world seems to be lusting for me," she told a jealous Judy Garland. "Even though I'm married, the Hollywood wolves won't give up the chase."

"Lana Turner is now a full-fledged star," reported Hedda Hopper. "Talk about *oomph!* She oozes it."

If Lana had her wish, she'd go nightclubbing every night. When he wasn't doing a gig, Artie Shaw wanted to stay home and read. She said, "We lived in this hilltop cottage that fitted into my romantic fantasy, except for one thing: It didn't have what it really needed, and that was a man and woman in love."

Occasionally, Shaw would take her out for a night on the town, usually criticizing her for dressing too provocatively. His oft-repeated remark was, "I don't want you to look like some cheap whore."

Once, he invited her to Ciro's. Within the hour, Greg Bautzer entered with Dorothy Lamour on his arm. "The Sarong Girl" was herself becoming a Hollywood sex symbol.

"I see Bautzer's swinging high, swinging low in a hurricane with the jungle princess," Shaw told her. He was referring to three movies that had each featured the former Miss New Orleans: *Jungle Princess* (1936), *Swing High* (1937), and *Hurricane* (also 1937).

Hollywood was a small town in those days, and Ciro's had become the hottest spot for celebrities, so it was not much of a coincidence that Lana would patronize the same club as Bautzer and his new romance.

Lamour later commented on her affair with Bautzer: "I made him forget all about Lana Turner," she said.

She might have been jealous of Lamour, but Lamour was also jealous of Lana.

"Before Lana shot to fame as 'The Sweater Girl,' in *They Won't Forget*, my director, Henry Hathaway, came up with the idea of putting me in a sweater without a bra," Lamour said. "He took pictures of me which were published in the press. When Lana put on a similar sweater, she created a *Hurricane* of publicity. Forgive me for pushing one of my movies. But, lest the world forget, I was the first to don that damn sweater."

"As for Greg, he was a real Beau Brummel and an incorrigible flirt," she continued.

Years later, Lamour said she encountered Lana at a Hollywood party. "I admitted to her that I'd fallen in love with Greg. But I came to realize that whereas he was not a one-woman man, I was a one-man woman. I finally had to tell him that I couldn't go on seeing him"

"Well, dear," Lana told her, "you are right, of course. I came to the same conclusion. However, I also decided that a girl needs a good lawyer to get her out of a jam from time to time. As for me, I'm not a one-man woman…'the more the merrier,' I've often stated. Hollywood is the best hunting ground in the world. I think per square mile, it has the best-looking guys on the planet, most of them dreaming they'll become the next Errol Flynn or Tyrone Power."

According to Lamour, "Lana and I were both after Bautzer, and, later, she was brazen enough to go for my handsome husband, William Ross Howard III, a captain in the U.S. Army. One night at a party, I saw her giving Bill the eye. All the girls wanted him. When I spoke to her, she admitted it. 'Dottie,' she told me. 'If you and I weren't such great pals, I could really go for that stud you've bagged.' I thought nothing of it until later that night when Bill *[i.e., William Ross Howard III]* and I were undressing. Lana had slipped her phone number into the pocket of his coat."

***

On another occasion, Shaw escorted Lana to a club where his friend, Billie Holiday, was singing. "Lady Day," as she was nicknamed, was a jazz musician and singer-songwriter known for her "shading, phrasing, dark tones, light tones, and bending notes," as Frank Sinatra phrased it.

In 1937, she'd had a brief stint as a big band vocalist with Count Basie and his band, traveling from town to town, often in harsh living conditions because of segregation. A recurring theme in her music involved women unlucky in love.

After a few months, Count Basie fired her. Hearing of this, Shaw tracked her down to an address in Harlem, where she was staying in her mother's modest apartment.

"Her mother fried chicken for us as part of an early breakfast, and before the morning ended, Lady Day had packed her bags and was taking off with me in my car," Shaw said.

Shaw, his newest vocalist, and his band created a sensation at the jam-packed Madison Square Garden in Manhattan when they were configured as part of the evening's entertainment at the Harvest Moon Ball.

Trouble arose, however, during later gigs in the segregated South. Holiday was one of the first black singers to be featured against the background of an all-white band. Sometimes, racial tensions arose, with angry shouts from the audience. Holiday "exploded" (her words) when a redneck loudmouth in Louisville, Kentucky, called her a

"Dear little Lana: What Billie Holiday and I did before I married you is no one's business but our own," Artie Shaw said.

115

"nigger wench."

After touring for several months with Shaw and his orchestra, Holiday could take it no more. They were booked into the Lincoln Hotel in St. Louis. "The white guests complained when I took the elevator with them, and after that, the manager asked me to use the freight elevator. I wasn't allowed in the bar or in the dining room. That was the last straw. I finally had to tell Artie, 'I'm getting the hell out of here.'"

Lana, in vivid contrast, defined Holiday as a mesmerizing performer, and shared her husband's belief that she was one of the most original and stylish singers in the country.

After her performance, Holiday joined Shaw and Lana at table, and they talked until around 3AM when the club closed its doors.

At that early morning hour, Holiday kissed Lana on both cheeks, and delivered to Shaw a deep, passionate goodbye kiss.

As they drove together back to their hilltop home, Lana asked Shaw about Holiday. "You guys seemed very friendly, very intimate. She's most attractive. It causes a wife to wonder. Just how close were you two during those lonely nights on the road? I couldn't help but notice that lingering kiss."

In her memoirs, Holiday would later write, "There aren't many people who fought harder than Artie against the vicious people in the music business or the crummy state of second-class citizens which eats at the guts of so many black musicians. He didn't win, but he didn't lose, either."

Years later, in the late 1940s, after Lana had become a big star, she met for a drink at the Beverly Hills Hotel with Shaw. During their dialogues, he spoke of Holiday, saying he'd gone to see her in her "comeback concert" at Manhattan's Carnegie Hall in March of 1948. That was after she'd served a nine-month sentence at the Federal Reformatory for Women in Alderson, West Virginia. She'd been charged and convicted for possession of heroin.

"I went backstage to visit Billie after her concert," Shaw said. "The guys she'd hung out with had turned her into an addict and all the shit that goes with that. I was stunned when I saw her up close. She was no longer the twenty-three-year-old Harlem beauty I knew. Her rough living showed in her face, and she was hanging out with some gigolo who was just using her. Seeing her in that condition was no damn fun. After some talk, we said goodbye. I kissed her and made off into the night—and that was that."

"After that, I heard that she was shacking up with Tallulah Bankhead," he said.

***

As June of 1940 neared its end, Lana—visibly nervous and constantly smoking—would sometimes break into sobs. Living with Shaw was growing worse by the day, and the frequency and intensity of his temper fits had increased. She'd heard rumors that he was seeing other women on the side. Some nights, he didn't return home until two or three in the morning.

When she demanded information, he'd tell her that he'd been rehearsing with the boys in the band.

One night was worse than any that had preceded it. After a brutal fight, during the course of which he'd denounced her as "a whore" and "a slut," she became hysterical. He could not control her, and when she continued to scream, he summoned his doctor to their home on Summit Drive. After a cursory exam, the doctor injected her with some form of sedative.

When she awakened the next morning at a hospital in Beverly Hills, a nurse was in the room with her. "Are you feeling better, Mrs. Johnson?"

Shaw had registered her as "Mildred Johnson." She asked that a phone be installed in her room. When it was in place, she called Mildred with the address where she had been hospitalized.

About an hour later, her mother arrived. Without informing Shaw, Mildred checked her out of the clinic.

Back at her mother's home, her nerves more or less restored, Lana gave Mildred a key to the house she'd been sharing with Shaw on Summit Drive and asked her to retrieve her possessions, especially her clothing and jewelry.

To her surprise, her mother urged her to give the marriage one more try. "Breaking up is a bad idea after such a short marriage. The publicity might hurt you. You might be depicted as a silly movie star who doesn't take marriage seriously. I forgave Virgil and took him back many times after each of our many blow-ups."

Eventually Mildred's point of view prevailed, and Lana returned to Shaw's house on Summit Drive.

He didn't return home till well past midnight, with the scent of marijuana emanating from his breath and clothes. Instantly belligerent, he wanted sex, but she wasn't willing. Eventually, he forced himself on her.

As she later confided to Greg Bautzer, "He was brutal. He hurt me, and then he raped me. When I resisted, he slapped my face really hard. Finally, he got off me. I ran into the bathroom and locked the door. Fortunately, he fell asleep and did not try to break down the door."

"That morning, without sleep, I preceded him into the kitchen and prepared his breakfast. When he came downstairs, he was very hostile, hardly spoke to me."

As he prepared himself for

WHO'S THE MOVIE STAR? Despite her miserable marriage and signs of an impending breakdown, Lana "made nice" in this MGM-staged publicity photoshoot.

It portrayed her as a domesticated housewife who was subservient to the crushing emotional insecurities of her demanding husband.

work, he turned to her and said, "What kind of wife are you? I looked in the closet at the shoes I own. All of them need polish. Take them to the shoeshine man down the hill. When I get home tonight, I want to see my reflection in each of them." Then he stormed out, slamming the front door.

Immediately, she phoned Bautzer. "I want you to start divorce proceedings at once. I don't want to spend another night with this bastard."

"Pack your bags," he told her. "I'll be there within the hour, baby. You never should have married the shit. Greg to the rescue."

When Bautzer arrived, he held her in his arms, kissing her passionately. "My baby's come back to me."

Then he drove her to Mildred's, where he escorted her upstairs and put her to bed. Mildred agreed to nourish and take care of her.

At 8PM, as promised, Bautzer returned and spent the night with her, presenting her with white roses, a signal that their romance had resumed.

She didn't hear from Shaw until about a week later, when he called her unexpectedly. She felt that he was phoning to protest her petition for a divorce, but what he wanted was a favor. He needed her to pose with him for press and publicity photos of his debut on the *Burns and Allen Show*. "I want you to pretend that we're a loving couple."

She reluctantly agreed. Two hours later, she arrived at the Burns & Allen studio wearing a black dress inspired by Coco Chanel.

He kissed her lightly on the cheek before they began the business of posing for photographers together. After a few shots, a reporter from *Variety* called out to her, "Give Artie a big kiss, Lana!"

Impulsively, she shot back, "To hell with that. I've left him!"

The word was out. The morning papers carried the story, "LANA TURNER TO DIVORCE ARTIE SHAW."

Later, as an explanation, she told the press, "I'm divorcing Artie because I've become tired of being spoon-fed Nietzsche."

***

Lana couldn't sleep at night, and to an increasing degree was edgy, unhappy, and nervous. She phoned Louis B. Mayer at MGM and asked if she could meet with him. In his office, the following day, she pleaded with him to give her a few weeks' off to recuperate from the after-effects of her break-up with Shaw.

He agreed to send her on a cruise to Hawaii and told her why: "You're about to appear in *Ziegfeld Girl*, a picture in which you've got to look your most beautiful. Your looks will be compared to those of Hedy Lamarr, and there are those who consider her the most beautiful woman in the world. You don't want to look like a hag beside her."

Visible within the ranks of MGM during that era was Betty Asher, an MGM handler and troubleshooter, usually responsible for keeping the studio's bad girls—especially Lana and Judy Garland—out of trouble.

Lana's cruise ship was scheduled to depart for Hawaii in four days. Unaware that Lana had moved out of Shaw's home on Summit Drive, and with the intention of discussing details of her upcoming trip, Asher drove there when she couldn't get anyone on the phone. She assumed that Lana was there, but that she wasn't answering the phone.

It wasn't until Lana returned from Hawaii that she learned the events that had unfolded that afternoon after Asher rang the doorbell of Shaw's house.

According to Shaw, "I answered the door, and there stood Betty Asher, looking awfully good to me. The next thing I knew, I was in bed with her. She stayed for three days and nights before sailing away across the Pacific with Lana. We spent most of that time in bed. I got enough sex to last a month."

[As their time as shipmates passed, Lana learned more about her traveling companion. It turned out that Asher was a bisexual, having previously sustained an affair with another bisexual, a teenaged Judy Garland.]

Alone and unhappy, and recuperating from the after-effects of her marriage to Shaw, during the days immediately preceding the departure of her cruise ship, Lana impulsively phoned Desi Arnaz and invited him to join her on the cruise. Arnaz had two weeks before he was to report to work at RKO on *Too Many Girls* (1940). He seemed eager to join her.

In her memoirs, Lana "whitewashed" her link to Arnaz, writing that she met a group of college boys on board and "danced my way through the rest of the voyage, having the time of my life."

Only part of that statement was true, the part about having the time of her life. Her partying, however, didn't occur in the company of "college boys," but with Arnaz, in his cabin, night after night, during the ship's eastbound transit to Honolulu. During the day, they spent time together, lounging on deck, followed by dancing at night. On a few occasions, Arnaz agreed to sing for the passengers.

He discussed his childhood in Cuba. He claimed that when he was only fifteen, his papa had ushered him into La Casa Marino, a famous brothel in Santiago, Cuba.

He also revealed details of his visits to the bordello run by Polly Adler, Manhattan's most famous madam. "I didn't leave her joint until I'd sampled all the women," he confessed to Lana.

With Lana, at least, Arnaz's reputation as a sexual athlete had preceded him. She had heard plenty of stories about him from the boys in the band who played with Shaw.

His friend, actor Cesar Romero, claimed, "Desi just loved sex and couldn't get enough."

[Rumors had it that when a girl wasn't readily available, Arnaz took advantage of Romero's legendary skill at fellatio.]

One of Shaw's band members said, "Desi doesn't know the difference between sex and love. To put it bluntly, love to him is a good fuck. He can get that anywhere he goes."

A fellow actor, Roger Carmel, said, "Desi is a lech. Anything in a skirt from thirteen to thirty, he'll go after."

After the ship docked in Hawaii, Arnaz phoned RKO and was instructed to return to Los Angeles in two days for the filming of *Too Many Girls*. After kissing Lana goodbye, he boarded a morning flight, with the promise that he'd rendezvous with her the moment she returned to California.

Later that afternoon, Lana told Asher that she'd missed her period. An appointment was immediately scheduled with a local gynecologist/obstetrician. A pregnancy test revealed that she was pregnant.

That evening, when she phoned Shaw at his home, an unknown woman picked up the receiver. When Shaw was summoned to the phone, Lana told him, "I've got wonderful news, darling."

His reaction to the sound of her voice was brusque. "Why in hell are you calling me?"

"I found out today. I'm pregnant, and I'm coming back to you. I know I can make our marriage work. "

His answer infuriated her: "Who's the father?" Gene Krupa? Tommy Dorsey? Buddy Rich? Or did Arnaz knock you up during that stupid cruise to Honolulu? I heard all about it."

"The baby is yours, you bastard!" she shouted into the trans-Pacific phone line.

"Like hell it is. Maybe the kid belongs to some grip at MGM. Maybe even Louis B. Mayer!"

In her memoirs, she described how she then exploded. Before slamming down the phone, she called him a "no-good, rotten son of a bitch! You are the dirtiest, the lowest—I can't even call you a man. You're a creep. I hate you!"

The moment she returned to Hollywood, she met with Johnny Hyde, delivering nothing but praise for Arnaz as a seducer. "He doesn't just make love to a woman, he kisses and laves her body, driving her wild with excitement. Never before has any man attacked me like that. I can't wait until my divorce comes through, so I can marry Desi."

"Did he propose?" Hyde asked.

"Not exactly...but he will any day now."

She convinced herself that if Bautzer would speed up her divorce from Shaw, and if Arnaz would propose to her, there was still hope for a scandal-free birth of her child. As for the public at large, she and Arnaz, she told herself, could always claim that the birth of their baby had been premature.

As events evolved, she'd be cruelly disappointed.

***

After Arnaz reported to RKO for filming, he'd been introduced to Lucille Ball, who had just completed a fight scene with red-haired Maureen O'Hara during her filming of *Dance, Girl, Dance* (1940). Both O'Hara and Ball had been cast in that film as burlesque dancers.

Arnaz later wrote in a memoir, "Ball looked like a two-dollar whore who had been badly beaten by a pimp, with hair all over her face and a black eye." Her dress had been ripped.

Based on her appearance, Arnaz was skeptical, he revealed later, about her ability to portray the *ingenue* in *Too Many Girls*.

But when he met her again, three hours later, he thought she looked young and beautiful. "She caused a stirring down below."

"Hi, Daisy," she said to him.

"No, honey," he answered. "Daisy is a flower. The first name is D-E-S-I, the last name Arnaz. You'd better learn to pronounce it, 'cause you're gonna become Mrs. Desi Arnaz."

The rest is Hollywood history, especially television history.

As Lana told Hyde during her recitation of her pregnancy-related woes, "Desi said he prefers well-stacked blondes, yet I've heard that he's suddenly engaged to a redhead with no tits, and he isn't returning my calls."

"There's only one way out for you," Hyde told Lana: "Mayer doesn't like his stars to have babies without a daddy. That's strictly taboo. I hate to tell you this, kid, but you already know exactly what you must do."

***

A decision about ending her pregnancy would have to be made soon. One of Lana's options involved salvaging her marriage to Shaw. Mildred suggested that for Lana, but she adamantly refused. "I want a divorce. That's my final word."

Lana spent the next few days *incognito* and in disguise, wandering into undiscovered neighborhoods of Los Angeles where she'd never set foot before. She drove into the Hollywood Hills, and walked the lonely stretches of Malibu beaches. She wanted her baby, but to an increasing degree, she accepted the fact that giving birth without a husband would probably destroy her career.

Mildred kept urging her to return to Shaw, but she could never reach him on the phone. Lana became convinced that even if she begged him, he wouldn't take her back.

Finally, she woke up one morning and decided to make an appointment with an abortionist. Without telling Mildred, she drove to a seedy-looking private townhouse in downtown Los Angeles. As she entered, she smelled something like burnt cabbage.

She confessed in her memoirs that she expected knives "scraping away at my insides," but that did-

At the Trocadero, Lana (left) has a roving eye, as Mildred looks on. Her mother was flattered when people mistook her for Lana's sister.

121

n't happen. The doctor, whom she defined later as a quack, injected some kind of fluid into her cervix.

"The fetus will be aborted later," he told her. "You'll pass it like urine."

Still without telling Mildred what had happened, she returned to the home she shared with her and retired to her bedroom.

As her mother was preparing a light supper for her, the pain began. "At first, the cramps were minor. Then they came like a giant hand gripping my insides," she claimed.

By the time Mildred ascertained the problem, Lana was doubling over in pain. "It came over me like an ocean wave, then receded again, coming back with more pain than before. One cramp after another. I curled up into a ball of pain."

Mildred got the abortionist on the phone, but all he could recommend was lots of black coffee and walks—"plenty of walking. It will pass if you walk."

Lana tried walking, but collapsed, almost immediately, onto the floor, crying out as sharp pains convulsed her body.

She later asserted that she'd spent the most horrific night of her life, each hour saturated with impossible suffering. She sobbed and screamed and tried to walk as the doctor had instructed. By morning, she phoned the doctor. "My baby is still inside me. I can't stand it anymore. I'm dying."

Since she was unable to travel, the doctor eventually came to her home, where he confronted her angry mother, who told him, "You've threatened the life of my daughter—I should have you arrested. You're a bastard!"

He pulled off Lana's robe and without an anesthetic, he at last "scraped me out," she later wrote. Mildred remained by her side, reacting to every painful move. At one point, she placed her hand over her daughter's mouth to muffle her agonized screams.

The white towels her mother had brought from the linen closet became soaked with blood. "I felt like he was removing my guts. When I could take it no more, I passed out."

When she regained consciousness three hours later, the doctor was gone, his lingering aura a nightmare. As a departing insult, he had presented a bill for five-hundred dollars "for services rendered."

"Your baby was not meant to be," Mildred said. "Someday, with the right man as your husband, you'll have kids."

"I never want to go through the agony of childbirth," Lana answered. "That will never happen. I'll see to that."

Mildred brought her some freshly made chicken broth and coaxed her into drinking it. "You've got to get your strength back. Mayer wants you to begin filming *Ziegfeld Girl* next week and he expects you to look your loveliest."

"For the first time, I'll be facing the camera with my teenaged years behind me. I'll be a twenty-year-old woman."

***

MGM's plan at the time involved configuring *Ziegfeld Girl* (1941) as a sequel to *The Great Ziegfeld* (1936), a blockbuster that had brought a Best Actress Oscar to

Luise Rainer, with whom Lana had worked during the filming of *Dramatic School.*

William Powell had been cast in the original 1936 version as Florenz Ziegfeld, the flamboyant show-business impresario. Myrna Loy, Frank Morgan, and Virginia Bruce, who had been married to John Gilbert, rounded out the original cast.

The Great Ziegfeld had won an Oscar as Best Picture in the year of its release. Robert Z. Leonard, who had helmed the original 1936 version, was hired by producer Pandro S. Berman for the sequel two years later. *[The sequel would not include an actor attempting to impersonate Ziegfeld.]*

Before filming began, Lana studied long and hard with MGM drama coach, Lillian Burns. "This is my big chance, and I'm not going to fuck it up," Lana vowed.

Although she had never been drunk before, she was cast as a showgirl, Sheila Regan, who during the course of the film becomes an alcoholic. "I was known at the time as the Queen of Nightclubs, but I was no boozer. I went to the clubs to dance with handsome men, not to soak up liquor."

To prepare her for the role, Burns had Lana watch Bette Davis' performance of an alcoholic in *Dangerous* (1935). "I sat through it eight times," Lana said.

By the time she showed up on the set for filming, Lana told Leonard, "I think I know Sheila's every thought, how she walks, how she moves. I know everything about her, even how she feels at any given time."

As the weeks went by, the director appeared to agree with Lana. After seeing the rushes, he ordered scriptwriters Marguerite Roberts and Sonya Levien to expand Sheila's role. In one scene, the writers added a bemused, bittersweet comment that became Lana's all-time favorite line: "All the things I like are illegal, immoral, or fattening."

The original script of *Ziegfeld Girl* had been created by William Anthony McGuire. Although Flo Ziegfeld's showgirls were showcased as the most important visual element of the film, and although his legend itself was celebrated as one of the pre-suppositions of the script, the showman himself never appeared.

In 1938s proposed sequel, three leading male roles were cast with Walter Pidgeon, George Murphy (with whom Lana had worked before), and Frank Morgan. In 1940, these roles were awarded to James Stewart, Tony Martin, and Charles Winninger. However, before Stewart signed on, Leonard had asked Glenn Ford to play Sheila's truck driver boyfriend, Gilbert Young, who later becomes a bootlegger and goes to prison. His bootlegging had derived from his passion for Sheila, and his intention of buying her the expensive baubles she demanded.

When Lana was signed, Glenn Ford was still part of the cast. He called her and arranged a date, telling Leonard, "Ever since I saw those tits bouncing in *They Won't Forget,* I've been wanting to fuck that broad. What knockers!"

Lana, too, had been attracted to this handsome Québec-born actor ever since she'd seen him on the screen in *The Lady in Question* (1940), in which he'd co-starred with Rita Hayworth.

Over the years, many of the top female stars in Hollywood would desire and win his affections: Margaret Sullavan, Bette Davis (in spite of her denial), Joan Crawford, Barbara Stanwyck, and even Marilyn Monroe.

As Lana later told Johnny Hyde, "On three different dates, I got to know every inch of this gorgeous man. He liked to insert his thing in every orifice and between my breasts. He whispered sweet nothings in my ears. He's great at pillow talk. If I have any criticism of him at all, it's that he seems to be a character on the screen, not quite real. But his love-making makes up for that deficiency."

[Even after he didn't get the role in Ziegfeld Girl's *1938 reprise, Ford phoned Lana again during his filming of* Texas *(1941), with the equally handsome William Holden, who became his best pal.*

"Talk about two gorgeous guys new to Hollywood," Lana told Hyde. "Glenn talked to Bill Holden about me. Those guys wanted me to join them for a three-way in Palm Springs." Then with a pout, she added, "But I refuse to tell you if I accepted their tantalizing offer."

***

Flo Ziegfeld had been the most flamboyant showman in the American theater. Night after night, he glorified "The American Girl" (or the American concept of beauty) in glittering, glamorous settings, with an armada of female pulchritude attired in stunning, artfully outrageous, extravagant costumes. His *Ziegfeld Follies*, a lavish annual revue, attracted vast audiences during their heyday *[roughly speaking, from 1907 To 1931]*. In his glory years, he seduced as many of his actresses as he could get around to.

William Anthony McGuire had written the original Oscar-nominated *The Great Ziegfeld*, (1936) and he was called back to write a new script, but he died before shooting began in September of 1940.

Censors from the Breen Office cracked down on many of the lines from the 1940 script. In what they considered a generous concession, however, they allowed the character played by Dan Dailey to refer to Sheila as a "tramp."

As filming advanced, Lana, Garland, and Lamarr became very competitive. At one point, Garland complained to Leonard. "When Lana bounces by, the electricians whistle; when Hedy sweeps in, the grips stare lasciviously. But when I go by, it's 'Hi, Judy!'"

One day, Joe Pasternak, the film producer, perhaps during the period when he was debating whether he should officially migrate over to MGM, visited the set. On site, he closely observed the interactions of Garland, Lamarr, and Lana. "Judy didn't realize how much talent she had or that she had more to offer than Hedy or Lana, or even Joan Crawford. Judy never believed that she had the strength, I mean feminine strength. She felt she was a failure in her private life. Talk about failures! In their private lives, Lana, Hedy, and Joan were each disastrous, despite their triumphs on the screen."

Mickey Rooney arrived to visit Garland on the set. Although Lana did not exit from her dressing room to see him that day, he talked animatedly to Garland, his frequent co-star.

"If I looked like Lana," Garland said with more than a touch of envy, "I could have any man I wanted. Mostly I have to dream about them: Clark Gable, Tyrone Power, Errol Flynn, even Robert Taylor—I mean *especially* Robert Taylor. Lana represents the epitome of female beauty. As for me, men call me pretty and give me a pat on the chin."

On the set, although Garland and Lana pretended to be friends, Garland could hardly mask her jealousy. Lana had already snatched Artie Shaw from her arms, and now she was making a play for Tony Martin, even though Garland also had a crush on the singer, in spite of David Rose being in her life.

Garland's biographer, Gerald Clarke, wrote, "If Lana Turner could club-hop every night, why couldn't Judy? She was tired of being regarded as the kind of girl a boy might safely take home to the family. What she wanted was to be a seductress, a temptress who could look into a man's eyes and cause him to reel with lust and longing, abandoning everything for just one delirious night with her. She wanted to smile at Artie Shaw, as Turner had done, and cause him to tootle to her tune and her tune alone. She wanted, in short, to be Lana Turner."

At last, Lana was working with producer Pandro S. Berman, who, during his reign at RKO, had produced the Fred Astaire/Ginger Rogers musicals and was a prime fixture in the rise of Katharine Hepburn at the studio. He'd also just released such classics as *Gunga Din* and *The Hunchback of Notre Dame* in 1939. She later referred to Berman as "a darkly handsome dynamo, gruff and irascible."

Berman felt he really had to succeed in producing *Ziegfeld Girl* as a means of proving to Mayer that he could make spectacular films for Metro, the same way he had for RKO. He told Lana, "Pull this one off, baby, and you'll have a breakthrough film. If you do, it will mean only starring roles for you in your future."

[Berman came close to casting Lana in another film, Madame Bovary (1949), based on the Flaubert classic. He met with director Vincente Minnelli, and they agreed that Lana might be perfect for the role.

However, the Breen Office objected, sending a memo: "The classic French novel is about adultery, and Lana Turner in her private life carries sexual implications of an adulterous life. You will stay within the Production Code if you cast another actress of more digni-

Ziegfeld Girls are, left to right: Lana Turner, Judy Garland, and Hedy Lamarr. The film traces the triumphs and tragedies of these three showgirls: Lana as Sheila Regan, Garland as Susan Gallagher, and Lamarr as Sandra Koller. The trio was billed as "the three B's," a blonde, a "bronzetta," and a brunette.

fied appeal, perhaps Greer Garson or Jennifer Jones."

Jones got the role.

For creation of the film's lavish gowns, Berman hired the well-known costume designer, Adrian, knowing that he'd devise some of the most spectacular outfits ever seen on a movie screen.

Adrian opted to dress Lamarr in "high camp" costumes long before that term was invented. In her most famous scene, she appears in show-stopping headgear so heavy she could hardly walk, despite instructions from the director to appear, at least, to "float down the steps."

Lamarr later lamented to Lana, "I couldn't see where I was going because of the blinding lights. To keep me from falling over with that elaborate headdress, a board was fastened to my back and my bosom was taped from behind. I felt like some religious penitent in the 10th Century walking in a torture procession."

As choreographer for the spectacular musical numbers, Berman hired the well-seasoned Busby Berkeley.

Lana met Berkeley just at the time that his outsized musical numbers, which had enthralled Depression-era audiences, were becoming *passé*. She culled a lot of smart performance tips from him, especially about how to present herself regally as a showgirl. According to Lana, "Garland detested him, but I found him very sympathetic and deeply troubled."

Lana's former high school boyfriend, Jackie Cooper, was assigned the role of her younger brother, although they were the same age. Their young romance was not discussed, and he was going steady with her girlfriend, Bonita Granville.

At the beginning of the film, Sheila (Lana) was working as an elevator girl. She is plucked "out of the elevator shaft" to become a glamorous

Lana's final scene in *Ziegfeld Girl* depicts a boozy Sheila descending a grand staircase with all the majesty she can muster.

Midway down the stairs, she hesitates for a moment with her fragile hand on the banister. At the newel post, she collapses and takes a fatal downward plunge to her death.

Preview audiences, however, didn't like her dying. In the re-edited version, it's left up to the audience to determine her fate.

showgirl, and the movie traces her rise and fall through lavish production numbers in which she struts like a peacock.

She was assigned many dramatic moments, including one in which she's beaten up by a former boxer. In another, she accidentally plunges from the stage into the footlights in full view of the (horrified) opening night audience. There's even a sickbed scene during which it becomes clear that her illness is a result of chronic alcoholism.

After Sheila is fired from the *Follies*, she goes from bad to worse. To survive and to pay her liquor bill, she's forced to sell her jewelry, after which she's reduced to populating the seediest and filthiest of speakeasies.

In her interpretation of a showgirl (Susan Gallagher), Garland gets to belt out four numbers, including her most memorable song from the film, "I'm Always Chasing Rainbows." She also gets to perform a spunky tropical number, "Minnie from Trinidad."

Many critics lamented the fact that *Ziegfeld Girl* had been shot in black and white. An oft-repeated line in reviews was that the movie "screamed out for Technicolor." *Time* magazine asserted that the film was a "glorification of Lana Turner."

"The part of Sheila is Lana Turner's big chance—and she takes it," wrote the critic for *Kinematograph Weekly*. "All the hopes, disillusionment, and the follies of youth are crystallized in her vital, memorable, glamorous, and appealing performance." *The New York Times* reviewer claimed, "It is the perilously lovely Lana Turner who gets this department's bouquet for a surprisingly solid good performance as the little girl from Flatbush."

***

In her role in the film as showgirl Sandra Kolter, Hedy Lamarr was married to Franz Kolter (as played by Philip Dorn), a struggling violinist. She is snapped up by the *Follies* and becomes the breadwinner of the family.

Their marriage becomes complicated when she's attracted to the show's handsome headliner, Tony Martin, cast as Frank Merton. His marvelous voice rings out, with the approval of thousands of fans, much to the chagrin and jealousy of Hedy's unemployed husband.

Martin's show-stopping musical hit, which became an American classic, is "You Stepped Out of a Dream."

Lamarr would become a formidable rival of Lana's both on and off the screen. One reporter wrote, "The so-called friendship between Hedy Lamarr and Lana Turner is cordial on the surface, but hostility lurks under the skin."

Lana had been fascinated by the background of the Austrian beauty ever since she burst into fame after her appearance in the notorious German film, *Ecstasy* (1933), in which she runs nude through a forest.

In her distant past, Hedy Kiesler (her original name) had been married to Fritz Mandl, the Austrian munitions magnate, a friend of both Mussolini and Hitler. Although a closeted Jew, he supplied munitions to the Nazis.

Rumors circulated that Mandl had pimped his gorgeous wife to both dictators. Unknown to Hitler, Lamarr was also Jewish, the daughter of a wealthy Viennese banker.

Fame in America came for Lamarr when she co-starred with Charles Boyer in *Algiers* (1939). Sleek, slim, and chic, with her jet-black hair parted in the middle, her stunning face framed by picture hats, snoods, and turbans, she photographed beautifully.

The friendship between Lana and Lamarr might have been different if Lana had not rebuffed her sexual advances. Lamarr was bisexual, as she admitted candidly in her latter-day memoirs, *Ecstasy and Me*.

Lana told her, "I'm not that kind of girl."

In New York City in the 1970s, Lamarr and author Darwin Porter had each hired the same literary agent, Jay Garon, and occasionally ran into each other at parties. Once, she discussed Lana, though in veiled terms. "I told her that my bosom was not as large as hers, but I also reminded her that Venus de Milo had small breasts. Lana was very hostile to me, calling me distant and reserved, although those terms might also be applied to her. I tried to be friends with her, but she was always chasing after some man. On the set of *Ziegfeld Girl*, they included both Tony Martin and James Stewart."

In the 1940s, Lana and Lamarr would often co-star together with the same male stars: Robert Young, Clark Gable, Spencer Tracy, Robert Taylor, Bob Hope, and Ray Milland. "On the set of *Ziegfeld Girl*, I was having an affair with James Stewart," Lamarr said. "He and I had just made *Come Live With Me* (1941). Lana lured him away before she fell for Tony Martin."

"I think Lana got really mad at me," Hedy continued, "when I practically pulled that handsome devil, Errol Flynn, from her arms. I also kept luring George Montgomery and Clark Gable from her. Then, Howard Hughes told me that I was much better at oral sex than she was. That was his favorite sexual expression."

"I also seduced John Garfield when we made *Tortilla Flat* in 1942. That was three years before Lana got him when they co-starred together in *The Postman Always Rings Twice*."

***

Even though he'd been given star billing in *Ziegfeld Girl*, James Stewart was disappointed with his minor role. "Lana Turner should have had star billing instead of being in fourth position. My role as her bootlegging boyfriend should have assigned me to fourth place, following Judy Garland and Hedy Lamarr. Any number of actors could have played my part."

"However, on reflection, it did have the greatest fringe benefits of any movie being shot at MGM," he told Cary Grant, Henry Fonda, and others.

No doubt, he was referring to his seduction of both Hedy and Lana during the filming of *Ziegfeld Girl*." The director, Robert Z. Leonard, said, "I know for a fact that he spent three hours in Hedy's dressing room one afternoon when I didn't need them on camera. Not only that, but I saw him driving away from the studio an hour or so later with Lana. They returned the next morning in the same car. There was little doubt he'd spent the night with her, and that satisfied grin on his face proved my case."

It may have seemed unlikely to his fans, but this lanky actor, who stood six feet three and weighed only 140 pounds of mumbling, stammering flesh, was one of the great Lotharios of Hollywood, perhaps even topping the record of Errol Flynn over at Warner Brothers.

Hailing from the town of Indiana, Pennsylvania, and before he settled down and married *divorcée* Gloria McLean, Stewart had blazed a trail of seductions through Hollywood.

His affair with Lamarr had begun after their completion of the 1941 picture, *Come Live With Me.*

Hedda Hopper didn't publish the fact in her column, but privately told friends that over a period of time, Stewart had kept a diary of his conquests. Before he finally got married, the diary contained entries on 263 (the exact number) of glamor girls he'd seduced, including many of the extras and bit players in his movies.

"Those were the years," Stewart recalled in later life. "Jean, Rita, Marlene, Grace, Loretta, Hedy, Lana, to name a few. My bachelor years, let me tell you, were wonderful, just wonderful. Boy, did I have a good time polluting myself." *[That was his word for having a sexual climax.]*

In addition to her offscreen role as his lover, Lana found she could confide in Stewart. At times, she treated him like an older brother instead of a lover. She spoke of the pain of aborting Artie Shaw's child, and he shared his own experience of having "a kid of my own," also aborted. *[While making Destry Rides Again (1939), with Marlene Dietrich, she became pregnant, and their child was later aborted.]*

While filming *Ziegfeld Girl,* Stewart was also simultaneously making another film, *Pot o' Gold,* forcing him to run from one set to the other. One day, when he arrived to film a scene in *Ziegfeld Girl,* director Leonard told him

Lana onscreen (top photo) and offscreen (lower photo) with James Stewart. Rumors of an affair between James Stewart and Lana swept Hollywood when they co-starred in *Ziegfeld Girl.* There was even speculation that the couple might get married after her divorce from Artie Shaw was finalized.

129

that Lana's character of Sheila had been killed.

In his stammering way, he asked Leonard, "Bring me up to date on the script, would you? Did I kill her?"

Lana telephoned Louella Parsons to deny the story of her romance with Stewart. "I admire Jimmy very much as an actor," she said. "He's always marvelous in every scene he's called upon to play. What a fine actor. But, romantically speaking, he is just not the type of man that I go for—at least not in *that* way."

She had a reason for calling Parsons to deny any involvement with Stewart. Actually, when she made that call, "Hedy was taking care of Jimmy's needs. I had moved on."

She had fallen in love with the fifth lead in the picture: Tony Martin.

***

Lana's involvement with Tony Martin began one afternoon when Milton Weiss, from the MGM Publicity Department, approached him and asked if he'd accompany one of two MGM beauties to a world premiere. "Your options include either Hedy Lamarr or Lana Turner," Weiss said. "The one you pick is entirely up to you, kid."

"That's like asking a cat if he'd like a white mouse or brown," Martin later wrote in a memoir. "They're both tasty. It's just a question of which flavor he prefers. I could have the most beautiful brunette in the world or the most beautiful blonde in the world. What the hell...I'll take Lana."

Later that day, he discussed his choice with Lillian Burns, MGM's drama coach. "I hear you're taking out the blonde bombshell. Watch yourself! Don't get hung up on her."

"I can take care of myself," he vowed.

"Of course you can," she answered. "That's what Napoléon said before he marched off to Waterloo."

As flashbulbs popped that Saturday night, Lana and Martin made a glamorous appearance at the premiere. After the screening, and after a visit to Ciro's nightclub, he spent the night on her satin sheets. "By Sunday morning, when I woke up with her, I forgot my depression about how another blonde, Alice Faye, had recently divorced me."

He wrote, "If you have a bruised ego, like I did following my divorce, let Lana Turner tend to you. She's the best little ego-builder I've ever seen. She had a way of looking at you, her eyes never wandering from yours. You could drown yourself in her blue eyes. She swept me off my feet, and I mean that, literally."

Lana had been attracted to Martin ever since she and Mildred had seen him in the 1936 movie, *Follow the Fleet*, starring Fred Astaire and Ginger Rogers, in which he'd been cast as a sailor. Lana had also purchased some of his recordings, marketed through Decca records.

A bachelor again, Martin had become a member of what a loosely organized group of single, promiscuous men collectively known as "The Stud Farm" in Hollywood of the early 1940s. "The Studs" randomly included, among others, Henry Fonda; the playboy prince Aly Khan (who later married Rita Hayworth); the gigolo, Pat DiCicco (who was once famously married to heiress Gloria Vanderbilt); Cubby Broccoli (later, the producer of some of the James Bond films); or roommates Bruce Cabot and Errol Flynn. The notorious playboy of the Dominican Republic, Porfirio Rubirosa, was a sometimes member, too.

"Members of The Stud Farm got pursued by girls as much as we pursued them," Martin said. "We weren't hard to get. All of us were gay blades."

Before he started going steady with Lana, there was an encounter at the men's urinal in Los Angeles' CBS Building with Artie Shaw, who was still in the process of divorcing Lana.

Shaw later revealed what happened that afternoon. "Tony and I were doing a show at the same radio network at the time Lana and I had decided to split."

"I was already at the urinal taking a piss when Martin came into the room," Shaw said. "There was a row of eight empty urinals, but he decided to stand next to me when he whipped it out."

"Hi, Artie," Martin said. It quickly became obvious that the two men were checking out each other's equipment. "I say, would you mind if I started to data Lana since you guys have broken up? Out of respect, I wanted to ask your permission."

"I didn't like him asking me like that at the urinals with our two Jewish cocks hanging out. But then I figured that at least Lana with either of us wouldn't have to cope with foreskin."

"Sure, do anything you god damn like," Shaw told him. "It doesn't make any difference to me."

Lana was seen on two occasions lunching with Martin and her best friend, actress Virginia Grey, on the set of *The Big Store* (1941), a Marx Brothers comedy in which they were cast together as sweethearts. Later that afternoon, Lana heard Martin sing "Tenement Symphony" with a children's choir.

During the white heat of their affair, Lana and Martin flew together to San Francisco, where he'd been sched-

"It was more than just sex with Lana," Tony Martin later said. "Many women I'd met when I was a member of the Stud Farm were good at that. She was a total woman. She was warm and tender and thoughtful and unselfish."

"When you were Lana's guy, you were king. She never looked at another man. She was always there ready to love you. While you were with her, it was as if she'd been put on earth for one purpose—to serve you and to love you."

uled to sing at the World's Fair. It was here that he introduced the Jerome Kern song, "All the Things You Are," which became a standard.

Judy Garland with her new husband, David Rose, joined Lana and Martin for dinner that night. Lana suspected that Garland still had a crush on Martin based on the way she gazed lovingly at him, annoying Rose.

After his first night in a San Francisco hotel suite with Lana, Martin ran into Victor Mature, the muscular actor, in the lobby. He had met him casually before. "Hi, Vic," he said. "I didn't know you were in town."

"I decided to check out the World's Fair," Mature said.

No mention was made of Lana. Martin had heard rumors that she might be involved with this handsome hunk, who was new to Hollywood, but he had opted not to believe them. "Lana looked at me with those dewy blue eyes, and they were so worshipful, that I knew I had to be the only man in her life, past, present, or future. I had even proposed marriage to her as soon as her divorce from Artie came through."

That day, from outside the hotel, Martin made several attempts to telephone Lana at their suite, but no one answered the phone. When he returned there at six o'clock, she still was not there and had left no note.

At around 8PM, she came in. He asked her where she'd been all day.

"A little sightseeing, a little shopping," she said, although she carried no packages with her.

At the end of their holiday, when Lana and Martin flew together back to Los Angeles, he decided to drive directly to her home to spend a long weekend. As they pulled into her driveway, he spotted Mature leaving her home with two overstuffed suitcases. Lana and Martin got out of his car, and Mature gave her a quick kiss on the lips. "Hi, everybody," he said. It was an awkward moment.

She quickly retreated inside her house, leaving Mature and Martin to face off in the driveway. Mature quickly placed his suitcases into the trunk of his car and then pivoted to face Martin. "Well, old buddy—this is goodbye."

"How's it going?" Martin asked.

"Just fine," Then, before getting behind the wheel of his car, Mature said, "Look, Tony, all I can say is that I want to wish you kids a lot of luck. With a war coming on, we'll need it. Both of us will probably end up in the service. I'll see you guys around."

Then he drove off.

***

In her memoirs, Lana wrote, "After my breakup with Artie Shaw, I did go out a lot and with many different escorts. Victor Mature, I saw once, I think."

In another memoir, Lana's daughter, Cheryl Crane, stated things more accurately. "Both mother and Victor Mature did a lot of dating in 1941."

In truth, the Kentucky-born actor, son of an immigrant Austro-Italian knife sharpener, had once moved in with Lana for a few weeks. At the time, he was already well-known in Hollywood for his dark good looks, his muscles, and his mega-watt smile.

Before meeting Lana, Mature had been cast as a fur-clad caveman in *One Million B.C.* (1940). His co-star in that film was Lana's rival, Carole Landis, with whom he'd sustained an affair.

In her column, Hedda Hopper had described Mature as "a sort of miniature Johnny Weissmuller."

"Hedda pissed me off by writing that," he said. "There's nothing miniature about me."

In 1941, he co-starred once again with Landis, and with Betty Grable too, in the crime drama, *I Wake Up Screaming.* "I seduced both of these blondes," he later boasted. "In the 1940s, I did quite a few blondes: June Haver, Veronica Lake, Betty Hutton, and Alice Faye, Tony Martin's ex. I can't help that I've got a powerful set of muscles, but I want to prove I'm something more. I'm tired of being nothing but a striptease act."

In time, he would cut a romantic trail across the Hollywood landscape, marrying five different times, and seducing an occasional brunette such as Elizabeth Taylor and Gene Tierney. He even dated actress Wendy Barrie, the girlfriend of gangster Bugsy Siegel, when she was not otherwise engaged by the gangster himself or by Greg Bautzer.

Artie Shaw remembered the night he escorted his estranged wife, Lana, before their divorce to a Hollywood party where she ran into Mature.

"She had this technique," he said. "When a stud entered the room, and he interested her, she would straighten her back, thrusting out her breasts like a pouter pigeon, and head straight to her target. I often knew who her conquest for the night would be before she did. When Mature entered the room, she glided toward him. An hour or so later, she was gliding out the door with him."

Mature became famous in Hollywood for his endowment. So far as it is known, only one actress, the very promiscuous and very outspoken Liz Renay, described his penis in any detail. "Victor was very thick and measured six and a half inches soft, rising to 10½" when aroused. And that's what I did to this magnificent hunk of beefcake. I aroused him time and time again. He hit the spot. What a man!"

"He told me he was a mean kid when growing up," Renay said. "On the first day of school, he bit his teacher. He hit Hollywood with a stash of candy, which he sold to pay his weekly rent of $8 for a burnt-out garage in someone's backyard."

What Renay and Lana didn't know was that during his first lean months in Hollywood, he hustled homosexuals along Hollywood Boulevard, charging them ten dollars for sex.

At one point in their relationship, Mature flew to Washington with Lana to attend one of Franklin D. Roosevelt's wartime charity balls to raise money to fight polio.

She'd received a special invitation to visit the White House a bit in advance of the other guests there, along with some other stars (not Mature), she was ushered into the room where FDR delivered his fireside chats.

A limousine had transported Lana to 1600 Pennsylvania Avenue. For the occasion, she wore a silky white lace dress over a flesh-colored petticoat, her ensemble cloaked with a white fox fur.

When it was time to meet the president, who was seated behind his desk, she admitted, "I was trembling with fear." He reached out for her hand, and she claimed, "I saw recognition in his eyes."

"You are none other than Lana Turner!" Roosevelt said.

"'Yes, Mr. President,' I said. He looked me over, and I think he saw everything I had, at least when I opened by coat to show him how I was dressed. He gave me a long, wistful look, perhaps remembering an earlier day, before he came down with polio."

"My, you are one beautiful young lady," he told her.

"Thank you, Mr. President."

"I predict you'll be the belle of the ball tonight, dancing around the floor."

"I don't know—the competition is rough."

Then he flashed his celebrated grin at her. "Oh, that I could be the one whirling you around."

She later admitted, "I was choking back tears, and was made painfully aware of his semi-paralyzed condition."

She wished him a happy birthday and gave him a light kiss on his forehead. "Here I was in the presence of the most powerful man in the world, far more powerful than either Hitler or Churchill."

After exiting from the White House, outside its gates, she was mobbed by screaming fans, who tore at her white fox coat. She begged the mob not to tear it as it was being ripped from her shoulders.

When White House security guards retrieved her coat, it was, indeed, ripped. "I hadn't even paid for it yet," she said.

That night, at the ball, she had danced not only with Mature, but with a number of top government administrators, including members of the Army brass.

***

Mature was "too big" a prize not to attract other Hollywood beauties. In *My Gal Sal* (1942), he was cast with both Rita Hayworth and Landis, who, along with Betty Grable, were Lana's chief rivals for the title of Pinup Girl of World War II.

"For a while, I was kept busy satisfying both Rita and Carole, with not a lot of time off. But even-

According to Victor Mature, "When I hit Hollywood in the early 1940s, I was in such demand that my datebook was constantly filled. Lana Turner was among my first conquests." She claimed, 'Vic was my greatest thrill.'"

tually, I settled for Rita."

"Call it a wartime romance," Hayworth said. "My shacking up with Vic really pissed off Lana Turner."

In July of 1942, Mature attempted to enlist in the U.S. Navy, but was rejected because of his color blindness. He then enlisted in the Coast Guard.

During his stint in the Coast Guard, while lying nude and uncovered on a cot, with his cock dangling over the side of the bed, a picture was snapped of him and widely distributed through the underground. Among homosexual men, and based to some extent on that photo, Mature became the Pinup Boy of World War II.

When author Gore Vidal saw the picture, he wrote: "If the Nazis had seen that picture of Victor Mature, they would have surrendered much sooner."

When Mature was away at war, Hayworth had promised to wait for him. But she didn't. Along came Orson Welles.

When Mature returned home on leave, she told him, as justification for her shift in loyalties, "Wartime promises are rarely kept. They're made on the impulse of the moment."

Lana had reason to be jealous of Hayworth. When they'd co-starred together in *Music in My Heart* (1940), Hayworth had sustained an affair with Tony Martin. She'd also seduced Lana's former lover, James Stewart, and she'd snared Lana's all-time crush, Tyrone Power, when they had co-starred in *Blood and Sand* in 1941.

Despite Lana and Mature's breakup as lovers, they continued as friends. In 1943, Lana released *Slightly Dangerous*, co-starring Robert Young. When it turned out that he was not available for the radio version, Mature filled in for him.

Lana also attended the premiere of Mature's most famous movie, Cecil B. De-Mille's *Samson and Delilah* in 1949. The seductress was portrayed by Hedy Lamarr. DeMille described the role of Samson as "a combination of Tarzan, Robin Hood, and Superman."

Groucho Marx had another point of view. "I never like a movie where the hero's tits are bigger than those of the heroine."

Lana heard that Mature had imported a concrete imprint of his buttocks in a location just outside the entrance to his dressing room when he became annoyed that Grauman's Chinese Theater had not invited him to leave an imprint of his hands and feet in the cement in front of their movie palace.

In 1954, when Lana was cast with Clark Gable and Mature in *Betrayed,* she celebrated a "working reunion" with two of her lovers from the early 1950s.

In 1960, facing a career in decline, Mature announced his retirement after filming *The Tartars* in Italy.

"Making movies wasn't fun anymore," he told the press. "I thought what the hell, since I was okay financially. I said goodbye to Hollywood. Let those jerks call me what they would—a 'Technicolor Tarzan,' a 'Lush Lothario,' an 'Overripe Romeo.' Fuck it all! I made money and I had a blast, and I screwed as many dames as I wanted to, from Lana Turner to Rita Hayworth. Not bad, wouldn't you say?"

***

In 1940, Mildred knocked on Lana's door as she was applying her makeup for another glamorous night on the town. "Joan Crawford is on the phone."

At first. Lana was tempted not to take the call. Since she was no longer sleeping with Greg Bautzer, she wondered what new boyfriend of Crawford's she'd been moving in on.

"Darling," came Crawford's voice over the phone. "I just heard that MGM is considering a remake of my 1928 silent, *Our Dancing Daughters,* with you in the lead."

"This is the first I've heard of it," Lana said.

"Dear heart, you're not good enough as an actress to lie to me. Of course, you know all about it. But I wanted you to know that if you try to replicate my role as 'Dangerous Diana' Medford, you might be laughed off the screen."

"I never saw your movie," Lana said, "and I know nothing about it. I was just a little girl when it was released. Mother didn't let me go to filthy pictures."

"In that film, I had to tear loose with one Charleston after another," Crawford said. "The part requires tremendous skill as a dancer. Of course, I can pull it off, but from what I hear, you have to rehearse and rehearse to perform the simplest steps. *Our Dancing Daughters* made me a big star. Perhaps you can find some other vehicle better suited to your limited talents."

"Miss Crawford, I really must go," Lana said. "Thank you for your career advice. The next time I need such advice, I'll phone you. Heaven knows, you've been in the industry long enough to know everything about it." Then she slammed down the phone.

MGM eventually shelved plans to remake *Our Dancing Daughters.*

John Carroll, the Clark Gable wannabe, ultimately struck out with Lana after a two-night fling, yet succeeded with another famous blonde, Marilyn Monroe, in 1947.

He and his wife, Lucille Ryman, head of new talent at MGM, took in this "stray waif and sex kitten."

Carroll seduced her, the first of many times, when he found her walking around nude in his house while Ryman was away at MGM. After he'd finished, she wanted to know, "Was I as good as Lana Turner?"

Ryman later revealed, "At the time John and I took Marilyn in, she had been prostituting herself on Hollywood Boulevard in exchange for meals. Say what you want about the notorious Lana Turner—she never stooped that low."

***

During his tenure as Lana's agent, Johnny Hyde continually worked to get her the right movie roles.

Such was the case with the projected film, *Little Working Girls.* Based on a story by Bradford Roper, it was slated to be filmed with Lana and a handsome actor named John Carroll.

Born in New Orleans, Carroll was a mustachioed actor who had been making films since

1936, none of them memorable.

Lana had seen only one of them, *Susan and God* (1940), and that was because Joan Crawford had been its star. She'd played a flighty society lady who becomes entranced by a new movement in religious thought.

Carroll had been awarded fourth billing after Fredric March and Ruth Hussey. To her surprise, Lana had spotted Rita Hayworth interpreting a small part in that film. "Tomorrow's competition," she told Mildred.

When Carroll learned that MGM had cast Lana in *Little Working Girls*, he phoned her and arranged a date. Having recently divorced his first wife, he was a bachelor-at-large.

As her escort, Lana found him courtly and attentive. He was one of several actors billed at the time as "the next Clark Gable."

As Lana described to her friend, Virginia Grey, "Since I can't get the real Gable, why not settle for merely the mock?"

Their first night out was spent together at Ciro's. The next day was Saturday, and he invited her to join him at the home of his friend, actor Ben Lyon, at his beach house in Santa Monica.

It was at the beach house that Saturday afternoon that Lana's "two-day affair," (her term) with Carroll began. He confessed to her, "I'm famished for blonde goddesses, and in Hollywood, you're the blonde goddess of them all—forget Betty Grable and Carole Landis."

The following week, when Carroll phoned to invite Lana for another weekend at Lyon's beach house, she refused to take the call, informing Mildred, "Tell Johnny boy I'm not in. I've got other plans."

Since their previous weekend together, Hyde had called to inform her that MGM had shelved plans to film *Little Working Girl*. Lana had responded, "Leave all those shopgirl roles to Crawford. Get me something glamorous with Clark Gable or Robert Taylor."

***

With the arrival of the 1940s and America's entry into World War II after the December 7, 1941 bombing of Pearl Harbor, Lana was on the dawn of her greatest stardom.

America's G.I.s, fighting on battlefields in both the Pacific and in Europe, named her, "The Girl We'd Like to be Stranded on a Desert Island With." She was also called "The Most Gorgeous, Spectacular, and Pulse-Stirring Thing on High Heels."

As America went to war, the 18th Bomb Squadron of the U.S. Air Force painted her image on the nose of one of its B-17s. In her honor, the flying fortress was nicknamed "Tempest Turner."

Her look, her taste, her fashion accessories, and her style were subsequently imitated by young women across America, many of them working in defense plants.

She was not a mad egotist like Hedy Lamarr, who she considered more beautiful than she was.

She told the press, "Jobs are landed in Hollywood through brains, ability, beauty, talent, hard work, or through a combination of features that stack up to a photogenic accident. I was one of the photogenic accidents."

Mervin LeRoy, the director who had discovered her, relinquished his personal contract with her to Louis B. Mayer at MGM. Thus, the way was paved for her to become the undisputed Queen of Metro-Goldwyn-Mayer. She would sit on that throne for eighteen years.

***

Following her divorce from Artie Shaw, and before her second marriage to Stephen Crane, Lana was plunged into the most promiscuous and randomly romantic period of her life.

SMITTEN, this serviceman is, as were thousands of his counterparts, with the spontaneous charm of lovely Lana, at a Navy party in 1940.

Lana Romances
Dr. Jekyll, Rhett Butler, Bugsy Siegel,
& a Galaxy of Other Celebrities

The Luscious Blonde Makes Music with
The Boys in the Band

Years later, Lana recalled the first time she walked onto the set of the 1941 film, *Honky Tonk,* her first really big starring role. In it, she'd appear with Clark Gable, The King of Hollywood.

"I was intimidated, knowing that I would be the latest in a stream of his leading ladies who had already included Greta Garbo, Jean Harlow, Mary Astor, Joan Crawford, Carole Lombard, Myrna Loy, Vivien Leigh, Hedy Lamarr, Loretta Young, Norma Shearer, Helen Hayes, Claudette Colbert, Rosalind Russell, and Jeanette MacDonald."

Salesman, lumberjack, truck driver, telephone repairman, and newspaper reporter, Gable, a native of Cadiz, Ohio, became a bigtime movie idol in spite of his large ears. Jack Warner looked at one of his early screen tests and said, "Those ears will doom his career as a leading man." In another test, his physique was defined as "not impressive enough to play Tarzan."

Gable, of course, was one of the major seducers of Hollywood, estimated to have "conquered" some of MGM's biggest stars plus hundreds of starlets or women in other professions, such as carhops.

Before Lana Turner started wildly dating almost a new man every night, Artie Shaw came back into her life. He was pleased that during their divorce, she had not asked for alimony.

It was Christmas Eve, 1940. After an exhausting road trip, he had returned to the home they had shared on Summit Hill in Brentwood. He turned the key in the front door, entered his living room and turned on the lights. To his amazement, a Christmas tree positioned in the center of the room was suddenly illuminated. Presents had been positioned around the base of the tree.

Then, as if in a dream, a seductive Lana emerged from behind the sofa, wearing a sexy black lace *négligée.* "Merry Christmas, darling," she said, even though he was Jewish.

"What a surprise," he said. "I'm worn out, but you've inspired me to new life."

At the peak of her fame in the early 1940s, Lana reigned supreme as the cover girl of movie magazines. In one month alone, her glamorous picure appeared on the covers of eighteen magazines.

She'd ordered a champagne dinner, which arrived at ten o'clock. That was followed by a night of lovemaking.

He awakened at 11AM on Christmas morning, completely exhausted, but satisfied. "What a hot damn homecoming that was!"

Over a late breakfast, she proposed a remarriage. "Let's get back together. I've missed you."

"I've missed my blonde goddess. Let's think about it."

Remarrying was not a decision that either of them wanted to rush. In the coming months, they saw each other only sporadically. There was no more talk about it. Eventually, plans to remarry were abandoned, buried as each of them were by heavy dating schedules, especially Lana. "Artie and I became friends," she said. "Even the rolls in the hay stopped."

"There was a time I actually did consider remarrying her," Shaw said. "But there was something preventing that. I couldn't stand the thought of her one hundred pairs of shoes crowding me out of my closets."

There was another, even more serious reason. Before her 21st birthday, Lana went on a nymphomaniacal rampage, dating almost every handsome hunk who caught her eye.

She shared the most intimate details of her adventures with Virginia Grey, who became intrigued with the graphic descriptions. In distinct contrast, Shaw himself never really wanted to hear about them.

"Yet she filled me in whether I liked it or not," he said. "Perhaps she was showing off, letting me know she could get on very well without me. She'd phone and say, 'Guess who I did last night?' She would then transmit the most intimate details of her latest conquest, even his penile measurements. She must have kept a ruler under her pillow. Virginia was much more intrigued by all these physical descriptions than I was. Frankly, I'm not turned on by men and could care less about their love-making techniques or their pillow talk."

"Without meaning to, I may have aided her conquests in an indirect way," Shaw continued. "In those days, I went to a lot of movies. When we talked about them, I often mentioned an actor who I thought was going to get hot in films."

"Some of these guys were just making their debut in films. Others had been kicking around Hollywood for a while in the 1930s, but were suddenly becoming box office draws now that the former male stars had been shipped off to the Pacific or wherever. Guys like Sterling Hayden come to mind. Perhaps 'come' is the wrong word. Within a week or so after talking about an actor, I'd get a call from Lana."

"We did it," she'd say.

"'Did it!' was the way she described intercourse. Then I'd hear a play-by-play description of her conquest. Many times, she never had these guys after their one-night stand. She was too busy in most cases for repeats. Of course, some of her lovers were already married. A few also had boyfriends—that's pretty common in Hollywood."

***

Lana's radically renegotiated MGM contract called for an increase in her salary to $1,500 a week. "I was on my way to being a big star. At that time, my salary was a heady sum for a twenty-year-old."

In her next three pictures, she would be co-starring with the three biggest box office attractions at MGM. Those stars, in descending order of the profits they generated at the box office, included Spencer Tracy, Clark Gable, and Robert Taylor.

To millions of her male admirers, she was acclaimed as "The Most Desirable Woman in the World." Her star power not only extended to her roles at MGM, but to her private life, too. "Unless the guy was a homosexual, I could have virtually any man I wanted in Hollywood."

"Even if he's married?" asked Grey.

"Especially if he's married," Lana boasted.

During the opening months of America's involvement in World War II, Lana's fame grew monthly to the point where she eventually evolved into the unofficial "Sweetheart of the Navy." And although marines and soldiers in the Army dug her, too, she remained a special favorite with sailors throughout the duration of the war and for years after it ended.

Life magazine published a poll of sailors aboard the *S.S. Idaho*, and Lana emerged the clear favorite. Minor votes were cast for runners-up Betty Grable, Ca-

141

role Landis, Rita Hayworth, and Dorothy Lamour. Hedy Lamarr also garnered numerous votes, although the men seemed to prefer actresses with larger busts.

Based on her new status as "The Queen of Metro-Goldwyn-Mayer," Lana, along with Mildred, moved into a movie star mansion in Beverly Hills. For the first time in her life, she hired a staff of servants, including a housekeeper and a cook. As Shaw claimed, "Lana was spending every cent of her weekly paycheck."

***

At the beginning of the 1940s, Lana entered a romantic period of her life that daughter Cheryl Crane later called "The Boys in the Band." She'd met dozens of musicians through her link to Artie Shaw.

Her favorite—"and the best looking and the best lover" (her words)—was Gene Krupa. The ninth son of Polish parents, Krupa had been born in Chicago and was thirteen years older than Lana. Although a hell-raising, drug-taking musician, composer, and bandleader, he was originally reared for the priesthood.

He'd been playing drums since the 1920s. By December of 1934, he was a member of Benny Goodman's band. During his time there, he became famous across the country. "No one could beat the drums like Gene," Lana said.

During the time she dated him, he invited her to the set of *Ball of Fire* (1941), starring Barbara Stanwyck, the wife of Robert Taylor. Stanwyck didn't seem to want to have anything to do with her—"and I hadn't even met her husband," Lana protested.

Stanwyck's co-star was Gary Cooper. "I really don't think he even remembered having an affair with me," Lana said. "Imagine forgetting that you went to bed with Lana Turner! Of course, I was a bit young in those days."

When Lana met Krupa, he was working with Glenn Miller's swing band. Howard Hawks had cast Krupa in *Ball of Fire*. He performed an extended version of "Drum Boogie," a number that Stanwyck, cast as a burlesque dancer, pretended to sing, her voice dubbed by "the songbird," Martha Tilton.

While Krupa was beating his drums on camera, Lana wandered off with actor Dana Andrews, who had the fourth lead in *Ball of Fire*. After studying acting at the Pasadena Playhouse, he was just breaking into films, having earned his living as a gas sta-

Lana had a fling with sweat-soaked Gene Krupa in the 1940s. She had nothing but praise for his "boudoir antics. He pounded a woman like his tom-tom, even when he was high on what he called weed."

tion attendant. When she met him, he had just appeared in *Tobacco Road,* based on that controversial Erskine Caldwell novel. In *Ball of Fire,* he played the villain bemused by Cooper's timidity.

Andrews looked very masculine, solid, and reliable, giving off a virility that seemed in some ways uninspired. Nevertheless, after the sometimes overly energetic Krupa, she was drawn to Andrews' masculinity.

At one point during their dialogues, he asked for her phone number, and she gave it to him. "It can't be tonight," she said. "I'm involved with Gene."

"I can see that," he said. "But that's subject to change."

She soon discovered that Krupa was heavily addicted to drugs and always seemed stoned on marijuana, even though it didn't seem to harm his musical performances.

During her brief marriage to Shaw, she came to believe that all musicians smoked pot. "Artie wasn't an addict, but no day went by when he didn't have a smoke or two. When Artie and the boys in his band got together, everyone was always going up in smoke."

Their romance ended long before Krupa was arrested in 1943 for possession of marijuana. His habits contributed to the breakup of his own band, and he later rejoined Benny Goodman's Music Makers.

***

It was through Krupa that Lana met a future lover, Benny Goodman. Another son of Chicago, Goodman was a clarinet player like Artie Shaw, and both musicians vied for the title of "The King of Swing."

Goodman was the ninth of a dozen siblings born to Russian Jewish immigrants. He was a boy—not even a teenager—when he made his professional debut during the early 1920s in Chicago, a city addicted to jazz at the time.

One night on a date with Goodman, Lana was introduced to trumpeter Harry James, who had "a thing for blondes," and even married one, Betty Grable. "He made a pass at me, but I didn't receive it," Lana said.

"I loved dancing to Benny's music," she said, "especially the bebop and the cool jazz that America was listening to as it went to war. I think he was a greater clarinet player than Artie, but don't tell my former husband I have that view."

"He was a smooth lover in bed," she told Grey. She never admitted to Shaw that she was having an affair with his chief rival.

Lana asked Grey a question: "Benny

"I will always say this about Benny Goodman," Lana said. "He knew how to use his mouth in bed with a woman, perhaps from years of holding that mouthpiece between his front teeth and his lower lip."

might be a smooth lover, but does a woman really want a guy that smooth in bed?"

Years later, in an interview, Lana claimed that both Goodman and Shaw were instrumental in removing racial segregation among black and white musicians. "When a drunk once approached Benny and me at the Trocadero, and asked him, 'Why do you play with niggers,' Benny stood up, threatening him."

"I'll knock you out if you say that word around me again," Goodman said to the racist drunk.

"Although I admired Benny in so many ways, especially his talent, I had to move on," Lana said. "To be really frank, my game back then was called 'playing the field.'"

***

Of all the boys in the band that Lana dated, Tommy Dorsey didn't quite meet her demand for good looks in a man. He was charming and reasonably attractive to her, at least enough so that she dated him for a while. "Perhaps it was his smooth-toned trombone playing that won me over," she recalled.

Her daughter, Cheryl Crane, later wrote, "One of mother's prized possessions was a trombone from Tommy Dorsey that read: "Lana, Happy New Year, The Boys in the Band."

The son of a bandleader from Pennsylvania, Dorsey was a master musician—jazz trombonist, composer, conductor, and one of the leading bandleaders of the wartime Big Band era. He was known as the "Sentimental Gentleman of Swing." And he was the younger brother of another bandleader, Jimmy Dorsey. Tommy recorded one of Lana's all-time favorite songs, "I'll Never Smile Again," with vocals by Frank Sinatra.

Throughout his career, Tommy Dorsey worked with some of the biggest names in music: Glenn Miller, Dick Haymes (Lana's former lover), Nelson Riddle, Paul Whiteman, the Pied Pipers, Buddy Rich (another of Lana's lovers), and such female vocalists as Jo Stafford and Connie Haines.

Sinatra achieved his greatest success as a singer in Dorsey's Band, making eighty records from 1940 to 1942. The singer claimed that he learned breath control watching "Tommy play the trombone."

Lana was instrumental in getting Dorsey

Tommy Dorsey was always saying goodbye to Lana, as he headed out for another gig or else for a rest at his 21-acre estate in Bernardsville, New Jersey.

One photographer snapped a picture of one of their goodbyes at the railroad station. She is glamorously dressed as he looks lovingly at her. But that very night, after their farewell, she fell into the arms of Buddy Rich. As she told Grey, "Why waste time?"

to hire her ex-husband (Artie Shaw) in 1942 when he broke up his own band. Dorsey employed Shaw and his string section.

When Lana dated him, he was already married, but away from his wife, "Totts" Kraft, for weeks at a time. He was only 17 when he took the 16-year-old as his bride.

Lana was quick to point out that she was not the cause of Dorsey's divorce in 1943 from his wife, but it was his affair with singer Edythe Wright.

***

Born in Brooklyn of Jewish-American parents, both of whom were vaudevillians, Buddy Rich grew up in the world of music. At the age of one, he surprised his father by keeping a steady beat with spoons. At the age of 18 months, he was playing drums on stage in his parents' vaudeville act.

In time, he became known as the greatest drummer in the world, celebrated for his virtuoso technique, power, and speed. He performed with Tommy Dorsey and Harry James, even with Count Basie, eventually conducting his own band.

"For a while, I adored Buddy," Lana told Grey. "When I dated him, I was making *Dr. Jekyll and Mr. Hyde*. I soon learned that Buddy could have played both roles. That guy sure had one short fuse. He could be charming one minute, then Mr. Hyde the next."

"One night at this club, he accused me of making goo-goo eyes at Sinatra." Lana said. "When Frank joined our table for a while, he and Buddy talked like old friends. Then Frank said something that pissed off Buddy, and he struck him. Frank didn't hit him back, but two days later, two goons—no doubt Frank's chums—beat up Buddy in an alley."

At one time, both Rich and Sinatra were members of Tommy Dorsey's band. They frequently got into brawls even back then, but somehow managed to make up and be friends once again.

"Finally, after a fight one night, I knew I had to end it with Buddy," Lana said. "I told him, 'I love your music and our love-making, but my face is my fortune. I fear that you might cause me real damage. So I'm out of here. Save your pounding for the drums!'"

"Buddy Rich was a very satisfying and most competent lover, but I had to be careful around him," Lana said. "I never knew when I was going to piss him off and get struck by him. He frightened me, even though I was attracted to him."

***

As the venue for his first date with her, Dana Andrews invited Lana to a cast party for the actors in the romance film *Ball of Fire* (1941). The party was hosted at

145

Café Formosa. A favorite gathering place for actors, it stood across from the entrance to Goldwyn Studios.

Its host was mobster Benjamin ("Bugsy") Siegel, a Jewish-American gangster from Brooklyn, one of the founders of Murder, Inc.

Lana had heard of the joint, but had never visited it.

Set for a December, 1941, release, *Ball of Fire* had cast Gary Cooper as Bertram Potts, a professor who falls in love with Sugarpuss O'Shea (Barbara Stanwyck), a burlesque dancer.

Andrews had been cast as the gangster, Joe Lilac, who is involved with Sugarpuss.

The actor told Lana that he was modeling his character after Siegel himself, who was known for his thousand dollar suits, his smooth talking, and his good looks.

In addition to his involvement with the British actress Wendy Barrie, Siegel took for his mistress Virginia ("Sugar") Hill. Born in a backwater of Alabama, Hill was a bosomy, auburn-haired, green-eyed beauty. She had persuaded director Howard Hawks to give her a role in *Ball of Fire*. Per-

Lana liked being escorted by Dana Andrews, whom she felt was a strong, macho figure. Indeed, he would in time be cited as "*film noir*'s masculine ideal of steely impassivity."

She was a bit put off, however, by his excessive drinking, which made him stand out even in a heavy-drinking crowd.

haps coincidentally, Stanwyck's character in the movie was named "Sugarpuss."

Gene Krupa, who was also in the cast, could not escort Lana anywhere that night since he was scheduled for a gig out of town.

At the party, Andrews introduced Lana to the film's director, Hawks, who told her he'd like to direct her in a movie.

However, when she ran into Stanwyck, the actress turned her back on Lana, who would soon be co-starring with her husband, Robert Taylor, in *Johnny Eager.*

The highlight of the evening occurred when Andrews introduced her to the charismatic Siegel, whom she found "extraordinarily handsome." Although he was accompanied with his girlfriend Sugar, she was called away by Hawks to meet the people at his table while Andrews was otherwise occupied at the bar.

Alone together, Lana flirted shamelessly with Siegel. Perhaps she did it for vengeance against Greg Bautzer. [*As part of a complicated romantic rondelay, Bautzer had once canceled a date with Lana for a tryst with Wendy Barrie, and perhaps in some perverse way, she was getting back at Bautzer for tossing her over, if only for a night.*]

When Andrews returned from the bar, Siegel invited them, as a couple, to one of his lavish Hollywood parties scheduled for the upcoming Saturday.

After their exit from the party at Formosa, Lana took the wheel of his car, driving Andrews to her home, where she suggested that he spend the night. "You've had too much to drink," she told him, "and I think you'll be safer in my bed."

She later discussed her night with Andrews with Virginia Grey. "Dana certainly has the equipment to satisfy a woman, but he drinks too much. I'm convinced he wasn't half as good as he would have been if he'd been reasonably sober."

After a late breakfast, Andrews assured her that he'd retrieve her at 8PM on the designated night to escort her to Siegel's party. But when he showed up at Lana's doorstep, he was already intoxicated.

Surmising that there was no way she could sober him up, she devised a scheme, offering him a series of three more drinks, even though before he drank them, he looked as if he were close to passing out on her sofa.

He eventually did that (pass out) before 9PM, at which time she put a blanket over him and left him to sleep it off. Then she drove to Siegel's party alone.

***

Arriving alone that Saturday night at Siegel's party, Lana was ushered into the lavishly furnished Holmby Hills home of Bugsy Siegel. Over the decades, she would attend countless Hollywood parties, many of them spectacular, but Siegel's big bash would stand out in her mind "It was the first real A-list party I ever attended," she said.

Seeing her from across a crowded room, the gangster rushed to her side and greeted her warmly, kissing her on both cheeks. She found him likable and ingratiating, even though she knew he was a murderer.

The guest list stunned her, particularly when she chatted with her boss, Louis B. Mayer. He warned her, "You should be home getting your beauty sleep."

She also ran into Jack Warner, one of her former bosses. "I was wrong about you, girl," he said. "I thought you didn't have what it takes to make it. But you've got it, baby."

She spoke with Clark Gable, with whom she briefly discussed their upcoming picture, *Honky Talk*, until he was rescued by his wife, Carole Lombard.

Frank Sinatra approached and gave her a passionate kiss on the lips before introducing her to his friend, Cary Grant, who had recently married, after breaking Randolph Scott's heart, the Woolworth

Lana had never seen a man as expensively dressed as Bugsy Siegel, beginning with the best-tailored suit she'd ever seen a man wear. With it, he wore a red silk shirt in an era when men tended only to wear white shirts. From his alligator shoes to his red silk tie, he looked like he'd stepped out of some gentlemen's style magazine.

heiress, Barbara Hutton.

Before the night was over, as she was standing alone on his moonlit terrace, Siegel approached her from behind. Within a few minutes, he'd arranged a date with her for the following Monday night.

"I can't wait, baby," he whispered in her ear.

At 8PM on that scheduled night, a bulletproof limousine pulled up in her driveway, conducted by "the handsomest chauffeur in the history of the world," as she recalled. "I never saw or heard of him again. Perhaps he couldn't act, but he would have lit up the screen."

For her night with Siegel, "Everything was champagne-colored—my hair, my shoes, my gown, even my undergarments."

As if he'd known in advance what she'd be wearing, he'd arranged a catered champagne supper. "Even the sofa was made of champagne-colored fabric, so I blended in."

Throughout dinner, Siegel never seemed to take his eyes off Lana. He was a fascinating host, relaying tales of his life without mentioning the criminal elements.

"Jean Harlow went wild over me. Of all the blondes in Hollywood, I think you're the only one who has what it takes to replace her."

"Tell me that and I'll follow you anywhere."

"Even to my bedroom?" he asked.

"Perhaps if you give me just a little more champagne," she responded, coquettishly.

Then he retrieved five gold lockets and opened them for her, describing their contents as pubic hair "harvested" from the nether regions of Jean Harlow.

"I didn't collect them personally," he said. "Another mobster did when Harlow had some emergency surgery. They were plucked off without her permission, and I paid $500 each for five of these."

In his bedroom, as he was undressing, Lana wasn't surprised when he removed his trousers to reveal monogrammed, red silk underwear. As she'd later relay to Virginia Grey, "Bugsy looked even better with his clothes off. He was one of those men that wives dream about when their dull husbands are screwing them."

[Another mobster, Abe Zwillman, had already spread the word that, "Bugsy is God's gift to women." When Lana heard that, she chimed in, "I second the motion. Before me, and before Harlow, Bugsy had brought joy to the likes of everybody from Sophie Tucker to Mae West."]

During a chat with Grey, she said, "The only surprise about this he-man is that before he goes to sleep, he puts on a chin strap to keep his perfect profile intact, and blue shades over his eyes. Otherwise, he sleeps in the nude, as befits God's gift to women. And the next morning, he told me that even if I become a big star, making a lot of money, he'd never ask me for a loan."

"Why would you need a loan from me?" she had asked him. "It looks like you've got more money than God Herself."

"It's a sideline for me. Mayer and Warner pay me off so I won't cause problems at their studios and disrupt production. I also borrow money from stars like Cooper, Gable, and Grant. Although they know that I'll never pay them back, they come through for me. During my first year in Hollywood, I pocketed $400,000 in loans from stars."

"Thanks for excluding me," she said. "But I'll make a deal with you. I'll give you five pubic hairs and I won't even charge you $500."

"It's a deal," he said.

Before she left that morning, she heard him on the phone with his lawyer, Jerry Giesler.

When he came back into the breakfast room, he said, "This Giesler is a great guy. He's the best lawyer in Hollywood. If you ever commit murder, call Giesler. He'll get you off."

She didn't think a lot about that remark at the time, but years from that date, she'd place an emergency call to Giesler during the pre-dawn hours of a blood-soaked Hollywood morning. Her call originated from within what the press would loudly define as "the murder house."

***

Lana's second film for 1941 was a prestige production, Hollywood's third reprise of *Dr. Jekyll and Mr. Hyde*. It was, of course, based on the 1886 novella by Robert Louis Stevenson, *The Strange Case of Dr. Jekyll and Mr. Hyde.*

In 1920, John Barrymore had been cast in the silent version of this classic, turning it into one of the most famous of the silent horror films. His co-star was Nita Naldi, a well-known actress and vamp during her heyday.

Barrymore was able to replicate the monstrous Mr. Hyde wearing almost no makeup, relying on his uncanny ability to contort his face.

This was in radical contrast to the 1931 Talkie with the same name. It had starred Fredric March as the doctor/monster. His Mr. Hyde was a hairy simian with canine fangs. The role brought March an Oscar as Best Actor the year of its release.

Since the second version was crafted during the Pre-Code era of rela-

Director Victor Fleming had directed Vivien Leigh as Scarlett O'Hara in *Gone With the Wind* before tackling Lana in this horror movie.

149

tively loose censorship, it allowed Miriam Hopkins, cast as Ivy Peterson, the tarty barmaid, to be more sexually provocative than either of the other two.

Like Barrymore, Spencer Tracy, co-starring with Lana in the classic theme's third (1941) incarnation, did not rely on heavy makeup, but used facial contortions to establish his character.

The familiar story, known to most school children at the time, reveals that Dr. Jekyll is motivated by the battle raging in his soul between good and evil. His experiments, which involve ingestion of a serum, transforms the kindly Dr. Jekyll into the cruel, evil, and violent Mr. Hyde.

Victor Fleming was assigned to helm the 1941 remake of *Dr. Jekyll and Mr. Hyde* with Tracy and Lana.

[The son of a truck salesman from Wisconsin, Tracy had made his film debut in Up the River *(1938). He'd gone on to win two Best Actor Oscars (for Captains Courageous (1937) and again for his portrayal of Father Flanagan in Boys Town (1938).]*

He was at first reluctant to accept the role of Dr. Jekyll until his best friend and sometimes lover, Katharine Hepburn, persuaded him to do it.

Hepburn's advice was motivated by reasons of her own. After reading the script, she became intrigued with each of the two roles it contained for women. One was that of Jekyll's prim, ladylike *fiancée*, Beatrix Emery.

The other role that appealed to her was that of a slutty barmaid, Ivy Peterson. It was Hepburn's idea that she would star in both roles, interpreting "the good girl" who (in a transformation similar to that of Dr. Jekyll himself) mutates into "the bad girl" through makeup and talent. Both Mayer and Fleming vigorously rejected the idea.

For a while the mogul and his director considered casting the virginal *fiancée* role with either Ruth Hussey or Maureen O'Hara. Finally, in an agreement with David O. Selznick, it was decided that Ingrid Bergman—the beautiful and soft-spoken Swedish actress—would be ideal as Dr. Jekyll's elegant *fiancée*.

But when Bergman read the script, she decided that she wanted to play the slutty barmaid who is terrorized by Mr. Hyde.

"I'm tired of playing good girls," she said. "I want a role with some meat on it." Secretly, without Selznick's knowledge, Bergman made a screen test whose results Fleming had interpreted as powerful.

By that time, however, Lana had been offered the role of the amoral barmaid. But after she read the script, she protested to

On screen, Lana played Dr. Jekyll's virginal *fiancée*, Beatrix, who was "Victorian sweet, but spirited."

Off screen, Tracy added Lana to his long lists of A-list movie star conquests that ranged from Joan Crawford to Nancy Davis (aka Nancy Reagan).

Mayer at a meeting where she told him that she was too young and inexperienced to portray the battle-hardened Ivy, survivor of many a seduction. "That role is so deep, I don't know if I could trust the director enough to let me try to reach those emotions."

Consequently, she convinced him that she'd be better cast as Beatrix, a polite well-mannered Victorian girl. As such, Mayer acquiesced to Bergman's wish to interpret the role of the prostitute.

When Lana first met Bergman, the Swede thanked her for surrendering the role of the bad girl barmaid, Ivy Peterson, for the demure role of Beatrix. "I want to show the bastards in Hollywood that I can play a sexy whore," Bergman said.

Lana responded, "In Adrian's billowy, 19th-century gowns, I'm sure I'll look virginal. Me, Lana Turner! Isn't that a hoot?"

Whereas Lana had not bonded very well with her female co-stars in previous films, such as *Ziegfeld Girl*, where her rivals had included Hedy Lamarr, on the set of the Jekyll & Hyde movie, she and Ingrid bonded and shared long talks with each other.

Bergman, who was married at the time to the Swedish doctor, Petter Lindstrom, shared with Lana her theory about how to be authentic and convincing on screen with her leading man.

Lindstrom later revealed that his wife had asserted, "I can't work well as an actress unless I'm in love with either the leading man or the director."

"Your romance," Bergman suggested to Lana, "will not necessarily continue after the picture is finished, except in some rare cases."

Lana took Bergman's advice to heart, and followed the Swede's example in her future pictures, as many of her leading men could later testify.

***

Since the debut of his career in Hollywood, Fleming had been known mainly as a man's director, and Lana was intimidated by the idea of being helmed by him.

When she had first met him, he'd said, "So I didn't get to direct you as Scarlett O'Hara in *Gone With the Wind*, as I got stuck instead with Vivien Leigh."

"I'm sure you're teasing me, Mr. Fleming," Lana responded.

As filming progressed, Fleming suffered through several blow-ups with her, at one point referring to her as a "no-talent, bosomy bitch."

One scene called for her to shed tears, but none would emerge from her dry eyes. Exasperated, Fleming grabbed her by her arm and sharply twisted it behind her back. In the aftermath, he got his tears streaming down her face.

Within the first week of filming, she saw firsthand that Ingrid practiced what she preached, as it applied to falling in love with either her leading man or director. In this case, it involved them both.

"Ingrid was juggling both Tracy and Fleming," Lana said, "keeping both of them satisfied, or so it seemed to me."

Although Ingrid frequently appeared onscreen during the course of her career as innocent, serene, and pure, her future director, Alfred Hitchcock, once said, ungallantly, "Ingrid would do it with a doorknob."

Indeed, as the years passed, Bergman continued to practice her theory about the benefits associated with seductions of her leading man of the moment. Her love affairs seemed to dovetail neatly with her filmmaking schedule, beginning with Leslie Howard and moving on to Spencer Tracy, Humphrey Bogart, Gary Cooper, Gregory Peck, Yul Brynner, Joseph Cotten, Bing Crosby, Anthony Quinn, and Omar Sharif.

Spencer Tracy posed for this publicity shot with Ingrid Bergman (left) and Lana. The tarty barmaid, Ingrid, and Lana, his fiancée, had switched roles before filming began because Ingrid had wanted to play "against type," in an attempt to broaden her range of acting skills.

Offscreen, Tracy seduced first Bergman, then Lana. At some point, Bergman left Tracy altogether in her pursuit of the film's director, Victor Fleming.

Despite his ongoing cohabitations with Katharine Hepburn, Tracy stayed married to the former actress, Louise Treadwell. Hepburn showed up only once on the set of *Jekyll & Hyde*, where she was polite but not especially friendly, to both Bergman and Lana.

"Hepburn obviously didn't demand fidelity from him," Lana speculated. "Judy Garland told me that Tracy had seduced her when she was an underaged teenager."

Near the end of filming, after Fleming apparently fell in love with Bergman, she paid less attention to Tracy.

"But I filled in for her," Lana confessed. On at least five different occasions, she was spotted exiting from Tracy's suite at the Beverly Wilshire Hotel at 5AM, presumably on her way to an early-morning appointment with makeup at the studio. Insofar as these writers know, she never revealed any of the details of her intimacies with Tracy, but she did tell Fleming, "Spence makes the best cup of morning coffee I've ever had."

On the final day of filming, Fleming threw a cast party which Lana attended. She asked Bergman what would be next for her.

"I'm doing this cheap little melodrama at Warners, *Casablanca* (1942), with Bogart. I don't want to do it, but it'll be shot rather quickly. I'm just biding my time until I get to co-star with Gary Cooper in Ernest Hemingway's *For Whom the Bell Tolls*" (1943).

Dr. Jekyll and Mr. Hyde became one of MGM's biggest grossing films of the year it was released (1941). But although Tracy usually got rave reviews for his movies, reactions to his dual role in this one were mixed. Some critics asserted, "Tracy is hamming it up too much."

Lana didn't expect rave reviews for herself. "I was mostly an adornment in the film, beautifully made up and gowned, sitting in opera boxes or at dinner tables."

One critic noted, "Lana Turner has too much carnality to be effective as a symbol for Victorian purity."

Life magazine claimed: "Pictorially, *Dr. Jekyll and Mr. Hyde* is well worth a look at such moments when the purity of Lana Turner, who plays Jekyll's *fiancée*, is symbolized by white flowers, and Ingrid Bergman lies in a mud puddle to indicate the baser nature of Hyde."

The review that Lana disliked the most was when a critic called her "colorless and wooden in her nice-girl role."

Reviews of Ingrid as a slutty tart were so effusive that they aroused Lana's jealousy. But the envy she experienced in 1941 was different from the rage she suffered years later, when it became clear that two of her beaux, Greg Bautzer and Howard Hughes, were each in pursuit of Ingrid.

***

For years, Robert Stack remained Lana's on-again, off-again lover. As he said later in life, "Occasionally, for old time's sake, we made it but what emerged in our last years was enduring friendship. We started out as kids and eventually grew old in Tinseltown, where age most often is a liability, especially for women."

"In the late 1940s, I had a roving eye," he said. "I seduced one Hollywood beauty after another, often with my friend, John F. Kennedy, when he was in town. Sometimes as a favor to Lana, I served as her 'beard,' covering up some affair she was having with a good-looking guy, especially during her marriages. My guest room was always available to her and her *beau du jour.*"

One Sunday afternoon, Stack hosted a pool party and invited some of his friends, especially the girl of his dreams, Carole Lombard (Clark Gable was out of town). The guest list also included Ronald Reagan and his wife, Jane Wyman, as well as Andy Devine, Ann Rutherford (Lana's friend), Bruce Cabot, and Dan Dailey. Stack's guest list was short on women that day until Lana arrived with her best girlfriend, Virginia Grey, who, years later, remembered that hot, long-ago afternoon before Hollywood went to war.

According to Grey, "It was the afternoon that Lana met George Montgomery." *[Fox had recently changed the actor's name. Throughout the 1930s, he'd been billed as George Letz.]*

"Lana and I first spotted Montgomery poised on a diving board as he was about to make the plunge into Stack's swimming pool. He was wearing a male bikini briefer than any I'd ever seen before," Grey said. "How can I put this delicately? It was white and did little to conceal his ample merchandise. We watched him swim three laps before he came up. He emerged like Neptune from the waters. That white bikini, when wet, became almost transparent. That's how he introduced himself to us. I think Lana stared at his crotch before looking into that gorgeous, masculine face. The man was a dreamboat. Even Jane Wyman was giving him the eye, much to the annoyance of Ronald Reagan. Lana told me that she and Reagan had gotten it on back in the late 1930s, when both of them were contract players at

153

Warners."

"For George Montgomery and Lana," Grey continued, "it was the beginning of a beautiful friendship."

Born on a remote ranch in northern Montana, Montgomery was five years older than Lana. Rugged, soft-spoken, and incredibly good-looking, he was the youngest of fifteen children born to immigrants from the Ukraine.

Ironically, during his early 20s, he had studied interior design while earning his living as

One of the then-novel photographic innovations pioneered in *Dr. Jekyll*, a nightmare sequence with Bergman (left) and Lana.

a boxer, showing off his splendid physique. Stack told Lana, "George is the only guy I've ever heard of who was an interior decorator as well as a boxer, a stunt man, a cattle puncher, and a college athlete."

Tired of ranch duties in Montana, Montgomery hitched westbound rides that eventually landed him in Hollywood. Within a few days, he was working as a stunt man at MGM on a film starring Greta Garbo, *Anna Karenina* (1935). He continued as a stunt man in many westerns, including in Gene Autry's *The Singing Vagabond* (1935). Autry used him in several other western films after that, too.

Standing 6'3", with a muscular, 210-pound body, he attracted attention from many Hollywood beauties and cut a streak through their boudoirs while fending off dozens of homosexual advances. When he made *The Cisco Kid and the Ladies* in 1938, he also had to fend off the sexual advances of its star, Cesar Romero.

In the early 1940s, when many leading stars (including Henry Fonda and Tyrone Power) went off to war, Fox decided to transform the former George Letz into the leading man henceforth known as George Montgomery. He was cast in *Cadet Girl* (1940), starring Carole Landis, Lana's rival. During the shoot, he spent a lot of time in her dressing room.

Other Hollywood beauties were waiting in line to "audition" him, as news of his sexual prowess had by then surged through the Hollywood grapevine. He received the inevitable call from Joan Crawford, who wanted to be the first of the really big stars to seduce "Fox's answer to Clark Gable."

At Fox, Montgomery co-starred with some of the leading actresses of Hollywood, and sometimes became their lover. These included Ginger Rogers, with whom he co-starred in *Roxie Hart* (1942), Gene Tierney in *China Girl* (also 1942), and Maureen O'Hara in *10 Gentlemen from West Point* (in 1940, his peak year). Betty Grable, the biggest female star in Hollywood at the time, nailed him for *Coney Island* (1943), in more ways than one.

Beside Stack's pool, Montgomery wrapped a bath towel around his midriff and spent the rest of the afternoon talking to Lana. As the sun was setting, after Grey had exited with Bruce Cabot *[perhaps for a communal rendezvous with Errol*

Flynn], Lana invited Montgomery to her home.

The next morning, Stack and Grey were among the first persons Lana phoned. "I've met the man I'm going to marry," she said, repeating the same line to each of them. "Should I propose to him, or should I wait for him to pop the question?"

"The wonderful and most enduring thing about George, aside from the obvious, is that he doesn't seem to realize just how good-looking he is, unlike every other male star in Hollywood who spends half the day looking at publicity pictures of themselves or else staring at their image in the mirror. George has a magnificent physique, although he told me he doesn't go near a barbell."

"I think he wants to design furniture or be an architect more than he wants to star in films."

"He told me on those long, cold nights in northern Montana, he would stick by the warm stove in the kitchen whittling on a stick of firewood. He said his dream was to build his own ranch house and make all the furniture for it himself."

Lana said, "God didn't create all men equally. He created regular men, and then he conceived his masterpiece, George Montgomery. When he strips down, his socks are among the first to go. Then those shorts come down. It's not only big but beautiful. I thought two sessions would be enough to satisfy him, but I woke up at 6AM when he piled on top of me for a divine encore. I can't wait for a repeat."

"During the days to come, George was often a breakfast guest," Lana said. "I had to buy hominy grits and learn how to make them the way he liked. He taught me to play tennis. You should see him on the court in his white tennis shorts. Betty Grable's legs—at least her left one— were voted the loveliest in the world. I disagree. George's legs are the most beautiful in the world, especially that stunning third one."

Years later, on reflection, Lana said, "George and I might have made it, had not every other beautiful hussy in Hollywood chased after him. I would have married him had not the so-called 'world's most beautiful woman' spotted him shirtless and then *that singer* came along to take him from me. But more about those ravenous bitches clawing his flesh some other day."

***

Montgomery, as well as Robert Stack, would each enter and exit, time and again, from Lana's life throughout the 40s and 50s. Thankfully, for the sake of her career, neither Hedda Hopper nor Louella Parsons ever "uncovered" the ongoing nature of their secret trysts.

***

Honky Tonk (1941) was the first of the Gable/Turner pictures, followed by *Somewhere I'll Find You* (1942), *Homecoming* (1948), and Betrayed *(1954).*

Jack Conway was one of Gable's most trusted directors. The Minnesota native was both a director and film producer as well as an actor. Beginning with D.W. Griffith's silent film stock company, he had more recently helmed Gable in *Boom Town* (1940), which had co-starred Spencer Tracy, Claudette Colbert, and Hedy Lamarr.

Both Gable and Conway were great friends and heavy drinkers, spending a lot of time together. Lana feared that as the female lead (i.e, her role) might be sacrificed to show off more of Gable. "An actress has to think of such things," she told co-star Claire Trevor.

Lana worked smoothly with Conway. "He was not a creative genius, but very competent. He stayed within the budget and brought the picture in on time. When I wanted more lavish costumes, he said no, citing budget considerations."

For *Honky Tonk,* Conway assembled a talented cast for the minor roles. The roster was led by Frank Morgan, who had recently interpreted the title role in *The Wizard of Oz* (1939). Other stars included Claire Trevor, Marjorie Main, Albert Dekker, Henry O'Neill, Chill Wills, and Vera Ann Borg.

Gable was cast in the film as an engaging con artist, "Candy" Johnson, who arrives in Yellow Creek, Nevada, during the Gold Rush. On the westbound train, he meets Elizabeth Cotton (Lana), who takes a dislike to him…or is she secretly attracted by his roguish, masculine charm?

Waiting to greet her at the railway station is her drunkard father, "Judge" Cotton (Morgan), who, unknown to her, is also a crook.

In the film, at Yellow Creek's town saloon, Gable hooks up with an old friend. "Gold Dust" Nelson (as portrayed by Trevor) who plays a hooker with a heart of gold.

Trevor, a blonde from Brooklyn, was cast as Lana's rival for Gable's affections. "If they want to cast a hard-boiled blonde, they call *me*," Trevor told Lana. "If they want a soft-spoken, beautiful blonde, they call Lana Turner."

In *Honky Tonk,* melodramatic complications become rife, as Gable tangles with Lana and gets involved in all sorts of intrigues that include gunfights, murder, and pregnancies. Love eventually wins out.

In 1938, in the aftermath of Jean Harlow's death and in the rush for her replacement, Louis B. Mayer had asked Gable to read out loud, with Lana, lines from the script of *Red Dust,* the movie he'd made with Harlow in 1932.

At the time, Gable was filming *Too Hot to Handle* (1938) with his co-star, Myrna Loy. Mayer had the idea that the seventeen-year-old Lana could be groomed to replace Harlow on the screen.

Lana was very nervous when she appeared for the reading with Gable. "I know I was very bad. I flubbed two or three lines. Clark was very kind to me, but I disappointed him."

When director George Cukor had suggested Lana as a possible Scarlett O'Hara, Gable had been disdainful. "Oh, yeah, the blonde Turner dame. She's too cute for Scarlett. As for Tallulah Bankhead, Selznick must have been out of his fucking mind. Your best bet for Scarlett is Carole Lombard."

Months later, when Conway told Gable that he was going to co-star him with Lana in *Honky Tonk,* he asked, "Can't you find someone better? She's got the looks but she can't act."

"I found out that Clark had never seen one of my movies, not even *Ziegfeld Girl,*" Lana said.

"In our first scene together, I was determined to impress Clark—and apparently I did," Lana said. "After I finished and returned to my dressing room, a box of yellow roses arrived from him. Through some source, he found out that I preferred yellow roses to red. The box included a note from him that read, 'I'm the world's worst talent scout.' Later, he poked his head through my dressing room door and said, 'Baby, you sure have learned a thing or two!'"

Lana later spoke of her admiration for Gable during the shooting of *Honky Tonk.* "He was very kind and considerate to me. When I fluffed a line, he'd say, 'That's all right, baby. Now don't you worry about it.' Whenever I did that, he'd blow a couple of lines himself, so I wouldn't feel inept. He also played practical jokes on me because he said I was a good sport. He would tease me and joke with me to put me at ease."

Scenes from *Honky Tonk,* each actor, both Lana and Gable, pumping up his or her allure.

Lana had never been sexier on the screen. In some scenes, she paraded in front of the camera in black corsets, with diamonds in her hair, and black lace stockings. Almost evoking the rape scene of Scarlett O'Hara in *Gone With the Wind*, on their wedding night, Gable as Candy breaks down her bedroom door. He's determined to have her.

"From the moment we rehearsed our first scene together, there was a wonderful rapport between Clark and me," Lana said during an interview. "The sexual chemistry was definitely there. We were very close without intimacy. I had a great love for him, but there was no affair."

But as she later told her co-star, Claire Trevor, "What else could I have said? Of course, you don't believe the shit I throw to the press. Clark fucked me every chance he got during the making of *Honky Tonk*. He said I had feline sex appeal, and he labeled me his sex kitten. If I were a sex kitten, he was one hell of a tomcat."

Despite her coy and coquettish statements to the press during the shooting of *Honky Tonk*, journalists were speculating wildly about their possible affair.

"Imagine the combustion at MGM when two powerful sex symbols come together on the screen, or off the screen," wrote one reporter.

Conway asserted, "Lana and Clark were instantly attracted to each other. To put it bluntly, they had the hots for each other. She had youth and beauty, and he had this powerful image of masculinity. Call it sexual chemistry. Love is not the right word. He loved Carole Lombard but that didn't stop him from cheating on her."

"The electricity between our two screen lovers was so hot that it sizzled," Conway continued. "It was definitely a physical attraction. On camera, they weren't just acting...It reminded me of John Gilbert and Greta Garbo in *Flesh and the Devil* (1926)."

Robert Stack was friends with both Gable and Lana. Once, after he asked why she found Gable so attractive, she answered, "I always had this fantasy of being violated by a lumberjack...in Gable's case, a former lumberjack."

Conway later claimed, "Clark and Lana went at it every chance they got. When I asked him about it, he told me, 'We are merely rehearsing our upcoming love scenes to make them more authentic, particularly where I tear down her bedroom door. I know that rape can't be depicted on the screen, but we wanted to capture the spirit of it.'"

"Oh, Clark," Conway muttered skeptically..."Oh, Clark."

"During filming," Lana said, "I learned that Lombard had gone ballistic when she heard that I'd been assigned as Gable's co-star. She even appealed to Louis B. Mayer to fire me before shooting began. I understood that she and Clark had many fights over me, and that she threatened him that if she found out that he was screwing me, she'd come onto the set and kick ass."

"Lana Turner is supposed to play this sweet little Bostonian virgin," Lombard told Conway. "But I hear the blonde bitch fucks anything in pants."

After meeting with Lombard, Mayer called Conway. "Except for the lezzies," Mayer said, "Gable has fucked nearly every leading lady at MGM. Make sure he stays out of the hot pants of Turner. I don't want any scandal or any trouble from

Lombard. She's threatened me that if Gable gets involved with Lana, she'll mess him up so bad that he'll stay home sick for a week or two, running up production costs."

In the middle of one of her love scenes with Gable, Lana looked up at the vindictive, disapproving face of Lombard, who had been hawk-eyeing them. When the scene was ruined and the cameras stopped, Lombard had addressed her harshly: "Don't mind me, Lana," she said. "Pappy's not very good in the clinch."

"I became so flustered, I had to flee to my dressing trailer. I stayed there trying to pull myself together. Within the hour, Conway came to get me. He told me that Lombard had been kicked off the set and that shooting could begin again."

On several other widely witnessed occasions, Lombard had ridiculed her husband's prowess as a lover. "If Clark had one inch less, he'd be the Queen of Hollywood."

When Lana heard about these remarks, she informed Virginia Grey and others, "Even Clark admits he's a lousy lay. But that's missing the point. Studs are a dime a dozen in Hollywood, but there's only one Clark Gable. When you're getting screwed by him, you're not just getting Clark, but Rhett Butler, with all the fantasies that unleashes in a girl. I'm crazy about him. He makes me go to pieces. He's like a dream come true. We really click. Lombard's too old for him anyway. He wants a gal who's young and vital. Like me. When he first seduced me, he told me he preferred blondes to brunettes. 'Most brunettes look dirty to me,' he said."

As Gable's biographer, Warren G. Harris, stated, "Lana bragged to friends that she was going to break up the marriage of Gable to Carole Lombard."

That statement was not as heartless as it seemed. Lana was emphatically aware that one of her best friends, Robert Stack, had occasionally seduced Lombard during periods when Gable was off on some other fling.

"She's not the doting, faithful wife she makes herself out to be," Lana claimed.

Before the release of *Honky Tonk*, billboards across the country read: "Clark Gable kisses Lana Turner in *Honky Tonk*—and it's screen history."

Honky Tonk became MGM's biggest grossing film for 1941, the year America entered World War II.

Life magazine splashed Gable and Lana across one of its front covers and wrote: "The colorful Wild West is the setting for a series of sizzling bedroom scenes in which, in a variety of dress and undress, Clark Gable and Lana Turner make love. For Turner, now graduated from sweaters to nightgowns, it means the topmost rung in her meteoric four-year climb to success. For cinema fans, it means the birth of a hot new screen team."

***

On Gable's arm, Lombard attended the premiere of *Honky Tonk*. As reporters noted, she was "touchy-feely" throughout the event, as if wanting to demonstrate that she possessed him. Once journalist referred to her behavior as "overly doting in public."

No reviewer seemed to think that *Honky Tonk* was a great film, but nearly all of them praised the on-screen charisma of its co-stars, Lana and Gable. *Newsweek* asserted, "Miss Turner never falters in her presentation of Miss Cotton."

Photoplay found that the movie "rambles and rambles but in its circling, it does manage to gather up Lana Turner and Clark Gable and give them a twirl in the usual sexy old merry-go-round."

Variety wrote that "Miss Turner, who is graced by tremendous sex appeal, proves that she also can act as well as turn the boy on. Gable and Turner click together in a lively, lusty Western that makes you wish you had been there."

In her memoirs, Lana devoted less than a page to co-starring with Gable in *Honky Tonk*. That caused columnist Sheilah Graham, the former lover of F. Scott Fitzgerald, to remark: "I wish movie queens would tell the truth or shut up. Reading Lana's memoirs, I got the impression that she was a candidate for the convent."

Lana's statements about her affairs, both during interviews and as published in her memoirs, have generally been discredited. In 1982, while on a tour touting one of her books, she constantly denied having had an affair with Gable. In a TV interview, she claimed, "I had a reputation for being a sexpot, but I never was one. In fact, I never had much feeling about sex at all."

This spectacularly disingenuous comment was greeted with "mocking laughter that echoed from the Hollywood Hills down to Laguna and north to Santa Barbara," said catty Shelley Winters.

Jimmy Fiddler, the Hollywood columnist, said, "It's amazing to see stars like Lana Turner interviewed on television. Take the very suggestion that one of them might have had sex with one of their leading men. The likes of Lana Turner or June Allyson suggest that no handsome hunk ever crawled between their sheets. Although hundreds of eyewitnesses have testified to Lana's affairs, she remains virginal between marriages, at least in a memoir."

As late as the early 1960s, Lana would agree with Marilyn Monroe's assessment of Gable during the filming of what emerged as his last movie, *The Misfits* (1961): "When Clark kissed me," Monroe said, "all I wanted was for it to go on and on and on. I got goose bumps. I'd have followed him anywhere, done anything. It was a miracle just to be in his arms."

***

During the filming of *Honky Tonk,* Lana joined a luncheon in the MGM commissary. Included in the venue were her friend, Virginia Grey, and one of the movie's co-stars, Chill Wills. Also present was another MGM star, the studio's Tarzan, Johnny Weissmuller, impressively attired in a double-breasted suit. An ethnic German, he had been born in 1904 in what is now part of Romania.

Although one day, Lana would marry a screen version of Tarzan, Lex Barker, she had never seen one of Weissmuller's jungle adventures. She had heard that he was the world's fastest swimmer, the holder of five gold Olympic medals. Still looking in topnotch form, he had been married to the notorious Mexican actress, Lupe Velez, and was currently wed to Beryl Scott, the San Francisco socialite who had been born in Canada. Gossip columnists speculated that the marriage was coming apart.

As Lana would later tell Grey, "Johnny is not only an athlete and the King of the Jungle, but, except for Gable and Robert Taylor, one of the handsomest men at MGM"

The lunch meeting had a purpose, as Weissmuller, Grey, and Wills had signed to star together in the *Tarzan's New York Adventure* (1942), the last of the Tarzan franchises at MGM.

As Lana later stated: "I was expecting some muscle-bound lug, but discovered a romantic, kind, and considerate gentleman. He was imbued with chivalry and treated me like I was the Queen of Sheba."

There was speculation about how his fans would react to a movie where he appeared in a suit. Grey told him, "Men go to see you battle lions in the jungle, but women attend your movies to enjoy your magnificent body, hoping that loincloth will blow upward in the breeze."

He laughed at that, claiming, "That's happened a few times already. One shows me in all my manly glory after I forgot to wear a jockstrap that morning. On my first day at MGM, I was given a G-string and asked if I knew how to climb a tree," he said.

Lana kept abreast of Hollywood gossip, and was aware that Joan Crawford, among dozens of other stars, had already seduced Weissmuller. The ever-indiscreet Tallulah Bankhead had widely boasted about her conquest. *"Dah-ling,"* she told him. "You're the kind of man a woman like me must shanghai and keep under lock and key until both of us are entirely spent. Prepare for a leave of ten days."

Weissmuller, a gifted athlete, was known for seducing "lots and lots" of chorus girls, starlets, and barmaids.

"What do you find most annoying about playing Tarzan?" Lana asked.

"Every homosexual at MGM seems to want to take turns making me up as Tarzan and fitting me for my skimpy wardrobe. No one is satisfied until I've been fitted with at least a dozen jockstraps before they settle on the right one. I'm also tired of how every greeting I get tends to be the same: '*Hiyah, Johnny, I didn't recognize you with your clothes on!'*"

That afternoon, Weissmuller also said that he had met Elmo Lincoln, the screen's first Tarzan, the day before. "He's reduced to playing a minor role, a circus roustabout, in this latest version of Tarzan."

Lana described to Virginia Grey her weekend with Johnny Weissmuller in Palm Springs:

"He was everything I'd dreamed about in a man. Now I know why wardrobe designs that loincloth to hang low. I've never seen such an elongated foreskin on a man. But once his 'charger' bursts forth, it's one of the greatest thrills a woman can know, a pounding, like the beat of a Tom-Tom. He's a fabulous lover. At his climax, he lets out the Tarzan Yell."

"I was there when they met," Wills said. "Lincoln was not as impressed with Johnny as we are. He called him a sissy."

Wills said, in reference to his own role in *Tarzan's New York Adventure,* "I play the good guy, but I get murdered."

Grey said that she had been cast in their upcoming film as a torch singer, Connie Beach. "My big scene is when I do this number, 'I Must Have You or No One.'"

In reference to the action/adventure aspect of his upcoming film, Weissmuller said, "I have to perform a number of stunts. In one scene—it's faked, of course—I climb a skyscraper. In another, I'm shown jumping 200 feet off the Brooklyn Bridge. I told those jokers that they'd have to use a dummy for that scene. The funniest scene will be when I take my first shower with indoor plumbing. I keep my suit on, surprising Maureen O'Sullivan, who plays Jane."

After Wills and Grey departed, Lana remained at table in the commissary with Weissmuller. "This is a bit sad for me. Mayer is cutting off the series, and I'm moving over to RKO. Maureen told me that this will be the last time she'll ever play Jane."

Lana reached for his hand. "What about me as your new Jane?" Then she paused. "At least off screen."

"I thought you'd never ask," he said. "A friend of mine *[Weissmuller never named him specifically]* has this villa in Palm Springs with an Olympic-sized pool. I'm driving there tonight. I need to do a lot of laps to get into shape for the camera. I have to be back at MGM early Monday morning. Come with me. But I have to warn you: I swim in the nude."

"I have a feeling I'm in for a big treat."

On Friday, after twilight, Weissmuller headed east with Lana through the desert to Palm Springs. The following Monday, when Grey met up with Lana at the studio, she was eager for a play-by-play description of how their weekend together had been spent.

"If we'd filmed it, it would be known as *Tarzan's Palm Springs Adventure.*"

***

Lana would later refer to "the most bizarre fan letter I'd ever received." It had arrived at MGM in 1942.

The letter had been postmarked in London, but, as was later revealed, it had been written in Germany and somehow passed to someone who had mailed it from a London post office.

It was from a mysterious woman, Eva Braun, who had written its original version in German. It was accompanied by an English-language translation.

Lana did not know who Eva Braun was, only learning after the war that she had been the mistress of Adolf Hitler and then, for a period of less than 40 hours, his wife before their joint suicide in April, 1945 in an underground bunker in Berlin.

World War II had already ended by the time someone briefed Lana on the saga and symbolism of Eva Braun. Born in 1912 into a bourgeois German family and convent-educated, she had worked in Munich as a model and photographer's assistant for Heinrich Hoffmann, who would become the official photographer for the Nazi Party.

It was at Hoffman's studio that seventeen-year-old Eva met Hitler in October of 1929. He was a rising power in the National Socialist movement and 23 years her senior. Hitler enchanted the nubile, not particularly brainy Eva, and she became his mistress.

When Hoffman saw that Hitler was fascinated by his assistant, he warned the leader, "Eva is a feather brain, interested only in clothes, sports, and the cinema."

Of course, at the time, it was beyond her wildest dreams to imagine Hitler as the dictator of Nazi Germany and a threat to the very foundation of Western Civilization.

Although concealed from both the German and international press, Eva became the *Führer's* official hostess at Berchtesgaden and an "up front and personal" eyewitness to some of the major events of the 20th Century. "There are frequent showing of movies at the Berghof," Eva wrote. "We are avid movie fans."

In her letter addressed to Lana via MGM, Eva had revealed that the great dream of her life was to visit Hollywood "and become the next Lana Turner." She had seen every movie that Lana had made. Even during the war years, many of them were smuggled into Berlin, perhaps by Goebbels himself, and many had been screened for the entertainment of Hitler's entourage. Eva had been particularly "enthralled" with *Ziegfeld Girl*.

[Originally, Eva had wanted to star in German films and, with that agenda in mind, appealed to Josef Goebbels, the Nazi minister of propaganda. Hitler, when he learned of her intention, would not allow it.]

In her fan letter to Lana, Eva had enclosed a picture of herself snapped during a picnic at Obersalzberg. Her pose evoked a cheesecake-inspired stance evocative of Betty Grable. The implication was that she was wearing a bathing suit, but her torso was coyly concealed behind a flower-patterned parasol.

According to Lana, in her letter, Eva stated that it would be "inevitable" that the Nazis, with their powerful, well-equipped armies, would one day subdue America. "There will be many persons slated for death, including the execution of the Roosevelts." Eva's letter continued with the prediction that "traitors" like Marlene Dietrich would also be killed, along with "all the Jews who had fled to Hollywood from Europe."

Eva went on to promise Lana that when the Nazi conquest of America was finished, "I will appeal to Wolf *[her nickname for Hitler]* to spare your life because of how much your films have meant to me."

Apparently, Eva had already screened a copy of *Honky Tonk* which had been smuggled

To Eva Braun, Hitler's mistress, Lana was an inspiration. Actually, she wanted to become "the Lana Turner of Nazi Germany," but the Führer had other plans for her.

into Germany, and she'd found Lana's scenes with Clark Gable "sizzling."

"Regrettably," Eva had continued, "Wolf has horrendous plans for Gable. When he is captured, he will be stripped naked and exhibited in a cage that will tour throughout Germany."

[Ironically, with the understanding that the cage and its contents would be hauled across the Soviet Union, this was Stalin's plan for Hitler, if he'd been captured alive.]

Assuming that the bizarre letter had derived from some crank, Lana, after reading it, had destroyed it, recalling its contents after the war, when she realized who Eva Braun had been.

Years later, she said, "I wish I had saved that letter from Eva Braun. Had I known who she was, I certainly would have. I bet it would be worth a lot of money today."

***

In 1941, Lana was slated for roles in movies than were never actually filmed and/or completed. Some of them never emerged from their talking stages; others had evolved into fully developed shooting scripts, but later abandoned for various reasons.

In 1941, Louis B. Mayer met with Lana and told her that the studio was preparing a script specifically gauged and crafted for her. Its working title was *The Flying Blonde*. It called for her to play a female pilot who grapples with romantic adventures with a handsome pilot.

Paramount had already signed Stirling *[an actor later billed as Sterling]* Hayden as the male lead. They were billing him at the time as "The Most Beautiful Man in the Movies."

"I think we could sex up this film by co-starring you in it as 'The World's Most Beautiful Blonde,'" Mayer said. "On screen together, you'd be dynamite. Paramount owes me a favor, and they'd actually make money by lending Hayden to us, since he's contracted over there with a low salary. Before shooting begins, I want you to go out with him. Perhaps dinner together at Ciro's, where we can get our photographer to snap pictures for the papers."

"Mr. Mayer, this is a project that really excites me," Lana said. "I want to meet this gorgeous dreamboat. I suspect that Joan Crawford, as usual, has already phoned him."

"I've been in the business long enough to know that all actresses are hussies," Mayer responded. "For most of them, anything in pants will do."

"Not really, Mr. Mayer," she answered. "We do have one requirement. It's how the man fills out those pants."

***

Based on Mayer's directive, Hayden phoned Lana for a date. When she suggested the names of some nightclubs they might visit as a background for getting their names in the paper, he rejected the idea. She was struck by his fierce inde-

164

pendence and his disdain for Hollywood.

"I'm not some pretty boy who poses for pictures in a nightclub," he said. "I'm a sailor. How about sailing over to Catalina for the weekend?"

By then, she'd seen some of the publicity pictures of him released by Paramount. He did indeed look like a Viking god. She accepted his invitation and packed all-white sailing clothes. That afternoon, she talked with his agent, who told her, "Sterling was born in the wrong century. He should have been a sea captain in the 19th Century."

Born in 1916 into a working-class family in Montclair, New Jersey, Hayden as a boy haunted public libraries. There, he would sit for hours devouring such seafaring stories as Jack London's *Call of the Wild* or Herman Melville's *Moby Dick*. Inspired by these adventures, he left home at age seventeen and was hired as a "ship's boy." That led to problems. The pretty boy attracted rough sailors who'd been at sea too long without a woman, and Hayden sometimes had to fight off their sexual adventures.

Edward Griffith, an executive at Paramount, although admitting that Sterling Hayden was "wooden" in his screen test, saw something of value in him.

Even before his first picture, Paramount publicists set out to hype him as "The Most Beautiful Man in the World," and as "The Blonde Viking God."

Then, after trysts with some of the leading ladies of gossipy Hollywood, word spread about his "stupendous package."

His adventures on the oceans of the world were more improbable than any screenplay he would ever star in. At the age of 20, he become first mate aboard the *Yankee* during its around-the-world voyage. In 1938, when he was 22, he'd advanced to the role of skipper aboard a 90-foot square-rigged sailboat, the *Florence B. Robinson,* during its transit from Gloucester, Massachusetts, to Tahiti.

Many of Hayden's admirers suggested that he should monetize his towering physique and movie-star good looks and migrate directly to big-money acting contracts in Tinseltown. There, unable to find work, he posed nude for gay photographers. Nude pictures of Sterling Hayden are highly valued today as collector's items. As one devotee said, "His god damn whopper hangs down all the way to Tijuana."

Their weekend odyssey to Catalina was remembered by Lana as "one of the most memorable of my life." After her return to Hollywood and lunch with Virginia Grey, she had nothing but praise for Hayden.

"He's 6'5", and if you add those two numbers together, you'll get an idea of how long it stretches," Lana said. "And oh, boy, is he great with a woman, treating her like a lady even as he devours her. I'm leaving next weekend unscheduled, waiting for him to call."

That weekend came and went, and Hayden didn't phone. The gossip columns later revealed what happened to him.

Even before Lana heard that the script for *The Flying Blonde* had been rejected and shelved, he'd already learned other news from Paramount. He was told that he'd been hired as the star of his first movie, *Virginia* (1941), and introduced to its co-star, Madeleine Carroll, the classically cool blonde from England.

She had already risen to fame as the heroine of two imported English thrillers, both directed by Alfred Hitchcock: *The 39 Steps* (1932), and *Secret Agent* (1936).

After the actress rejected Hitchcock's sexual advances, he never hired her again, referring to her as an iceberg.

Hayden, however, managed to heat her up.

When Lana heard that Hayden had been "coupling" with Carroll, she said, "Isn't he old enough to be his mother?"

[Carroll, born in 1906, was ten years older than Hayden.]

As Lana lamented to Grey, "I thought Sterling and I had something cooking before Carroll got him. But with a war on, life is moving too swiftly."

"Carroll came along to lure him from me. As for me, Robert Taylor arrived on the set of *Johnny Eager*. After Clark Gable, he was the second leading matinée idol at MGM that I wanted to work with...and perhaps pursue other diversions. Of course, he *is* married to Barbara Stanwyck, but I wouldn't examine that marriage too closely."

As it turned out, Lana would never work with Hayden, releasing him instead to such leading ladies as Bette Davis and Joan Crawford. But they did meet again in 1952, when she was divorcing Bob Topping, and he'd been asked to replace Lex Barker *[Lana's future husband]* as the screen Tarzan. He rejected the role.

***

The next time Lana was called into Mayer's office, he made a very different offer. "There's a war on, and as you know, Hitler wants to gas Jews like me. I want my leading stars, when they're not working—to join in the war efforts—war bond drives, volunteer work at the Hollywood Canteen, broadcasts on the Armed Forces Radio. I know you like to kiss men, and I'm sure men like to kiss you. Some of the stars are selling their kisses to raise money to buy war bonds. I want you to join them.

"It's a date!" she answered. "I can just see the headlines: LANA TURNER GOES TO WAR!"

Chapter Eight

Wartime Lana

Servicing the Men in Uniform Who Won World War II

In their hit picture, *Johnny Eager,* Lana Falls for Robert Taylor On and Off the Screen.

During its promotion of *Johnny Eager,* MGM billed its co-stars as "HOTTER THAN T-N-T." In years to come, movie buffs like Norman Lear, creator of TV's *All in the Family,* would define its love scenes as "the sexiest ever performed on celluloid."

Years later, Taylor shared with a reporter his impressions of working with Lana: "She wasn't very career minded. She preferred men and jewelry over everything else. She should call her memoirs *Hearts and Diamonds Take All,* since that would reflect her main interest. Her face was delicate and oh so beautiful. I've never known such succulent lips on a woman."

"Personally, I was never one to go that much for blondes—give me Elizabeth Taylor any day," he said. "But Lana was the exception. I couldn't take my eyes off her. There were times during our love scenes in *Johnny Eager* that I thought I'd...*how shall I put this?*...erupt. She had a voice like a breathless little girl. She couldn't say 'good morning' without giving me a hard-on. There was a downside, though. She wasn't as busty as I had been led to believe, since she had that reputation for being 'The Sweater Girl.'"

When she wasn't on any of the MGM sound stages or sets, looking blonde and gorgeous in front of cameras, Lana pursued aggressive romantic pastimes which she usually conducted at night. And it was those romances—launched during the intensely emotional context of the wartime 40s—which massively contributed to the Lana Turner legend.

It was an era marked by almost manic-depressive waves of hope, fear, and tenuousness, when millions of individual Americans endured some of the greatest upheavals in their personal and national history.

Lana's staggering numbers of romantic and sexual conquests involved male movie stars who, within months,

would either join the military; or future movie stars whose careers wouldn't flourish until after their return from the battlefields. She also dallied with dozens of good-looking "civilians" (that is, non-movie stars) who, if they managed to survive the war, returned to towns like Lawrence, Kansas; Homestead, Pennsylvania; or Elkin, North Carolina, to spend the rest of their lives coasting on and boasting about one major claim: "I fucked Lana Turner."

In these emotional and high-strung war years—before, during, and after her marriage to Stephen Crane—Lana allowed herself to be conquered by a string of virile young men, who with some justification were described by columnist Sheilah Graham as "the handsomest, sexiest, and hottest that America would ever turn out."

At parties, with a glorious sense of cattiness, Graham remarked, "Lana is to be forgiven if she missed a few hundred men before they were shipped off to battle, yet she managed to seduce her fair share, giving many of them a farewell fuck before sending them off with a glorious memory of an American bombshell."

Journalist Adela Rogers St. Johns observed: "The real Lana Turner is the same Lana Turner you see on the screen. She always wanted to be a movie star, and now she's the Queen of MGM. Her personal life and her life as a movie star are one and the same. The same Lana Turner who gets up at 5AM to put on her makeup is the same Lana who, later in the day or night, crawls under the sheets with Errol Flynn, Clark Gable, or Robert Taylor."

The last sentence was struck from her copy by a blue-nosed editor.

To Hedda Hopper, Lana pointed out the downside of fame. "The more famous an actress, the less she's allowed to eat, unless she wants to play mothers in baggy clothes. Instead of exercise in a studio gym, you can burn off more calories between the sheets. Don't print that. If you do, I'll deny it."

To Louella Parsons, Lana confessed her goal to become the most famous movie star on the planet, and "The Playgirl of the 20th Century."

To her dear friend, columnist Sidney Skolsky, she shared a secret at Schwab's Drugstore. "You may not know this, since you're not a homosexual, but every man's dick is different. I've never known one dick that is the same as another man's. There are certain similarities among some men, for sure, but nothing identical unless they're twins, I guess. I noticed the difference between a Jewish man and a Gentile. Take Artie Shaw or Johnny Weissmuller. It's all a matter of a bit of skin at the end of the prick."

Skolsky later told friends, "There's a good reason that men in blue voted Lana as the most desirable woman on earth during World War II. Each of them had sampled the wares and knew what in the hell they were talking about."

"One thing about Lana," Parsons told her confidantes, "is that she never lets a marriage get in the way of her pursuit of outside male flesh. Having just one husband at a time has never been enough to satisfy her. No one man is adequate for the task. Lana is a hot firecracker. Ask Clark Gable. Ask Mickey Rooney. Ask Greg Bautzer."

***

Lana didn't devote all her time to making movies and men. She also developed dialogues and friendships with a number of girlfriends over the years, although Virginia Grey remained her most trusted confidante. "At least *some* women like me and weren't too jealous," Lana said. "Two of my best girlfriends in the early 1940s were Linda Darnell and Susan Hayward."

Darnell's sultry beauty appealed to Darryl F. Zanuck at Fox, who for almost a year and a half summoned her to his office, locking the door behind her, at 1PM every day.

A hard life had toughened Darnell, and Lana admired her fighting spirit when she met her at a party. "I've got more balls than most men do!" she told Lana. "If it's anything I hate, it's a weak

The Yellow Rose of Dallas" (Texas), Linda Darnell was two years younger than Lana.

Aggressively promoted by her stage-struck mother, the former Pearl Brown, Linda had been a child model, dreaming of movie stardom for herself. Her mother became committed to the belief that Linda was the only child she had produced with potential as an actress. Subsequently, while pushing and prodding Linda and her stage training, she virtually ignored the rearing of her other children.

When Linda was in her teens, a talent scout spotted her, which in time led to a contract with 20th Century Fox.

man."

Over the years, Darnell would sustain an unusual array of lovers, including Lana's former beau, Donald ("Red") Barry; Milton Berle; and even a chicken farmer, Rudolph Sieber, the estranged husband of Marlene Dietrich.

Darnell would not marry until 1944, when she wed J. Peverrel Marley, a studio cameraman. In the meantime, she dated a lot, even attracting the amorous attentions of the then high-flying aviator, Howard Hughes. "That was no distinction," Lana said. "He's been after all of us whenever he isn't chasing after Jack Beutel."

[Beutel was the handsome stud he'd cast as Billy the Kid in The Outlaw (1943) opposite Jane Russell.]

Lana concealed it rather well, but she was jealous of Linda who, almost from the beginning of her career, had been cast in pictures that co-starred Tyrone Power. "He was one man I dreamed about," Lana said.

Darnell had originally been a strong contender as the female co-star with Power in *Johnny Apollo* (1940), but the role was ultimately assigned to Dorothy Lamour. However, that same year, Darnell was given the female lead opposite Power in *Day-Time Wife,* a light romantic comedy. That led to an affair with Power, which, between giggles, she'd reported to Lana. As a promotional quote associated with the release of that film, *Life* magazine pronounced Darnell "The most physically perfect girl in Hollywood."

Lana bit her lip and only smiled when Darnell told her, months later, that she had also been slated to co-star with Power in three more films: *Brigham Young* (1940), *The Mark of Zorro* (also 1940), and *Blood and Sand* (1941). In the latter picture, in which Power made a striking figure clad in a bullfighter's "suit of light," she had to compete onscreen with Rita Hayworth.

"Ty looked so dashing, so sexy, so romantic," Lana said after she went to a screening of *Blood and Sand*. She never missed one of Power's films.

Word spread that even though Power had married the French actress, Annabella, neither had remained faithful to the other. Louella Parsons, in private, claimed theirs was an arranged marriage designed to throw off an unsuspecting public to the fact that Power was bisexual. He might indeed, be known, underground, for sexual liaisons with Darnell, Hayworth, and Judy Garland, but he also had a reputation for sharing his bed with Hughes, Robert Taylor, and Errol Flynn, each—like himself—a bisexual.

***

One night, another contract player at Fox came into Lana's orbit, a man who was attractive and beguiling enough to allow Lana to forget about Power—at least temporarily.

She liked to host parties back then, and to one of them, she invited Darnell, instructing her to "bring any man you want."

She opted to invite John Payne, with whom she was appearing in the 1940 *Star Dust,* directed by Walter Lang.

"When Linda dated Payne, he was still married to the actress Anne Shirley, but that marriage was in its final stages. *[Their divorce would become final in 1943.]*

Two nights after she met him, Payne phoned Lana for a date, and she eagerly accepted. Because he was still married, he suggested a discreet dinner at some remote, out-of-the-way place.

That night marked the beginning of a long and enduring friendship during the course of which, each would endure multiple triumphs and tragedies.

Payne had already studied drama and journalism at Columbia University in New York City, "where I lost my magnolia Virginia accent," he said.

To support himself with his muscled and well-developed physique, he became a professional wrestler, billed as "The Savage of the Steppes." Later, he morphed into "Tiger Jack Payne," a quasi-celebrity boxer.

John Payne, Fox contract player, posed for this "crotch shot," which made him a pinup boy of World War II for horny women and gays.

"Tyrone Power may be the prettiest boy in Hollywood, but John Payne is the handsomest masculine male," Lana said. "My friend, Linda Darnell, has all the luck. both men have had affairs with her."

"Many of the gals in New York came to see me in a pair of boxing trunks," he confided to Lana.

One night it was not just women who were impressed with Payne in his boxer trunks, but a homosexual talent agent for Samuel Goldwyn. After he "auditioned" Payne, he advanced enough money to allow Payne to take the train to Hollywood. There, he was given a screen test and later a contract from producer Samuel Goldwyn.

Among other jobs, he had been a radio singer in New York, and his smoother, harmonious tenor voice was spliced into such early movies as *Tin Pan Alley* (1940), co-starring Alice Faye (Tony Martin's former wife). Payne also appeared in movies with two other blondes, each sexually voracious, Betty Grable and that ice-skating tramp from Norway, Sonja Henie, whom he described as "a nympho. She needed it seven times a day."

As Lana reported to Virginia Grey, "John has a captivating voice, a strapping physique, movie star looks, and an eye-catching cleft in his chin. He stands six feet four, but it's those other inches that he has which can thrill a woman, along with his broad chest and slender waist."

In addition to his marriage and his ongoing affairs, Lana also learned that he'd been seducing Jane Wyman ever since they had appeared together in *Kid Nightin-*

gale (1939).

"Jane told me my legs are more muscular and my chest better developed than Ronald Reagan's."

"That's true," Lana replied, "and I speak from firsthand experience."

According to Lana, years later, "I would have married John, but he never asked me. Along came the war, but we continued to see each other for years to come."

On October 13, 1942, Payne joined the military as a student aviator. For a while, he was stationed in Arizona. In 1944, still in the military, he returned to L.A., to a post at Ferry Command at Long Beach, California.

Lana saw him on rare occasions, from 1944 on, even though at the time, he was married to the actress Gloria DeHaven.

As Lana later told Darnell, "What's a gal supposed to do? The best men are either in the Army or they join the Navy, the Air Force or the Marines. Uncle Sam gets the gravy, and we get the leftover mashed potatoes."

"Dear Heart, you'll manage to find the few gold nuggets left behind," Darnell said. "Perhaps they'll be classified 4-F for no other reason than color blindness or flat feet, but you'll find 'em."

***

Whenever Hedda Hopper or Louella Parsons phoned a star for an interview, he or she usually came to their homes as part of the venue.

One afternoon, Hopper summoned Lana, and seemed eager for information about her experience with Clark Gable in *Honky Tonk* and her upcoming movie, *Johnny Eager* with Robert Taylor. She wanted a column that focused on Lana's interactions with MGM's leading men.

During that interview, Lana strenuously denied an affair with Gable. "After all, he's married to Lombard. Likewise, nothing will happen with Mr. Taylor and myself on the set of *Johnny Eager*. As you, of all people know, he's married to Barbara Stanwyck."

Hopper listened impatiently, not believing a word Lana was telling her, but promising to give her "a vanilla writeup," instead of blasting readers with a scandal-soaked *exposé*.

As Lana later told her mother, Mildred, "When a woman like Hedda has 32 million readers, we hasten to her door when she calls."

After the interview, Hopper asked Lana to stick around, since she was hosting a small cast party for a film in which she had recently appeared, and she wanted Lana to attend.

[Before she became a gossip columnist, Hedda had acted in films. In the early 40s, her long-term friend, the director Cecil B. DeMille, assigned her a small role in the movie version of the novel, Reap the Wild Wind *(1942).*

In it, Paulette Goddard was cast as a fiery Southern belle, with Ray Milland and John Wayne fighting over her. The cast also included Robert Preston, Raymond Massey, Charles Bickford, Louise Beavers, and a fiery redhead from Brooklyn who had recently changed her name to Susan Hayward.]

That afternoon, the only person at the party that Lana knew was Goddard.

Also among the celebrants were two of her future co-stars, Ray Milland and John Wayne. Lana spent time with each of them, and also with Hayward, with whom she formed an unlikely friendship, instead of a fierce rivalry.

After Hopper's cast party, Lana and Hayward began to see each other on occasion, their favorite topic being men. The granite-hard Brooklyn-born actress gave Lana her opinion. "Men...I'd like to fry 'em all in deep fat."

Her toughness reminded Lana of Barbara Stanwyck.

As stated by Hayward's first agent, Ben Medford, "Susan was a terrible actress, just terrible. Nobody liked her since she was a real bitch. But I saw hidden talent there, and in time, I would be proved right."

Instead of playing Scarlett at MGM, Hayward ended up with a contract from Warner Brothers, where she was cast in campy, melodramatic Grade B flicks, a good example of which is *Girls on Probation* (1938).

During its filming, she met a handsome young actor, the heroic male lead, from Tampico, Illinois, Ronald Reagan. She fell in love with him, and they began a passionate affair.

That same year, he made *Brother Rat*, on the set of which he met another promising young actress on the rise, Jane Wyman. She, too, fell for him.

The race for Reagan was on, and when both actresses went on a promotional tour that had been organized with (and nominally chaperoned by) Louella Parsons, they even fought over him. Eventually, Wyman got him, marrying him in 1940. Begrudgingly, Hayward moved on to other conquests.

Just a few weeks before Lana was introduced to Howard Hughes, Hayward told of her own experience with the aviator. His pimp, Johnny Meyer, brought Hughes and Hayward together for some vague conversation about making a film about Billy the Kid. *[It eventually became* The Outlaw *(1943).]*

"Howard was obviously looking for an actress with boobs, and I had those. And I was proud of them," Hayward told Lana, who was also celebrated for her breasts.

Lana learned that Hayward had

A sexy, gutsy redhead, Susan Hayward, then known as Edythe Marrener, the daughter of a Coney Island carnival barker, had been born into poverty. As a girl, she'd hawked copies of the *Brooklyn Eagle* on street corners before graduating to employment in a stenographers' pool.

In time, she became a photographer's model and landed on the cover of *The Saturday Evening Post*. It was seen by director George Cukor during his casting of *Gone With the Wind* (1939). He brought her photo to the attention of David O. Selznick, who agreed to test her for the role of Scarlett O'Hara.

told Hughes that "redheads make better actresses than blondes because their emotions are much closer to the surface and better reflected in their faces."

A lot of Hayward's self-promotion didn't work. As she related, bitterly, to Lana, "Then he met Jane Russell, a girl whose boobs were bigger than mine, and I lost the part."

***

During a trip to New York in 1941, Lana became the victim of the most vicious rumor ever spread about her. It was so repulsive to her fans that no reporter dared publish it, although some hinted at it.

Biographers Joe Morella and Edward Z. Epstein vaguely aired Lana's link to the Red Rooster nightclub in Harlem, yet released no details about what "Broadway insiders" were gossiping about.

News of her alleged indiscretion traveled along the grapevine from Harlem to Hollywood, where gossips found the tale a salacious delight, especially Louella Parsons and Hedda Hopper, who could not print it.

Finally, in the 1950s, a tabloid magazine alluded to it, again without releasing details of exactly what the scandal involved. Cryptically, the magazine published this enigmatic blurb:

> "Lana in the early 1940s visited Gotham. She would don slacks and dark glasses and scurry off on a nightly jaunt to the Red Rooster, a wild little joint in Harlem. She was known to take several trips to the club to hear the music of Billy Daniels, its owner."

What is known is that when Louis B. Mayer heard that Lana, his profit-generating white goddess, was frequenting a notorious, fast-emerging nightclub in Harlem, he sent Johnny Meyer, a member of his security team, to escort her. [Meyer later became a pimp for Howard Hughes.]

Mayer had been Lana's escort on the night the rumor had originated. Allegedly, a drunken Lana asked Meyer to stand guard at the entrance to the men's toilet. She was said to have requested that he send the biggest and handsomest "bucks," one by one, each of them black, into the toilet.

Before the night ended, and again, only according to an unsourced rumor, she was said to have fellated nine African-American men before she was seen stumbling out of the club.

Meyer later claimed that the rumor was true.

The rumor was given greater credence when an African American waitress, Fannie Pennington, who at the time was working at the Red Rooster, verified it. Later, she became a well-known activist, organizer, and fundraiser in the Civil Rights Movement, and a coordinator in Harlem for Adam Clayton Powell, Jr., then the most famous black congressman in America.

Pennington would eventually interact with such illustrious figures as Eleanor Roosevelt, Dr. Martin Luther King, Jr., and Malcolm X. In 2015, she was designated as one of the NAACP's "History Makers."

She claimed that the fellatio story about Lana and the black men was true, and that she saw the young studs coming and going from the men's room where Lana waited inside for them. The rumor would have been long ago discounted were it not for the reliable credential of Pennington.

Billy Daniels, the club's owner, was there on the night of the alleged incident, but he always refused to comment on the accusation. In fact, he became a friend of Lana's, and the two of them would become embroiled in a scandal that was reported in *Confidential* magazine during Lana's marriage (1948-1952) to Bob Topping.

Lana become enraptured by Daniel's voice on radio in 1941, when she had heard him sing, "Diane." His all-time greatest hit, "That Old Black Magic," would not be recorded until 1948.

After the fellatio rumor became widespread, Lana radically curtailed her visits to the Red Rooster.

***

As reported above, MGM had appointed Johnny Meyer as Lana's escort (some said "chaperone," others said "security guard") during some of her visits to the Red Rooster. But weeks later, he was hired by Howard Hughes as his pimp.

Meyer's duties included setting up dates for Hughes with whomever he fancied in Hollywood. That included, in addition to Lana Turner, Veronica Lake, Rita Hayworth, and Ava Gardner.

In her memoir, Lana devoted scant attention to Hughes, presenting their relationship as relatively benign and harmless. Actually, it was far more complicated, not only her sexual liaisons with him, but his trysts with some of her girlfriends (notably, Susan Hayward, Ava Gardner, and Linda Darnell).

Meyer arranged for the introduction of Lana to Hughes when both of them happened to be passing through Chicago. Through Meyer, a dinner was arranged for them in Hughes' hotel suite, with the understanding that she'd spend time with him there the evening before the departure of her train to New York the next morning.

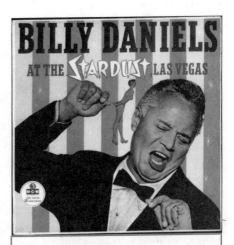

The son of a postmaster in Jacksonville, Florida, Billy Daniels was the product of a mixed heritage, part Portuguese, part Choctaw Indian, part African-American, and a direct descendant of that trail-blazing frontiersman, Daniel Boone.

Daniels had sung at various clubs before he was discovered by big band leader Erskine Hawkins, who made him his band's leading vocalist. After long tours across the country, Daniels became a radio singer in Manhattan. His performances at a club in Manhattan on 52nd Street attracted the attention of such stars as Billie Holiday, Frank Sinatra, and Benny Goodman.

As she confessed, "I found him likable enough, but not especially stimulating. He was also hard of hearing." Their encounter included a bizarre incident that she didn't write about.

Two hours after dinner, following pleasant but unremarkable conversation, he invited her into his bedroom. She assumed it was for the same reason pursued by dozens of other men. But Hughes was different. She was shocked to see a scaled-to-life rubber copy of herself lying nude on the bed. "It looked so real, I thought I was seeing double," she later told Robert Stack, another occasional stud within Hughes' roster of male lovers. "That thing had my breasts, and a reasonable replica of my vagina."

She stood back in stunned disbelief as Hughes, face to face with the life-sized rubber doll, pulled down his trousers and produced an erection. "I want to show you what I do to this dummy of you, since I haven't had the real thing."

She watched for only about a minute as he mounted the rubber copy of herself. Then she fled from his suite.

After her return to Hollywood, she related what had happened in Chicago to Stack.

"It seems harmless enough," he said. "Don't be afraid of him. He's not violent, and he has many troubles. But he's a powerful figure in this town, and you'd be wrong to turn him down if he calls you for another date. He told me that one night, he plans to buy a big movie studio in Hollywood. If things don't work out for you at MGM, you may want to reign as the queen of whatever studio he's eyeing. I know he's considering RKO."

"Then perhaps I'll reconsider," she answered, primly.

"I'm having this pool party Saturday afternoon," he said. "I'll invite both of you. You're to arrive separately, of course."

Three days before the pool party, she set out to learn whatever she could. To her, Hughes was just another big and very rich name. She met with Hollywood columnist James Bacon, who knew Hughes quite well. He seemed to delight in sharing Hughes stories with her, revealing that he preferred divorced women such as Lana herself, referring to them as "wet decks."

"Howard once told me that he'd lost his virginity to his uncle, Rupert Hughes, when he was only fifteen

Howard Hughes dancing with Lana, avoiding the camera. This is the only known picture of them ever taken.

176

years old."

In his capacity as a journalist, Bacon kept a dossier on Hughes' lovers, dating from his early days as a movie producer. The list he had compiled was long and amplified with dates and circumstances of their sexual assignations and implications. ("I'd call Howard Hollywood's greatest swordsman," Bacon had gloated.) Names on his list included Carole Lombard, Bette Davis, Billie Dove, Olivia de Havilland, Paulette Goddard, Jean Harlow, Katharine Hepburn, Fay Wray, and Ginger Rogers. According to Bacon, he had also "dated" actors from the A-list, some of whom had included Errol Flynn, Gary Cooper, Cary Grant, Tyrone Power, Robert Taylor, and Randolph Scott.

Stack later devised a plan that would render Lana more alluring to Hughes. With a sense of ironic self-deprecation, he said, "Imagine *me* telling the love goddess of Hollywood how to be more alluring."

During the planning stages of this scenario, Stack informed her that "Howard is a man for boobs," and with that in mind, they devised a plan.

Alluringly clad in a bathing suit, Lana positioned herself near Stack's swimming pool for what seemed like a long time before Hughes finally arrived in a battered old Chevrolet. He was shabbily dressed, as usual, and would not appear in bathing trunks, probably because he was embarrassed by his skinny frame. He sat beside the pool sipping lemonade, closely observing both Lana and Stack, each of whom, clad in swimwear, looked movie-star and camera-ready.

It was time to put her plan into action. After executing a running dive from the diving board into the pool, the straps holding the upper half of her bathing suit "malfunctioned," and came (deliberately) undone, exposing her breasts. Then she swam around a bit, later admitting, "It was hard to swim and keep my breasts covered at the same time.

When Lana emerged from the water, Stack (who had gallantly retrieved the top of her bathing suit from the waters of his pool) was waiting with the soggy garment and a large pink towel.

Her pre-choreographed striptease seemed to do the trick. Hughes invited her to get dressed and to have dinner with him.

The next morning, she phoned Stack to thank him for the party and to tell her friend—and sometimes lover—what she later recorded in her memoirs, "Hughes confessed a preference for oral sex, but I wasn't interested."

***

On other occasions, Lana asserted that she did not indulge in fellatio. However, many of her lovers—former and future—suggested otherwise.

[Some insiders suggested that her denial of fellatio was a demure attempt to squelch rumors about her "performances" within the men's toilet at the Red Rooster in Harlem.]

Lana and Hughes began to date, but she downplayed her involvement with him. In her memoirs, she wrote, "I saw him from time to time, and occasionally, he'd come to the house just to sit and talk with my mother. She liked him and sympathized with his partial deafness."

Having already dated such fancy dressers as Greg Bautzer, Lana had never been escorted anywhere by a man as sloppily dressed as Hughes. During their shared outings to Trocadero, he'd arrive unshaved and wearing clothes he'd lived in for most of the previous week. He'd have a stubble of beard, and he wore shoes but no socks. His shirt, which he hadn't removed in a while, usually had buttons missing and traces of body odor. He always wore a battered gray hat that looked like he'd purchased it in 1933. Before sexual intimacies, she'd insist that he shower.

She told Stack that Hughes revealed to her that he was the regular client of a Hollywood bordello populated with prostitutes who, in their dress, makeup, and clothing, evoked specific movie stars. Sometimes, Hughes maintained, the women had submitted to plastic surgery as a means of reinforcing their similarities to "the real thing."

Howard Hughes: There was always a problem with his shabby dress code.

"If men can't get the real thing, they settle for the mock," he said. "You should be flattered: The most requested 'working gal' there is a Lana Turner lookalike," he told her. "Next in line, based on the number of requests, is Betty Grable, followed by Rita Hayworth and Ava Gardner. There aren't that many requests for Hedy Lamarr, perhaps because the rumor still persists that she slept with the *Führer*."

Once, when Hughes arrived, as planned, to escort Lana to dinner, he entered her living room but refused to sit down. Then he revealed to Lana and to Mildred that he'd ripped his pants.

Her mother told him to remove his trousers and that she would sew them up.

"I can't," he answered. "I never wear underwear."

Consequently, after Mildred's coaxing, he retreated to the bathroom, removed his pants, and returned to the living room with a towel wrapped around his midriff.

Mildred sewed up his pants.

Then, with the intention of procuring him some underwear, Lana went to one of her wardrobes and retrieved an old pair of Artie Shaw's shorts, which she gave to Hughes. "You shouldn't go around with dirty pants next to your body," she lectured him.

Although Mildred professed to like Hughes, and urged Lana to marry him ("Think of those millions!"), behind his back, she called him "a strange bird."

***

178

One night, inspired by her belief that there would be good roles in postwar films for women pilots, Lana asked Hughes to teach her how to fly an airplane.

Consequently, Hughes escorted her to an abandoned airfield outside Los Angeles, the same place where he had taught Katharine Hepburn basic lessons in flying. Taking time out from work he should have been completing on his experimental plane, the XF-11, he gave Lana lessons.

On another occasion, he picked her up in another equally old, equally battered Ford and drove her out beyond Culver City to an airfield, where one of his planes was waiting. As she later relayed to Stack, "Within the hour, we were flying to Las Vegas."

"Lana doesn't need a bed on which to make love," Hughes confided to Stack. "The floor of my Sikos, while we were on autopilot at 12,000 feet, was bad enough. Call it an airborne fuck, apparently her first."

On another occasion, Hughes flew Lana to New York, where he'd booked suites for them at the Sherry-Netherland Hotel. It was later revealed that J. Edgar Hoover of the FBI instructed his G-Men to bug Hughes' suite.

Their stay lasted for twelve days and nights. She remembered the occasion with fondness. "On the streets, the women were wearing their wartime finery, and most of the men looked gorgeous in their military uniforms parading up and down Fifth Avenue. Howard invited me to go into any store and buy anything I wanted. Although I loved diamonds, I felt it would be too brazen to take him into Tiffany's."

Years later, she told a reporter, "Those who walk the streets of New York today would never realize how glamorous it looked back them. There was an excitement in the air we no longer have."

After their stay in New York, whereas she returned immediately to Hollywood, he flew to Louisville for the Kentucky Derby. He was soon back in New York, where he filed a $5 million lawsuit against the Motion Picture Producers and Distributors of America for interference in trade. They'd censored his movie, *The Outlaw*, starring Jane Russell. In Lana's words, *The Outlaw* "introduced the breasts of Jane Russell."

The press was filled with speculation that Lana and Hughes were going to get married. It was even reported that she had ordered that her new towels be embroidered with the initials of "H.H."

Publicly, she denied any marital plans with Hughes. Likewise, Hughes told Johnny Meyer, "I'm not going to marry her. As for those towels, she can always marry Huntington Hartford."

[Ironically, by the end of the war, Lana would be dating the A&P heir.]

***

After Hughes' return to California, she waited and waited for him to call. But for eight months, he disappeared, and only a few trusted aides knew where he was. The whereabouts of this eccentric, mysterious, at times frightening, and always unpredictable man remained unsolved. In time, he would return and play a major role in Lana's life.

Once again, Lana's mentor, Mervyn LeRoy, was assigned to direct her in another picture, in this case, the crime drama, *Johnny Eager*. Developed and conceived as an MGM release for 1942, it was wrapped six weeks before the Japanese attack on Pearl Harbor (December 7, 1941), playing in movie houses just as America had gone to war.

Like *Honky Tonk*, which had teamed her with Clark Gable, Lana once again was featured with one of her alltime "dreamboats," the dashingly handsome Robert Taylor, who was billed at the time as "The Heartthrob of America."

"From the first day I introduced Bob to Lana, love was in the air," LeRoy said.

One of the claims in the title of Lana's memoir contained the words, "The Truth." Yet within its pages, she (inaccurately) denied having had an affair with Taylor during the shooting of *Johnny Eager*. She wrote, "Bob had the kind of looks I could fall for, and we were attracted to each other from the beginning. I'll admit I flirted with him, but for me, it was no more than that, since he was married to Barbara Stanwyck."

She also claimed, "Certainly our mutual attraction didn't harm our love scenes. I wasn't in love with Bob, not really. Oh, we'd exchanged romantic passionate kisses, but we'd never been to bed together. Our eyes had, but not our bodies."

That assertion was accurate during the first few days of the shoot, but as LeRoy later said, "By the fourth day, those two gorgeous creatures were really going at it. You could almost hear the sounds of love-making coming from her dressing room. I hated to interrupt them to call them back to the set."

In the film, Lana portrays the adopted daughter of Edward Arnold, who was cast as John Benson Farrell, the crusading prosecutor who's responsible for having sent Johnny to prison. Lana's father is now the District Attorney, who at first is not aware of Johnny's dog-racing scams.

As an actor, Lana worked smoothly with Arnold, who was a formidable character actor who had grown up in New York, the son of German immigrants. He'd made his first stage appearance at the age of 12. By 1935, he was cast in the pivotal title role of *Diamond Jim* (1935), a

A son of Oklahoma, Heflin was one of the most talented actors Lana would ever work with. After *Johnny Eager*, she would co-star with him in two more movies, *Green Dolphin Street* and *The Three Musketeers*.

"Van is a reasonably attractive man," Lana told LeRoy, "but he's definitely not my type."

part he would reprise in 1940 when he starred in *Lillian Russell*.

He told Lana, "I gave up losing weight and went after character roles. The bigger I get, the better parts I receive."

The best acting in the picture was executed by Van Heflin, who was cast as the drunken attorney, Jeff Hartnett, the only real friend Johnny Eager has. For his brilliant portrayal, he won the Oscar that year as Best Supporting Actor.

Heflin had made his film debut in 1936 in *A Woman Rebels*, with Katharine Hepburn. He'd later appear on Broadway with her in stage version of *The Philadelphia Story*, but he lost out on the role when it was adapted into a movie. His career would be interrupted by the war, when he joined the U.S. Army Air Corps as a combat cameraman assigned to the Ninth Air Force in Europe.

During their first week of shooting, LeRoy congratulated Lana on how she'd grown as an actress. "If you want to survive in this wicked business, you have to learn the ropes fast," she said. "I had to hold my own against Spencer Tracy, Clark Gable, and now Robert Taylor. A girl has to learn the tricks of the trade."

Robert Sterling was cast as Jimmy Courtney, Lana's high society boyfriend. In a few weeks, Lana would find herself working with him again on her next picture, *Somewhere I'll Find You* with Clark Gable.

As the film unfolds, when Johnny Eager's childhood friend, Lew Rankin (as interpreted by Barry Nelson), gets fed up being a second stringer in the gang, and defies Johnny in an attempt to replace him, the gangster has him murdered without the slightest regret.

One of the most dramatic moments in the film occurs when Johnny frames the character played by Lana for murder. He orders Julio (Paul Stewart), one of his underlings, to burst into their quarters and pretend to try to kill him. During the fake struggle, Julio drops his gun, only to have Lisbeth (Lana) retrieve it and shoot him in an attempt to save Johnny's life. She is hustled out of the room before she can determine that the gun she used had been filled with blanks.

Lana's affair with Robert Taylor, both on and off the screen, was doomed. At the film's conclusion, Johnny is shot dead in the street by a policeman, proving once again, that crime doesn't pay.

***

Both Lana and her closest friend, Virginia Grey, compared notes on the lovemaking techniques of Robert Taylor, as he had already been sexually intimate with each of them. His affair with Grey transpired before he met Lana. Robert Stack, another of Taylor's lovers, was also kept abreast of Lana's new affair.

"A lot of women dream about finding a patient, totally giving lover like Bob, but they rarely find him," Lana confided.

Stack told her, "Bob is probably the handsomest man alive, and the least actorish actor, without any feeling of being the matinee idol that he is. What he looks like is not what he is. He's just a guy who looks like a god with a widow's peak."

Actually, his hair had originally "squared" in a straight line across his forehead, but Mayer had ordered makeup artists and hair stylists to give him his famous

181

widow's peak.

Among his early seductions was a bit player on the set of his 1936 film, *Small Town Girl*, starring Janet Gaynor. In addition to seducing Gaynor, Taylor took the virginity of Thelma ("Pat") Ryan long before Richard Nixon married her and, as Pat Nixon, she became First Lady of the United States.

Taylor had also seduced Greta Garbo, with whom he'd appeared in the 1936 classic, *Camille*. Both Ava Gardner and Elizabeth Taylor lay in his future.

A bisexual, Taylor was known among Hollywood insiders for his sexual conquests of John Gilbert, Tyrone Power, Errol Flynn, and Howard Hughes.

"I had to have Lana Turner if only for one night," Taylor told LeRoy. "A man would risk being sent up for rape for just one night with her."

When Louis B. Mayer heard this, he dispensed his MGM press agent, George Nichols, to tell Taylor "to keep it soft and in your pants."

Nichols later recalled, "Lana went from the bed of Clark Gable to the bed of Robert Taylor. I used to kid Clark and Bob for seducing some of the same women— Joan Crawford and Norma Shearer come to mind. Sometimes, Clark gave women's telephone numbers to Bob when he wanted to dump some broad."

One day, unannounced and without warning, Taylor's wife, Barbara Stanwyck, appeared on the set of *Johnny Eager*. Seeing her, Lana fled to her dressing room, an act that evoked the scene she was shooting with Clark Gable in *Honky Tonk* when his angry wife, Carole Lombard, suddenly appeared during one of his love scenes with Lana.

This time, Lana refused to come out of her dressing room until LeRoy assured

Lana's role in *Johnny Eager* evolved into one of the most glamorous of her career. She was cast as a society beauty, Lisbeth Bard, who falls in love with the gangster, Johnny Eager, as portrayed by Taylor. Whereas he pretends to be a cab driver, reporting to a parole officer, he's really running a murderous gang.

her that Mayer had ordered that Stanwyck be escorted away from from the lot.

One evening at midnight during the shooting of *Johnny Eager*, when Taylor had still not returned home, Stanwyck placed an angry call to Lana. He had left her home less than a half-hour before. As Lana described to LeRoy the next day, "That Stanwyck woman can curse like a truck driver. She called me everything bad that you can call a woman, from bitch to slut."

Many Hollywood biographers have suggested that the Taylor/Stanwyck union was a "a lavender marriage" with its participants committed to a relationship devoid of sexual intimacies. Stanwyck was known for having affairs with Marlene Dietrich and her dearest friend, Joan Crawford, each of whom was also a bisexual.

It was rumored that Stanwyck harangued her husband so much about his secret status as a homosexual that he had become impotent, but only with her.

Before that, he had told Gable, "Ah, that wife of mine…She always wants to run the fuck."

By mid-production of *Johnny Eager*, Taylor seemed to have fallen in love with Lana, enough so that he went home one night and informed Stanwyck that he was divorcing her to marry Lana. The next day, he told a (horrified) Lana what he had done.

For four days, Stanwyck disappeared. It was later learned that after a suicide attempt *[she slit her wrists]* she'd checked into Cedars of Lebanon Hospital. She'd registered at the hospital under the pseudonym of "Sarah Bruce." For days, Taylor didn't know where his wife was or what had happened to her.

***

Johnny Eager did well at the box office, and the reviews were fair, with lavish praise going to Heflin for his performance. Most critics cited Lana and Taylor for their star power and their on-screen chemistry.

Photoplay wrote, "Frankly, we like Lana Turner better in 'slitchy' roles, but, even so, her performance here is proof that she can act."

One critic got carried away: "I'm not sure what this story about a cold-blooded gangster was about. All I know was that fans just wait for Taylor and Turner to make love on screen. His sheer male beauty and her luminous face are something to see. The love scenes lack subtlety, but who wants subtlety?"

The New York Times wrote that *Johnny Eager* was "a tight tale of underworld hor-

Johnny Eager had a "sock" ending, with Taylor planting a solid right on Lana's chin, as if knocking some sense into her and paving the way for her to return to her society boyfriend.

ror that drives hard, even in the clinches, and though not a serious drama, the movie moves at a turbulent tempo. Taylor and Turner strike sparks in their distraught love affair."

Critic Emanuel Lewis complained that the plot failed to make any sense and that Heflin "stole every scene he was in."

Variety reported that, "Johnny Eager is an underworld meller *[melodrama]* with a few new twists to the usual trappings. But by and large, it's the familiar tale of a slick gangster vs. an innocent rich girl."

Sometime in February of 1943, Taylor dropped in for a "drink" at Lana's house that lasted for five hours. He had recently joined the U.S. Naval Air Corps under his original Nebraska name of Spangler Arlington Brugh.

In the Navy, he had become a flight instructor, but by the time he was discharged late in 1945, he was a full lieutenant.

During his first week back, he lunched with Lana in the MGM commissary, lamenting that in his absence, "all the good men's roles had gone to Van Johnson, Peter Lawford, and Frank Sinatra."

She assured him, "You'll come back bigger than ever."

***

On Sunday, December 7, 1941, "that date that will live in infamy," Lana threw a party, inviting former lovers who included Tommy Dorsey and Buddy Rich, as well as a future lover, Frank Sinatra. She also invited two of her girlfriends, Susan Hayward and Linda Darnell.

The party lasted well past midnight, at which point her mother, Mildred, arrived home from a trip to San Francisco.

She immediately chastised Lana and her guests for "partying at a time like this. Haven't you turned on the radio all day? You fools don't even know that the Japs attacked Pearl Harbor? Turn on the damn radio!"

Lana and her guests gathered around the radio to listen to the latest news from Honolulu and Washington. America was at war. In one way or another, each of them, including Lana, knew that the war would forever alter their lives.

In the weeks ahead, she would say goodbye to many former lovers headed off to war, including Robert Stack, Robert Taylor, Wayne Morris, Victor Mature, Glenn Ford, and Spencer Tracy.

When not making a picture, Lana vol-

When Barbara Stanwyck saw this publicity photo of herself, she said, "That's what I'd like to do to Lana Turner for fucking Robert Taylor during the filming of *Johnny Eager.*"

unteered for railroad tours, visiting town after town for rallies to sell war bonds.

Every American in the 1940s knew what a war bond was, less so today. *[In essence, a war bond was a debt security issued by the government to finance military operations and other expenditures.]*

During the tour, one of Lana's first stops was Wallace, Idaho, her birthplace. The whole town turned out to greet their hometown girl who had gone to Hollywood and become world famous. The mayor gave her the key to the city, and she was escorted on a tour of familiar sites, including the house where she had lived with Virgil and Mildred.

In October of 1942, Lana became a regular volunteer at the Hollywood Canteen at 1451 Cahuenga Boulevard, a club that would entertain servicemen until it closed on Thanksgiving Day in 1945, following the Japanese surrender that September.

The canteen had been founded by Bette Davis and Lana's future co-star, John Garfield, along with Jules Stein, President of the Music Corporation of America. During the war, Lana, during most of her visits to New York, also paid visits to the Stage Door Canteen, a venue with R&R for servicemen in mind, and the regular lair of such Broadway stars as Tallulah Bankhead.

The Hollywood Canteen offered music, free food, and a chance to dance with a bevy of on-site movie stars, some of whom might on any given evening have included Lana, Bette Davis, Betty Grable, Marlene Dietrich, and Rita Hayworth.

Not just movie stars, but industry grips, musicians, singers, comedians, writers, and other entertainment venues signed up as volunteers. Entertainers ranging from Dinah Shore to Bob Hope performed for the servicemen, including those in Allied armies in Europe and Canada.

On any given night, a serviceman might be dancing in the arms of Lucille Ball or Ava Gardner, perhaps Carole Landis, while being served food by Errol Flynn and listening to songs by Peggy Lee.

One night, Davis caught Dietrich and Lana in the kitchen together washing dishes. She shouted, "Get that Kraut and Turner out front dancing with the men. We can always get Ethel Barrymore and Cecil B. DeMille to wash the dishes."

On a few occasions, Lana was behind the grill, preparing her specialty—juicy porterhouse steaks smothered in onions. In cooler weather, Lana showed up in her most dazzling gowns and a mink coat. She told Davis, "The men expect me to look like Lana Turner, not Elsa Lanchester, the *Bride of Frankenstein* (1935)."

Davis skeptically noted that Lana was free with her kisses, "especially if a guy were good-looking. The rules were that our volunteer women were not supposed to fuck the enlisted men. But Dietrich and Turner never followed the rules. Nor did Hedy Lamarr, for that matter."

Lana often encountered Ronald Reagan, who talked about the politics of the war. At the time, both of them were solidly behind President Franklin D. Roosevelt.

A special surprise awaited the millionth serviceman who checked in at the door of the Canteen. A Texan, he was kissed by the singing star, Deanna Durbin, Marlene Dietrich, and by Lana herself. The soldier reported, "Eddie Cantor was there, and gave me a big wet one right on the lips. I loved the kisses from the gals, but could have done without the liver lips of Cantor."

When the Canteen had been operating for some time, Artie Shaw showed up, and Lana went home with him. She told him that the men she'd met at the Canteen fell into two different categories. "A certain type of man has a brave heart, filled with courage as he goes off to war, to land on some god-forsaken island in the South Pacific where the Japs are waiting to shoot him."

"Or else a young man is afraid to die, not ready to give up his life. After spending a night with me, he wants me to hold him in my arms the next morning like a loving mother. Over an old-fashioned American breakfast prepared by Mildred, we both reassure him of a safe return. He wants to believe us."

***

During the war, Lana also performed in shows for the Armed Forces Network. Even before America entered the war, Lana, on September 22, 1941, had appeared on the NBN show, *Salute of Champions*, a special tribute to men serving in the armed forces.

The cast brought her together for the first time with Rita Hayworth, who during the war would vie with her as the pinup girl most favored by GIs. Betty Grable remained the Number One favorite.

After posing for photographs, the two screen goddesses had little to say to each other. Yet on many a night in the 1940s, "Lana & Rita," as they were called, showed that they had the same taste in men.

Lana had seduced Hayworth's future husband, singer Dick Haymes, before she did. In addition, both Lana and Rita were each "deflowered" by many of the same beaux: Tony Martin, Peter Lawford, Robert Mitchum, Tyrone Power, James Stewart, and inevitably, Howard Hughes.

Lana did not like to be compared to Hayworth, and was outraged at the remarks bandleader Fred Karger made. "When I first spotted Rita in 1939, I had never seen such a beautiful woman. She had tremendous magnetism about her, walking into a room, an aura really. Lana Turner was gloriously beautiful, too, but didn't have Rita's magic."

Karger would later become the mentor and lover of Marilyn Monroe. He would in time marry Jane Wyman, the ex-Mrs. Ronald Reagan, who would divorce him, then remarry him, then re-divorce him after realizing that their romance was a lost cause.

At another rally before the war, in November of 1941, Lana arrived in New York for an appearance at Madison Square Garden, where Eleanor Roosevelt was the featured speaker, alongside an array of stars ranging from Groucho Marx to Danny Kaye. Lana found the First Lady "a warm-hearted, charming old soul."

Lana ended 1941 by appearing again on NBC Radio on the *Chase & Sanborn Program* starring Edgar Bergen and his talking dummy, Charlie McCarthy. Bud Abbott and Lou Costello were also slated to attend, but at the last minute, Costello caught the flu. Mickey Rooney, Lana's former beau, filled in for him.

She was still in New York for the New Year's Dancing Party broadcast coast to coast, with Lana pitching the virtues of the USO.

***

186

During the months ahead, Lana continued her rivalry with Hedy Lamarr, often for men or perhaps for the same roles. She resented her co-starring with Robert Taylor and Clark Gable. Mostly, she resented how Lamarr defined herself as "The Queen of MGM," a title that Lana felt she owned.

The rosters of men who roared through each of their lives during the war, were similar: Errol Flynn, Jean-Pierre Aumont, Howard Hughes, John Garfield, and then Navy lieutenant John F. Kennedy, appeared on both lists.

Lana had always considered Lamarr an empty-headed beauty. She was later shocked to learn that she also had a brain.

Along with George Antheil, the composer and pianist, Lamarr had invented a secret communication system that was adapted into a radio-controlled torpedo guidance network.

As detailed by Lamarr's biographer, Ruth Barton, "The procedure involves sending a series of signals from a transmitter to a receiver in a manner that can-

Movie stars such as Lana, Hedy Lamarr, and Carole Lombard were instrumental in promoting war bond sales. In one day, Lana raised $5 million for the government, even giving away a kiss for $50,000. Lamarr topped her, garnering $7 million in war bond sales, also in one day.

not be intercepted, thus allowing for a torpedo to be dropped remotely. It was crucial that the message cannot be jammed by a third party."

In June of 1941, Lamarr and Antheil formally registered their invention with the U.S. Patent Office. Today, it's credited as an essential part of everything from military weapons to cellphones. Encountering Lana after news of her invention became widely publicized, Lamarr told Lana, "Just because a woman is beautiful does not mean she is stupid."

***

Lana remained friends with Artie Shaw throughout most of the duration of the war. In fact, she spent her final night with him before the bandleader enlisted in the Navy, following the attack on Pearl Harbor. He was assigned to Staten Island in New York, where he was trained aboard a minesweeper.

He wrote her every month, telling her he had been transferred to Newport, Rhode Island, where he had been promoted to the post of Chief Petty Officer. "Not only that," he wrote," but I've been given a band to lead, consisting of the world's most untalented musicians."

Using the power of his famous name, he persuaded the military brass in Washington to allow him to recruit extremely talented musicians who had been drafted into the Navy.

By the summer of 1943, he informed Lana that he was the leader of a "real band," and would be sailing from Pearl Harbor aboard the battleship, USS *North Carolina,* touring the Pacific theater to perform for servicemen. He visited such outposts as New Caledonia and the Solomons. Venues for the band ranged from on-board concerts to makeshift stages hastily erected in jungles.

Lana, with Rita Hayworth, raising morale. Their joint appearances always seemed to spark debates about the relative merits of blondes vs. redheads.

When Shaw arrived on battle-torn Guadalcanal, there remained some pockets of Japanese resistance. "My tent was so full of bullet holes, it looked like Swiss cheese," he said in a letter to Lana.

He also described how he began the musical lineup of his concerts with "Begin the Beguine," and that the boys had almost cried with glee to hear American music, "since they were homesick in this cesspool of horror."

Shaw learned via short-wave radio that his fourth wife, Betty Kern, the daughter of songwriter Jerome Kern, had given birth to a seven-pound boy. But they would soon divorce.

He wrote to Lana that Tokyo Rose, the infamous Japanese propaganda broadcaster, often played recordings of his hits, asserting that the music was being broadcast live from the ballroom of the St. Francis Hotel in San Francisco.

"Hear this, Yankee soldiers," she would announce to U.S. servicemen who had gathered around their radios, swatting away bugs in the sweltering jungle heat. "After the show, the boys in the band are making out with your girlfriends, even though they promised to wait for your return."

As the war progressed and as Shaw's USO tours through the Pacific continued, he suffered from (and was diagnosed with) exhaustion, and was subsequently shipped back to a Naval Hospital at Oak Knoll, California.

When Lana arrived to visit him, she saw that he'd lost a lot of weight and was looking weak and pale, enough to keep him in the hospital for three months. He'd picked up some "bug" in the South Pacific, he'd told her.

In 1944, he was discharged from the Navy, and there was some talk that he and Lana might remarry. But then into his life came Lana's new best girlfriend, Ava Gardner, who, in 1945, married him herself, with disastrous consequences.

***

In October of 1942, the month it opened, Lana made her first conquest at the Hollywood Canteen. Her friend, Linda Darnell, had arrived with her at the Canteen that night.

"Robert Moseley was the best-looking guy I've ever seen in a sailor's uniform," Lana recalled. He told her that he'd become an apprentice seaman, having been assigned to the U.S. Naval Reserve Station in Los Angeles.

As she danced with him, she said, "Where are you from, sailor boy?"

She almost laughed at his answer: Pumpkin Center, California. Before the night ended, she also learned that he was a few months younger than she was.

From a faraway corner of the room, she pointed Moseley out to Darnell. "Don't you think he's a living doll? What a divine physique. I've already learned that he grew up on a ten-acre ranch, and that he was an athlete in high school."

When she danced with him again, he told her, "I attended this junior college at Bakersfield, and the guys in the locker room called me the male version of Lana Turner."

"I guess I should be flattered," she said. "Or else you should be flattered. I think you should be in pictures, and I know just the right agent for you. I'm no longer his client, but we're still good friends. His name is Henry Willson."

"I'm no actor."

"Darling, I'm no actress," she said. "To be a movie star, you really don't need to know how to act. You could light up the screen with your looks."

Although it was against the rules of the Canteen, she invited him to her home that night. As she later told Darnell, "I was thrilled with his love-making."

The next afternoon, she asked him to escort her to Willson's Saturday afternoon pool party. Her homosexual agent was enthralled by Moseley, telling her, "I'll have to change his name." Then he rattled off about ten proposals for new names. Of them all, she preferred "Guy Madison."

Alone, over drinks with the just-renamed Guy Madison, she explained to him, "Henry has this thing for men in uniform."

"You mean, he's *that* way?" he asked.

"Exactly," she answered. "You've got that right. Actually, I think it's only fair that handsome young men have to lie on the casting couch in Hollywood just like women have. How do you feel about

Lana met the handsome Guy Madison at the Hollywood Canteen, suggesting that, based on his looks, he should be in pictures.

She warned him that with Henry Willson as his agent, he might have to spend some nights on the casting couch.

that?"

"If this Willson guy can get me into the movies, I guess it's okay," he said.

Henry operates an Adonis factory," she said. "When you get out of the service, I bet he can get you a contract with David O. Selznick."

"You mean the guy who produced *Gone With the Wind?*"

"One and the same," she said.

"Hot damn!" Being a star sounds a lot better than shoveling cowshit out of a barn on the family ranch."

Before they left the pool party, Willson called Lana aside. "Thanks for introducing me to the newly christened Guy Madison. He looks like a real-life version of one of Tom of Finland's wet dreams."

She didn't know who he was referring to.

[Tom of Finland was the pen name of the Finnish artist, Touko Laaksonen (1920-1991), who developed an international reputation for his erotic drawings of super-masculine males with monstrous endowments. Many of his homosexual fans referred to him as "the King of Beefcake."]

Willson wanted Madison to remain behind, but Lana said, "He's taking me to the Mocambo tonight. Ganymede is mine."

"Ganymede? Since when did you start using such a classical reference?

"I learned it from Artie Shaw," she said.

At the Mocambo, Madison was awed, telling Lana, "The decorations here make me feel like I'm inside a coffin."

"You're a hit," she said. "When we walked in, more eyes were trained on you than on me." Before the night was over, she'd introduced him to both Veronica Lake and Dorothy Lamour.

"You're more beautiful than those hussies," he told her.

Even during Lana's second marriage to Stephen Crane, Madison became a reliable date whenever he visited the Canteen. When she personally rendezvoused with him, it was usually upstairs within one of Willson's bedrooms. Also, during the course of his first year in the service, Willson also got to "audition" the young sailor several times.

For three years he served in the Navy, eventually moving on to the Transition Training Squadron of the Pacific Fleet in San Diego. At one point, he injured his back and was transferred to the U.S. Naval Special Hospital at Banning, California, from which he was eventually discharged.

Stardom, through Henry Willson, awaited him. As Lana recalled to Alexis Smith, who had met Madison at the Canteen, "Guy is the kind of young man who can satisfy both men and women in equal measure."

In time, his fan clubs would dub him, "The World's Most Desirable Male."

Television's future Wild Bill Hickock was on his way to stardom.

***

Scheduled for a 1942 release, *Keeper of the Flame* was a story about the pitfalls of hero worship. As its stars, Louis B. Mayer and director George Cukor cast Spencer Tracy and Katharine Hepburn.

One of the supporting actors was Forrest Tucker, a ruggedly handsome farm-boy who had arrived in Hollywood financed by a wealthy male "mentor," in whose home he lived for several months.

Tucker was said to "ooze masculinity," and his wavy blonde hair, his photogenic good looks, and his height of 6'4" soon attracted attention. At the age of 14, Tucker had entered show business, singing at the 1933 Chicago World's Fair. He later worked at the Old Gaiety Burlesque Theater in Washington, D.C., where the big teenage boy created a "sensation:" among the burlesque dancers and the male drag queens.

In Hollywood, Tucker came to the attention of a talent scout at MGM, Wesley Ruggles, who ordered a screen test for him. "He's a hunk all right. I thing he could be MGM's answer to John Wayne." Ruggles would soon direct Lana's next big picture with Clark Gable.

Tucker came to Tracy's attention when he appeared with his friend, Gary Cooper, in *The Westerner* (1940). Tucker has stood out in a fight scene. Within weeks, the bisexual Tracy became Tucker's new "mentor"

During the filming of *Keeper of the Flame,* Tracy invited Lana to lunch in the MGM commissary. They had become friends since making *Dr. Jekyll and Mr. Hyde* together, and would co-star with each other in the future.

She later confided to Susan Hayward that not since Sterling Hayden had she met such a "walking streak of sex. I went for Forrest in a big way, although I hope he has something left after Cukor and Spence finished with him for the day."

Fortunately, Hepburn wasn't at lunch that day. She'd had a fight with Cukor and had stormed off. Tracy told Lana about her blow-up:

Hepburn had been feuding with the movie's scenarist, Donald Ogden Stewart, demanding that his script follow more closely I.A. R. Wylie's novel. In that book, Steven O'Malley (the character played by Tracy), was depicted as an "impotent eunuch."

In front of the cast, Tracy had ridiculed Hepburn's suggestion. "You want me to play the role with no balls! No way!"

Hepburn was also angry that Cukor was devoting more time to getting Tucker's scenes right than he was to her

Spencer Tracy introduced Lana to the studly Forrest Tucker. "We were going to dinner," Lana told Susan Hayward. "But he never left my house all weekend. He calls that monster thing of his 'The Chief.' It's his pride and joy, and does he ever know how to use it!"

In the weeks ahead, news of "The Chief" swept through Hollywood. George Cukor jokingly said that an impression of it should be pressed into wet concrete along Hollywood's Walk of Fame.

character. She noted that Tucker disappeared with the director for almost two hours every afternoon, bolting his door behind him.

During lunch, when Tracy was called to the phone, Tucker asked Lana for a date, and she accepted.

As Lana discovered, Tucker was not another John Wayne, but a man of sensitivity and feeling. He spoke of going to "the school of hard knocks." His father had died of mustard gas during World War I, and his mother worked as a burlesque dancer. During the worst years of the Depression, he'd ridden the rails with other hobos looking for work, or at least food.

Lana had never seen Tucker on film, not even the movie he'd made with Gary Cooper. One afternoon, he arranged a screening for her at MGM of his 1941 release, *Honolulu*, in which he'd co-starred with the Mexican spitfire, Lupe Velez. She had once been married to the screen Tarzan, Johnny Weissmuller, Lana's former flame.

After Tucker seduced her, the outspoken Velez had spread the word that "Before Tuck, I thought either Gary Cooper or Johnny were my greatest thrills."

Three years later, Velez would commit suicide.

***

Lana and Lupe Velez were not alone in spreading the "big news" about Tucker's self-styled "Chief."

James Bacon, the Hollywood columnist, even wrote about Tucker's endowment after he joined the Lakeside Country Club. Members there included Bob Hope, Bing Crosby, Weissmuller, W.C. Fields, Mickey Rooney, and Humphrey Bogart.

Bacon wrote, "Tuck's heavy endowment would become the chief tourist attraction at the club. As he lay passed out drunk in the locker room, a stream of members with guests would slowly and quietly file in. The towel would be lifted for an unveiling, and there would be many gasps."

While Lana was dating Tucker, an even greater legend grew up around him. The comedian Phil Harris told Lana and countless others that one afternoon he was playing golf with Tucker at the club. "On the 7th hole, Tuck teed off, his ball hitting the green only a foot from the hole. I came within four feet of the same hole. Since he was so close to winning, he asked me if he could declare victory."

"Hell, man!" he told Harris. "Even the Chief can hit that hole."

"I bet you can't," Harris responded, reaching into his pocket and removing five $20 bills.

"You're on," Tucker said. He unbuttoned his pants and fell to a position on his hands, his knees above the turf, and "The Chief" scored a perfect bull's eye. Word of that feat soon spread across Tinseltown.

In spite of his budding stardom, Tucker was drafted. He told Lana goodbye two days before he left for boot camp. He'd joined the U.S. Army, where in time he'd earn a commission as a second lieutenant.

After the war, she saw him periodically and only at parties. After he'd made *The Yearling* (1946) with Gregory Peck and Jane Wyman, he shot *Never Say Goodbye* with Errol Flynn that same year.

At a party in Flynn's home, Tucker asked Lana if she'd retreat to Flynn's bedroom with him.

"Not me," she said. "He's got a two-way mirror for voyeurs."

"I don't mind staging an exhibition," Tucker said.

"Give me a raincheck, Tuck," she said. "Some things are best kept private."

After that, she was pleased for him for his big breakthrough role in *The Sands of Iwo Jima* (1949) with John Wayne. She was mostly delighted with his role as Beauregard Burnside, the first husband of Rosalind Russell in *Auntie Mame*, the biggest-grossing film of 1958.

***

All the gossip columnists, even those at *The New York Times*, wrote of the up-coming marriage of Hedy Lamarr and George Montgomery, although no specific date had been set for the ceremony. A *Times* writer reported, "For an ex-cow puncher, Montgomery isn't doing badly at all. He recently sealed his intentions of becoming Hedy Lamarr's next husband. What it all adds up to, in short, is that Mr. Montgomery has arrived."

Lana wondered about his commitment to Lamarr. She had learned that he was slipping around and dating a beautiful MGM starlet, Kay Williams.

[As Kay Williams Spreckels, then best-known as a socialite, she would become the fifth and final wife of Clark Gable.]

As Lana told Virginia Grey, "I still have a special place in my heart for George Montgomery. He's not the kind of man a gal gets over easily. All the papers, as you know, are filled with news of his engagement to Hedy Lamarr."

"His nickname for her is Penny," Lana said, "but I wouldn't call her that. My nickname for her rhymes with witch."

One afternoon, Lana encountered Lamarr at MGM. To judge from her talk, the Austrian star was unaware that Montgomery had ever dated Lana.

[At the time, Lamarr and Lana were still pretending a surface friendship.]

"I am so happy with George I'm dizzy," Lamarr confided. "It is unbelievable that one girl could be so much in love. I have never been in love like this before. Last night, George gave me a $100 bottle of *Shalimar.*"

"That's what I call true love," Lana said, disguising the sarcasm in her voice.

"He also gave me a clay Popeye he'd won throwing baseballs at a fun arcade," Lamarr said.

"That's even better than a diamond ring," Lana said.

"Don't be catty, dear," Lamarr cautioned her.

Three months later, Montgomery called Lana. "Penny *[his nickname for Lamarr]* and I are through. We broke off our engagement last night. You may not want to take me back, but I was wrong to leave you like I did."

It was 1943 and he'd just joined the U.S. Army Air Force after he'd played the lead in *Bomber's Moon.*

"Of course, I'll see you," she said.

He picked her up that night and drove her to a small Italian restaurant out in San Fernando Valley, far removed from the glitter of Tinseltown. They ate pasta and drank two bottles of wine by candlelight. He drove her back home, and she invited him in to spend the night with her before reporting for duty.

During the war, that penchant for "sending a soldier to war with a smile on his face" became a familiar routine for Lana.

Her rival, Carole Landis, remarked, "Lana Turner could always be counted on to give the boys a farewell fuck."

When Lana heard that remark, she responded, "Unlike Landis, I don't charge. Once a hooker, always a hooker."

She never heard from Montgomery again, but read in the *Hollywood Reporter* that he'd been assigned to the Army Signal Corps and stationed in Alaska.

During his visits to Los Angeles, he didn't call her, but had not taken up with Lamarr again either.

It came as a shock to her to read that in December of 1943, he'd married the singer, Dinah Shore. According to the report, she had staked him out as her husband the first day she'd met him.

But whereas Lamarr remembered Montgomery in her memoirs, Lana did not.

"George is one of the men whom I almost married," Lamarr wrote. "Everybody thought I was going to marry him, and perhaps I should have. He was so versatile and handsome. When he went off to war, he was even more attractive in uniform than in any of his Hollywood roles. Once we had made some vows, but we both had a faculty for seeing through sham and hypocrisy. We couldn't fool each other, and we both realized deep inside that we weren't sure enough about each other."

***

At a party at Errol Flynn's home on Mulholland Drive, Lana was introduced to Jorge Guinle, the movie star's house guest. He was the scion of Brazil's richest family, called "The Rockefellers of Rio de Janeiro." In fact, when Franklin D. Roosevelt once visited, the president of Brazil asked the Guinle family to house him, since their residence was the most spectacular in the country.

When Guinle visited New York, he was a guest of Nelson Rockefeller. During the war, Nelson had used his influence to get Guinle a "soft job" in Hollywood, reviewing scripts to ensure that the countries of South America weren't wrongly depicted. In the middle of a war, the United States needed its good neighbors

Jorge Guinle, a wealthy Brazilian playboy, didn't look like the typical Hollywood stud, but he seduced some of the most famous stars in Hollywood, including Lana and Marilyn Monroe.

In his heyday, he ranked up there with Aristotle Onassis, Howard Hughes, Prince Aly Khan, and Porfirio Rubirosa ("Rubber Hosa").

to the south.

Years later, Guinle would recall the first time he saw Lana enter Flynn's living room. "She was all in white, furs, diamonds, high heels, and a white gown with plunging *décolletage*. She was a dream walking."

Lana recalled that she was surprised at how short Guinle was, but was impressed with his penetrating blue eyes and his suave South American charm. He immediately won her over, and their brief fling would begin one weekend in Palm Springs.

She was not alone. His other conquests included Veronica Lake, Hedy Lamarr, and Jane Russell, Howard Hughes' big-busted discovery and the star of *The Outlaw*.

During their courtship, both Lana and Guinle shared a fascination for jazz. He had, in his capacity as a very wealthy investor, already financed some of the recordings of Charlie Parker and Dizzy Gillespie.

When he wasn't pursuing the most glamorous women of Hollywood, Guinle went nightclubbing with an array of male friends who included Orson Welles, Ronald Reagan, and Lana's mentor, Mervyn LeRoy.

During a visit to New York, Guinle introduced Lana to another friend of his, Huntington Hartford, the A&P heir. Lana would begin dating him in 1945.

At one point when she was dating Guinle, Lana learned that he was also spending some of his evenings with her girlfriend, Susan Hayward.

In 1946, when Lana attended a party hosted by Hartford, she shared a reunion with Guinle. He described his experience on the night Paris was liberated. "I attended a party thrown by Elsa Maxwell," he said. "Cole Porter played *La Marseillaise*, and I kissed and hugged Greta Garbo, Frank Sinatra, Charles Boyer, Maurice Chevalier, and Marlene Dietrich."

With the arrival of the 1950s, Guinle engineered new conquests, including Jayne Mansfield and Marilyn Monroe.

Guinle lived to be 88 years old. Before his death in 2004, he told the press, "Thanks to Viagra, I've continued with my love making. I'm still floating and not sinking."

Along with his youth, through bad investments, his wealth had long ago disappeared. "The secret of living well is to die without a cent in your pocket."

"The days of all my old friends like Prince Aly Khan have gone. At times, I feel that glamor itself has disappeared from the world. On cold, windy nights when I'm alone, I relive my illustrious past. I seduced Lana Turner during the war and Marilyn Monroe in the 1950s. Not bad for a little short guy from Brazil."

***

After dumping George Montgomery, Hedy Lamarr wasted no time in linking herself to Jean-Pierre Aumont. He was a French Jew and had been forced to flee from his native France after its Nazi takeover.

Aumont was a fast worker. As he later wrote in his memoir, *Sun and Shadow*, his affair with Lamarr began at a party at her wooden house, a building whose architecture reminded her of equivalent buildings in her native Austria. "She appeared, dressed in red, her black hair flowing. She was a vision of sensuality, with her nose upturned just enough to keep her from being too beautiful. During dinner, she pressed one of her knees, the lovelier of the two, against mine. The following week, we were engaged."

Later, as he would explain to Lana, the engagement ended when he was driving her home from a concert. "I braked a little too quickly. Hedy became hysterical, claiming that I had purposely tried to throw her against the windshield because I was jealous of her beauty."

The next day, their engagement was canceled.

As was her custom, Joan Crawford had been the first to discover and seduce Aumont. In his own words, "During World War II, a young Frenchman who wasn't bad looking, who owned a dinner jacket, and could babble a few words in English was received with wide open arms. Such was the case with Miss Crawford and myself."

"Everything about her seemed immense: Her eyes, her mouth, her shoulders, her greeting."

"The first night she invited me to her home, she didn't let me go for three days. My agent, Charlie Feldman, finally figured out where I was and came to rescue me."

It was at a house party at Crawford's that Aumont made his next conquest. She was Gene Tierney. "I was trying to flirt with her until Charles Boyer took me aside."

"Watch your step," Boyer cautioned. "She's a married woman. It's simply not done here."

"What a strange country," Aumont said.

In the days ahead, he did not follow Boyer's advice.

Although Tierney was married to Oleg Cassini, the fashion designer, at the time, he was often away for design and fashion commissions in New York. Neither Tierney nor Cassini was faithful to the other, and Tierney's affairs were wide-ranging. In addition to a dalliance with JFK, they included intimacies with Howard Hughes, Mickey Rooney, George Sanders, Victor Mature, Tyrone Power, and Darryl F. Zanuck.

Before arriving to deflower Hollywood actresses, Aumont had seduced Vivien Leigh in London. Grace Kelly was another goddess who lay in his future.

Lana once proclaimed the glories of the French actor, Jean-Pierre Aumont.

"He was France's great gift to the love-starved women of Hollywood—perhaps in gratitude for their help in World War II. From Hedy Lamarr to Gene Tierney, he was much appreciated, especially by myself."

"Gene Tierney had skin made of gold," Aumont claimed, "with green-blue eyes. Her hair came down to her shoulders, and it curled at the ends. Her shoulders were broad, but not so much as Crawford's, and she spoke a bit with the Connecticut accent of Miss Katharine Hepburn, but far more seductive, of course."

"When I did get to talk to her, we spoke in French, since she'd learned how to speak it in Switzerland.

"How very nice to meet someone who is civilized," she said to him.

Within days, their on-again, off-again love affair, had begun, especially when her husband, Oleg Cassini, was away in New York.

Lana's affair with Aumont had begun on March 29, 1943, when they had co-starred in the dramatization of *Crossroads* for CBS's Lux Radio Theatre. After the broadcast, he'd invited her to dinner, which she followed up with an invitation to her home.

Little is known of their brief fling, except for one detail, which she shared with Mervyn LeRoy:

"Before Jean-Pierre gets excited, he needs his ass spanked. Apparently, he had developed this sexual fetish when he was enrolled in a boarding school in France. Every morning, he told me, his one-armed professor would order the boys to pull down their pants while he gave their bare butts a good spanking. Whether they did it or not, he spanked them for having masturbated the night before. From this punishment, Aumont seemed to have developed his fetish. After the spanking, he delivers the goods, and he's really fantastic. It's easy to understand why women are attracted to him."

Despite Aumont's affair with Lana, he would marry Maria Montez that year. A native of the Dominican Republic, she had gravitated to Hollywood, where she became "The Queen of Technicolor" after making a series of pictures that included *Arabian Nights* (1942), *Ali Baba and the Forty Thieves* (1944), and *Cobra Woman* (also 1944).

Montez was in the Dominican Republic when Aumont was invited to Cole Porter's much-anticipated annual Hollywood party, so subsequently, he attended without her. "I felt like I was on top of the world," he said. "Everybody, including Lana, was congratulating me on my film, *Assignment in Brittany* (1943), in which I posed as a Nazi leader conspiring with the French Underground. The role had originally been slated for Robert Taylor."

"That night, Lana made me feel like I had invented the electric light bulb," Aumont said. "I was the center of attraction, and Porter seated me between Gene (Tierney) and Lana."

"Everything was perfect that night...too perfect. The caviar followed the *foie gras*. Violins were playing Viennese waltzes. I was surrounded by beauties, riches. But my stomach was tied in knots."

"Here I was, enjoying the good life while my countrymen in France were starving to death or being killed by the Nazis," Aumont said. "I suddenly got up and headed to the terrace without excusing myself."

Fearing he might be suddenly ill, Lana followed him into the garden trying to comfort him. "I just can't go on living in this fake world," he told her. "My heart is in France, and my country is bleeding."

197

He later told friends, "Lana was very tender to me, very loving, not some fake glamor queen. Apparently, she'd had much experience in sending men off to war."

Leaving the party, he drove her through the Hollywood Hills, where he found a secluded parking space at a belvedere. Both of them would remember that night's breezes and the lights over Los Angeles.

Holding on to her, he pleaded, "I don't want to be alone tonight."

After a night with her, he told her the next morning that he'd made up his mind. He was going to send a telegram to Captain de Manziarly, the head of *France Libre*, and volunteer his services. *[France Libre and Forces françaises libres were names for the government-in-exile spearheaded by Charles de Gaulle during World War II. Designated as an official ally of the UK and Britain after the collapse of France, it continued to fight against the Nazi governments of France's Vichy régime and Germany throughout the remainder of the war. France Libre began operating from a base in London in June 1940 and organized and liaised, from their base in London, the French Resistance in Nazi-occupied France.]*

The day after that, Aumont visited Louis B. Mayer at MGM, informing him of his decision to fight with the forces of *France Libre.* "I'll be spending some time in England," Aumont said. "When I return, I'll speak English better."

"Whatever you do, don't lose your accent," Mayer warned him. "It's your major asset. I'd rather you come back without a leg than without your accent."

For his final visit to MGM, he went to Lana's dressing room and remained inside for two hours.

In New York, at the moment of his departure for the battlefields of Europe, it wasn't Lana, but Maria Montez who bid him *adieu.*

In North Africa, he joined the Free French forces fighting with the Allies to drive the Nazis out. In battle, he was wounded twice. For his bravery, he was made a member of the *Légion d'Honneur* and received *La Croix de Guerre. [The National Order of the Legion of Honor* (L'Ordre national de la Légion d'honneur) *is the highest French order for military and civil merits, established in 1802 by Napoléon Bonaparte.]*

***

Even though it was against the policy of the Hollywood Canteen, Lana sustained a number of affairs with enlisted men before they were shipped to the Pacific. One of them was on the dawn of major stardom, and another, somewhat lesser-known, would become a leading man in pictures.

Their names were Alan Ladd and Scott Brady.

Born in Arizona in 1913, Ladd had grown up in the Depression era, as he and his mother had struggled to survive in a kind of *Grapes of Wrath* scenario. His father had died of a heart attack when he was four years old.

Mother and son moved to California, where Ladd attended school, excelling in athletics in spite of his short stature. *[He would eventually reach a height of five feet, four inches. Some of his future leading ladies, including Shelley Winters, would have to stand in a shallow ditch for their love scenes with him.]*

His schoolmates mocked him, nicknaming him "Tiny." He perpetuated that name when, as a hard-working teen entrepreneur he opened Tiny's Patio, a hamburger joint and malt shop across from his school.

Along the way, he met Marjorie ("Midge") Harrold when she was a seventeen-year-old senior in high school. They would marry in 1936 and give birth to Alan Ladd, Jr., who one day would become President of 20th Century Fox.

Ladd's early days in Hollywood evoked scenes from that haunting novel of Tinseltown, *The Day of the Locust*. In 1932, he signed with Universal, which cast him in bit parts. The title of his 1933 film, *Island of Lost Souls*, could have described his personality.

He later described to Lana how Universal let him go within a few months. "I was told I was too short and too blonde. I was booted out the same day they dismissed another actor, Tyrone Power. He was told he was not masculine enough to be a leading man."

After that, Ladd got hired by Warner Brothers as a grip, getting an occasional bit part in films. In the 1939 *Citizen Kane,* he makes a brief, shadowy appearance playing a reporter at the end of the movie during its famous "Rosebud" scene.

His life changed when he met actress Sue Carol, who had become his theatrical agent. When she first spotted the handsome, blue-eyed actor, she said, "He looked like a Greek god and was unforgettable." She aggressively took over management of his career and married him in the aftermath of his divorce.

Carol was determined to make him a star, which finally came with the 1942 release of *This Gun for Hire,* in which he played a hired killer opposite Veronica Lake with her peek-a-boo hairdo. Although fourth-billed, he became the overnight sensation of the picture, enough so that Paramount would reteam him in other pictures with Lake. *[In private, the duo detested each other.]*

The year of his first big success, 1942, was the year that Lana met him at the Hollywood Canteen. Fortunately for Lana, Carol had gone to New York for business meetings and would be away for a week.

After dancing with him at the Canteen, Lana invited him home with her. He shared his dream of becoming a bigtime movie star. "I have the face of an aging choirboy and the build of an undernourished featherweight. If you can figure out my recent success on the screen, you're a better person than I am."

As Lana would later relay to Susan Hayward, "Alan was filled with self-

Lana met Alan Ladd at the Hollywood Canteen before his career took off.

"I usually go in for men tall in the saddle, but sometimes short men need love, too. Alan and I had just a brief fling, but June Allyson went ape-shit over him, even though both of them were married."

doubt, even after we did it. He asked me a question no man had ever asked: 'Did I do it right?' he wanted to know."

"I assured him that he did and was so convincing that he wanted to do it again."

During *après sex*, he shared memories of his past. The most traumatic occurred when his beloved mother committed suicide by swallowing large amounts of an over-the-counter insecticide then being marketed as "ant paste".

He said they'd had a hard time putting food on the table. "It was always weak soup and cheap cuts of mutton. Today, I can't stand the smell of lamb."

Eventually, Ladd slipped away and paid a final call on Lana during February of 1943 before he left for service in the U.S. Army Air Force. Originally, he'd been classified 4-F because of a chronic stomach ailment. But he was eventually assigned to the Army's Motion Picture Unit, and even starred in a U.S. military propaganda film, *Letter From a Friend*.

For a while, Ladd was stationed at the Walla Walla Air Base, serving in their film unit, where he attained the position of Corporal.

He was given permission to attend the March, 1943 Academy Award presentations, where he shared a reunion with Lana. By December of that year, he would be voted the 15th Most Popular Star in the United States. *The New York Times* wrote, "Alan Ladd has built up a following unmatched in the film industry since Valentino skyrocketed to fame."

After the war, Lana and Ladd remained good friends. She was often entertained at his home, with Carol present as hostess. It is not known if his wife ever uncovered their long-ago affair.

Lana was amazed at the success of Ladd in films that included his memorable *Shane* (1953) with Jean Arthur. For a while, he and Marilyn Monroe were voted the most popular stars in the movies.

Lana saw a lot more of the Ladds when all of them were living in Europe, taking advantage of the 18-month tax break the Internal Revenue Service granted to stars who lived and made pictures abroad.

She recalled going to parties hosted by director Tay Garnett. "These parties were for homesick exiles," Lana said. "One night, Clark Gable showed up with Ava Gardner and Robert Taylor. Ava rolled up her sleeves and cooked Carolina fried chicken for the gang."

In a talk between Gable and Ladd, Ladd revealed that he had been an extra in a Gable picture, *They Met in Bombay*, which was originally to have starred Lana as the female lead.

"Clark and Alan represented the vagaries of Hollywood," Lana said. "When he made that Bombay picture, Clark was the King of Hollywood. Now, years later, Alan was the leader in the popularity polls and at the box office."

In the years that followed, Lana saw less and less of Ladd as he sank deeper and deeper into depression and alcoholism. He also suffered from a gunshot wound that had been self-afflicted, although reported in the press as "accidental."

In his last picture, *The Carpetbaggers* (1964), he portrayed, with irony, a broken down former movie star.

***

[Death came to Lana's friend, Alan Ladd, on January 29, 1964. An autopsy revealed that his blood was saturated with a lethal combination of sedatives and alcohol.

The funeral was scheduled for February 1. Fans and friends showed up within the solid stone walls of the Church of the Recessional in Forest Lawn Memorial Park.

Her face partially concealed by large sunglasses, Lana appeared dressed in black, five minutes after the service began. Not wanting to be recognized or acknowledged, she left before the end of the service.

The next day, she phoned June Allyson, who had been one of the great loves of Ladd's life, even though he had been married to Carol throughout most of the duration of their affair.

"I was shocked at Alan's death," Lana said. "At the funeral, so many memories came rushing back of life in the '40s and '50s. For the first time in my life, I felt old. From now on, what's left for all of us?"]

***

Another up-and-coming star who Lana seduced after rendezvous at the Hollywood Canteen was the handsome and strapping Brooklyn-born Scott Brady. That was his screen name.

Two years younger than Lana, he had been born Gerald Kenneth Tierney. His father had been the Chief of New York's Acqueduct Police Force.

Brady's motivation for changing his name derived from the fact that his older brother, Lawrence Tierney, migrated to Hollywood before he did, and had already been indelibly associated with the name "Tierney."

Brady's one-night stand with Lana might have faded from her memory had he not become a movie star after his service in the military.

Before stardom, he'd been a prize fighter, a lumberjack, and a cab driver. When Lana met him at the Hollywood Canteen, he had already studied acting at the Beverly Hills Drama School.

Lana had spent a night with Brady before he became a naval aviation mechanic overseas, serving aboard the USS

"My fame in the boudoir spread like wildfire when I landed in Hollywood to stay," boasted Scott Brady. "The first big star I seduced was Lana Turner. I met her at the Hollywood Canteen."

"When I returned from the service, my leading ladies went for me—take Joan Crawford in *Johnny Guitar* (1954) and Anne Bancroft in *The Restless Breed* (1957)."

"Hollywood gays also went for me big time, especially Rock Hudson at the Finlandia Baths. Before he became a bigshot movie star, Rock and I made two movies together—*Undertow* (1949) and *I Was a Shoplifter* (1950). All I would do is let him service me. Scott Brady is no fag!"

201

Norton Sound. After the war, he returned to Hollywood, where he appealed to his brother (Lawrence Tierney) to help him break into pictures.

By then, Tierney had evolved, through a series of well-publicized scandals, into one of Hollywood's most flagrant bad boys. During the course of his career he would be arrested twenty times for drunkenness or assault. As one columnist phrased it, Tierney was a "rowdy screen actor who has been decisioned, knocked out, and fouled by John Barleycorn."

Brady also became reckless, cutting a path of seduction and scandal across Hollywood, although not of the sort to get himself arrested.

Lana became aware of the rumors flying through Hollywood about these naughty brothers. One afternoon, during her filming of *Mr. Imperium* (1951) at MGM, Tierney managed to reach her on the phone. He sounded drunk. "My brother, Scott, still talks about that night he spent with you. I'm told that if a gal goes for one brother, she might also have the hots for his other brother, too."

"You've been misinformed, Mr. Tierney," she said.

"Perhaps not. Why not get together with Scott and me? Just ask Joan Crawford for a recommendation. The two of us can really show a gal a good time."

"The invitation sounds enchanting, but count me out. Why not give Marilyn Monroe a ring instead?" Then she slammed down the phone.

***

Director Wesley Ruggles was the first to call Lana with the good news. "Mayer thinks reteaming you again with Clark Gable is as good as money in the bank."

"And what have you guys come up with for us?" she asked.

"It's a movie called *Red Light*."

"Are you kidding? That suggests a 'Red Light 'district. Will I play a prostitute?"

"No way. You'll play a newspaper gal."

"That sounds somewhat better."

After a long chat with her new director, Lana put down her white phone in her all-white bedroom with a sense of elation. She was thrilled that she'd be making another movie with "The King."

If only she knew of the tragedy looming.

Chapter Nine

How Many Affairs?
Can a Married Woman Have?

Hot Sex but Cold Love

During its planning stages, Louis B. Mayer called *Somewhere I'll Find You,* starring Clark Gable and Lana Turner, as "money in the bank." Released after the Japanese attack on Pearl Harbor, it was a big hit at the box office, as America faced its darkest year of the war, with much of its Pacific fleet destroyed. Production was almost suspended when Gable's wife, Carole Lombard,died in an airplane crash, and her husband, the film's male lead, virtually collapsed in grief.

After the film was wrapped, Gable delivered Lana a kiss on the cheek. "Someday, we may meet again...perhaps." As she remembered later, "He had this sense of his own impending doom."

In mourning for his dead wife, and perhaps in the throes of a major midlife crisis, Gable left Hollywood, enlisting in the Air Force, where he progressed through the ranks and was appointed First Lieutenant. By 1943, he was serving in England with the 351st Bomb Group. There, he was promoted to the rank of Captain. He flew combat missions and was eventually awarded an Air Medal and Distinguished Flying Cross. At the time of his discharge from active duty in June of 1944, he'd achieved the rank of Major.

One newspaper reporter nailed it: "Clark Gable is to Lana Turner as flint is to steel."

He was speaking of the recasting of the romantic team who had electrified *Honky Tonk*, Gable and Turner. He was also referring to what was then being discussed as their upcoming release, *Red Light*, a film that was later reconfigured, retitled, and released in 1942 as *Somewhere I'll Find You*.

Louis B. Mayer assigned Wesley Ruggles to direct it, knowing what a veteran he was. Ruggles had broken into silent films in 1915, when he was an actor working on occasion with Charlie Chaplin. Before Talkies, he made 50 forgettable films, most of which are lost to history. His best work was *The Age of Innocence (1924)*, based on the Edith Wharton novel. His first acclaim came when he directed *Cimarron* (1931). The Edna Ferber novel was the first Western to win an Oscar.

Ruggles had directed Gable before in the light comedy, *No Man of Her Own* (1932), co-starring his future wife, Carole Lombard. A year later, he helmed Mae West and Cary Grant in *I'm No Angel* (1933).

In *Somewhere I'll Find You,* both Lana (as Paula Lane) and Gable (as Jonny Davis) were cast as war correspondents. The plot was based on a magazine series that had run in *Cosmopolitan*. Marguerite Roberts had written the film scenario, which was filled with sexual innuendo.

The movie would be Gable's last before he enlisted in the Army Air Force during World War II. His absence from the screen lasted for three years.

Cast as Jonny's brother, Robert Sterling was Kirk Davis, who is in love with the character played by Lana. Jealous rivalries arise when Jonny begins pursuing Paula too.

Somewhere I'll Find You was one of the first pictures to use the December 7, 1941 Japanese attack on Pearl Harbor as part of a movie plot.

When Lana, as a war correspondent, is sent to the Pacific theater, she disappears, and both Sterling and Gable go in search of her. She's located in the Philippines on the eve of its Japanese invasion, rescuing children from the battlefield and taking them to safety. The action ends up in war-torn Bataan.

The script called for Gable to get the girl in the final reel, and as a plot device, Sterling's character dies in action. The film closes as Lana and Gable are pounding away at their respective typewriters, filing correspondence from the battlefield, ending their dispatches with, "MORE TO COME."

Successful at the box office, the film was released during the darkest days for America in World War II, when the outcome of the war was uncertain.

***

Before facing the cameras again, Lana had continued with her excessive night-clubbing and wartime dating, becoming a regular at the Hollywood Canteen. Her pattern of seductions led to inevitable disagreements with Mildred. They occupied the same house, but Mildred had been assigned (or banished) to her own wing, and Lana barred her from her part of the house at night.

Almost on a daily basis, Mildred confronted her errant daughter, and their quarreling grew bitter. "You seem to bring home a different man every night," Mildred scolded. "You'll soon be known as the Whore of Babylon."

She also objected to Lana's heavy drinking. "Well, lemonade, mother dear, does not quench my thirst." The tension between mother and daughter grew so tangible that Lana eventually rented an apartment for her mother and moved her out.

After script conferences, Gable began to meet secretly with Lana, arousing the suspicions of his sharp-tongued wife, Carole Lombard, who suspected they had resumed the affair they'd indulged in during their time co-starring together in *Honky Tonk.*

During one of their arguments, Gable was said to have informed Lombard, "If my affairs outside the house mean nothing to *me*, why should they bother *you*?"

Robert Taylor, Lana's most recent lover and one of Gable's best friends, said, "She is a very special lady. I knew Clark was nuts about her, but I knew he'd never divorce Carole to marry Lana. Clark just couldn't help himself. He was a serial seducer."

Ruggles agreed with Taylor. "I think Clark was falling in love with Lana. She was young and pretty, and he felt he was getting old. For a while, Lana seemed to give him a sense of renewal of his youth. He told me, 'My old virility has returned.'"

Filming on *Somewhere I'll Find You* began in mid-January of 1942. Reporting to work on the first day, Lana met each member of

The story of two brothers falling in love with the same woman had long been a theme in drama. In *Somewhere I'll Find You*, Robert Sterling (left) and Clark Gable appear as foreign corespondents, Kirk (Sterling) and Jonny. This publicity still reveals who's going to get Lana in the final reel.

the cast and graciously welcomed them to the picture. Gable did not show up that morning.

The leading hairdresser at MGM at the time was a Londoner, Sydney Guilaroff. During his long career, he would dress the hair of stars in some 2,000 movies. Joan Crawford had insisted on him for almost every picture she'd been in.

For *Somewhere I'll Find You,* Guilaroff and Lana decided to "crown" her with a shorter hairstyle, a perky, more manageable cut which became known as "The Victory Bob." MGM announced that Lana's new hairstyle was better (and less hazardous) for women working in munitions plants, soon, "The Victory Bob" swept through America, and the style was even adopted by women working in factories in war-mangled Britain.

[Their decision to shorten Lana's hair had been influenced by the government's request during the early months of the war that Veronica Lake get rid of her peek-a-boo hairdo. In imitation of her hair style, many women working in the war plants were getting their long hair caught, sometimes with disastrous results, in machinery.]

In the movie, Kirk (that is, Robert Sterling) becomes part of a detachment under the command of Lt. Wade Hall (as played by Van Johnson). Their duty is to repel a Japanese amphibious landing. Johnson, a red-haired, freckle-faced, and somewhat naïve Rhode Islander, was new to films, and he and Lana bonded from the beginning of filming.

Johnson would later emerge as one of the biggest stars at MGM in the late 1940s. Eventually, he would co-star with Lana in *Week-End at the Waldorf* (1945).

Somewhere I'll Find You was a milestone in Johnson's life. It was there that he met and fell in love with character actor Keenan Wynn, who also, as his Hollywood debut, made an uncredited appearance in it.

In sophisticated ways that evoked such actresses as Joan Crawford and Carole Lombard, Lana was one of the most indulgent actresses in Hollywood regarding homosexuals. Lana and Johnson became confidants, exchanging gossipy tidbits about their respective male lovers.

He told her, "The moment I walked through the gates of MGM, I felt I'd arrived at my new home. I'm terrified having to do a scene with Clark Gable. As a star-struck teenager, I used to write him fan letters…well, they were really love letters. I'm terrified to have to play a scene with him, since I still have this big crush on Rhett Butler. I saw *Gone With the Wind (1939)* four times."

***

Shortly after the U.S. entry into World War II, Henry Morgenthau, the Secretary of the Treasury, assigned Howard Dietz, the Hollywood publicist, the task of promoting the sale of war bonds. To this end, it was understood that he'd enroll movie stars and other entertainers as a promotional tool.

With that in mind, in advance of a major bond rally in Indiana, Dietz had invited Carole Lombard to appear. At the time, she was the most celebrated Hoosier in the world.

He advised her to travel by train, thereby avoiding the risk of an overcrowded plane, most of which had been overbooked by the military anyway.

Lombard pleaded with Gable to go with her, but Louis B. Mayer, preoccupied with the production of *Somewhere I'll Find You*, refused to grant him leave.

On the day of her scheduled departure, Gable and Lombard had one of their most violent confrontations. She'd accused him of resuming his affair with "that blonde whore," an unkind reference to Lana.

"So what?" he'd shouted at her. "Maybe I want some young pussy for a change." Then he'd stormed out the door, never to see her again.

He'd be gone all day, meeting with military brass who wanted him in the U.S. Air Force, promoted immediately to officer status. Gable rejected their offer. "Thanks, but no thanks. I want to be a regular enlisted man, an average Joe, without any officer stripes."

Later that day, in lieu of returning to the home he shared with Lombard for the night, he remained at Lana's throughout the evening and night, departing from her house early the next morning and heading directly with her for MGM.

Soon after their wedding, newlyweds Clark Gable and Carole Lombard continued their bonding as part of Hollywood's most publicized romances.

Sterling recalled what Gable had done that day. He'd gone to the special effects department at MGM with an order that shocked the staff.

At around 6PM, he knocked on Sterling's dressing room door. "Come on, Junior," he said. "I want you to help me get this dummy into my car."

Sterling was flabbergasted to see a rubber dummy that resembled Gable except for its erect twelve-inch penis. [*When she'd been drunk at parties, Lombard had continually told her friends, "I love Pa, except for his less than average prick."*]

Sterling later informed his friends, "The dummy was amusingly vulgar. I helped him put this sex toy into his car, and he drove off. We were careful not to endanger the erect penis and those grapefruit-sized balls. When Carole returned, she would be in for a big surprise. Clark told me, 'I just wish I had what that god damn dummy has. But with what god gave me, I've fucked every hot broad at MGM from Jean Harlow to Loretta Young.'"

After great difficulty, because of the war, Lombard finally reached Gable via telephone. "Ma & Pa," as they called each other, made up. Once again, Gable denied that he was having an affair with Lana, lying to Lombard by maintaining that it was Sterling whom Lana had fallen in love with, and that they were having a torrid affair.

In Indiana, the war bond rally was a great success, and Lombard was proud to learn that she had sold $2 million worth of bonds. Her mother, Elizabeth Peters, was with her at the time.

Carole told her mother that she wanted to rush back to Hollywood as a means of ending her husband's affair with Lana. Even though he'd denied it, Lombard had continued to surmise *[with uncanny accuracy]* that Gable was spending every night in Lana's arms.

Ignoring previous advice, Lombard decided to fly back to Los Angeles, taking her mother and MGM's publicist, Otto Winkler, back with her.

The doomed flight left Indiana, heading west for a refueling stop in Albuquerque, New Mexico. It was here that military personnel asked Lombard and her two guests to relinquish their seats aboard the plane to make room for servicemen. *[This was common practice during the war.]*

Lombard, however, manically applied a high-octane acceleration of her star power. She insisted that she'd just "scored a killing in Indiana, $2 million in war bonds. I think we've earned our seats." Eventually, she won, and, with her entourage, she remained aboard the plane.

Flying out of New Mexico, Transcontinental & Western Airlines DC-3, designated as Flight 3, set itself on a course to Las Vegas.

Flight 3 landed at Las Vegas for another refueling before flying out *en route* to Burbank. On board were Carole Lombard, her mother, Winkler, and 19 other passengers.

It took off at 7:07PM, Pacific Time, on its last flight.

Twenty minutes later, the plane crashed into the arid, rocky side of Potosi Mountain, one of the six high points surrounding Las Vegas, about 30 miles west of the city. Its wreckage was scattered, and the bodies of the victims were buried in waist-high snow. Lombard's body, it was later discovered, had been decapitated and then ignited in flames after the plane hit the steep incline of the mountain. Everyone aboard was killed.

The ten-month-old plane had been piloted by Wayne Williams, at the time, one of TWA's most experienced pilots.

In his book, *Fireball*, Robert Matzen, a former contractor for NASA, convincingly argues that the plane crashed because of a combination of factors. "A slightly erroneous flight plan, a blackout of a warning beacon because of wartime restrictions, and the pilot's vision being obscured by cockpit lights at a critical

Lovely, foul-mouthed Carole Lombard. The blonde star was known in Hollywood as "The Queen of Screwball."

After a successful war bond tour, she lost her life in an airplane crash, becoming the first movie star victim of World War II.

208

juncture during a black night."

Matzen writes, "Clark only learned how important fidelity was in his relationship with Lombard when it was too late. She kept trying to get through to him, including in that final flight. Then she did get through to him and proved how important this marriage was to both of them by dying in an effort to rush home to save it."

From his base in Burbank, Howard Strickling, head of publicity at MGM, had assembled fifty photographers and reporters at Burbank for the arrival of Lombard's plane. Expected arrival time was 8:45PM. But in Nevada, miners working a remote hillsite west of Las Vegas reported a bright orange flash near the summer of Mount Potosi. The plane had flown seven miles off course and on a trajectory that was 750 feet below the summit of the mountain.

Strickling was the first to hear the news. He chose not to call Gable, but notified Louis B. Mayer and his publicity assistant, Eddie Mannix, instead.

He finally phoned Gable, but didn't tell him what he already knew: That Lombard and everyone aboard had died. Aboard a hastily summoned charter flight, Strickling, with Mannix and Gable, flew to Las Vegas.

Mannix's telegram was flashed, sometimes as a newspaper headline, around the country: "NO SURVIVORS. ALL KILLED INSTANTLY."

Buster Collier, a close friend of Gable's, later reported how "The King" received the news of Lombard's death: "He put on the greatest act of his life, trying to keep everyone else from crumbling. He saw this old-time cowboy trying to eat a steak with no teeth. He gave him a hundred-dollar bill, 'Get some teeth, cowpoke,' he ordered the stunned man."

Returning to Los Angeles by train, Gable accompanied Lombard's body back to her final resting place, along with the corpses of his mother-in-law and Winkler.

Sympathy notes from around the world, everyone from Franklin D. Roosevelt to the King of England, flooded into MGM. Gable was inconsolable.

Immediately, word spread that Lana had been the incentive for Lombard's rush back to Burbank aboard what had evolved into a fatal flight.

According to Ruggles, "Lana came to me in tears. She feared rumors would harm her career. She didn't know what to do."

"I knew that Robert Stack had been screwing Lombard," Ruggles continued. "So I advised Lana to throw off the bloodhounds by being seen constantly with Stack. I told her,

Lombard has always been cited for her ability to charm, way beyond her glamour. Shown here, with Gable, chewing watermelon, she proves she's just a Hoosier farm girl.

'Go everywhere with him. Spend the night with him. Don't hide your affair! Make it public!"

From Stack, Lana learned that Lombard, in an attempt at revenge against her philandering husband, had also sustained an affair with Stack. She'd even arranged a role for him in her latest film, *To Be or Not To Be* (1942), co-starring Jack Benny.

As Manzen wrote in *Fireball*, "By no coincidence, the presence of Stack—handsome as the devil—served as a constant reminder to Clark about how it felt to watch your spouse in close quarters with a younger and very attractive co-star for days on end."

Lombard and her mother, Elizabeth Peters, were buried at 4PM on January 21, 1942 in Forest Lawn's Hilltop Church of the Recessional. Gable, wearing very dark sunglasses, conversed with no one and left after the service, disappearing into the back of a limousine that quickly hauled him away.

After the funeral, Gable spent almost every night at the home of his longtime lover, Joan Crawford. She later described his condition to friends such as Barbara Stanwyck and William Haines. "He would come over and break down and cry. I'd never seen him cry before. He would drink almost a quart of booze before dinner, and then eat only enough to keep himself alive."

Crawford admitted that after two weeks of this, he turned to her for sex. "I tried to lure him away from the bedroom, because he'd be drunk and it offered little satisfaction for me. On at least three occasions, he called me Carole. It was an awful experience, but because I had always loved him, I endured this ghoulish form of sex."

"After every night he spent at my house, Clark would send me a dozen long-stemmed roses the next day," she said. "For about four months after Carole died, Clark would stop in at my house every day, if only for a quick drink. He wasn't the gay romantic I'd known in the 1930s when we made films together. He was no longer the easy-going Clark. He'd turned into a moody alcoholic who needed my love, support, and friendship more than he needed any hanky-panky. Unlike Miss Turner, I was there for him. She was there for half the men in Hollywood, especially those in uniform."

Shortly before her death, Lombard had signed to star in *They All Kissed the Bride* for Columbia Pictures, on a loan-out from MGM. In the aftermath of that plane crash, Crawford stepped in and agreed to star in the picture, donating all of her $125,000 salary to the American Red Cross.

***

After only three days of shooting, production on *Somewhere I'll Find You* ground to a slow pace, as only scenes without Gable could be shot. When Lana and their director, Ruggles, visited Gable at his home, they found him too drunk to appear on camera. He had to have more time to mourn the loss of Lombard before facing the cameras again.

Mayer tried to keep Gable from enlisting in the Air Force. He even went so far as to announce an upcoming film in which he'd star, *Shadow of the Wing*. To lure him, he claimed that Victor Fleming, who had directed Gable as Rhett Butler, would sign on as his director once again. But Gable turned the mogul down.

Word reached Lana that *Somewhere I'll Find You* might even be shut down because Gable was such an emotional wreck he might not be able to perform. Since so little footage had been shot, MGM could suffer the loss without too many financial difficulties. It was also suggested that Walter Pidgeon might replace Gable as the romantic lead.

But then, as a point of honor and as a dedicated professional, Gable announced that he would continue filming and finish the movie.

Before he reported back to the studio, Mayer summoned Lana into his office. "When he comes back, it will be very trying for Clark. Be patient with him if he flubs every line or two. If he wants to work right through lunch, go for it. If he wants to have dinner with you at his ranch, accept his invitation and do what you can to comfort him." Then he stared at her. "WITHIN REASON!"

When Gable reported to work, Lana found that he looked pale and—other than an aggravated weariness—showed almost no emotion. "It was like a part of Clark had died with Lombard," Lana said. "In many ways, he was a stranger to me. Some of the workers were afraid to go near him. I tried to offer what sympathy I could, but he didn't want to hear it. He was filled with this inner tension I felt would burst out at any minute."

"Before Lombard's death, he had this wonderful boyishness to him. But before filming of *Somewhere I'll Find You* ended, I knew that the boy in Clark had died along with his wife."

"Clark was inconsolable throughout the rest of the shoot," Lana said. "I feared he would not be able to complete the picture. He told me that it was all he could do to get out of bed and put one foot in front of the other. He was filled with rage and suffered from guilt. He was tortured over having argued with Lombard about me the last time he saw her."

"He became an aimless wanderer," she said. "I heard he drove up the West Coast toward Canada all by himself," she said. "He even bought a motorcycle and rode it at night, tearing up into the canyons."

Gable did invite Lana out for dinner one night. She later told Ruggles, "There was no talk of Lombard. We spoke about the picture, the war, his upcoming enlistment. There were long periods of silence."

"He showed me his gun collection. I always respected him, since he was the consummate professional and deserved

Even during the peak of her bad-girl rivalry with Lombard, Lana still managed to steal magazine publicity from her and every other actress in La-La Land.

to be called 'The King.' I just knew he'd pull himself together. I left early and was taken home in a studio limousine. I found Robert (Stack) asleep on my sofa."

At one point, Gable asked Lana if she would fill in for a live performance, broadcast over the radio that Lombard had committed herself to: a radio adaptation of *Mr. and Mrs. Smith*, a movie, released in 1941, that Lombard had made with Robert Montgomery. Lana accepted, with delight. Errol Flynn would be her radio co-star.

After the broadcast, she invited Flynn to spend the night with her. "But not at *your* house," she told him. "Not with Bruce Cabot or David Niven watching us."

***

When Lana heard that Gable was back in Hollywood, she thought he might call her, but he didn't. Their reunion lay in the future, when they'd once again co-star in the aptly named *Homecoming* (1948).]

Gable later claimed, "I did not read the reviews of *Somewhere I'll Find You*."

But Lana did, interpreting her second picture with "The King" as a career milestone.

Photoplay praised the performances of both Gable and Sterling, adding, "Lana Turner, the beautiful corner of the triangle, looks too beautiful and continues to amaze with her seasoned performance."

Newsweek wrote, "Miss Turner stamps her part with passionate intensity and that unsmiling conviction which set her love scenes and dramatic high levels apart from those of any other screen actress."

Writing in the *New Yorker*, critic John Mosher claimed, "The sensuous tug and talk between Gable and Miss Turner is powerfully dramatic, and is counterbalanced with serious things, including life-and-death matters."

After hailing Gable's performance, the critic for *Time* wrote: "Lana Turner is superbly toothsome for Gable's masterful routines. She can tilt her chin that, in any posture, suggests that she is looking up from a pillow."

Variety hailed Lana as "the modern Jean Harlow of celluloid—a sexy, torchy, clinging blonde who shatters the inhibitions of the staidest male."

***

After *Somewhere I'll Find You* was completed, Lana learned that MGM had no immediate plans for her next picture.

She went on another bond tour, riding the train to San Francisco, then continuing northward for war bond rallies in Portland, Seattle, Spokane, and Tacoma.

Returning to Brentwood, she was clearly bored and restless. Many of her beaux had already been snared by Uncle Sam and shipped off to war. For a while, she quit visiting the Hollywood Canteen altogether.

Late one afternoon, Johnny Meyer called. She immediately recognized his voice and braced herself for a solicitation of another date with Howard Hughes. But that wasn't the case. Instead, he invited her for dinner at Mocambo's with three of his business associates.

At table with them a few nights later, their talk bored her. All of them seemed to work for Hughes, who was having trouble with wartime Washington about airplane production. She couldn't have cared less.

But as the band started up for the next dance, a handsome young man appeared at Meyer's table. He ignored Meyer and the other male guests and instead, he focused intensely on her. "Hi, I'm Steve Crane, and my greatest dream in life would be to dance with the forever gorgeous Miss Lana Turner."

"You're on, buster," she said, rising to her feet. She was swept onto the dance floor, where they encountered Marilyn Maxwell with Frank Sinatra. Crane held her close, pressing his body intimately into hers. "I think he wanted me to get a feel of him, and I did," she later told Linda Darnell. "He was terrific, and did he ever smell nice."

She never returned to Meyer's table, but took a seat at the bar, where Crane stood close by her side. She learned that his full name was Joseph Stephen Crane III. *[Lana spelled it "Stephan" in her memoirs.]*

He was vague about who he really was, but appeared to be some tobacco heir from Indiana, who had arrived in Hollywood to try his luck. To judge by his tailor-made suit, he appeared to be well off, although he had some vague dream of becoming an actor.

After slipping out of Mocambo's together, he drove her home, where she sat talking with him until 3AM. Since it was Saturday morning, and she hadn't been needed at the studio in weeks, she didn't mind the late hour. He made no move to leave. Finally, she stood up, announcing that both of them had better get some sleep.

As she later told Darnell, "He kissed me passionately and slowly, ever so skillfully, and guided me into the bedroom. He even helped me out of my clothes before removing every stitch of his own. He was charming and ever so skilled as a lovemaker. So adorable and gifted by nature in all the right places. I could tell from his seduction that I was not his first woman."

[In Hollywood, Crane had just had an affair with the French actress, Simone Simon. There was a certain irony here. During the most heated weeks of her romance with attorney Greg Bautzer, he had put Lana on freeze while he, too, had run away with Simon.]

For the next three weeks, Crane began to date Lana intensely, al-

"One night across a crowded room, I met a handsome stranger (Stephen Crane)," Lana said. "But why did I fall in love with him and marry him, depriving Joan Crawford of his studly duties?"

though he'd sometimes disappear for several hours, not telling her where he'd been other than that he had some business to attend to.

It was only months later that Bautzer told her that when Crane had met her, he was having an affair with Joan Crawford—that is, when Crawford wasn't occupied with Bautzer himself, or else with Phillip Terry, an actor whom RKO billed as "a combination of Clark Gable and Cary Grant."

[Crawford had married Terry in July of 1942.]

Through his link to Bugsy Siegel, Louis B. Mayer had become aware, almost from the beginning, of Lana's emotional involvement with Crane. Consequently, Mayer called her into his office at MGM and warned her to drop him, hinting that Crane had underworld connections.

According to Lana, "I didn't listen to Mayer because I was already falling in love with Stephen. At the time I met him, he was just coming down from an affair with that Norwegian ice skater. What is her name now? Oh, yes, Sonja Henie. I don't go to her silly movies."

On July 17, 1942, Crane arrived with a dozen roses and an engagement ring. "I want to marry you. Elope with me to Las Vegas. We can't get a conventional flight because everything is booked by the Army. So I've chartered a plane."

[Two weeks later, Lana got the round-trip bill for the private airplane he had chartered.]

I'll need a maid of honor," she said.

"That means you'll accept?" Then he grinned, grabbed her, and kissed her passionately.

Within the next thirty minutes, she was on the phone to Linda Darnell. "Drop everything! I want you to fly to Las Vegas at eight tonight with Stephen and me. We're eloping. The press doesn't know."

That appealed to the romantic in Darnell, who telephoned her boyfriend, Alan Gordon, a Hollywood publicist. Even though he had never met him before, he agreed to fly with them, even to serve as Crane's best man,

En route to Las Vegas, Lana sat in the airplane's front row seats with Darnell, pinning pink orchids on themselves. Crane and Gordon chatted amicably in the seats behind them. Lana whispered to Darnell, "I'm the happiest I've ever been in my life."

A tale that morphed into a legend was generated by the elopement. Lana was said to have been married by the same justice of the peace who had presided over her marriage to Artie Shaw. She was alleged to have told him, "Judge, this time tie the knot a little tighter."

She later denied that story as "a press agent's invention. It was a different justice of the peace."

After a late dinner in Las Vegas, the party of four flew back to Los Angeles. After their plane landed, Crane drove them to Brentwood in his Lincoln coupé. The moment they walked into her home on McCullough Drive, they were greeted by guests who included Judy Garland and David Rose, Ann Rutherford, Bonita Granville, Frank Sinatra, Marilyn Maxwell, Susan Hayward, and Robert Sterling. Mildred had arranged a champagne brunch for the newlyweds.

"Stephen possessed charm by the bundle," Lana told Susan Hayward. "He's so debonair. He says he's from a small town in Indiana, but he has such poise and grace that he's almost like an American version of Jean-Pierre Aumont, Hollywood's favorite Frenchman."

After the first three nights in a row that Crane spent in Lana's bed, she heard from Darnell, who asked her, "How's it going, you old married lady?"

"I'm heels-over-chin, pinwheels-on-fire-in-love," she answered.

"What a quaint way of phrasing it," Darnell said.

When Lana first spoke to the press after her elopement, she said, "I'm lonely unless I have someone to love. Along came Mr. Crane."

***

The first weeks of summer, 1942 were among the most idyllic of Lana's life. As she told her girlfriends, "I'm blissfully happy. Stephen is a great lover. But there may be problems in the future. We've agreed to share household expenses, but so far, I haven't received any contribution from him. He doesn't have a regular job, but seems to have plenty of money to spend. Maybe it's from his tobacco inheritance."

Finally, six weeks into the marriage, she came face to face with the source of Crane's finances: There was an unexpected knock on her door. When Lana answered it herself, she encountered Virginia ("Sugar") Hill, the girlfriend of the notorious gangster, Bugsy Siegel.

Lana herself had had an affair with the Mafia Don, and she feared that Hill had arrived to confront her, based on this indiscretion.

Hill did not introduce herself, but Lana knew who she was, having seen her pictures in the paper. "Is Mr. Crane at home?" she asked in a voice frigid as ice. "I haven't heard from him in days, and I'm getting worried."

"No, he isn't," Lana answered. "But I'm Mrs. Crane. May I help you?"

"Can I come in? I'm not used to conducting my private business on doorsteps." Then, without waiting for an invitation, she barged into Lana's living room. There, she refused an offer of tea and didn't want to sit down. "I'll get right to the point. Your husband is my boyfriend…that is, whenever Bugsy isn't around."

"That can't be," a shocked Lana protested. "He's married to me!"

"Listen, sweet cheeks, who in the fuck do you think pays his bills? I finance the gigolo with money I get from Bugsy. I even paid for his plastic surgery."

"He's had plastic surgery? I wasn't aware of that."

"He's had his nose repaired, and been given a new chin, although that stuff is still in the experimental stage. In twenty years, when plastic surgery has been perfected, maybe you and me will be having it done to erase time."

Finally, Hill sat down for a girl-on-girl talk. Lana learned that Crane had arrived with his brother in Hollywood in 1933 to become an actor, but so far, no job had ever emerged. "Let's face it. He's charming but no Clark Gable. He even admitted to me that he's a lousy actor."

Six years older than Lana, Hill, in Alabama, never owned a pair of shoes until she was seventeen. After running away with a stranger, she'd arrived in Chicago, where her beauty soon got her initiated into her new and very profitable life as a gun moll.

One newspaper reporter in Chicago described the bosomy would-be actress: "She is more than just another set of curves. She has considerable flair for hole-in-the-corner diplomacy, enough to allay the suspicions of trigger-happy killers. She remains close-lipped about gangland slayings."

Years later, in Hollywood, after Crane met Siegel, the gangster had liked him a lot, even trusting him to escort Hill out on the town in both New York and in Chicago. "Be her escort, and nothing else, or I will personally cut off your balls," he had warned him.

With Siegel's money, Hill was known to spend anywhere from $3,000 to $7,000 a night at such clubs as the Mocambo or the Trocadero, ordering lots of champagne for her gangs of hangers-on.

In her living room that afternoon, Lana learned more about her husband during a brief chat with Hill than she'd ever heard from the man himself.

From the back roads of Alabama to the lavish boudoir of the trigger-happy gangster, Bugsy Siegel, Virginia ("Sugar") Hill arrived on Lana's doorstep to tell her that Stephen Crane was her "kept boy."

Overwhelmed with emotion and with information, Lana soon became eager to bring the confrontation to an end. "If you don't mind, I prefer to keep your visit a secret. Stephen will be back tonight. If he wants to phone you, that's entirely up to him. Now, may I show you to the door? It isn't necessary to call on me again."

An ominous feeling came over Lana after Hill left. She sensed that more trouble, perhaps lots of it, would be coming from this stranger she'd married. In contrast, Sugar Hill seemed like only a minor annoyance.

Darnell later speculated, "By the time of her confrontation with Hill, Lana had been around Hollywood long enough to learn how we play the game out here. Instead of facing Crane that night and behaving like a jealous wife, she must have done some calculation. Crane's screwing around gave her a license to make off with the next available guy who crossed her radar screen. She told me he could go off and have his fun, never telling her where he was. But she, at least, wasn't going to wait for him in the kitchen baking an apple pie for the bastard's return."

***

Lana's only major film release during that dreadful wartime year of 1943, when America's young men were dying by the thousands, was a fluffy little comedy for MGM

At first, it was *Lawless*, before its name was replaced with *Careless Cinderella*. Then, before it finally opened in 1943 in theaters across the country, it was retitled

Slightly Dangerous.

The director who cast her was Wesley Ruggles, who had just helmed Clark Gable and her in *Somewhere I'll Find You*. He came by her home to discuss the script.

Her first question was, "Who's my leading man? I hope he's someone as handsome as John Payne or George Montgomery." Her face did not conceal her disappointment when he told her it was Robert Young.

"Don't expect any hot love scenes like those I had with Bob Taylor and Clark. Young just doesn't inspire me."

"I admit that the movie is just a comic piece of fluff," he said. "But it could be a milestone in your career. For the first time, you'll have star billing—no more playing second fiddle to Spencer Tracy, Clark Gable, or Robert Taylor. You'll carry the film on your own box office power. Lana Turner billed over Robert Young."

Young didn't have the male beauty of some of Lana's former co-stars, but she was impressed with his output of films and with such leading ladies as Katharine Hepburn, Margaret Sullavan, Joan Crawford, Luise Rainer, Hedy Lamarr, Greer Garson—even Helen Twelvetrees.

Between 1931 and 1952, although Young would appear in some 100 films, he became a more widely recognized name after his debut on TV in *Father Knows Best*. Lana had several talks with him, finding him different from his screen *persona*. He was bitter about the way in which he had, throughout the course of his screen career, been cast.

"When producers can't get Gable or Taylor, or some other big star, they cast reliable ol' Bob, especially if the part has been rejected by the biggies."

Her lack of sexual chemistry with Young dated back to the 1938 release of *Rich Man, Poor Girl*, in which she had played a small role. Of the two leading men in that film, she had opted to pursue handsome Lew Ayres, husband at the time of Ginger Rogers

"I was never interested in Mr. Young. Nor did he ever show the slightest interest in me."

In *Slightly Dangerous*, Lana was given the lead role of Peggy Evans, who first appears as a brunette when she's a "soda jerk" at the luncheonette of a department store in the small town of Hotchkiss Falls, in the Hudson Valley of New York State. There, she tangles with Bob Stuart, her boss, as played by Young. She's frankly bored with her job and longs for a more glamorous life. She boasts that she can make a banana split with her eyes blind-

folded. Someone dares her, and she takes up the challenge and, with panache, succeeds.

The "Lana, blindfolded" scene involved many technical challenges. It was directed by Buster Keaton, a friend of Ruggles.

Keaton, of course, had been one of the most inventive comics of the silent screen before falling into the depths of alcoholism. She later claimed that the blindfold scene was the hardest in the film to shoot. "The bright lights kept melting the ice cream before I got it right. Buster was very patient with me."

The customers treat Lana's "blindfold act" as a charming conceit, and business increases as Lana perfectly executes her tasks, even with the handicap.

But Young, as the store's newly appointed general manager, is not amused. He calls her into his office and fires her, prompting her to run away from him and out of the store. It's instantly assumed by the other store employees that he had made sexual advances to her.

He, too, then loses his job, after Lana (as Peggy) writes what appears to be a suicide note and disappears.

Young, incentivized by wanting to bring her back to their small, gossipy town as a means of salvaging his reputation, will eventually track her down.

In Manhattan, Lana spends all her savings, $150, on a new wardrobe and a blonde dye job. As she is passing a newspaper office, an overhead maintenance man drops a bucket of red paint on her head.

Feigning amnesia, but in total control of her thoughts, she convinces the publisher of the local newspaper that she's the long-lost daughter of Cornelius Van Burden, an industrial mogul played by Walter Brennan. He's a veteran of many of John Wayne movie, and he becomes convinced that she is his long-lost daughter, Carol.

Young learns of Lana's whereabouts and follows her to Manhattan. Since it's a movie, the pair fall in love, and at this point, Brennan is so fond of Peggy that he doesn't care if she's his daughter or not.

Lana liked crusty, irascible Brennan, who usually played eccentric old-timers and had been nominated for Best Supporting Actor roles in 1936, 1938, and 1940.

Ruggles told the press, "Lana is the best replacement for the 'It Girl,' the label worn by Clara Bow in silent

Lana was "discovered" as a customer at a soda fountain.

Shown here in *Slightly Dangerous* with Robert Young, she reverses herself by actually playing a "soda jerk."

films." He had directed the flapper in *The Plastic Age* (1925).

For his supporting cast, Ruggles assembled a team of what were arguably the most talented character actors in the movies that year (1943).

These included Dame Mae Whitty, Eugene Palette, Alan Mowbray, Florence Bates, Millard Mitchell, Ray Collins, Ward Bond, and Kay Medford.

Since the picture had been made during the deprivations and rationings of World War II, Louis B. Mayer ordered his photographer, Eric Carpenter, to "take some of the hottest cheesecake pictures of Lana ever shot. I want her pictures to compete with Betty Grable and Rita Hayworth. Let our boys abroad know what they're fighting for!"

Lana was most cooperative, putting on her sexiest pout, moistening her lips, and sticking out her breasts. She wore revealing outfits that included a black sequined gown that became one of the most famous fashion statements of the war years.

Carpenter's pinup shots of her became some of the most popular of World War II. American troops carried them inside their uniforms during some of their bloodiest assaults against the Nazis and the Japanese.

In the *New York Daily Mirror,* Lee Mortimer pronounced *Slightly Dangerous* as "thin on plot but saved by Ruggles' directorial pacing and the talented supporting players' ability to overcome any plot handicaps. When they falter, Lana Turner's chassis does the rest."

Family Circle evaluated *Slightly Dangerous* like this: "This new builder-upper for its No. 1 glamor gal should do just that for both MGM and Lana, if slightly less for audiences in general. The picture affords cash customers an opportunity to view Lana in repose and in hysterics, in love and out, dark-haired and blonde, dressed and not dressed. Despite certain distractions, it must be conceded that the girl has the beginnings of the making of a trouper."

Viewed through the sexually sophisticated lens of today, *Slightly Dangerous* had at least one ironically humorous and memorable line: Young tells Lana, "I couldn't hate you, darling, not even if you turned out to be a female impersonator, and I bet my bottom dollar you're not."

When *Slightly Dangerous* opened in theaters, author Anita Loos wrote, "Lana Turner is the vamp of today as Theda Bara was of yesterday. She doesn't look like a vamp, however. She is far more deadly because she lets her audience relax."

***

In two other films released in 1943, Lana

made only brief cameo appearances.

In *The Youngest Profession*, she joined other A-list stars also making cameos, including Greer Garson, Walter Pidgeon, Robert Taylor, and William Powell.

The star of the picture was the young actress, Virginia Weidler. Born in 1927, and only sixteen the year the film was released, she'd been cast as a star-crazed autograph hunter.

Other cast members in *The Youngest Profession* included Edward Arnold (one of the most talented of the lot), plus John Carroll and Jean Porter.

On the first day Lana showed up to work, Carroll made a final attempt to rekindle something by visiting her dressing room. She turned him down.

Lana made yet another cameo appearance in *Du Barry Was a Lady* (1943),

starring Red Skelton, Lucille Ball, and Gene Kelly, along with Tommy Dorsey and his band.

In addition to Dorsey, singer Dick Haymes was another of Lana's former lovers cast in the movie, but because of her own brief involvement in that film, she did not encounter him. "If you blinked, you missed me," she said. "I think I was on the screen for only fifteen seconds, *but I looked lovely.*"

[For her cameo appearance, she wore a form-fitting white lace gown. It marked the first time she was presented in Technicolor.

As a footnote in Hollywood history, Ava Gardner, Lana's future best friend, appears uncredited in that film as a character designated as "Perfume Girl."]

***

Lana and Crane's marriage started to unravel after only five weeks of marriage. She sometimes ran into him on the threshold of her house at 5AM as he was returning home from a night of revelry, just as she was rushing off to work at MGM.

One afternoon, as Lana recalled, "The news hit me like a ton of bricks. I know that's a *cliché*, but a good one to describe how I felt."

It was a windy day in the Los Angeles area on that fateful day in November when Crane entered the dressing room of her Brentwood home. "I don't know where to begin," he said. "Our marriage was a big mistake...a big one."

"Is this your way of telling me you want a divorce?" she asked. "Who's your new girl?"

"It's not that. I was married before to a girl back in Indiana, a little brunette by the name of Carol Kurtz. We got a divorce, but I've just received a call from her.

220

She's read about our marriage. Trouble is, there's a technicality. I'm a bigamist. The one-year waiting period for our interlocutory divorce has two months to go."

She later revealed that she almost fainted. As she started to keel over, he caught her in his arms, but she revived and broke away, pounding on his chest.

"How could you do this to me? I can just see the headlines: "LANA TURNER MARRIES BIGAMIST."

Eventually, after a lot of rending of garments, Lana agreed to a tense meeting at Kurtz's apartment. It did not go well. At one point, Lana accused both Crane and Kurtz of collaborating in a blackmail scheme. Before the end of the afternoon, she agreed to give Kurtz a check for $5,000 if she'd keep quiet.

In defiance, however, the next day, Kurtz betrayed Lana and sold her story to the press. Despite her payment of $5,000, Lana was now confronted, publicly, with the embarrassing revelations.

It was reported in the press that, "During her marriage to Stephen Crane, Lana Turner has been living in sin, so the saying goes. According to California law, the marriage does not exist, since Crane was already married. Lawyers may disagree, but some legal sources claim that in such a circumstance, there is no need to annul a marriage that never existed in the first place."

Completely confused about what to do, Lana phoned Greg Bautzer and set up a meeting. The attorney advised her to kick Crane out of her home, change all the locks, and seek an immediate annulment.

Louis B. Mayer was furious, threatening to fire her for violating some of the morals clauses in her contract.

Around this time, she'd begun feeling nauseated most mornings, so she decided to visit her doctor. He confirmed her worst suspicion: She was pregnant. In her just-defined role as a co-bigamist in a now-illicit marriage, it meant that her hoped-for child would be born

During her brief cameo appearance in *Du Barry Was a Lady*, Luscious Lana made her Technicolor debut with Red Skelton, who would do about anything for a laugh.

Lana, looking luscious, in a publicity shot for *The Youngest Profession*.

Undoubtedly, one has heard of the oldest profession. But what is the youngest profession? According to the Lillian Day novel, it was the collecting of movie star autographs.

illegitimate.

On December 8, 1942, Lana announced that she was pregnant, telling Louella Parsons, "Both Stephen and I want a son."

Crane, as the father, spoke to the press. "I deeply regret the unhappiness brought about by these circumstances. It was all a misunderstanding on my part. There was no attempt to deceive. Miss Turner is an innocent suffering through a legal tangle, of which she had no prior knowledge."

On February 4, 1943, a red-eyed Lana, her eyes concealed by large, very dark sunglasses, appeared before Judge Roy B. Rhodes, who listened to her heartfelt predicament. After ten minutes of her testimony, he granted her an annulment and custody of "my unborn son," as she referred to her unborn baby.

Outside the courthouse, reporters mobbed her. Each of them asked the same question: "Do you plan to remarry Stephen Crane?"

In every instance, she refused to answer. Two security men hired for the day pushed a path through the crowd so that she could get inside a waiting limousine.

The news that blasted across America indulged in mostly speculative reporting, asserting that she'd remarry Crane, "if only to legitimatize her child."

When she reported to MGM, Mayer sent word for her to come to his office for another of his lectures. "I demand that you remarry the whore-mongering bastard. Since you locked him out of your house, I hear he's been fucking everybody from Virginia Hill to Susan Hayward and Joan Crawford, maybe with Ann Sheridan thrown in as a sideline."

Crane phoned her every day, urging her to remarry him so that he could become the father of their unborn child. "Remember, it is not just your child, but mine, too."

Despite his pleas, she continued to resist him.

Five days after her annulment, Lana collapsed onto the floor of her living room. Mildred, who'd been in the kitchen at the time, rushed in to discover her, and immediately phoned for an ambulance. On the way to the hospital, Lana drifted in and out of consciousness.

After an examination, doctors discovered that her white blood cell count "is so high you might die." They diagnosed her condition as "anemia in the extreme."

She was warned to have an immediate abortion as a means of preserving her own life. When she protested, her doctor said, "It is almost 99 percent certain that if you persist in giving birth, the baby will be a stillborn, and you may not survive childbirth."

Despite that, and despite the hysterical urgings of Mildred to abort the child, she refused to follow his advice.

Four nights later, after she'd delivered yet another rejection of remarriage, she was awakened at 2AM by the sound of a loud crash outside her bedroom window.

Before leaving his apartment, Crane had swallowed a bottle of barbiturates and then positioned himself behind the wheel of his Lincoln *coupé*. He'd perilously maneuvered the car to Brentwood, going along the cliff-fronting road almost directly uphill from Lana's house.

Suddenly, attempting suicide, he turned the wheel and steered it off the unfenced road. His Lincoln lunged forward, careening down the slope, stopping abruptly in the heavy underbrush that functioned like a big net to entrap his car. Hurled forward on impact, he was badly bruised, but without any broken bones.

In another incident, an emergency call came in from a nearby hospital, informing Lana that Crane had overdosed on sleeping pills as part of yet another attempted suicide. She rushed to his side, where she found him under supervision, guarded by nurses on a suicide watch.

Crane was finally allowed to return to Brentwood where, as Lana told Darnell, "He arrived with flowers and bushels of that old Crane magic. Even so, I refused to remarry him, although I did let him go to bed with me."

"I just don't feel I could go through another marriage ceremony. I didn't tell him the real reason: I had stopped loving him. The sex thing was still OK. It was hot sex but cold love."

A month after Crane was released from the hospital, he received his draft notice. Finally, for the sake of her unborn child not having a father, she agreed to drive to the seedy border town of Tijuana to marry him once again on March 15, 1943.

"I stood before this little man whose office sign read, 'Legal matters adjusted,'" Lana recalled. "Once again, I became Stephen's wife. He rounded up this Mexican on the street for a few pesos. He agreed to be our witness."

As a wedding gift, he brought home a two-month old lion cub as a house pet. She was stunned. "I've got a baby on the way. We can't have such a creature here. He'll grow up to look like the MGM lion."

She called security at MGM, and two men arrived that afternoon to take the lion cub away. She said, "I don't know what happened to it."

Crane reported to Fort MacArthur for a physical examination from an Army doctor. That night back in Brentwood, he complained to Lana about it. "The doctor was an obvious homosexual. He examined most of the guys and passed them on. Not so with me. He spent a lot of time juggling my balls and touched my dick several times. He was practically giving me an erection."

Because of an old knee energy, and perhaps a back ailment, Crane was accepted into the Army as a noncombatant: That meant he would not have to be shipped overseas. Since Fort MacArthur lay close to Los Angeles, he could drive home most evenings.

During his gig at Fort MacArthur, Crane, almost every night, brought home Army captains and lieutenants to show off Lana to them. "It really increased my standing at the base," he claimed.

He refused to wear the regular uniform, claiming that the rough material caused skin rashes. To deal with his needs, Lana ordered her dressmaker to design three new, custom-tailored uniforms for him in gabardine. "Stephen Crane was the best-dressed man in the U.S. Army," Lana said.

Because of a knee injury, Crane was never sent abroad and was discharged after only six months of service. Louis B. Mayer may have used his influence to get him relieved of his duties.

With medical bills mounting, and with Crane draining her resources, Lana was almost broke. She needed work, and eagerly accepted the first job offer. It paid $5,000, and involved her participation in a radio broadcast for the Philip Morris Playhouse for CBS on October 1, 1943.

It was a televised re-dramatization of the 1942 movie, *The Talk of the Town*, a film that had originally starred Cary Grant and Ronald Colman. Lana was to reprise the Jean Arthur role.

In advance of her performance, Crane and Lana headed by train for New York City. But he wanted to stop first at his hometown of Crawfordsville, Indiana. What he really wanted to do, other than to share a reunion with his mother and grandmother, was "to show off my blonde bombshell of a wife to my fellow Hoosiers."

After she arrived in Crawfordsville, at its railway station, Lana hired a local driver as their chauffeur. She fully expected to be taken to his ancestral home and to visit the tobacco factory to which he was an heir. Or so he had said.

She was terribly disappointed when the highlight of their stop turned out to be a dingy little cigar store attached to a rundown pool hall filled with shady characters. Then, the ancestral home turned out to be a modest, two-story frame house that looked like it hadn't been painted since its original construction in 1903. Mother and grandmother were pleasant and friendly, looking like local factory workers in faded patterned dresses made from feedsacks.

Back in his hometown, Crane—who was known as "Joe" by the locals, based on his first name, "Joseph"—began a routine of bringing locals back to their "ancestral home," to meet his beautiful movie star wife.

In desperation, she finally retreated upstairs to the bedroom that his mother had set aside for them.

***

During the seventh month of her pregnancy, she imminently feared either a miscarriage or a premature birth. She had painful contractions and was rushed once again to a hospital. She later wrote about spending an agonizing twelve hours on an examination table with a needle inserted into her spine. With fluid dripping into her, the pains eventually went away. Had they continued, her baby would have been born prematurely and stillborn, her doctor told her.

On July 24, 1943, Mildred and Lana went for a walk outside her home when suddenly her water broke. Clutching Lana, Mildred immediately returned to the house. Crane was at home at the time, and he hustled Lana into his car and, breaking speed limits, drove her to Hollywood Hospital.

She'd later tell Darnell that the next eighteen hours, as waves of pain kept shooting through her body, were the most horrific of her life. "I've never been stabbed, but it must be like I felt, getting stabbed and stabbed again without letup."

The doctor gave her a spinal anesthetic and waited for the baby to come out. Although she experienced great pain, she was still awake as it emerged. "It's a girl!" Lana heard the nurse say.

She later said, "The first thing I thought of was that Stephen and I had wanted a boy."

Cheryl Crane "was the most anemic baby I've ever seen," the doctor recalled. Amazingly, and true only in rare cases, the blood of the baby and the blood of its mother were not compatible.

Since the Hollywood Hospital was not adequately equipped to handle a case of erythroblastosis, the newborn was transferred to the Los Angeles Children's Hospital three blocks away.

Lana's Rh-negative blood was producing antibodies to destroy Cheryl's Rh-positive blood cells. As Lana later wrote, "I was killing my daughter even as I was struggling to give her life."

Blood transfusions were urgently needed, as it would be necessary to pump out every drop of Cheryl's blood and then replace and reinforce them with transfusions. Riddled with needles, the baby survived the ordeal. She had entered the world weighing seven pounds, four ounces.

Lana herself had to remain in the hospital for nine more days. Before leaving, she was allowed to hold her endangered infant—so fragile and delicate—in her arms. Cheryl's life remained in jeopardy. For two months, Cheryl hovered between life and death before she was appraised as healthy enough to join her mother in Brentwood.

For child care, Lana relied on the loving care of Mildred, whom Cheryl would later call "Gran," and the expert wisdom of Margaret MacDonald, an older but still vital Scottish woman.

After the birth of her baby, on the nights Crane was away, Lana began to date other men at private residences or in secluded, out-of-the-way places.

Meanwhile, Crane was stationed at nearby Fort MacArthur. She was already aware that on many nights, when he might have returned to Brentwood to join her, he did not. That alone, to some degree, seemed to justify her intimacies with other men.

***

As a Civil Rights activist, Lena Horne, a star of stage, music, and film, had already blazed a trail for other African American performers, having broken down racial barriers from the 1940s and 50s. Eventually, she rose to the top of her profession, as part of a life filled with triumphs and tragedies.

Lana had heard of a hole-in-the-wall *boîte* "The Little Troc," which had become the "in" place in Hollywood during the early 1940s. John Barrymore was a frequent visitor, arriving drunk. Marlene Dietrich for a while adopted the place as her nighttime rendezvous, sometimes appearing with her lover, Claudette Colbert.

When Lana read that Horne was performing there, she asked Stephen Crane to escort her there one night. As an example of

Lena Horne: "Think of me as a sepia version of Hedy Lamarr."

those quirky coincidences that were frequently swirling around her, she spotted her former husband, Artie Shaw, in the audience waiting for Horne's act to begin.

When he saw her, Shaw jumped to his feet, kissed Lana and shook Crane's hand, inviting them to sit at his table to watch the show.

Almost immediately, she sensed that her first husband was having an affair with the singer.

After the show, Shaw introduced Horne to Lana. Surprisingly, the two women didn't seem jealous of each other—in fact, they began a friendship that would last for years and in time become the subject of some nasty rumors.

"Hello, darling," Horne said, kissing Lana on the cheek.

Lana already knew that MGM had signed Horne to a contract. "I look exactly like every other gal at MGM, except I'm bronze," Horne said, in an ironic observation of her skin tone.

"I read in Elsa Maxwell's column that you're a honeypot for the bees, and it seems that Artie here agrees." Lana said.

"It's nothing serious," Horne said. "I've separated from my husband, Louis Jordan Jones, and Artie is a change of pace from Paul Robeson, Joe Louis, and Duke Ellington."

At the age of sixteen, Horne, from her base in Brooklyn, had joined the chorus of Harlem's Cotton Club. She'd made her film debut at MGM in *Panama Hattie* (1942), in which she'd performed her most memorable song, "Stormy Weather."

Later, when Crane and Shaw disappeared together into the alley to smoke marijuana, Horne said, "Girl, let's talk."

She then preceded to relay some insight into her affair with Shaw: "What I like most about him is that he understands the obstacles I face as a black entertainer. As you know, he took Billie Holiday out on the road, so he knows what I'm up against."

"The one thing about Artie is that he seems without prejudice," Lana said.

"I fell for him when I heard his recording of 'Star Dust,'" Horne said. "It was in June of 1941 at the Café Society in New York."

"It appears that many women find my former husband irresistible," Lana said. "Judy Garland among them. He's also literary, hanging out with Hemingway and his ilk."

Shaw later told Crane and others, "I'm trying to convince Lena that she is the most beautiful creature in the world, even more beautiful than Greer Garson, and, if I dare say so, more beautiful than Lana herself."

"Don't get THAT carried away," Crane cautioned.

[Decades later, at the age of 94, a curmudgeonly Shaw talked with a reporter about his long-ago affair with Horne. "She was quite pretty and a lot of the guys were after her, both white and black, Frank Sinatra among them. I liked her looks, so I went after her. After all, some men can like both vanilla and chocolate. Her singing was okay, not great. At least she could carry a tune."

"We did more than date. We fucked a lot. Our affair lasted for several months, and she was always pestering me to marry her. I warned her that such a marriage would destroy both of our careers."

"Lena was always protesting the white man's treatment of blacks," Shaw said. "She

screwed a few black guys, but I think she really went for the white men. If that sounds too racist, don't print it."]

One night when Crane had to (or chose to) overnight at Fort MacArthur, Lana arrived at the club with Virginia Grey. Horne introduced the actresses to her estranged husband, Louis Jordan Jones.

Horne later said, "Louis seemed enchanted by Lana, like she was the gal of his wildest dreams. I don't know what happened at the club that night. I know he left after the show with both Lana and Virginia."

It might have come as a shock to Lana's fans, but in James Gavin's definitive biography of Horn, entitled *Stormy Weather*, he reveals that Jones was a womanizer. Some of his movie star lovers included two blondes, both Sonja Henie, Crane's former girlfriend, and Lana herself.

Jones was considered a highly desirable "catch" on the night he disappeared with Lana after Grey had retreated to her home. He was twenty-eight years old, working as a press and publicity agent for the Cleveland Indians. He was quite handsome, a light-skinned mulatto with straightened hair parted and slicked back. He frequently appeared in well-tailored, double-breasted suits and had a reputation as a playboy.

"At the time I took up with him," Lana said to Grey, "I wasn't really getting back at Lena for screwing my former husband. I was actually getting back at Stephen, because I learned that he was still dropping in at Joan Crawford's house at least once a week."

Lana later told Grey at one point she discussed Jones with Horne.

"I found sex with him very dirty!" Horne said. "He's a god damn animal in bed."

"Lena, darling, you must realize that what you view as dirty, another woman might find thrilling. Just because a man likes to do everything in bed—and I mean *everything*—doesn't necessarily mean that it's dirty."

"That's why they print menus, Lana, darling," Horne replied.

Months later, when Lana encountered Horne, the singer told her the news. "Artie has dropped me and taken up with Jerome Kern's daughter. But don't feel sorry for me. I'm shacked up with Orson Welles. How about you, darling?"

"How much time do you have?" Lana said. "I'll tell you, but it'll take all night."

***

During her last and final war bond tour, Lana made a secretive, off-the-record stopover in New Orleans. She'd been invited to visit the city by two former lovers, Victor Mature and Errol Flynn, who had booked a suite there, and—as a team—invited her there as their date.

Before the war, both men had seduced her, separately, and she had enjoyed their company and their love-making.

After her "before-the-war" affair with Mature, she had lost touch with him. She was aware, however, that during their filming together of *My Gal Sal*, released in 1942, he'd begun a torrid affair with its co-star, Rita Hayworth.

Mature had originally wanted to enlist in the Navy, but was rejected because of his colorblindness, even though he insisted, "I can see red, white, and blue."

Finally, he ended up in the Coast Guard, patrolling the war-torn North Atlantic aboard the ship he'd been assigned, *Storis*.

By 1944, he'd been granted shore leave to star in the film version of the film version of the morale-boosting musical revue, *Tars & Stripes*, which—in addition to providing entertainment to sailors—had also been conceived as a recruitment campaign for the Coast Guard. As a film, it had opened in Miami in April of 1944, traveling through the States, playing at movie houses and old vaudeville theaters. During his time in New Orleans, Mature visited defense plants and shipyards.

Flynn, who was involved at the time with a war bond tour, was making some of the similar rounds when he ran into Mature. These two bisexuals had been sometimes lovers before the war, and Flynn invited Mature to share his hotel suite in New Orleans. The two handsome hunks didn't emerge from the suite for twenty-four hours.

The following day, they encountered a war-based lack of transportation, as most of the buses and what had been taxis had been commandeered into the war effort.

Fortuitously, immediately across the street from their hotel, they spotted a used car lot, where a battered taxicab was available for $600. Agreeing to split the cost between them, they bought it.

Just for fun, Flynn also acquired the uniform of a taxi driver, complete with hat. Then he and Mature drove through the wartime streets of New Orleans, picking up horny, sweaty servicemen and inviting them back to their hotel suite for an orgy.

Once in New Orleans, Lana was delighted to be reunited with Flynn and Mature, considering both of them among the most skilled of her lovers. Soon, she was riding around with them in their taxi, enjoying the sights, the jazz, and the cuisine of New Orleans, especially its gumbo dishes.

The Hollywood threesome, in the words of one restaurant owner, "consisted of the two handsomest men and the most beautiful woman ever to set foot in our fair town."

It was wartime, and shortages were prevalent, but restaurateurs always made exception for Lana, Mature, and Flynn, slipping them special treats.

During the short time Lana occupied a suite with Mature and Flynn, champagne was on hand every night. It was a time not just to make love, but to talk about all the changes the war would rapidly bring to

At the end of a war bond tour, Lana stopped off in New Orleans to share the beds of both Victor Mature and Errol Flynn (above).

"Why not?" she asked. "They're the two hottest men in California...or elsewhere."

Hollywood and on the type of films it would produce.

When the men stripped down, Lana, one of the great judges of the male physique, noted that Mature was in his body beautiful shape, whereas Flynn, because of his dissipation, had developed a slight paunch.

In the three days she spent with the two actors, Lana was brought up to date on what they'd been doing.

She also discussed her crumbling marriage to Stephen Crane and the difficulties she'd had during childbirth. "I don't think I'm cut out to be a wife and mother," she confessed. "Here I am carrying on with two of Hollywood's leading horndogs."

"And enjoying every minute of it," Flynn said. "Admit that it's true, ol' girl!"

"What red-blooded female would turn down an invitation for love in the morning, love in the afternoon, and love at night? You guys are sex machines!"

Flynn had just emerged from one of the worst ordeals of his life. Two under-aged girls, Betty Hansen and Peggy Satterlee, had hauled him into court on a charge of statutory rape. The tabloids had gone wild in tarnishing his reputation, creating a new term for the American vernacular: "In like Flynn."

Lana had been impressed with Flynn's defense by attorney Jerry Giesler, who had impugned the accuser's character and morals, a tactic that eventually led to the star's acquittal. Eventually, Lana would desperately need Geisler's services for herself.

Flynn's marriage to actress Lili Damita had ended in divorce in 1942. The following year, he'd married eighteen-year-old Nora Eddington, a worker at a cider stand.

Flynn had filmed *Northern Pursuit* (1943), directed by Raoul Walsh. He told

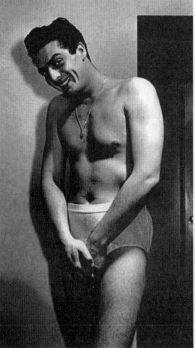

"Victor Mature almost invented the word 'beefcake,'" Lana said. "I'm not sure if I invented the word 'cheesecake,' but I'll take credit."

229

her of the many fights he'd had with his director. In the movie, he'd been cast as a Canadian Mountie with "links" to the Fatherland in Germany."

When Flynn was at the bar having a drink, Mature brought her up to speed on the gossip. Flynn's co-star, Helmut Dantine, a dashing young Austrian actor, had fled to California after the Nazi takeover of his country. As a Jew, he had escaped just in time.

When making *Edge of Darkness* in 1943, Flynn had made sexual advances to him. The handsome blonde actor had declined, claiming that he was "saving myself for Tyrone Power."

But with Power away at war, Flynn, according to Mature, finally succeeded in seducing Dantine during the making of *Northern Pursuit*. "If Flynn doesn't succeed the first time," Mature claimed, "he tries again and again until he gets his man. Of course, Flynn had Ty Power years ago. As for women, they stand in line for Robin Hood."

When Lana returned to California, she told Virginia Grey, "Millions of women dream of going to bed with Errol Flynn or Victor Mature. Imagine me, little Miss Lana Turner, going to bed with both of them at the same time! I don't want to make the gods jealous. They might punish me for having such luck."

"I loved my time in New Orleans with those guys," Lana said. "If I have one regret, it's that Errol got Ty Power, that living doll, before I do."

***

During the shooting of David O. Selznick's *Since You Went Away* (1944), Lana visited the set. That film was slated to become one of the most popular of the "Homefront Movies" of World War II.

Ostensibly, she was there to see her friend, actor Robert Walker, who had had bit parts in two of her previous films, *Dancing Co-Ed* and *These Glamour Girls*.

Directed by John Cromwell, *Since You Went Away* starred Claudette Colbert, Jennifer Jones, Shirley Temple, Joseph Cotten, Monty Woolley, and Hattie McDaniel.

Lana's former agent, Henry Willson, invited Lana to go with him to the studio. He had persuaded Selznick to cast Robert Moseley (later known as Guy Madison) into a brief role as a sailor.

Willson also introduced Lana to "Dare Harris," his latest discovery. Later, as John

The strikingly handsome Guy Madison had appeared in sailor whites, chatting with Robert Walker and Jennifer Jones, during a three-minute segment of *Since You Went Away* (1944).

When the David O. Selznick film was released, his appearance created a sensation. Selznick's office was flooded with fan mail from bobbysoxers across America.

Derek, he, like Madison, would become a matinee idol and the future husband of such beauties as Ursula Andress, Linda Evans, and Bo Derek.

Willson maintained, and Lana agreed, that Harris and Madison "would become celebrated as the most striking of the pretty boys of the 1940s...and beyond." This time, his prophecy came true.

The future John Derek seemed very impressed with Lana, telling her, "You're like a goddess to me. My favorite movie star. I have your picture hanging on my bedroom wall. The first thing I see in the morning, and the last thing I see at night."

Lana realized that Willson was already "dating" (some said "molesting") each of these handsome actors, but she wanted to continue her affair with Madison and to get to know Derek better. She was worried about Derek's age since, "He looks seventeen," she told Willson.

"He's only four years younger than you, my dear. He looks gorgeous with his clothes on and heavenly bare-assed."

"You should know," she said. "I always trust your judgment in these matters."

Originally, Willson had renamed Madison "Guy Dunhill," but later reconsidered his choice. Across from Selznick's studio was the Dolly Madison Bakery, named after the former First Lady. [*Serving in that capacity from 1809-1817, she actually spelled her name "Dolley."*]

Since [*Guy*] Madison was getting off work that day at 4PM, Lana invited him to drop in at her home, the interior of which he already knew well, with the understanding that later that evening, he'd be her escort at a party Willson was hosting.

He arrived with a passionate kiss. "Let's get re-acquainted. I haven't seen you in weeks."

Later that night, he took her to Willson's mostly male party. At around midnight, Madison told her he wouldn't be able to escort her home because Willson was demanding a "sleepover."

The next day, Willson phoned Lana: "YOU BITCH!" he said. "Guy told me you drained him dry before I got a chance at him. Thankfully, Frank [*Frank McCowan, later renamed "Rory Calhoun,"*] was in working order, so my night wasn't a complete waste. Frank is going to be a big star. I'll have to change his name, of course. He'll need some publicity, so I want him to date you and take you to all the places where photographers are waiting. Alan Ladd...how shall I put this?...has already discovered this handsome hunk of male flesh."

Willson eventually flew Madison to the New York premiere of *Since You Went Away*. He later told Lana, "He was a sensation. The bobbysoxers went after him like he was Frank Sinatra. Crowds followed us everywhere."

"I tipped off the press that we'd be arriving on Broadway by limousine to see Judy Holliday in *Born Yesterday* (1950). Screaming fans were waiting *en masse* for Guy. Before exiting from the limo, my hand, concealed with a blanket, made a grab for Guy's crotch. 'You're a star, baby, you're a star!' I told him."

Lana later said, "Henry took all the credit for making Guy a star, but I was the one who really discovered that incredible beauty at the Hollywood Canteen. If God had made me a boy instead of a girl, I would want to look like Guy."

During one of her visits to the set of *Since You Went Away*, Lana renewed her friendship with Robert Walker.

The director of the picture, Tay Garnett, joined them for lunch. He would later helm her in what is arguably her most famous picture, *The Postman Always Rings Twice* (1946).

That afternoon, as she was preparing to leave, she encountered David O. Selznick, who had, years before, rejected her screen test during try-outs for the role of Scarlett O'Hara in *Gone With the Wind* (1939). "Too bad, kid," he had said at the time. "You're just not the Southern belle type, growing magnolias out of your butt. But you'd be great as a *femme fatale* blonde in a film noir."

Thanks for your advice, Mr. Selznick," she said, passing on. Her revenge would eventually be exacted from Selznick, but not until years in her future.

Before exiting from the film set that day, she had invited Walker for a drink. A few days later, he'd been seated in her living room for less than thirty minutes when he confided to her what had been going on in his life:

His marriage to Jennifer Jones had come unglued. Selznick was pursuing her, and Walker suspected that the film mogul and his wife were already deep into an affair.

"Thank god for Peter Lawford," Walker said. "He's become my best friend. In fact, he told me the other night, he'd like to meet you. You're his favorite actress."

She would later report to Willson the mental anguish that Walker was enduring.

Walker had told her, "Everyone has problems, but I can't live with mine. God knows I can't compete with Selznick. He's one of the biggest producers in Hollywood, and Jennifer is very ambitious. She talks about him all the time. Considers him a genius. Is always bragging about the great things he's going to do for her career. For her, the sun rises and sets on David O. Selznick."

"What can I do? He has this obsession for my wife. He's a powerful man. He could cut me to pieces in a minute. I'd be finished in this town. Actually, I hate Hollywood. I've never felt com-

As Robert Wagner's marriage to Jennifer Jones was crumbling, he formed a bond with Lana, a relationship that would last until his untimely death.

Both of them found sympathy and comfort in their shared anxieties over the failure of their respective marriages. Unlike many of Walker's friends, Lana accepted his love affair with Peter Lawford and didn't judge him.

fortable here."

"What you can do," Lana advised, "is to fall in love with someone else. You're a good-looking boy. Many women could go for you."

"Is that an offer?" he asked, provocatively.

"Perhaps it's a proposal for an affair, but nothing really serious," she answered. "I'm getting rid of my second husband, and I don't want to be tied down anytime soon. After my last pregnancy, I'm also determined not to go through that kind of hell ever again."

Walker spend the night in Lana's bed. She would never rank him among the greatest of her lovers, but she agreed with Garnett when she later worked with him. The director told her, "Bob is a talented, sensitive guy who has a little boy lost quality about him that some find appealing—at least those who aren't attracted to the John Wayne type."

In the weeks and months ahead, Walker and Lana did not see much of each other, but they often talked on the phone. He shared frustrations from the set of *Since You Went Away*. One of them involved the fact that Selznick insisted that he shoot his love scenes with Jones over and over again, even though they were estranged, and on some days, belligerent with each other.

Lana felt that Walker was sinking deeper and deeper into alcoholism and mental illness, and she feared that he might be contemplating suicide.

Their lovemaking had ceased almost as soon as it had begun, yet she still maintained a friendship with him. Later, she learned that he was seducing Judy Garland on the set of a film in which both of them were co-starring, *The Clock* (1945).

***

Johnny Meyer phoned one night to extend to Lana an invitation from Howard Hughes, who had disappeared for almost a year. No one seemed to know where he was or where he'd been. Apparently, he had "resurfaced" in Idaho and wanted her to fly there for a few days of R&R.

She was tempted by his offer for her to return to the state of her birth, and she accepted. She was under a severe strain from her unraveling marriage, and wanted to escape from Hollywood.

After her big hits with Robert Taylor and Clark Gable, she had wanted to star in bigger and better films, but the scripts for the remainder of the war years seemed lack-

Smokin' Joe Petrali, the "King of Dirt," was a demon on his motorcycle and a demon in bed. Just ask Lana Turner, Ava Gardner, and Joan Crawford.

luster to her.

At 7AM the next morning, Meyer arrived at her house, finding her ready with suitcases fully packed with resort clothes. He drove her to the Burbank airport, where he introduced her to Hughes' favorite pilot, Joe Petrali, known to his friends as "Smokin' Joe." He did not have a pretty face, but was ruggedly masculine. Errol Flynn had defined his appearance as a "dime-store version of Humphrey Bogart."

Lana had never heard of him, but she would later learn that he was a legend among motorcycle racers. Between 1925 and 1937, he'd consistently been a champion, eventually establishing the world's motorcycle speed record, clocking one of them at a speed of 136.183MPH at Daytona Beach, Florida. You name the motorcycle venue—board track racing, hill climbs, speed records, dirt track—Petrali had been his era's champ, sometimes nicknamed (affectionately) as "The King of Dirt." Although his birth certificate had been lost in the 1906 earthquake, his contemporaries usually concluded that he was a year older than Hughes.

After Petrali's retirement from motorcycle racing, he became an airplane engineer. In 1947, he became a footnote in aviation history when he rode aboard Hughes' first and only takeoff of the legendary "Spruce Goose," with the entire world looking on.

[The H-4 Hercules, developed at staggering expense by Howard Hughes, was a prototype for a transatlantic "flying boat," conceived for military use during World War II. It was not completed in time to be used for heavy transport during the war.]

***

A few minutes after her arrival in Sun Valley, in an airplane piloted by Joe Petrali, Lana and her luggage were hauled by limousine to an elegant chalet, either rented or owned by Hughes. She expected that he would be there to greet her, but found that he had not yet arrived.

When she asked about it, Petrali told her, "I never ask questions about where Howard is or where he goes. Frankly, he seems to be showing more and more signs of paranoia. But how do I know—I'm not a psychologist."

She later told her girlfriends that Petrali, for such a rough, macho guy, was actually a spiffy dresser, and spent great amounts of time getting dressed. "As much as I do," she claimed.

For dinner at a local restaurant, at a table positioned near a blazing fireplace, he appeared in spit-shined dress shoes, an immaculate black and white sweater, and a hand-tailored shirt emblazoned with his initials, a gift from Hughes.

As she later claimed, "I think there was a lot more going on between Howard and Joe than I was aware of. In other words, I think he was more than Howard's pilot. After all, let's face it: The Aviator flies both ways."

Although she enjoyed the companionship of Petrali, who was devoted to outdoor activities, she was tempted to leave by the third day, as Hughes had still not arrived.

Then, one night, Petrali, who occupied the suite of rooms next to hers, entered her quarters fresh from his shower, clad only in a bath towel wrapped around his waist.

"Like the Walls of Jericho, that towel fell to the ground," she recalled. 'What can I say? Seeing is believing. I have known better-looking men, but never a powerhouse like Joe. He braced his hands on his thighs and stood before me for inspection. Without touching himself, his most prized possessions began to rise and rise, then rise some more."

"My stay in Sun Valley stretched out for more than a week. God made men and was pleased with his creation. He then decided to create his masterpiece. The end result was Smokin' Joe."

Years later, a rather drunken Lana, sitting with Merv Griffin in the bar of the Beverly Hills Hotel, spoke of Petrali when he was quizzing her about Hughes.

"After a while, I passed Smokin' Joe on to Ava Gardner, who was dating Howard at the time. She got to see a lot of Joe…I mean, *all* of him. When Ava moved on to her next dozen men, Joan Crawford heard about him and went after him. Usually, Joan beats me and Ava to the prize, but this time, she got sloppy seconds, or, in his case, fourth or fifths. Ava and I beat her to him, and I'm sure Howard beat all of us to Joe. After Crawford, or so I heard, Joe made the rounds of Hollywood beauties. I never knew if he were married or not. Why would I care about a thing like that?"

***

Almost as a parting gift before divorcing Crane, Lana used her connections to the movie industry to get film work for her husband. He kept pressing her to do something to get his career as an actor launched, even though he admitted that he had little talent. "As you, of all people know, I'm God's gift to women. I think I can project some of that male magic onto the screen."

Finally, a minor contract from Columbia came through. Lana told Ann Rutherford, "I almost had to promise to sleep with Harry Cohn to get Stephen work at Columbia."

Crane's first movie for the studio was the 1944 *Cry of the Werewolf*, alongside the Dutch-born Nina Foch cast as the lead. Sometimes released as *Daughter of the Werewolf*, the film cast Foch in the unlikely role of a Gypsy cursed by lycanthropy. She didn't look like a female Werewolf. When photographed from a certain angle, she resembled Marlene Dietrich.

Director Henry Levin was an eyewitness to the sexual chemistry between Stephen Crane and Nina Foch.

"I think part of Nina's reason for seduction is that she wanted to see what 'ladykiller' Steve Crane was like in bed. An added inducement was that he was Lana Turner's husband. I think Nina wanted to be Lana Turner."

Crane was cast as a scientist who discovered that his father has been killed by a werewolf.

Arriving from the Netherlands, Foch epitomized the cool, aloof, blonde sophisticate. She would not marry until 1954. At the time she met Crane, she had launched her film career in Hollywood with horror films such as *The Return of the Vampire* (1943).

Foch told Levin, "Lana is very cruel to Steve, marrying him, divorcing him, threatening not to remarry him—even after she got pregnant. She practically drove him to suicide after it was discovered that he was a bigamist. And as it was widely known, she sleeps with other beaux. He is a wonderful lover and smells so clean. Even on a hot day, it's like he just emerged from the shower. Frankly, I will marry Steve if his divorce comes through and he proposes."

The Crane/Foch romance lasted only until the end of the filming of *Werewolf*. As a Hollywood Romeo, "Steve went on to bigger game, namely Joan Crawford and Rita Hayworth," Levin said.

For his next film, a 1945 mystery, *The Crime Doctor's Courage*, Crane was reduced to seventh billing. Its star was Warner Baxter, an old-time actor born in Ohio in 1891. He was usually cast as a scowling leading man with a pencil-thin mustache. In 1926, he been assigned the title role in Hollywood's first attempt to bring the F. Scott Fitzgerald novel, *The Great Gatsby*, to the screen. That movie is now lost to history.

Baxter also played the hard-as-nails director in the 42nd *Street* (1933), in which he delivers that immortal line to dancer Ruby Keeler, "You're going out there as a youngster, but you've got to come back a star!"

Crane met Baxter as he was recovering from a nervous breakdown. He'd fallen on bad days as he'd aged, and was now reduced to roles in B pictures at Columbia. He'd go on to make nine *Crime Doctor* films.

Director George Sherman was not impressed with Crane's acting, and, although Baxter liked him, Crane wasn't offered a role in any of the other films within the series.

***

The most support for Crane's movie career derived from Mildred, not from Lana herself.

In her memoirs, Crane's daughter, Cheryl, wrote, "My grandmother had grown fretfully supportive of her son-in-law. She found his courtly manners irresistible, and she believed that he still offered some hope for stability in her daughter's madcap life. Gran was appalled that before mother's second marriage had been dissolved, she was always out at night with other men."

Some of those men over the course of the next few years were famous: Gregory Peck, Robert Mitchum, Robert Hutton, John Derek, Guy Madison, Victor Mature, Errol Flynn, John Hodiak, James Craig, Peter Lawford, Robert Walker, Turhan Bey, Rory Calhoun, and Tyrone Power.

Lana referred to some of the "regular guys" (i.e., non-movie stars) she dated, most often through encounters at the Hollywood Canteen, as "the nameless ones, the guys who went home after the war and settled down, often with their high school sweetheart. They sold insurance or else joined the baby boomer construction industry as plumbers or carpenters."

***

Eventually, Crane got cast in a small part at Columbia, in a film starring Rita Hayworth, *Tonight and Every Night,* released in 1944.

Victor Saville cast the musical which was set in wartime London, and loosely modeled on the Windmill Theatre in Soho (UK), which became legendary for not missing a single performance during the Nazi blitzkrieg of London.

Hayworth looked glamorous in Technicolor, playing an American showgirl who falls in love with an RAF pilot (Lee Bowman). Crane had a few lines as Leslie Wiggins, Bowman's best buddy in the RAF.

On the first day of work, Crane's manly charms met approval from lusty Shelley Winters, a future movie star. She had just filmed a bit part in Hayworth's *Cover Girl,* and had been cast in another minor role in *Tonight* as "Bubbles," a ditzy showgirl.

When Winters published her 1980 autobiography, *Shelley,* Crane was still alive. Perhaps she didn't want to embarrass him, since he was still married to Lana when Shelley seduced him. However, after his death in 1985, she became more outspoken.

"The first night Steve took me out, we went to Ciro's and then later dropped into his apartment," Winters claimed. "I knew we were going to make love, and I also knew that Lana was going to divorce him. So I figured, 'Why not?'"

"I was pretty experienced at this time," Winters continued. "I'd lost my virginity when I was fifteen. I'd used Southern Comfort and potato chips to seduce him."

"Over the course of many years, Lana and I would share many of the same guys: William Holden, Errol Flynn, Clark Gable, Sean Connery, John Garfield, Howard Hughes, Sterling Hayden, Anthony Quinn—you name 'em. I don't know if she ever fucked Marlon Brando. We both got plowed by Frank Sinatra—that was before he got pissed off at me and denounced me as a 'bowlegged bitch of a Brooklyn Blonde.'"

"Steve Crane was a real gentleman, very courtly and proficient in bed," Winters claimed. "His equipment was similar to that of Lancaster. Our affair wasn't really that. Call it a fling. It didn't last long."

"He soon discovered this shy little girl, very pretty. She used to hang around a lot at Columbia, watching us but not saying much. When she did speak, it was barely a whisper. She always wore halter dresses one size too small and carried around a big book like a dictionary or encyclopedia." Winters wrote that in her first memoir.

"It wasn't long before Steve discovered 'Norma Jean something or other.' He stopped dating me and took up with her. I ran into them one night at Schwab's Drugstore, where Lana was allegedly discovered."

[In time, Norma Jean renamed herself Marilyn Monroe. She not only had a brief fling with Crane, among others, but became Winters' roommate.]

Eventually, the star of the picture, Rita Hayworth, discovered Crane's seductive skills. Suddenly, they became "an item."

"I don't know the exact moment Rita took notice of Steve," said director Saville. "But she sure did. It was the talk of the set. I suspected it might be Rita's way of getting back at Lana, her main rival as pinup girl, during the war."

"Rita had eloped with Orson Welles in 1943, but he was never around and still playing the field," Saville claimed. "Rita's affair with Victor Mature was over. She and Lana both went for him. Steve was just the tonic for Rita at that troubled time in her life."

"After such dragon ladies as Joan Crawford and Sonja Henie, I found Rita a very nice lady," Crane told Saville. "She was very kind, very loving. She should never have married Orson Welles…He led to disaster for her."

"Rita's figure wasn't as great as Lana's, though she had the world's most beautiful breasts," Crane said. "Her arms and hands were lovely, but her legs were a bit on the thin side. She had the cutest little belly, which her cameraman was ordered to conceal."

"One day, she came to me," Crane said. "She'd just been in the office of Harry Cohn *[the notoriously abusive president of Columbia pictures]*, and he'd called her 'a tub of shit.' I brought her comfort. She needed love that night. Welles was away, and Cohn had made her feel worthless. I restored her to her throne as a love goddess."

"My romance with Rita didn't last long," Crane admitted. "She was pregnant at the time *[with her daughter, Rebecca]*. On looking back, I think that Rita, unlike Lana, didn't really want to be a movie star."

"In her heart, she was just a simple dancing gypsy girl, who could have settled down with an average Joe and had children. I don't know if Lana ever found out about my affair with Rita—perhaps she did. It was never mentioned."

***

In August of 1944, Lana divorced Crane for the second time. "I was disillusioned during my second marriage to Stephen," Lana told Linda Darnell, who had been her maid of honor during her first marriage ceremony to Crane.   "He was always accusing me of keeping late hours, drinking too much, and whoring around."

Before a judge, Lana presented her case in seven minutes. She claimed that

Crane made her irritable all the time, and created nervous anxiety in her. She accused him of causing her to have frequent colds, and she blamed him for a drastic weight loss. "I've been forced to turn down important pictures because of the turmoil in my life," she claimed in open court.

"My health has been seriously damaged because of him, and I've actually contemplated suicide," she maintained.

The judge granted her divorce and awarded her custody of their daughter.

Lana gave her version of the breakup to Louella Parsons. "Stephen and I sat down for a heart-to-heart talk. We were no longer quarreling. We knew it was time to go our separate ways. I willingly gave my permission for him to visit Cheryl at any time."

[That wasn't exactly accurate: Crane had actually sued Lana for custody of his daughter, but lost in court.]

Lana and Crane remained friends even after their divorce, and many of their subsequent reunions concerned Cheryl. Insiders such as Darnell said that on rare occasions, they continued to have sex together.

As biographer Joe Morella wrote: "Lana's reputation was growing, not only as an offscreen sex symbol, but also as a young woman who could more than hold her own with the hard-drinking Hollywood crowd and match their expletive-peppered vocabulary word for word. Magazine stories carried such headlines as LANA TURNER'S SENSATIONAL LOVES."

Darnell said, "Rumors were rampant about Lana's all-night revelries at clubs along Central Avenue, which was known as 'The Harlem of Hollywood.' Parties there were pretty wild, or so I heard. I never went there myself."

Lana told her girlfriends, many of them envious, "Millions of men consider me the most desirable woman in the world. But my greatest moments, my greatest love affairs, my greatest thrills, lay in my future."

Perhaps to erase memories of her troubled life with Crane, Lana sold her house and moved into a rental property. "I want a fresh start."

In the meantime, Crane became one of the most sought-after bachelors in Hollywood, even taking Lana out on occasion.

The manager at Ciro's reported that on three nights in a row, Crane showed up with Lana Turner, Ava Gardner, and Rita Hayworth. "It was amazing. What did this Hoosier boy have?"

The Intangible, Snake-Oil Charm of Lana's Third Husband, Hollywood's Lothario, Stephen Crane

Whatever Special Combination of Male Charm and Pizzazz Did He Have That We Don't Know About?

Stephen Crane, on three nights in a row, dated Rita Hayworth, Ava Gardner, and his former wife, Lana. As a trio, they were known as the most desirable women inhabiting the planet. What special gift, one wonders, did he have?

Chapter Ten

How to Be a Hot Pants Movie Star

"I Can Fall in Love for Only One Night"

The manly endowments of John Hodiak had been widely discussed after his co-star, Tallulah Bankhead, seduced him during the filming of Alfred Hitchcock's *Lifeboat* (1944). He'd started out being billed as "the next Clark Gable," but didn't get far with that moniker. He'd been classified as 4-F by the Army.

Lana, too, succumbed to the sex appeal of Hodiak on the set of *Marriage Is a Private Affair*, where he was somewhat wooden as an actor.

"He might have been wooden on the screen," Lana told Virginia Grey, "but he's wonderful in bed, and he has a formidable weapon indeed. Tallulah was right."

During World War II, customers could walk into a drugstore and discover the glamorous face of Lana Turner on at least six or seven movie magazines on any given month. Commercial products, such as Woodbury Soap, courted her endorsement, whether she used the product or not. She was one of the most publicized blondes—along with Veronica Lake, Betty Grable, Carole Landis, and Betty Hutton—who adorned the screen during the war years, adding glamor to an otherwise dreary world.

James Robert Parrish, a Hollywood biographer, wrote: "With her voracious sexual appetite, Lana Turner dated incessantly. "I find men terribly exciting," she once said. "Any girl who says she doesn't is an anemic old maid, a streetwalker, or a saint."

"If it were for a quick bedroom tussle, she wanted well-endowed beefcake," Parrish claimed.

Turner shared her philosophy of a man and a woman. "A successful man is one who makes more than a wife can spend. A successful woman is one who can find such a man."

An edition of *Current Biography* wrote: "It is said that Lana Turner has dated 150 members of the opposite sex, and she has been reported to have become engaged to marry five different men at the same time, and was actually on the verge of going to the altar with a dozen."

Even so, she also got publicity about being a mother, with stories appearing under the headline of LANA'S LITTLE DIVIDEND.

The *Hollywood Reporter* wrote, "Whenever Lana is seen with her daughter, she seems very fond of the little one. But she isn't particularly maternal by nature, by instinct (lots of women aren't) or by circumstance. It takes a remarkable character to be a hot pants movie star and an adequate mother. Lana's sex life was always sinning. She had all those troubles, plus her career, plus her own not-very-sound character to cope with."

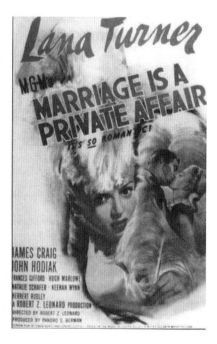

Lana reached the peak of her beauty in the mid-1940s. Even so, she considered Hedy Lamarr more beautiful than she was. "Blondes are more fun. They're bubbly with personality and are pretty like Betty Grable and me, but brunettes are the really sultry beauties of the screen."

She never went out of the house unless she was "camera ready." She didn't know what photographer was sneaking around to take her picture in what she referred to as "one of my off moments."

She announced to advertisers, "I will sell only beauty products—not spark plugs like Rita Hayworth."

Most of the men she dated were actors, or musicians, especially during her early days as a film star. Often, her dates lasted only for one night, perhaps dancing at Ciro's. Sometimes, she continued an affair for three weeks to a month. On occasion, she took up with former lovers, getting together for "a reunion in my boudoir."

"For the most part, I like men tall, dark, and handsome. I think I invented that phrase which became a *cliché.*"

"I was impulsive when it came to men," she said. "I could fall in love for just one night. But then morning came and the man in bed with me didn't look so hot."

She concluded by saying, "My definition of love is believing in your dreams."

***

The war years of 1941 and 1942 had been spectacular for Lana, playing opposite Robert Taylor and Clark Gable in *Honky Tonk, Johnny Eager,* and *Somewhere I'll Find You.* They were followed by her 1943 release of *Slightly Dangerous,* which was like some warmed-over script in the late 1930s before America went to war.

Lana was not pleased, however, with her film output in 1943 and 1944. Her marriage to Stephen Crane, the bigamy charge, and a pregnancy that almost killed her and her child, had interrupted her career at the time when she was about to take the crown as Queen of MGM.

Now, after an eighteen-month absence from the screen, she was hoping that her newest film, set for a 1944 release, *Marriage Is a Private Affair,* would be big at the box office.

She desperately wanted the script to be good, since she would be billed as the star, her name appearing before the title. Never before had she involved herself to this degree in the early creation of a script.

Her director, Robert Z. Leonard, who had helmed her in *Ziegfeld Girl,* had been assigned to bring Judith Kelly's best-selling novel to the screen. In it, Lana was required to transition from a frivolous society girl to a wartime bride and mother.

She was disappointed to learn that MGM had signed an unknown writer, Tennessee Williams, to craft the adaptation. She had wanted an established, thoroughly seasoned Hollywood pro.

Williams had landed in Hollywood in 1939. The only job he could get was as a feather plucker on a squab ranch outside

A pre-fame Tennessee Williams sits in a cubbyhole at MGM, trying to create "a celluloid brassiere for Lana Turner."

243

the city limits of Los Angeles.

As stated years later to his reporter friend from *The Miami Herald*, Darwin Porter: "My time of dread was when a group of young men, most of them boys, came over three times a week to commit mayhem in a place known as 'The Killing Shed.' Here, they would murder the squabs by slitting their throats with sharp knives. The poor birds would frantically twitch as these killers would hold them by their legs over a bucket to bleed them. My share of the squabs was delivered to me, along with my mostly Mexican co-workers. I had to pick the feathers off these dead birds. I was meagerly paid by the number of squabs I plucked."

Tennessee was rescued from this bloody horror by his literary agent, Audrey Wood, who informed him one afternoon that she'd gotten him a job as a scriptwriter at MGM for a salary of $250 a week, the most money he'd ever received.

His first assignment involved adapting a romantic novel, *The Sun Is My Undoing,* for the screen. However, when he reported to work that Monday, he was informed that Pandro S. Berman, its producer, had reassigned him to adapt a different novel, *Marriage Is a Private Affair,* into a sort of "comeback" film for Lana Turner.

According to Tennessee, "I think that was one of the funniest and most embarrassing things that ever happened to me. That I should be expected to produce a suitable vehicle for this actress. I feel like an obstetrician required to successfully deliver a mastodon from a beaver. I've been assigned to create a celluloid brassiere for Lana Turner."

Tennessee never understood the individualized allure of Lana, nor did he appreciate the spellbinding image she could bring to the screen, attracting millions of fans, not all of whom were men. "She couldn't act her way out of her form-fitting cashmeres," he said, referencing her nickname of "The Sweater Girl," a moniker which she was hoping to live down at this point in her career.

Leonard sent him word that if the leading male role he was crafting were strong enough, it might also be used as a starring vehicle for Clark Gable's return—after his service in the U.S. Army Air Force—to the screen.

A memo Williams read revealed that the character he was trying to create required twenty separate scenes, each infused with drama, plot advancement, and characteriza-

Here comes the bride, portrayed by an actress eventually associated with seven real-life husbands—not a particularly good role model for a virginally white wedding.

244

tions. It was clearly understood that during the course of these twenty scenes, she'd be glamorously clad in a different piece of *couture*—one of them a dazzling wedding dress, and each of them unique—created by "Irene."

"MGM doesn't want a movie script," Williams complained. "They're putting on a fashion show starring Lana Turner as the model."

For the third lead, he was instructed to write a dramatic, non-dancing role for Gene Kelly, who wanted to try his luck performing in a drama. Running like a thread through all his communications with Berman and the studio chiefs was enormous pressure to get *Marriage is a Private Affair* before the cameras.

Surpassed only by Betty Grable over at Paramount, Lana continued to be the second most popular pinup girl of World War II. MGM's mail department was deluged with fan letters, asking when Lana would return to the screen. Even though its script was still uncertain, Mayer had already announced that *Marriage* would be shown "in all the theaters of war around the world."

Williams was also asked to write a short and cheerful prologue for Lana, with the understanding that it would be inserted early in the film as a morale booster for the troops. In reference to the prologue he agonized over, he quipped to his gay friends, "I'll suggest that both Lana and I will each be available to service the troops. But whereas Lana gets to seduce them with spotlights and makeup and razzmatazz, I'll promise to service them with my oral talents after dark, in the fog, on the piers of San Francisco, before they're shipped off to war."

For days, Tennessee sweated and bled over her script, complaining loudly, "It's not my kind of story." He grew so frustrated that he once said, "I can almost hope that Lana Turner will die in childbirth."

[The star was pregnant at the time.]

Late one morning, the lesbian film director, Jane Loring, showed up unannounced at Tennessee's small office at MGM. She told him that she was assisting producer Pandro S. Berman, and that she'd come to check on the script. "Pandro wants me to help you invent some sexy situations that will pass the blue-nosed censors."

Loring wore white flannel pants, a beret, and large aviator glasses—very mannish attire. "She did not conceal the fact that she was a lesbian," Williams said. "I'd heard rumors that she was the lover of Katharine Hepburn. My suspicion was confirmed when I had lunch in the commissary with

"The dyke bitch, Katharine Hepburn, held me in utter contempt," Lana said. "I made two movies with Spencer Tracy, and she accused me of making a play for him. That was true only when he was Mr. Hyde.

Let's face it: He wasn't getting anything from Miss Hepburn."

them."

[Hepburn had arrived thirty minutes late and was introduced to Tennessee, who later recalled, "Back then, she regarded me as a little minnow in a fast-flowing stream. The women ignored me and talked about how difficult it was for them to work in a male-dominated industry called Hollywood."

When Lana's name came up, Hepburn flashed anger. "That god damn bottle of bleach practically threw herself at Spencer (Tracy) when they made that movie."

She was referring to the 1941 release of Dr. Jekyll and Mr. Hyde.

The irony of Hepburn's snub of Tennessee Williams was that in years to come, he would create two of her most memorable roles—that of Violet Venable in Suddenly Last Summer, and that of Amanda in the televised version of The Glass Menagerie.]

***

One afternoon, the love goddess herself, Lana, showed up at William's office at MGM. According to Tennessee, "She poured out her marriage woes to me, talking about her difficult times with Stephen Crane. She even suggested that I work some of her troubles into the script, particularly an episode inspired by when she discovered he was a bigamist. She also suggested that I have the soldier in the script try to commit suicide by driving his car over a cliff after she refused to marry him."

"It happened in real life with Stephen," Lana told Tennessee, "and it would be a very dramatic scene."

That day, Tennessee shared his own opinion about marriage with her: "I think no woman divorces a man who's great in bed. If he delivers in bed, a woman, so I am told, can endure a lot."

"That's not the problem with Stephen," she said. "He's very good in bed. Just ask Joan Crawford or Rita Hayworth. Frankly, I'd like to date Frank Sinatra and marry him, but his Nancy seems like such a clinging vine."

She also revealed that she was almost flat broke. "Bills are piling up."

Before leaving his office, she asked if she could read some of the script he'd labored over. When he revealed that he had only five minor pages of screenplay to give her, she seemed disappointed.

The next day she called him, complaining, "I was dumbfounded by a lot of the dialogue. I'm playing a spoiled society girl, not a poetess. Can't you make her speak like the character I'm playing?"

He later claimed in his memoirs that he had avoided "any language that was at all eclectic or multisyllabic. But the dialogue was beyond the young lady's comprehension."

Years later, when he wrote the play Small Craft Warnings, he arranged for the character of Quentin, an elderly writer, to comment about his experience in Hollywood: "They found me too literate on my first assignment, creating a vehicle for the producer's doxy, a grammar school dropout."

[Synonyms for doxy include bimbo, floozy, hoochie, hussy, minx, slut, tramp, wench, and whore. Tennessee, through the character of Quentin, was referring to the producer of Marriage Is a Private Affair, Pandro Berman, and its star, Lana Turner.]

Late one Monday morning, Berman phoned Lana, telling her that Williams had been removed from his job as a scriptwriter, and that two experienced writers, Leonore Coffee and David Hertz, had been hired to replace him.

He also informed her that Gene Kelly had dropped out of the picture, and that "Your handsome leading men will be John Hodiak and James Craig. Both of them are Louis B. Mayer's best hope to replace Clark Gable, who may never regain his pre-war acclaim. It's been a while since he's played Rhett Butler."

[Rounding out the supporting cast were Hugh Marlowe, Frances Gifford, Keenan Wynn, Natalie Schafer, and Tom Drake.]

***

Just before the filming of *Marriage Is a Private Affair*, as Lana was looking for a way to escape from her divorce-related traumas, she eagerly accepted the invitation of Frank Sinatra to occupy his vacation home in Palm Springs while he was in New York.

[During his rounds of Manhattan, Sinatra was frequently seen with the blonde actress, Marilyn Maxwell.]

First, Lana phoned one of her girl friends, either Linda Darnell or Susan Hayward (perhaps both), asking them to accompany her. "We'll find something on the hoof when we get there," Lana promised.

Both actresses, however, had other commitments.

Finally, she called Henry Willson, knowing that from his stable of boys, he could provide a handsome, well-endowed escort for her.

He suggested that a suitable escort might be Derek Harris (later billed as John Derek). "He's been ranting and raving about you ever since I introduced you."

"He might be ideal," she said "I thought he was ever so handsome."

"He's a winner, baby," Willson said, "and usually hot to trot."

The next morning, Derek, clad in a T-shirt and a pair of tight-fitting shorts, was behind the wheel of her Lincoln Continental driving them into the desert toward Palm Springs. *En route*, he confided to Lana that Willson was having a hard time getting him launched.

[Derek had just finished an uncredited role in Since You Went Away, *which film critic Bosley Crowther had appraised as overcomplicated: "Selznick's first screen production in four years features a script with an excess of exhausting emotional detail," one of which might have involved Derek's brief on-screen emotional involvement with the character portrayed by Shirley Temple.]*

After a weekend with John Derek in Palm Springs, Lana reported back to Willson: "If a contest were held tomorrow, Derek would win as having the most beautiful penis in Hollywood, and, as you know, other than you, I'm the best judge of that."

"I've seen the rushes of *Since You Went Away.*" Derek told her. "I play Shirley Temple's boyfriend. If you blink, you'll miss me."

He went on to tell her that he'd been assigned another small role in David O. Selznick's upcoming new film, *I'll Be Seeing You.* Ginger Rogers, temporarily on parole for the holidays, falls in love with a disturbed soldier (Joseph Cotten).

According to Derek, "Once again, I've been cast with Shirley Temple. That brat is growing up, and Selznick doesn't seem to know what to do with Miss Lollipop. With all these scene-stealers, who will notice me?"

"Sounds like more of Selznick's famous *schmaltz* to me," Lana said. "But I'll notice you, no matter how small the part. You're very distinctive."

"You're a gal after my own heart."

She glanced flirtatiously at him. "Actually, I invited you down for something else."

He smiled at her. "You'll get that...and a lot more."

"I can hardly wait," she claimed.

***

On the morning of her return to Los Angeles from her weekend in Palm Springs with Derek, Lana phoned Willson, as he had demanded a full report, and said, "Thank God you haven't ruined him for women. In fact, he seems to worship beautiful women. He treated me like a goddess."

"We got there right after lunch, and I retired to my bedroom for a while. He said he wanted to swim in Frank's pool. When I woke up, I put on my suit and went to join him. What I saw amazed me. He was standing stark naked beside the pool, with his hands on his hips. He was absolutely gorgeous...and nude."

"I agree with you," Willson told her. "Been there, done it."

"I know you have," she said. "You're a dirty old man, but I adore you. At Christmastime, I want you to strip Derek naked, tie a ribbon around it, and place it under my tree."

"Okay."

Word about Lana and Derek spread among the young beauties at MGM. Elizabeth Taylor heard about it and invited Lana for lunch in the commissary. "I developed a crush on Derek in school, even though he was six years older than me—and not in the same class," Taylor said.

In a later memoir, entitled *Elizabeth Taylor,* she wrote about Derek: "There was this most beautiful boy—to me, then, like a god. One day, we were going down the corridor, and he tripped me, then picked me up. 'Hi there, beautiful,' he said. Oh, you can't imagine. I was in such ecstasy. I went to the girl's room and just sat there dreaming about him."

She confessed to Lana that her closest friend, Roddy McDowall, the British actor, taught her to satisfy a man without getting pregnant. "I was told to pretend that it was a lollipop. I was one of those devotees of childhood sexuality."

Lana's dates with Derek were cut short by Selznick, who ordered him, for publicity purposes, to start escorting Shirley Temple to various events, including premieres and parties.

Another disincentive to Lana's interest in him came when McDowall, who was also her gay friend, told her that Derek worked as a male prostitute on the side. "He needs the money and charges ten dollars a session. Spencer Tracy is his best customer, although Derek adores beautiful women like you."

"I guess a guy has to make a living," she said. "But there's something about him that troubles me. I suspect he has a dark side I know nothing about. He's also a bullshitter. Would you believe that he told me that he's the bastard son of Greta Garbo? He tells everybody that, although his mother is that very minor actress, Dolores Johnson."

"Derek wants to paint me in the nude," she said, "but I turned him down. 'Why put me on canvas when you can see the real thing in the flesh?' I asked him."

There were rumors in the press that Temple was going to marry Derek, but she went for John Agar instead, much to her later regret.

In 1988, Lana read *Child Star*, Shirley's memoirs, and didn't like what she'd written about Derek. Shirley referred to him as "a self-important young man who had pleasant features, perhaps a little too sensitive for my taste. With a shock of dark hair cascading artfully over his forehead and his suit shoulders padded to disguise a delicate frame, he made a highly photogenic companion."

"To hell with her," Lana said. "I've been over every inch of Derek's body. He doesn't need to pad anything."

In *Child Star*, Shirley also made a shocking revelation, claiming that Derek would often use a dangerously sharp knife to furiously stab the air, aiming the weapon at some invisible enemy. Summing up, she wrote, "Not every girl gets to neck with a knife-wielding bastard."

"My god," Lana said. "Little Miss Rebecca of Sunnybrook Farm makes him out to be psychotic. I don't believe a word of it."

After their weekend together in Palm Springs, Lana met Derek again at a party at the home of Humphrey Bogart and Lauren Bacall. Both men had just completed their 1949 film, *Knock on Any Door*, in which Derek played a juvenile delinquent being defended on a murder charge by an idealistic lawyer, as played by Bogart.

That same year, Derek had also been cast in the Oscar-winning *All the King's Men*, playing the adopted football-playing son of Broderick Crawford. Derek's character ends up in a wheelchair in the aftermath of trying to please his image-conscious father.

Both Bogie and Lana predicted great things for Derek in the 1950s, but lived to see him make a string of lackluster movies. Ultimately, he became famous not as an actor, but for marrying beautiful women and becoming a Svengali-like mentor to Bo Derek. He directed some of the films she eventually starred in, which were reviewed as some of the worst movies ever made.

***

Lana was invited to the premiere of David O. Selznick's *Since You Went Away*. Much to the delight of photographers (they weren't known as *paparazzi* yet), she showed up on the arm of the young British actor, Peter Lawford. The verdict was that the handsome star and the beautiful blonde goddess looked "absolutely ravishing together."

Although Peter was attired in a well-tailored tuxedo, Lana was the standout. With her long blonde tresses, she made a spectacular entrance at the Carthay Circle Theatre, at the time one of the most spectacular movie palaces in L.A.

She wore an unusual ensemble that night: A wide-skirted black strapless gown of sheer net sprinkled with sequins. The long black gloves were mandatory, as well as the diamond jewelry and mink wrap. Even her shoes were unusual: A pair of lace satin slippers. After the premiere, the glamorous couple were photographed at the Clover Club with Lawford nibbling at her ear.

At the premiere, she was greeted by Ingrid Bergman, who had befriended her on the set of *Dr. Jekyll and Mr. Hyde*. Bergman was escorted by Gregory Peck, her upcoming star in *Spellbound* (1945).

She had heard rumors that the established star and the upcoming star were lovers, even though each was married. Peck was dashingly handsome and kissed Lana on both cheeks.

"Lucky Ingrid," Lana said to Lawford when the pair was out of hearing distance.

"Lucky me to be out with you," he answered.

She greeted Jennifer Jones again, and the two were polite but not particularly friendly. Lana didn't know if Jones had heard rumors about Robert Walker and her.

Jones had already achieved stardom in *The Song of Bernadette* (1944), for which she'd won a Best Actress Oscar. She had separated from Walker in the autumn of 1943, and began living with Selznick, whose wife, Irene Mayer Selznick, daughter of Louis B. Mayer, eventually divorced him in 1945. Jones divorced Walker that same year, too.

On occasion, at future gatherings, Lana and Jones came face to face, although they were never friends.

They were two very different types of actresses, but on rare occasions, they were each considered for the same roles. When Jones turned down the female lead in *Cass Timberlane* (1947), co-starring Spencer Tracy, the role went to Lana.

[Ironically, when Lana campaigned for the title role in the film adaptation of Flaubert's Madame Bovary *(1949), the role was assigned to Jones.]*

Both Selznick and Jones raged against both Lana and Kirk Douglas when they co-starred together in *The Bad and the Beautiful*. All of Hollywood was buzzing about who the film had been based on. Louella Parsons nailed it in print: Lana's role of Georgia Harrison was based on the

When Lana made *The Bad and the Beautiful*, her character of Georgia Harrison was said to have been based on Jennifer Jones.

Mortified by the gossip, Jones cattily responded, "The last actress I would want to depict me on the screen is the notorious Lana Turner."

250

real-life story of Jennifer Jones, and Kirk Douglas' character of Jonathan Shields was inspired by a real-life episode in the life of David O. Selznick.

**

Peter Lawford and Lana saw each other during an eight-month period in 1944. Since she was in a deteriorating, highly publicized marriage to Stephen Crane, each of their rendezvous was kept for the most part under wraps.

Lana had met the handsome British actor at a party at the home of his friend and sometimes lover, Keenan Wynn. Secretly, when no one was looking, he made a date for the following evening. In the words of one writer, he was "part suave, part smarmy, with thick brows and lounge lizard looks."

In 1954, Lawford would achieve worldwide fame when he married Patricia Kennedy, the younger sister of Massachusetts Senator John F. Kennedy. During his troubled later years, he became known more for his celebrity than for his acting.

Before, during, and after his marriage, Lawford racked up a series of "gender neutral" seductions to rival those of almost any other actor in Hollywood.

In addition to Lana Turner, Lawford's sexual intimates included June Allyson and Van Johnson (both of whom were celebrated at the time as "America's Sweethearts"). Lucille Ball joined Anne Baxter on the list, as did director George Cukor *["Peter was a lousy lay."]*, Noël Coward, the African-American singer/actress Dorothy Dandridge, Judy Holliday, Tom Drake, Rhonda Fleming, socialite Sharman Douglas, Ava Gardner, Judy Garland, Rita Hayworth, Janet Leigh, Marilyn Monroe, Elizabeth Taylor, Robert Walker, Nancy Davis (later known as Nancy Reagan), Clifton Webb, Jane Wyman, and Lee Remick. He also seduced unknowns, including college cuties and hookers, male and female, who viewed him as a reliable $50 "oral trick" who required little more than their permission for him to service them orally.

Lana also succumbed to his allure, at least for a while.

He'd been having sex since the age of ten, when he was fellated by his English governess. Like Howard Hughes, he was known for his predilection for oral sex. Sal Mineo in the 1950s would refer to him "as the best cocksucker in Hollywood."

In London, in 1930, Lawford made his film debut at the age of seven, when he was assigned a role in *Poor Old Bill.* In 1938, he co-starred with Roddy McDowall and Freddie Bartholomew in *Lord Jeff,* and then later lived in Florida.

Back in Hollywood, he landed small roles in two big hits, *Mrs. Miniver* and *Random Harvest,* each released in 1942, and each starring Greer Garson.

In the years ahead, he became one of MGM's bobby sox idols, appearing in films that included *Easter Parade* (1948) and *Little Women* (also 1948.)

In time, Lawford would be included in Frank Sinatra's Rat Pack and become a confidant of Marilyn Monroe, even being controversially linked to her death in 1962.

When his mother, Lady May Crawford, found out that he was dating Lana, she objected almost violently, calling Lana a slut. *[Lady May's memoirs were aptly entitled* Mother Bitch.*]* As time went by, the more her son saw of Lana, the more loudly Lady May objected, publicly referring to the blonde goddess as "all boobs and no brains."

Vindictively, his mother made an appointment with Louis B. Mayer, revealing to him that she suspected that her son was a homosexual, and accusing him of being intimately involved with both Van Johnson and Keenan Wynn. She went on to ask Mayer if he could arrange for some form of "treatment" to cure her son of homosexuality.

When Lawford heard about this, he exploded in humiliation and fury. His relationship with his mother would never recover.

In the aftermath, Lawford asked Lana to meet with Mayer and to reveal the details of her affair with him as a means of convincing him that he was not a homosexual. Temporarily, the mogul might have been persuaded, as, apparently, he'd never heard of bisexuality.

Despite Lana's gallant defense, Lawford was dragged out of the closet when he was arrested for fellating a teenage boy in the men's room at Will Rogers State Park.

"The Fixers" at MGM, Eddie Mannix and Howard Strickling, were called in to suppress the story and to see that it wasn't published in the papers. In time, thanks to the intervention of MGM, the record of Lawford's arrest was discreetly removed from police files in Los Angeles.

During a heated confrontation, Mayer met with Lawford, demanding that he submit to a radical new treatment. He claimed that several of his other male stars at MGM had already taken the treatment, receiving injections of extract from monkey glands…"And they never sucked another cock again."

Lawford never submitted to the treatments, and continued his status as the fourth member of a *ménage à quatre* consisting of Van Johnson, Keenan Wynn, and Robert Walker, all of them friends of Lana. They rode motorcycles, went on trips to the desert together, and were highly visible fixtures at all-night beach parties at Malibu.

On many a night, Lawford drove Lana to the same moonlit beach at Malibu, or else he'd take her dancing at the Mocambo, which became their favorite hangout. The evening would end at her house, not at his. "My tarantula mother would eat Lana alive for getting her hands on her darling boy."

Lawford told his friends, "For such a big, glamorous movie star, Lana has

James Spada, Lawford's biographer, wrote: "Peter Lawford at twenty-one was one of the most attractive and charming young men to be found in Hollywood since Errol Flynn became a star in 1935. His success with women would soon be almost as legendary as Flynn's. Few could resist his boyishly open face, dazzling smile, and tight physique or his charming English accent, impeccable manners, and quick wit."

simple tastes except for her love of diamonds. On some afternoons, when it wasn't too hot, we'd play tennis, or else go riding along bridle paths in the Hollywood Hills. She told me that Ronald Reagan had taught her how to ride a horse."

One night, he explained to her why he never had to enter military service. At 14, he had severely injured his right arm when it went through a glass door. That injury and the irreversible nerve damage it had caused forever compromised the use of his hand and lower arm. As the years went by, he concealed that, at least from the camera.

That injury was a boon for his career, since heartthrobs like James Stewart and Clark Gable were already off to war. In lieu of those bigger but faraway stars, Lawford was able to nab some romantic leads at MGM.

As Lana's daughter, Cheryl, wrote, "Lawford seemed to be more enamored of my mother than she was of him." At the time, more or less liberated from her husband, Lana wanted to play the field. She did not want to tie herself to another man, especially to one as immature and impetuous as Lawford. Once, he proposed marriage to her. Ever so politely, she rejected his offer.

Henry Willson, as a voyeur, wanted a "blow by blow" description of Lana's affair with Lawford. He may have been among the first to learn that Lana was tiring of oral sex. She confessed to him that one night she exploded in fury, shouting at him, "God damn it, Peter. I want you to fuck me. If you want a blow job, call one of your beach boys."

As Lana's eight-month involvement with Lawford was coming to an end, so was World War II, though it had a few more horrific months to go.

"I like Peter and at times, he's very entertaining," Lana told Willson. "But he's still a boy, and I want a man. Besides, I always wonder, when he's in bed with me, whether he really wants to be in bed with Van Johnson."

Lawford wasn't always fun-loving, as she soon discovered. He had a dark side. "I have these frightening depressions," he confessed. "I have great days, then the dark days descend like the Bubonic plague. Why? I have everything. Good looks, Money, Fame. And my pick of any gender."

Keenan Wynn had such a crush on Lawford that he became jealous of Lana. One night, when Lawford's car was parked in her driveway, he came by at around 3AM and let the air out of all four of the tires on Lawford's car.

One Saturday, when Lawford came by her house to pick her up for a date, Mildred was there to announce to him, "Lana is gone," before refusing to provide any further details about her whereabouts.

Only the day before, he had told Frank Sinatra, "Lana and I are really hitting it off. I am her man, and she is my woman."

Sinatra eyed Lawford skeptically. "Since when did a British fag like you become a man?" Then he grabbed his ample crotch. "Let's face it, pal, this is what you really want."

"Frank, I love you dearly, but those put-downs, even if you're joking, are hard to take."

During the frantic week that followed, Lawford could find no trace of Lana. No one at MGM knew where she was, since she wasn't shooting a film at the time. Up till then, she and Lawford had been in daily contact, if not in person, then via phone.

One night at around midnight, Lana phoned Lawford at his home. She was calling from Boston. He had angry words with her, but she remained calm. "I thought you'd been kidnapped. What in hell are you doing in Boston?"

"It's over between us," she said. "But I want you to know that it's been fun. I did care for you...at least a bit."

"It's over? What in hell are you talking about? Only a few days ago, you made passionate love to me!"

"I've fallen for someone else."

"Who is it now?" he asked contemptuously. "Some busboy with a big dick?"

"Gene Krupa." Then she abruptly put down the phone.

***

Two weeks later, when Lana returned to Hollywood, she did not call him. Instead, he read in Louella Parsons' column that she was dating the Turkish actor, Turhan Bey. Jealous and infuriated, Lawford, throughout the remainder of his life, referred to that actor as "Turban Bey."

The publicist, Milton Ebbins, who was Lawford's greatest mentor, said, "Peter's breakup with Lana changed the way he treated women. After that, he seemed to just drop them the moment he was finished with them. Take Judy Holliday, for example. He could be cruel, heartless. It was Lana who taught him that."

***

Bored and riddled with anxiety, Lana was anxious to return to work at MGM. She was smoking too much, drinking too much. Late one morning, she received a call from Mervyn LeRoy. She was delighted to hear from her former mentor.

"Lana, my dear, it's been too long," he said. "I've come up with a fabulous new idea for casting you. After watching the final version of my latest picture, *Thirty Seconds Over Tokyo* (1944), I realized that I'd directed three of your friends in it: Spencer Tracy, Van Johnson, and Robert Walker. Those guys are doing just fine, but I made a discovery. *I think I've found a star of tomorrow!* His name is Robert Mitchum, and he's been kicking around Hollywood a bit, going nowhere until now. I think you two would make a dynamic screen team. I can just see the marquee now: LANA TURNER AND ROBERT MITCHUM STARRING IN...well, whatever."

"I like the billing. When do I meet God's gift?"

"First, I'd like you to come over to MGM tomorrow afternoon at three o'clock. I'll arrange a screening of *Thirty Seconds Over Tokyo* (1944) so that you can see what I'm talking about."

The next afternoon, she arrived on time and sat through the screening with LeRoy. It was a dramatization of the April, 1942 American bombing of the Japanese capital.

She, too, was impressed by this "dynamic hunk of man," as she called

Mitchum.

"Before I signed him, I put him through thirty screen tests," LeRoy said. "I told him that he was the best actor I'd ever seen…or the worst."

The director set up a luncheon meeting with Lana and Mitchum the following day. LeRoy had intended to join them, but he was called away at the last minute to report to the office of Louis B. Mayer.

That left Lana to eat alone with Mitchum, whom she found "amazingly appealing," as she'd later report to LeRoy.

"Bob—he told me I could call him that—is utterly fascinating," she said. "Too bad he's married."

"When did that ever stop you?" LeRoy quipped.

"I hope you aren't turned off by my looks," Mitchum told Lana over lunch. "Some guy wrote that I look like a shark with a broken nose."

Despite his barrel chest and cleft chin, he was not traditionally handsome, but she found him sexy nonetheless. His hooded eyes became known as "bedroom eyes," and he possessed an insolent gaze and fearless veneer, a look that seemed to say, "Baby, I don't give a damn."

He spoke to Lana about his publicity build-up: "I don't give a fuck what they write about me. Booze, brawls, and broads—I represent the three Bs of life."

In time, she'd learn about his background. Of all the actors she knew, his was the most colorful. He'd been a gang member growing up in Hell's Kitchen in Manhattan. He was partially descended from Blackfoot Indians and, as a youth, had led a gypsy-like existence. As a homeless roustabout during the Depression, he'd ridden the rails with the other hobos, migrating from town to town.

A series of thefts landed him in a chain gang in Georgia, from which he eventually escaped. One random job after another awaited him—boxer ("That's where I got this broken nose"), beach bum, ("I rolled drunks"), ditch digger, dishwasher, fruit picker, stevedore, a ghost writer for Carroll Righter (Lana's astrologer), stagehand, poet,

[In 1940, Robert Mitchum married Dorothy Spence, to whom he'd been attracted since he met her when she was thirteen. She was pretty, slender, brunette, sweet and soft-spoken.

Over the years, she must have been the most understanding wife in Hollywood, overlooking or forgiving her husband's affairs not only with Lana, but with Rita Hayworth, Ava Gardner, Lucille Ball, Anne Bancroft, Jane Russell, Jean Simmons, Sarah Miles, Jane Greer, Gloria Grahame, Carroll Baker, Shirley MacLaine, and, lest we forget, Marilyn Monroe, with whom he co-starred in *The River of No Return* (1954).

Of all these women, only Marilyn gave him a bad review. "He's a lousy kisser and should watch that bad breath."

an extra in *Hopalong Cassidy* Westerns, and a machine operator for Lockheed Air-craft.

The afternoon he met Lana, he was on his way to becoming filmdom's first hipster anti-hero. "I was one wild boy of the road," he confessed. What he didn't tell her was that when he'd arrived broke and hungry in Hollywood, he'd hustled homosexuals, including Clifton Webb, who for a time was his best customer.

Lana would later tell LeRoy, "Bob has this sense of self -mockery. He told me that he started out as a sex fiend, but couldn't pass the physical."

Later, Howard Hughes, their mutual friend, told Lana, "There's not a dame around who won't drop her britches for Bob. To make it worse, he doesn't give a damn if they do or not."

"For me, it's hard to articulate Bob's sex appeal," Lana said to LeRoy. "It's there, just there, very immediate. You feel it the moment he looks at you."

As the afternoon wore on, she invited him to go home with her. "Even back then, he was a hard drinker," she claimed. "But no matter how much he drank, he was still in control, still coherent." For dinner, she ordered a lavish meal from Chasen's, which was delivered to her doorstep.

He told her amusing stories of his life, some of which had unfolded during his work with her friends on the set of *Thirty Seconds Over Tokyo*. Some of the scenes had been shot at the Naval Air Station in Pensacola, Florida.

"I got cruised in the communal shower and had to take a shit in group latrines. We stood in the mess line for rotten food."

Mitchum's biographer, Lee Server, wrote that the actor "got a reputation for dropping his pants in front of officers and other dignified types."

The fake (Hollywood) soldiers and the *bona-fide* enlisted men invariably clashed. The crew from California was referred to as "Hollywood fags."

"A drunken sailor one night was beating the shit out of Robert Walker, and I stepped in," Mitchum said. "I grabbed the son of a bitch and beat him so badly he had to be rushed to the hospital. After that, the guys let us alone."

"Mitchum spent the night with Lana. "He got on top and plowed and plowed," she confessed to Virginia Grey. "What a man! I was definitely not his first time at the rodeo."

When she met again with LeRoy, she told him that she thought Mitchum would be ideal as her screen lover. "Or off screen as the case may be."

When she was offered the lead female role in *The Postman Always Rings Twice*, Lana lobbied for her director, Tay Garnett, to cast Mitchum as the male lead, but he rejected her idea. Instead, he preferred "bad boy" John Garfield for the part.

***

On the set of *Marriage is a Private Affair* (1944), director Robert Z. Leonard grandly welcomed Lana. She was eager to meet her two leading men, James Craig and John Hodiak, neither of whom was there that day. She'd read in the papers that Hodiak was being positioned as "the successor to Clark Gable." The Pittsburgh-born actor, of Ukrainian and Polish descent, was touted as the "one man who best could fill the shoes of 'The King.'"

His rival contender, also at MGM, was James Craig, a son of Tennessee, who had lost his Southern accent. Of all the Gable wannabees, he most resembled Gable, mustache and all.

Louis B. Mayer had signed him to a seven-year contract, based to some degree on MGM's understandable fear that Gable, after his discharge from the Air Force, would look far older than Rhett Butler in *Gone With the Wind* (1939).

Leonard told Lana that the success of this upcoming film rested entirely on her shoulders. She would be on the screen for 116 minutes, and that she'd have sole billing above the title.

She was delighted that her favorite hairdresser, Sydney Guilaroff, had been assigned to her, and that the fashion designer, "Irene," was preparing a vast wardrobe for her. Irene had long ago learned that Lana's left shoulder and hip were higher than her right.

Lana had been cast as Theo Scofield West, a society girl who "spends her winters in Palm Beach, her summers in Reno." Actually, that description directly applied to the society actress, Natalie Schafer, who had been assigned to play Theo's (i.e., Lana's) mother in the film.

Schafer's character, the script revealed, had, by this point in her (screen) daughter's life, already maneuvered her way through what seemed like an endless series of divorces.

Theo (as played by Lana) has no intention of marrying anyone—at least not at this point in her life—until she meets Lt. Tom Cockrane West, an Air Corps lieutenant.

Without really taking time to get to know him, she accepts his proposal. During the period of adjustment that follows, a baby is born and Theo is embroiled in a matronly domestic life, yearning for a return to her status as a party girl.

Along comes James Craig, cast as Miles Lansing, who is far more attractive and appealing than her husband. Theo had dated him before her marriage, and he seems to be carrying a torch for her.

Lana would work with Natalie Schafer again. The veteran actress would become a household word when she later appeared (brilliantly) as the gadabout society matron, Eunice Wentworth Howell (aka "Lovey") in CBS's hit sitcom, *Gilligan's Island* (1964-1967). She'd been married (1933-1942) to the famous actor, Louis Calhern, but had divorced him.

Schafer would repeat her role as Lana's mother twenty-five years later in a 1969

Natalie Schafer never revealed her age. However, when she died in 1991, it was learned that she'd been born in 1900. She gave Lana some advice: "Men come and go when a woman is young. But to comfort her in her old age, she needs to have collected diamonds."

She took her own advice. At the time of her death, she was a multimillionaire, having made a fortune in real estate.

episode of *The Survivors*, a TV series.

Until the last minute in the casting process, it had not been certain that Lana would star in *Marriage*. The script had been owned by Warners, but Jack Warner feared trouble with the censors. Especially provocative were the conversations it contained about abortion and adultery. He had sold it to Mayer, who originally intended it as a vehicle for Myrna Loy and Robert Taylor, with George Cukor set to direct.

At the beginning of the film, as an introduction, and with the understanding that it would be shown to servicemen worldwide, Lana appears on screen to deliver a morale-boosting pep talk. "Well, here we are, having a world premiere of our picture for the Armed Forces overseas. And if you think this isn't important, you've got another thing coming. But, seriously, you should see all the best pictures, and you should see them first because...well, because you're you. Because you're the first in our hearts, our hopes, and our thoughts. Thanks for coming to the show. I hope you like it. So long and good luck."

Marriage Is a Private Affair had its world premiere on September 23, 1944, at the Teatro Della Palme in the recently recaptured city of Naples, Italy. An Army newspaper wrote: "Miss Lana Turner's fine points are revealed to advantage in a few idyllic sequences which suit the GI appetite. However, one scene in which the newlyweds are shown sound asleep in twin beds in the morning after the wedding drew some strange noises from the audience."

After the film opened in Los Angeles, a critic for *The Los Angeles Times* wrote: "This picture is unimportant except as a vehicle for Miss Turner, but it is effective as such, and it demonstrates her ability to act, to project a soft and appealing femininity, which, of course, comes with that pronounced loveliness which has always been hers."

A critic for *The New York Times* wrote: "Lana Turner is a lovely, appealing little thing, and mankind was fashioned primarily to make her happy and supreme."

***

In *Marriage is a Private Affair*, James Craig was cast as Lana's former beau before her (onscreen) marriage to John Hodiak.

Before Lana ever seduced Craig, he'd already been auditioned by some of the *femmes fatales* of Hollywood.

Off screen, his conquests had included Marlene Dietrich during their filming of *Seven Sinners* (1940); Ginger Rogers during *Kitty Foyle* (also 1940); Lucille Ball during *Valley of the Sun* (1942), and Hedy Lamarr during *The Heavenly Body* (1944).

On the set of *Marriage*, Natalie Shafer, cast as Lana's mother, said. "Lana is such a darling, I just adore her. But as if Hodiak wasn't enough, the dear thing also had to bed James Craig... Not that I blame her, mind you...."

Craig had never planned to be an actor. On a chance encounter, he had met Oliver Hinsdell, a talent scout, who was struck by his resemblance to Clark Gable. Craig's career got off to a slow start, as he drifted from one lackluster movie to another, from Paramount to Columbia, and on to Universal before landing at MGM.

In 1942, he was cast in *Northwest Rangers*, a Westernized reworking of *Manhat-*

tan Melodrama in which Gable himself had been cast in 1934.

In *Lady Without a Passport* (1949), Hedy Lamarr, still Lana's rival, faced the same dilemma that Lana had confronted when she'd made *Marriage Is a Private Affair*. Her leading men were the same as Lana's: John Hodiak and James Craig.

She followed in Lana's footsteps, sustaining affairs with both actors. "I was already familiar with the charms of Mr. Craig," she told her director, Joseph H. Lewis.

***

John Hodiak first tried for a job as a radio actor, but was rejected because of his Ukrainian accent. As a caddy, he practiced his diction and studied hard, until finally, he was accepted for a job on radio in Chicago, playing the comic strip character, L'il Abner.

But his major recognition didn't come until *Lifeboat*. Bankhead spread the word—"it's like getting fucked by a beer can, *dah-ling.*" News like that spread fast, and soon, Hodiak was pursued in Hollywood by a coven of sexually voracious females.

"When I first went to bed with John Hodiak, I imagined his love gift sprinkled with sapphires and diamonds," Lana said. "I couldn't wait for him to recover so we could go another round."

"Who needs Clark Gable when you've got his replacement?" Virginia Grey asked Lana. "Maybe you'll leave Clark for me when he comes marching home from the Air Force."

In the months to come, after they finished their picture, Lana and Hodiak became a "sometimes thing" (her words).

Years later, Hodiak confessed to Lana that it was not only women who sexually pursued him, but an occasional male, including two of her friends. He cited Van Johnson, with whom he had co-starred in *Command Decision* (1948), and Robert Taylor in *Ambush* (1949).

In Gore Vidal's most controversial novel, *Myra Breckenridge*, there is a glowing passage concerning the sexual allure of actor James Craig.

"I practiced self-abuse thinking of James Craig's voice," Myra proclaims in Vidal's novel. "Those broad shoulders, those powerful thighs thrust between your own. No matter what condition James Craig is in today, decrepit or not, Myra Breckinridge is ready to give him a good time for old times' sake."

She used her affair with Hodiak to goad Stephen Crane into granting her a second divorce. As her daughter, Cheryl, later wrote, "She told Dad a baldfaced lie—that she was in love with another man. She named Hodiak."

Lana may not have been in love with Hodiak, but she certainly was smitten with him. She told him that she had blamed him for the breakup of her marriage.

"What the hell?" Hodiak had said. "Now Crane will come gunning for me."

"He's house broken," she responded. "He never kills my lovers."

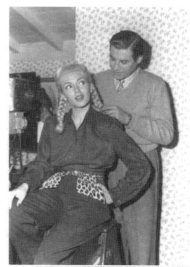

Photographs snapped during the filming of *Marriage* reveal Lana with Hodiak during the blossoming of their romance. At one point, he was photographed braiding her hair; in another picture, she sips afternoon tea from his cup.

She used her influence to get him a number of lucrative radio jobs, wherein, from recording studios, they each read their lines into microphones. Their first dramatization together was *Once Upon a Honeymoon,* a Screen Guild Players Presentation that aired on November 20, 1944.

Originally conceived as a romantic comedy/drama that was released as a film in 1942, it had starred Cary Grant and Ginger Rogers. Both of them, however, had rejected proposals to get them involved in the radio-broadcasted reprise.

On April 11, 1946, Lana and Hodiak costarred in a CBS presentation of the Lux Radio Theatre. The radio play was *Honky Tonk,* the film she had made with Clark Gable before America went to war.

The Screen Guild Players reunited Hodiak and Lana again in their radio rendition of *Marriage Is a Private Affair,* which was broadcast on June 17, 1946.

The Guild hired Lana and John Garfield to do the original radio broadcast of *The Postman Always Rings Twice* on CBS Radio on June 23, 1947. The show was so well-re-

Two views of John Hodiak: (top photo) braiding Lana's hair; (lower photo) shirtless and adrift at sea with Tallulah Bankhead in *Lifeboat.*

ceived that the Screen Guild recycled it for another radio adaptation, eventually broadcast through ABC on February 8, 1951. This time, however, Garfield was not available, so Hodiak was substituted, with Lana reprising for radio her original film role.

During the last years of his life, Hodiak slipped around for an occasional private rendezvous with Lana. After he'd made *Marriage* with Lana, he was cast in the 1944 film, *Sunday Dinner for a Soldier,* in which he co-starred with Anne Baxter. The two actors fell in love and were married in 1946.

As the years passed, Lana was saddened by the decline in Hodiak's career. After he was heavily promoted for his roles in a series of lackluster films, movie exhibitors across the country labeled him "box office poison."

On October 19, 1955, Lana was listening to the radio when a bulletin was announced. Hodiak had suffered a fatal heart attack in the bathroom of his home [*a refuge he had originally built for his parents]* in Tarzana, California. He was only forty-one years old.

"In some of his *film noir* roles, John was a brute," Lana recalled. "But not in real life."

***

John Hodiak and James Craig weren't the only men Lana dated during the course of her marriage to Stephen Crane. During that period, an especially exotic male also entered her life. Urbane and dapper, Turhan Bey became her lover, too.

With his dark good looks, swept-back hair, and Continental charm, he had been born in Vienna, the son of a Turkish diplomat and a Jewish-Czech mother.

Bey was typecast as a dashing, bare-chested foreigner who often played a Turk or an Arab in period pictures that included *Raiders of the Desert* (1941), *Arabian Nights* (1942), and *Ali Baba & the Forty Thieves* (1944).

At the time Lana met him, he was filming *Dragon Seed* (1944), playing the Chinese husband of Katharine Hepburn, whose performance called for her to appear throughout the film in pseudo-Asian makeup. The film had been based on Pearl S. Buck's saga of a Chinese town torn asunder by the Japanese occupation.

In all these movies, *Screen Guide* magazine found Bey "cultured, suave, and inscrutable—made to order for moviegoers."

Before she ever met him, Lana appeared one day to watch the rushes from *Dragon Seed.* She told the director, Jack Conway, "I fancy this young Turk."

Eventually, she met Bey at the home of Jean-Pierre Aumont. Her French former lover was married at the time to Maria Montez, with whom Bey would eventually co-star in several Technicolor escapades. The press had already nicknamed him, "The Turkish Delight," and his reputation had preceded him by the time Aumont introduced them.

Lana's first words to Bey were, "I think the newspaper gossip columns are all wrong calling you the 'Poor Man's Valentino.' I think you have more going than he did."

He thanked her, as he hated that label himself. The Valentino comparison would be recycled when he starred in *Sudan* (1945). *The New York Times* wrote:

"Turhan Bey gives a boyish imitation of Rudolph Valentino as the desert sheik."

One night at a party in Beverly Hills, Lana was dancing with Bey when Stephen Crane entered the room. He approached the couple and pulled them apart. Then he made an attempt to remove from her finger the diamond ring he'd given her, loudly asserting that it was a family heirloom.

She protested, "But I've had it reset!"

Ever the gentleman, Bey invited Crane to step outside into the garden to settle the dispute. Once they were there, the two men began to fight as Lana rushed out. In her frustration, she threw the ring into the shrubbery. Two other men from the party pulled Bey and Crane apart, but not before Bey had given Crane a black eye. Bey sustained only minor bruises.

The last that Lana saw of Crane that night was watching him crawl around in the bushes looking for the three-carat diamond ring.

The scandal made the papers, and in the weeks to come, pictures of Lana on dates with Bey were widely distributed in the gossip columns.

Gardner and Lana often shared the same man, including Peter Lawford. Such was the case with Bey. Although he rarely

Bey recalled, "At the time I met Lana, World War II was winding down. The really big male stars such as Clark Gable and Robert Taylor were away, and some of us younger actors were taking over their roles. It was a good, glorious time in my life. My career was going great, and I had Lana Turner, with Ava Gardner just around the corner."

gave interviews after his flight from Hollywood, Bey did talk to a reporter in Vienna about the era when he was sustaining simultaneous affairs with both Gardner and Lana.

"They were very different," Bey asserted. "Lana was more in control. She never went wild. I can't say the same for Ava. She was untamed, and would do almost anything if you dared her. Lana never let you forget that she was a goddess. Ava, on the other hand, would kick off her shoes and become the life of the party."

"Lana and Ava did have something in common. You might take one of them out on a date, but that didn't mean you'd come home with them. If Lana or Ava saw someone more tempting than me, perhaps a waiter in tight black pants, they would ditch me and run off with that other guy. One night, Ava and I double-dated with David Niven and her friend, Peggy Maley. David and Ava practically seduced each other at table and on the dance floor. At one point, David whispered to me, 'Dear Boy—be a good chap and take Peggy home for me. Ava and I are heading out.'"

[A Hollywood-bred playgirl, Maley was and would be Gardner's roommate, dreaming

of a stardom that never came. She immortalized herself on the screen, however, in The Wild One *(1954), starring Marlon Brando. In that film, she feeds him the line, "What are you rebelling against?"*

He replies, "Whaddaya got?"]

***

Katharine Hepburn encountered Lana on the set of *Cass Timberlane* (1948) months later, when she was visiting her friend, Spencer Tracy, Lana's co-star. She recalled appearing in Chinese makeup with Bey in *Dragon Seed.* "Both of us looked pretty silly." At one point, she asked Lana about what had happened to her romance with Bey.

Lana looked at her squarely and bluntly said: "He gave me the clap." Then she turned and walked away.

In 1953, as Bey's film career was about to end, the rumor mill in Hollywood was working overtime. Gossip had it that he was about to become embroiled in a major scandal that was set to be aired in the exposé magazines. It was never proven, and no charges were ever filed, but gossip had it that he had raped a twelve-year-old girl. The case did not go to court because the mother of the girl preferred to blackmail Bey instead of filing formal charges.

Consequently, Bey fled from Hollywood and returned to his native Vienna, where he became a photographer for both high fashion and for girlie magazines.

He did give one interview in Vienna about his abrupt departure from Hollywood. "I could have stayed and fought the charges, but I chose not to defend myself from those salacious rumors. I was innocent of all charges, but I finally decided it wasn't worth it to stick around."

After staying away for decades, Bey slipped back into Hollywood in 1993. Jobs were scarce, but he nonetheless found a gig for a guest appearance on *Murder, She Wrote*, the hit TV series starring Angela Lansbury. He also nabbed a starring role in a B-movie, *Healer.*

One night, he had a chance encounter with Cheryl Crane, Lana's daughter, at a party hosted by George Sidney. He said, "Your mother was so, so beautiful, and I imagine she still is. Would you ask her if she'd consider going out with me again?"

She conveyed the invitation, but by that time, Lana was in the throes of throat cancer. She said she was flattered by the offer, but that she must turn it down. "It's best to keep old memories locked inside your heart. Yesterday is dead and gone."

Bey remained a bachelor throughout his entire life, dying in Vienna on September 30, 2012, at the age of ninety.

***

By this time, although Henry Willson was no longer Lana's agent, he called her from time to time whenever he wanted her to publicize "one of the boys in my stable," or when he was trying to set up a management contract for yet another young actor's career.

Lately, he'd been captivated by John Dall, a young New Yorker who was about

Lana's age. Dall had grown up in Panama, where his father, before committing suicide in 1929, had worked as a civil engineer.

After his return to New York, the tall, thin young man with a slightly superior air, had briefly enrolled at Columbia University, but he was eventually drawn into acting, ending up in Los Angeles at the Pasadena Playhouse.

Lana agreed to go out with him because he had received rave reviews for his portrayal of Morgan Evans in *The Corn Is Green* (1945), starring Bette Davis. He would later be nominated for an Oscar as Best Supporting Actor. Although Warners had signed him to a contract, they were planning to let him go in 1946, and he needed publicity to rekindle some interest in himself as an actor.

Dall told her that as a teenager, he'd acted on the stage in Panama, but she learned later that he left that country to return to New York at the age of ten. He also told her that he'd been married in 1940, "but it didn't work out." *[Later, it was revealed to her that he'd never been married.]*

After three dates with him, Lana put her foot down, saying, "I've done my bit for Henry," and she moved on to other, more "connected" liaisons.

As John Dall was one of "Henry's boys," Lana knew in advance that he was either homosexual or an "indulgent bisexual," so she wasn't expecting much in the way of romance.

"He sort of put on the straight act with me," she later told Willson. "He was practically inventing a background for himself."

Believing, nonetheless, that he had the makings of a star, she did, however, run into Dall from time to time in his future. That was particularly true when Alfred Hitchcock cast him as a cool-minded intellectual killer in *Rope* (1948), co-starring James Stewart and Farley Granger.

[John Dall and Granger sustained an affair during the making of the film. Hitchcock later revealed, "I wanted to cast Rope *with two genuine homosexuals."]*

***

Ava Gardner, a barefoot North Carolina Tarheel girl, and the auburn-haired blonde, Julia Jean Mildred Frances Turner, of Wallace, Idaho, each took Hollywood by storm. They should have been rivals—and indeed, they were—but through all the turmoil of their lives, they retained a strong female bond. Each of them survived countless men, broken marriages, scandals, and the ups and downs of a movie career at MGM.

Lee Server, in *Love Is Nothing*—his biography of Ava Gardner—wrote:

"Lana Turner and Ava had much in common: They had both been teenagers when

plucked from nowhere without experience or education. Lana was Metro's hot sex symbol, and so was Ava. They often fell for the same guy. Some of them, like Artie Shaw, Howard Hughes, and Frank Sinatra, had been Lana's first; others, like the racketeer Mickey Cohen's sleek thug, Johnny Stompanato, were Ava's cast-offs. At times, Ava found Lana a bit of a bore, humorless except unintentionally funny, as when, with the manners of an accountant, she reviewed the genital size and ability of her various lovers."

The parallel courses of their lives were striking: Years before Gardner married Mickey Rooney in 1942, Lana had had an affair with "The Pint-sized Wonder" during the late 1930s and had aborted his child. Gardner stayed with him for only a short time, later asserting, "It was the mistake of my life."

After their divorce, Gardner and Lana became lifelong *confidantes*. Howard Hughes went first for Lana before succumbing to the charms of luscious Gardner. Their highly destructive relationship often turned violent.

Both Lana and Gardner were "Queens of the Night," dancing until dawn at many of L.A.'s late-night clubs. Although the former Mrs. Artie Shaw had warned Gardner not to become the next Mrs. Artie Shaw, Gardner did not take Lana's advice and lived to regret it.

They certainly doubled up on the same men, often dating Turkish actor Turhan Bey at the same time. Likewise, Gardner had an affair with Stephen Crane, Lana's second husband. Only a partial list of their shared lovers included the attorney, Greg Bautzer, Richard Burton, Howard Duff, Clark Gable, Fernando Lamas, Peter Lawford, and the "Three Roberts:" Mitchum, Taylor, and Walker.

Gardner warned Lana not to take the notorious gangster, Johnny Stompanato, as a lover. Lana rejected her advice, later admitting, "Stompanato was the worst mistake of my life."

Frank Sinatra seduced Lana long before he married Gardner.

Years later, on reviewing her life, Gardner admitted, "Lana and I did some acting, but our real dramas occurred off screen," Gardner said. "We should write a joint bio, and entitle it *Tales of Two Lurid Lives*."

Gardner and Turner, as nymphomaniacal, dyed-in-the-wool night owls, prowled Los Angeles after dark, winding their ways in and out of boudoirs, but on a few occasions ending up in sleazy motels, especially if their assignations were with dishwashers or garage mechanics. "Lana and I dazzled the fuckers with our beauty," Gardner said.

Both of them denied that they'd arrived in Hollywood as ambition-crazed starlets determined to make it at any cost. Gardner said, "When I hit town, I came looking for a paycheck. I knew that Hollywood was filled with hundreds of gals willing to peddle their pussies for an acting job. They were straining every nerve to become a star. But, for me at least, it was a joy ride. Lots of fun. Lots of night clubs, and the world's most beautiful men. I was like a girl on the vacation of a lifetime. I had no real acting plans, and no more ambition than a flea."

"Some assholes called Lana and me whores," Gardner said. "*Honey chile*, we weren't whores. We never charged. We gave it away."

Lana and Gardner had more or less the same point of view, especially when it came to men and glamor. Lana told Gardner, "Life is what happens to you while you're waiting for the appearance of crow's feet to fuck up your looks. In time, I would name every god damn wrinkle in my face."

Like Lana, Gardner was also defined and promoted as "the most irresistible woman in the world," sultry, tempestuous, and ravishingly beautiful. Columnists proclaimed that "Ava and Lana sizzle both on and off the screen. They serve up a plate of glamor with passion as the main course. Their breasts are world-renowned. Lana virtually invented the tight-fitting sweater. Rooney proclaimed that "Ava's big brown nipples, when aroused, stood out like some double-long golden California raisins."

"We were hard-living and hard-drinking broads, Gardner said. "Right from the beginning, we recognized that fact in each other. Life played us wild cards. In spite of all the scandals, the disastrous love affairs, the tragic, costly mistakes, Lana and I lived life to the hilt."

In a candid admission to Virginia Grey, Lana said, "I was drawn to Ava because she was the most liberated woman I'd ever known. She went through life following her own rules, not those dictated by some man. She chose her own men. She didn't lie on any casting couch. Ava often pitched sex to a guy before he got around to it. She followed Mae West's advice: 'When you hit town, don't keep it a secret.'"

"Ava projected sex appeal. According to rumor, so did I. Men flocked to us. We rejected most of them, but gave a few hundred the thrill of their lives. We ruled as queens over the heyday of movie making, a time that Hollywood will never see again. We seduced and discarded men like Kleenex."

***

Lana released two films in 1945, the year World War II ended. The war was in its final stages when she reported to work on *Keep Your Powder Dry*, with co-stars Susan Peter and her least favorite actress, Laraine Day. Lana had worked with Day before on the set of *Calling Dr. Kildare*, and neither actress was fond of the other. Lana had always referred to Day as "The Ice Queen."

In *Keep Your Powder Dry*, director Edward Buzzell said, "Lana and Laraine played antagonists in the movie, and they weren't acting. It was the real thing."

Joan Crawford had been slated to play the lead, in which she'd impersonate a WAC [*i.e., a member of the Women's Army Corps, a subdivision of the U.S. Army created for women during World War II.*]

George Bruce and Mary McCall wrote its original story as a tribute to the

WACS and the fighting spirit of American womanhood. *[The theme was in vogue at the time: Paramount had released So Proudly We Hail (1943). MGM had shot Cry Havoc (1943) and Universal made Ladies Courageous (1944).]*

In this movie which hovered between comedy and drama, Lana was cast as Val Parks, a spoiled society girl who must join the WACs to save her inheritance. Natalie Schafer, who had played her mother in *Marriage Is a Private Affair,* was cast this time as her parasitic best friend, Harriet Corwin.

Lana's fellow WACs included Day as "Napoleon" Rand, and the ill-fated Peters as Annie Darrison, who suffers the loss of her soldier husband in the movie.

In the beginning, Lana's character of Val didn't take being a WAC seriously. "Napoleon" (Day), an army brat since birth, is a thorn in her side, strictly maintaining military discipline. One reviewer appraised Day's performance as "pathologically bossy." Despite the venom they release at each other, the women triumphantly reconcile before the end of the final reel. *[Hey, it's a movie!]*

Peters, acting as peacemaker, interpreted her sympathetic role with great sensitivity, providing a luminous presence on the screen. If a tragic gunshot hadn't ruined her life, she might have become a star.

Before the movie's release, Peters was accidentally shot during a duck-hunting trip with her husband, Richard Quine. After the accident, she was permanently paralyzed from the waist down, spending the remainder of her short life in a wheelchair.

After a few unsuccessful attempts at a comeback, she lived in seclusion. On October 23, 1952, wracked by almost constant pain, she died at the age of thirty-one, having virtually starved herself to death.

On the set of *Keep Your Powder Dry,* Lana worked well with the film's Brooklyn-born director, Edward Buzzell, who had once been married to Ona Munson, the whorehouse madam, Belle Watling, in *Gone With the Wind* (1939).

***

In the film, in addition to the role essayed by Schafer, Lana's other martini-soaked "sponger" friend was Jess Barker, cast as a sleazy gigolo. In the year (1944) that Lana met Barker on the set, he'd married Susan Hayward, who

Three WACs in a row: Laraine Day, Lana Turner, and Susan Peters star in a wartime propaganda film.

Cast as a New York playgirl, Lana found her role unusual in that "there was almost no romantic element for me in the script. That forced me to go after Susan Hayward's husband off screen."

was still, at least on the surface, one of Lana's best friends.

For some reason, Lana had never broken from Hayward, even after she learned that she was sleeping with her husband, Stephen Crane.

There is no record that Lana ever confronted Hayward for having an illicit affair with her husband.

During the making of the film, it was Barker who pursued Lana. He turned to her for comfort, as he was having lots of difficulty with Susan. Their nights often ended in arguments, leading to violence.

"I felt sorry for him," Lana confessed to Buzzell. "Susan seemed to be castrating him. Of course, she's the big star, and he's a nobody. He was tired of being known as Mr. Susan Hayward. He turned to me for comfort, and perhaps things got a bit out of hand."

It became obvious to the entire cast and crew that Lana was inviting Barker to her dressing room for sex whenever there was a break in filming.

If she's a WAC, she's the best-coiffed, most manicured GI in military service. Some soldiers said that this is photo of Lana—a credit to the U.S. Armed Forces—is even sexier than those in which she appears in ribbons and lace.

"There sure must have been something hot going on in there," Schafer said. "I feared that word would get back to Hayward, and that she'd storm onto the set for a catfight with Lana. Fortunately, that didn't happen."

"At the end of filming, Barker went back to Hayward, and Lana was off to her next conquests," Schafer said. "That happens a lot while films are being shot. That's Hollywood for you. I don't want to judge Lana too harshly. Barker is a handsome man. If I'd been a few years younger, I would have gone after him myself."

Keep Your Powder Dry opened at the Capital Theatre in Washington, D.C. on March 8, 1945. The highlight of the evening was a personal appearance of Lana, who looked far more glamorous than she had in any of the film's WAC uniforms.

Virginia Wilson in *Modern Screen,* wrote: "When you see Lana in uniform, you'll probably rush right out and join up for yourself."

In the *Los Angeles Times,* critic Philip K. Scheuer wrote: "Even when it turns to the severities of military discipline, MGM managed to pour on the glamor. The film somehow emerges as a high-powered vehicle for the studio's stable of beauties, notably Miss Turner herself, who at first appears as a playgirl specializing in highballs and high heels."

The film's most scathing review was published in *The New York Times.* "The writers dashed off the script on the doorstep of the studio beauty shop."

Most of Lana's personal reviews concentrated on her beauty, not on her acting.

***

Henry Willson, the gay talent agent, phoned Lana once again with another request. He wanted her to take as her escort a young actor he was promoting. He needed both of them to show up at the world premiere of *Spellbound,* the 1945 movie co-starring Ingrid Bergman and Gregory Peck.

"His name is Rory Calhoun—for two weeks I'd named him Troy Donahue," Willson said. "I can see you making an entrance in all your platinum blonde glory. It'll be a perfect match, Rory with his raven-black hair and dark, feral look. The photographers will go wild."

Willson's prophecy came true.

The son of a professional gambler in Los Angeles, Rory Calhoun (born Francis Timothy McCowan), was the same age as Lana and exceedingly handsome. "He was oozing with masculinity," she later told Willson. "Unlike John Dall, he does women, too, and how! And he can go all night."

In his promotion, Willson didn't mention that Calhoun had spent much of his young life in prison, mostly on convictions for robbing jewelry stores. As Calhoun himself later admitted himself, "I skipped high school and grew up in a federal penitentiary."

After meeting Susan Hayward's handsome husband, Lana told her director, "Jess Barker sure looks delectable. Susan always raves about his performance in bed, which she considers better than anything he does on the screen. Dare I go where angels fear to tread and find out for myself what causes Susan such joy?"

"Don't go there," the director warned her. "You're inviting trouble."

"I think it's fair play," she answered. "I know for a fact that Susan slept with my husband."

"I'll say it again. Don't go there."

Before his "discovery" the rugged young man had been a firefighter, lumberjack, miner, and cowboy. When he first arrived in Hollywood, he was a male hustler. "I had a weapon that all the homos went for," he accurately boasted.

Calhoun had first been discovered by the bisexual actor, Alan Ladd (Lana's former lover), who doted on Calhoun's perfect physique before turning him over to Willson. Ladd had spotted him while horseback riding in the Hollywood Hills. Willson soon added him to "my stable of boys," and even got David O. Selznick to sign him to a movie contract.

When Lana first met this striking young man, he had recently signed to star in *The Great John L* (1945), based on the life of the turn-of-the-20th-Century heavyweight champion, John L. Sullivan. Its producer was Bing Crosby. *[In an earlier version, Errol Flynn had played the boxer in* Gentleman Jim *(1942).]*

The Great John L gave Calhoun a chance to show off his impressive physique and athletic prowess, which earned him a devoted following among horny teenage girls and ravenous gay men.

After his first night with Lana, Calhoun gave her an anklet, which she often wore, according to her daughter, Cheryl. Before he dated Lana, Willson had already phoned Louella Parsons, hawking Calhoun "as the next Clark Gable."

By this time, Willson's lust for Guy Madison had dimmed, somewhat, and he began revealing to his entourage that he was "mad about the new boy," as he said, meaning Calhoun. To Lana, Willson confessed that "Rory is the most exciting man I've ever met."

"Henry demands that I spend three nights a week in his company," Calhoun told Lana, "but I'm free on the other nights of the week."

The day after Calhoun seduced her, Lana delivered a rave report to Willson. "He's six feet three and all man," she said, "and I'm sure you've explored every foot."

"My job has been to transform this thug into a movie idol," Willson said. "Thanks for helping to get his picture in the paper. I plucked his eyebrows...too hirsute."

"After those pictures of Rory and me appear, I'm sure Joan Crawford will have him on the phone."

When he wasn't dating Lana, Calhoun was often seen on the town with Willson and Guy Madison. There was talk of a *ménage à trois*. As a trio, they were seen dining at

At the premiere of *Spellbound*, Lana spent at least ten minutes chatting with its co-stars, Ingrid Bergman and Gregory Peck.

She later told Henry Willson, "When Ingrid finishes with Greg, I'm next in line. I don't know if I can hold out that long."

The premiere of *Spellbound* marked Calhoun's first public appearance.

With Lana, looking her most glamorous, on his arm, the couple was a sensation, their photograph appearing in most of the nation's newspapers the next morning.

Chasen's and at Romanoff's, and night clubbing at Ciro's and the Trocadero. It was only later that she learned that Madison had fallen in love with Calhoun.

As the years went by, Calhoun didn't confine his charms to Willson or Lana, but shared them with Betty Grable, Yvonne De Carlo, the French actress Corinne Calvet, Susan Hayward, and Marilyn Monroe.

In *That Hagen Girl* (1947), Calhoun competed with Ronald Reagan for a very young Shirley Temple.

In 1948, he married the Mexican actress, Lita Baron. In 1970, when she divorced him, she named seventy-nine women, including Grable and Lana, with whom her husband had committed adultery. When the actor was asked by a reporter if that charge were true, Calhoun said, "Heck, she didn't even include half of them."

Lana stayed in touch with Calhoun, even as both of their careers declined. She spoke to Virginia Grey about him. "Time goes by, and my phone doesn't ring as often as it might. But, sitting home on a rainy night, without a date, I could always give Rory a ring. Even as he got older, it was forever steel hard. Or, as he often boasted, 'In my day, I've re-arranged a few guts.'"

***

For another 1945 release, director Robert Z. Leonard cast Lana in *Week-End at the Waldorf*, a radical "refurbishment" of Vicki Baum's *Grand Hotel*, a novel, published in 1929, which MGM had first adapted in 1932 with an all-star cast headed by Greta Garbo, John Barrymore, and Joan Crawford.

Lana was disappointed when she was told that she'd have to relinquish first billing, in the 1945 reprise, to Ginger Rogers.

In their version of the film, Crawford and Garbo had had no scenes together. Likewise, Rogers and Lana didn't either, which was just as well. Rogers was "seriously pissed off at Lana" for the affair she'd had with Lew Ayres during the years she'd been married to him.

Envisioned as film that would dovetail neatly (and glamorously) with America's Victory celebrations, *Week-End at the Waldorf* assembled an all-star cast that included Van Johnson, Walter Pidgeon, Edward Arnold, Phyllis Thaxter, Keenan Wynn, Robert Benchley, Leon Ames—even Xavier Cugat and his Orchestra. Irene, when sober, was in charge of Lana's gowns, and Sydney Guilaroff tended to her "Victory Bob" tresses.

The movie focuses on various guests lodged at the famous New York landmark, the Waldorf-Astoria Hotel. Rogers, who handled the role previously made famous by Greta Garbo, was cast as the lonely screen star, Irene Malvern, in town for the premiere of her latest movie.

In contrast, Lana as Bunny Smith, the hotel's stenographer, followed in the footsteps of Crawford, who had originated the role.

Walter Pidgeon played war correspondent Chip Collyer, who is mistaken for a jewel thief.

Van Johnson was cast as Captain James Hollis, a wounded hero who's scheduled, within a few days, for some perilous surgery.

Lavishly produced and brilliantly directed by Leonard, *Week-End at the Waldorf* became the sixth-highest-grossing film of 1945.

This scene at the desk of the Waldorf-Astoria showed the four major stars of *Week-End at the Waldorf* checking in.

(Left to right), Ginger Rogers, Walter Pidgeon, Lana Turner, and Van Johnson. It was just a publicity still, not actually a scene from the movie.

Leonard was already adept at handling temperamental stars, having been married to the silent screen diva, Mae Murray. Her most famous movie had been the silent version (1925) of *The Merry Widow,* in which Lana would star in the 1950s remake. Adding to his "skill set," Leonard had directed Lana before in *Ziegfeld Girl.*

Edward Arnold, who had co-starred with Lana in *Johnny Eager,* was cast as Martin X. Edley, a bull-headed businessman trying to sign the Bey of Aribajan to a shady oil deal.

Many reviewers pointed out that *Week-End* would have been a better movie if Lana and Rogers had reversed their roles.

Week-End at the Waldorf was released in October, 1945, about a month after the Japanese surrender. In the movie, the war was still slogging on.

Variety noted that "there is never a dull moment in this Week-End." *Cue* praised the film as "an elaborately frothy three-corner comedy drama."

***

During the filming of *Week-End at the Waldorf,* Lana was introduced to the famous hoteliers, Conrad Hilton and his son, Nicky, who was four years younger than she was.

When Lana checked into the film's namesake hotel, she was assigned to the best suite at the hotel. She found it filled with roses. And before fifteen minutes had passed, three bottles of chilled champagne, each in an icy silver bucket, were delivered to her suite.

When she was introduced to Conrad, the founding father of the chain that bore his name, she found him deeply suntanned and quite handsome for a man born in 1887. As she later said, "He'd held up well, despite his (1942) marriage to Zsa Zsa."

The founder of Hilton Hotels and author of the bestselling promotional bio, *Be My Guest*, Conrad was a tall, powerful Texan, who started out with nothing. A bellhop in Dallas once lent him money to buy himself a hamburger and a Coke. From such lowly beginnings, he'd created an empire.

He was Lana's first overnight guest in the suite he had provided for her. And he seemed delighted that MGM was making a movie that featured his hotel as the backdrop. He expressed only one disappointment: He had wanted Louis B.

Walter Pidgeon and Ginger Rogers bond with each other before a panoramic view of New York, a city in the throes of celebrating the end of World War II.

The character she played was that of a lonely movie star, he a foreign correspondent.

Mayer to film the (black & white) movie in Technicolor as a means of better "showing off the glories of my hotel."

Lana interpreted Conrad as "a Gary Cooper type," rather rugged, a real "ride 'em cowboy" type. Was that her reference to him in bed?

That night, Conrad danced with her downstairs. "He held me so close I could hardly breathe. I felt the State of Texas rising, if you get my drift." All of this she confided to her director, Robert Z. Leonard.

Back in her suite, Conrad invited her to fly to Texas with him for the weekend. "Instead of a *Week-End at the Waldorf,* why not in Dallas?" He went on to confide that his favorite sport was shooting rattlesnakes and then having his chef *sauté* the reptiles for supper, serving them with his Lone Star hot sauce.

"I think I'll skip that and have an omelet," she said. She also turned down his invitation for the holiday in Dallas, but graciously thanked him anyway.

She found him blunt but amusing, and filled with colorful anecdotes from his early days, claiming, "Before I started buying every deluxe hotel in America, I sold coffins. And when I was growing up, Indians were still a problem. I lived in fear that

Lana is seen with Van Johnson, whose character faces surgery so dangerous his life is in peril.

Off screen, she noted that he had resumed his affair with character actor Keenan Wynn, cast in the film as a cub reporter.

out on the trail, they'd abduct me and turn me into a squaw. They often did that to young white men they captured. At our homestead, I slept with a gun under my pillow. If a redskin broke into our house, I'd send the bastard to that happy hunting ground in the sky."

Zsa Zsa had already spread the word in Hollywood that in spite of his age, her husband *"vas a vonderful lover, virile, vell-endowed, and masterful in bed. It's more than ten inches long and ever so thick. Getting banged by him is like having a baby come through your womb."*

The next morning, instead of telling her what a wonderful night he'd had with her in bed, Conrad complained about the failure of his marriage to Zsa Zsa.

"She is the world's most self-centered woman. She expects me to indulge her every whim. She has never forgiven me for putting her on a budget, a very strict budget."

"I don't know what kind of husband Conrad would make," Lana said to Grey. "According to his reputation, he has a girl in every port. In his case, those "ports" include El Paso, San Francisco, Houston, Chicago, and New York."

He shared a late breakfast with her that morning in the lobby of his hotel. Finally, he got around to discussing their intimacies of the previous night. "That time with you was what I had expected when I married Zsa Zsa, who I plan to divorce."

"Will you be looking for another wife any time soon?" she asked.

"Not right away. I don't want to put down Zsa Zsa too much. Being wed to her brought me, in many ways, more laughter and gaiety than I've ever known. But it brought me more headaches and heartaches as well. It was a little like holding a Roman candle—beautiful and exciting, but you were never quite sure when it would go off. And it is surprisingly hard to live up to the Fourth of July every day."

Although he had promised to take her dancing that night at the Stork Club, some emergency suddenly manifested itself in Texas, and he informed her of it with the news that he'd be flying away to the southwest that afternoon. Then he told her that his son, Nicky, would arrive at the hotel later that day. "I'm

When Lana met Conrad Hilton, his marriage to Zsa Zsa Gabor was crumbling. According to press reports, Conrad, a devout Catholic, had a lingering guilt about having married "such an international hussy," and even insisted that they sleep in separate bedrooms.

During their courtship, Conrad one night had presented Zsa Zsa with her choice of either of two small gift boxes, each containing a diamond ring, from Tiffany's. Apparently, he had configured the episode as a test that would determine if she were "the diamond-drenched caricature of a fortune-hunting blonde," as depicted in the newspapers.

Clever fox that she was, Zsa Zsa opted for the smaller diamond during her acceptance of his proposal of marriage.

sure the kid would love to escort the ever-gorgeous Lana Turner out for a night on the town. He specializes in movie stars."

Unknown to both Lana and his father, Nicky had spent the previous night in Bel Air (California) in the bed of his stepmother, Zsa Zsa, who had told him—and later everybody else, too—that "He's even better in bed than Connie, and I thought he was the greatest stud. I guess it's his youth. He did, however, inherit his equipment from his father—and does he know how to use it!"

[After Lana's return to Hollywood, Lana told Virginia Grey, "I knew Conrad was still burning to have me. I was flattered by his attention. After all, he was the most famous and one of the richest men in America. If I married him, I could continue my movie career, reign as Queen of MGM, and also become Empress of the Hilton Hotel chain, with free suites wherever I went."]

***

The evening after her intimacies with his father, Nicky Hilton arrived in her suite at the Waldorf with the intention of escorting her to the Stork Club. Even though he had a reputation for violence against women, Lana was impressed with Nicky Hilton's courtly manners and good looks.

Speaking in a soft Texan drawl, with a reputation as a playboy and for seducing movie stars, he was tall and broad-shouldered, wearing a tailor-made suit from London's Savile Row.

In their usual race to see which woman got him first—a game that Lana was playing with Joan Crawford—Crawford had already won, having seduced Nicky during one of her previous visits to Manhattan. She had booked a suite at the Plaza Hotel in Manhattan. As he told friends later, "We did it on the living room floor. It would have been a memorable experience, but she had the most awful breath."

Nicky candidly admitted to Lana that he'd fallen in love with her after her appearance with Clark Gable in *Somewhere I'll Find You.* "I fell asleep that night and dreamed that, in real life, I was the one holding you in my arms."

She found Nicky a "clean-cut All-American boy. His wild eyes seemed to undress me, but I couldn't hold that against him, now, could I?"

Although they dined on caviar and the world's most tender steaks at the Stork Club, both of them admitted that they'd have happily settled for a hamburger smothered with onions at some joint.

They didn't agree on everything. He named Ezio Pinza as his favorite singing star. She detested both him and his voice. In her future, she would display her utter disdain for Pinza when, in 1951, she co-starred with him in *Mr. Imperium.*

She knew very little about Nicky's background He had dropped out of Baltimore's Loyola College at the age of nineteen and joined the Navy. After some gay sailors spotted him nude in the shower, he attracted lots of propositions and an occasional lover. As he told Cary Grant, "I'm not really that much into guys. But I like it when they worship me and service me. They do all the work."

He also told Grant, "My father is called 'the man with 100,000 beds. My goal in life is to try each of them with a different partner."

Even though the Hilton heir looked like he'd just graduated from college, he

275

was a man of the world, having launched affairs with members of both sexes since he was fourteen years old. He was at ease with famous people, having spent his teenage years meeting (often seducing) industrial tycoons, presidents, senators, Texan oil men, movie stars, and fading members of the European aristocracy.

Although he almost never worked, he held two important positions—one of them Vice President of the Hilton Corporation; and the other as manager of the swanky Bel Air Hotel, an upscale jewel that he referred to as "my fuck pad."

In time, either before or after Lana, Nicky spread his charms among Jeanne Crain, French actress Denise Darcel, Mamie Van Doren, Joan Collins, Natalie Wood, and such socialites as Kay Spreckles and Hope Hampton. Terry Moore reportedly said, "Making love to him was like fornicating with a horse. And such stamina!"

After a night of passion, Lana admitted to Virginia Grey, "I was ready to take him as my next husband, but Van Johnson warned me that he was a *Dr. Jekyll & Mr. Hyde* kind of guy. He's a gambler, a woman-beater, an alcoholic, a closeted heroin addict, and a sex maniac."

Nicky never wanted to date Lana exclusively. Each managed to fit the other into their schedules during his visits to the West Coast. They were seen together riding along Bel Aire's bridle paths, or at exclusive Hollywood parties. He escorted her to lavish dinners thrown by his rich and powerful friends. At one party, she met a rising politician, Richard Nixon. She would soon meet another rising politician, John F. Kennedy.

"Daddy Conrad" never dated her again, but was often seen out with her friend from MGM, tap-dancing Ann Miller. In her memoirs, Miller wrote, "Conrad and I were just good friends."

"If that's what she wants to call it," Lana quipped. "Such good friends, they sleep in the same bed in the same suite."

Nicky would ultimately marry another friend of Lana's, Elizabeth Taylor, in a "fantasy wedding" in 1950.

Lana was very cynical about the nuptials: "Perhaps I was a little jealous," Lana said. "After all, Nicky was a great lover and the most eligible bachelor in America. Every woman he took out, he screwed, and each of them, including Elizabeth, was a great

After Lana's "Weekend at the Waldorf" with hotel heir, Nicky Hilton, he later became the first husband of Elizabeth Taylor. The photo above depicts them at their wedding in 1950, a marriage that lasted less than a year.

During the course of his first date with Elizabeth's blonde competitor, in Manhattan, Nicky couldn't stop praising Lana's looks. Adorned with diamonds, she wore an Irene-designed, magenta-colored gown with towering high heels in a style referred to in 1945 as "Joan Crawford fuck-me shoes."

beauty. He was wild with women and with the Hilton money."

After eight months of marital horror, Elizabeth admitted to Lana, "The fucker often beats the shit out of me. He's a big gambler, heavy drinker, a monster. We're great in bed, but our troubles begin when I'm on the way to the bidet."

That was a line she might have borrowed from Ava Gardner.

"I'm divorcing him," Elizabeth, meeting with Lana in the makeup department at MGM, told her early one morning. "If you want him back, you can have him."

"Thanks for the offer, dear, but I've moved on. As is obvious to all of us hapless gals, Nicky is just not husband material. Even if he marries again, he'll never be true to one woman."

"You and I should follow in Nicky's footsteps," Elizabeth said. "Why should we be faithful to just one man? That's so old-fashioned. People call me a scarlet woman. I'm not...Color me purple!"

***

For a brief time during April of 1946, Lana told friends that Charles P. Jaeger, an executive of the American Broadcasting Company, "is my one and only." A picture taken of them nightclubbing was published in newspapers across the country, and rumors persisted that marriage was imminent.

Back from a trip to New York, Lana phoned Louella Parsons. "Charlie is tall, very handsome, and oh so wonderful," she gushed. "He really knows how to treat a lady. He's just what I've been looking for all my life. Yes, he has proposed to me, but I haven't made up my mind. I'm still thinking it over."

On April 14, passengers spotted Lana and her infant daughter, Cheryl, aboard a TWA Constellation flight leaving Los Angeles heading for New York. Jaeger accompanied her.

After they arrived in Manhattan, Cheryl was transferred to the care of a nanny, as Lana made the rounds of the chic spots, including the Stork Club. Jaeger, ever so attentive, was at her side.

She had claimed that he proposed to her. But when questioned by reporters, he answered, "We're just friends."

On at least two separate occasions, they were seen theater-going together in New York, attending a performance of *Born Yesterday*, which

At the Stork Club in Manhattan, Lana is seen dining and nightclubbing with ABC executive Charles P. Jaeger.

Hollywood insiders, most of them seeing pictures of Jaeger for the first time, didn't quite consider him the male beauty Lana raved about. He was reasonably attractive and well-groomed, but hardly the matinee idol Lana had described to her friends.

would, in 1950, be adapted into a movie in which Judy Holliday would beat out frontrunners Gloria Swanson and Bette Davis for the coveted Oscar.

Jaeger also took Lana to a performance of Tennessee Williams' *The Glass Menagerie*. At this point in his career, Williams was no longer an unknown, struggling over script details for *Marriage Is a Private Affair*. At this point, he was Broadway's overnight sensation, and the most sought-after playwright in the entertainment industry. In her future, Lana would campaign for two coveted roles in plays he'd write, *Cat on a Hot Tin Roof* and *Sweet Bird of Youth*.

Lana and Jaeger didn't seem on the same page about their upcoming wedding. On yet another occasion, he admitted that marriage might be in the offing, but it might take place "anywhere from a week to five years from now."

However, when Lana was questioned, she said that the marriage was scheduled in less than a month. "I have always wanted to be a June bride."

She made those remarks in New York. When questioned, after her return to Los Angeles, she said, "Mr. Jaeger and I know each other, but we're not even engaged."

Suddenly, Jaeger exited from Lana's life, and Lana, the next week, was seen dating Huntington Hartford, one of the richest men in America and heir to a vast A&P fortune.

***

If Lana had married Huntington Hartford in 1946, she would have a choice of places where she could live. She would also be marrying a man who dated from the A-list. Before her, he'd bedded the two richest women on the planet: tobacco heiress Doris Duke and the Woolworth heiress Barbara Hutton.

After Lana, Marilyn Monroe would loom in his future. As he said when he was dating her, "If I went for Miss Turner, the blonde bombshell of the 1940s, why not the blonde bombshell of the 1950s, too?"

Hartford not only dated powerful women, but he forged friendships with powerful men, too. Among them were Errol Flynn, Richard Nixon, Aristotle Onassis, Howard Hughes, Charlie Chaplin, and John Jacob Astor VI. He was also "pals," as he called them, with the Duke and Duchess of Windsor.

Hartford's homes included villas at Cap d'Antibes and in Palm Beach, a flat in London, an apartment in Paris, a 24-acre

In 1946, photographers caught up with Lana and Huntington Hartford together at a nightclub in Miami. Again, as with Jaeger, there were rumors that marriage was imminent.

[One of them mocked her with rumors of having previously monogrammed her towels with "HH" when she thought that Howard Hughes was going to marry her.]

estate outside Los Angeles, and a roomy duplex on Beekman Place in Manhattan. In time, he would own Paradise Island (formerly Hog Island), across from Nassau in The Bahamas.

He confided to Lana that he planned to spend his millions while he was still alive and could enjoy the rich lifestyle. "I prefer to be a man of leisure—sailing, partying at the best of clubs, and surrounding myself with beauty, not only the world's most beautiful women, but the world's most stunning art treasures."

He had very strong opinions about art, both painting, sculpture, and even writing. He considered Picasso, Tennessee Williams, and William Faulkner "vulgar."

He was also interested in becoming a Broadway producer, and pitched a project to Lana. He wanted her to consider appearing in an adaptation of Charlotte Brontë's *Jane Eyre*, with her in the title role. He told her that the play would be perfect if Errol Flynn were cast opposite her as "The Master of Thornfield."

Alas, her affair with Hartford ended about as abruptly as her affair with Jaeger. There was no fight, no formal parting of ways. She described her last night with him as "a lot of fun." At breakfast the next morning, she sensed no farewell.

Mildred had wanted her to marry Hartford, telling her daughter that he would bring her the financial security she'd need when her beauty faded. When she didn't see him calling on Lana again, she asked, "What happened?"

"I don't know," she answered. "After our last breakfast, he kissed me passionately at the door, the kind of kiss a soldier gives the girl he's leaving behind before going off to war. He never called again."

She later read that Hartford had been seen out and about with Gene Tierney.

With contempt in her voice, Lana told Mildred "that Tierney woman usually takes my sloppy seconds: Howard Hughes and Victor Mature come to mind."

Unknown to Lana, Tierney would soon appear in *The Razor's Edge* (1946) with Tyrone Power, a man ("Lana's greatest love") who would loom in her future.

After moving on from Tierney and Lana, Hartford spent the rest of his life squandering his vast fortune. He said, "The golden bird, coming to life, has somehow wriggled out of my hand and flown away."

At the age of 97, the former tycoon died on Lyford Cay in The Bahamas. He had outlived Lana by thirteen years.

***

As if Lana couldn't find her own men, her best pal, Ava Gardner, often fixed her up with one of her cast-offs. Hollywood's most beautiful blonde and Hollywood's most beautiful brunette often shared lovers—and not just Frank Sinatra. Gardner even married Lana's first husband, Artie Shaw. As Lana told Mildred, "Now Artie won't be hanging around me all the time."

Lana had also sampled the charms of Mickey Rooney before Gardner was foolish enough to marry him.

She had just co-starred with Burt Lancaster in *The Killers* (1946), based on the famous short story by Ernest Hemingway.

[Hollywood footnote: in 1964, Ronald Regan would play a brutal crime kingpin in a remake of The Killers. It would be his last motion picture before he found a new profession.]

279

Gardner had had a torrid affair with Lancaster, but it was time for her to move on. She extolled his male beauty and after-midnight charms to Lana, who said: "Tell me more. I'm more than interested in auditioning him."

Lancaster was a well-muscled athlete, having been a circus acrobat before his gigs in Hollywood. Filled with robust energy, he was strikingly handsome, with an intense glare. The author, Norman Mailer, said, "His grip could crush, and I never looked into eyes as chilling as his." Lana used an odd word to describe his smile…"piercing."

Lancaster had grown up on the tough streets of Manhattan's East Harlem. His most traumatic experience had come when he was twelve years old. Six neighborhood toughs had overpowered him and repeatedly raped "the pretty boy," as they called him.

Lancaster might have been pretty, but he was also street fighter. Three months later, he trapped the

To publicize *The Killers*, Burt Lancaster and Ava Gardner were driven to Malibu, where they strutted for photographers on the beach in their bathing suits. They took turns posing piggyback atop each other.

According to Ava, "Burt was such a marvelous athlete, he seemed able to make himself pounds lighter. That's how he could ride my back…no pun intended."

gang leader in a back alley and slashed his face with a switchblade, but didn't kill him. He was never arrested.

He was also smart, winning a scholarship to New York University. Before joining the circus, he worked as a singing waiter.

In 1942, as America went to war, he joined he 21st Special Services Division, a military group of talented young soldiers who provided the troops with entertainment as a means of keeping up morale. From 1943 to 1945, he served in General Mark Clark's Fifth Army in Italy, as the Allies chased the Nazis north.

Tall and muscular, Lancaster was a "babe magnet" before the term was invented. As a teenager, he posed for nude photos. One of them was later reprinted and widely distributed, eventually published in books and underground newspapers. He became the first movie star male pinup, though not nearly as widely distributed as his female counterparts, Betty Grable and Lana.

"Burt and I were just kids starting out," Gardner told Lana. "We were enjoying ourselves and discovering each other. Of course, I was married to Artie at the time, even though that marriage started to fall apart on our honeymoon."

She warned Lana, "You might be disappointed when Burt strips and exposes his uncut glory. Of course, his body is magnificent, but it appears that Mother Nature wasn't too generous. But that's only a first impression. He's a grower, not a show-er."

She also revealed that producer Mark Hellinger had first tested Lancaster and her in a love scene. "His passion was real. I felt his erection pressing up against me. I knew then I had him, or soon would. Just to make sure that everything was in order, I slipped my hand down there for a good feel. I thought he'd climax right on the spot."

"He's everything a lover should be," she said, "both sensual and passionate. I'll let you in on one of his sexual secrets. He likes his balls jiggled."

On his first date with Lana, Lancaster told her that he had been discovered in an elevator in Manhattan. "This guy got on the elevator with me, and kept looking at me with X-ray vision. It was like he was undressing me. I get off and this guy follows me. I turn around and grab him by the necktie like I'm going to choke him. I said, 'Listen, you pansy, keep that up and I'll beat the shit out of you!' Then I head for this job interview in the next office, and this same guy puts in a call, telling me he's a producer casting a play. And he wants me for an audition. I'd heard that line before. Turns out he was legit. That play eventually led me here to you tonight. Hollywood AND Lana Turner! What more could a man ask for?"

On his first date with Lana, he took her to a boxing match, showing her to a front-row seat. She was dressed all in white and feared her outfit might get splattered with blood.

That night in her boudoir, as she later reported to Gardner, "He was all you said with your advance billing…and a bit more. He also likes to nibble your toes, calling them 'delectable morsels of shrimp.'"

A writer for *Cosmopolitan*, describing Lancaster in *The Killers*, wrote: "It was an extraordinary debut for an unknown. Overnight, Burt Lancaster was a star with a meteoric rise faster than Gable, Garbo, or Lana Turner."

Over the next few years, Lancaster and Lana often encountered each other at parties. During the 1940s and early 50s, both of them had moved on to others, and Lana got married to Bob Topping.

Lancaster's longtime companion, Jackie Bone, told her, "Burt loves to take his leading ladies to bed, and he's had quite a few of them, everyone from Yvonne De Carlo to Shelley Winters.

Lancaster told Lana, "I know what you've heard about me, that I'm difficult to work with and grab all the broads. That's not true. I'm difficult only some of the time, and grab only some of the broads."

Louis B. Mayer had not signed Lancaster, and one night at a party, he asked her how she would describe him. "He's compulsive, dynamic, memorable. His friends call him a vulgar hot-head, yet he loves opera and the ballet."

"Funny that you should say that. I keep hearing that he's a fag."

***

Lana had known Virginia Mayo for several years, ever since she and Ava Gardner had agreed to be cheerleaders for a charity baseball game, billed at the time as

"Stars vs. Stars."

They had never known each other well, but occasionally, they ran into each other at premieres or at parties, when they "air-kissed" their way past each other.

Lana had just seen Mayo in William Wyler's drama, *The Best Years of Our Lives* (1946), in which Mayo had played the unsympathetic gold-digger married to a returning war veteran, Dana Andrews, another of Lana's previous "flings." It would become the highest-grossing film in the United States since *Gone With the Wind* (1939).

As a fellow blonde goddess, Lana was rather jealous of the victories Mayo had recently scored with the press. One fan magazine said "she looked like a pinup painting come to life," and the Sultan of Morocco declared that her beauty "was tangible proof of the existence of God."

As Mayo related to Lana, she had a problem: During the filming of *The Best Years of Our Lives*, she had become involved with Steve Cochran, who had been cast as her sleazy boyfriend. Their affair continued after the filming ended. However, she'd met a minor B-list actor, Michael O'Shea, whom she would marry in 1947.

After listening for a few minutes, Lana asked, "In other words, you want me to take this Cochran boy off your hands? I've already heard quite a lot about him. He's dynamite."

"That he is," Mayo answered. "In more ways than one. You won't be disappointed. Joan Crawford, or so I've heard, hasn't gotten around to him yet.

[Hollywood footnote: Crawford's affair with Cochran would not begin until they co-starred together in The Damned Don't Cry *(1950).]*

Cochran, the son of a logger, had grown up in Laramie, Wyoming. During his teenage years, he'd had a number of run-ins with the police.

Once in Hollywood, Cochran confessed that his ultimate dream fantasy involved being a Sultan controlling a harem staffed with girls aged 13 to 14.

He arrived the following night at Lana's house, and from her first observation, she realized that casting directors would interpret him as the ultimate "sleazy pretty boy" for *film noir*. She served him dinner, but halfway through the meal, he couldn't wait, and dragged her off into the bedroom.

The next morning, she called Mayo after Cochran had departed. "It was a big thrill all right. I'd hate to have been a virgin broken in by him. He's a walking streak of

During his first months in Hollywood, Steve Cochran had earned a reputation as a womanizer, and Lana's gossipy girlfriends were touting his male assets. He was "The New Boy of Tinseltown," and was already being referred to as "Mr. King Size" when he wasn't otherwise being labeled "The Schvantz."

sex, and he can go all night. But he's far too violent for my taste. My body is bruised. I was afraid he might injure my face. It's a good thing I don't have to confront the camera tomorrow. After all, you and I get by on our looks. Neither of us is Sarah Bernhardt."

"Don't worry about Steve," Mayo answered. "I just heard that Mae West has contacted him and wants to audition him to go on a road trip with her in *Diamond Lil.*"

[Cochran, in reference to West, later admitted, "I threw the stuck-up bitch a few mercy fucks. That was almost written into my contract. When was the broad born? No doubt in 1880."]

After Mamie Van Doren filmed *The Beat Generation* with Cochran in 1959, she described him in a memoir. Her experience with this rough guy was similar to what Lana's had been years before: "He was the rough-hewn, sexy, perennial movie tough guy. What I discovered about Steve after we had been dating for a while was that his behavior was frighteningly erratic. He had a violent temper reminiscent of my first husband. In bed, he became increasingly rougher, until one night he very nearly beat me up."

Many of Cochran's conquests claimed that he pumped up his excitement by slapping a woman during intercourse, and spitting into her mouth.

***

Eddie Mannix, from MGM's publicity department, phoned Lana with a request. He wanted her to appear, accompanied by Peter Shaw, at the premiere of *The Yearling* (1946). Starring Gregory Peck and Jane Wyman, *The Yearling* was set in the early frontier wilds of Florida.

"Who the hell is Peter Shaw?" Lana asked. "Never heard of him."

"He's a Limey that we're putting under contract. He's even handsomer than Errol Flynn. Lately, he's been going out with Joan Crawford."

"Leave it to that bitch to get him first," she said.

"Not only Joan, but he's also been seen taking out Rita Hayworth and Ava Gardner."

"For the new boy in town, this guy is sure devouring the frosting off the cake."

"From what I hear, Peter is an apt name for him," Mannix told her.

Lana agreed to the date, but phoned Gardner to see if Shaw were worth pursuing after the screening.

"He's an absolute doll in and out of bed," Gardner claimed. "He's not stuck-up at all. He even told me that as an actor, he can't even act. MGM wants to market him as their new celluloid heartthrob. If he attends the premiere with you, looking absolutely gorgeous, the two of you are sure to hit the morning papers."

Then Lana asked about Crawford. Gardner said that she'd started dating Shaw after her divorce from Phillip Terry had been finalized. "But that's over now. Peter told me that he's too strong a man to be prince consort for the Queen of Hollywood."

"So now, Crawford—The San Antonio Beauty Queen of 1904—is the Queen of

Hollywood?" Lana said, with strong contempt in her voice. "Who the fuck crowned her that?" *[Lana was referencing the year and the birthplace of Crawford.]*

At the glittering premiere, Shaw and Lana, dressed all in white, made a spectacular appearance. There were immediate rumors of a romance.

A highlight for Lana occurred later, at a private VIP reception associated with the premiere. There, she got to talk to the star of the film, Gregory Peck. She still wanted to date him, but somehow, had not found it possible, barring a full-frontal assault.

During their dialogue, she made overtures about seeing him alone, but he didn't pick up on them. Treating her graciously, he moved on to talk to Wyman and then to Bette Davis.

That left Shaw, and he lived up to Gardner's advance billing as "being the most gorgeous thing walking on two feet." He stood six feet three, with thick dark hair, broad shoulders, and narrow hips. "He did look a bit like Errol Flynn, but without his hangups," Lana said.

That night, and over the course of the two weeks that followed, she got to know this dashing young Brit who had gone to school in London's Westminster section with another actor, Peter Ustinov. When England entered World War II, he'd joined the British army.

Along the way, he'd met a model, Mercia Squires, and after some intense dating, had married her. When he left for Belgium in 1944, she was pregnant. In Hamburg, during the days immediately flanking the end of the war, he worked as an aide to Field Marshal Bernard Montgomery. News arrived that he was the father of a son named David.

However, when Shaw eventually returned home to Britain, he found that his new wife was living with another soldier. Heartbroken, he wanted to leave England He found a theatrical agent who pitched his good looks and British charm to MGM. In a surprise

Two views of Peter Shaw: (top photo), with Lana, with whom he did not find happiness, and (lower photo) with Angela Lansbury, with whom he (presumably) did.

move, he was awarded a contract and hired at $350 a week.

After Lana's first few nights with Shaw, she reported to Gardner about her latest beau. "The first night he stayed over, I woke up. It was a Saturday. He was not in the bed with me. A few minutes later, there was a rap on my door, and he entered with a breakfast tray. He'd cooked it himself and had even placed a red rose on the tray. My God, in addition to being a heavenly lover, he can cook, too!"

"We'll work out some arrangement," Gardner said. "I need Peter at least two nights a week. The rest of the time, he can freelance."

"Ava, darling Ava. It's more than that. Based on my first morning's glow, I'm thinking of marrying this darling man."

"Tomorrow, you'll feel different," Gardner predicted.

As it turned out, her words were prophetic.

Shaw's film career was slow to launch, as one producer after another told him that he looked "too much like Tyrone Power."

Then, instead of Shaw, the REAL Tyrone Power walked into Lana's life.

The British actress, Angela Lansbury, also had her eagle eye trained on Shaw, and, she too, considered him marriage material. By 1949, they had wed.

When Lansbury learned that her future husband had seduced Lana, she cattily said, "Lana Turner is a good example of what an acting coach can do with completely incompetent material."

Lansbury had wanted the role of Milady De Winter in the upcoming remake of *The Three Musketeers,* but ended up cast in a smaller role as France's Queen Anne instead.

She later said, "Miss Turner got the coveted role. The film gave her a chance to show off her chest."

***

Lana had been a big hit throughout World War II, especially with the men who fought that war, but during the postwar year of 1946, with the soldiers returning home and Hollywood's product moving rapidly into new arenas, she worried about her future. Would she become one of those over-the-hill blondes, like Veronica Lake or Carole Landis, whose allure ended with the peace treaty with Japan? Even her chief rival, Betty Grable, didn't expect to retain her wartime fame as the leading pinup beauty.

Would the boys who had returned from the battle fronts adore Lana as much as before? Every day, she studied her nude figure in a full-length mirror, searching for that first wrinkle, those first tiny sags of flesh. Both her hairdressers and makeup artists assured her that she was at the peak of her beauty. Eventually, she believed them.

She was having numerous affairs and continued to do so, based on the slogan she had so often repeated: "So many men, so little time."

Anxious to learn what 1946 held, she arranged "readings" with two separate fortune tellers in Los Angeles. Somewhat generically, both of them predicted "great tragedy" looming in her faraway future.

She couldn't worry about that, as she was living for the here and now.

But if either of the fortune tellers had been genuinely clairvoyant, they would have predicted that, indeed, BIG events lay in her immediate future:

ONE:
She'd have an affair with a young Naval lieutenant who would one day become the most powerful man on earth; and

TWO:
She'd meet the love of her life; and

THREE:
She'd make what many critics consider her finest motion picture, and

FOUR:
She'd enter into a loveless marriage, her third.

Chapter Eleven

The Postman Rings Twice for Lana

And Then Again...and Again...and Again

Tyrone Power Becomes the Love of Lana's Life

"If only one Lana Turner film could be placed in a time capsule to be seen by future generations, then I would select my role as Cora in *The Postman Always Rings Twice*. At first, I had protested casting John Garfield in the role. I was wrong. I later learned in a motel room that a man didn't have to look like Robert Taylor or Errol Flynn to be a great lover."

In most accounts, Lana's brief fling in 1946 with the British actor, Rex Harrison, was not detected on the radar screen. However, her daughter Cheryl, in her memoirs, listed him as one of the men that Lana was seeing at the time, along with several other beaux: Greg Bautzer (their affair never really ended); Tony Martin (who on rare occasions made an overnight stopover at Lana's home); Peter Lawford (who slipped back into her good graces on three occasions after she'd dropped him); and Howard Hughes (making an unexpected appearance now and then). Even Huntington Hartford phoned her when he flew to Los Angeles one night.

As she boasted, "These guys can't seem to get Lana out of their blood."

Ever since Harrison had scored big in the U.K. on both the stage and on screen, Hollywood had been trying to lure him to its inner sanctums. Then, as he was weighing various offers, World War II began, and he joined the RAF.

Finally, at war's end, he was lured to Hollywood after being offered a contract at 20th Century Fox. Newspapers were packed with news of his arrival in Tinseltown.

As a "young gent," studying in Liverpool, Harrison had been introduced to sex by a black prostitute from Kingston, Jamaica.

By 1934, he was seasoned for marriage to fashion model Collette Thomas, the union lasting until 1942. That didn't stop him from adulterous affairs, including one with Vivien Leigh. In 1943, he married the German actress, Lilli Palmer, although he wasn't faithful to her, either.

The Australian actress, Coral Browne, nicknamed him "Sexy Rexy," and the label had stuck.

One afternoon, Paulette Goddard phoned Lana and invited her to a dinner party. "My seating calls for man, woman, man, woman. I've invited Rex Harrison, and I need him to show up with a date to make my dinner seating come out evenly. Would you allow him to escort you to my dinner? Every guest is strictly A-list."

"I'd be honored," she answered.

"I'm looking forward to seeing you again. He'll pick you up at 7:30. You and I have come a long way since we starred together in *Dramatic School.*"

"And how! Can I assume, darling, that you've already enjoyed Rex—if you hadn't, I guess you wouldn't be recommending him."

"Yes, darling," Goddard answered. "You and I on occasion have sampled the same mer-

After her one-night stand with "Sexy Rexy" (Rex Harrison), Lana told her friends that she found him "dangerously attractive, but nothing but trouble for a woman."

chandise. Gable comes to mind. So do Gary Cooper. Greg Bautzer. David Niven. Spencer Tracy."

"Don't leave out my former husband, Artie Shaw."

"Oh yes, and him, too. In case you ever have the chance, skip John Wayne. Get him out of the saddle and a gal has got very little to work with."

[Goddard had co-starred with Wayne in Reap the Wild Wind *(1943). Lana would co-star with him in* The Sea Chase *(1955).]*

"I must warn you," Goddard said. "Rex is such a cad, very snobbish, very conceited. But I think you'll find him amusing. His wife is out of town, so he's free to escort you."

The actor might have agreed with her assessment of him. He once told an interviewer, "Off stage, I can be far from charming. I am acid. *ACID!* I have a direct tongue, and I say what I think is the truth. I don't give a damn for the consequences."

He had also expressed his view of marriage. "I would never fit into the life of some woman. She has to fit into mine. The happiest married men I know have a wife to go home to, not to go home with."

Later in life, Alan J. Lerner, who wrote the lyrics of Harrison's biggest hit, *My Fair Lady,* claimed, "It's a melancholy fact, but Rex and I, between the two of us, have supported more women that Playtex."

During their transit to Goddard's home, Harrison did not live up to his awful advance billing. He was the perfect English gentleman, with impeccable manners and a clipped English accent that amused her. Yet during odd moments, he could be wickedly provocative. Noticing that she was very, very blonde and dressed all in white, including her fur, he raised an eyebrow. "Are you blonde all over?"

"That's for you to find out, but only if you get lucky," she shot back.

Goddard's dinner party was a success. Through it, Lana got to meet some of the leading members of the British expatriate colony.

Lana was also introduced to Goddard's third husband, whom she'd married after leaving Charlie Chaplin. Burgess Meredith was five feet seven inches tall, with ginger-colored hair. She did not find him particularly attractive, but his reputation "as a Casanova and a cocksman" on Broadway and Hollywood had preceded him. He admitted, "God knows I'm not a dashing swain, but a kind of mongrel, the way I chase the foxes."

Those "foxes" included Tallulah Bankhead, Ingrid Bergman, Olivia de Havilland, Marlene Dietrich, Hedy Lamarr, Ginger Rogers, and Norma Shearer.

While Harrison was talking with Goddard and Douglas Fairbanks, Jr., Meredith asked Lana to walk out onto the terrace for a moonlit preview of their well-manicured garden. In the middle of their talk, he reached for her free hand and placed it on his crotch. "Does that answer the question about why I'm sought after by the ladies?"

"It does so *amply,*" she answered, before turning to go inside. "When you break up with Paulette, which seems in the cards, come up and see me sometime."

En route back to Lana's house, Harrison told her, "I have no idea who I am at any given time. I have six different personalities. When I wake up each morning, I never know which personality will take over."

"Which of the many Mr. Harrisons is driving me home tonight?" she asked.

"A combination of Cary Grant and Laurence Olivier," he said, "without the homosexual overtones. I'm also a bit of Noël Coward and John Gielgud. Again, without the homosexual overtones."

"Are all great English actors homosexual, or at least bi-?" she asked.

"Most of them are, even Richard Burton, who frequently admits it."

"I'm not familiar with this Mr. Burton."

"You soon will be," he predicted. "He's a Welsh actor with a magnificent speaking voice, ideal for stage and screen. I know it sounds far-fetched, but you might one day be co-starring with him."

[Ironically, that is what happened in 1955 when Burton and Lana co-starred together in The Rains of Ranchipur. *Fourteen years after that, Harrison, in the grotesquely campy* Staircase *(1969), would play Burton's gay lover.]*

On her doorstep, Harrison took her in his arms and kissed her passionately, but she refused his request to come in for a nightcap.

Goddard phoned the following morning for an update on what had happened with Harrison after she left the party.

"I found him very suave, very charismatic. A bit aloof, self-enchanted. He is *oh so veddy* English. A real arrogant bastard, but in some way strangely appealing."

"Did Rex carve another notch on his belt?"

"Not at all…although he tried."

***

After that "kiss-off" on her doorstep, Lana didn't expect to hear from Harrison again. But he called two days later to invite her to a party at the elegant home of Merle Oberon. The beautiful actress with the porcelain skin had been born in Calcutta, the daughter of a British father and a woman of India.

Lana had always been intrigued by her reputation, especially that she was now making a film at Universal, a somewhat confusing and silly historical fantasy with a then-massive budget of $1.6 million. Entitled *A Night in Paradise* (1946), it was being shot with Lana's former lover, Turhan Bey.

Oberon had just emerged from an affair with James Cagney. It had been sparked during their collaboration in a war bond drive that had toured the country. Her other lovers had included three men whom Lana knew well—Clark Gable, Gary Cooper, and David Niven. She would soon seduce Prince Philip before his marriage to Princess Elizabeth.

The photographer and designer, Cecil Beaton, claimed, "Merle (Oberon) is almost a nymphomaniac. She makes love because she likes it, or because of the money. She is as promiscuous as a man enjoying a quick one behind the door."

290

At Oberon's party, Lana had an amusing chat with Cecil Beaton, the gossipy photographer and designer. She emerged from it somewhat surprised that Greta Garbo had, for a period, taken him as a lover. "He seemed '100 percent homosexual' to me," she had said.

Lana chatted briefly with Darryl F. Zanuck, who had also been one of Oberon's lovers. To Lana, Zanuck said, "I regret that I let you slip through my fishing net and land in the lap of that asshole, Louis B. Mayer. I could have turned you and Tyrone Power into the hottest screen team since Harlow and Gable."

"I regret that, too, Mr. Zanuck," Lana answered.

"I'm probably the straightest guy who ever set foot in Hollywood. I take a steambath with Power every day. At times, he's so fucking pretty that I've considered raping him myself."

Ava Gardner had forewarned her, "The only thing bigger than Zanuck's cigar is his cock, which he's not too shy to show or put to use. He gets turned on by watching two starlets make love to each other before ravishing one of them."

After Oberon's party, Harrison drove Lana home again, and this time, did the inviting, suggesting that he should come in for a nightcap. As her mother, Mildred, learned the following morning, Harrison evolved into a surprise guest for breakfast.

This time, Lana phoned Goddard to deliver a gossipy report: "In a word, he's proficient. Although I prefer the George Montgomery type, I find Rex wickedly amusing. Last night at the party, he wore a rather forbidding monocle over his right eye and had a long cigarette holder clenched between his teeth. He has the aura of an English aristocrat. A temporary diversion for me—nothing else."

***

Intent on playing the field, Lana did not accept Harrison's third invitation for a night in his hotel suite. Robert Stack had introduced her to a young navy lieutenant, the son of one of the richest men in America, an Irish mogul whose fortune was based partially on bootlegging. It was clearly understood that the ex-Navy man would not remain in Hollywood for long, and she wanted to be with him.

It came as little surprise to her that Harrison was soon sustaining an affair with Carole Landis, another blonde and a longtime rival of Lana's, although they kept up some pretend friendship. "Landis and I are acquaintances, not friends," Lana said whenever her name came up.

At the time Harrison began his affair with Landis, she was twenty-nine years old and at the rocky end of her fourth marriage, this time to a businessman, W. Horace Schmidlapp. The former call girl from San Francisco had also had a lesbian affair with author Jacqueline Susann, who would go on to write the mega-bestseller, *Valley of the Dolls*.

At this point in her career, Landis had become known in Hollywood for prostituting herself, making her sexual favors available to studio executives at both Warners and at 20th Century Fox, hoping to get better roles.

Although still married to Lilli Palmer, Harrison continued his affair with Landis until the night of July 4, 1948. By then, she had fallen madly in love with him, but her passion was not reciprocated. He was using her only for sex.

On his last night with her, he told her that he was leaving her. He didn't stop there, perhaps wanting to say something so provocative that she would drop him for good and not pester him with recriminations. "You know," he told her, "Lana Turner and I had this thing when I first came to this boring town called Hollywood. Well, we've resumed our affair, and I've fallen in love with her, even though she's seeing this guy Bob Topping. That doesn't matter to me. I'm leaving you for Lana."

[Actually, Lana was doing more than "seeing" Topping. She went on to marry him in April of 1948.]

Yet long before Lana married him, Landis had had an affair with him. In Walter Winchell's column of October 12, 1944, appeared this item: "The humidity felt over the weekend in New York can be traced to Carole Landis and her latest love, Bob Topping, heir to a tin-plate fortune."

Three years later, in December of 1947, Landis rented her house to Topping, with the full understanding that by then, he was deeply involved with Lana. He wanted use of her house for four months while another home was being restored and renovated for Lana and himself in anticipation of their upcoming marriage.]

After the completion of some final business arrangements, Landis arrived back at her home late on the morning of July 5th, 1948. She was morbidly despondent over Harrison walking out on her. Up to that point, he had misled her, telling her that he was on the verge of divorcing his German wife (Lilli Palmer) so that he could marry her.

Landis sat down, took out a sheet of her blue stationery, and wrote a suicide note to her mother. She then swallowed some fifty Seconal tablets, known at the time as "red devils."

[Lupe Velez had committed suicide this way in 1944.]

Did Lana inadvertently figure into the suicide of her rival, Carole Landis?

On the night he dumped her, Rex Harrison told his mistress that he was leaving her for Lana Turner. Landis was found dead the next day.

Harrison arrived at her home later that day and was let in by the maid. He wanted to remove his belongings. The maid had not ventured upstairs that day, but Harrison did, discovering Landis' corpse sprawled out across her bathroom floor.

Before calling the police, he phoned Harry Brand at 20th Century Fox, who worked in the studio's publicity department. Nicknamed "The Fixer," he occupied the same position as Eddie Mannix at MGM.

The news of Landis' death could not be suppressed. Her adulterous liaison with Harrison was splashed across every frontpage in America.

The scandal was so damaging that Fox terminated its contract with Harrison, who fled back to England. For many years, he was blacklisted in American films. Lilli Palmer would wait another decade before divorcing him.

As Harrison later told Noël Coward and others, "Carole went to her death thinking I had returned to Lana Turner."

***

During Landis' brief career, she was often compared to Lana, and in many cases, she appeared on the same lists together. Such was the case in 1947 when each of them made "The Top Best Undressed List." Cited were Marie ("The Body") Mac-Donald in a bathing suit; Rita Hayworth languorous in a *négligée,* Lana prettiest in a slip; and Landis loveliest in a night gown.

Lana and Landis were linked on their final list when gossip writer Bob Thomas published his annual "Best and Biggest" roster for 1948:

BEST PICTURE: Hamlet
BIGGEST SOCIAL EVENT: The Lana Turner/Bob Topping Wedding;
BIGGEST FEMALE DISCOVERY: Betsy Drake (the wife of Cary Grant); and
BIGGEST SHOCK—the Carole Landis suicide.

***

Robert Stack had met John F. Kennedy in 1940 during his first visit to Hollywood. They became immediate friends. "Jack told me he wanted to fuck every big star in Hollywood," he said. "He called it 'celebrity poontang.'"

Alfredo de la Vega had introduced the two bachelors-at-large. During their first dinner together, Stack had told him about his secret hideaway, which he called "the Flag Room." It was within a small apartment that lay at the end of a cul-de-sac, Whitley Terrace, between Cahuenga and Highland in the Hollywood Hills. Here stood a jumbled mass of apartments stacked on top of each other like a set of warped building blocks about to tumble over. Many of them opened onto balconies draped with wisteria.

Stack told JFK that within the Flag Room, he learned about "the birds, the bees, the barracudas, and other forms of Hollywood wildlife."

The small, cramped room contained a double bed, which took up almost the entire space. The ceiling was only five feet above the floor, making standing fully upright impossible for both Stack and for JFK too. On the ceiling, Stack pinned flags of various nations. When he took a girl there, he demanded that she identify all the flags or else "pay the piper," which meant "surrender to seduction." JFK

293

thought that that was a fun game. Stack jokingly told Lana, "Jack is the only man in town better-looking than I am. All the hot tamales out here are taking notice."

One night, Stack phoned Lana, as he often did between girlfriends, and asked her to lunch.

Stack later said, "Unlike me, Jack was versatile in his taste in women—blondes, brunettes, redheads, young ones, mature ones, gals with large breasts, gals with lemons for breasts. But regardless of the dame, he wanted one with shapely legs."

He said that within the "humble portals" of the Flag Room, he and Jack seduced a gamut of women ranging from members of chorus lines to Oscar winners. "I can't name names,"

On his first visit to Hollywood, JFK had seduced Betty Grable. But on his second visit in 1946, he wanted Lana Turner, having seen her in three of her movies, beginning with *The Ziegfeld Girl*.

After the war, and for a brief time, JFK and Stack were "the two hottest dates in town." In the words of Judy Garland, "Robert served as Kennedy's guide to the hottest pussies. Lana Turner topped the list."

Stack claimed that JFK inherited his womanizing from his father, Joseph P. Kennedy, who had seduced a bevy of stars, notably Gloria Swanson, but also Constance Bennett and even Marion Davies, the mistress of press baron William Randolph Hearst. His surprise seduction was Greta Garbo.

One night Stack phoned Lana, as he often did between girlfriends, and asked her to lunch with him that following midday. He was entertaining John F. Kennedy, "the son of the ambassador," at his home. He told her than "son John" had been newly elected to Congress from Massachusetts. She had heard many stories about his father, but knew absolutely nothing about the son. "He's very rich, very handsome," Stack said. "He was a military hero in the Navy."

That previous morning, Lana had learned that June Allyson was eagerly awaiting an invitation from Stack to visit. Gene Tierney was also getting in on the act.

"This guy must be something special," Lana told Allyson.

"He can literally charm the panties off any gal," Allyson claimed.

Stack suggested that Lana arrive at his home at 11AM, so all three of them could get into swim trunks before lunch. She arrived on time, and Stack, in bathing trunks, escorted her out to the pool.

There, she met a handsome, rail-thin young man who wore a pair of white shorts. He was resting on a *chaise longue*, but jumped up as she entered the patio.

"My God, you're even better-looking than you are in the movies," JFK proclaimed.

As they chatted over coffee, she said, "I heard you performed heroically in the Navy."

Guess who?

294

"Are you kidding?" He flashed a smile. "To hear Bob tell it, I single handedly beat the Japs." The twinkle in his eyes revealed that he was satirizing his own exploits.

After lunch, as they returned to the pool, it was JFK who suggested that all three of them go for a nude swim.

JFK was the first to remove his shorts. As his future wife, Jacqueline, would say, "Jack was not shy about nudity. He seemed to pull off his trunks every chance he got."

Stack quickly dropped his trunks, too, but Lana took her time. "I knew I was putting on a show for the boys."

As she confided to Virginia Grey, "One thing led to another. After frolicking in the pool, we ended up in Bob's bedroom. The boys wanted a three-way, and I didn't disappoint. Bob was familiar terrain for me, but JFK was new and fresh. He didn't stay long in the saddle before he blasted off to the moon. I guess he found me so delectable he couldn't hold back."

When Stack phoned the next day, he said, "Jack thought you were terrific. The word he used was *BOOOOOM*. He wants to see you tonight."

"I was drawn to his quick wit and Irish charm," she told Grey. "He's very handsome, but it's his humor combined with his personal magnetism that I find so appealing."

As she revealed, "I'd known men with better builds. He is very lanky and rather bony. I bet he weighs less than I do. He's not only very thin, but has this yellowish cast to his skin. Maybe he came down with malaria in the Navy."

[Throughout his life and into his presidency, JFK would perpetuate the myth that he had had malaria. Actually, he was suffering from Addison's disease, which destroyed his adrenal glands and immune system, making him relatively defenseless to infections.

She saw him on three separate nights, when he preferred to be alone with her.

When Grey wanted more specifics, Lana was forced to admit that it was his personality that drew her to him. "The sex isn't all that great. He prefers to lie on his back. I suspect he's in some sort of pain. He's very fond of oral sex. But once he's done, things come to an abrupt end, with him heading off to the nearest phone, talking either to Boston or to Washington.

"One thing I found out, Jack's a funny man. He doesn't pinch, but he pats like crazy. I nicknamed him, the 'Pat-a-Cake Man.'"

***

In the years to come, Lana would make herself available to JFK whenever he phoned, perhaps in New York, but more often in California.

Once, when he was President, and when Jacqueline was away in Virginia horseback riding, he arranged for the Secret Service to slip her into the White House. "That night, he seduced me in Abraham Lincoln's bed. At first I was afraid to lie down on it, but he made me feel comfortable. I think it wasn't the first time he'd used Lincoln's bedroom for sex. It was a big, intricately carved rosewood bed. I bet Lincoln turned over in his grave that night."

"Before he left that morning, he told me that legend had it that if I made a wish on Lincoln's bed, it would come true. He wanted to know what I wished, but I never told him."

Actually, as Lana related later to Grey, "I wished that he would divorce Jackie and marry me so that in his second term in office, I'd be First Lady."

***

During a phone call to Lana, director Tay Garnett led off with his best opening line. "Lana, dear, I want to cast you in what is sure to be the role of your lifetime, the female lead of Cora Smith in *The Postman Always Rings Twice* (1946). Years from now, your unborn fans will idolize you for your glamorous interpretation of a murderess."

"I'm not sure what a postman has to do with this story," she said. "Do I go for him instead of the milkman?"

"No, silly, this is the part of a seductress who's involved in a loveless marriage. After she falls for a roguish drifter, she plots her spouse's murder."

"Some hardboiled crime writer named James M. Cain wrote it as a novel in 1934, and Louis B. Mayer acquired its movie rights for $25,000. But because of those god damn blue-nosed censors, no one has touched it for more than a decade."

"MGM tried to film it with Jean Harlow, but the Breen office rejected the script, interpreting it as 'thoroughly objectionable.'" But when the same author *[James Cain]* wrote a crime thriller called *Double Indemnity* and adapted it into a film with Barbara Stanwyck, it ushered in a new era of *film noir*. And that's not all that Cain devised: Warners recently adapted his *roman noir* called *Mildred Pierce* into a film with Joan Crawford, and it's set for a release soon."

"In this *Postman* caper, who will play the drifter?" Lana asked.

"John Garfield,"

She did not conceal the disappointment in her voice. "C'mon, Tay, why can't you find some attractive male? Someone who looks like Burt Lancaster or James Craig. And I bet that if you could borrow him, that Robert Mitchum would be ideal. I'd look forward to doing torrid love scenes with any of those hunks. I've already auditioned each of them."

Carey Wilson, the writer-producer of *Postman,* had worked with his screenwriters Niven Busch and Harry Ruskin, and had devised what Garnett thought was a script that could get a pass from the censors.

[Before Postman, *Wilson had written screen plays for* Ben-Hur *(1925), starring Ramon Novarro, and* Mutiny on the Bounty *(1935) with Charles Laughton and Clark Gable. He would eventually write the screenplay for Lana's historical melodrama,* Green Dolphin Street *(1947). He was one of the thirty-six Hollywood pioneers who had founded the Academy of Motion Picture Arts and Sciences in 1927, and he had also collaborated with Jean Harlow on her novel,* Today is Tonight.*]*

Although it had been interpreted as too sizzling for a Hollywood film during the 1930s, the plot of *Postman* was acceptable for Broadway, where censorship standards were more lenient. In 1936, a stage adaptation of *Postman* opened in New York. It starred Richard Barthelmess and Mary Philips, who had been married to Humphrey Bogart.

[As a novelist whose works were in vogue for filmmakers, Cain even became popular abroad. In 1939, in one of the last French films made before the Nazi takeover of that country, Le Dernier Tournant (based on Cain's The Postman Always Rings Twice) was released. It starred Fernand Gravet, Michel Simon, and Corinne Luchaire.

In a brazen move in 1943, in the middle of World War II (supposedly when an armed belligerent didn't care about trespassing a U.S. copyright), the Italian director, Luchino Visconti, ignored Cain's copyright and filmed Ossessione, starring Massimo Girotti, Clara Calamai, and Elio Marcuzzo. Since the film rights belonged to MGM, the studio prevented prints of the movie from entering the United States. Critic Arthur Knight called the Visconti film "a true masterpiece."]

After reading the script for *Postman*, Lana was reluctant to play Cora, claiming, "It will blemish my screen image."

In a meeting with Mayer, he urged her to accept the role. "You need to alter your screen identity. You're no longer 'the Sweater Girl.' With this film, you can be as glamorous as ever, but it will show the world you're also an accomplished actress. I see an Oscar in your future."

She accepted the role after Garnett assured her, "I'll order Irene to dress you sexily in virginal white."

Shooting began in May of 1945, as victory was declared by Allied forces at the surrender of Nazi Germany. Before filming began, Irene had designed a wardrobe for Lana that *Life* magazine would later predict "would become historic." Her hair had been dyed a snowy white.

Garnett said, "The world didn't have 'hot pants' back then, but you couldn't tell that by looking at Lana." Except on two occasions, including at a funeral, Lana wore white throughout the movie.

The revised plot, toned down from the novel, depicts a drifter, Frank Chambers (Garfield), who stops at the Twin Oaks roadside diner for a hamburger. It advertises a chicken dinner for $1.25. In the window, Garfield spots a MAN WANTED sign.

He meets the affable late middle-aged owner of the café, Nick Smith (Cecil Kellaway).

But it is the appearance of Cora Smith (Lana) who fascinates him. Her entrance in the film is viewed as the most stunning of any other actress in the 1940s. She drops a tube of lipstick, which rolls across the floor of the diner. The camera then opens onto her open-toed white high heels and follows upward to encase her perfect figure, beginning with her shapely tanned legs and taking in her white shorts and white halter top to showcase her insolent but stunningly beautiful face that's offset with a white turban.

Lana's entrance ignited a fashion vogue around the country of women wearing shorts and, on occasion, turbans.

As Garfield takes in her image, she says, "You won't find anything cheap around here." She also tells him, "The harder the wind blows, the hotter it gets."

Critic Hollis Alpert labeled her "the quintessential sex object—the woman to be had at *any* cost."

Gone was the kittenish Lana Turner of those late 1930s films. This is Madame

Satan herself, with arched eyebrows, half-parted succulent lips, protruding breasts, and a body oozing with sexual tension. Her silvery magnetism would shock post-war movie audiences.

Almost from the first, Garfield becomes obsessed. He accepts the low-paying handyman's job that had been advertised in the window, and assists in the day-to-day running of the diner.

Soon, he and Cora are locked into an adulterous love affair, which really heats up when she suggests that they could find happiness together if only her husband were out of the way.

As the plot unfolds, Nick is hit over the head with a wine bottle and pushed off a cliff in his car. The lovers are booked on a charge of murder, but a clever lawyer gets them off. Cora discovers that she is pregnant, and marriage is contemplated.

Back from making love on a moonswept beach, she gets into a car to drive back to the diner with Frank. *En route*, they are involved in an accident, which kills her.

The last we see of Cora in the film is at the site of the fatal car crash. Her dead hand reaches up, dropping that tube of lipstick we'd seen during her dramatic entrance at the debut of the movie.

A trial ensues, and Frank is convicted of her murder, which, ironically, had been an accident. He is sentenced to die in the electric chair and stoically accepts his fate, realizing that justice has been carried out, even though he's about to be electrocuted for the wrong murder.

He contemplates what happens when a person is expecting a letter. He feels it is no concern if at first the postman only rings the doorbell once, because he will always ring it a second time.

Lana and Garfield, as the protagonists of *Postman,* were backed up by a well-chosen supporting cast, notably Cecil Kellaway in the third lead. Although the character she played detested the character he played on screen, she said that off-screen, between takes, she "adored him."

Born in South Africa in 1890, he was usually cast as a jovial, stocky, silver-haired character, with a kindly speaking voice. Before meeting him, she had seen several of his films, notably *Wuthering Heights* (1939), with Laurence Olivier, and *The Letter* (1940), starring Bette Davis.

Hume Cronyn, the husband of actress Jessica Tandy, was cast as Arthur Keats, a slyly sleazy and unscrupulous criminal lawyer, with Alan Reed cast as Ezra Kennedy in the role of a "gumshoe."

Leon Ames, who had starred with Lana in *Week-End at the Waldorf,* had a very different role in *Postman.* As Kyle Sackett, he was the local prosecutor who suspects Lana and Garfield of murdering her husband.

Another blonde, Audrey Totter, was no rival for Lana. She was cast as Madge Goland, Garfield's cheap pickup girlfriend, and was one of the best of "the tough-talking, hard-edged broads" of f*ilm noir* in the late 1940s. Her career faded in the early fifties when that style of dame went out of fashion.

In her memoirs, Lana revealed that Garnett almost didn't finish the film. Trying to shoot the beach scenes in Laguna, the cast and crew encountered day after day of heavy fog. Although their director had been "on the wagon" for three years, the pressure from MGM and the long delays caused him to sink into deep bouts of alcoholism where he often became violent, even threatening, at one point, to beat up Garfield.

"No one could control him," Lana wrote. "He was a roaring, mean, furniture-smashing drunk. The girlfriend he'd brought with him stayed for a while, then gave up."

MGM sent nurses to tend to him, and Garfield tried to get him to sober up, but to no avail. He told Lana, "The bastard was so drunk, he didn't even know who I was."

Lana herself intervened, begging him (and eventually prevailing) to enter a clinic in Los Angeles for a quick rehab. Garfield and Lana resisted a proposal for MGM to assign another director, because they'd seen the rushes and felt that he'd wangled a "dynamic performance out of us."

Miraculously, the day Garnett returned to the set from Los Angeles, the fog lifted and shooting resumed. At the end of filming, Lana presented Garnett with a fur-lined jockstrap. "Don't let anyone say to you that you don't go first class."

As 1946 came to an end, Lana was named one of the highest-paid women in America, earning $226,000, a staggering amount at the time.

The Postman Always Rings Twice opened at Manhattan's Capitol Theater on May 2, 1946, as both a critical success and as a box office hit. Lana had never received such glowing reviews.

The *New York World-Telegram* wrote, "One of the astonishing excellences of this picture is the performance to which Lana Turner has been inspired."

In the *New York Post*, Archer Winsten wrote: "Before *Postman*, all Lana had to do was look good in front of the camera. If it is possible not to be dazzled by her beauty

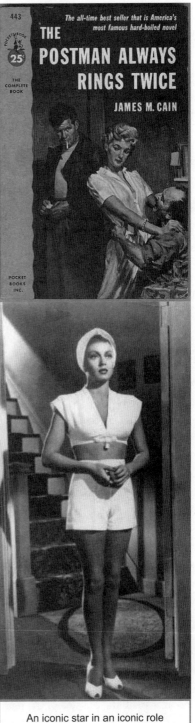

An iconic star in an iconic role

299

and pile of taffy hair, you may agree that she is now beginning to roll in the annual actresses' sweepstakes."

Newsweek reported, "Within the limits of movie medium, the film is as explicit as it can be." *Life* critiqued it as "a catalogue of the seven deadly sins. We recommend that the faint of heart stay away."

Time weighed in, too: "The hideous story of *The Postman Always Rings Twice* features reptilian bits of legal chicanery, characters as amoral as zoo exhibits, and dialogue paced and keyed like an erotic discussion between a couple of cats."

Writing in *The New York Times*, critic Bosley Crowther said, "Too much cannot be said for the principals. Mr. Garfield reflects the crude and confused young hobo who stumbled aimlessly into a fatal trap. And Miss Turner is remarkably effective as the cheap and uncertain blonde who has a pathetic ambition 'to be somebody,' and a pitiful notion that she can realize it through crime. Cecil Kellaway is just a bit too cozy and clean as Miss Turner's middle-aged spouse."

In this movie still from *Postman*, John Garfield in the back seat is about to knock out happy Cecil Kellaway with a wine bottle. Lana's face reflects the impending doom of her husband.

Critic Stephen MacMillan Moser, no great fan of Lana's, credited her with being a star, but not necessarily an actress. However, he pronounced *Postman* "a stunner—a cruel, desperate, and gritty James Cain vehicle that sorely tested her skills. But she succeeds marvelously, and from the first glimpse of her standing in the doorway in her white pumps, as the camera travels up her tanned legs, she becomes a character so enticingly beautiful and insidiously evil that the audience is riveted."

Years later, the *Saturday Evening Post* asked Lana who her favorite character had been in all the films she'd ever shot. She chose Cora. "Playing a wicked woman makes the audience more aware of you as an actress. The role gave me something to work with. Cora was not the usual heroine. I thought I understood the odd, twisted reasoning that made her yearn for a small piece of property out in the hills—for what she considered respectability and security—and yet, at the same time, led her to do things which ruined her chance of getting what she wanted."

***

As John Garfield, Lana's highly promiscuous co-star in *The Postman Always Rings Twice,* candidly admitted, "I was in Hollywood for a full week before I got laid. I don't know—that may just be a record."

Artie Shaw, Lana's first husband, told a reporter, "He loves being John Garfield because of all the pussy and the perks."

Garfield's list of seductions was long and impressive, ranging from A-list stars to cheap pickups. The more distinguished women he bedded included Hedy Lamarr, Ann Sheridan, Anne Shirley, singer Margaret Whiting, Shelley Winters, Frances Farmer, Ida Lupino, Eleanor Parker, and, surprise, even the legendary French singer, Edith Piaf.

To that list could be added dozens of script girls, extras, starlets, and "all the female students at the American Laboratory Theatre in Manhattan (at least he claimed that)."

Author Truman Capote once said, "He was one of the nicest people I've ever known. My mother saw him just once and tried to get him into bed with her. She did not succeed. But I did."

Tough, edgy, street-smart, and cynical, Garfield grew up in the 1920s on the streets of the Bronx and Manhattan's Lower East Side. Born Julius Garfinkle, he was the son of Russian Jewish immigrants. His father was a clothes-presser and part-time cantor.

"In the streets of New York, I learned all the meanness, all the toughness it's possible for kids to acquire. If I hadn't become a movie star, I would probably have become Public Enemy Number One."

As he matured, he became a gang leader in the Bronx until he contracted scarlet fever, an affliction that left him with permanent heart damage.

Gradually, he drifted into acting, eventually migrating from New York to Hollywood. When the war came, he was rejected for military service because of that heart condition. Along with Bette Davis, he helped found the Hollywood Canteen. Long before she became intimate with him, Lana knew him during the war because of her own involvement with the Canteen. "I left the dirty dishes for the other stars and danced with the servicemen."

She had protested the casting of Garfield in *Postman* because she did not find him attractive as a male animal, and feared they would not have the sexual chemistry that the script demanded. She obviously underestimated his male allure, as the first rushes of *Postman* revealed.

Film critic Lou Valentino wrote: "John Garfield and Lana Turner depicted in this beach scene, worked surprisingly well together. Her blonde, angel-faced sexuality contrasted brilliantly with his dark, brooding features, and they created one of the most exciting star combinations of 1946."

After seeing those rushes, Garnett said, "There was a special chemistry between my two stars. I don't know if they had anything going on the side, but on film, you were rooting for them, even though they played murderers. John had

301

his share of girls, but he had a bad heart and that might have frightened Lana off. He teased her about sex, which tends to make me believe that nothing happened. They sizzled on the screen, though."

During those long days and nights at Laguna Beach, waiting for the director to sober up and for the fog to lift, Garfield knocked on Lana's door one night. Lonely and bored, she invited him in. The next morning, he was seen leaving her suite. They spent the following day together, waiting for the cameras to roll, and he spent another night in her suite, and then another and another.

John Garfield should have kept his eyes on the road—and not on Lana. In this pivotal scene, Lana, as Cora, is about to meet her tragic ending.

At the time of their affair, Lana and Garfield had to be very discreet. After all, he had been married to Roberta Seidman, a member of the Communist Party, since 1935.

After being seduced by the actor several nights in a row, Lana had to agree with the assessment of columnist Sheilah Graham. "He made love like a sexy puppy, in and out, huffing and puffing in quick gasps."

After the shooting of *Postman*, Lana saw very little of Garfield, as she had by then launched a torrid affair with Tyrone Power. However, she did meet him one night at a party when he was making his next picture, *Humoresque* (1946) with Joan Crawford.

"When I was introduced to Crawford," he told Lana, "she extended her hand to me. Instead of taking it, I reached to pinch her nipple. At first, she looked angry, but that soon faded into a seductive smile. She told me, 'You and I, buster, are going to get along just fine. I just hope you're good in the sack, and that that arrogant act of yours isn't faked.'"

At the time of Garfield's death on May 21, 1952, he was planning to divorce his wife. He died of a heart attack in the apartment of actress Iris Whitney in New York City. Having sustained great stress because of having been blacklisted for allegedly being a member of the Communist Party, he finally surrendered to the burdens of a troubled life.

Lana was greatly distressed to learn about his death and discussed him with her friends: "John had a penchant for picking up girls, sometimes two at a time, and a reputation as a demon lover. He died young, which was understandable."

"He once told me that an actor doesn't reach maturity until he turns forty. We'll never know what future greatness he had in him. He was only thirty-nine when he died. He never lived long enough to become a screen legend like Bogie."

"I was moved to learn that some 10,000 people gathered in the Riverside Memorial Chapel in Manhattan to pay their final respects to this most talented young man. That was the largest turnout of fans since the death of Valentino. I will always have a special place for him in my heart, remembering the times he and I had making our most memorable movie, the picture in which I ended up smashed to death, and he faced the electric chair."

***

During the filming of *The Postman Always Rings Twice,* Lana began an affair with a tall, handsome actor from New York State, Robert Hutton. She'd met him at the Hollywood Canteen in 1944. *["Hollywood Canteen" was also the title of a movie he made that year.]*

They didn't start to date right away until he escorted her in December of 1945 to the premiere of *Leave Her to Heaven,* the movie that brought Gene Tierney an Oscar nomination.

[At the end of the film, Lana whispered to Hutton, "I could have played that part, and I wish I had."]

Hutton, the son of a hardware merchant, was famous for being the cousin of Barbara Hutton, the Woolworth heiress who had been married to Cary Grant.

During the period that Lana dated Hutton, Warners was promoting him as its newest heart-throb, since some of their matinee idols were beginning to fade a bit. Columnist Walter Winchell wrote about Lana's dating of Hutton, calling him "her biggest thrill."

That remark brought laughter to her many friends in Hollywood, who asked her, "Is Bob really your biggest thrill?"

Hutton later complained, "I hated that rumor. Every time I went to a urinal to take a leak, I was followed by some queen who wanted to check me out."

When she started dating Hutton, he was divorcing Natalie Thompson and had become a free agent like herself.

One of the highlights of her dating schedule was when he took her to the lavishly decorated home of his mega-wealthy cousin, the Woolworth heiress, Barbara Hutton. *[When she'd married Grant, the press had collectively dubbed them "Cash and Carry," but they had since divorced, although remaining friends.]*

At a party, Lana talked to Grant, who asked her, "Why haven't we made a movie together?"

"It's about time," she agreed.

Lana thought Robert Hutton bore a strong resemblance to Jimmy Stewart, to whom he was often compared.

He confessed that his wartime career had depended on what was called "Victory Casting," meaning that he and other actors who didn't have to go into military service stayed in Hollywood, taking roles that might have otherwise gone to Stewart, Clark Gable, Robert Taylor, or others.

During Lana's talk with the heiress, Hutton said that she preferred to date European men such as Prince Frederick Hohenzollern. "Except for the one I married, they are more sophisticated, more aware."

She was referring to Count Kurt Haughwitz-Reventlow, a Danish nobleman. A story was making the rounds in Hollywood that, following an argument, he had forced her into the bathroom, where he made her sit nude on his lap while he relieved himself.

She also dated movie stars, not just Grant. Her lovers had included two of Lana's former beaux, David Niven and Errol Flynn. She had also been involved with the English actor, Michael Wilding, before he married Elizabeth Taylor.

Lana found Barbara indiscreet during a discussion about her former lovers, as if satirizing herself. "One night, I visited Michael Rennie. He was gone for a while and then emerged from his bathroom wearing a rubber diving suit. He had a bullwhip in one hand, and a jar of Vaseline in the other. I won't go on. I was also involved with

Barbara Hutton—rich and wistful. When Lana met her, she was regally seated on a throne-like chair receiving her guests.

In the 1930s, the subject of custody battles among feuding factions within the Hutton clan, she had been dubbed "The Poor Little Rich Girl."

In reference to her later life, author Truman Capote called her "the most incredible phenomenon of the 20th Century."

the playboy, Fred McEvoy. He kept the preserved body of his dead baby on display at his villa in Mexico City."

She told Lana, "I won't say that my husbands thought only of my money, but it held a certain fascination for them."

What she didn't tell Lana, but what she had learned through gossip, was that her on-again, off-again lover, Howard Hughes, was having an affair with Grant during her marriage to him.

At the last party Lana attended at Barbara's residence, the heiress took her hand and held it tenderly as she said goodbye. "Remember, my dear, money can't buy you happiness."

Lana continued to date Robert Hutton until she went on an extended trip to South America. Upon her return, she learned that he had fallen for Cleatus Caldwell and was soon to marry her.

Like so many men that Lana dated, Hutton's life ended in tragedy. He broke his back in an accident at his home and spent his last days in a nursing care facility, dying on August 7, 1994.

In the 70s, she recalled, "If Robert had any grudge against me, he took it out on me by writing the script for my 1974 film, *Persecution,* one of my worst movies. I can't bear to watch it."

***

For months, Howard Hughes had lived up to the label that Errol Flynn had bequeathed him: "The Lone Wolf." But near the end of the war, after a long disappearance, Hughes flew to Los Angeles, landing at the airport at Burbank. A reporter spotted him and leaked word that he was back in town to the newspapers. At least three screen beauties, perhaps a lot more, awaited his phone call. Lana, Rita (Hayworth) and Ava (Gardner) topped the list.

Having emerged from his self-imposed exile, he re-inaugurated, once again, his pursuit of some of the world's most alluring women. During the autumn of 1945, he was seducing actress Jane Greer and flying to Canada to make love to Yvonne De Carlo. He told his aides, "Yvonne is my hot new flame, but I don't want to confine myself to just one woman."

The months immediately following the end of the war seemed to bring renewed energy to him. He had survived, more or less intact, his wartime airplane production scandals, including the furor over his ill-fated, way-over-budget, plywood-sheathed "Spruce Goose."

He ordered a screening of Lana's latest film, *The Postman Always Rings Twice.* After watching it with Meyer, he told him, "Lana is the hottest platinum blonde in Hollywood since I first fucked Jean Harlow. She's compellingly sexy in this film, although I usually prefer bosomy brunettes. I might contact her again."

That is exactly what he did, and in April of 1946, Lana and Hughes checked once again into Manhattan's Sherry-Netherland Hotel, occupying different suites. When she walked into her elegantly furnished lodgings, she found it filled with her favorite flowers: rare white orchids, ivory roses, and gardenias.

It was sometime during her stay with him there that he proposed marriage. After thinking it over for a tantalizing minute, she said "yes." He seemed so delighted by her acceptance that he immediately hauled her off to bed.

But a complication emerged almost immediately. The very next night, Hughes phoned Linda Darnell, who had remained a close friend of Lana's. "You have no idea how much I love you," he told Linda. "I can't wait for us to get married." Darnell enthusiastically supported the plan, promising that she'd immediately divorce her husband, cameraman Peverell J. Marley.

After Darnell transmitted this information to her then-husband, Marley imposed a condition on what soon emerged as a plan to facilitate Hughes and Darnell's marital "reshuffling": Marley wanted the billionaire to pay him an annual salary of $25,000 for the remainder of his life.

Darnell discreetly decided not to inform Lana of Hughes' proposal.

With a mind-numbing duplicity, Hughes simultaneously, and despite his promises to Darnell, continued the plans he had set in motion to wed Lana, defining May 8 in Las Vegas as the venue for their upcoming wedding. He even commissioned a $5,000 wedding dress for Lana from Oleg Cassini, with instructions that

305

it be delivered to her house for a fitting.

Hughes' elaborate "Lana" plan included an agreement that at 9AM on the morning of the wedding, he would retrieve her in a limousine for transport to the airport, where a private plane would be waiting to haul them off to a civil ceremony and honeymoon in Las Vegas.

To her consternation, by 10AM on Lana's big day, neither Hughes, nor his car, nor his driver, had arrived. Worried and fretful, Lana called Johnny Maschio, one of his chief aides. He told her that he had not heard from Hughes since the previous night.

"Find out where in hell he is," she demanded. She then called back every thirty minutes.

Finally, at 4PM, Hughes finally contacted (by phone) Maschio, not revealing his location or his intentions.

"Lana is enraged," Maschio reported to his boss. "What should I tell her?"

"Absolutely nothing," Hughes said before abruptly hanging up his phone.

The next day, a stunning diamond bracelet from Tiffany's arrived. Because of her love of diamonds, Lana decided to forgive him.

***

After the humiliating collapse of their marriage plans, Hughes phoned Lana only occasionally, meeting with her even less frequently. She reported to Susan Hayward, who also dated him, that "Howard seems deeply troubled. He's like a man searching, searching, for something, but never finding it."

One night, he dropped by Lana's house, telling her that at long last, he was ready to be the sole test pilot aboard his experimental new aircraft, the XF-11.

She urged him not to do it, and to select one of his trained pilots instead. She later told Hayward, "I had this incredible intuition, I smelled trouble before it happened. I just knew that that damned XF-11 was heading for disaster."

On Sunday morning, July 7, 1946, Hughes—at the controls and alone in the cockpit—set out on his daring test flight. Before boarding the aircraft, he told his aides, "It's the most beautiful plane I ever built."

Subsequently, his plane crashed into a private home in Beverly Hills, which resulted in legal implications that dragged on for years. An emergency ambulance rushed to the rescue, and with its red dome light flashing, sped him to the nearest hospital. Blood ran from his nose, mouth, and ears, and his leather jacket had ignited into flames. Doctors gave him a fifty-fifty chance of survival.

Lana had switched on the radio that morning. She was shocked when bulletins about Hughes and his unlucky aircraft began dominating the news broadcasts.

In the days that followed, Hughes struggled for life. Recovering from burns and injuries, he was in great pain, his doctor shooting him with morphine to ease his agony.

Days and days went by before his condition began to improve. America was waiting, since at that time, he was a household word.

The hospital was overrun with visitors, a few of whom included former girlfriends Ginger Rogers and Olivia de Havilland, and a horde of people Hughes hardly knew, including James Cagney, David O. Selznick, and Danny Kaye. Johnny Meyer was ordered to turn most of them away.

Linda Darnell, who had apparently recovered from the pre-marital embarrassments she'd suffered, showed up too. Dressed in black, she was refused entry. The next morning, the *Hollywood-Citizen* ran a blaring headline—LINDA DARNELL REFUSED PERMISSION TO SEE HUGHES.

The next day, also dressed in black, Lana appeared. Because of her friendship with Johnny Meyer, she was allowed access, although he warned her, "Make it quick!"

She was horrified by what she saw. As she later confided to Meyer, she offered to marry him, in spite of his broken promise and his disastrously embarrassing no-show on the infuriating morning of their aborted wedding. "But you've got to promise me you'll never fly another plane."

Enigmatic, as always, about his commitments, he thanked her and falsely soothed her with the promise "I'm through with aviation."

The following day, as Hughes continued his recuperation in the hospital, Meyer granted access to Jean Peters, a fresh-faced, green-eyed farm girl from Ohio, another of the actresses whom Hughes had been dating. She was under contract to 20th-Century Fox.

Although he could have dated far more glamorous stars, he'd perceived a particular affinity for her. She had wanted him to marry her, but, as with Lana, he stalled.

[Eventually, by 1954, she abandoned any hope for marriage to him, and married Stanley M. Cramer III, a Texas oil executive, instead.

In 1957, Peters divorced Cramer and, in a secret wedding ceremony in Tonapah, Nevada, married Hughes. Abandoning her film career, she subsequently became a virtual recluse.

As for Lana, her relationship with Hughes was far from over, and would soon veer off the highway with a radical left turn into chaos.]

***

Frank Sinatra had met Lana when each was relatively new to Hollywood.

In the months to come, Lana—who was always with one of her many *beaux*— often encountered Sinatra and his wife Nancy at Hollywood parties or premieres. He knew her well enough to visit her on the set of her film, *Keep Your Powder Dry.* Showing up there with Gene Kelly (one of her future co-stars), they each wore sailor uniforms.

In 1944, she appeared on the *Frank Sinatra Show* for CBS, and later that night a photographer snapped their picture together at the Clover Club.

Daughter Cheryl remembered "Uncle Frank" calling on her mother at their marvelous home in Bel Air overlooking the local country club.

[According to Hollywood lore and the singer's own boastings, the notoriously promiscuous Sinatra had—based on his screening of The Postman Always Rings Twice—*moved her from "Number 8" to the top of his "list of actresses to seduce."]*

"I've got to have Lana," Sinatra told Tommy Dorsey. "I know you've already

307

had the pleasure."

Swimming star Esther Williams had been assigned the dressing room next to Lana's at MGM. She spotted Sinatra slipping in and out for secret rendezvous. "My dressing room was modest, but Lana had a king-sized bed in hers, complete with pink satin sheets. She also had a lot of mirrors so she could oversee the action. From the sounds of things, he was having one big explosion. Why not? At the time, Lana was hailed as the most desirable woman on the planet."

At the time that Sinatra became involved with Lana, she was one of the most widely publicized sex goddesses of the silver screen. Many of her friends, including Linda Darnell, agreed that, "Lana tries to live up to that title. She told me that a variety of men add spice to a girl's life. No sooner would *Photoplay* herald one of her romances and run a picture of the two of them, she would be dating some other man. Gossip columnists were always out of date where she was concerned. Sinatra went through women, and Lana went through men, as fast as commercials on the radio."

An aide to Louis B. Mayer told him that he had spotted Lana and Sinatra together in the back seat of his car "smooching." Actually, "smooching" was not the right word for it. Mayer was horrified, eager to avoid a scandal based on the fact that Sinatra was still married to his first wife, Nancy.

Esther Williams remembered the afternoon that Nancy Sinatra arrived, unannounced, and loudly knocked on the door to Lana's dressing room, which, as mentioned, was immediately next door to Esther's. Hearing the knock, and with the understanding Lana was away from MGM that day, Williams invited Nancy into her own dressing room instead.

According to Esther, "She looked distraught. Shaking all over. In tears, Nancy told me that Frank had fallen in love with Lana, and that the night before, Frank had told her that he wanted a divorce. I tried to comfort her as much as I could. That night, I attended a party at the home of Sonja Henie. Frank was there with Lana. They had eyes only for each other as they danced crotch-to-crotch. When Lana went to powder her nose, I told him that I'd seen Nancy. He confirmed that he'd asked her for a divorce so that he could marry Lana."

Without informing Lana, Sinatra rented a duplex apartment in Hollywood for them. He filled it with $50,000 worth of new furnishings, and even purchased several sets of pink satin sheets. *[He also maintained a more modest apartment about fifteen blocks away for assignations with other women.]*

When it was sparkling and "prepped" for its role as their love nest, Sinatra drove Lana to the duplex. He later said, "She wasn't impressed. She called it a dump and told me that she wouldn't sleep one night in such a joint. So I took her to the Beverly Hills Hotel where I rented a bungalow, and we spent the rest of the night making love."

Sinatra authorized publicist George Evans to announce that he and Nancy had separated. It came as a shock to his fans. When it was revealed that Lana, as his lover, had played a role in the separation, she was denounced as a home-wrecker.

After news of the breakup appeared in the newspapers, Sinatra and Lana were seen together at a resort in Palm Springs.

Back in Hollywood, when Lana read the horrible press she had generated, she phoned Louella Parsons. "I am not in love with Frank Sinatra. Nor is he in love with me. We're just good friends. I have never broken up a home and I don't intend to."

Within a span of about two weeks, Sinatra had obviously changed his mind about marrying Lana. He had purchased an expensive diamond bracelet for her, but decided not to give it to her. He told Phil Silvers, "I've had a change of heart. I will not marry Lana. That doesn't mean I'm giving up fucking her. She really gets off being plugged by my whopper."

That diamond bracelet was eventually presented to another blonde actress,

Lana had known Frank Sinatra since 1940, but didn't have an affair with him until right after she'd filmed *The Postman Always Rings Twice*.

When she'd first met him, she told Ava Gardner that she thought, "He's all skin and bones."

But Gardner later revealed his allure: "There may be only ten pounds on the guy, but there are 110 pounds of cock."

Marilyn Maxwell, instead, but not before Nancy had discovered it (and presumably registered its value), after finding it concealed in a drawer at home with his underwear.

Later, at a party hosted by Nancy and Frank at the Sinatra home, Maxwell indiscreetly showed up wearing that bracelet. After the party had been rocking along for two hours, Nancy approached her and demanded that she relinquish the bracelet and give it to her. At first, Maxwell resisted, but, fearing a fight and horrendously embarrassed, she reluctantly surrendered it.

Later, at a New Year's Eve party in Hollywood, Lana was introduced to Nancy. The other guests backed away, warily expecting fireworks, but the two women gossiped and seemed to enjoy each other's company.

In a corner of the party, a very handsome actor, under contract to MGM, was holding forth, surrounded by three starlettes. "Boy, the gal he selects tonight is in for a big disappointment," Lana said. "That's the only thing *big* about him. He must need a pair of tweezers to jerk off."

Nancy laughed. "That's hardly Frank's problem."

To Nancy, Lana expressed her disdain for Hollywood. After defining it as "a boiler factory," she said, "The men here are either fairies or hounds. Women out here like to slit each other's throats. Take Joan Crawford and me, for example."

Weeks later, both Lana and Nancy were in New York at the same time, each of them for, among other reasons, Sinatra's opening at the Waldorf Astoria.

Whereas Nancy attended the 10PM show and then retreated to her suite, Lana showed up for the midnight show and wildly applauded Sinatra. At the end of his concert, he rushed over to her table. Embracing her, he whispered in her ear. "I've missed you, baby. Can't live without you."

She told him she'd rented a suite at the nearby Plaza, a few blocks from the Waldorf. Within the hour, he was there, knocking on her door.

A bellhop saw him leaving the Plaza at 7AM the next morning, on his way back to his suite at the Waldorf…and Nancy.

Perhaps caught up in the sexual excitement of a reunion with Lana, Sinatra proposed marriage to her once again. This time, she accepted.

"I'm making wedding plans," Lana told Linda Darnell after her return to Hollywood. "Frank has again promised to marry me, and I've accepted. He's definitely going to leave Nancy this time. There can be no turning back. He said the spark is gone between Nancy and him."

When this photo of Sinatra feeding Lana a popsickle appeared in the newspapers, gossips quipped: "That's not the only popsickle Frankie's feeding Lana."

Yet after his own return to Los Angeles, he changed his mind again. Phil Silvers was performing at Slapsie Maxie's Club, and Sinatra showed up. Although Nancy was in the audience that night at a table with friends, Sinatra did not acknowledge her. Silvers invited Sinatra up onto the stage, and he sang a beautiful rendition of "Going Home." At the end of the song, he received wild applause when he walked over to Nancy's table and took her in his arms and kissed her. Reunited, the couple left the club together. The next day, *Variety* announced: *FRANK SINATRA BACK WITH WIFE.*

Lana's maid delivered her the morning paper. When she read the headline, she shouted at her maid and hurled her breakfast tray against a mirror. "How dare that son of a bitch! That fucker!! How could he do this to me?"

Storming out of her bedroom, she ordered her maid to "clean up this god damn mess."

Years later, that maid spoke to a reporter. "I never understood why Miss Turner got so upset about Sinatra. Only the night before, she told me that she'd fallen in love with Tyrone Power."

After Sinatra's reconciliation with Nancy, their marriage would struggle along for four more unhappy, turbulent, scandal-soaked years.

Even though he'd returned to hearth, home, and Nancy, Sinatra confessed something to Peter Lawford, with whom he had co-starred in *It Happened in Brooklyn* (1947).

"Because of my involvement with Lana, I now have great expectations from a woman, one that Nancy can't fulfill. I need variety in love-making, not the same

310

old missionary position night after night. I fear I'll never find another Lana Turner…that is, unless I start banging Ava Gardner."

Sinatra told Dean Martin, "I like brunettes. Ava Gardner proves that. But when a blonde like Marilyn Maxwell, Lana Turner, or Marilyn Monroe comes along, I get as erect as the Empire State Building."

Although Lana and Sinatra maintained their sexual involvement during many years of his marriage to Nancy, Lana ended their affair when he married Gardner. She said. "I'm not going to have sex with my best friend's husband." But Lana's vows didn't mean a lot.

In a memoir, Cheryl admitted that Lana and Sinatra were romantically involved on and off for many years. She recalled seeing them dancing together in 1970 at the Candy Store on Rodeo Drive. She also claimed that over the years, Sinatra presented her mother with many gifts, including diamonds.

"Keep Betty Grable, Lamour, and Turner," Sinatra sang in his first recording of "Nancy," that reference having been inspired by his daughter, Nancy, and not to his wife.

In her memoirs, Lana denied ever having had an affair with Sinatra. Her book editor later revealed, however, that the original manuscript contained a "blow-by-blow" description of their romance. By the time of its publication, Lana and Sinatra, both now aging, had had a row. In its aftermath, Lana demanded that her romantic passages about the singer be removed. "I don't want to give him the satisfaction."

Ava Gardner's autobiography contained the passage, "Lana had a very serious affair with Frank. We once met in the ladies' room during a Hollywood party many moons ago. She told me her story, that she was deeply in love with Frank, and so, she thought, he was with her."

***

In Argentina, a small-time actress, call girl, and radio announcer, Eva Duarte (later known, worldwide, as Evita Perón), had forged the most fascinating and frightening political partnership in South America. Hooking up with a military commander, Juan Perón, whom she was romancing at the time, she had worked behind the scenes to win for him, in 1946, the presidency of Argentina. From the power base she helped him establish and reinforce, they would rule together with an iron, anti-colonial fist.

She and Perón were ruthless power grabbers, even working behind the scenes with the Nazis, to secure financing for various development and military projects in Argentina. As history revealed, they picked the wrong side during World War II, and—after the war—were severely ostracized by many of the Allies, especially since their country had become a post-war haven for Nazi refugees in hiding.

From dire poverty, Eva in time became one of the most powerful women in the world, a blonde goddess like Lana, swathed in furs and draped with diamonds. Most of her politidal support derived from her *Los Descamisados [aka* "the shirtless ones"*]*, legions of impoverished blue collar laborers.

What was not widely known at the time was her obsession with the image projected by Lana Turner. Eva's lover and Lana's future lover, the Argentine actor,

Fernando Lamas, said, "Eva Perón wanted to be Lana Turner. She modeled her wardrobe, her makeup, even her hair styles to emulate Lana. As such, she became one of the most fashionable women in the world and the first to appear in public in Argentina wearing pants."

***

In 1946, as part of a publicity tour and in need of a long vacation, Lana flew to Buenos Aires with her paid companion, Sara Hamilton, paying her expenses and lending her money. Hamilton was a magazine writer who had befriended Lana. According to Lana, "I trusted Sara, but she betrayed me. When she got back home, she fed unflattering gossip about me to the fan magazines, for which she was paid."

Before flying out of L.A., Lana met with Greg Bautzer, having long ago forgiven him for breaking what she viewed as an engagement. She had a problem she asked him to solve: She wanted Mildred out of her house, complaining that she had become a nuisance. Instead of living in her quarters, she had "expanded her turf" and commandeered Lana's living room, remaining there, often half the night, for her daughter's return. Invariably, Lana came home with a young man, and Mildred was very vocal with her disapproval of her daughter's stream of pickups. She often complained, "Where did I go wrong? I wanted you to grow up to be a good girl, not the whore of Babylon!"

Lana had a solution. She instructed Bautzer to sell her large house and to move her into a smaller one, with just enough room for Cheryl and herself. "I was a twice-divorced woman in my mid-twenties, and I didn't need parental guidance for myself."

The attorney promised Lana that he'd take care of her real estate problems and that he'd move Mildred into a separate apartment.

When she arrived in Buenos Aires, Lana was greeted at the airport by hundreds of fans who turned out to welcome her. An MGM publicist helped her fight her way through the crowds. "Latins love blonde movie stars," she later proclaimed.

Outside the airport's terminal, a near-riot ensued. People were pushing and shoving. "They wanted a piece of me," she said. At one point, a woman grabbed for her pearl necklace, but Lana fought her off.

In the rear of a limousine, she complained to the publicist, "Make sure I get all of my jewelry back." She had made it a special point to accessorize herself in Argentina with her beloved diamonds, along with sapphires and emeralds. Much to her distress, Argentine Customs had confiscated her jewel case with a promise to return it to her.

"Those shitheads went over every piece of my lingerie, paying particular attention to my silk panties."

Lana's jewels were safely returned to her, delivered to her hotel under armed guard two nights later. It was months before she learned that Eva Perón had ordered that the jewels be temporarily confiscated so that her jeweler could copy the designs in advance of preparing absolute duplicates of Lana's adornments.

The next day, Lana spoke to the press about the near-riot at Buenos Aires' airport. Commenting on the hysterical reaction to her arrival, she said, "People will risk a broken arm or leg, even serious injury, to get a closeup look at a big Hollywood star."

As they toured the Argentine capital, their maroon-colored sedan was followed by a car filled with four dark-suited men. Lana later referred to them "as the Argentine version of Edward G. Robinson, James Cagney, George Raft, and Paul Muni."

She had a friend in Buenos Aires, Betty Dodaro, who hosted a lavish *haute* society party for her, inviting Eva Perón, who had expressed a desire to meet her.

Eva sat in a far corner of the room in a gold chair, looking like royalty. Dodaro brought Lana over for introductions.

In a memoir, Lana recalled that she was shocked to discover that the dictator had dyed her hair as pale as hers. Even her gown was the same as the one Lana had worn for an MGM publicity still. Eva had on long, ruby-colored gloves, and a strapless gown, the same ensemble Lana had worn to pose for pictures advertising Lux Toilet Soap before the release of *The Postman Always Rings Twice*. "I felt I was looking at my twin sister…sort of. Madame Perón did not really have my beauty, in spite of copying my makeup."

Before flying south, Lana had posed for photos. Her presentation had included an elaborate hairdo into which flowers and a diamond necklace had been interwoven. She was shocked to see Eva with that same coiffure.

When Lana went to the powder room, Eva got up and followed her in. She ordered everybody else out and posted a security guard at the door.

"Welcome to Argentina," she said. "You are even lovelier than in your pictures."

As the two women chatted, and as her English-speaking Argentine bodyguard remained posted attentively nearby, Eva asked Lana for some beauty tips.

Lana freely shared some of her secrets, suggesting that she remove all makeup before going to bed. "Never sleep with it on." She also advised that before leaving her house, she should check her image in a full-length mirror to see how she looked from the rear. "Remember, more people will see you leave than see you arrive."

She also suggested a diet that included hot chili peppers to cleanse her body of toxins. "I don't need to tell you never to wear anything off the rack. When in doubt about wardrobe, ermine and silk brocade will do. Since we're both world famous, it's important never to step out the door unless you're camera ready."

Eva Perón, a Lana Turner impersonator.

313

The night that Lana talked to Eva, "Madame Perón," in the words of her biographer, Mary Main, "had reached the most opulently ostentatious period of her career. In appearance, she was the apotheosis of the *demimondaine:* There was a voluptuousness about her that did not come from the prodigal display of ornament alone, but from a lushness of the flesh itself. She displayed a softness and womanliness in her face. To the discriminating, her appearance was vulgar. Beautiful as her clothes were, they might have been chosen for the star of some super-colossal Hollywood production."

Eva thanked Lana for her beauty tips, and offered to do anything she could to make her sojourn in Argentina pleasant. Before departing from the powder room, she grabbed Lana and kissed her passionately on the lips.

Lana later said, "I was stunned…absolutely stunned. Was Madame Perón a closeted lesbian? Or just an effusive Argentine woman showing her thanks?"

At the end of her trip, Lana was relieved to be flying away from Argentina. There had been political rallies and protests, some of them violent. Perónista guards had appeared with drawn sabers. The night before she left Buenos Aires, a bomb had been thrown into the lobby of her hotel. Shaking and terrified, she and Hamilton had sat up all night. Their itinerary called for her to make an appearance next in Brazil.

***

Landing in Rio de Janeiro, Lana and Sara Hamilton were met by the same tumultuous crowds that had greeted them in Argentina. They had arrived in time to join in the annual Carnival festivities. The whole city seemed to be celebrating. As just-arrived VIPs, the two women were invited to lavish parties where the hosts never seemed to spare any expense. Wherever Lana went, she was mobbed by adoring crowds. She danced the night away with what she called "the world's most beautiful men. All of them propositioned me. Did I respond? That's for me to know and for you to try to find out…maybe."

Somewhere in Rio, a spectacular party was hosted in Lana's honor, and, as she admitted herself, "I never looked more seductive." She'd made a grand entrance in a black satin halter dress, set off with diamonds and flowers in her hair.

At the end of the party, back at her hotel suite, she hung up that satin dress in her closet. The next morning, her entire wardrobe smelled of ether.

[According to Lana, the party that night was punctuated by the consumption of diethyl ether as a recreational drug, either through inhalation or through drinking. Brazilians would soak their handkerchiefs, inhaling it through the fabric to induce a head-spinning and hallucinogenic high.]

Night after night of partying and casual seductions "of only the handsomest and most well-built of Brazilian men" left her exhausted. When it became clear that she was coming down with a ferocious cold, her doctor, fearing that she was developing pneumonia, sent her for a ten-day rest at the mountain resort of Quinadita, where she languished until she recovered.

***

314

Saying goodbye to South America, Lana and Hamilton flew from Rio to Miami, where she stayed in a suite at the Roney Plaza on Miami Beach.

While in Florida, she was rumored to have had an affair with John Alden Talbot, a rich socialite who had a lavish villa in Palm Beach and was known to Joseph and Rose Kennedy.

The first time she met Talbot, she told him, "You're so handsome, you should be in pictures." Palm Beach society had dubbed him as one of America's "top ten playboy-bachelors." At the time she dated him, he had recently married, the previous April, Nancy Rheem Talbot.

Then Lana flew from Miami to New York for a stay that lasted for two weeks. She lodged within the same accommodation at the Sherry-Netherland where Howard Hughes had made love to her. This time, another former suitor with the initials "HH" was seen coming and going from her suite at all hours of the day and night. She'd resumed dating Huntington Hartford, the A&P heir. When reporters asked her about him, she (rather grandly) quipped, "If only those A&Ps sold champagne and caviar."

Talbot followed her to New York City, where they were seen dancing cheek-to-cheek at the Stork Club. To complicate matters, his wife apparently found out and allegedly threw a jealous fit, flying to Washington, D.C. to be with her mother.

After Lana's return to California, after learning that the Talbots had agreed to a trial separation, she had a reunion with her daughter after an absence of many weeks.

Immediately after her return, she learned that Bautzer had arranged for her to live in a smaller house on Crown Drive in Brentwood, a move that had been deliberately orchestrated as a means of "evicting" Mildred, who was transferred into a small apartment nearby.

Lana would never live with her mother again.

On December 5, Talbot and Lana, with daughter Cheryl, were seen aboard the 20th Century Limited, as it pulled into Manhattan's Grand Central Station. Headlines announced: LANA AND YALE MAN ARRIVE. One columnist wrote, "Her escort was handsome as a collar ad and just as inarticulate."

"Is he your new flame?" one reporter yelled out at her.

"I wouldn't know," she said before disappearing into a limousine.

Once again in Los Angeles, gossip mongers painted her as a heartless *femme fatale* who had broken up yet another home. To counter the rumors, she wisecracked with reporters who gathered around her on the MGM lot: "I have dinner with a fellow a couple of times. Suddenly, I'm a home wrecker. Great big lecherous Lana, that's me."

***

During the second week of August of 1946, Tyrone Power, "the man of my dreams" in Lana's words, also flew to Buenos Aires as part of a Good Will Tour of South America sponsored by 20th Century Fox. Along with a pilot-navigator and a Fox publicist, he was accompanied by César Romero, a fellow actor long billed as "the Latin from Manhattan." Romero's long homosexual attachment to Power was well known by insiders in Hollywood.

In a twin-engine Beechcraft named *Saludos Amigos*, the two stars arrived together at the airport in Buenos Aires to discover that hundreds of Argentines had turned out to welcome them. Something resembling a riot broke out, discord that evoked the tumultuous reception that Lana had received.

Both Eva and Juan Perón, who ruled Argentina, were their hosts at a lavish banquet they gave for the two stars at their palace. Both Power and Romero were awed by the extent of their reception, as no head of state had ever been received as tumultuously.

Eva's obsession with Lana—her clothes, her style, and her looks—was an "open secret" among the extended members of her enormous entourage. What wasn't known, except to her direct confidants, was that she had developed a powerful crush on Power. Whenever she spoke of him, she called him "the most beautiful man on earth."

On his third night in Buenos Aires, she made a secret visit to his suite after he'd booted Romero out of it. After their assignation, at 4AM, she'd slipped out of the hotel through a rear exit, hurrying into a curtained limousine driven by a member of her security team.

As Power confessed at breakfast to a jealous Romero, "Eva and I made love all night. She couldn't get enough of me. I felt I was being devoured instead of devouring her. I'd heard that she got her start working as a *puta* in a bordello. That's probably where she picked up some of those sexual tricks in the art of how to satisfy a man. Lucky Juan."

As Romero later revealed, years after Power's death, "Eva Perón paid three more visits to our suite for trysts with my handsome roommate. In every instance, she adopted the hairstyle, clothing, and makeup styles of her favorite movie star, prompting Power to exclaim, 'I felt I was fucking Lana Turner.'"

Romero feared that if the dictator Juan ever found out, he might order that Power be killed.

"Frankly, I don't think he cares all that much," Power responded. "I heard some gossip that he has two underaged mistresses on the side, and about two nights a week, he pays a visit to a secret hideaway where keeps a pretty, twelve-year-old boy."

***

Lana had known Power since 1940, often encountering him at lavish parties or premieres. But after his return from Argentina, she was invited to a party at the home of Edie and Keenan Wynn. At the time, Power was still married to the French actress who billed herself only as "Annabella." He had married her in 1939, when they co-starred together in *Suez*. Although the couple had, by this point, legally separated, they were still married.

At the Wynn party, Power spent most of the evening talking to Lana and avoiding the other guests. She, too, according to Keenan, "Had eyes only for Ty. And who in her right mind wouldn't? The guy is gorgeous!"

Before Power left the party, he invited Lana to his home the following evening for a drink. She eagerly accepted.

He followed her out to her car. Opening the door for her, he took her in his arms and kissed her passionately. She later wrote about that moment, claiming, "I went weak in the knees."

[Columnist Hedda Hopper later disputed Edie Wynn's claim that it had been she who brought Lana and Power together. Hopper printed her own version of their meeting: "Lana Turner was sitting alone in a booth at Romanoff's when Tyrone Power walked into the restaurant. She smiled at him and patted the empty seat beside her. He sat next to her as a sexual combustion set in."]

A matinee idol in the late 1930s and early 1940s, Power was known for his striking good looks, appearing in a series of romantic leads or as a swashbuckler in the style of Errol Flynn. He had played a bullfighter in *Blood and Sand* (1941), when he was sustaining affairs with both of his beautiful co-stars, Rita Hayworth and Linda Darnell.

He was the son of the English-born stage and screen actor, Tyrone Power, Sr. In Hollywood, Darryl F. Zanuck had helped Power, Jr., launch his film career at Fox, casting him in hit after hit, including *In Old Chicago* (1938) with Alice Faye; and *The Rains Came* (1939) with Myrna Loy. Zanuck, however, refused to lend him to MGM for the role of Ashley Wilkes opposite Vivien Leigh in *Gone With the Wind* (1939). Zanuck also turned down Warners, which wanted to cast Power opposite Ronald Reagan in his most prestigious film ever, *Kings Row* (1942).

Almost from the first year of his arrival in Hollywood, insiders at Fox learned of his bisexuality. Howard Hughes wanted to take advantage of it, and invited him to fly to Miami for a lavish vacation. The Ohio-born actor at the time was living up the reputation of the character he'd developed for his latest movie, *Ladies in Love* (1936), and as such, was having affairs with both of his co-stars, Janet Gaynor and Loretta Young. His on-and-off affair with Young would continue after his return to Hollywood when he made three more pictures with her: *Love Is News* (1937); *Safe Metropole* (1937); and *Second Honey-*

Throughout his career, Tyrone Power had almost as many lovers as Lana did (well, not quite that many). They ranged from Joan Crawford to Noël Coward, from Betty Grable to Doris Day, from Rita Hayworth to Loretta Young and Sonja Henie.

He once said, "For anyone truly interested in the theater, like me, it's a tragedy to be born handsome and such a sex object to both women and guys."

317

moon (also 1937).

Hughes told gay actor William Haines, "This sun-bronzed god got off the plane in Miami, where I was waiting for him at the airport. He was just too good-looking to be real."

A fan magazine at the time expressed it differently: "Tyrone Power is actually as good-looking as Robert Taylor is supposed to be."

According to one of Power's closest friends, actor Monty Woolley, "Howard and Ty became lovers on Miami Beach, and their affair on and off continued for many years. At the time, the press was comparing him to Robert Taylor and Errol Flynn. He later confessed to me that he had sexual liaisons with both actors, justifying it with: 'I wanted to size up the competition.'"

As proof of Hughes' attraction to Power, Johnny Meyer said that his boss often supplied Power with extra cash. For years, even though he was a star at Fox, he drew a relatively meager salary, based on the terms of his original contract.

Woolley claimed that Hughes was not just a lover "but a kind of father figure to Ty."

As for Power's true sexual preference, his longtime "trick," Scotty Hanson, said, "Ty was basically gay, but liked a girl from time to time, marrying three of them, but jilting Lana Turner."

When Power joined the military in 1943, it was not Annabella who said farewell to him, but Judy Garland, who was in love with him at the time. She was also pregnant, and he advised her to have an abortion because he was a married man. He later told Cesar Romero, "I loved Judy very much, and wanted her to have my baby, but it was impossible."

Garland was heartbroken when he was ordered to Saipan. *[The second largest island in the South Pacific's Mariana Islands archipelago, after Guam, it was defined, strategically, as the last defense against the U.S. invasion of the Japanese homeland, and as such, fiercely contested during one of World War II's longest and costliest battles there in June and July of 1944.]*

Louis B. Mayer told her to get over it. "You're not in love with Power. Only with his picture on the cover of *Photoplay*."

When Power was discharged at the end of the war, he returned to Hollywood, where he found Garland married to the first of her gay husbands, Vincente Minnelli.

For Lana, what began as a cocktail in Power's living room on the first night she was ever alone with him, developed into a sleepover. She left the following morning, but returned again that same night and the night thereafter.

At the time that Henry King was getting ready to helm Power in *Captain from Castile*, the director recalled seeing Lana and Power together on the beach at Malibu.

"It was near sunset, and both of them wore white bathing suits, each of them looking glorious, almost like a mirage in the fading reddish glow. They were holding hands and laughing as they ran along the sands. It was one of the most memorable sights of love I've ever seen."

She christened her affair with Power as "richer and more mature" than what she'd had with her two previous husbands, or with any of her fleeting romances, most of which she'd called "fly by night" or "ships which pass in the night."

Mistakenly, she thought she could overwhelm Power with the fruits of the $5,000 she'd spent on clothing, or with the $1,000 worth of expensive hats she'd acquired from the collection of the *haute* milliner, John Frederics, in New York. That kind of money could buy a lot of wardrobe in 1946.

Power would actually have preferred her in a simpler array of outfits.

In many other ways, they were not compatible, except that he had painted all his rooms as white as the wardrobe she wore in *The Postman Always Rings Twice*. In almost every room of his house were floor-to-ceiling bookshelves, and whereas he'd read dozens of books, it had been difficult for her to wade through *Gone With the Wind*.

Power's biographer, Fred Lawrence Guiles, wrote, "Lana and Ty were both sensualists. Touch and proximity were as important to them as sex. After their first date, which ended in bed, he became a regular at her home in Brentwood, spending night after night there, although he felt awkward being around her three-year-old daughter, Cheryl."

Actually, Lana praised the warm, fatherly relationship Power had with the little girl. "Real husband material," she told friends. "And I bet he'd make a great daddy for Cheryl."

She told Linda Darnell, Power's former lover, "He is the first man who makes me really happy." In spite of that, she often succumbed to bouts of deep depression, worrying about the direction of her career, her affair with Power (who kept stalling his divorce from Annabella), and the understandable fear that her beauty would eventually fade.

In Beverly Hills, she found her own "Dr. Feelgood," who got her addicted to amphetamines. She was so hyped up from his dosages that she could party all night, even when Power wanted to go home. But, as Guiles revealed in his biography, "There were times when she (Lana) was clearly out of control, her laughter too shrill, and her moods irrational." Her chain smoking also increased.

The more she urged Power to divorce Annabella, the more he stalled, making up excuses. They lived apart, but occasionally got together, ostensibly to discuss their career choices and even the terms that a divorce might entail. The more he put off marriage, the more Lana's chances of marrying him diminished.

During the white heat of her affair with him, she was shooting *Green Dolphin Street*, where he became a frequent visitor to the set.

On the MGM lot, in a dressing room adjoining Lana's, Esther Williams said, "From the sound of things, Ty and Lana must be setting fire to those pink satin sheets of hers."

Victor Saville, directing *Green Dolphin Street*, said, "Ty had so much charm it

319

should be outlawed. Did Lana really love him? I don't know. Had she really loved anyone before? Frankly, I think she fell in love with Ty because he was the male version of herself."

Helen Young, an MGM hairdresser and close friend of Lana's, said, "If I had to choose the most important event in Lana Turner's life, I would have to say it was her love affair with Ty Power. He was thirty-three years old when he became involved with her. He still had his good looks and, as always, could charm both men and women. In fact, he once admitted to me that even straight men propositioned him."

When Zanuck informed Power that he'd have to fly to Mexico for location shooting on *Captain from Castile* (1947), he met with Romero, who would be co-starring with him in the film. Power surprised his companion when he told him, "I'm glad to take a breather and get out of Hollywood for a change. Lana is so in love with me she is smothering me to death, and I need some breathing room. To inhale some fresh air. My god, she seems to want reassurance every minute that I love her!"

"Don't worry," Romero assured him. "I'll take care of all your needs down in Mexico."

Edie Goetz, the daughter of Louis B. Mayer, once tried to explain Lana's "suffocating kind of love."

"She knows no other way to love. She's a clinger, seemingly wanting proof of her lover's devotion every minute. That was not Ty's way. He often wanted to be alone for days at a time. He liked to lock himself in his house and read books, always searching for the right kind of story that might make a great film. He told me that he had never actually proposed marriage to Lana, even though she begged him almost every day to marry her."

In contrast, Lana told such friends as Linda Darnell, Virginia Grey, and Susan Hayward that, "Ty and I are officially engaged. He's searching for an engagement ring for me right now, I suppose."

According to Goetz, "Of course, I had to admit that physically—not emotionally—they were perfectly matched. When I first saw them together, they took my breath away with their stunning beauty. Her Jean Harlow platinum hair contrasted with his raven black locks. One evening, they were planning to co-star in a film together, called *Forever*. I told him that my father, Mayer, would never agree to lend Lana to Fox, and I'm sure Zanuck didn't want my dad to get his hands on Ty."

On many a night, Power talked with Lana about making a film out of his favorite novella, *Forever*. Written by Mildred Cram in 1934, it was a fragile, 60-page story, whose theme was that love reaches beyond the borders of life and death. The plot involved Colin and Julie, who in this otherworldly story, meet before they are born and finally find each other in this life and in this world.

Originally, Janet Gaynor had purchased its film rights as a vehicle for herself and perhaps Robert Taylor. Later, MGM acquired the rights as a possible project for Norma Shearer with Clark Gable. Ultimately, however, a film adaptation of the novella was never made.

Unknown to Lana, when Judy Garland was in love with Power, he read her the story one night by the fireplace and intrigued her into co-starring with him in this supernatural tale of enduring love. Someone wrote that Garland memorized the novella "word for word," but that seems unlikely.

Even though Zanuck would not green-light *Forever,* he and Power still remained best friends. With Lana, Power spent two weekends every month at the Zanuck estate in Palm Springs.

***

In mid-November of 1946, Power left for the scenic village of Morelia, near Pátzcuaro, Mexico, for location shooting on *Captain from Castile.* The next day in Hedda Hopper's column, she wrote, "Beautiful Lana Turner and beautiful Tyrone Power pledged their love and devotion to each other before he flew south." Privately, Hopper had asked him, "Are you really in love with Lana?"

"It's the nearest I've come to it," he confided to her. "But don't print that. It would hurt Lana's feelings."

She remained behind, filming *Green Dolphin Street.*

Arriving in a bone-bare Mexican outpost, the prospects looked bleak for Power, who faced a three-month shooting scheduled. His co-star was Jean Peters. But Hughes had warned him to stay away from her, because he had staked her out for himself. He would eventually marry her.

Errol Flynn, Power's former lover and a frequent visitor to Mexico, had arranged for Power to have a Mexican "guide." It turned out to be Carlos Francisco, who was eighteen. He'd been born in Juarez to a Mexican mother and an American sailor from San Diego who had spent only one night in the town.

Flynn had discovered Carlos when he was only fourteen years old, and had him delivered to the location shooting. In his note to Power, Flynn defined Carlos as "a party favor. He's the most beautiful boy in Mexico, and I'm sure you'll agree."

Power did agree, and moved Carlos into his modest living quarters, booting out a jealous Romero, who had, by now, gotten used to being ejected.

At MGM, Lana had missed spending Christmas with Power. During the shooting of *Green Dolphin Street,* MGM had warned her not to fly anywhere until the film was wrapped. She was so desperately lonely, however, that she decided to fly to Mexico City anyway during her three-day vacation so that she could "bring in" 1947 with her lover. She had been told that it was urgently necessary for her to report back to work at MGM at 9AM on January 2.

She opted not to alert Power, but planned to show up unexpectedly on the set.

In Mexico City, she learned that Morelia was some 85 miles away. There was no train service, not even a bus to this remote location, which was reached via bumpy roads better suited to a donkey than an automobile. The roads often washed out, she was told.

She placed an emergency call to Power, and, after about ten attempts, was finally able to reach Henry King, the film's director, who summoned Power to the phone.

"Hi, baby!" he said. "How's the weather in L.A.?"

"How in hell would I know?" she asked. "I'm in Mexico City."

To his shock, he learned that she had flown there to pay a surprise visit to him on the set. He promised to get back to her, claiming that he would try to charter a small plane to bring her to the nearby landing strip at Pátzcuaro.

He came through for her, and she boarded the rickety airplane with great trepidation. In the meantime, Power had time to move a very disappointed Carlos out of his shack.

Lana later said, "I was very upset by the sound of Ty's voice. He didn't seem exactly elated that I was in Mexico. I suspected that he had shacked up with some Mexican spitfire like Lupe Velez in my absence."

"There I was, stranded in Mexico City feeling god damn foolish. I was trying to pull off this big romantic fling with Ty, but I feared that I was like a school girl with a crush on the football captain. I was making a fucking nuisance of myself."

In spite of his initial reservations, Power welcomed her to the set and to his modest abode. She later told Darnell, "We made love all afternoon. It was worth the horrendous trip just to be in his arms once again."

"Romero, however, gave me a chilly reception, as did his co-star, Jean Peters. I heard that she was dating Howard, so I think she was jealous of me." She also noted that a very good-looking Mexican boy kept following Power and her around at a safe distance. She said, "If looks could kill, I'd be dead."

To Mexico, she had brought all the equipment, accessories, and wardrobe to make herself look glamorous on New Years' Eve.

She wore an Oriental dress with a high mandarin collar, her skirt slit up one side to show off her shapely legs. Under the nighttime sky, "I was a vision of seed pearls and rhinestones with a diamond necklace woven into my hair by a fat Mexican woman."

She recalled "It turned out to be the most romantic night of my life. The whole town was celebrating New Year's Eve, as the strains of music wafted across the cobblestoned town square where everybody gathered to hear the ringing of the church bells, signaling the new year."

In front of the church, as the bells were ringing, he kissed her at the stroke of midnight. She later claimed, "It was the single greatest and most passionate kiss of my life. And I've been kissed by some of the greatest smoochers on the planet."

But on the morning of her return, the skies opened up and "each raindrop seemed to contain a pint of water," she said. "The roads were washed out and all planes were grounded."

She did not show up for work at MGM on January 2 at 9AM. Saville, who had already shot the scenes where she wasn't needed, had no alternative but to shut down production. From 9AM to noon, he waited, and finally her call came in, informing him that she was grounded by bad weather, based on her impulsive weekend jaunt to a remote corner of Mexico to be with Power.

Mayer had to be informed of the delay, which he said would cost MGM $100,000 a day. Even if he exaggerated that figure, it would be very costly to the studio.

He asked Saville, "Does the bitch have to fly to Mexico to get fucked? There are plenty of dicks to go around in Hollywood. She should sample this new guy, this actor, John Ireland. I was told yesterday that he had the biggest dick in town."

Finally, the weather cleared, and Power arranged for her to fly to Mexico City.

She gave him a long, lingering kiss before boarding. "I'll be back and the next time, we won't have to rush."

That did not work out. She never returned to the location.

From Mexico City, she flew back to Los Angeles, where she showed up the next morning to find the set completely dark. Her first fear was that Mayer had shut down the picture and would sue her for the cost of the film so far.

Nevertheless, she put on her makeup and costume and walked onto the set. Not a soul was in sight. Suddenly, the lights were switched on, and she heard the sound of Mexican music. Saville emerged leading the cast and crew. Everyone wore a sombrero, and all of them were singing "South of the Border."

In spite of the serious breach of her contract, she was not sued, although her paycheck was docked.

Lana completed *Green Dolphin Street,* and Power eventually finished location shooting for *Captain from Castile* and then returned to Los Angeles for interior shots.

Shortly after his return, he and Lana were seen on the nighttime circuit, popping up at Ciro's or the Mocambo. Once again, Lana brought up the subject of divorce. He put her off, telling her that Annabella was in Paris filming *Éternel Conflit* (*The Eternal Conflict*, 1948), and that nothing could be done until she returned to California.

In Paris, the actress announced to the press, "I have no intention of divorcing Mr. Power."

***

Hughes had been surprised when his aide, Johnny Meyer, reported to him that Lana was having a torrid affair with Tyrone Power, and that they may even have fallen in love. He was no longer as infatuated with them as he'd been when he'd first met them, but he was still intrigued. He ordered Meyer to put both of them under 24-hour surveillance and to report back to him with full details.

"From the beginning, Howard wanted to be in on the affair," Meyer claimed, years later after Hughes had died. "He wanted to be part of the action, or so I thought. It was almost like, 'How dare you two fall in love without getting my permission first?'"

Hughes had also put actress Jean Peters under surveillance during the time she co-starred with Power in *Captain from Castile.*

Early in 1947, columnist Florence Muir reported that Lana had packed ten glamorous bathing suits to take with her to Acapulco for a vacation with Power. Muir knew only half the story. The invitation from Hughes had been collectively extended to them both, as a committed couple, in love.

The aviator/movie czar had arranged for "these two lovebirds" (as he called them) to stay in luxurious comfort in a villa within the then new, glamorous, and to some degree, semi-private resort of Acapulco.

Their host would be Teddy Stauffer, a Swiss-born big band leader whose tireless promotion of his luxury retreat (and the resort that contained it) had earned him the nickname "Mr. Acapulco."

Fleeing from the Nazis in 1940, Stauffer had settled in Mexico. Before that, he'd introduced American-style swing to pre-war Europe. He'd owned a night club and had been a small-time actor, but mostly he was known as an international playboy.

Like Hughes, he was a world-class seducer and had even married two of Hughes' former girlfriends, Hedy Lamarr and actress Faith Domergue.

In Mexico, Stauffer was on hand to welcome Lana and Power, giving the couple his most luxurious villa, which was filled with flowers and had a refrigerator overflowing with champagne.

The next day, Hughes showed up to take Lana and Power on a sailing expedition aboard a luxurious yacht he'd rented, complete with crew. When the yacht returned at 6PM, its "cargo" included a 210-pound swordfish. "Ty and I caught it together," Lana told Stauffer.

Years later, Stauffer revealed additional details of Lana's trip to biographer Charles Higham, but asked him not to print any of the graphic details. "I was in on Howard's plan right from the beginning. I set the whole thing up for him. He planned to make a grand entrance in the nude in the bedroom that Lana occupied with Power. I told him I thought the couple might be accommodating for a three-way, although I feared that Lana might hesitate. Even though sleeping with every Tom, Dick, and Harry in Hollywood, she sometimes made cooing sounds that she was a lady."

"Howard had left the lovebirds alone for their first night," Stauffer said. "But on the second night, he stripped down in front of me and headed bare-assed into their villa. I stayed nearby in case of trouble. He took the lovers by surprise. I heard a lot of loud talk, then everything settled down."

"The next morning over breakfast," Stauffer said, "I personally squeezed Howard's juice from blood-red oranges. He always insisted it be done right in front of him. He reported to me, while Lana and Power were still sleeping, that the previous night had been a success. Howard claimed that he had gone down on both of them while they kissed each other passionately. Later, as Power fucked Lana, he fucked Power, who was 'Lucky Pierre' caught in the middle of the sandwich. Howard confessed that, 'It was the best orgasm I ever had.'"

***

After she had finished shooting *Green Dolphin Street*, Lana had been set to co-star with Spencer Tracy in *Cass Timberlane*.

In the meantime, she sat night after night with Power, who claimed that he wanted to escape from adventure stories and prove to critics that he was a serious actor, especially in the wake of good reviews he'd gotten for *The Razor's Edge* (1946). He'd discovered a controversial script entitled *Nightmare Alley*, a compelling story about life—morbid but fascinating—as experienced by workers in an itinerant carnival.

In his role, Power becomes entangled with mind-reading Joan Blondell and assorted sideshow weirdos. He ends up as a sleazy, somewhat demented carnival geek eating raw chickens.

Darryl F. Zanuck did not want his leading matinee idol to play such an unromantic role, but Lana backed Power, earning a tongue lashing from the Fox mogul.

Finally, and very reluctantly, approval was granted. Even though *Nightmare Alley* (1947) failed at the box office, Power got some of the best notices of his career, and it eventually became an cult classic.

After a weekend with Power, Lana, alone in her house on a Monday afternoon, was overcome with nausea and set up a five o'clock appointment with her doctor. After an examination, he informed her that once again, she was pregnant.

That night, when Power came over, she told him the news. "With me as the boy's mother, and you as its father, it'll be the most beautiful little baby ever born."

In the months to come, columnists followed the romance of Lana and Power. Sidney Skolsky reported that "Tyrone Power and Lana Turner continue to be the most romantic couple in town."

Sheilah Graham informed her readers that Lana had gone on a diet and had lost seven pounds. "And, lest I forget, she's still in love with Tyrone Power, in spite of her reputation—or his—of being fickle."

She also reported that Power was still married to Annabella.

He wasn't so sure, pointing out that since he was still married, news of the pregnancy might destroy both of their promising careers. He urged her to consider an abortion.

She suggested that she might go away for nine months and disappear like Loretta Young had done when Clark Gable had impregnated her on the set of *The Call of the Wild* (1935).

"What if the boy is the spit image of me?" he asked.

He said that he was going to leave the decision of an abortion up to her. "I'll respect your wishes."

[She objected to his attitude. That was not the reaction she had wanted. In her fantasy, she had expected him to grab her, kiss her, and hold her, showing his delight that she was going to be the mother of his baby. She had also wanted him to promise he'd arrange a quickie divorce from Anabella and marry her at once as a means of making their baby legitimate.]

The night of the following day, she was even more horrified when he told her that he was going to fly aboard a converted DC-E during an upcoming two-month Good Will Tour of Africa. Although she didn't confront him with it directly, she felt he was abandoning her to solve the dilemma of an unwanted baby by herself. She had hoped to announce her engagement to the press before his trip, but he balked. "It would not be discreet," he said.

Nonetheless, she threw a $10,000 *bon voyage* party for him at Ciro's. Its theme was "Cupid & Love," and as a decorative logo on display, the letters "L&T" were entwined with an arrow. She announced that night that she would be joining him in Africa as soon as *Cass Timberlane* was wrapped.

That's not what Power told Romero the following day. "For me, my romance with Lana is on life support."

She drove him to the airport on the morning of his departure. The pilot of his plane was Robert Buck, and, among others, Power was accompanied by his secretary, Bill Gallagher.

The plane was scheduled to leave Los Angeles *en route* to Miami. From there, Power and his entourage would fly south to Brazil and from there, they'd cross the Atlantic for the west coast of Africa.

Before departure, he and Lana devised a secret code whereby she could inform him of her decision about the abortion. Motivated by the fear that an overseas operator might be listening to their conversations, she instructed Power that if she'd opted to abort the child, she'd say, "I found the house today," and that if she opted not to abort the child (and presumably to raise him or her as her own), she would say, "I haven't found the house today."

At the airport, she give him a long, lingering kiss, saying, "I will miss you, darling, and will count the hours until you are back in my arms."

She had already discussed an abortion with her most trusted *confidante*, Virginia Grey. She warned Lana that having the baby out of wedlock would destroy her career and possibly harm Power's, even though men were judged by a different standard.

Lana said, "I desperately want to have Ty's child. But after pondering it for a week, I decided to go ahead with the abortion."

Unlike a previous abortion, this one was performed without complications on a clean operating table with an anesthetic. She said, "The abortion took the fetus from me, but it did more than that. I took a piece of my heart."

***

One night in Africa, Power confessed to Buck, his pilot, that he wanted to "break it off with Lana."

He had already told Cesar Romero, "I find it much harder to break off a love affair with a woman than with a man."

"So you're calling it quits with Lana?" Buck asked.

"I already have. I just haven't told her yet. I want to be free as a bird, going where the wind takes me. Having new adventures, new, exciting conquests."

Chapter Twelve

The ManWho Got Away

Lana Weds a Tin Plate Heir
"Whose Figure Is Less Than Greek"

In a costume drama based on the Dumas classic, *The Three Musketeers*, Lana in Technicolor had never looked more dazzling or more beautiful.

"I sank my teeth into my first truly villainous role. Of course, I get beheaded for my evil deeds. But what a lovely head it was. I was playing a murderess and a thief, enough to make Lucretia Borgia look like Mary Poppins. My character was a wily and arch schemer. I'm imprisoned for my treachery. But I feign illness to win the sympathy of my jailers. Then I coldly murder them."

After 1945, despite her ongoing romantic problems with Tyrone Power, Lana forged ahead with her career, pouring cinema magic, scandals, and interviews out onto the fast-evolving postwar scene.

Columnist Dorothy Kilgallen wrote: "Lana Turner is a super-star for many reasons, chiefly because she is the same off-screen as she is on. Some of the great stars

327

are magnetic dazzlers on celluloid and ordinary, practical, polo-coated little things in private life. Not so Lana. No one who adored her in movies would be disappointed to meet her in the flesh. The flesh looks the same. The biography is as colorful as any plot she has ever romped through on the screen. The clothes she wears are just like the clothes you pay to see her in on Saturday night at the Bijou. The physical allure is just as heavy when she looks at a headwaiter as when she looks at a screen hero."

Lana spoke to the press, commenting on success in Hollywood, defining it as "the most dangerous thing that can happen. There is nothing more devastating."

In 1947, after being off the screen for a full year after the success of *The Postman Always Rings Twice,* she released *Green Dolphin Street* and *Cass Timberlane.*

The director of *Green Dolphin Street,* Victor Saville, had lined up a strong supporting cast, headed by Van Heflin, who'd played a

The the costume drama, *Green Dolphin Street,* Lana was cast as Marianne Patourel, who was stronger and more dominant than her sister, Marguerite (Donna Reed).

"Donna had the easy role, and did it well, but I had the major acting challenge--a real gutsy woman who stands by her man through earthquakes and a native Maori uprising."

drunken lawyer in her film, *Johnny Eager.* Heflin had not been designated as the romantic lead, that role going to Richard Hart. Donna Reed played Lana's sister, backed up by Frank Morgan, Dame May Whitty, Edmund Gwenn, Reginald Owen, and the formidable Gladys Cooper.

Although Lana as a blonde had created a sensation in *The Postman Always Rings Twice,* for *Green Dolphin Street* her hair was honey brown. Since her role demanded several different coiffures, her hairdresser, Helen Young, devised thirty-four different hairpieces for her, some of which were never used. Her fabulous costume wardrobe was created by Walter Plunkett, who had dressed the stars of *Gone With the Wind*.

In September of 1943, MGM had offered a $200,000 prize for the writer who developed the best story for adaptation into a film. The honor went to Elizabeth Goudge in 1944. Her romantic novel, *Green Dolphin Street*, had already sold 1.5 million copies.

MGM's filming of this 1840s-era drama included staggering costs and major challenges, including the hiring of hundreds of extras; the creation of background settings for New Zealand, China, and the Channel Islands; and the building of full-scale replicas of clipper ships. The biggest challenge was for the special effects technicians, who had to simulate a major earthquake. For their efforts, Warren Newcombe and A. Arnold Gillespie received an Oscar.

Originally, Saville thought the strong role of Marianne Patourel

During the filming of *Green Dolphin Street*, Lana related well to Del Armstrong, a genius when it came to makeup. She formed a friendship with him that would last a lifetime.

They had first met when he applied her makeup for *Marriage Is a Private Affair*.

"I could always trust him," she said. He'd see her through suicide attempts, a murder, and all her various love affairs. "If I ever had a man who was a best friend, it was Del. He never betrayed me, like so many others. He was always there for me."

required the arresting presence of Katharine Hepburn. But in the wake of her stunning performance in *The Postman Always Rings Twice*, Louis B. Mayer wanted to give Lana a chance to shine once again—this time in the Channel Islands seaport of St. Pierre. Donna Reed was cast as Lana's sister, Marguerite. Originally, that role was to have gone to June Allyson.

Richard Hart played a dashing naval captain, William Ozanne, who arrives unexpectedly one day in port. Both of the Patourel sisters fall instantly in love with him, although he prefers Marguerite, perhaps finding Lana's character of Marianne too strong for his tastes.

Later, while serving in the Royal Navy in China, he hooks up with Timothy Haslam (Heflin). Together, they plot their future and decide to travel to New Zealand and launch a lumber business.

One night, a drunken William writes to Marguerite, asking her to come to New Zealand and become his wife. In his stupor, he addresses the letter to Marianne instead.

Imagine his shock and surprise when Lana, instead of Reed, arrives in New Zealand, as instructed. The irony of the plot is that Timothy (i.e., Heflin) has been in love with her since his boyhood days in St. Pierre, but now sees her slipping off for marriage to his best friend.

As the plot unfolds, Lana (as Marianne) becomes a strong and powerful wife, virtually the backbone of her husband through all his triumphs and tragedies. As for poor Donna Reed (aka Marguerite) left back in the Channel Islands, she enters a convent.

Many of the exterior shots were filmed beside the banks of the Klamath River in Oregon. In a bit role, starlet Linda Christian was cast as Lana's maid, "Hine-Moa." She would later tell the press that Lana offscreen was very abusive to her.

Lana countered, "I hardly remember the girl and certainly was not abusive to her. I treat all my fellow actors with respect." At the time, she could not have conceived what a major and disastrous role Christian would play in her future.

As was her style, Lana worked well with the supporting cast, who included Edmund Gwenn, cast as her father, the wealthy Octavius Patourel. The oldtime London-born actor had immortalized himself that year playing Kris Kringle in the Christmas film, *Miracle on 34th Street*, which had garnered him an Oscar for Best Supporting Actor.

Reed had just finished making *It's a Wonderful Life* (1946) for Frank Capra. James Stewart played the male lead. [*This picture is taken out of mothballs every year and reshown during the Christmas holidays.*]

Generating fair to good reviews, *Green Dolphin Street*

A handsome Rhode islander, Richard Hart, who spent much of his acting career on a stage, would appear during the course of his career in four films.

During lunch with Hart and Lana, Donna Reed told them, "No one who watches this film is going to believe that you'd fall in love with me—and not with Lana."

[*In 1951, at the age of 35, like so many actors with whom Lana worked, Hart died young—in his case, of a heart attack.*]

"In his role of Timothy Haslan, Van Heflin is secretly in love with me," Lana said. "Our hardest scene was that god damn earthquake sequence where he heroically comes to my rescue."

eventually emerged as MGM's biggest hit of 1947.

Leo Miski, writing in the *New York Morning Telegraph,* described the movie's elephantine approach and treatment, claiming that it was impressive by its sheer weight more than anything else.

In the *Los Angeles Times,* Edwin Schallert praised the beauty of both Lana and Reed as well as the costumes of Walter Plunkett, but he noted that the film "screamed out for Technicolor."

Cecilia Ager in *PM* said: "No matter what the century Miss Lana Turner is assigned to, she brings her own firm-fleshed contemporary glamor. Wherever she is, she stands out as Lana Turner, unquestionably photogenic, one of Metro's most glittering productions all by herself. In a movie dedicated to ponderous production values, Miss Turner right or wrong is eminently right."

***

In 1945, the closing year of World War II, Sinclair Lewis (1885-1951) released a novel, *Cass Timberlane,* a saga of husbands and wives and a May-to-December romance. It was a meditation on themes that included love, marriage, trust, heartache, and redemption in a small town in Minnesota. Although Lewis had won the Nobel Prize for Literature in 1930, most critics pounced on *Cass Timberlane,* defining it as "second rate."

Even so, Louis B. Mayer purchased its film rights for $150,000, with the intention of adapting it into an MGM feature for a 1947 release.

Arthur Hornblow, Jr. was designated as the film's producer and George Sidney its director.

Sidney was an odd choice, based on his previous association with the *Our Gang* shorts, the *Crime Does Not Pay* series; and Pete Smith's popular comic specialties. Later, despite a reputation as a third-rate director, Sidney was assigned the job of helming the MGM musical hit, *Anchors Aweigh* (1945), casting Frank Sinatra and Gene Kelly as sailors. When Lana met Sidney, he had just directed Judy Garland in *The Harvey Girls* (1946). He would not only helm Lana in *Cass Timberlane,* but later, he'd be her director in the Technicolor extravaganza *The Three Musketeers* (1948).

In the beginning, it was not at all certain that Lana would be assigned the lead in *Cass Timberlane.* Ava Gardner had made a pitch for the role, but was rejected. She later complained "MGM already has a sex symbol *[she was referring to Lana],* and those guys don't know what to do with another one."

For a brief time, Vivien Leigh and Jennifer Jones were also under consideration. In the end, Sidney, with Mayer's blessings, decided to cast Lana in the role, based on her previous acting in *The Postman Always Rings Twice.*

She interpreted her acquisition

331

of the role with a certain irony: "Vivien took Scarlett O'Hara from me, not that I really had that role, and Jones made off with *Madame Bovary (1949)*. Now I'm taking something from those two."

As the male lead, Sidney toyed with the idea of casting Walter Pidgeon. But that didn't work out.

[Actually, Pidgeon did make a surprise cameo appearance in Cass Timberlane, encountering Lana's character at a party in Manhattan. MGM had a custom of casting some of its major stars in brief, sometimes unexpected cameos. Lana had been pleased with the casting of Pidgeon because the two of them had performed so well together in Week-End at the Waldorf.*]*

Sidney phoned her late one afternoon to announce that Spencer Tracy had accepted the lead role, and that Zachory Scott would be playing the second male lead. *[She had not only worked with Tracy in* Dr. Jekyll and Mr. Hyde, *but had had a brief fling with him then as well.]*

When she lunched with Tracy one day in the MGM commissary, he complained about the choice of directors, not wanting Sidney. "I preferred either my pal, George Cukor, or that other fag, Vincente Minnelli, but was

Spencer Tracy was cast as the highly respected Judge Cass Timberlane, an ethical man moving deeper into middle age. Up to that point, he'd been viewed as incorruptible. The most controversial thing he ever did involved taking Virginia ("Jinny") Marshland as his young bride. Lana got the role.

Sinclair Lewis, in his novel, had described her character as "a half-tamed hawk of a girl, twenty-three or -four, not tall, smiling, lively of eye."

Jinny was definitely from the wrong side of the tracks, and she shocked the judge's more conservative friends.

voted down. Maybe Sidney will turn *Cass Timberlane* into another *Our Gang* comedy."

The scriptwriter, Donald Ogden Steward, was known at the time for his golden age comedies and melodramas. He was brought in to devise a film script based on the Lewis novel. His big hit had been *The Philadelphia Story* (1940), starring Katharine Hepburn, Tracy's companion.

In spite of Steward's credentials, Sidney wasn't pleased with his final script. He complained to Lana that although he had strengthened Tracy's role as the judge, he had reduced her character's presence. Subsequently, he brought in scriptwriter Sonya Levien to beef up the role of the young bride.

Lewis was known for exposing the hypocrisies of Main Street America. In the script, Lana's marriage to the judge, as hawkeyed by everyone in town, doesn't run along an even course. As Jinny, Lana encounters disapproval from Tracy's staid friends, usually older couples, with one exception. His best friend is lawyer Bradd Criley, the role that Zachory Scott would play.

Joan Crawford had already spread the gossip among the women stars and starlets at MGM that Scott was a closeted homosexual, despite his recent marriage to Elaine Anderson. *[She would later divorce him to marry John Steinbeck.]*

Scott and his wife were frequently seen in public with Angela Lansbury and her husband, Richard Cromwell. Lana picked up more gossip: Cromwell was Howard Hughes' sometimes lover, and, it was also said, that Scott and Cromwell were engaged in a torrid love affair behind the backs of their wives. Lansbury later publicly admitted that her husband was a homosexual, as she'd learned painfully.

Finally, Lana learned more scandalous information about Scott during her reunion with her friend, Tom Drake, who'd been cast in *Cass Timberlane* in the small role of Jamie Wargate, and with whom she'd worked on *Week-End at the Waldorf.* He brought her up to date on all the latest gossip about Van Johnson and Peter Lawford. Over more than a few drinks, Drake confided that he had only recently begun an affair with Scott himself.

On the sets of many of her pictures, she had often pursued her leading man, but in this case, she didn't mind that Scott was off-limits. Her current lover, Tyrone Power, was a frequent visitor to the set during filming.

In *Cass Timberlane,* Lana's hair was dyed blonde again. Bored with her existence in this small town, Lana is intrigued with the charm of Bradd Criley, who is the town's most handsome, most charismatic playboy. He helps her relieve her boredom, especially when she goes to New York to lighten her spirits after her baby dies during childbirth.

She wants to remain in Manhattan, but her husband, the Judge, refuses. Defiantly, however, Bradd agrees to show her the town.

During filming and on at least two occasions, Tracy visited her dressing room and pressed her for sex, but each time, she refused.

Cameron Mitchell, the son of a Pennsylvania pastor, played a minor role of Eino Roskinen. Lana became very impressed with him as an actor, telling Sidney, "I think you've cast the next John Garfield."

One slow afternoon, Cameron had consumed a few beers during his wait for the next take. When Sidney informed him that there would be another delay, he whispered to Lana, "Wanna fuck?"

She whispered back, "Wanna not?"

Ever since Zachory Scott had co-starred with Joan Crawford as her sleazy love interest in *Mildred Pierce* (1945), Lana had been intrigued with what she described as Scott's "lizard-like appearance, the perfect villain."

The year she worked with him, he'd been voted the "third most promising star of tomorrow."

In the years ahead, she watched Mitchell star in so many movies that she wondered when he ever slept. Today, audiences see him on the late show playing an incognito millionaire in pursuit of a gold-digging Lauren Bacall, in *How to Marry a Millionaire* (1953) with scene-stealer Marilyn Monroe.

Both *Green Dolphin Street* and *Cass Timberlane* were released in October of 1947, and Lana found that she was competing with herself for movie audiences. She need not have worried, as each of them emerged among MGM's high grossers of that year.

Many of the reviews for *Cass Timberlane* were tepid, but that didn't seem to affect movie attendance. Lana herself, in several cases, got better reviews than the movie itself.

Kate Cameron, writing in *The New York Daily News*, said: "There is no doubt about it. Lana Turner screens more beautifully than any other blonde in Hollywood. She literally illumines the screen with a glow that is soft, warm, and altogether feminine. That she is able to hold the spotlight while Tracy is on the screen is a test of her ability as an actress and a charmer."

Many critics felt that Lana and Tracy improved on Sinclair Lewis' original characters, making the judge and his young wife warmer, more human, and more likable than they'd been in the original novel.

Tracy phoned Lana a few days after their picture was released. "I'm pissed off at you," he said. "I just read a review of *Cass* in *Variety*. The asshole who wrote it claimed that in scene after scene, you stole them from me, and I came across as wooden. What did you do? While I was emoting, did you pull out one of your tits behind my back? I used to be a friend of Sinclair Lewis. I knew him well enough to call him 'Red.' He's seen our movie. Now he refuses to take my calls."

***

During the long weeks that Tyrone Power spent in Africa on his Good Will Tour, Lana used her coded message to tell him that she'd aborted his child, a baby she had desperately wanted to keep. The secret codewords they'd developed privately had been necessary, based on their fear that an overseas operator would listen to their conversations and break the news of their aborted "love child" to the press.

During Power's tour, she didn't disguise the contempt in her voice when she told Ava Gardner, "Good Will for whom? Certainly not for our relationship."

During Power's absence from Hollywood, columnist Harrison Carroll wrote, "Lana Turner was seen nightclubbing at Ciro's with her old flame, Peter Lawford."

Later, when Carroll ascertained that Power would not return to Hollywood until November 10, he wrote, "I still wouldn't make any bets that he and Lana will ever make it to the altar."

On October 8, 1947, columnist Sheilah Graham reported that Lana had abruptly canceled her trip to join Power in Africa. When he decided to stop over in Rome during his transit back to New York, there was speculation that she'd fly there to meet him. Graham later revealed that Lana's trip to Italy had been canceled for reasons unknown.

Later, in advance of Power's flight from Europe back to New York, Lana flew to New York to meet him there. Checked into the Waldorf-Astoria, she received a call from Frank Sinatra, who had flown East for a performance in New Jersey. He, too, had checked into the Waldorf, and invited her for a drink "for old time's sake."

The next morning, a room service waiter delivered two breakfasts to Lana's suite. Later, for fifty dollars, the waiter tipped off columnist Walter Winchell. The news of Lana's reunion with her former lover made the international gossip circuit.

During the weeks that Power spent in Rome, the Italian capital was fast becoming "Hollywood on the Tiber," and no doubt, the news of Lana's sleepover with Sinatra reached him.

She made several attempts to contact Power in Rome at the Hotel Excelsior on the Via Veneto, but could not get through, even though she called at random hours of the day and night. Again and again, she was told, "Mr. Power is not available to take calls."

She finally got him on the phone and chastised him for being out of touch. She informed him that she'd wait for him in New York at the Waldorf-Astoria, ready, willing, and able to receive him the moment he arrived at Idlewild Airport.

In Manhattan, perfumed and accessorized, she waited and waited. Still no Power.

Finally, she was informed that he had shuffled his westbound flight to avoid a stopover in New York altogether, and that he'd transited to Kansas City. From there, after refueling, he flew directly to Burbank in California, arriving there on November 25.

From New York, Lana placed an urgent call to his home, and this time, her call was connected right away. "What in hell happened?" she asked, not disguising the anger in her voice.

He explained that he had urgent business on the West Coast and that he had to get back to Los Angeles immediately. He'd been gone too long, he informed her.

"I'm taking the next plane to L.A.," she said. "I'll cable you my flight number and its expected arrival time, and I want you to pick me up at the airport. It's been far too long for me, too."

When her flight landed in Los Angeles, he was not at the airport to meet her. She waited around for an hour for him to show up. Finally, he did.

Driving her home, he was almost silent throughout the ride. She invited him in for a drink. Inside, the tension was obvious.

As she would later tell Ava Gardner and others, "I finally got enough courage to ask him what had gone wrong between us. At last he confessed. He said that during his stay in Rome, he'd met Linda Christian and had had an affair with her. "We've fallen in love," he said. "We may even get married. I'm sorry. You may remember her. She played your maid in *Green Dolphin Street.*"

"I remember the bitch all right," Lana screeched at him. "An international whore. I can't believe you'd fall for such trash like that. She's fucked everybody from Errol Flynn on down.

"She's really a sweet girl," he protested, "when you get to know her."

"Like hell I'll get to know her," she yelled at him. "I don't even know you anymore. Get the hell out of my house. And stay out!"

He slammed his drink down on her coffee table and quickly headed out. At the door, he paused. "Let's be friends. I'll invite you to my wedding."

"Get out!" She picked up his cocktail glass and threw it at the door, narrowly missing him.

It was over.

***

After Power left, she phoned Virginia Grey, asking her to come over at once. She'd later recall, "Lana was suicidal when I got there, or at least I thought she was. I agreed to stay over with her because I seriously believed she was ready to do herself in. She would hardly eat for three days and nights. All she'd do was drink and smoke. At one point, in a drunken stupor, she fell down the steps. Fortunately, she didn't injure herself. Just bruises and stuff. I phoned a doctor, who heavily sedated her. I stayed there like a nursemaid for a week. I don't know where her kid was. I think she'd been shipped off to her grandmother's, but I'm not sure. I didn't ask."

The following week, Lana spent hours working on her looks before appearing in public again. On December 2 came the announcement from MGM publicity that Lana and Power had ended their widely publicized romance. The release claimed, "They met over the weekend and decided to relegate their romance to the vault of sweet memories."

At MGM, she was confronted by Hedda Hopper who wrote, "Mr. Power has returned to Hollywood from Africa, and is determined to join Ronald Reagan, Clark Gable, and Robert Taylor in the battle against the communists infiltrating Hollywood. These Reds are the scourge of the world."

"Personally, Mr. Power and I have gone our separate ways," Lana told the columnist. "At no time did we ever talk about getting married. We were just good friends."

"As you know, when I saw him very infrequently, he was married to Annabella, a fine lady and actress. I always steer clear of married men in spite of what the press reports."

"I read that his divorce is coming through and he will no doubt remarry, but not to me. The press invented a romance between us. None existed. I'll carry my chin higher and get on with making movies. I have no serious romance in my life at the moment."

In an overview of Lana's life, it's clear that Tyrone Power became "the man who got away."

Years later, Lana said, "No man except possibly Ty took the time to find out that I was a human being. Not just a pretty, shapely little thing. That could have been my fault. I didn't know myself back then. How could any man understand me?"

***

It was heartbreaking for Lana to read about Tyrone Power, the lover who had abandoned her, and his new girlfriend, Linda Christian, whom she only vaguely remembered from having played her maid in *Green Dolphin Street*.

She was learning more and more about her rival every day, and Lana felt humiliated that a star of her stature would be jilted and that the cad who rejected her would then opt for the company and sexual favors of an even more notorious starlette.

When Power first got involved with the then-23-year-old Christian, she was having a fling with Turhan Bey after Lana had dumped him. One night, Lana said. "Christian is taking my sloppy seconds."

When she heard that Power was stopping over in Rome, Christian flew there at once, also checking into the Hotel Excelsior where, on her first night there, she ran into him in the luxurious lobby. What happened after that earned her a place in the saga of Lana Turner.

Wedding Bell Blues: Lana wept uncontrollably when word reached her from Rome that Tyrone Power, the love of her life, had married Linda Christian.

"Imagine taking a handsome devil like Tyrone Power from the famous, the celebrated, the luscious Lana Turner," Christian said. "My friends said it couldn't be done. Honey, I had him the first night."

The next day, after leaving the Excelsior for an appointment with a hairdresser, she told an unidentified female companion, "I've bagged Ty Power. He told me last night that he was once in love with his wife, and on another occasion, with a bigtime Hollywood movie star. I knew that he meant Annabella and Lana Turner."

The press dubbed Christian "The Anatomical Bomb," because of her international affairs that had begun after Errol Flynn first discovered her in Acapulco and brought her to Hollywood. Soon, she was dating famous racing drivers, bullfighters, financiers, politicians, and playboys.

The daughter of a Dutch engineer and his Mexican-born wife, Christian had learned seven languages, even "haphazard Arabic," because of the nomadic lifestyle of her parents.

Power's biographer, Hector Arce, called her, "Madame Du Barry born two hundred years too late. All her life, she'd been trained in the ways of pleasing a man. She was bright and shrewd, fevered with a desire to be somebody. The chief blind spot in her makeup was her inability to distinguish fame from notoriety."

Lana certainly didn't expect Christian to be faithful to Power. Word reached Lana that her former lover, Johnny Weissmuller, was dropping his loincloth for her when both of them were starring together in *Tarzan and the Mermaids* (1948).

In time, the starlet would become the first James Bond girl when she appeared in the 1954 TV adaptation of Ian Fleming's *Casino Royale*.

At long last, on January 26, 1948, Annabella divorced her husband. He told his friends, "The French bitch cleaned me out. I'm now flat broke and stuck with a monstrous alimony."

Much to Lana's chagrin, the venue for the wedding of her former lover to Linda Christian took place in Rome. The assembly there of more than 10,000 fans degenerated into a riot.

Theirs would become a marriage fragmented by enormous tension, many of them based on his serial adulteries with both genders, and their frequent separations based on their respective work commitments.

During the months to come, Lana derided the marriage to her friends. "I hear that Ty is keeping her barefoot and pregnant all the time. It's been reported that for most of their marriage, she walks around with a big belly. I know Ty. That's a big turn-off for him."

Actually, Christian admitted herself that she had three miscarriages during the course of her marriage to the actor. Yet she eventually gave birth to two girls. In fact, she was pregnant in 1952 when Power first asked her for a divorce.

[He did not divorce her until 1956. Yet three years before that, Christian became genuinely enraged when Power rejected an offer to co-star with Christian in the 1953 blockbuster, From Here to Eternity. *"It was my big chance, and Tyrone fucked it up for me," Christian protested.*

The roles eventually went to Montgomery Clift and Donna Reed, who won a Best Supporting Actress Oscar for her performance.]

During periods when she wasn't recovering from either her miscarriages or her childbirths, Power and his new wife became notorious in Hollywood for their pool parties, wherein both of them indulged in serial adulteries. The early hours of these parties were devoted to heavy drinking, but by midnight, guests were indulging in orgies or else pairing off and heading for the bedrooms upstairs.

Since, as a bisexual, he seduced either gender, Power doubled his chances of conquest. Once, he was seen ascending the stairs with Rock Hudson. On another occasion, he and a former lover, Howard Hughes, competed for the affection of a handsome young actor, Robert Francis. *[Later, Power used his influence to get Francis cast with him in his 1955 film,* The Long Grey Line.]

Christian would marry again, but not until 1962. The scope of her conquests was vast. "I've always been the pursuer," she once told the press. "Only once did I fail to get the man I went after. Cary Grant. But I learned later that he was a homosexual."

She had affairs with Miguel Alemán, the president of Mexico, and with Prince Aly Khan, despite his marriage at the time to Rita Hayworth. When she met Mexico's most famous painter, Diego Rivera, he said, "You will pose nude for me." It was not a request, but a command.

Lana, for reasons of her own, followed the almost daily reportage of Christian's affairs, including with the playboy, Richard Schlesinger. When Schlesinger was hauled into court for nonpayment of a million dollars' worth of jewelry he'd given Christian, she refused to return the diamonds, rubies, and emeralds.

She proclaimed to all the world that the then-married Marquis Alfonso de

Portago, the celebrated Spanish racing driver, was "the love of my life." In 1957, at the Mille Miglia race, she was photographed kissing him. Minutes later, he crashed his Ferrari, dying instantly. The press, in news flashes that went around the world, dubbed it "The Kiss of Death.'

[The Mille Miglia (aka the "Thousand Miles") was an open-road endurance race between Brescia to Rome, round trip. Between 1927 and 1957, with an interruption during World War II, it took place in Italy twenty-four times, captivating the attention of millions of fans.]

Christian also traveled the world with Francisco ("Baby") Pignatari, the Brazilian millionaire, making an occasional film.

During the shooting of *House of Seven Hawks* (1959), she seduced Robert Taylor, another of Lana's former lovers.

Christian went on to play Rod Taylor's gold-digging girlfriend in *The VIPs* (1963) with Elizabeth Taylor and Richard Burton. During its filming, she slipped around and seduced Burton. When Taylor heard about it, she ordered that Christian's best scenes be cut from the film.

In 1964, during the filming of a documentary about bullfighting, Christian seduced Luís Domínguez. Even though his affair with Ava Gardner had ended before their encounter, Christian boasted, "I took away a matinee idol and a world-famous bullfighter from two of Hollywood's reigning love goddesses, Lana Turner and Ava Gardner. Not bad for a little Mexican spitfire, wouldn't you say? I must have something they don't. There are things a man likes done to him that Ava and Lana just wouldn't do. I will!"

In the immediate aftermath of her abandonment by Power, Lana thought that her link to Linda Christian was over. To her rage and fury, it resurfaced again in 1955 in a most infuriating way.

***

Although Lana never got involved with Power again, she followed his career and private life with avid interest. He was still in his early forties. Based perhaps on his high-drama affairs and his all-night partying in California and abroad, he was beginning to lose his matinee idol good looks. As he moved into middle age, the dissipation was reflected on his face as his smoking and drinking accelerated. He ignored his doctors, who warned him that, like his father, he had a weak heart.

The last movie he attempted was *Solomon and Sheba* (1958), in which, on location near Madrid, dressed in heavy armor in record-breaking hot temperatures, brandishing a heavy sword during a dueling scene with George Sanders, he collapsed and suffered a fatal heart attack.

It was November 15, 1958. He was only 44 years old. Bulletins immediately flashed the news around the world.

News of his death reached Lana during a vacation in Acapulco as the guest of Ted Stauffer at his luxurious resort, the same venue that had sheltered her during her three-way with Power and Howard Hughes. Stauffer called her to the phone to hear about Power's death.

In her memoir, she recorded her reaction: "Tyrone, that beautiful, sensitive man, so in love with life. I sat disbelieving and numb. I didn't cry, not then, and not later, when the numbness wore off, and I realized that it was true. Tyrone Power was dead. My tears had been shed years before, when that door closed. Now it was truly closed forever. In my life, I loved other men, but Tyrone was special. He was the one who broke my heart."

***

At long last, MGM reteamed Lana with Clark Gable in a post-war film, aptly entitled *Homecoming* (1948) in which Louis B. Mayer hoped to replicate the success of their pair of pre-War movies, *Honky Tonk* and *Somewhere I'll Find You*. Mervyn LeRoy, Lana's long-ago mentor, was set to direct her once again. Although he had never directed Gable in a film, he'd also been a mentor to him when he first hit Hollywood.

More than a decade earlier, the director had recognized Gable's potential as a future matinee idol during his screening of *The Last Mile* (1930), wherein Gable interpreted the role of "Killer Mears." Meeting Gable for the first time, LeRoy tried to get him screen tested, with hopes of configuring him as a contract player, but Jack Warner said, "His ears are too big. I think he'd become airborne in a head wind."

The director continued to try to open doors for the actor, and eventually Gable and LeRoy became close friends. Leroy had tried unsuccessfully to get the unknown stage actor cast in a role in *Little Caesar* (1931), and later, he urged his colleague, director Howard Higgin, to assign Gable the fifth lead in *The Painted Desert* (1931), a film that otherwise starred William Boyd and Helen Twelvetrees.

Although LeRoy never directed Gable in a movie until *Homecoming*, he took pride in his discovery. He watched Gable become the King of Hollywood, the leading man to Greta Garbo, Joan Crawford, Jean Harlow, Norma Shearer, Barbara Stanwyck, Helen Hayes, Claudette Colbert, and Hedy Lamarr. "I seduced most of them," he confessed, "except for the lezzies." He also starred with Loretta Young and Myrna Loy before landing the role of Rhett Butler in the classic, *Gone With the Wind*.

Until *Homecoming* came along, both Lana and Gable had rejected scripts sent to them, finding none of them suitable for his post-war comeback film. In 1944, Sidney Kingsley had devised a drama, *The Homecoming of Ulysses*, specifically as a vehicle for

Gable. In 1934, Kingsley had received the Pulitzer Prize for Drama, based on his play, *Men in White*. It had been made into a movie starring Gable and Myrna Loy.

Paul Osborn wrote the final screenplay for *Homecoming*. He had just written the screenplay for the highly successful *The Yearling* (1947), which had co-starred Gregory Peck and Jane Wyman.

In the drama, cast in the role of Col. Ulysses Delby ("Lee") Johnson, Gable plays a New York society doctor who's married to Penny (Anne Baxter). He's so caught up in the social whirl of Manhattan that he can't help an old schoolmate, Dr. Bob Sunday (John Hodiak), tackle a malaria epidemic from decimating a tribal village. Gable's character is eventually "converted" to good causes after his designation as a major in the Army Medical Corps.

En route to Africa, Ulysses meets the very lovely Lt. Jane McCall (Lana; nicknamed in the film as "Snapshot"), who will become his inspiration and assistant. Slowly, amidst a torrent of bickering, the couple fall in love.

During the course of the film, ostensibly during the infamous Battle of the Bulge, "Snapshot" dies from fragments of an exploding bomb. After the war, a chastised man, Gable returns to Penny, despite confessing his love for the dead nurse.

It seems that Ulysses and Penny will patch up their differences and live happily ever after in post-war America.

Stripped of her usual glamor girl wardrobe, Lana, as "Snapshot," comes across as a kind, good-hearted nurse with quiet, sincere good judgment. No longer was she interpreted by moviegoers as the murdering Cora in *The Postman Always Rings Twice*. Even without her usual accessories, Lana's beauty still shined through.

Lana related an embarrassing incident in her memoirs: To keep her mouth fresh, she chewed gum. During one of the takes, she stashed the gum away with her tongue, moving it into the recesses of her cheek. During her heavy kissing scene, the gum came loose and wound up sticking to Gable's false teeth. No one was amused. "From then on, I used Listerine to keep my mouth fresh," she said.

Lana concealed her shock about how much Gable had aged. He looked heavier, more jowly, a much older and sadder man. Somehow, for her, at least, the sexual magnetism was no longer there, although they still held onto their easy camaraderie. No longer was she a

There was no chance of Lana reviving her long-ago romance with Gable. "He had moved on, and so had I," she told Virginia Grey.

Unlike Lana, Grey had already resumed her own pre-war romance with Gable.

starlet in the making. Instead, she had morphed into a full-fledged box office attraction in her own right.

Lana shared a reunion with John Hodiak, but by now, he was married to Anne Baxter. A few decades later, at her home in Easton, Connecticut, Baxter told author Darwin Porter, "I knew Lana still had the hots for my John (Hodiak), so I watched her like a hawk. I didn't trust the two of them alone for a minute. She knew what John was carrying around in his pants, and I can't blame her for wanting a rematch. But it didn't happen. I saw to that."

Lana and Gable between takes on the set of *Home-coming.*

Ever the realist, Gable was very candid about his physical appearance, confessing that he was using hemorrhoid ointment to shrink the bags under his eyes. His jowls were pulled tight behind his ears with rubber bands.

Likewise, during the early weeks of making *Homecoming,* Tyrone Power (who had not yet departed on his African Good Will Tour) visited the set.

Lana was emphatically aware that Power had had an affair with Baxter when both of them had co-starred with Gene Tierney in *The Razor's Edge* (1946).

LeRoy described the sexual intrigue on his film set like this: "Anne Baxter was keeping Lana from John Hodiak, and Lana was seeing that Tyrone Power remained off limits to Anne."

In one of the ironies associated with changing partners and bisexuality in Hollywood, Lana learned through LeRoy that Hodiak had stopped "servicing" Cesar Romero, Power's longtime lover.

Leroy selected a strong supporting cast to back up his screen duo. Lana had worked with Gladys Cooper (playing Mrs. Kirby) before, as she had with Cameron Mitchell (playing Sgt. Monkevickz). Once again, Mitchell told her, "I still want to fuck you."

"Sorry," she said. "Ty put a chastity belt on me while he's away."

Lana met and talked with character actor Ray Collins. Although he would appear in some 75 films, he became better known on TV for playing the irascible Lt. Arthur Tragg in the long-running *Perry Mason* series.

One day, his best friend, Orson Welles, came to visit him. Welles had cast Collins in *Citizen Kane* (1941).

Lana later told LeRoy about her introduction to Welles in her dressing room. "After Ray left, I was alone with him. Welles put his hand up my dress and I wasn't wearing panties. He dug in deeper, and I had one hell of a time ejecting him. I don't know how Rita Hayworth puts up with him. He's outrageous."

***

In the words of newspaper columnist Lee Mortimer, "*Homecoming* is an exhibitor's dream and a theater patron's paradise."

MGM's publicity department billed its cast as "*The Team That Generates Steam.*"

Columnist Adela Rogers St. Johns wrote, "I thought Lana Turner gave one of her greatest performances ever. I was burned because I thought she did not get enough credit. I remember a gal named Clara Bow who every once in a while used to turn a heart-twisting bit like that."

Wanda Hale in the *New York Daily News* wrote: "Clark Gable and Lana Turner take up where they left off before the war. MGM's big money team, their screen romance followed the routine—man and girl meet, they dislike each other on first sight, they fight, they hate each other, and then they fall in love. All of which was, and still is, thrilling to those who rate such a love affair higher than the story. Gable and Turner are Gable and Turner—and that's all their fans want."

New York film critics described *Homecoming* as one of the worst films of 1948. Gable's reaction? "A bunch of snobbish faggots."

***

Lana received an unexpected call from David Niven, with whom she'd had a brief fling. At the suggestion of his close, swashbuckling friend, Errol Flynn, he wanted to ask her if he could escort her to a private party at Flynn's home the following night. "Clark Gable will be there, and several others—maybe thirty in all."

She eagerly accepted the invitation as a distraction from having been recently deserted by Tyrone Power, and was surprised that Gable and Flynn had become such close friends, seeing each other several times a week. After his return from the warfront, Gable seemed to have evolved into a bachelor-at-large with a roving eye.

Upon his homecoming, he had resumed his affair with Virginia Grey, and almost daily Lana's friend articulated her heartfelt desire that Gable would settle down and propose marriage.

To Lana, that didn't seem likely.

He was seducing Paulette Goddard, but had complained to Lana that "she's too strong- willed for me, and keeps hinting that some diamonds might be in order." He was also dropping in on occasion to see his long-time flame, Joan Crawford, and was also seen escorting Anita Colby to functions. Dolly O'Brien had rejected his proposal of mar-

A savvy cad—David Niven, defying wartime frugality.

riage. He told Flynn and others, "Dolly said I didn't satisfy her in bed.:"

The press had also linked Gable to Betty Chisholm, the Jones Sausage heiress, and to Millicent Rogers, the Standard Oil heiress.

Before making *Homecoming* with Lana, he'd filmed *The Hucksters* (1947) in which Ava Gardner had one of the roles. In their girl-to-girl chats, Lana and Gardner often sliced up men, and both of them agreed that Gable was a self-admitted "lousy lay."

On a Friday night, Niven arrived at Lana's house, and, as always, he was the courtly British gentleman. When they appeared on the doorstep of Flynn's home for a party, as planned, both of them were surprised when two young girls, no more than teenagers, opened the front door. "They were incredibly beautiful and absolutely nude," Lana said. She tugged at Niven's arm, suggesting, "This isn't my kind of party."

But he insisted that they go inside and greet Flynn, who had become aware of their arrival and was heading to greet them with one of his warm kisses on each of their lips.

Once inside, Lana entered a room of strangers, except for a few familiar faces. Bruce Cabot and Gable sat on Flynn's sofa, receiving guests like royalty. Most of the party-goers were grips, studio technicians, budding starlets, and cameramen.

When she turned around, she encountered Ann Sheridan who whispered to her, "Watch what you say in the powder room. It's bugged."

Like the exuberant and spontaneous host he was, Flynn worked the room, occasionally stopping beside Lana to give her a kiss. When a seat on his sofa became available, Gable patted it and signaled to Lana to sit down. She noticed that "The King" was visibly shaking, although his weakened condition did not stop him from all-night partying and numerous conquests. He admitted to her that his tremors were caused by the Dexadrine he was taking "to lose all these pounds I've put on from too much boozing."

Suddenly, Shelley Winters rudely squeezed herself into a position on the couch between Gable and herself. Niven jumped to Lana's rescue, inviting her onto the moonlit terrace where he stood with her, looking back into the living room at both Gable and Flynn. "Looks like Yvonne De Carlo has staked out Errol for the night," she said.

"Take a good look at those two once-handsome legends," Niven said. "You'd better look now, because those two are about to fall apart with all this boozing, high living, constant fucking and wenching until dawn. It's a bloody shame!"

"I agree," she said, taking his hand and lightly holding it against her lips. "Let's get the hell out of here. Since it's Friday and I'm not scheduled to be at the studio until Monday morning, why not let me entertain you this weekend?"

"That's the best offer I've had since Merle Oberon asked me to enter through the rear door."

"Oh, David, you're so vulgar! I love it! Let's head for the door."

She already knew what to expect from Niven, as did every star from Mae West to Hedy Lamarr, from Rita Hayworth to Ginger Rogers. The allure of David Niven was legendary.

It would be Monday morning before Niven told Lana goodbye after breakfast.

Later that day, she phoned Gardner to compare notes on their respective nocturnal activities over the weekend. Each seemed obsessed with the subject of male genitalia. "David Niven and John Hodiak have the two thickest cocks in Hollywood," Lana claimed. "Not the longest, but the thickest. When I first saw them, nude and erect (and separately, of course), I wondered what I could do with such appendages other than to bring them gifts. But somehow, I managed."

"Lately, I've been coming up short-changed in the male department," Gardner said. "However, Porfirio Rubirosa, the playboy from the Dominican Republic, just called me. He's known in restaurants as 'Mr. Peppermill.' I hear he can balance a chair with a telephone book on the tip of his erection."

"My dear, it sounds like you're heading for the hospital to be sewn up!"

"But what fun I'll have in the meantime," Gardner said. "A little advice from a friend. Time for you to get back into circulation, more than just a weekend fling with Niven. Perhaps find Husband Number Three, or should I count four since you married Stephen Crane twice?"

"Great idea!"

The two stars went on to discuss Gable, Gardner maintaining, "I have my stable of stud horses, and he has his harem." She admitted to an affair she was sustaining with Robert Walker, her co-star in *One Touch of Venus* (1948). She had also met with Robert Taylor for a fling before they began filming *The Bribe* (1949).

"Clark Gable, Robert Walker, Robert Taylor," Lana said. "Sounds like you're following in Lana Turner's footsteps. Been there, done all of them! You even married my first husband"

"I've got a new one you haven't done yet," Gardner said. "A sleek thug who works for Mickey Cohen. His name is Johnny Stompanato. He's a boy wonder who compares his thing to the length of the Oscar."

"I've never heard of him," Lana said.

"You will. He's making the rounds of all the beauties of Hollywood."

[Gardner would go on to make two more pictures with Gable, and Lana, after Homecoming, would star with him in one final movie. During interviews, both of the love goddesses denied having had any sexual liaisons with Gable. "We're just good friends," was their standard refrain.

Whereas Lana's affair with Gable had too many eyewitnesses for her to convincingly deny it, Gardner squeaked by, sowing confusion, based on her frequent denials of any romantic links to Gable.

Gardner's platform was shattered, however, in 1953, when veteran reporter Ruth Waterbury visited her at her flat in London. She found Gardner cooking a batch of bacon and eggs. From the bedroom, Waterbury heard a familiar voice: "Hey Ava, my bacon and eggs ready yet?"

"To my great surprise," she said, Clark Gable appeared at the door coming from the bedroom. He wore nothing but a mischievous grin."]

***

A new man was about to enter Lana's life, even though at first she didn't think he was worth a second look. She eventually came to view him as marriage material—that is, if she wanted financial security and not a hot sex life.

To escape from Hollywood and its memories of Power, she had fled to New York. She kept asking herself: "Was the breakup my fault? Where did I go wrong?"

To complicate matters, she was also under a rigorous audit from the Internal Revenue Service. Her accountants had routinely deducted "movie star items needed for work," including tailored gowns, expensive furs, closetsful of shoes, even her chauffeur-driven limousine. Many other female stars were doing the same, but suddenly, the IRS cracked down, ruling that these were not deductible items, labeling them as personal expenses.

The audit went badly for her, and she found herself owing the IRS thousands upon thousands of dollars in back taxes. She reminded the IRS that she'd made millions for the U.S. Treasury during her war-bond tours, but that didn't matter.

She was forced to meet with the legal department at MGM, where an agreement was reached that a hefty percentage of her weekly paycheck would be deducted and mailed directly to the IRS.

She was fortunate to have been recently granted a pay raise, so that now she was drawing the same salary as Clark Gable. Nonetheless, her accountants warned her to stop being so extravagant and to live within her means.

In Manhattan, as a vehicle for escaping from the pressure, she threw herself into the city's chic nightlife, going out with a different man every night. Most of the rendezvous were set up through MGM's publicity department, often with wannabe movie stars hoping to become matinee idols of the 1950s to replace Tyrone Power or Clark Gable. She hoped that inviting them back to her suite to make love to her would help her forget Power. Even after their intimacies, none of them did.

There was one exception: Howard Keel, a handsome actor from Illinois "with a great set of pipes." Oscar Hammerstein II had awarded him the lead in the London production of *Oklahoma!,* and he had emerged as the macho baritone par excellence.

Keel met Lana as he was contemplating a divorce from his first wife, actress Rosemary Cooper. Lana was hoping he'd help her get over the loss of Power, and he did—at least for a weekend. *[The venue for their time together was the Plaza, not the Waldorf, as might have been expected, based on the title of Lana's earlier film.]*

On their first date, Keel escorted her to the Stork Club. ("I paid the bill.") and then she

During time he had spent working in an aircraft factory in California, Howard Keel was said to have taken the virginity of 13-year-old Norma Jean Baker, who eventually changed her name to Marilyn Monroe. At the time of his seduction of this underaged girl, she was trying to fashion herself after Lana.

When Keel had first dated her, he was twenty-three years old. She had developed a crush on him, claiming, "I like older men." However, he ultimately opted to reject her because of her age, defining her as "jailbait."

invited him to her suite, from which he did not exit until Tuesday morning. Room service catered their meals, including plenty of champagne on ice.

She'd later relate the thrill of it all to Virginia Grey. "He has long legs, especially his 'third leg," a narrow waist, and broad shoulders. He doesn't just seduce a girl, he transports her to paradise."

She wanted him to stay, but he had to fly to Hollywood to begin his film career. Very soon, she learned that he'd been cast as the cocky marksman, Frank Butler, in *Annie Get Your Gun*. He was to play opposite Judy Garland, but she was fired, the role of Annie Oakley going to Betty Hutton.

With Keel gone, Lana continued with her whirlwind nightlife. She shuddered to think of Power making love to Linda Christian, against whom she continued to rage.

During her recent filming of *Cass Timberlane,* her dressing room had been swamped with white orchids and red roses. Every day, a deluxe box of chocolates arrived. The card that accompanied these gifts read Henry J. Topping. He usually signed "Bob" below the printed version of his formal name. "I fed the candy to the crew and felt intoxicated by the roses, enough for a funeral," she said.

Bob Topping's name was vaguely familiar to her, based on her avid pursuit of the era's gossip columns. She knew that he'd had an affair with her former rival, Carole Landis, who had committed suicide over Rex Harrison.

When Topping finally got Lana on the phone, she demanded that he stop sending flowers and candy to her dressing room. She also told him not to call her again.

However, during her installation at the Plaza, Topping's offerings of flowers, candy, and expensive trinkets that included costly bottles of French perfume, began reappearing. He finally got her on the phone through a connection he made to someone on the hotel's switchboard. As he said, "It's amazing what a fifty-dollar bill can do to an underpaid telephone operator."

After much persuasion and much rejection, she finally agreed to go out with him. In the meantime, she made a few calls to in-the-know friends for some background on her upcoming blind date.

Topping was known as "the tin plate heir." His family's wealth, estimated at $140 million, derived from their grandfather, Daniel G. Reid. Most of the fortune came from tin plate, but he also made millions in steel, tobacco, railroads, and banking.

About six years older than Lana, Bob had been born in New York, one of three brothers. His brother Dan was famous in the city as the part owner of the New York Yankees.

At the age of twenty-one, Bob had married actress Jayne Shadduck, following her divorce from the playwright, Jack Kirkland. Their marriage lasted three years before he divorced her to marry Gloria ("Mimi") Baker, a much-publicized café society woman related to members of the Vanderbilt family.

Bob's most recent marriage had been to actress Arline Judge, whom Lana had met briefly at Hollywood parties. As part of a somewhat unsavory rondelay, Judge had first married Bob's brother Dan, which made her the sister-in-law to her ex-husband and Bob the stepfather to his nephew, Dan Topping, Jr.

Since the 1930s, Judge had appeared in several low-budget B movies, but, in time, she would become more famous for her seven marriages, even though she'd been educated in a convent. Her first husband had been director Wesley Ruggles, who had helmed both Clark Gable and Lana in *Somewhere I'll Find You*.

When Topping, as part of their first date, arrived to retrieve Lana at the Plaza, with the intention of escorting her to an important premiere in a chauffeur-driven limousine, he was in the process of divorcing Judge after only a few months of marriage.

Lana concealed her disappointment. Topping was gracious, well-dressed, and had impeccable manners, but, as she'd admit later, "He was certainly no Tyrone Power in either looks or physique, and he looked like he needed to lose more than a few pounds."

They were on their way to an MGM publicity event. The studio had asked Lana to fill in for Loretta Young, who had been slated to deliver a welcome speech before an invited audience attending the premiere of her latest film, *The Bishop's Wife*. Young had fallen ill. The 1947 release co-starred Cary Grant and David Niven, along with Monty Woolley, the notorious homosexual actor who was one of Power's closest friends.

In the back of his limousine, *en route* to the premiere, she opened her purse to retrieve a cigarette. As she did, he dropped into it a small jewelry box emblazoned with the gold-lettered imprint of Cartier. She opened it to discover a stunning pair of diamond earrings. Hesitant to accept such a lavish gift from a stranger, she pointed out that she was already wearing her own pair of diamond earrings.

"A beautiful woman can't own too many diamonds," Topping responded. "Just ask Zsa Zsa Gabor."

She removed her earrings and replaced them with his gift to her.

At the premiere, after greeting dozens of people she knew from Hollywood, she delivered a brief welcoming speech, receiving loud applause.

About an hour later, midway through the screening of Loretta Young's film, Lana nudged Topping's arm and whispered, "I can't stand this lousy movie. Let's get the hell out of here."

"I agree," he said, as he discreetly escorted her to the nearest exit.

He had his chauffeur drive her to a lavish apartment on Park Avenue, the domain of Mrs. Evander Schley, who was hosting a party. The doyenne of society, Elsa Maxwell, chatted with Lana as she surveyed the roomful of New York's elite, the women dressed in gowns from Christian Dior or Hattie Carnegie and purchased through such outlets as Saks or Bergdorf's.

Maxwell said, "Lana, my dear, you'll have to adjust to Park Avenue because Park Avenue will never lower itself to Hollywood."

She took her over to introduce her to the chicly dressed Duchess of Windsor. Lana later said, "I find the Duchess incredibly polite but also stuffy and cold."

Lana made the rounds, greeting Mrs. Henry Payne Bingham, Mrs. Carol Carstairs, and Mrs. Harrison Williams, among others.

On leaving, she spoke again with the Duchess of Windsor. "You seem like such a beautiful young lady," the Duchess said. "I must get the Duke to take me to one of your movies."

Lana dated Topping for the next five nights in a row, turning down his request to come into her suite for a nightcap. On the sixth night, he was invited inside for more than a nightcap. As she'd later confide to Virginia Grey, "He hardly looks like Mr. America. He could pass for any rich man on the golf course at Palm Beach. As the saying goes, his physique is less than Greek. Average cock, missionary position, and one lousy kisser, but rich men can get away with their physical inadequacies."

For the Christmas holidays, he invited Lana and her daughter to the 600-acre Topping estate, Dunellen Hall, a palatial replica of an English manor house with more than 50 rooms for the Topping family and their guests, plus another 20 rooms in a separate wing for an armada of staff.

[Dunellen Hall, at 521 Round Hill Road in Greenwich, Connecticut, built in 1918 by the founder of the Topping's family fortune, has been described by real estate agents in The New York Times *as "among the most famous of the region's 13 (great) estates, with the 'ultimate' location on 'the most famous street' in the 'best town in Connecticut.'" A previous occupant, cattle heiress Lynda Dick, articulated her belief that misfortune, like that associated with the Hope Diamond, had always befallen whomever owned it.*

The manor house, partially assembled from stones and masonries salvaged from 16th-century manor houses torn down in England, included stables, tennis courts, horses, ducks, sheep, a working farm, a scenic lake, and greenhouses that evoked tropical gardens. In 1968, the house was the setting for a A Lovely Way to Die, *starring Kirk Douglas.*

In 1983, after multiple owners of varying degrees of tragedy, dissipation and misfortune, Dunellen Hall and its furnishings were bought by Harry and Leona ("The Queen of Mean") Helmsley for $11 million. Subsequently, their lavish enlargements and restorations, each defined, for tax reasons, as business expenses, were later challenged (and denied) by the IRS. The Helmsleys' widely publicized trials exposed Leona to nationwide humiliations and time spent in jail. (At the time, even Leona's defense attorney referred to her in public as "a tough bitch.") Leona died at Dunellen Hall in 2007, aged 87, bequeathing a large block of her fortune to her dog.]

That night at dinner, Lana met Bob's brother, Dan Topping, whose previous wives had included Arline Judge and Sonja Henie, the Norwegian skating star and movie queen on ice. Henie and Tyrone Power had once been lovers.

Shortly thereafter, Topping invited Lana to ring in the New Year of 1948 at El Morocco in Manhattan.

About an hour after their arrival, she excused herself to go to the powder room. When she returned, she picked up her martini only to notice something flashy at the bottom of the glass.

"Fish it out," Topping told her. She did, and discovered a fifteen-carat marquise diamond engagement ring. "If there are two things I know, it's men and diamonds," she later said. "This was a

Lana's first date with Bob Topping. Heavy drinking was part of their dynamic as a couple.

349

true Cartier gem, the most beautiful diamond ring I'd ever seen."

"What's this for?" she asked, feigning innocence.

"You know what it's for," he said. "I want you to become my wife."

Before putting the ring on her finger, she warned him, "You know I'm not in love with you, don't you?"

"You will be," he predicted. "Not today, not tomorrow, nor even the next day, but in time, you'll love me night after night for the rest of our lives."

Later that evening, an alarming note was sounded, as she noticed what a heavy drinker he was. Of course, it was New Year's and everyone was drunk. But even at the Topping estate during everyday "non-holiday" gatherings, the family began heavy boozing at five o'clock, the hard and heavy drinking continuing through the evening. She could not keep up, although on occasion, she tried.

The press had begun to take Lana's romance with Topping seriously. However, a New York columnist wrote, "Lana would give up anything, certainly Bob Topping, should Tyrone Power come back, kiss her, and make up."

Louella Parson's last column for 1947 reported, "Bob Topping gave Lana a Christmas present of a pair of diamond earrings. Could this soon follow with a diamond ring...and marriage?"

Parsons was a little late with her report. Lana was already wearing that diamond ring in New York.

On January 2, Lana received a telegram from MGM to report to work on her latest picture, *The Three Musketeers*.

"I'll fly back with you," Topping told her.

***

During the first week of the New Year, Hollywood gossip columnists carried reports of the upcoming marriage of Lana to Topping. It was revealed that their engagement would be announced at a lavish party at Mocambo, and that invitations to that announcement party would be sent to 400 *invités*, including the Duke and Duchess of Windsor.

Mayer exploded when he read the news, and received his own invitation: "Get Eddie Mannix *[from MGM's publicity department]* on the phone," he shouted at his secretary.

When they established telephone contact, Mayer ordered him to contact Lana at once and demand that she cancel her engagement party. "For God's sake, the guy's married. Lana's name has been linked to too many married men—and that includes Tyrone Power. She has a morality clause in her contract. I want no more of this lurid publicity about her getting engaged to married men."

Reluctantly, and humiliated, she had to notify the hundreds of invited guests that there would be no party.

During her first visit with Virginia Grey since her return home, Lana said, "If you want a blueprint of a woman's life, here's one. Lose a lover, snap right back, catch another one, perhaps not as exciting as before, but what the hell? Even if he's not handsome, you might settle for rich."

***

No novel in the history of the movies, worldwide, has been dramatized on screen more frequently than *Les Trois Mousquetaires (The Three Musketeers)*, by Alexandre Dumas, *père*, first published, in French, in 1844.

Amazingly, its first film adaptation, a French production, was released in 1903, more or less at the dawn of the movies.

[It would require a separate book to document the many screen and cartoon treatments the novel has received since then. The 1921 silent adaptation of the novel by a French studio became a blockbuster hit, as did a Hollywood version starring Douglas Fairbanks, Sr., that same year. Swashbuckling Fairbanks was known for his athletic ability: His one-handed handspring grabbing a sword during a duel was later interpreted as one of the great stunts of the silent era.

His son, Douglas Fairbanks, Jr., tried to persuade Louis B. Mayer to cast him as D'Artagnan in 1948, but the studio boss at MGM turned him down.

A little-known fact is that in 1933, Mascot Studios filmed a serial set in North Africa, where three musketeers became French Foreign Legionnaires. The serial featured a little known actor by the name of John Wayne, Lana's future co-star.

RKO filmed its own version of The Three Musketeers in 1935, starring Walter Abel. His interpretation of D'Artagnan was denounced "as the dreariest of the many film versions of the Dumas novel."

In 1939, the year of release of some of Hollywood's greatest movie classics, Don Ameche as D'Artagnan teamed with the Ritz Brothers in a comic version of Dumas' characters. Binnie Barnes starred as Milady de Winter, with Gloria Stuart cast as Queen Anne.

In 1942, during World War II, Cantinflas, the famous Mexican comedian, released his own version of the story, turning it into farce.]

By 1948, Mayer had decided to adapt *The Three Musketeers* into a top-notch Technicolor spectacular, the greatest version of the classic ever made.

As funding for the remake, Mayer green-lighted a budget that was considered massive at the time and which

351

placed special emphasis on costumes and scenery. Robert Ardrey, best known for his scholastic writings on sociology, was hired to write the screenplay. Mayer wanted Robert Taylor and Ricardo Montalban in the male leads, with Lana Turner cast as Milady de Winter. George Sidney, who had recently helmed Lana in *Green Dolphin Street*, was hired to direct.

When Taylor and Montalban were not available, the director cast Gene Kelly in "an acrobatic version" of D'Artagnan. The other two musketeers were cast with Van Heflin as Athos and Richard Coote as Aramis. Coote was unknown to Lana at the time.

As for Heflin, ever since they had co-starred together in *Green Dolphin Street*, Lana had never considered him as a "romantic leading man," but she greatly admired him as an actor, and their scenes together went smoothly. In contrast, Gene Kelly had been her friend ever since his arrival in Hollywood.

[When news leaked out about MGM's big film for 1948, it became clear that the independent producer Edward Small had already been working on his own version of The Three Musketeers, *with the intention of starring the dashing Louis Hayward. As part of a sideshow that erupted simultaneously with MGM's plans for an equivalent film of its own, Small soon realized that he couldn't compete with MGM's more lavish version, so, with regrets, he put his screenplay into mothballs.]*

With Mayer's approval, Sidney rounded up a strong supporting cast, notably Angela Lansbury as Queen Anne, with June Allyson in the second female lead as Constance Bonaclieux. Other players include Frank Morgan as King Louis XIII, Vincent Price as Richelieu, Keenan Wynn as Planchet, John Sutton as the Duke of Buckingham, and Ian Keith as Rochefort, chief henchman to Richelieu.

Lana was excited that for the first time, she would appear in a feature film in Technicolor, having been told that color would highlight her beauty as never before. *[The only time she'd been photographed in color up to this point was during a brief camo in* Du Barry Was a Lady *(1943).]*

She had been promised star billing above the title of her newest project, and it had been understood that her name would appear more prominently than those of the four other featured players: Kelly, Heflin, Allyson, and Lansbury.

Yet in spite of that star billing, Lana reported that she was horrified after reading the script. "I was not the star. Gene was. My role as Milady was just a supporting part. I called MGM and refused the role. I was immediately put on suspension."

During the next few weeks, she refused to come to the studio, not answering urgent calls from MGM. Mayer negotiated with Alida Valli to replace Lana in the film. An Italian actress, she had been born a baroness, and was viewed as most capable of playing a French aristocrat. Film critic Frédéric Mitterand had hailed Valli as "the only European actress equal to Greta Garbo and Marlene Dietrich."

The news reached Lana, who lived in dread that Valli might play the role more convincingly than she could have. "What does a little barefoot girl from the wilds of Idaho known about how a French countess acts?" she asked Kelly.

[When Lana's suspension ended, based on her agreement to participate in the film, Mayer dismissed Valli. That was just as well for Valli's career, since she was soon after cast as the mysterious Czech refugee wanted by the Soviets in Carol Reed's The Third Man *(1949), co-starring Joseph Cotten and Orson Welles. That movie went on to be hailed as*

one of the greatest film classics ever made.]

During Lana's suspension, a rival actress, Angela Lansbury, loudly expressed her wish to be re-cast as Milady de Winter, as she was not satisfied with her part as the villainous, older, and stodgier Queen Anne. "I'm too young for the role," she protested. She finally got Mayer to agree to meet with her. She remembered the long walk down the carpeted hallway to his office, where he sat behind a big round white desk.

She appealed to him to switch her role. He listened patiently until he'd heard her pitch. Then he rose to his feet, signaling that the meeting had come to an end: "You'll be wonderful as Queen Anne," he assured her.

Years later, Lansbury retraced her steps along that long walk back from his office and reflected, "I knew that from now on I would not get to the top of the class at MGM. My best roles were behind me. I was right. The studio was changing. Even Mayer himself would be booted out, as would the most stellar names on its big roster of stars, and that included both Lana Turner and Clark Gable. The MGM I knew would be no more."

The Associated Press, on January 14, 1948, leaked the news of Lana's suspension. Mayer threatened to charge her from $300,000 to $400,000 for pre-production costs generated because of her absence.

Topping flew Lana back to Dunellen Hall to ride out her suspension.

Hedda Hopper offered advice: "If you care for your movie career, you'll get your shapely ass out of New York and appear on the set at MGM."

She had lawyers negotiating with MGM, demanding that her role get beefed up. Not only that, but she was asking the studio to give her a year's vacation with pay and $25,000 up front. Although she finally agreed to return to Hollywood to participate in filming with a revised script, with a meatier part for her, all of her other demands were rejected by Mayer.

On the set once again, she praised the camerawork of Robert Planck, who would win an Oscar nomination for his work. She was reunited with costume designer Walter Plunkett, who was considered the best in his field ever since he'd designed the antebellum costumes for *Gone With the Wind*.

Critic Jeanne Basinger described Lana's first appearance in the film, the scene where she emerges from a darkened horse-drawn carriage into the light: "Lana Turner looks like an apparition beyond life, a mysterious creature. She is unreal, a proper goddess."

Allyson told Lana that she never wanted to play Lady Constance. "I don't feel comfortable in a period piece. I think I am only convincing as the girl-next-door in a skirt and blouse, or else as the perfect wife in apron and skirt. I don't think any fan will believe me as Lady Constance. Mayer has seen the first rushes, and he told me I'll be fine. 'Finish the damn picture,' he said, 'and stop your bellyaching.'"

Allyson recalled a memorable scene with Lana when Milady was imprisoned, and begs her to bring her a knife so that she can commit suicide. "Lana was daring, playing the scene without makeup, a first for her. She did the scene beautifully, shedding real tears. I was mesmerized. Actually, I didn't know that Milady wanted that knife to stab my (character's) heart."

Over lunch in the commissary, Lana and Allyson discussed their former boyfriends. Both of them were surprised that each had shared a brief fling with Ronald Reagan, Peter Lawford, and John F. Kennedy. But when Lana revealed that she'd had a fling with Alan Ladd, too, Allyson's face dimmed.

"Oh, no, not him, too!" Allyson said. She went on to confess that Ladd had been the love of her life, even though she was married to Dick Powell during the peak of their affair.

Allyson maintained a sense of humor about herself and her success. Mayer had told everyone, "June Allyson isn't pretty. She certainly isn't sexy. She sings fairly well. She doesn't dance all that well, either. But she's got something, including a raspy voice like that of Jimmy Durante."

Kelly enjoyed co-starring in *The Three Musketeers* with Lana, claiming, "It was like being a kid again, playing cowboys and Indians. The action sequences, all that dueling, were like extensions of the dance. Lana complimented

In *The Three Musketeers*, Lana as Lady de Winter threatens to stab Gene Kelly as D'Artagnan. Within a decade, Lana would become more famously involved in a real-life stabbing.

Meet the merry band, all for one and one for all.

From left to right: Lana Turner, Gene Kelly, Van Heflin, June Allyson, Angela Lansbury, Frank Morgan, and Keenan Wynn.

me on my agility. While I was shooting the picture, I ran into my good pal, Frank Sinatra. He asked me if I were taking leading man privileges and fucking the hell out of Lana like most of her leading men did. I firmly denied it."

Kelly relayed this to Vincent Price, adding in a confidential whisper, "After I denied messing around with Lana, Frank kidded me and said, 'I forgot. You're the one who likes to take it up the ass.'"

In one scene, the athletic Kelly had to fling Lana across a bed. He used too much force and pitched her all the way over to a point beyond the bed's far side. She hit the floor with such force that she broke her elbow, delaying production on her scenes for two weeks.

Lana and her other co-star, Van Heflin, never became friends. "I think he viewed me as a vapid blonde actress with noodles forming my brain matter."

Lana enjoyed meeting and talking with Robert Coote, born in London in 1909. She told him something he didn't know: Had casting gone differently, she would have appeared with him in *Forever Amber (1947)* instead of her friend, Linda Darnell. The actor would also star with Lana in her upcoming film, *The Merry Widow* (1952).

She liked working with Vincent Price, viewing him as "the master of high camp," a term she used in later years to describe him. *[At the time, that term did not exist.]* He challenged her with his scene stealing, forcing her to develop new techniques of her own—the flap of a glove, the turn of her head—to distract the viewer.

"Vincent and Clifton Webb were two of the gayest men in the movies, and they got away with it, although homosexuality was illegal at the time and absolutely forbidden on the screen," Lana said. "I adored Vincent. He could play any role: *film noir,* thriller, horror, drama, mystery, comedy. I told him that I had desperately wanted to play *Laura,* his 1944 movie in which he co-starred with Gene Tierney in a part that should have been mine."

As one of her facial accessories, Lana demanded that makeup fit her with a beauty mark. They came up with three "moles"— one shaped like a star, the other two a moon and a heart.

She liked all three of them, and appeared on camera at various times and in various scenes with one or another of them positioned on various parts of her face.

***

Bob Topping was almost a daily visitor to the set for lunch with Lana. He was getting a lot of coverage in the press. His wife at the time, Arline Judge, vowed during an interview with the entertainment columnist Earl Wilson, "He won't get a divorce from me for any amount of money." Later, she had obviously changed her mind, telling Sheilah Graham, "When I divorce the bastard, I'll ruin him, take every cent he has."

Topping told Lana that he had decided to divorce Judge after she broke a bottle of champagne over his head, giving him a concussion. "A vintage year at that."

After months of legal wranglings, Topping's divorce from Judge became final on April 23, and he was at last free to marry Lana. Judge had been awarded a lump sum of $500,000, plus her lawyer's fees.

In court, she claimed that on two occasions, Topping had threatened to kill her. "He is insanely jealous," she testified. "Miss Turner better watch out that this lout doesn't do her harm, perhaps damage that pretty face of hers."

She also testified that in the immediate aftermath of her appendix operation, he had flown into a rage and kicked her directly on the site of her incision.

***

MGM promoted *The Three Musketeers* with slogans that *included "LANA TURNER! FIRST TIME IN TECHNICOLOR!"*

Bosley Crowther, writing in *The New York Times,* said, "*The Three Musketeers* is a splendiferous production with dazzling costumes, more color, and more of Miss Turner's chest than has ever before seen in a picture like this one."

Cue magazine pronounced her film "The best movie version yet of a Dumas novel to come out of Hollywood."

Cosmopolitan claimed that "This is Leo the Lion's most successful houseparty, with its background of romance and swordplay and Lana's lethal beauty. As the lovely, lethal Milady, she is the only really inspired casting in the film."

Once again, Lana scored a big box office success.

***

By March, Lana was getting such bad press for her marital misbehaviors that she made attempts to soften the attacks by letting reporters interview her on one of the sets at MGM.

One journalist had written, "Stuffing a black wasp-waisted gown that squeezed a good deal of Miss Turner out the top, she declared people can stop making wedding plans for her and Bob Topping because they have no plans themselves. She also denied being involved with John Alden Talbot, the wealthy Palm Beachite, whose wife has named Miss Turner in a temporary maintenance suit."

That was on March 5.

On March 21, she issued a different statement, claiming "Now that *The Three Musketeers* is finished, Bob [*Topping*] and I plan to fly to New York." She went on to announce that she was going to marry the tin plate heir and would in the future divide her time between Hollywood and the East, living in California only when making a movie.

356

***

By mid-April, the national press was carrying stories about Lana's upcoming marriage to Bob Topping, who was described as a "wealthy sportsman."

The press also revealed that the newly married couple would fly to London for the opening of his new midget auto-racing venture.

[Midget cars (aka Speedcars), typically have four-cylinder engines, roll cages, and a very high power-to-pound ratio, usually with up to 400 horsepower and weights of only 900 pounds. They're intended to be driven only on racetracks for short distances of no more than 25 miles at a time, at very fast and very dangerous speeds.]

She objected to holding their wedding ceremony on the East Coast at Dunellen Hall.

In lieu of that, Billy Wilkerson, the publisher and night club owner who had discovered Lana at a soda fountain years before, offered his luxurious home in Bel Air. As an extravagant gesture, Topping cleared out at least three florist shops, filling the Wilkerson home with gardenias, daisies, gladioli, and delphiniums.

She chose Sara Hamilton as her maid of honor (the journalist hadn't betrayed her yet), and Wilkerson was best man for Topping. Lana's daughter, Cheryl Crane, was designated as the flower girl.

On Wilkerson's arm, Lana descended his curving stairway carrying a bouquet that contained four large white orchids. Mendelssohn's wedding march was performed by a string band hired by Topping.

A drunken Errol Flynn turned up with actress Anita Louise. When it came time to kiss the bride, he stuck his tongue down Lana's throat and pinched her left nipple.

A retired pastor, the Rev. Steward P. McLennan, officiated. Later, headlines blared: *MINISTER IN LANA TURNER WEDDING FACES PRESBYTERIAN CHARGES.* According to church law, he was not to officiate at the marriage ceremony of a divorced person until an entire year had passed since that person's divorce had been concluded. In the case

Lana was said to have spent $30,000 on a new wardrobe, including her wedding gown, which she described as "cocoa lace over nude satin." The designer, Don Loper, described it more formally as "champagne Alençon lace from France over champagne satin."

She wore it while posing for this photo with Bob Topping.

In addition to new suits, hats, coats, dresses, and shoes, she spent $5,000 on lingerie—panties, brassieres, and see-through nightgowns, including a half-dozen crafted from flowery chiffon—at an exclusive store in Beverly Hills.

357

of Topping, his divorce from Arline Judge had just been finalized.

The guest list at the reception that followed the Topping/Turner wedding was packed with A-list Hollywood. Greg Bautzer was invited, but Lana disapproved of him showing up with an uninvited guest, Joan Crawford. Louis B. Mayer and Eddie Mannix were there from MGM, and her director, George Sidney, also attended, as did George Jessel and Ben Cole.

Albert ("Cubby") Broccoli showed up. Later, he would become fabulously wealthy by adapting Ian Fleming's James Bond "007" character to the screen.

Unlike Hedda Hopper, Louella Parsons had usually run friendly items about Lana. At the reception, Lana noticed Parson's increasing deterioration. She was often drunk and rattled and would bring up perceived oversights in her past. "I will never forgive Clark Gable for not letting me have the scoop on his marriage to Carole Lombard." Often, when she sat on a sofa drinking for a long time, she left a large wet spot "the size of Brazil," according to Hopper, her arch-rival.

At the reception, top chefs from L'Aiglon and LaRue's opened lavish tins of Beluga caviar, served with exotic delicacies from America's fields and streams, such as smoked salmon or roasted pheasant. *Foie gras* and champagne had been imported from France.

The Beverly Hills police was called out to control the crowds, who broke through the barricades to trample Wilkerson's well-manicured gardens. It wasn't until 3AM that the police rounded up the last of the intruders.

By that time, Lana and her new husband had escaped to the most exclusive bungalow at the Beverly Hills Hotel for their honeymoon night.

When they woke up the next morning, room service had delivered an elegant breakfast to their enclosed veranda. It was being devoured by Hedda Hopper, who had persuaded the manager to admit her to the public areas of the bungalow in advance of their emergence from the bedroom.

Hedda desperately wanted to be the first reporter to receive an exclusive on the marriage. Lana and Topping cooperated, although she later told her new husband, "The bitch hates my guts."

Hopper's first question was both insulting and provocative, "Are you just marrying Topping here for his money? Or are you on the rebound from Ty Power?"

In her column the next morning, she crit-

Hedda Hopper had remained Lana's least favorite columnist. Imagine her shock when she woke up from her honeymoon night in bed with Bob Topping to encounter the (uninvited) gossip columnist downing sausages, scrambled eggs, and caviar in the next room.

"I'm beating Louella with the scoop," she told Lana. "How was Bob in bed?"

icized Lana's "excessive dating and multiple marriages. This time she did it not for the man's looks, but for his money."

The next day, Lana phoned Hopper and set up an appointment to see her at her home. When she got there, Lana protested Hopper's continuing attacks on her over the years, and the scenario degenerated into an angry confrontation. At one point, Lana screamed at her, "Time to tell you the truth, you old bag! I detest you!"

Hopper ordered her out of her house. The next day at MGM, Lana confessed to Eddie Mannix some of the details about what had happened. "I may be the only star in Hollywood with enough courage to tell Hopper off."

Mannix predicted an avalanche of critical columns, pointing out that Hopper had virtually destroyed the career of Ginger Rogers with her constant attacks.

To everyone's amazement, that didn't happen for Lana. All she heard from Hopper was silence. However, that changed when Lana married Lex Barker, who Hopper "adored."

Her post-wedding column set off an avalanche of bad publicity, as reporters picked up the thread of Lana's constantly changing partners or husbands. Pastors denounced her from their pulpits as a "Hollywood Jezebel."

When *Life* magazine published photos of her wedding, Lana flew into a rage. "The god damn photographer shot me at the worst angles. I look like Marjorie Main on a bad hair day, and as fat as W.C. Fields."

A reporter described her heavy coatings of pancake makeup, claiming that she was so nervous that her bouquet of white orchids trembled in her hands. For the next few years, she refused to cooperate with *Life*.

Cheryl later wrote about the *Life* coverage: "Mother looked bovine, Papa Topping looked chinless, and I looked intense."

For their honeymoon, Lana and Topping sailed across the Atlantic aboard the SS *Mauretania,* arriving at the Port of Southampton where "the press was waiting to ambush me." She greeted reporters in a sable furpiece and a sharkskin dress. The first question was, "Is that your real hair?" Her press coverage seemed to go downhill after that.

Londoners had not recovered from the war, and vast parts of the city, especially the East End, lay in ruins. Food was rationed. When Lana arrived with four large trunks of clothing, her arrival was written up as "vulgar and in bad taste," and the Toppings were accused of flaunting their riches. Word leaked out that he'd had steaks flown in from Boston and delivered to the kitchen of the Savoy. Most of the U.K.-based journalists writing about Lana at the time were getting by on kidneys and stale mutton.

Not only was Lana enduring a beating from the press in London, but several attacks on her appeared in America, too. "The bastards are threatening to destroy my image," she complained to Topping. Word reached her from Eddie Mannix that the studio brass was "grooming" Ava Gardner to take over roles previously earmarked for her.

Lana was putting on weight, some thirty pounds, and "the boys from Fleet Street" made a point of that in their unflattering coverage of her. "Why don't they go after Rita Hayworth?" she fretted. "She's fatter than me!"

When she and Topping walked up Bond Street in Mayfair, many passers-by hissed at them.

She appeared at the inauguration of Topping's midget racing cars at the London Stadium. She was driven around the arena in an orchid-colored car, waving at fans, but generating a lot of boos. The Lord Mayor of London had agreed to introduce her. Before his address to the crowd, he whispered to her. "Tell me something I can say about you. Frankly, old girl, I've never heard of you."

The U.K. inauguration of Topping's midget cars was a disaster. Many of them broke down on rough surfaces, the drivers' faces pelted with cinders and small rocks. Even worse, their tires developed slits and went flat. As expected, the British press attacked, stridently defining midget car racing as "a lunatic American sport."

That trip to London signaled the end of Topping's venture into midget cars. Lana remembered how, back in their hotel suite, he had to write $400,000 worth of checks, paying off his London debts and his backers in New York.

"All in all, our honeymoon in London has been one big fiasco," she told Topping. "Let's escape to the French Riviera."

She was delighted to flee from England, heading for Paris. She vowed, at least temporarily, that she'd never return to London.

In Paris, in her swanky suite at the George V, her mood improved, although Topping remained depressed because of his business failure.

Three calls came in for her from Prince Aly Khan, but she refused all of them, even though he was an authentic prince and the world's most famous playboy, a catch even more desirable than Porfirio Rubirosa from the Dominican Republic. Finally, on the fourth call, she accepted. He invited her to dinner.

"Please, Mr. Khan, Your Highness," she protested. "I'm a married woman on my honeymoon."

"Surely you can get away for one night. If you refuse, you're missing out on something big. The press calls me the world's greatest lover."

"Please, don't call me again," she said, putting down the phone.

Within a year, he'd marry Rita Hayworth, attracting worldwide attention.

After Paris, they were off to the Côte d'Azur, where Topping had booked suites for them at the Miramar Hotel in Cannes. Mildred and Cheryl were flown in to take over another suite.

Lana's spirits perked up considerably after Eddie Mannix called from MGM to inform her that *Modern Screen* had named her "Hollywood's Number One Box Office Star."

At long last, she felt like she was on a honeymoon, enjoying the beach, dancing under the stars, lavishly dining on an exquisite cuisine, often lobster, and downing the best of French wines and champagnes. She also got to spend time with Cheryl, whom she had been neglecting.

Topping had told her that he wanted to spend at least two months on the Mediterranean, yachting and simply enjoying life. But she was shocked one morning to learn that aboard their cruise he'd invited one of his best friends, Freddy McAvoy, a notorious international playboy. She wanted to conceal from her husband just how well she already knew McAvoy.

***

Born in Australia, Freddie McEvoy (aka "Suicide Freddie") was Errol Flynn's best friend. A sportsman and socialite, he was fodder for the tabloids because of his love for danger, both in his romantic, hell-raising life and in his devotion to daredevil sports.

As a visitor to Flynn's house on Mulholland Drive, Lana had already met the dashing racing driver, who was known for marrying heiresses. In 1940, he'd wed Beatrice Cartwright. Thirty years his senior, she was one of the heirs to the Standard Oil fortune. Although confined to a wheelchair, she had a ravenous sexual appetite and imported some of the world's studliest studs to her home.

McEvoy and Porfirio Rubirosa, the playboy of the Dominican Republic, were each celebrated for their "hideously large endowments."

When Lana met McAvoy, he was spending many evenings with Barbara Hutton, the Woolworth heiress, in the immediate aftermath of her divorce from Cary Grant. Hutton rejected McAvoy's proposal of marriage, but paid him $100,000 to arrange for her to meet Rubirosa, whom she eventually married, after his divorce from Doris Duke, the tobacco heiress.

[Even though she didn't marry McAvoy, Hutton told her friends, "He is the only man I've ever known who could give me an orgasm."]

When Tennessee Williams flew to Mexico during the shooting of the film adaptation of his play, *The Night of the Iguana,* he spent several evenings with Ava Gardner, who—with Richard Burton—was one of the co-stars of the movie. She told the playwright about how, during the roundelays that followed the promiscuities and marital shakedowns of Doris Duke and Barbara Hutton, "Lana got Freddie, and I got Rubi."

Lana's relationship with McAvoy began the first night she met him at Flynn's house. She was already aware that Flynn had previously installed two-way mirrors in each of his bedrooms, and that as such, they carried the risk of exposure, perhaps even to blackmailers. Based on that knowledge, she invited McEvoy to her home for further intimacies. After that, she slipped away with him whenever he visited Hollywood.

She modified Hutton's assessment of McAvoy's sexual prowess, claiming to Ava Gardner, "Freddie is the only man who has given me multiple orgasms."

During the war years, J. Edgar Hoover, Director of the F.B.I., kept both McEvoy and Errol Flynn under surveillance. When McAvoy appeared at the

Legendary *roués* at the same wedding: Errol Flynn and Freddie McEvoy (right)

361

1936 Olympic Games in Berlin, he had become acquainted with the Nazi hierarchy, and he was later accused of smuggling weapons to the Nazis.

To save Lana's reputation, McAvoy, when Topping introduced him to Lana, pretended he'd never met her before.

During their yachting vacation, McAvoy was the perfect gentleman and an amusing guest. But when Lana's new husband had to abandon his yachting party and fly to Paris from Nice, Lana did not spend her first night alone. After the other guests had retired for the night, McEvoy discreetly knocked on her cabin's door.

Wearing one of her new see-through nightgowns, she opened it and he slipped in, leaving early the next morning. She not only found McAvoy "great company, always moving and charming, but a man with more staying power than any other man alive. I think he could go around the clock. Truly amazing."

Within a few years, tragedy struck McAvoy, and she was sorry when she read about it. In November of 1951, McAvoy married Claude Stephanie Filatre, a French fashion model. Off the coast of Morocco, they drowned together in a shipwreck.

***

Back home in the United States, Lana settled into her life as a retired actress and the wife of Bob Topping. She was no longer a celebrated movie star, or so it seemed, but a "homebody." She tried to fit into Topping's lifestyle at Dunellen Hall, but felt more and more isolated.

At the family manse in Greenwich, there was a constant round of parties, sometimes drawing as many as 150 socialites. Nearly all of the Toppings' friends lived on inherited wealth. Often, all the bedrooms in the house were occupied, with guests sleeping in and around in various combinations, gay or straight.

As Topping told Lana, "Our grandfather made the money…now his offspring are spending it."

She could not help but notice that some of their houseguests would arrive late on Friday afternoon, and would often change partners before the end of the week-end. Bloody Marys were served *en masse* in the late morning, as guests tried to cure their hangovers from the night before. Most of them slept all afternoon, in antici-pation of the evening's bacchanals.

Lana complained to her friends in Hollywood, "All these East Coast people do is eat, drink, party, and fuck all night!"

Suddenly, Lana found herself pregnant again, although after Cheryl's birth, doctors had warned her that—because of the Rh factor of her blood, a hereditary trait which had almost killed her first born and her, too—it would be dangerous to have more children.

When her pregnancy reached its sixth month, doctors in New York told her, "Your child might not survive. There are complications."

On January 14, 1949, reporters emerging from Manhattan's Doctors Hospital reported that Lana had suffered a miscarriage. Her baby boy had been stillborn.

To help her recover, Topping suggested a Caribbean vacation. She later re-called, "This was the high point of my marriage. After that, our relationship was all downhill."

Back at the Topping manse, her spirits were enlivened when Dan and Bob Topping divided up their late mother's jewelry between them. Lana was presented with several pieces of heirloom jewelry, including a diamond-encrusted watch and an exquisite pearl necklace.

Bob seemed to be growing restless, missing out on all the changing partners and "switchhitters" that had punctuated his many house parties on Round Hill Drive.

Without explaining what she meant, Lana, during a phone call to Linda Darnell, told her, "Some of Bob's romantic suggestions are too erotic, too sophisticated for *lil' ol' me*."

What she omitted from her memoirs was a suggestion that her husband made to her one night: The inauguration of a three-way sex romp with his brother, Dan, and herself. He justified it with the assertion that, "We've done this before: Dan and I had many three-ways with Arline Judge."

"That's different," Lana protested. "At least both of you at one time or another had been married to her. My answer is a definite NO."

More and more, she was anxious to return to Hollywood to "get back into the movie business."

One afternoon, when she suddenly realized that the Topping fortune had its limits, that became less of a dream for her and more of a necessity.

Topping had made a series of bad investments on the stock market, and the cost of running Dunellen Hall, with its extensive grounds and battalions of servants, had become too burdensome. The Toppings would have to sell off their land and perhaps the house itself. Topping even suggested that Lana might start making movies again "to bring in some extra loot."

Faced with a possibility of a comeback picture, she went on a rigid diet with the intention of losing thirty pounds. The strict cutback in her food intake made her nervous and irritable. Through her self-imposed famine, she plotted her return to the West Coast.

Two weeks later, she packed her trunks, and he did the same, and together, they headed off to California.

He had arranged for them to rent a 24-room Georgian style mansion on Mapleton Drive in the perilously expensive neighborhood of Holmby Hills. Their next-door neighbors would include Humphrey Bogart and Lauren Bacall. Bing Crosby, Alan Ladd, and Sonja Henie lived on the same street.

The home required a staff whose salaries were paid by Lana. On the sprawling premises was a swimming pool, plus two tennis courts, a kennel, a greenhouse engineered for tropical plants, and a terraced garden.

As she told Virginia Grey, "I married a millionaire, and suddenly, I find myself the breadwinner, just like I was when I was married to Stephen Crane."

She was spending more and more time in the library reading scripts. Topping was gone a lot, claiming, "I'm playing golf." Often he returned home at 2AM, telling her, "I stopped off with the boys for some drinks." It was the same pattern of deception she had experienced with Crane.

Eddie Mannix phoned from MGM to inform her that according to the latest lists within *Modern Screen*, she was still the nation's top female star.

Late one afternoon, two policemen arrived at her doorstep, and she invited them into her living room. They looked grim when they told her that although they had recently arrested a man on an unrelated charge, it was learned from him that there was a plan afoot to kidnap Cheryl and hold her for ransom.

Lana was horrified and phoned Greg Bautzer after the cops had left. He swung into action, hiring security guards, disguised as gardeners, to maintain a 24-hour vigil over her house.

Bautzer also rented attack dogs to patrol the grounds. Lana warned her staff not to let Cheryl out of their sight, insisting that most of the time she'd be under the direct care and attention of either Mildred or her nanny. "At all other times, she is to be strictly supervised," Lana ordered.

***

It seemed inevitable that Lana would get involved in some sort of scandal after her return to L.A. from her honeymoon in southern Europe.

In spite of dwindling funds, Lana and Topping became known there for their lavish parties, on some occasions attracting more than a hundred guests.

Frank Sinatra was a regular, and sometimes, the Bogarts dropped in from next door. Susan Hayward was a guest on occasion, as were Linda Darnell and Ava Gardner. Johnny Ray or Sammy Davis, Jr. would show up and even entertain the guests. Often, a drunken Judy Garland would sing, accompanied by Oscar Levant on the piano.

The African-American singer, Billie Daniels, occasionally dropped in, too. Lana had heard him perform in New York in each of two different clubs along 57th Street.

Daniels had left the Big Band scene to pursue a solo career. One night, when he arrived at one of the Toppings' parties, he had recently recorded his signature song, a big hit entitled "That Old Black Magic" by Harold Arlen and Johnny Mercer.

On this occasion, Daniels showed up with five other musicians. Topping had gone to bed shortly after midnight, but Daniels and his musicians stayed on site, making music until way into the morning.

Billy Daniels

When word about it reached Robert Harrison, the publisher of *Confidential*, he ordered his writers to expose Lana's dalliance with Billy Daniels.

Harrison had published lurid stories about Lana before. One of them ran beneath headlines that trumpeted: *WHEN LANA TURNER SHARED A LOVER WITH AVA GARDNER.*

Now, another exposé from *Confidential* hit the newsstands: *THE NIGHT BOB TOPPING CAUGHT LANA TURNER WITH BILLY DANIELS.*

Although her private life had frequently been revealed in excruciating detail to the masses, the story brought a carload of new humiliations to Lana.

At around 3AM that night, Topping woke up and headed downstairs in his pajamas to look for Lana. He stumbled into the living room, where he heard noises. All the lights were out. Topping switched on the lights to discover Daniels fornicating with Lana on one of the sofas.

Topping rushed to engage himself in a fight with Daniels, and kicked him out of the house. Returning to the living room, he socked Lana and gave her a black eye. She screamed at him, "Don't injure my face, you bastard!"

She immediately fled from the house and sought shelter at her mother's apartment, where she remained for ten days. Topping phoned every day, asking her to forgive him. She did not ask him to forgive her for having sex with Daniels.

Finally, Topping arrived at Mildred's with more pieces of jewelry from his late mother's heirloom collection. After examining the jewelry, she agreed to return with him to their home.

Lana tried to explain her tryst with Daniels to Virginia Grey. "You know that ever since hooking up with Artie Shaw, I've had this thing for musicians."

She talked with several friends: Sinatra, Gardner, and Greg Bautzer. "I want to get revenge on Harrison. Hollywood stars should rise up and go after him, cripple him with lawsuits."

In his biography of Errol Flynn, David Brett reported that Lana eventually hired a hitman to kill the publisher of *Confidential*. According to the author, a marksman was to assassinate Harrison when he went on a hunting trip.

Details are unclear, but apparently, three shots were fired, but bounced off a large tree and never hit their mark. The hitman fled, and the publisher escaped with his life.

No other evidence has surfaced to back up that claim, but even though it sounds unlikely, it might, indeed, have happened.

As the columnist Sheilah Graham wrote, "In Hollywood, anything is possible, even the impossible."

***

Joan Crawford continued as a remote fixture in Lana's life, "hovering over me like some witch on a broomstick." *[Lana's words.]* Their primary channel of communication was Greg Bautzer, although soon, there would be a newer connection too.

Bautzer sometimes phoned Lana for "some intimate time" together, and she would slip out of her house to visit him, claiming to Topping that she was consulting him about a contractual issue with MGM.

Yet when he wasn't with her, Bautzer continued to seduce Hollywood beauties, including Joan Caulfield, and Merle Oberon. A new addition to his harem was the rising young actress, Marilyn Monroe.

Occasionally, Crawford would throw a jealous fit and kick him out of her bed. After one particularly violent fight, she refused to see him for a month. But he kept calling until she relented. To welcome him back, she gave him a gift of matching "his-and-her Cadillacs."

Bautzer drove his new car for three weeks before crashing it into a lamppost and mailbox. The papers reported that he was not seriously injured. Some unknown blonde in the passenger seat was seen fleeing from the scene of the accident.

Enraged, Crawford left Hollywood for a four-month stay at Manhattan's Hampshire House. Bautzer kept calling her, trying to get back with her, but she refused.

Crawford, in the meantime, began dating the very handsome British actor, Peter Shaw, who had already sustained an affair with Lana. Eventually, he would desert both Lana and Crawford to marry Angela Lansbury. "This time," he announced, "Angela is not getting stuck with a homosexual husband," a reference to her previous husband, actor Richard Cromwell.

Bautzer flew to New York and wooed Crawford back, at least temporarily. She had arrived at the Hampshire House with four densely packed trunks. But after Bautzer took her shopping along Fifth Avenue, especially to Saks, she left New York with eleven trunks.

Back in Hollywood, the Crawford vs. Bautzer truce didn't last. After he was seen dating Rita Hayworth, Crawford broke off from him yet again.

Sheilah Graham wrote, "Crawford and Bautzer quarrel in Hollywood and make up in New York. They enjoy a lovers' tryst in the Catskills, but have a big eruption in Malibu."

Crawford phoned Stephen Crane and invited him to her home. As he later claimed, "She took immediate possession of me."

One night, Crawford asked Crane to be her escort for a night of drinking and dancing at the Mocambo, still a number one spot in the area, especially for stars. By coincidence, Topping invited Lana that night to the same club.

As she passed by their table, Lana was shocked to see her former husband nuzzling the neck of the grand diva, Joan Crawford. She walked on by without acknowledging them, and didn't introduce Topping to Crane.

Later, when Lana went to the powder room, Crawford followed her. As Lana was refreshing her makeup at a vanity table, Crawford sat down at the table beside her, "to apply more warpaint."

"I see that Greg Bautzer, Clark Gable, and Peter Shaw weren't enough for you," Lana said. "So, now it's Stephen."

"I had no idea, dear, that Stephen still remained your personal property," Crawford answered. "Before you got him, I considered him marriage material for myself, but ended up with Phillip Terry, who told me that he once fucked you. I figured it this way: If you can fuck my husband Terry, I can fuck your husband Crane."

"I do concede the point," Lana answered.

As Crawford was leaving the powder room, she looked back with a smirk at Lana: "I enjoyed attending your wedding to Topping. Let me know when you divorce him."

Columnist Adela Rogers St. Johns wrote that Crawford once again was back with Bautzer. At the Farmers' Market, she removed a large pair of sunglasses, revealing "a big black shiner, a gift from Bautzer."

"She told me she'd broken up with Stephen Crane," St. Johns said. "Joan liked to be treated rough, and she felt that Crane was too much a gentleman in the sack."

"Crane just doesn't understand something," Crawford said. "He told me he doesn't go in for the rough stuff. He doesn't get it that even a lady likes to be treated like a whore from time to time."

***

After her marriage to Bob Topping, Lana paid little attention to the affairs of Stephen Crane, even though he was the father of her daughter. She was usually not at home when he came by to visit Cheryl.

After Columbia dropped him, Crane abandoned his hope of becoming an actor. "I was good looking, but not that good looking. Besides, the established stars had returned home from the war. Newer, younger male stars were also arriving in Hollywood daily. And many of them could act, which I could not."

Crane always managed to snare Hollywood beauties, not only Ava Gardner and Rita Hayworth, but the French sex kitten, Corinne Calvet, and even Olga St. Juan, who was trying to become "the next Mexican spitfire," following in the wake of the suicide of Lupe Velez.

After drinking too much, and wandering around Hollywood for a year, he decided to launch himself into the restaurant business. He'd saved up some money from gambling, but he needed a partner. He found one in Al Mathes, a well-known gambler at the tables in Las Vegas. The ex-boxer suggested they open a restaurant called Lucy's, across from the gated entrance to Paramount Pictures, close to RKO and Universal.

Within weeks of its opening as a steakhouse, Lucy's became a favorite watering hole for movie stars. Humphrey Bogart and Lauren Bacall became customers, and Judy Garland dropped in often, as did John Payne, Robert Mitchum, and John Garfield. On occasion, Peter Lawford showed up, even Nicky Hilton with Elizabeth Taylor. Regrettably, Nicky got into a serious altercation with Crane, who seemed to pay too much attention to Elizabeth.

Frank Sinatra refused to patronize the joint, claiming that Crane "is nothing but a cheap gigolo."

Welcoming guests at the door, Crane turned on "my fatal male charm," and quickly made a success of the place.

Along came love. Lila Leeds, a budding starlet, and a Lana Turner lookalike, showed up one night. She'd styled her blonde hair and her dress as imitations of Crane's former wife. Even columnist James Bacon noted the similarities: "She looks like Lana Turner—only cuter."

Coincidentally, Leeds had played a minor role in Lana's *Green Dolphin Street*. She had been cast as a Eurasian who drugs the leading man and rolls him for his money.

Crane took immediate notice of Leeds and began to date her, although the twenty-year-old was known as "Hollywood's budding bad girl." He soon discovered that she was addicted to marijuana, a drug unknown to most Americans at the time.

Like Lana, Leeds, too, had been seduced by Jackie Coogan soon after she hit town. He was married at the time to Betty Grable.

Robert Montgomery had assigned her a small role in *Lady in the Lake* (1947), a picture in which Lana, for a time, had been set to star. Montgomery had told Leeds, "You're going to become the new Lana Turner."

One night at Lucy's, another young starlet was "coming on too strong" with Crane. Leeds struck her, and a fight ensued, dubbed as "the battle of the blondes." The other starlet was Marilyn Monroe.

Lana visited Lucy's one night with Topping. Crane had already presented Leeds with a three-carat engagement ring and a proposal of marriage. "This is Lila Leeds," he said to Lana. "She's going to become the stepmother of Cheryl, so you should get to know her."

When she met Lana, Leeds said, "Stevie here is my hunky lunky."

Lana reached for Topping's arm and headed for their reserved table. "Perhaps some other time," she said.

At table, she turned to Topping: "This Leeds creature is merely the mock. You have the real thing."

***

On September 1, 1948, Leeds life was about to change. At Lucy's, she had become friends with Robert Mitchum, both of them having already discovered their fondness for "weed." She invited Mitchum to her home one night to smoke pot and to meet her female roommate. Unknown to the actors, her house had been staked out by drug agents who were planning a raid on it that night. Mitchum had walked into a trap.

Both Leeds and Mitchum were arrested, as the newspapers revealed with blaring headlines the next morning. Each of them received a jail sentence of sixty days.

Crane, not wanting to get drawn into the scandalous trial, made a deal with a friend to take over the administration of Lucy's. That left him free to fly to away to Paris with his reputation intact.

Ironically, Mitchum's career actually got a boost from the arrest, since he was already known as one of Hollywood's "Bad Boys." But it ruined the budding career of Lila Leeds.

Lana never heard of her again until she saw an item in *Variety*. In Chicago, in 1956, Leeds had been arrested for soliciting.

***

Lana's long suspension at MGM was lifted when she agreed to star in a melodrama, *A Life of Her Own*. Back on the lot, she got into an argument with its director, George Cukor, on the first day of filming. "You've chosen the wrong leading man. Under no circumstances can I pretend to be in love with that poker-faced Wendell Corey."

Chapter Thirteen

Another Divorce
Lana Emerges as The Merry Widow

She Becomes The Bad & The Beautiful

To publicize her "comeback" picture, *A Life of Her Own,* Lana posed for this strikingly dramatic photograph. It was taken by Eric Carpenter, who was the chief photographer in MGM's publicity department. It became Lana's favorite photograph of herself, and she kept it prominently displayed in her living room for more than a decade.

Lana's return to the screen was in a black-and-white melodrama, *A Life of Her Own* (1950), for MGM, the story of an aspiring model who flees her small town in Kansas for the bright lights of New York to seek her fame and fortune. She finds that, but also experiences an ill-fated love affair.

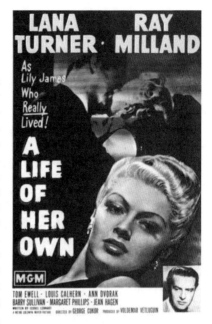

Disillusioned with her own marriage to Bob Topping, she was eager to return to the screen, fearing that her fans might desert her if she stayed away much longer.

She and Topping now occupied separate bedrooms, and often, he didn't come home at night. She had heard rumors that he was seeing another woman, an aspiring blonde starlet named Beverly Garland (aka Beverly Campbell). Four years younger than Lana, she had divorced her husband, Robert Campbell, and had not yet remarried.

Ironically, Lana was shocked to learn that Garland had been cast in a minor role, identified as "Girl at a Party," in *A Life of Her Own*. Previously, when Lana encountered Garland on the set at MGM, she had ignored her.

Although the plot for her new movie was loosely inspired on the novella, *The Abiding Vision*, by the famous novelist Rebecca West, Lana's film would be remarkably different in tone and texture.

A Life of Her Own dealt with adultery, a theme which was virtually forbidden in films by those guardians of public morality, the Joseph Breen Office. After reviewing the script, the censors wrote to MGM: "It is completely unacceptable, shocking, and highly offensive with its portrayal of adultery and commercialized prostitution."

A revised and much toned-down revision was then submitted to the Breen censors, who came back within a week, citing the script as having "insufficient moral values." Screenwriter Isobel Lennart was ordered to "show that adultery is wrong and that sinners must be punished." It was recommended that Lana's character of Lily Brannel James commit suicide before the end of the final reel.

George Cukor, the director, detested the suicide ending, and so did Lana, but they filmed it that way anyway. However, at the first preview of the movie in Burbank, the audience objected to it, as expressed on the notes they scribbled on their survey questions before exiting from the theater.

Consequently, Lana was summoned back to MGM to shoot another ending, one in which she was allowed to live, albeit with remorse, regret, and guilt. Approval for filming from the Breen office was finally granted, but most begrudgingly.

In the script, Lana, as Lily, goes to New York and becomes a highly successful fashion model. As a favor to her attorney, Jim Leversoe (Louis Calhern), she entertains Steve Harleigh (Ray Milland), the owner of a copper mine from Montana. The two fall in love, but she soon finds out that he is married. His wife, Nora (Margaret Phillips), is a paraplegic whose disability stems from an automobile accident for which her husband was responsible.

Lily's love for Steve grows stronger as the film progresses, until she summons the courage to confront Nora, asking her to divorce her husband. But when she encounters the disabled woman in a wheelchair, Nora is kind and polite to Lily. Seeing how totally dependent Nora is on her husband, Lily realizes that she cannot continue her affair with Steve. Leaving the apartment, she encounters him exiting from the elevator. She forces herself to inform him that their affair is over.

In the final cut, one of Lily's lines almost echoes the career of Lana herself. "All I want is to be somebody. All I have is myself and how I look." She makes a decision to go on with her life with courage, even though she faces a life of loneliness.

The new ending was a bit of a stretch for movie-goers. At the peak of her glamour and beauty, the character of Lily, a single woman on the loose in Manhattan, leaves the impression that she won't be lonely for long.

Even before Lana signed to make *A Life of Her Own*, there was a flurry of casting, both for the director and for the film's leading man. Originally, Vincente Minnelli—the gay director who had married Judy Garland—was assigned to helm the project. But after the many starts and stops, MGM reassigned him to direct Spencer Tracy and Elizabeth Taylor in *Father of the Bride*. George Cukor replaced him.

Cary Grant had been offered the role of the leading man, but rejected it as "too downbeat for me." When MGM sent over George Murphy as a replacement for Grant, Cukor rejected him, saying, "Ronald Reagan's best friend is just too wholesome a guy to play an adulterer cheating on his crippled wife."

Howard Keel was selected next. Cukor, who was fully aware

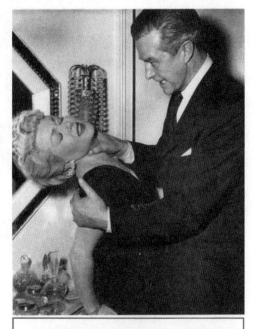

In *A Life of Her Own*, Lana and Ray Milland are supposed to play lovers, but in this publiciy still, it looks as if he wants to choke her to death. When Lana saw it, she said, "It should be the other way around. Before filming the ending, I wanted to choke him."

The scene depicted above does not appear in the final cut.

that Lana had previously sustained an affair with him, was physically attracted to the big, macho actor himself. But at the last minute, MGM withdrew him, fearing that the role was too dark for a star the studio was promoting as Frank Butler in *Annie Get Your Gun.*

MGM then offered the role to the British actor, James Mason, who was believable as an adulterer. He was attractive, suave, and had a melodious voice. "I know how to play an adulterer," he told Cukor. "I frequently cheat on my wife."

Despite Mason's acceptance of the role, he dropped out a week before shooting began. "I decided that no one would believe me as a Montana man, the owner of a copper mine. I'm too elegant for that. Get someone else."

Over Cukor's objection, MGM then designated Wendell Corey as the leading man. He had launched his career in 1947 as Burt Lancaster's closeted lover in *Desert Fury* with the lesbian actress, Lizabeth Scott. In spite of his ordinary looks, he went on to star with some of the silver screen's leading ladies, including Joan Crawford ("He's a dud in bed"), Margaret Sullavan ("It was like getting fucked by Henry Fonda, no great compliment"), and Barbara Stanwyck ("I could hardly stand him").

Forced to work with him, Lana admitted to Cukor, "Corey and I will have as much sexual chemistry on the screen as Pa Kettle and me," a reference to character actor Percy Kilbride.

It was not just *A Life of Its Own* that was having difficulties, but MGM itself. In the previous year, the studio had lost $6.5 million, and Dore Schary had been hired by the banking interests to take over production. It was rumored that Louis B. Mayer was on his way out the door.

Lana was nervous about meeting Schary, because in reference to her, he had told his aides, "I don't like that kind of popcorn blonde."

The first time she met Schary, she had loudly protested Corey's candidacy as her leading man. He listened for only a few moments before ignoring her plea. Unlike Mayer, Schary did not pay much attention to her concerns.

After her meeting with him, Lana grew more concerned about her career, and had a frank talk with Cukor one night when she visited his home. She'd become alarmed when columnists started referring to Marilyn Monroe as "the new Lana Turner" after her casting in *The Asphalt Jungle* and *All About Eve.*

Cukor advised her that she could still have some big box office triumphs in the 1950s "and perhaps beyond, depending on the scripts." She listened carefully. Although he'd been replaced as director of *Gone With the Wind* (1939), he'd made such screen classics as *Dinner at Eight* (1933) with Jean Harlow; *The Philadelphia Story* (1940) with Katharine Hepburn; and *Gaslight* (1944) with Ingrid Bergman. He also beat out some stiff competition to help Judy Holliday prepare for her role in *Born Yesterday* (1950), a part that Lana had wanted.

From the beginning, Lana did not like her leading man, Wendell Corey. After two days, she told Cukor, "Making love to Corey is like coming on to a stern Presbyterian deacon. I don't understand why he's even considered a leading man. Would you, a self-respecting homosexual, go to bed with him?"

Cukor told her he would not.

After a week of shooting, Cukor, Corey, and Lana sat through the rushes. Her opinion of him was confirmed.

Even Corey himself told them, "I'm completely wrong for this role. Before we shoot anymore, I want out."

The news was flashed to Mayer, who called executives at Paramount, which had lent the actor. A truce was worked out that morning. By 3PM, Mayer had personally phoned the agent of Ray Milland, who was out of work at the moment. "Do you want to be Lana Turner's leading man in an illicit love story?" the agent asked the actor.

"I've had worse jobs," Milland answered, sarcastically. "I'll take the god damn thing without even seeing the script."

Reporters converged around Lana and asked her why Corey had bolted. "I don't know," she answered. "If being a movie star doesn't work out for him, he can always go back to selling washing machines in a department store. His ancestors are very impressive: John Adams and John Quincy Adams."

***

In the late 1940s, when Ray Milland walked onto an MGM set to co-star with Lana in *A Life of Her Own*, he was at the pinnacle of his career, having already won a Best Actor Oscar for his portrayal of the alcoholic writer in *The Lost Weekend* (1945).

As the highest-paid actor at Paramount, he would have a long career, co-starring with other big name actresses who included Gene Tierney, Marlene Dietrich, Ginger Rogers, Barbara Stanwyck, Hedy Lamarr, and Loretta Young.

In the future, he would fall in love with one of his co-stars, Grace Kelly, during the filming of *Dial M for Murder* (1954). Their romance would threaten his long-enduring marriage to Muriel Weber, whom he had wed in 1932. He would ask her for a divorce until she reminded him that all the property they shared was in her name.

Back on the set the following Monday, Lana began to meet and work with the film's strong supporting cast, many of whom she knew.

Cast as her roommate, the fading model Mary Ashlon, Ann Dvorak had reached her peak in the Pre-Code 1930s. Groomed as a dramatic actress sponsored by Howard Hughes, she had previously co-starred with Bette Davis, Humphrey Bogart, Paul Muni, Spencer Tracy, Joan Blondell, and James Cagney.

She told Lana, "Like the character I'm interpreting, it's about time for me to make a graceful exit from the screen." In the year that followed the release of *A Life of Her Own*, Dvorak retired from movies.

Helen Rose was assigned to design Lana's super-glam wardrobe in a style that suited her character's definition as a Manhattan model. Quite recently, she'd designed the wedding gown of Elizabeth Taylor for her marriage to Nicky Hilton, and she was also designing Taylor's wardrobe for *Father of the Bride*. She'd soon be creating Lana's wardrobe for *The Bad and the Beautiful*.

Margaret Phillips delivered a sympathetic, convincing performance as Steve's pathetic, wheelchair-bound wife. The Welsh-born actress had trained at the Actors Studio, and had rehearsed with such actors as Marlon Brando and Montgomery Clift.

In a party sequence, Lana danced with Hermes Pan, Fred Astaire's choreographic collaborator in those 1930s movie musicals with Ginger Rogers. He'd previously appeared on film with both Betty Grable and Rita Hayworth in dancing sequences.

Barry Sullivan was cast as Lee Gorrance, an advertising executive whose romantic advances are spurned by Lana in the film. She had come close to working with him in *Three Guys Named Mike,* but the role she'd wanted was ultimately assigned to Jane Wyman. They would soon be working together in her next film, *Mr. Imperium,* and eventually, he'd play opposite her in *The Bad and the Beautiful.*

After his performances in *A Life of Her Own* were filmed, he told Lana that he'd been cast in *The Story of a Divorce* (later re-titled *Payment on Demand;* 1951) with Bette Davis, and then suggested, "I didn't get much of a love scene with you on screen. How about something off-screen?"

"Give me a raincheck, doll," she answered. "As for Miss Davis, I suggest you wear a jockstrap made of steel. She castrates her leading men."

As Lana's lawyer, Louis Calhern delivered his usual stellar performance. He'd already been nominated for a Best Actor Oscar for his performance as Oliver Wendell Holmes in *The Magnificent Yankee* (1950). "Louis was a dear old thing," Lana said. "He'd made his first film when dinosaurs roamed the earth." She noticed that his health was declining. In 1956, he made his last film, *High Society,* with Bing Crosby, Grace Kelly, and Frank Sinatra, a remake of Katharine Hepburn's *The Philadelphia Story.* He died shortly thereafter.

In the beginning, Lana and Ray Milland got along, and he entertained her between takes with stories of his early days in films. He revealed that when he'd made *The Jungle Princess* (1936) with Dorothy Lamour, "I indulged in water sports. We were in this swimming pool together, and the water was very cold. Somehow, it caused me to start to urinate, and soon, the Sarong Girl was enveloped in a sea of yellow piss."

That same year, he'd filmed *Beau Geste,* "with this beast of a man, Brian Donlevy, whom I detested, along with the rest of the crew. During a fencing sequence, I deliberately nicked his unpadded penis with the tip of my sword. He was rushed to the hospital, where it was discovered that I'd halfway circumsized him. Doctors competed the rest of the operation. Donlevy emerged from the hospital with a bandaged penis. He'd become a Jew overnight."

Milland also admitted that he'd suffered a permanent loss of a lot of his hair during the filming of *Reap the Wild Wind* (1942). "My character was supposed to have curly hair. Those shitheads in makeup gave me all these women's permanents and used electric curlers. The result left me with a receding hairline."

"In one of my early films, the makeup men destroyed my eyebrows," she admitted.

As for their love scenes, Lana agreed with the assessment of Marlene Dietrich. During the making of *The Golden Earrings* in 1947, she claimed that "Milland has a hygiene problem. He stank!"

As for whether or not she had sex with Milland, Lana, when asked by Cukor, said, "Forget it. The closest we came to getting physical offscreen was when he showed me this grotesque tattoo on his upper right arm. It was of a skull with a snake curled up on top of it with the tail of the reptile sticking through one of the eyes of the skull."

What ultimately turned Lana against Milland was his almost constant attack on homosexuals. "He was always making nasty remarks about Cukor, Hermes Pan, Tom Ewell, and others in the cast, calling them faggots and lurid names. Once, he grabbed his crotch in front of me, telling me, 'The bastards will never get a taste of this.'"

She had looked at him with contempt, saying, "I'm sure they'll survive the deprivation."

Eventually and off the set, as a woman who befriended homosexuals, she made a point of avoiding Milland whenever possible. In his autobiography, *Wide-Eyed in Babylon,* he made no mention of her, despite having described in detail his appearances with Paulette Goddard in that silly period piece, *Kitty* (1945).

Lana ultimately came to despise Milland, but she was still sorry to see how far a bigtime movie star could sink, an insight which ignited fears of her own. The last time she saw him onscreen was when he starred in *The Thing With Two Heads* (1972), cast as a bigot whose head was grafted onto a black man's body.

Although she'd eagerly looked forward to working with Cukor as her director, each of them was disappointed when they saw the final cut, agreeing that *A Life of Her Own* would eventually be judged as one of their weaker pictures.

Most critics panned it, *Cue* magazine writing, "All the plush and polish can't turn this gushing goo into a substantial drama."

One of Lana's most consistently negative critics, Bosley Crowther of *The*

Before filming *A Life of Her Own,* Lana went on a strict diet to slim down. She showed she was "camera ready" when she posed for this glamorous publicity shot.

As a high fashion model in *A Life of Her Own,* Lana wore her most dazzling headdress, studded with fake raindrop diamonds. Dressed like this, she would have looked more at home on the set of *Ziegfeld Girl.*

New York Times, wrote: "Two years' absence from the movies obviously didn't improve Lana Turner's talents as an actress, or her studio's regard for what she can do."

Variety reported, "The soap opera plotting has been polished to a certain extent, the playing by the *femme* cast members is topnotch, and the direction aids them, but it is still a true confession type of yarn concerned with a big city romance between a married man and a beautiful model. Script is spotted with feeling and character and also a lot of conversation that doesn't mean much. A decided asset is Turner's performance."

After production costs were deducted, *A Life of Her Own* suffered a loss of about $700,000, making it the only movie of Lana's that never paid off. She told Cukor, "I've got to succeed in my next picture, or they'll throw me out of MGM!"

In recognition of her past stardom, she was asked to put her hand and footprints into wet cement in front of Grauman's Chinese Theatre in Hollywood. She willingly complied. Fans gathered, many of them calling for her to (obscenely) immortalize those features of her body that had earned her a label as America's Sweater Girl. She demurred, claiming, "We must keep this event in good taste."

Nonetheless, columnists reminded her that Betty Grable had immortalized her leg in cement, Bob Hope his ski nose, and Monty Woolley his beard.

In her assessment of Lana Turner, columnist Adela Rogers St. Johns articulated why Lana Turner's legend lives on. "Lana is an exaggerated, unconventional, slightly mad, utterly enchanting creature unlike anybody else in the world, with plenty of brains and practically no sense at all. She drinks martinis and assorted beverages from 86 to 100 proof, collects elaborate *négligées* and embroidered nighties, loves Clark Gable movies, Palm Springs, sun-bathing, owns 250 pairs of shoes but roams her house barefooted, drives a robin's egg blue Cadillac convertible with red leather cushions, and lives in a $100,000 mansion on three rolling acres above Sunset Boulevard with daughter Cheryl, husband Topping (whom she calls Poppa), and six TV sets. She is a success story in search of an explanation, a love story in search of a happy ending, and an endless list of contradictory quotes."

***

While still a twelve-year-old schoolgirl, Norma Jeane Baker (also known as Marilyn Monroe), had begun to menstruate, and her breasts had developed rapidly.

She was mesmerized when she went to see Lana Turner in her screen debut, *They Won't Forget.* She both envied and was jealous when Lana, in a form-fitting sweater, walked down the street with her breasts the focus of the camera. Norma Jeane wanted to be like her, especially when Lana became known across America as "The Sweater Girl."

Inspired by young Lana, Norma Jeane transformed a red cardigan into a more form-fitting garment. She removed all her underclothing and wore only the sweater, buttoning it in back in ways that made it tighter in front so that it would emphasize the size and shape of her breasts. She described the cardigan as, "my magic sweater. I was a budding Lana Turner."

Wearing that sweater during her first year at Emerson School in Los Angeles, she was avidly pursued by older teenaged boys.

After that, Norma Jeane never missed a Lana Turner movie. Her favorite for glamour alone was *Ziegfeld Girl*, although she was also thrilled by Lana's love scenes with Robert Taylor in *Johnny Eager* and by Clark Gable in *Somewhere I'll Find You*. Often, she'd schedule her arrival at a movie house for the first screening of a Lana Turner movie and remain there until that day's last show, surviving on a coke and a bag of popcorn.

Later, when Norma Jeane began to model, photographers didn't like her curly hair, suggesting that she should style it smoothly like Lana Turner, whose coiffure was then in vogue.

When she was hired to pose for a shampoo ad, the representative for the product suggested that she dye her hair blonde and have it straightened to more closely resemble Lana Turner's.

Norma Jeane, who needed the money from the modeling gig, straightened and dyed her hair accordingly. In the aftermath, she looked more like Lana than ever.

When Marilyn went to work for Columbia in the spring of 1948, Harry Cohn, the studio executive, hired her because he wanted to groom a possible replacement for Rita Hayworth, should she prove unreliable. Makeup men went to work on Marilyn, raising her hairline through electrolysis to emphasize her widow's peak. In the aftermath, she looked more like Lana than Rita Hayworth.

That was the year she gravitated into the orbit of Johnny Hyde, who had been Lana's agent before she dumped him. He took Marilyn under his wing, demanding sex from her daily, with the promise that he was going to turn her into the next Lana Turner.

Hyde was able to get Marilyn cast in MGM's *The Asphalt Jungle*, in which she was a success in a minor role. He tried to get Louis B. Mayer to give Marilyn a contract, but he turned him down, informing Hyde, "We're already grooming other blondes to replace Lana. We don't need another one."

In his book, *The Private Diary of My Life With Lana*, Eric Root, her longtime companion later in her life, wrote how Marilyn first approached Lana. She sent her two rare photographs of herself, requesting that Lana autograph them on the back and return them. "Your signature will be immortalized in my heart."

Lana didn't return the pictures, but Marilyn had included

Keith Andes and Marilyn Monroe were lovers in the 1952 *Clash by Night*. But it was the star of the picture, Barbara Stanwyck, who actually put Marilyn on the casting couch.

her phone number, so Lana phoned her and set up a meeting that following afternoon.

Marilyn dressed as sexily as she possibly could. She'd heard rumors that Lana had a lesbian streak in her and that she was the possible lover of Ava Gardner.

Joan Crawford had already made a pass at Marilyn, and Barbara Stanwyck had seduced her when they'd co-starred together in *Clash by Night*. Marilyn figured that Lana also might be sexually attracted to her.

Arriving at the designated time, Marilyn was graciously received by Lana. There would be no sexual come-ons. Instead, with the understanding that Marilyn desperately wanted to be a movie star, Lana decided to offer some beauty tips.

Lana didn't mean to hurt Marilyn's feelings, but she pointed out that her makeup was all wrong, "unless you've been cast as a streetwalker along Santa Monica Boulevard." Lana also objected to the way Marilyn dressed, interpreting her outfit as vulgar. "You've also got to get rid of those unfortunate bulges."

She promised Marilyn that she'd be allowed to visit her again. According to Root, Lana agreed to teach her "how to walk, how to act, what to say, and what not to say."

During the coming months, although Lana had very little time to coach Marilyn in the art of becoming a movie star, she spoke to her on the phone whenever she could.

As Marilyn's fame grew, *Confidential* began to link Lana, Marilyn, and Ava Gardner as "the unholy trio of Hollywood." Each of the three women were exposed in one scandal after another, either real or invented.

At first, Lana did not realize what a legend Marilyn would become. She'd grouped her with Jayne Mansfield, Mamie Van Doren, and the British bombshell, Diana Dors. "They all copy me," she told Root. "They all have the same toner in their hair like I do, and use the same bleach. But there's only one Lana Turner, and that's *moi.*"

In time, however, Lana sensed that Marilyn was different from the rest, although she could not quite understand what made her so. She told Virginia Grey and others: "I don't know what it is, but Marilyn has this certain quality. She's one of the few Hollywood blondes who might become a really big star like me. All the other blondes can only imitate me."

In time, though, Lana became disillusioned with Marilyn: "I gave men a hard-on by wearing a sweater," Lana said. "Marilyn posed for nude pictures that are all over town. She and Mansfield dress so sexily that their tits are spilling over."

Ultimately, Lana grew jealous of Marilyn, especially after she seduced some of her former lovers (Frank Sinatra, Howard Hughes, Peter Lawford, Robert Mitchum, and Rory Calhoun).

After Marilyn's mysterious death in August of 1962, Lana was flabbergasted by the publicity it generated, the books and articles written, even fictionalized films of her imagined life.

She was also amazed at how Marilyn's sexual liaisons with John F. Kennedy became familiar to millions. "I had an affair with Senator Kennedy, and no one knew it at the time," she told June Allyson, who had also had an affair with the future president.

One night over drinks, Lana told Virginia Grey, "I think the secret of becoming a blonde movie legend like Jean Harlow and Marilyn is to die young. Had I succeeded when I tried to commit suicide, I'd be a much bigger legend."

***

After filming *A Life of Her Own,* MGM ordered Lana to star in *Mr. Imperium* (1951) with the celebrated opera singer, Ezio Pinza. After reading the script, she reported back that, "It's stupid. I don't want to star in it." She had heard that Greer Garson had already turned it down.

Her attack on the script proved embarrassing to her. It had been written by Don Hartman, who was slated to direct it. He would later become the head honcho at MGM. His co-writer was Edwin H. Knoff, who eventually emerged as its producer.

Because she needed the money, Lana accepted the role. What she didn't tell MGM was that she was three months into her second pregnancy, and she knew she wouldn't be able to work for some time. Her doctor gave her a series of injections which he said would help save the baby, but warned her "these shots are going to hurt like hell." Because she desperately wanted her second child, she agreed to endure them.

Production began on a hot summer day, June 18, 1950. It was the story of a European prince, Alexis, who falls in love with an American nightclub singer while vacationing in Italy. He learns that his father, the king, has died, and he must now rush back to his country to be crowned as its king. After their burgeoning romance is sabotaged by affairs of state and members of his political entourage, the presumptive king disappears from her life for twelve years.

When he'd first met her, she'd been Frederika Brown, a charming but run-of-the-mill nightclub singer. Now, a dozen years later, she has now blossomed into a major-league movie star, Fredda Barlo. Reunited with her in Palm Springs, the king realizes that he is still madly in love with her. In the meantime, her producer, Paul Hunter (Barry Sullivan), has fallen

Lana and opera star Ezio Pinza seemed filled with love, joy, and delight when they posed for this publicity still.

Privately, she called him, "Old Garlic Breath. He made me sick."

in love with her, too, and also wants to marry her.

Fredda and Mr. Imperium, now a king on the verge of exiling himself because of his love for her, enjoy a weekend tryst in Palm Springs. The movie ends when, with tenderness and shared expressions of ongoing loyalty, he departs from her life once again, assuring her that he'll return for her one day.

An Italian opera star, Pinza was known for his rich, smooth, and sonorous voice. For nearly a quarter of a century, he had been a star at New York's Metropolitan Opera House.

His biggest Broadway success involved his co-starring role with Mary Martin in the 1949 stage version of Rodgers & Hammerstein *South Pacific*. In it, he introduced his hit song, "Some Enchanted Evening," which helped transform him into a matinee idol and a national celebrity.

Eddie Mannix, from MGM's publicity department, had billed Pinza as "The Great Lover," but he later regretted it. According to Mannix, "I think he came to believe his own publicity."

Pinza told Mannix, "I hear Lana even propositions handsome men from among the film crew, inviting a stud to her dressing room. I bet she's going to be an easy conquest for me."

After Lana met him, she later complained, "He treated me like a tramp. He seemed to want to sleep with every woman involved in the film, including me. He made all these florid attempts to woo them, along with myself, into his bed."

Based on her scenes with him, she nicknamed him, "The man with the Roquefort teeth. Before coming onto the set, he downed all these cheese pastries and endless cups of espresso."

In her pregnant state, she found the odor so offensive that she often had to run to her dressing room and vomit. Not only that, but at one point he openly groped her. "He was one crude beast," she claimed. "He even tried to rape my pretty stand-in, Alyce May, who had to fight him off."

From the beginning, she complained to Hartman that she and Pinza as screen lovers could not be convincing. "I've got to do love scenes with my grandfather." At the time he made the movie, Pinza, born in Italy in 1892, was already fifty-eight years old. "If Greer Garson had accepted the role, she would have been more convincing," Lana said. "After all, she was born in 1903, which makes her only two years younger than Clark Gable."

Lana had to sing one song in the movie, part of a nightclub act, "My Love and My Mule." MGM hired singer Trudy Erwin to dub her voice.

Pinza was given three songs, "Let Me Look at You," and "Andiamo," both by Harold Arlen and Dorothy Fields. His third was the standard, "You Belong to My Heart," which British exhibitors used as the title of the movie when it was released in that country. [*They objected to the title*, Mr. Imperium.]

Reunited with Barry Sullivan, after having finished *A Life of Her Own* with him, he was most cordial, using his most seductive voice. "I tried to get lucky with you on our last picture. What about this time around?"

"You're a very attractive man, but I'm spending all my nights in the arms of Mr. Garlic Breath."

"Yeah, right," he answered. "We'll meet again."

Sullivan was right about that. He would be her co-star in *The Bad and the Beautiful.*

The distinguished English actor, Sir Cedric Hardwicke, was cast as Bernand, the manipulative prime minister of Pinza's mythical kingdom. He told Lana, "I believe that God felt sorry for actors, so he created Hollywood to give them a place in the sun and a swimming pool. The price they had to pay was to surrender their talent."

The only bright spots in the finished product were the appearances of Marjorie Main, as Mrs. Cabot, the owner of a resort hotel, and her meddlesome helper, Gwen, played by Debbie Reynolds. This marked the beginning of the long friendship between Reynolds and Lana.

"Many of the MGM glamour girls I worked with liked their sex rough," Reynolds said. "Elizabeth Taylor liked it rough. So did Lana Turner, who often came to the makeup room with bruises or a black eye. Sometimes, they would have to reshoot things after one of her boyfriends knocked her around."

Reynolds was also aware of the violent fights between Frank Sinatra and Ava Gardner. "Once, Ava shot Frank. Lucky for him her aim was lousy. She hit him only in the leg."

Reynolds remembered Main as "so much fun," and also as a performer who had trouble with her bladder. In the middle of a take, she'd suddenly bolt for the toilet. "Between Marjorie's pee breaks and Lana's fighting with Pinza, it was a pretty tense set," Reynolds wrote in a memoir.

Without pre-screening it in advance, executives at Manhattan's Radio City Music Hall, had pre-booked *Mr. Imperium* for a long-term run. But when they were finally allowed to screen it, they canceled their commitment. Overall, the film was a flop.

Reacting to the gloom that prevailed in the aftermath of *Mr. Imperium,* Lana feared that she was slipping and that her contract at MGM would not be renewed. Adding to her humiliation, many movie houses that presented it as part of a double feature positioned *Mr. Imperium* in the second slot—a first for a Lana Turner movie, especially one with big production values and Technicolor.

Nonetheless, Lana's contract was renewed only two months after *Mr. Imperium* opened. Even though dozens of other big stars under contract to MGM were fired, MGM, even under Dore Schary, still believed in her box office appeal.

As anticipated, critical reviews of *Mr. Imperium* were terrible. The *New York World Telegram* wrote, "Mr. Pinza had better stay away from Hollywood unless he takes his own writers with him next time."

Photoplay struck an especially sour note: "Despite the grandeur that sweeps from the Mediterranean shores to Palm Springs' gardens, the story itself never jells. Lana Turner, who is seldom given material worthy of her, looks beautiful and does more than her share to tote this bale of nonsense. Pinza is just another middle-aged actor, trying to prove himself as far as this film is concerned. Certainly, his magnificent voice is woefully neglected. The few songs given him are far below his vocal ability."

One critic wrote that "the man who decided that pickles and ice cream made a delightful combination must have cast Lana Turner with Ezio Pinza. He is the musical version of Edward Everett Horton."

The New York Times found that "Lana Turner and her wardrobe were beautiful, but it's hardly likely that anyone would ever envy her dialogue." Other critics found that the much older Pinza in his love scenes with Lana came across as "a dirty old man."

MGM thought so little of the movie that in 1979, it did not renew the copyright. Subsequently, the film entered the public domain.

***

For Lana, it was not a question of if she would divorce Bob Topping, but when? She was finding it costly being married to a millionaire, both financially and personally. Because of problems with the Topping estate, he had been reduced to receiving only $1,000 a month, leaving her to pay all the bills. "My god!" she told Benton Cole, her business manager. "Bob will bet $2,000 on a god damn golfing putt!"

She'd had to make the $35,000 down payment on their $100,000 house in Holmby Hills and then stay current with the mortgage payments. At dizzying speed, Topping had already decimated his personal fortune, running up big gambling debts, which perpetually went unpaid despite the fact that his creditors were practically pounding on his door. Some of them contacted Lana with personal death threats.

Frank Sinatra warned her, "When you run up big gambling losses to the boys in Vegas, they get paid one way or the other."

She became worried for her own safety and for that of Cheryl, fearing once again that she might be kidnapped and held for ransom.

On top of everything else, MGM was deducting a hefty chunk of her paycheck every week for payment of her ongoing back taxes to the IRS.

Every business venture that Topping launched ended in failure, beginning with his midget racing car venture in England. He ended up losing the remainder of his personal fortune in an ill-fated attempt to manufacture fiberglass boats.

One afternoon, right before Christmas, he took her to one of the most expensive and exclusive jewelry stores in Beverly Hills. Optimistically, and for the first time, she began to suspect that one of his investments had paid off. He had her inspect a series of diamond necklaces until she selected one that she particularly liked. It just happened to be the most expensive.

She eagerly waited until Christmas morning when she gathered with Topping and Cheryl to open their presents. As his gift to her daughter, he'd presented her with a black French poodle, which she named "Tinklette."

Lana opened her carefully wrapped gift, expecting the necklace. Instead, she found only a little gold pin. Trying to mask her disappointment, she turned around as Tinklette ran into the room barking. Around his neck was the diamond necklace she'd admired. "It was a joyful Christmas," she recalled, in spite of Topping's morbidly heavy drinking throughout the course of the holidays.

To her chagrin, within the month, a bill arrived from the jewelry store in Beverly Hills. She painfully learned that he had charged the necklace and didn't have the funds to pay for it.

The more her bills piled up, the more collectors hounded them, and the more Topping drank. When she saw him hitting the bottle at eight o'clock in the morning, she knew he'd become a chronic, wildly over-the-top alcoholic. She became afraid every time he took the wheel of her car.

She admitted to Mildred that she'd married him not for love, but for financial security—and now she had neither. "My dear," Mildred said. "You have to face facts. You can no longer afford to keep a millionaire."

Lana knew she had to cut down on expenses, and with that in mind, she began to eliminate all but the most essential servants.

Coupled with her own financial problems, her career at MGM was in jeopardy.

In 1951, Mayer was fired from MGM. Bitterly, he packed up his belongings and—without a goodbye to Lana—left the studio that he'd co-founded.

Dore Schary took over as president. But whereas Mayer had favored splashy, wholesome entertainment, Schary was promulgating dark, post-war "message pictures," grim movies like *Battleground* (1949) and *The Red Badge of Courage* (also 1949).

The rise to power of Dore Schary also marked MGM's decline and the rise of its new enemy: Television. Little black boxes were being installed in living rooms across the nation. Americans were staying home watching it, abandoning their once deeply entrenched habit of going to the movies two or three times a week.

Schary was not impressed with MGM's stable of glamour queens: Lana, Ava Gardner, and swimming star Esther Williams. Williams defined him as "rude, cruel, and even more imperious than Mayer."

After he assumed power at MGM, Schary told his aides, who passed the word down the line, that he was tired of MGM's glamour girls of the 1940s, including Ava and Lana, and that he was banking on new talent, such as the emerging *femme fatale*, Elizabeth Taylor.

On Lana's homefront, Topping increasingly disappeared for long periods of time, returning after prolonged absences with no explanation of where he'd been.

She hired a private investigator to trail him, and within days, he reported back to Lana. Topping was seeing not only other women, but attending a series of stag parties where failed starlets, out-of-work Las Vegas showgirls, and unemployed and broke young women had been hired as short-term companions and prostitutes.

Tragedy struck again in October of 1950 when Lana slipped on a polished floor at her home and suffered her second miscarriage. It had resulted from complications associated with her Rh blood factor. She had hoped that a new baby might save her marriage, but now, she saw how hopeless that was.

She rarely confronted Topping about the other women in his life, running up bills in her name, or his long absences from the house.

When she did confront him, he often flew into an alcoholic rage, in some cases in full view of her guests when she was hosting a party. Kathryn Grayson once said something that antagonized him, and he picked up a lamp and threw it at her. It narrowly missed her head and face, crashing loudly into a mirror behind the bar.

On one occasion, Topping disappeared for two weeks with no word about where he was. Eventually, a letter arrived from his attorneys in Manhattan, revealing that he intended to sue for a legal separation. Allegedly, he'd gone on an extended fishing trip to Oregon and might, after that, proceed to Alaska to fish for salmon.

Lana phoned Greg Bautzer, asking him to begin divorce proceedings and to work out a settlement with Topping's lawyers. After much bickering, Lana was allowed to keep the house in Holmby Hills, on which she was making the payments. Very reluctantly, she agreed to return the heirloom jewelry from his mother's estate. She refused, however, to relinquish the marquise diamond ring he'd dropped into her martini glass at Manhattan's "21" when he'd proposed marriage.

On September 11, 1951, MGM announced that Lana and Bob Topping were divorcing. She was quoted as saying, "Bob wants me to give up my film career, but it means too much to me and my fans. I've worked too hard to become a movie star to abandon it at this point. I wish him all the happiness in his new life."

At the time of the announcement, Topping was shacked up in Sun Valley, Idaho, with Mona Moedl, an ice-skating instructor.

What Lana defined at the time as "my fourth and last marriage" survived for 4½ troubled years. Cheryl was nine years old the day he left for good.

He predicted trouble ahead for Lana. "Your daughter is dangerous," he warned her. "You tend to believe her, but she's full of complexes and prone to lie."

[Lana waited until the autumn of 1952 to start divorce proceedings. Before they could begin, she had to spend time in Nevada as a means of establishing residency in that state.

In 1953, after the legalities of their divorce were finalized, Topping married Moedl. He continued to drink heavily, dying fifteen years later at the age of fifty-four.]

***

Confronted with yet another failed marriage, and living in fear for her career, Lana admitted she'd wandered down a stairway to a dark gulf, and she wanted to escape from her emotional pain and anguish. Partly because she had adequately provided for both Cheryl and Mildred in her will, she left more and more of the day-to-day supervision of her daughter to her mother.

At this point in her life, she sometimes contemplated suicide. As unbelievable as it sounds, she actually attempted it when both Benton Cole (her business manager) and Mildred were with her in the house.

She went into her bathroom and locked both doors. "There was nothing else left for me to do," she wrote in her memoirs.

Then she opened her medicine cabinet, removed a bottle of sleeping pills, and swallowed every one of them. Fearing that that would be insufficient, she took out a razor and, in one sharp movement, she slashed her left wrist as blood spurted out. Within minutes, she passed out, collapsing onto the marble floor.

Having heard the crash, and fearing that something was wrong, Cole pounded on the bathroom door. When he got no answer, he kicked it in, finding her unconscious in a pool of blood. As he applied a tourniquet, he shouted for Mildred to summon a doctor

Dr. John McDonald, from his home nearby, rushed over and immediately carried Lana to his car and rushed her to the Hollywood Presbyterian Hospital, where doctors saved her life by stopping the bleeding, sewing her up, and pumping out her stomach.

The doctor later described her self-inflicted wound as "a jagged laceration across the lower quarter of her left forearm." Two tendons had been cut, but only halfway through.

She remembered lying alone in her hospital room, sobbing for hours in shame for what she'd tried to do to herself.

MGM's Eddie Mannix denied that Lana had ever attempted suicide. Although no one believed him, he announced that she had fainted in the shower and had fallen and cut her arm as it shattered a glass door. This was the same story that had been invented for Barbara Stanwyck a decade earlier.

On her way out of the hospital, Lana denied that she had attempted suicide. "I plan to live to become the oldest woman in America," she said.

After her divorce from Topping, Lana greeted her new neighbor, Judy Garland, and was introduced to her husband, Sid Luft. "Judy had faced suicide herself," Lana said. "We promised to keep each other from killing ourselves. I needed some strong feminine support at the time. Both Judy and I had pre-adolescent daughters to deal with. Liza Minnelli in her case. The question was, which daughter would cause her mother the most grief?"

During her recovery, Lana began to throw parties with a ratio of guests that was eighty percent male, twenty percent female, "the latter as unattractive as possible."

***

In the course of Stephen Crane's self-imposed exile in Europe, his daughter, Cheryl, learned that he had married actress Martine Carol, an elegant blonde goddess and one of the most beautiful women performing in films on the Continent.

After a suicide attempt and two days in the hospital, Lana, with her wrists bandaged, was released. She immediately faced an armada of reporters and photographers.

To help prepare her for her exit, Mildred had hauled in an all-white wardrobe that included a babushka, slacks, and an ankle-length overcoat.

Pictures of her in this outfit appeared on frontpages of newspapers across the country.

385

By the late 1940s, when she became Cheryl's new stepmother, she had become the leading actress in French cinema. She would keep that reputation until the mid-1950s, when she was upstaged and more or less replaced by the "sex kitten," Brigitte Bardot.

During her father's time away, Cheryl had been virtually out of touch with him, with almost no insights into the gilded life he was leading as a *bon vivant* on the Continent.

As Crane's memory had receded, one Sunday afternoon, Bob Topping had called out to Cheryl, summoning her to approach him. She was resting by the pool, and he was at the breakfast table on the patio. He immediately got to the point: "Your father is dead. Stephen died in a car accident in Paris." He held up the Sunday newspaper with a blaring headline—LANA'S EX IN PARIS CRASH. That horrible news was highlighted with a photo of a sports car that had been demolished in an accident.

"I am so very sorry," Topping told his stepdaughter. "You've got to be brave. Stephen would have wanted that. This is not the time for you to fall apart. Please let Lana adjust to this in her own way, and not make it an issue to cause her more grief. From now on, you can call me Daddy, even though you've resisted doing that until now."

Cheryl had not seen her biological father in two years. The only mention Lana had made of him was when she'd told her, "Your father has married a French actress. You are not going to see your new stepmother."

In her memoirs, Cheryl noted, "There was little time to mourn."

This incident illustrates a strange gap, or "disconnect" in the life and times of Lana Turner. If Stephen Crane were indeed dead, why didn't Lana talk about it with her daughter? Apparently, she did not. Neither did her grandmother, Mildred.

Months later, when Mildred was shaking her granddaughter awake from a deep sleep, she said, "I have wonderful news for you, dear. Your father is back in California. I talked to him last night. He's coming over to see you today."

Cheryl immediately became hysterical. "That's a lie! He's not coming! He's dead!"

In an attempt to calm her down, Mildred asked, "Where did you hear such an awful thing?"

"Papa told me," Cheryl answered. "My daddy died in a car crash in Paris. I'll never see him again."

"You must have misunderstood," Mildred said.

Cheryl had not misunderstand, and she never knew why Topping had perpetrated such a lie. Having kept her grief to herself, she had never discussed Stephen's (presumed) death with either her mother or her grandmother.

That afternoon, another Sunday, Cheryl waited at the bottom of the steps for the arrival of her father. At 2PM sharp, he showed up, loaded down with presents.

He looked as handsome as ever, but had "gray dustings around his temples. He walked with a slight limp from the time he'd wrapped his sports car around a telephone pole. He told her that he'd spent a month on the critical list in a Paris hospital, but that he had pulled through.

She was anxious to hear about his life during his long absence. After tears of joy, hugs and kisses, he took her for a ride in his new limousine. Over a late lunch, he thrilled her with news of the glamorous months he'd spent in Paris, on the French Riviera and in north Africa. He had hung out with Woolworth heiress Barbara Hutton, King Farouk of Egypt, Prince Aly Khan (married to Rita Hayworth, with whom he'd had an affair), Prince Rainier of Monaco, and with Aristotle Onassis and his mistress, Maria Callas. She wondered how he could have afforded such a lavish lifestyle.

He admitted that he'd smuggled contraband such as luxury products, into post-war France, which was trying to recover from the nightmare of its long occupation by Nazi armies.

He discussed his new wife, Martine Carol, admitting that she had led a reckless life before meeting him. Her first love had been Geôrges Marchal, who had abandoned her, deserting her to go off with actress Dany Robin. Distraught, Carol had ripped off her clothes and jumped into Paris' Seine river near the Pont d'Alma. A taxi driver had plunged into the river and rescued her.

Stephen claimed that he had brought stability to her life as a movie star. For a while, they had lived in chic Monte Carlo near the villa of Prince Aly Khan and Rita Hayworth. Without admitting it, Cheryl may have gotten the impression that he had resumed his affair with the lonely Miss Hayworth whenever her errant prince was away in the arms of some other woman.

His life sounded far more glamourous than Lana's, now that she'd married Bob Topping.

During the subsequent months, Stephen faithfully arrived to retrieve Cheryl, according to a pre-arranged schedule, for afternoon bondings. At no point did Lana ever appear to greet him.

Years later, Cheryl recalled attending a pool party with her father and his friends. In a distant corner sat a beautiful blonde starlet who had recently signed with 20th Century Fox. Cheryl later found out that the starlet had recently changed her name to Marilyn Monroe.

Darryl F. Zanuck was at the party. After Cheryl was taken home, he'd seen Stephen return to the party, where he then escorted Monroe out the door. The couple disappeared for three days and nights.

Zanuck said, "Marilyn not only wants to be the new Lana Turner, but she wants to seduce her ex-husbands as well. Her next conquest will probably be Artie Shaw."

Stephen, before and after his divorce from Martine Carol, would continue seducing the glamour queens of Hollywood. He was even rumored to have had an affair with another blonde beauty, Mamie Van Doren, who was often dubbed in the press as "a Marilyn Mon-

The leading actress in French cinema, Martine Carol, became the next Mrs. Stephen Crane. But which was she? "The next Lana Turner?" or "France's answer to Marilyn Monroe."

roe clone."

After Crane's divorce from Carol in 1953, he launched Luau, a Polynesian-themed restaurant on Rodeo Drive in Beverly Hills. It quickly became a celebrity hot spot, known for its innovative décor and movie star clientele. Guests included an impressive roster of celebrities: Robert Mitchum, Joan Crawford, Loretta Young, Marlene Dietrich, Shelley Winters, Clark Gable, Robert Taylor, Bing Crosby, Errol Flynn, Gary Cooper, Burt Lancaster, and William Holden.

In time, he would expand his "Kon Tiki Empire" with theme restaurants stretching from Honolulu to Portland, Oregon, and from Chicago to Boston.

There is a saying in Hollywood that a star is only as commercially valuable as his or her latest picture. In Lana's case, that was not true. Her two previous pictures had each flopped at the box office. But based on her casting as the lead in a big Technicolor musical, *The Merry Widow* (1952), she was hoping for a triumph.

On December 30, 1905, in *beaux-arts*, pre-World-War I Vienna, *Die lustige Witwe* (*The Merry Widow*) was performed for the first time. The operetta became the most famous creation of Franz Lehár, the Austro-Hungarian composer of light operas. Its theme song, "The Merry Widow Waltz," became an international standard.

In the decades that followed, interrupted by both World War I and II, Lehár's operetta remained a witty, popular, and escapist vehicle on stages worldwide. In 1907, Broadway discovered the operetta, which opened with Donald Brian and Ethel Jackson—two big but now forgotten stars of yesterday—in the romantic leads. It reached the screen for the first time in a 1912 two-reeler starring Alma Rubens and the doomed actor, Wallace Reid.

Its greatest exposure came in 1925 when the tyrannical film director, Erich von Stroheim, adapted it into a silent movie co-star-

"My God, had I succeeded in commiting suicide, I would have denied myself the pleasure of kissing Fernando Lamas," Lana said.

"He had a wonderful technique, giving only a flicker of his tongue as a tantalizing prelude of more to come. I don't mean that as a pun."

ring the self-enchanted Mae Murray and John Gilbert, the movie making him a matinee idol of the silent screen. Murray was cast as the dancer Sally O'Hara, with Gilbert playing the romantic Prince Danilo. Unknown to even some of their most ardent fans, Clark Gable and Joan Crawford each appeared in it as uncredited extras. She shot to stardom quicker than he did.

The Merry Widow would be adapted for the screen four more times: In 1934, 1952 (Lana's version), and again in 1962 and 1994.

When Lana starred in the film, she had to wear heavy bracelets, gloves, or a fur piece to cover the scars of her recent suicide attempt.

MGM cast a real singer into its '34 version, Jeanette MacDonald, who starred in it opposite the French actor/comedian Maurice Chevalier, under the direction of Ernst Lubitsch, who made it a bit of a bedroom farce. Ironically, Una Merkel appeared in both this, the '34 version of the film, and again, in the 1952 version with Lana.

During her time filmmaking with Lana, Merkel told her, "In 1934, I played Queen Dolores. Now I'm cast as your handmaiden pouring your bath water. How the mighty have fallen."

The Hungarian-born producer, Joe Pasternak, announced that he was going to reconfigure *The Merry Widow* as "a love story with music." Its stars would be Lana and Ricardo Montalban. In this latest version, scriptwriters Sonya Levien and William Ludwig took great liberties with Lehár's original libretto and score.

MGM wanted a Technicolor blockbuster, and raided Broadway for topnotch talent. Jack Cole, the dancer, choreographer, and theater director, known as "the Father of the Theatrical Jazz Dance," got involved. Such glamour queens as Rita Hayworth, Betty Grable, and Jane Russell had worked with him previously. His most famous gig focused on the staging of Marilyn Monroe's number, "Diamonds Are a Girl's Best Friend," in *Gentlemen Prefer Blondes*. In Lana's picture, Cole's naughty can-can at Maxim's, and his magnificent waltz finale, did much to launch the 1952 version of *The Merry Widow* as one of the hit movies of the year, luring viewers into theaters and away from their TV sets.

A key figure in its eventual success was its musical director, Jack Blacton. In 1943, Rodgers and Hammerstein had tapped him to conduct *Oklahoma!"* on Broadway, and he would later conduct Ethel Merman's two greatest hits, *Annie Get Your Gun* (1946), and *Call Me Madam* (1950).

The German-born Curtis Bernhardt was designated as the film's director. Before that, he had directed such stars as Bette Davis, Joan Crawford, and Jane Wyman before tackling Lana. For reasons he kept to himself, he dropped Ricardo Montalban as the male lead and substituted Fernando Lamas instead.

The strikingly handsome Lamas had been an established star in Argentina, where he was the secret lover of that country's beautiful dictator, Evita Perón. In 1951, Hollywood signed him to compete with Montalban as the town's Latin Lover. Born in 1920, he was younger than Lamas, who first confronted the world in 1915.

Lana's friend and confidante, Helen Rose, designed most of her spectacular costumes. Her *Belle Époque* accessories included peacock feathers, hourglass corsets, lavish ball gowns, stunning picture hats, and sexy *négligées*. As Lana told Rose, "Mae Murray may have been merrier, Jeanette MacDonald more melodious, but

Lana Turner's stunning appearance will be the most illustrious of all. Wow! Just looking at myself in one of your gowns practically turns me into a lesbian."

As backdrops for Lana and Lamas, Bernhardt assembled an all-star supporting cast. Richard Haydn as Baron Popoff was known for playing eccentric characters. Before joining the cast, he had starred as the caterpillar in *Alice in Wonderland* (1950).

Thomas Gomez, cast as king of the mythical nation of Marshovia, played a variation of the oily, fleshy character he had developed for earlier films. Gomez became the first Hispanic American actor nominated for an Oscar for his performance in *Ride the Pink Horse* (1947).

The English character actor,

Vienna's (strapless) *Belle Époque*, replicated in Hollywood by costume designer Helen Rose, as interpreted by lovely Lana.

John Abbott, was a noted Shakespearean actor who had worked with such formidable British stars as Dame Sybil Thorndike, Vivien Leigh, and Laurence Olivier.

Robert Coote, as the Marquis de Crillon, was already known to Lana, having appeared with her in *The Three Musketeers.*

In the midst of the shooting, Spencer Tracy paid Lana a surprise visit. He congratulated her for signing a new and better contract with MGM. "They're getting rid of most of us old-timers. We're worn-out horses headed for the glue factory. We golden oldies belong to yesterday. But your future lies ahead of you. Your greatest roles are yet to come. Mine belonged to another day."

When he left, she told Helen Rose, "Spence has really aged. I doubt if he'll live out the 1950s."

Despite his failing health, Tracy would go on to live until 1967, when he died after making his last film, *Guess Who's Coming to Dinner* with his co-star and long-time companion, Katharine Hepburn.

About halfway through the shooting of *The Merry Widow,* MGM announced that both Lana and Lamas would co-star together in an upcoming movie, *Latin Lovers.* Around the same time, another announcement was made: The U.S. Marines had voted Lana the number one star of "Orality"—that is, a woman desiring to be kissed often and thoroughly.

Runner-up was Jane Russell, with Faye Emerson coming in third. In fourth place was Ava Gardner, trailed by the stripper, Lili St. Cyr.

Lana rebounded from her two recent failures with a hit. *The Merry Widow* played from Lima, Peru to Edinburgh, Scotland, from Buenos Aires to Rome. The romantic combination of Lana with Lamas, on screen and off, was combustible.

Though praised for its production values, *The Merry Widow* received some nasty comments from critics. One of them defined it as "more fizzle than fizz."

Newsweek praised the performances of both Lana and Lamas, as well as the baroque scenery of Marshovia. "Lana Turner is a well turned and glowing widow."

Bosley Crowther, of *The New York Times*, wrote, "*The Merry Widow* has never had it so good."

***

When Lana met Lamas, he had been married twice, the first time in 1940 to Perla Mux, an Argentinian film star. After his divorce from her, in 1946, he married Lydia Barache, the daughter of a Uruguayan real estate tycoon. Joining the cast of *The Merry Widow,* Lamas was in the final throes of his second divorce.

He had gotten his start as a movie star in his home country of Argentina, appearing in *On the Last Floor* in 1942. In America, he'd made such films as *Rich, Young, and Pretty* in 1951, and *The Law and the Lady* the same year.

He was not as good an actor as Ricardo Montalban, but he could sing fairly well, and Bernhardt decided to use his own voice in the final cut of the song "Vilia," where Lana's voice had to be dubbed.

Helen Young said, "Lana was ripe for a new romance now that she didn't kill herself and had dumped Bob Topping. It was about time."

Many reviewers commented on the tight trousers Lamas wore in the film. A reporter asked him who his tailor was. He didn't answer, but said, "I believe it pays to advertise. Soon, Ava Gardner will be knocking on my door."

He was right.

***

Lamas was already thirty-six when he met Lana. He boasted, "I'd had a lot of loving under my belt, which I unbuckled a lot to give the gals a thrill, even Miss

"When Lana Turner met Lamas for the first time, the birds burst into song, the bells rang in the church tower, the roses burst into sudden bloom, and the vines produced tender grapes," said director Curtis Bernhardt. "It was love at first sight. And no wonder. He was a very sexy guy in tight pants that revealed his manly powers."

Perón herself. She told me, 'If only Juan could make love like you do.'"

[She was referring, of course, to Juan Perón, president (aka Military Dictator) of Argentina.]

Lana sounded like a love-sick schoolgirl during her ravings about Lamas to Virginia Grey. "Fernando is so gorgeous he should be arrested for causing a gal's heart to flutter dangerously," she gushed. "As you know, I've seduced the best-looking men on MGM's roster of stars, everyone from Clark Gable to Robert Taylor. But Fernando is the best. He has a bronze tan, pearly whites, and always wears a silk scarf around his neck…each day, a different color, perhaps marigold, perhaps pink rose."

Grey responded, "It's called 'gaucho charisma.'"

Esther Williams, who occupied the dressing room next to Lana's, was among the first to witness the budding romance between Lana and Lamas. She saw him walking by in a "skin-tight brown dancer's leotard, which made no secret of his masculine charm," she wrote in her memoirs.

She related how she was even a witness to the first time Lana seduced Lamas. She heard Lana shout, after opening the door to her dressing room, "Fernando Lamas! Get your Argentinean ass in here!"

Williams confessed to putting a glass to the wall to hear what was going on. "The first movement began with gentle strings and sighing woodwinds. The second movement brought in the whole brass section with trumpets and tuba blowing like crazy. The third movement was filled with pounding kettledrums and marimbas which reached a wild and ecstatic crescendo."

Then she heard Lana moan, "Oh, Fernando! *OH FERNANDO!*"

During the filming of *The Merry Widow*, the press was quick to pounce on gossip about the romance of the film's co-stars. Although neither of Cupid's afflicted delivered any extended details about their love affair, Lamas, at least, made some quotable quotes:

"It is a known fact that Latin men prefer blondes. There is a difference between Latin men and American men. Latins give you more of everything: More headaches, more temper, and more tenderness. I am a handsome Latin and a wonderful lover. I got into movies because it was a great way to meet broads."

"One of my goals in deserting the film colony of Argentina and coming to Hollywood was to seduce both Ava Gardner (left) and Lana Turner.

"I succeeded both times beyond my wildest dreams."

"When word got out about me, my phone didn't stop ringing all night. But I was always too busy to answer it."

Lana gave Lamas the key to her home. One afternoon, when he got off from work several hours before Lana was finished at the studio for the day, he came to her house to swim in her pool. Cheryl was already there, playing beside its edge.

He came out onto the patio wearing a terrycloth robe. He asked her, "Have you ever seen a nude man before?" She shook her head no, later writing, "All I knew was that men had short hair and wore a fig leaf over their thing."

He dropped his robe and exposed himself, revealing to Lana's daughter what men are made of.

After that visit, he often appeared in the afternoon, each time going skinny dipping. He warned her not to tell her mother about his exposing himself to her.

Lana took Cheryl and retreated to Lake Tahoe in Nevada for six weeks to establish residency in that state so that she could file for divorce from Topping. Lamas was a frequent visitor. However, when word reached her of some of the comments he was making to the press, she exploded in anger.

One remark in particular had infuriated her. Lamas explained to reporters how Latin men make love. "We grab a gal around the neck, grasp her arms until they are black and blue, and then rip off her dress, saving the panties for last."

When Lamas' divorce from Lydia Barachi came through, it was assumed by reporters that he would immediately propose marriage to Lana. He did not, announcing instead, "I have no plans to marry anyone again."

Rumors about Lamas' genitalia made the rounds of Hollywood. In 1969, when he married Esther Williams, he said, "I'm hung very high. Somehow, my genitalia have been placed high on my pelvic bone. So it looks like this thing of mine goes on forever. It's really quite normal, but, of course, it's very grand when erect."

Williams also claimed that Lamas never wore underwear. "He had a way of thrusting his hips forward that made it very obvious what was inside those pants," she said. "And what was there was very substantial. It was his way of letting people know that he had a tremendous package."

After her own divorce was finalized, Lana, too, announced to the press, "I'll never marry again." However, she told "gal pal," Ava Gardner, "Fernando Lamas is going to be my next husband."

Preparing himself for any gala event invariably became a major ordeal for Lamas. "He spent more time getting dressed than I did," Lana said. "He didn't want any wrinkles or lines showing in his tight pants. He explained that he couldn't wear jockey shorts because a 'panty line' would show where his ass and legs came together. Before getting into the car to go somewhere, he'd take off his pants and drive with it all hanging out. At some place along a street with bushes, he and his pants would get out of the car and he'd change behind the screening of the bushes. That way he could arrive at the party without any wrinkles in his pants."

One night, when Lana and Lamas had gone nightclubbing at Mocambo, an angry-looking Lucille Ball approached their table. She was furious at Lamas' comments about Latin lovers. "You're the god damn reason Desi is chasing after every woman in skirts. He's trying to live up to the reputation you've set for Latin men. You're a horrible role model, you son of a bitch." Then she stormed away.

One night, Lana hosted a dinner party, inviting eight of her friends, including Virginia Grey. Before the party, Lamas told her that he would not attend, complaining about one of his recurring migraines.

After the meal, Lana invited her guests into her living room, where she switched on the music. There was much drinking and loud talking.

Suddenly, with a burst of anger, Lamas was seen bounding down the steps from the bedroom upstairs. He was entirely nude, shouting for the guests to leave the house at once. Then he stormed back up the stairs.

With embarrassed apologies, Lana escorted her friends to the door. Then she went upstairs, where she found him lying nude on the bed, glaring at her.

"Do you know, sir, that when you yell and you're jaybird naked, you produce an erection?"

"I'm not angry now, and look what I'm producing for you."

Eager to sample it, she headed toward the bed.

***

Lana feared that her career would nosedive if she made another flop. The big Technicolor musical, *The Merry Widow,* had done well at the box office, but as a follow-up, she wanted a non-musical role since, "I view myself as a modern woman who can pull off a contemporary drama minus the lavish costume period pieces where I look like some mannequin."

She thought she'd found it in a proposed script in the Hollywood-on-Hollywood genre like Judy Garland's remake of *A Star Is Born* or like Gloria Swanson as the delusional silent screen has-been in *Sunset Blvd.*

The plot of Lana's newest film dates back to 1949 when it was published in the *Ladies' Home Journal* as a short story, *Of Good and Evil,* by George Bradshaw. It was later expanded and renamed *Memorial to a Bad Man* (later retitled as *A Tribute to a Bad Man).*

When the project was assigned to producer John Houseman, he wanted to change the venue from Broadway to Hollywood.

Bradshaw had based the lead character (producer Jonathan Shields) on the notorious Jed Harris, "the Terror of the Great White Way."

Houseman didn't want to make another movie about Broadway because of the recent success of *All About Eve,* in which its co-stars, Bette Davis and Anne Baxter, had each been cast as Broadway stars, generating performances that earned

Oscar nominations for each of them.

When Lana was signed, with the provision that she would receive top billing, Dore Schary, the new head honcho at MGM, wanted the film's title changed to reflect Lana's character. The revised title was *The Bad and the Beautiful*. At first, Houseman objected, but later, he came to like it.

Vincente Minnelli, as director, and Houseman each wanted to bring it to the screen, with Lana cast into the female lead of Georgia Lorrison. But the studio chief, Dore Schary, who had replaced Louis B. Mayer, needed to be convinced. He felt that even at best, the picture would be a "B," and consequently allocated it a modest budget of a million dollars. Contractually, he approved of Lana's services for only four weeks of shooting, because he wanted to cast her as a follow up in another Technicolor musical, *Latin Lovers*, alongside her current lover, Fernando Lamas, typecast.

Lana felt that her role of Georgia might be the equal of her portrayal of Cora in *The Postman Always Rings Twice*. "I didn't get the Oscar for that, but here's a second chance for me," she told Minnelli, who at the time was somewhat depressed, coming down from his divorce from Judy Garland.

"Many of my friends wondered why I wanted to make such an anti-Hollywood movie," Minnelli said. "I told them I didn't see the character of Jonathan Shields as an unregenerate heel—first, because we find out that he has a weakness, which makes him human, and second, because he's as tough on himself as he is on everyone else, which makes him honest. That's the complex, wonderful thing about human beings—whether they're in Hollywood or in the automobile business or in neckties."

In a nutshell, the plot of *The Bad and the Beautiful* centered around producer Jonathan Shields and how he used and abused his star, Georgia, his writer, James Lee Bartlow, and his director, Fred Amiel.

Minnelli originally offered the role of Shields to Clark Gable, hoping for another Gable/Turner co-starring package. But the King of Hollywood, whose box office allure was slipping, turned it down. Minnelli then presented it to Spencer Tracy, Lana's former co-star, but he, too, rejected it. But Kirk Douglas, when it was offered to him, accepted immediately. ("I can be ruthless.")

When Lana first heard a layout of the plot, and learned about her character, Georgia Lorrison, she said, "I play a soggy mess, the daughter of a world-famous actor, who is sinking into oblivion, until I am rescued by an unscrupulous producer who propels me into stardom. I make the big mistake of falling in love with him, the story of my life. I believe in Georgia. Besides, she's a better character than those in the other turkeys presented to me."

Minnelli told her that her character was clearly based on the alcoholic Diana Barrymore, daughter of "The Great Profile," John Barrymore.

But the buzz in Hollywood suggested that Georgia might be based on any number of stars, former and present. At one point, Jennifer Jones believed that the role was based on her because the part of Jonathan Shields was clearly identified as inspired by her husband, David O. Selznick. Many scenes taken from his own life were inserted into the script.

The producer of *Gone With the Wind* was not the only inspiration for the character of Shields. The Russian American producer and screenwriter, Val Lewton, was also an inspiration. He was known for making a string of low-budget horror films for RKO Pictures, and also notorious for his cost-cutting techniques, and his abuse of his low-paid actors. His biggest hits had been *Cat People* (1942), *The Curse of the Cat People* (1944), and *The Body Snatcher* (1945), based on a short story by Robert Louis Stevenson.

In *The Bad and the Beautiful*, Shields and his director, Fred Amiel, are depicted making a low budget quickie employing "cat people."

Charles Schnee was assigned, as a scriptwriter, to adapt Bradshaw's short story—hence, he had to remain within the Hollywood (as opposed to the Broadway) genre. He had been a former partner in New York's experimental Mercury Theatre, working with both Houseman and Orson Welles. Although primarily a film producer and production executive, he had nonetheless developed a few screen-writing credits, including *Red River* (1948), a hit Western starring John Wayne and Montgomery Clift.

In the development of her character, Minnelli told Lana that he had ordered Schnee to use some of the characteristics of his ex-wife, Judy Garland.

Dick Powell's role as the writer was said to have been inspired by Paul Elliot Green, an academic turned screen writer whose main credit had been *Cabin in the Cotton* (1932), starring a very young Bette Davis [*"I'd kiss ya, but I've just washed my hair."*]

Leo G. Carroll played director Henry Whitfield, modeling his character on Alfred Hitchcock, with whom he'd worked in several pictures, including *Rebecca* (1940) with Joan Fontaine and Laurence Olivier.

***

In his capacity as author of the short story that had inspired it, George Bradshaw had wanted to write the screenplay for *The Bad and the Beautiful* too, but Minnelli had turned him down. He was hired, however, to produce a fifty-page scenario of his original story with amplifications. Minnelli hoped to cull from the scenario some additional material to add to the screenplay already in production by Charles Schnee.

Bradshaw was gay, as was his closest friend, the TV producer, Rogers Brackett, who at the time had a live-in lover, the then-unknown James Dean. Brackett had been supporting him, and procuring minor jobs for him in TV. Before that, Dean had been a street hustler.

Although Bradshaw did not like Dean personally, feeling that he was exploiting Brackett, he ultimately relented to his friend's plea, "Please write in a small part for Jimmy."

Bradshaw followed through and created a small but pivotal role for Dean.

It was inserted into one of the key moments in the film: After a triumphant win at the Oscars, Lana's character of Georgia Lorrison arrives, uninvited and unannounced at the mansion of Jonathan Shields. There, to her horror, she encounters his new lover. According to Bradshaw's early vision of the scene, as tailor-made for James Dean, it is not a sultry female brunette who emerges from his bedroom at the top of the stairs, as was depicted in the film's final cut.

Instead, the culprit was obviously a gay male: James Dean, provocatively dressed only in a snug pair of white boxer shorts.

Bradshaw invited Dean and Brackett to his apartment for a presentation of the then-scenario of the movie, as he had composed it to that point. He justified the homoerotic aspect of Dean's brief insertion into the script as follows: "To pull off Lana's later hysterical breakdown in the moving car, I felt that the script needed something more startling than just a beautiful, seductive tart at the top of the stairs. A producer who's fucking a starlet…that's nothing but a big, boring *cliché*. Come on, guys…it's about time we started defying the Production Code. Let's face it: It's 1951, not 1934."

"Your character doesn't say a word," Bradshaw said to Dean. "Your face has to say it all. You're to appear triumphant. You've stolen the man she loves from the most desirable woman in the world."

"*I can do it! I can do it!*" Dean shouted.

Brackett warned that although the insertion of a gay context would make a great scene, he feared that the

Lana had a distaste for the emerging young actors of the 1950s. Many of them were from the Method school of acting. However, there was something about James Dean, perhaps the wicked gleam in his eyes, that caught her attention. "Don't tell me," she said. "Are you a Marlon Brando clone?"

"Hell, no!" he said. "I have my own style and technique. I can act rings around Brando. And I can make an audience actually understand my mumbling. Besides, my dick is bigger than Brando's.

"Good for you, dear boy," she answered. "Modesty, I see is not one of your virtues. To get ahead in Hollywood, you can never be modest about your attributes."

censors wouldn't allow it.

[As it happened, he was right.]

Dean said, "MGM will be swamped with fan mail, asking "Who's that boy?...namely, me."

At 9:30PM that same night, Lana arrived at Bradshaw's apartment, having been driven there by an anonymous, shadowy male figure who all three men later agreed was NOT Fernando Lamas. He remained outside, behind the wheel of her car, throughout the course of her dialogue inside with Bradshaw, Brackett, and Dean. .

She explained that she didn't want to bring her unnamed companion inside "because I know you guys will go ape-shit over him and try to take him away from Ava and me. We've got a date at her place later tonight."

Of course, all three men knew that she was referring to Ava Gardner. Lana accepted glowing tributes from both Brackett and Dean, each of them insisting that she was their favorite screen actress.

"You probably say the same thing to Bette Davis and Joan Crawford," she said.

Then she expressed her dislike of the crop of young actors who had emerged during the early 50s, specifically naming Montgomery Clift and Marlon Brando. "Give me Clark Gable or Robert Taylor any day, especially that handsome devil, Tyrone Power. Errol Flynn is a darling, or at least he used to be. Dare I mention Victor Mature with his sledgehammer?"

At some point, she seemed to take notice of Dean, appraising him seductively. He would later tell Brackett, "She looked at me like a juicy piece of steak about to be devoured."

***

Without Brackett's knowledge, Dean arrived unexpectedly the next afternoon at Bradshaw's apartment with his shirt unbuttoned. After he was invited inside, he made the motivation for his visit clear. "I believe in repaying my debts," he said. "One favor deserves another."

"Rogers is my best friend," Bradshaw replied. "In Hollywood, a town of dishonorable people, I retain a sense of honor. I do not seduce the trick of my best friend. Now scram!"

"Okay, I'm going," Dean replied. At the door, he hesitated. "One more favor. Can't you beef up my scene? Have Georgia Lorrison approach me later on and seduce me? It would be a revenge fuck, Georgia giving it to Shields for betraying her."

"That I know I can't get away with," Bradshaw said. "But I might deliver the real thing to you. I talked to Lana this morning, and she asked about you. Her exact words were, 'Who was that divine young man last night? Does he fuck women, too?'"

Bradshaw then continued: "If you want to meet her, it can be arranged. I won't touch you, but Lana will. She devours young men. Rogers must not know."

"So your honor extends only so far?"

"Of course it does. After all, this is Hollywood."

Bradshaw phoned Dean the next day, saying, "It's all arranged for 4PM sharp this afternoon. I've got her address for you."

After writing down her address, Dean said, "Thanks, pal. I'll owe you one when I bolt from Rogers. That's in the cards, you know."

Arriving on time, unusual for him, Dean was directed to her swimming pool, where Lana, in a one-piece sunflowery yellow bathing suit, was sipping an iced tea.

He never discussed in any detail what happened that afternoon. Lana, still madly in love with Lamas, certainly didn't either.

After midnight, Dean returned to Brackett's apartment, claiming that he'd met some of his old school buddies and that he'd gone drinking with them.

Months later in New York, Dean shared a reunion with his old friends, composer Alec Wilder and TV producer Stanley Mills Haggart.

"I'm keeping a list of the famous men and women I've seduced in Hollywood. I need all this for the memoirs I'm going to write when I'm seventy-four. That list already includes Marilyn Monroe. I met her through my fuck buddy, Marlon Brando. To the roster of notables can be added one Miss Lana Turner."

Although Minnelli liked Bradshaw's having written a "young man at the top of the stairs" into the script of *The Bad and the Beautiful*, Houseman rejected it as "too daring."

***

A second attempt by Dean to appear in a movie with Lana also fell through.

Vincente Minnelli and his producer, John Houseman, were teamed together again for production of "a mental film," (Houseman's words). The movie, entitled *The Cobweb* and released in 1955, was set in a mental ward. As originally conceived, the director had cast the three leading roles with an amazing selection of two blondes, Lana and Grace Kelly, emoting with Robert Taylor. Dean was to have been cast into a secondary role. Later, it emerged that his studio refused to lease him.

The final cast of *The Cobweb* starred Richard Widmark, Lauren Bacall, Gloria Grahame, and John Kerr, making his screen debut in the role briefly targeted for Dean.

Even though Dean never got to work with Lana, his fascination with her continued. Months later, when he was searching for a place to live, a local landlord, David Gould, showed him a fully furnished house (at 1541 Sunset Plaza Drive) that had once been occupied by Lana.

Gould directed him to the master bedroom, the first room Dean wanted to see. Gould pointed out an elegant four-poster. "Lana slept in this very bed, but never alone, night after night."

"You've convinced me. I'll sign the lease. Tonight, I'll be sleeping in Lana's bed…and never alone!"

***

Right before Lana reported to work on the set of *The Bad and the Beautiful*, rumors reached MGM that both Lana and Ava Gardner were about to become the victims of an *exposé* in the upcoming edition of *Confidential.*

According to the grapevine, Gardner had stopped off for gasoline at a notorious filling station in Los Angeles at the corner of Hollywood Boulevard at Fairfax. After serving in the Marines during World War II, Scotty Bowers, a handsome, strapping ex-Marine, pumped gas at the station. In time, he developed a scheme for the employment of other good-looking, well-built ex-military men who had returned from World War II to a landscape with no jobs.

He began to arrange "dates" among these men and members of L.A.'s burgeoning gay population. Walter Pidgeon, one of Lana's co-stars in *The Bad and the Beautiful,* was one of Scotty's first and best customers.

Scotty and members of his crew also serviced women. Their conquests included Vivien Leigh and occasionally men in drag, one of whom was J. Edgar Hoover of the F.B.I. Ostensibly, the other gas jockeys at the station were also for rent.

When Gardner pulled into the station, her tank was filled by Greg Tolson, a 6'4" former paratrooper with bulging muscles and tight pants. He immediately attracted Gardner's hawkeye. There wasn't much time for small talk as the pair got down to some fast negotiations. They led to Tolson's arrival at Gardner's house that night at 10PM. Fortunately, her very possessive lover, Frank Sinatra, was out of town that night, performing in front of an audience in Las Vegas.

According to rumor, Tolson left Gardner's house at 10AM the following morning. Right before noon, she placed a call to Lana, with whom she often "traded" men, even a shared husband (Artie Shaw).

She apparently went into lavish praise of Tolson as a lover, telling Lana, "He's the kind of guy who comes into a woman's life only once in twenty-five years. Better take advantage now. The likes of him will not come again."

Intrigued, Lana, looking her most glamourous, arrived that night at Gardner's home, where she was introduced to Tolson.

"Seeing was believing," she reported later to Virginia Grey. "If he were a book, he'd be a bestseller."

Word of Lana's sharing of the gas jockey with Gardner reached Dory Schary's office, along with news about the upcoming *exposé* of the scandal in *Confidential.* He summoned both actresses into his office for a severe reprimand.

"If you don't give a god damn about your reputations, think of MGM and its reputation. Think of the morality clauses in both of your contracts."

After a stern and humiliating lecture about "cleaning up your acts," he dismissed them.

On her way out, Gardner turned back. "Don't worry, *honey chile,*" she said. "Even if *Confidential* exposes us, who's gonna believe it?"

***

Lana was eager to work with Kirk Douglas, her co-star in the upcoming *The Bad and the Beautiful.* She told Minnelli, "I think we'd make a dynamic duo on the screen, perhaps generate as much body heat as John Garfield and I did in *Postman.*"

She'd been impressed with the actor ever since she'd seen him star opposite Barbara Stanwyck in *The Strange Love of Martha Ivers* (1946).

Born Issur Danielovitch, the Russian Jewish actor, with his powerful build, expressed his relentless spirit through his cold, fierce eyes. He was a sort of virile anti-hero in post-war America, his cleft chin familiar to American audiences through such hits as the grim prizefighter in *Champion* (1949), or "The Gentleman Caller" in Tennessee Williams' *The Glass Menagerie* (1950).

After the first week of shooting, Hedda Hopper arrived on the scene, interrupting a conversation between Douglas and Lana. "I hear you kids may have a potential hit on your hands."

Then she turned to Douglas. "But I still think you're a son of a bitch."

"I've always been a son of a bitch," he answered. "But what about Lana here? Who is she?"

"Drop of 'son of'…and you've nailed her," Hopper said, before turning her back on the stars of the picture and walking away.

***

Long before Lana met Douglas, his reputation had preceded him. Early in his career, he'd auditioned for Mae West as a member of her stage revue. She insisted that actors who wanted to appear with her model for her in skimpy, form-fitting briefs that made their manly assets (or lack thereof) obvious. After giving Douglas a thorough appraisal, she rejected him for her backdrop of musclemen. "Buster, you just don't make the grade," she told him.

Then she turned to the next actor in line. "What's your name, kid? Steve Cochran, I heard. Is that a pistol in those briefs of yours—or are you just glad to see me?"

Evelyn Keyes had already revealed to anyone who wanted to hear that "Kirk is just parlor-sized."

Commenting on his own erection, he once told a reporter, "An erection is a mysterious thing. There's always the fear that each time one goes, that you won't be seeing it again."

Whether a great Romeo or not, Douglas would go one to seduce some of the stellar lights of Tinseltown: Lauren Bacall, Pier Angeli, Rita Hayworth, Marlene Dietrich, Gene Tierney, Patricia Neal, Ann Sothern, and Princess Safia Tarzi of Afghanistan.

Lana also appears on those lists of Douglas' seductions, despite denials from each of them that they never had an affair during the filming of *The Bad and the Beautiful*.

When he met her, he had only recently recovered from a case of pneumonia, the result of overexposure during the filming of his previous film, *The Big Sky* (1952).

During his recovery, he was visited often by Marlene Dietrich. "She would come over and cook soup for me, cuddle me, affectionate sex. But that was less important than the mothering. Marlene is an unusual person. She seemed to love you much more if you were not well. When you became strong and healthy, she loved you less."

Over lunch with her in the MGM commissary, Douglas amused Lana with stories of his life. As a young man, he'd worked as a bellhop at a summer resort owned by a rabidly anti-Semitic woman who was unaware that he was a Jew. All summer long, he had tolerated her racial attacks on the Jews.

Near the end of his tenure at the resort, right before he departed, she summoned him into her suite, and seduced him. As he confessed to Lana, "Right as I was about to climax, I whispered in her ear, 'This is a circumcised Jewish cock inside you. I am a Jew. You are being fucked by a Jew.'"

Rumors became so rampant in Hollywood about their alleged affair that Lana placed a call to Louella Parsons, who had suggested, in print, many times that Lana tended to seduce her leading men. "I never see Kirk after we close down the set for the day. Yet items keep appearing in the press about us having an affair. I'm in love with Fernando Lamas, and no other man means a thing to me."

Douglas also denied any affair with Lana. "Lamas was going with her. He was terribly jealous. Always on the set hanging around, guarding her like a hawk. Nothing happened between Lana and me. I liked her a lot and she did one of her best acting gigs in our film."

Were Lana and Douglas telling the truth? After all, she regularly denied affairs with Clark Gable, Robert Taylor, and many others.

Witnesses on the set, including Minnelli and such observers as co-star Dick Powell, claimed that she did have an affair with Kirk Douglas "What Lana told Parsons was true: *i.e.*, that she never saw Kirk after working hours," Minnelli said. "But what about those long visits to her dressing room with its pink satin sheets, when they weren't needed on the set by me? Esther Williams always seemed to have that empty glass against the wall of Lana's dressing room. She said they did have an affair, but one far more subdued than the rowdy sex with Lamas."

***

Minnelli was known mainly for directing big-ticket musicals such as *Meet Me in St. Louis, Gigi,* and *An American in Paris.* On occasion, he liked to tackle drama, too.

Lana had long been aware that her director was gay, perhaps bisexual. When she had co-starred with Gene Kelly in *The Three Musketeers,* she learned that Minnelli was in love with

As a ruthless producer, Jonathan Shields (Kirk Douglas) turns an alcoholic, self-destructive extra, Georgia Lorrison (Lana) into a super glamourous movie star.

Her mistake is to fall in love with him.

him. From 1945 to 1951, he'd been married to Judy Garland. The union had produced a daughter, Liza Minnelli.

Minnelli's biographer, Emmanuel Levy, wrote, "He was openly gay when he lived in New York. But when he came to Hollywood, he made a decision to repress that part of himself, or to become bisexual."

Before directing Lana, Minnelli had been told, "She can't act."

"I soon discovered that wasn't true," he said. "I found she had great imagination. She could do things I had no idea she could do. She had great depth and color and rose to the part."

Some of the scenes at the beginning of *The Bad and the Beautiful* were among the most difficult. Lana had to play the depressed, alcoholic, chronically hostile daughter of a great actor.

Her role was clearly based on the tragic life of Diana Barrymore, whose dingy apartment walls were covered with pictures of her late father, once known as "The Great Profile." But the voice heard in the background, a recording of her supposed father, was actually that of Louis Calhern.

Early in the filmmaking process, the Breen Office had objected to at least ten scenes in the script, most of them involving sequences of Lana portraying Georgia. They were labeled as "too explicit" by the censors. However, Minnelli decided to defy "these blue noses" and filmed the scenes anyway. His move was a major decision in the long-term goal of reducing the role of these censors. By the end of the 1950s, their power had begun to erode.

Once again, Lana faced one of the most talented rosters of supporting actors with whom she'd ever worked. In his interpretation of a hard-boiled Hollywood producer, Walter Pidgeon had aged considerably since she'd last worked with him in *Week-End at the Waldorf*. She later told her hairdresser, Helen Young, "Walter and I have one thing in common: We both go for the boys."

Originally, Dick Powell had been assigned the role of the director, Fred Amiel. But he didn't like the part, preferring the role of the easy-going, pipe-smoking, tweedy professor, James Lee Bartlow, whose character, the plot reveals, wrote a best-selling novel purchased by Hollywood. The role of the director went to Barry Sullivan.

Lana had never worked with Powell before, but she had co-starred with two of his wives, both Joan Blondell and June Allyson. Lana told Minnelli, "Dick is a nice guy and very talented, but frankly, I never saw him as a leading man, neither in those silly 1930s musicals or even as the hard-boiled detective Philip Marlowe. Critics wrote about his 'gosh-and-golly ebullience,' but I prefer a man who is 'Wow!' or 'Oh Boy!' more suited to my taste."

In *The Bad and the Beautiful*, sultry Gloria Grahame, playing Powell's wife, defined herself as "Los Angeles born and bred. All the rest of you guys in the cast are carpetbaggers."

Blonde and seductive, with bee-stung lips, Grahame could speak volumes with her arched brow. She immodestly told Lana, "Except for you, I was the sexiest thing in *film noir*."

In the film, she played Rosemary, a social-climbing Southern belle whose life ends in a scandalous tragedy when she runs off with Gaucho (*Gilbert Roland*), the

Latin Lover of the movie. Minnelli instructed Grahame to interpret her role "with cutesy-pooh mannerisms."

Barry Sullivan kept cropping up in Lana's films as her would-be suitor, who struck out notably in *Mr. Imperium* and *A Life of Her Own*. She would co-star with Sullivan once again in *Another Time, Another Place* (1958).

"When will I get lucky?" he asked Lana.

"You've tangled with Bette Davis and Jane Wyman, so why do you need me?" she asked. "Surely Joan Crawford at least lies in your future."

As a movie star, Gilbert Roland, cast as Gaucho, had seen bigger and better days in the movies. He was the original Latin Lover until Ricardo Montalban and Fernando Lamas came along.

He admitted that his performance in *The Bad and the Beautiful* was "self-parody, like the role I played in that Cisco Kid series." He told Lana that he'd wanted to be a bullfighter, but that he'd been lured to Hollywood, where he'd seduced a string of glamourous women who included both Clara Bow and Norma Talmadge. Eventually, he married the screen's cool, serene beauty, Constance Bennett.

***

Playing a bit part in *The Bad and the Beautiful*, Steve Forrest immediately attracted Lana's attention.

He looked so enticing as a male animal that Lana invited him into her dressing room, where he got to interact with her celebrated body on her pink satin sheets. She was so thrilled with his technique as a seducer, that she "summoned" him back on two more afternoons. It was only later that she learned that he was the younger brother of the more established actor, Dana Andrews, with whom Lana had also had a fling.

In fact, until he appeared in Lana's movie, Forrest had been billed as William Andrews. He didn't want the same last name as his more famous brother.

When Virginia Grey visited her friend on the set, as was her custom, Lana described her latest discovery and his relationship to Dana. "Until Steve screwed me, I thought brothers always had very similar cocks. Not in this case. They're very different."

"Which one gives the most satisfaction?" Grey asked.

"Steve, of course," she answered. "He's marriage material."

On the set of *The Bad and the Beautiful*, Lana—a skilled seducer of handsome young actors—spotted a tall, ruggedly masculine newcomer, Steve Forrest.

He had only a small, insignificant part in the film, playing a role defined by the script as "Leading Man."

[When Lana met Steve Forrest, he was already married to Christine Carilas. He'd wed her in 1948 and was still married to her when he died in 2013 at the age of 87.]

Lana got to appear with Forrest again in 1954 on *Ed Sullivan's Toast of the Town,* broadcast on CBS Television. It was an hour-long tribute to MGM, celebrating the studio's 30th anniversary.   As part of the tribute, Forrest joined fellow actors Edmund Purdom, Richard Anderson, and John Ericson as her backup, as she performed the "Madame Cremation:" number introduced by Judy Garland in *Ziegfeld Follies (1946).*

Lana invited him for a "sleepover," which he willingly accepted after they'd finished their filming. She never hooked up with him again, but she followed his career, as he played Jane Wyman's son in *So Big* (1953).

***

The most dramatic sequence in *The Bad and the Beautiful* occurred when Lana, as the rejected Georgia Lorrison, becomes hysterical, while driving her car, in the wake of a revelation about Jonathan Shields and his infidelities.

As she pleads with him for a private party (just the two of them), Elaine Stewart, as the ambitious starlet, appears at the top of his stairwell. Kirk Douglas, as Shields, kicks Lana, as Georgia, out of his house.

What emerged on celluloid became one of the most iconic scenes in motion picture history.

In preparation for its filming, Minnelli had wrapped every other scene in the picture, with the exception of Lana's near-fatal car ride, where she's screaming, thrashing, and sobbing hysterically behind the wheel of a moving car. Minnelli allowed her three weeks off before he was ready to bring her back to the studio for the filming of that scene.

By then, Kirk Douglas had moved on to other projects, shooting *The Story of Three Loves* (1953); and Sulli-

Albert Johnson in *Film Quarterly* said it best: "Lana Turner emerges from the mansion in white ermine and drives away. Her sobs soon build to hysteria, and lights of cars send flashes across the windows as she reaches a moment of unbearable frenzy. She releases the steering wheel entirely, and screams in emotional agony. Her foot presses the brake. One hears only her screams, the honking of passing auto-horns, and, suddenly, it's raining."

"The car bumps along uncontrollably for a second, then comes to a standstill. Turner falls over the wheel, still sobbing uncontrollably as the sequence fades. It is superb theater, one of the great moments of human despair shown in cinematic terms and a prime example of the coordination of actress, director, and cameraman which can create a perfect moment of dramatic poetry upon the screen."

van had departed for the filming of *Jeopardy* (also 1953) with Barbara Stanwyck.

As part of her three-week holiday, Lana invited Fernando Lamas to accompany her to Acapulco, where a rented villa awaited them. During their time there, Lamas spent most of his time walking around the house and its pool area fully nude.

"Fernando gave the three Mexican houseboys, all of whom were gay, a real treat," Lana said.

In his own less-than-modest appraisal, Lamas told her, "If I had gone for boys instead of girls, the line would have formed outside my door."

At the end of her holiday, she returned to MGM, where Minnelli directed her to a car raised up on a contraption that simulated speed and motion. A crew stood by, some of them wearing heavy yellow slickers, with buckets of water, spray nozzles, and oversized sponges.

"Exactly what am I to do?" she asked Minnelli. "Give me some guidance."

"I don't have any," he admitted.

After sobering and cleaning her up, Shields (Douglas) is determined to make Georgia (Lana) into a major star. Here, he is seen directing "a movie within a movie."

This setting on a theatrical balcony is a testament to the visual compositions of director Vincente Minnelli.

"I really don't. You have to get into that car and pretend to drive away, gradually growing hysterical, knowing that Shields has left you for a younger woman. I have faith in you as an actress that you can pull this off."

Once seated behind the wheel of the car, she decided to draw upon her own life experience as a means of validating the scene. "It was my first stab at Method acting. Was I to become the female Marlon Brando or not?"

She later recalled that for inspiration, she drew upon the painful moments from her past when Tyrone Power had deserted her for Linda Christian. "Emotion welled up inside me as I pretended to drive. The water from a mock rainstorm began to hit my windshield. I was blinded through that, and my tears which came gushing were echoed by the gush of water against the windshield."

"Lana pulled it off in one take," Minnelli later asserted.

***

MGM didn't mind sounding a bit sleazy in its advertising of *The Bad and the Beautiful*. Included among its headlines was: *NO HOLDS BARRED IN THIS STORY OF A BLONDE WHO WANTED TO GO PLACES... AND A BIG SHOT WHO GOT HER THERE THE HARD WAY!*

After *The Bad and the Beautiful* was released, producer David O. Selznick was seen sneaking into a movie house in Pacific Palisades. He wanted to learn if he should sue Metro-Goldwyn-Mayer for libel.

As he sat through the movie, he did indeed recognize himself in the character of Jonathon Shields, including his habit of kicking off his shoes. John Houseman had also suffered working for Selznick, and in some respects, Selznick interpreted it as Houseman's revenge. "For John, it's payback time."

In a pivotal scene at the end of the movie, Barry Sullivan (left), Lana, and Dick Powell eavesdrop on a phone conversation that producer Walter Pidgeon is having with Jonathan Shields (Kirk Douglas).

Although the director has betrayed each of them in separate ways, it is sort of obvious that they are going to agree to be sucked into his whirlpool again—and work on his latest film.

David Thomson, Selznick's biographer, wrote, "He huffed and puffed, not sure whether to be flattered or offended. After thinking it over for several days, he decided not to sue MGM."

One critic defined the movie as "The most exacting detailed study of the dream factory ever presented in the movies from the grand homes of the stars to the funeral of Shields' father, where he pays mourners to show up."

One of her most consistently negative critics, Bosley Crowther of *The New York Times* wrote: "Lana Turner is an actress playing an actress and neither one is real. A howling act in a wildly racing auto—pure punk—is the top of her speed."

Many other reviewers disagreed, claiming that Lana's car scene was one of the most exciting sequences for a picture in a decade.

Author Jeanine Basinger wrote: "None of the sex symbols who have been touted as actresses—not Rita Hayworth or Ava Gardner or Elizabeth Taylor or Marilyn Monroe—have ever given such a fine performance as Lana did in *The Bad and the Beautiful*."

The *Los Angeles Times* wrote: "The film is *What Makes Sammy Run?* and has the bitter flavor of *Sunset Blvd.* and *All About Eve* and, like the latter, is told in flashbacks by Shields' victims."

***

The night before the Academy Award nominees were announced, Lana threw a party to celebrate *The Bad and the Beautiful*. She staunchly believed that it, along with her performance within it, would be nominated for Oscars. "I've waited a long time for this," she told Lamas and others.

But after the nominees were announced, and she was not included among them, she sank into despair. The other nominees included Lana's friend, Susan Hayward for *With a Song in My Heart*, as well as Joan Crawford for *Sudden Fear*, Bette Davis for *The Star*, and Julie Harris for *The Member of the Wedding*. Shirley Booth would ultimately walk off with the Oscar for her role in *Come Back, Little Sheba*.

Kirk Douglas had seen her before the nominations were announced. Whereas he'd been nominated as Best Actor for his performance in *The Bad and the Beautiful*, he lost the award to Gary Cooper for *High Noon*. The other nominees included Marlon Brando for *Viva Zapata!*; Alec Guinness for *The Lavender Hill Mob*; and José Ferrer for his stunning portrayal of Toulouse-Lautrec in *Moulin Rouge*.

The cast and crew of *The Bad and the Beautiful* had high hopes that it would be nominated for Best Picture of the Year, but it wasn't. That year's Best Picture was eventually awarded to Cecil B. DeMille's *The Greatest Show on Earth*, starring Betty Hutton, Cornel Wilde, James Stewart, Dorothy Lamour, and Gloria Grahame. Grahame did win the Best Supporting Actress Oscar, not for the circus picture, but for the character she portrayed in *The Bad and the Beautiful*.

The picture did, however, win a number of minor Oscars: Robert Surtees for Black and White Cinematography; Helen Rose for Best Black and White Costume Design; Charles Schnee for Best Adapted Screenplay; and Cedric Gibbons, Edward Carfagno, Edwin B. Willis, and Keogh Gleason for Art Direction and Set Decorations.

Lana complained to Minnelli and Houseman, "We might at least have been nominated, but Dore Schary was against us from the beginning. He doesn't think much of me as an actress, and he did absolutely nothing to sell our picture to the Academy, whereas other studios were wildly promoting their selections. It's not fair!"

***

In 1952, the gala event of the year in Hollywood was the big spectacular that Marion Davies, former mistress of press baron William Randolph Hearst, gave in honor of the gay crooner, Johnny Ray. *[Hearst had died in August of 1951. In the wake of his death, Davies had married Horace Brown.]*

During her preparations for the party, Davies had transformed her Beverly Hills mansion into five different nightclubs with an orchestra for each. Guests could choose which mock nightclub they wanted to sit in. They included replicas of New York's Stork Club and the Cocoanut Grove in Los Angeles.

Esther Williams attended the party with her husband, Ben Gage. They awaited three guests who were to be seated with them. Finally, they arrived: Fernando Lamas with Lana on one arm, and with Ava Gardner on the other. This helped fuel the persistent rumor that their communal friendship had evolved into a three-way.

Gardner's husband, Frank Sinatra, was appearing in Las Vegas at the time.

As Williams later revealed in a memoir, "The grouping that night may still hold Hollywood's alltime record for musical chairs and tangled libidos." Gardner had been the former lover of Lamas, and in time, Esther would marry him.

When Lamas excused himself to go to the men's room, he came back with a smirk on his face. "Guess what? Our guest of honor, Mr. Ray, followed me into the men's room."

"I trust you put on a good show for him?" Lana said.

"The biggest and the best."

During the course of the evening, although Lamas didn't exactly ignore Lana—he invited her to dance twice—he paid more attention to Gardner and to Williams. He said, "Too bad there's only one of me and three of you hot tamales."

Perhaps to get even with Lamas for this real or imagined slight, Lana provocatively eyed the entrance into Davies' party of the handsome, virile Lex Barker, Hollywood's most recent incarnation of Tarzan. Barker was immediately surrounded by five beautiful women. Although still married to the raven-haired beauty, Arlene Dahl, he'd come alone to the party.

"No wonder Lex was cast as Tarzan," Lana said. "I bet he has muscle in all the right places."

"It's not a muscle, darling," Gardner said. "If it was a muscle, it would grow bigger by exercise. That means Frankie's would stretch around the block."

Lamas, who heard Lana's off-color remark, looked furious but said nothing.

About half an hour later, Barker approached their table, temporarily deserting his colony of female admirers. Ignoring Lamas, he asked Lana to dance.

On the floor, he held her in a tight embrace, a style not unlike that of Lamas during his courtly waltzes with Lana that appeared at the beginning of *The Merry Widow*.

Back then, in his capacity as the film's director, Curtis Bernhardt had intervened. "Lamas, you're supposed to be doing the waltz with Lana, not fucking her. Move apart a bit."

Now, years later, having observed Barker and Lana dancing sensuously together, Lamas began raging to both Williams and Gardner: "Jungle Boy is fucking her right on the dance floor." Then, in anger, he rose from his seat and headed toward the couple. When he reached them, he grabbed Lana by the shoulder and spun her around. He then turned angrily onto Barker. *"WHY*

What this picture doesn't show is how handsome, muscled, well-endowed Lex Barker, the screen Tarzan, hugged Lana up close. He'd unzipped and invited her to "take a feel."

DON'T YOU JUST TAKE HER OUT INTO THE BUSHES AND FUCK HER?" he said. His voice was loud enough to be heard by several of the dancing couples, who stopped dancing and stared at them.

Lana became instantly furious, slapping Lamas as hard as she could.

"You fucking cunt!" he yelled at her, giving the impression that he was about to strike her.

She rushed from the dance floor, nearly tripping, and headed for the exit after grabbing her mink. Lamas was on her trail.

As he descended the steps of the Davies mansion, a starlet, Jane Denier, surveyed the situation and reactively threw her arms around Lamas, telling him what a handsome stud he was. "You don't need Lana Turner," she said. "You look divine and you've got me." Then she tried to kiss him, but he picked her up and tossed her into the swimming pool.

A photographer was on the scene, and he shot the actress emerging—soaking wet, furious, and humiliated—from the pool. The picture appeared in the tabloids the following day.

[Denier would later play Dulcinea in one of the Broadway productions of Man of La Mancha.*]*

With Lamas behind the wheel, the couple's ride home was in silence. Once inside Lana's foyer, he slapped her so hard that her diamond earring shot across the hall. She tried to deliver a kick to his groin with her sequined shoe, but before it landed, he grabbed her right ankle and sent her sprawling across the marble floor.

With his fiery temper unleashed, he kicked her several times in the ribs before bending over her and striking her face twice, bloodying her nose. She raised her hands to protect her face from his blows.

Before he could inflict any more damage, he stormed out of the house, slamming the door behind him—never to return. The next day, someone came by for his clothes and possessions.

The next morning, Lana arrived at MGM badly bruised. Production had already begun on *Latin Lovers,* a movie, eventually released in 1953, that she'd been filming with Lamas as her co-star.

She put through a call to Benjamin Thau, head of MGM's casting, asking him to come to her dressing room. Sensing serious trouble, Thau was there within fifteen minutes, finding Lana a mess of bruises and scratches.

She burst into tears, sharing all the trauma of her bitter fistfight with Lamas. "He said the most vile things to me that anyone has ever said in my life," she sobbed. "He told me my pussy's been used so much it's like a limp dishrag. He accused me of being a lousy lay and claimed that he had to jack off to achieve orgasm since I couldn't do it for him. Crap like that."

She finally delivered an ultimatum: "I will not do the picture with Lamas. Go back to your original choice: Ricardo Montalban."

Under the circumstances, Thau acquiesced.

In her column the next day, Louella Parsons wrote: "I assume Lana Turner was shocked, as all of us were, at some of the things that Fernando Lamas said to her last night."

Shooting was delayed for ten days. During that interim, Montalban agreed to co-star with Lana. MGM announced that he would be replacing Lamas in the movie.

Lamas' days at MGM were now numbered. It wouldn't be long before Dore Schary "pink-slipped" him.

In October of 1952, Lana spoke to the press about the breakup. "It was just one of those things, like a Cole Porter song. We're still friends, but as far as romance is concerned, that's out. From now on, I'm interested in only one person—and that's Lana Turner."

Lamas spoke to the press, too. "I am an ordinary man with the ordinary defects and faults. I am human, thank God. I suffer, I love, I hate. About Lana, I have nothing to say. Because there is nothing. It is over! You read a good book, a beautiful book. You come to the end. You close it. That's it! The end!"

***

Among a different trio of bigtime movie stars, it was a week that began with violence and ended with violence. In this incident, in addition to Lana, the threesome also included Frank Sinatra and Ava Gardner. Lana, of course, had seduced Sinatra before Gardner ever discovered his charms.

"Frank can turn deadly on a moment's notice," Lana warned her friend. "Once, when I angered him, he threatened to have one of his gangster friends scar my face."

"I adored Ava, but she was a very strong-willed woman," Lana said. "She didn't take my advice about Artie Shaw, my first husband, and she went on to marry him. That marriage was a fiasco. And she didn't take my advice about Frank and she married him, too. Another fiasco."

When Sinatra was on the East Coast, he'd heard rumors that Gardner had resumed her affair with Howard Hughes despite her many rejections of him. Sometimes, her interchanges with Hughes became violent. On one occasion, she threw a lamp at him, causing a concussion. Even so, he had never completely abandoned his

For Sinatra, before there was Ava (the love of his life, lower photo), there was Lana (upper photo.). He was not the only man "shared" by the two Love Goddesses.

attempts to entangle her in his web.

"In those days, Frank had spies all over Hollywood feeding him information on Ava's private life," said columnist James Bacon. "Count me as one of them. I was always hoping for a scoop—nothing wrong with that."

When Sinatra flew back to Los Angeles, he headed immediately to a confrontation with Gardner, to whom he was married at the time. He thought he'd catch her with Hughes. Instead, he found her with her shoes off, her feet propped up on a coffee table, listening to his records.

He quickly accused her of two-timing him with Hughes. She fought back, claiming that the aviator, who had spies of his own, had provided her with detailed evidence of his philandering with prostitutes in New York. She also admitted that it had been Hughes who had arranged for one of Sinatra's mistresses to send her an embarrassing and incriminating letter the day before she married him.

It was all too much for Sinatra. He'd been drinking heavily all day, and he wanted revenge on Hughes. In one of the worst rages of his life, he wrecked the living room, but didn't physically attack Gardner.

Then he grabbed a bottle of Jack Daniels from the bar and, with a .38 pistol in his jacket, he set out in a drunken rage to shoot Hughes. "I don't want to wound him. I want to kill him."

Immediately after Sinatra stormed out of the house, Gardner phoned Hughes, urging him to fly out of town at once. The billionaire accepted that as good advice.

Sinatra never found Hughes, and finally, at 3AM, he abandoned his search, spending the night in the home of a musician friend.

Three weeks passed before Sinatra attempted a reconciliation with Gardner. In early October of 1952, he finally reached her on the phone. "I'm crazy for you, honey," he said. She agreed to have dinner with him and, for two days and nights, as she related to her sister, Bappie, "We made love in every known position, even inventing a few of our own."

On October 18, they dined together at Chasen's. Under the influence of a bottle of Jack Daniels, he undiplomatically raised the subject of Hughes once again. Their fight raged all that way back to the house at Pacific Palisades where they were staying. Once inside, she didn't speak to him, as he fumed.

She decided to take a bubble bath and was relaxing and easing her tension when all of a sudden, he barged into her bathroom, denouncing her as "nothing but a Tarheel whore."

She ordered him out of the house. "Okay, doll, I'll get out. You can find me in Palm Springs. I'll be there fucking Lana Turner."

"Fuck Minnie Mouse for all I care," she answered, shouting.

The previous week on the MGM lot, he had encountered his old flame, Lana herself. She had maintained her friendships with both members of the battling couple. "What's up, doll?" Sinatra asked her.

"I'm taking a week off in Palm Springs. I'm calling a realtor about a rental."

"Forget it," he told her. "My place is yours. It's available this weekend, since I'm tied up with work here in L.A."

"That's wonderful, dear," she said. "I'll pay you what you think it's worth."

"Come on, Lana," he said. "We're friends from way back. Come to my dressing room. I'll give you the key."

That weekend, Lana decided that she didn't want to spend time alone in Palm Springs. Based on her recent experience with Greg Tolson and Ava Gardner, she knew that the best place to pick up a well-built young escort was at Scotty Bower's gas station at Hollywood Boulevard at Fairfax.

Desperate for non-judgmental male companionship, she drove her car to the gas station. The first gas jockey who approached her was good-looking enough, but she was more attracted to another well-built man, who sat on a nearby bench, seemingly waiting for a customer. He sat on that bench with his legs apart, his obvious sex appeal clearly visible—in pants far too tight.

The negotiations that ensued were successful. Within an hour, they were naked together and inside her house, sharing a bubble bath.

The twenty-year-old had been born in Minnesota and had served in the Marines during the war. She later defined him as, "a Guy Madison lookalike with blonde hair and a muscled body. He name was Don Johnson (not the future star of *Miami Vice*). He had come to Hollywood to break into the movies either as an actor or as a stage hand.

She invited him to spend a week as her guest in Palm Springs, asking him to be her driver. It was just assumed that his additional duties would continue within in her bed.

Feeling uneasy about spending an entire week with a strange man, she also

Either real or imagined, *Confidential* magazine, the leading scandal tabloid of its day, kept up with the indiscretions of both Lana and Ava Gardner when they were not otherwise writing about Marilyn Monroe.

invited her business manager and agent, Benton Cole.

The plot began to thicken as characters moved onto the stage to play out one of the most scandalous dramas in the scandal-soaked history of Palm Springs.

Before departing for the desert, Lana ordered her cook to prepare a large pan of fried chicken, with the intention of bringing it with them.

Johnson, Cole and their communal hostess, Lana, arrived early enough in Palm Springs that day to enjoy an afternoon beside Sinatra's pool.

Thinking that she had the house entirely to herself and her guests, Lana looked forward to days of rest and recuperation as her nerves were frayed. She delighted in the beauty of bikini-clad Johnson by the pool. Cole was usually off-premises, taking care of business.

Meanwhile, alone and fuming in Hollywood, Gardner began to stew over Sinatra's threat to shack up with Lana over the weekend. She telephoned her sister, Bappie, announcing, "I'm gonna go to Palm Springs, where I'm gonna catch that bastard in the act."

One account has Bappie driving with her sister to Palm Springs; another report has her staying in Los Angeles and warning her sister not to go.

Regardless, Gardner traveled to Palm Springs to a location near Sinatra's house. Removing her shoes, she scampered over the six-foot chain link fence behind the Sinatra villa, even though she knew it might be infested with deadly sidewinders (rattlesnakes). The curtains of her husband's house were drawn, but

One of the great scandals of Hollywood in the 1950s was what happened that weekend in Frank Sinatra's villa in Palm Springs.

Some of the most lurid gossip in the history of that resort was spun after Frank Sinatra barged in. What he saw erupted into a fight that prompted police intervention. They arrived with dome lights flashing.

as a jealously obsessed "peeping Tom," she tried to peek inside, hoping to catch Sinatra in a compromising position.

It was at this point that Cole exited through the Sinatra villa's back door carrying a container of garbage. He was surprised to see Gardner, his client, lurking there and immediately invited her inside.

Lana was startled to see her, too, explaining Sinatra's invitation. Gardner was introduced to Johnson, and she appraised his body. Out of earshot of the young man, she whispered to Lana, "Buy me some of that, momma!"

"I already have. From the gas station, of course."

"It's gonna be a fun weekend, *honey chile!*" Gardner said.

"No stranger to nudity, Gardner began shedding her clothes. "Let's go skinny dipping like I used to do in North Carolina."

During this nude romp with Johnson and Lana, Gardner waved Cole away. He wisely retreated to his bedroom to read a book and to listen to Sinatra recordings.

What happened after that only became known when Johnson later tried to hawk the details of the notorious weekend to *Confidential* magazine. Editors indeed published an article, but it was more or less "a vanilla account," since the publisher, Robert Harrison, feared a libel suit.

The hustler claimed that by 6PM, he was in bed with both Lana and Ava. "I was shocked that Ava had a lesbian streak in her. But most of the attention was focused on my best asset. They really worked me over. I was one lucky guy. Fortunately, I've always been known for my stamina."

"Later, we got out of bed and headed for Sinatra's bar," Johnson claimed. "All of us had had a little too much to drink, and we were feeling no pain. Cole wasn't part of the action. He stayed more or less by himself. At one point, we got really hungry. That's when Lana revealed that her cook had fried a mess of chicken. We headed to the kitchen. Needless to say, all three of us had almost nothing on. We finished off some chicken and two bottles of wine before heading back to the bedroom."

"About two hours later, Ava, Lana, and I were enjoying a daisy chain when suddenly the door was thrown open," Johnson revealed in his report to Harrison. "I lost my hard-on…and fast. There stood Sinatra in the harsh light he'd flipped on. There was murder in those fierce eyes of his."

"Many stories have been published about that night, but almost no one has got it right," Johnson continued. "I'm left out of most accounts. And Barbara Payton, that blonde actress who became a prostitute, later insisted that she was with Lana and Ava, and that she jumped out the window and ran when Sinatra barged in. Yeah, right!"

[In her memoirs, Gardner revealed that Lana had invited a "boyfriend" to Sinatra's house.]

"Get out of this house, you fucking dykes!" Sinatra shouted at Ava and Lana. "And take this two-bit hustler with you!"

"I'd heard that Sinatra always carried a gun, and I jumped out of bed and ran past the crazy fucker," Johnson said. "I managed to escape with just a pair of jockey shorts. I was too young to die. Out on the main highway, I flagged down the first car coming. Was I in luck!"

"A Cadillac stopped," he said. "In the front seat sat two queens of the lisping variety. Instead of looking at my face, they eyed the bulge, and invited me to hop inside. I spent the rest of the weekend with them and emerged Monday with two suits of clothes and five hundred dollars in my pocket, plus a steady gig with them in the future. So my weekend in Palm Springs wasn't a total disaster. At least Sinatra didn't shoot me. By the way, I hate all his romantic mood music. I'm a Hank Williams fan."

With Johnson gone, Sinatra stood over Gardner, threatening to strike her. Trembling but defiant, she blurted out, "You want to fuck Lana Turner? There she is. Go at it!"

"Are you kidding?" he answered. "I wouldn't fuck this broken-down blonde if she were the last woman on earth."

In tears, Lana ran from the bedroom into the living room, where Cole waited with a coat to cover her nude body.

At the sound of violence from the bedroom, they fled from the house. Unfortunately, Lana's baggage remained in the master bedroom, where Sinatra and Gardner were battling.

"Frank's got a gun," she warned Cole.

Racing out into the night, they got into her car and drove to a small resort that rented villas by the week. Fortunately, one of them was available, and they made arrangements to stay there, planning to return to Frank's house to retrieve her clothes later.

Meanwhile, back in Sinatra's bedroom, "with red face and blazing eyes," he assaulted Gardner, kicking her in the rear as she darted from the bedroom into an adjoining room where she had stashed her clothing.

"I want you out of this house...and now!" he shouted. "You fucking Tarheel dyke whore!"

In Kitty Kelley's biography of Sinatra, entitled *His Way*, Gardner was quoted as saying, "I'll get the hell out of the house, but since this is also my house, I'm gonna take out everything that belongs to me. I started taking down pictures from the wall and Frank exploded. He grabbed everything I said was mine and hurled it outside onto the lawn. He was hysterical."

As the finale of his farewell to Gardner, he raced upstairs to the bathroom and filled her douche bag with water. Back out on the front lawn, he poured water from it over her. "Have a great time fucking Grace Kelly and Clark Gable in Africa, you slutty bitch."

[She had signed to film Mogambo *(1953) with those two stars.]*

After checking into her rented villa with Cole, Lana feared for Gardner's safety and persuaded him to drive back to Sinatra's house with her. When they pulled up in front, they saw two police cars with dome lights flashing. Spotlights illuminated the villa.

The front door was open, and Sinatra was tossing out Gardner's possessions as well as Lana's luggage.

Lana remained inside the car as Cole identified himself and was able to retrieve Lana's belongings. When Cole returned to the car, Lana asked him to give the policeman the address of the villa where they were staying, inviting Gardner to join them.

To back up Johnson's revelation about what transpired that night, an F.B.I. report released after Sinatra's death mentioned an "unnamed young man who claimed that he had had sex in Sinatra's house with both Ava Gardner and Lana Turner."

When Sinatra finally retreated into his house, bolting the door, Gardner found herself surrounded by her possessions on the front lawn. She was informed of Lana's invitation as the policemen gathered up her belongings for transport to the villa where Lana and Cole had moved.

Once there, Hollywood's blonde beauty offered the sultry brunette a stiff drink—both of them needed one. Then it was off to bed for both of them. Cole slept in a motel nearby.

"Poor Ava," Lana recorded in her memoirs. "She was badly shaken, and after my own grim experience, I could sympathize with her humiliation. I also felt sorry for Frank. It was a bad time for him. His career had slipped badly…and he was losing Ava."

The next morning, headlines in the *Los Angeles Times* asserted SINATRA-AVA BOUDOIR ROW BUZZES. The *Los Angeles Daily Mirror* claimed BOUDOIR FIGHT HEADS FRANK AND AVA TO COURTS.

Sinatra tried to reach Gardner, but she'd changed her phone number. He never found out that by now, Fernando Lamas, Lana's discarded Latin lover, was warming her bed at night.

Desperate to reach Gardner, Sinatra was a nervous wreck, and he often vomited. In desperation, he called Earl Wilson, his columnist friend, and begged him to print his plea for a reconciliation in the wake of the Palm Springs scandal. Wilson published the item under the headline FRANKIE READY TO SURRENDER, WANTS AVA BACK.

Somehow, that won her over, and a reconciliation was arranged. When Lana heard about their getting back together again, she asked Cole, "How long do you think it will last?"

"Oh, a few days, maybe weeks, perhaps months, I seriously doubt a whole year. Soon Frank will be on the stage in Las Vegas singing to his loyal fans his rendition of "The Birth of the Blues."

***

With Fernando Lamas out the door, Lana was primed for a new love affair, almost demanding it as her "divine right."

She surveyed the field of possible lovers. Her playing field was very large, and she was receiving offers almost daily.

Late one afternoon, her maid called her to the phone. "Miss Turner, it's the Ape Man. You know…Tarzan, who's always swinging from a vine. He wants you. I wonder why?"

...and then, in Lana's life, there was Lex

Lex Barker, also known as Tarzan and/or "The Perfect Specimen," became the new man in Lana's life. His most devoted fans consider him "the reincarnation of Adam created by God himself as the ideal male animal."

As noted in the February 7, 1949 review of *Tarzan's Magic Fountain, The New York Times* wrote: "Johnny Weissmuller finally has swung down from his jungle throne after sixteen years. RKO is launching its new muscle king, Lex Barker. and score one for Mr. Barker. A younger, more streamlined ape-man with a personable grin and a torso guaranteed to make any lion cringe, he seems just what the witch-doctor ordered for this tattered series."

Chapter Fourteen

Tarzan, The Apeman, Swings into the Life of Lana Turner

The Loincloth Hid His "Biggest, Deepest, & Darkest Secret"

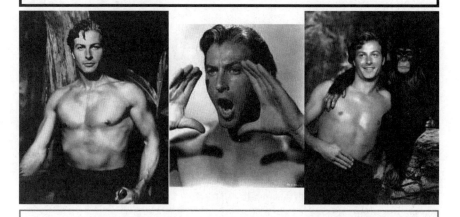

Lana found Lex Barker a male beauty, perhaps the sexiest man she'd ever met in Hollywood, all encased in a magnificent physique, an athletic, 6'4" sculpted frame.

He never achieved his dream of becoming the leading matinee idol of the 1950s, but his magnificent body and striking physique have given him a cult following that exists even as the world moves deeper into the 21st Century. Today, gay men keep alive his memory and continue to collect pinup pictures of him, often decorating the walls of their bathrooms.

His rival in love affairs was Fernando Lamas, hailing from Buenos Aires. Both of these hunks became embroiled in the lives of what was often called "the two most beautiful women in Hollywood: Flame-haired Arlene Dahl and the blonde goddess, Lana Turner. But whereas Dahl married both men, Lana only shacked up with Lamas before walking down the aisle with Tarzan himself.

At the debut of the Eisenhower era in 1953, "Lex & Fernando," although completely different types, were the two most sought after lovers in Hollywood. Women swooned over stories of their "fabulous endowments."

After Fernando Lamas was fired from *Latin Lovers* (1953), and replaced with his main rival, the Mexican actor, Ricardo Montalban, Lana reported to work at MGM.

Her former mentor, Mervyn LeRoy, had been assigned as its director. Joe Pasternak, who had produced *The Merry Widow*, was also producing *Latin Lovers*.

LeRoy greeted her with kisses on both cheeks and a strong embrace. He invited her into his office, where she expected him to discuss her breakup with Lamas, but he didn't mention it. Actually, he had other troubles of his own he wanted to tell her about.

He had brought her with him from Warners to MGM, but he had long grown disillusioned with Metro, mainly because of Dore Schary. LeRoy had worked relatively smoothly with Louis B. Mayer, but not with his replacement.

"Schary and I just don't see eye-to-eye on anything," he said. "We've bickered so much that by now, we're hardly speaking. After I finish a couple of films, I'm leaving MGM for good, abandoning my $5,000-a-week salary. Schary wants me to do a remake of *The Student Prince,* but I'm bolting. I can't take his constant nagging anymore."

This sexy dance with Ricardo Montalban in *Latin Lovers* was about as romantic as Lana got with the Mexican actor.

"Would you believe it?" she asked Mervyn LeRoy. "A leading man who's faithful to his wife?"

"I'm shocked," she said. "You've been so successful here. As for myself, I may be called The Queen of MGM, but I fear my crown is a little shaky."

LeRoy rose to his feet. "Come, let's meet your two leading men, Montalban and John Lund, and the supporting players. Most of them are here for a rehearsal."

A romantic musical comedy in Technicolor, *Latin Lovers* was written by Isobel Lennart, who had penned Lana's screenplay, *A Life of Her Own.* In this latest venture, Lana was cast as a rich girl, Nora Taylor, worth $37 million. She arrives in Brazil, where she fears men only want to pursue her for her money.

Her current suitor, Paul Chevron (Lund), wants to marry her, but hardly for her money. He has about $10 million more than she does.

In Brazil, she meets dashing Roberto Santos (Montalban), who sweeps her off her feet. His father, Eduardo, is played by her old friend, Louis Calhern, with whom she'd work again in the future.

During the making of the film, Debbie Reynolds gave a party to which she invited Montalban and Lana. The gathering was actually in honor of the dancing duo, Marge and Gower Champion. In a memoir, Reynolds wrote: "Lana Turner and Ricardo Montalban did the rumba in the center of the floor as Jennifer Jones sat on the floor observing."

That sexy party dance was about as romantic as Montalban and Lana ever got, except for on the screen, where she found him a good kisser. If she thought she had encountered another Latin lover, she was mistaken. He was a devout Roman Catholic, and he did not cheat on his wife. He had married Georgiana Belzer in 1944, the half-sister of Loretta Young. Apparently, he was faithful to his wife until her death at the age of 83 in 2007. The actor himself died in 2009.

When Lana met him, Montalban had been thrown off a horse during the filming of *Across the Wide Missouri* (1951), starring Clark Gable. The traumatic injury never healed, the pain increasing as he aged. He ended his life in a wheelchair.

Although Lana and the actor never became lovers, they did develop a friendship that lasted for many years.

She had a chance to work with Jean Hagen again, having appeared previously with her in *A Life of Her Own*. In *Latin Lovers,* she played Anne, Lana's secretary, who is secretly in love with Paul Chevorn (Lund). Lana congratulated her on her Oscar nomination for her performance in *Singin' in the Rain* (1952).

Referring to her role, Hagen said, "It takes talent to play a talentless movie star," referring to her performance in *Singin' in the Rain* as the silent screen star with the squeaky voice, Lina Lamont.

Lana was introduced to Eduard Franz, who had been a stage actor for twenty years, finally appearing in his movie debut in the 1948 *The Wake of the Red Witch,* starring John Wayne. Privately, Lana told LeRoy, "Franz is a nice guy, but rather nondescript, a second stringer."

She also was introduced to the aging character actress, Beulah Bondi, born in 1889. She'd begun her theatrical career as a child. She'd twice been nominated for a Best Supporting Actress Oscar, first in *The Gorgeous Hussy* (1936), where she was seen as the devoted, pipe-smoking wife of Andrew Jackson. Her other nomination came for *Of Human Hearts (1938),* when she played the compassionate, self-sacrificing mother of James Stewart.

"The plot of *Latin Lovers* was silly," Lana said. "But I looked gorgeous as a real clotheshorse, wearing those incredible gowns by Helen Rose."

421

"Beulah is definitely the hair-in-a-bun archetype of motherhood," Lana told LeRoy.

She merely shook the hand of Rita Moreno, not realizing that this talented young woman would go on to win an Oscar, a Tony, an Emmy, and a Grammy. She assured herself a position in film history when she played the role of Anita in the 1961 film version of *West Side Story*.

Romantically adrift, Lana had no sexual interest in her second leading man, John Lund, the son of a Norwegian immigrant and glassblower from Rochester, New York.

On the set of *Latin Lovers*, Lana confers with her two leading men, Ricardo Montalban (left) and John Lund.

"They pursued me romantically in the movie, but not off screen. Was I losing my sex appeal? Lex Barker didn't think so."

He didn't finish high school and worked at odd jobs: soda jerk, carpenter, timekeeper. Eventually, he made it to Hollywood and won a co-starring role in *To Each His Own* (1946) with Olivia de Havilland.

Although always saddled with a reputation as a second tier leading man, he appeared with such stars as Gene Tierney, Miriam Hopkins, Joan Fontaine, and Grace Kelly. He is remembered today mostly for playing the romantic interest of both Marlene Dietrich and Jean Arthur in *A Foreign Affair* (1948),

Originally, Lana had been slated to appear with Michael Wilding, the English actor married at the time to Elizabeth Taylor. He dropped out at the last minute, protesting that the role was "too stuffy and not real star material." Lund then won the part.

MGM promoted *Latin Lovers* with this ad: "*The Bad and Beautiful* girl is bad and beautiful again in a wonderful new musical. *The New York Times* praised the dancing of Lana and Montalban.

Most critics were fairly kind, although recognizing *Latin Lovers* for what it was—"a wonderful piece of fluff," in the words of one critic. "Gorgeous people, gorgeous gowns, beautiful Technicolor, dreamy surroundings…a parfait!"

***

Three days after Fernando Lamas stormed out of Lana's house, following his violent attack on her, Lex Barker phoned her for a dinner date. It was agreed that she'd have dinner with him at Chasens, followed by dancing at the Mocambo.

It was later revealed that Lamas might have had good reason for his harsh reaction to Barker holding Lana so tightly on the dance floor. As Barker told Sol

Lesser—the producer of his last Tarzan picture, *Tarzan and the She-Devil (1953)*—Barker had whispered to Lana while holding her close, "I'm unzipped. Reach inside to find out that I'm bigger than Lamas."

Lana and Barker had met when he was a free agent. His short marriage in 1951 to the raven-haired beauty, Arlene Dahl, had ended in 1952.

Before going out with Barker, Lana met with Eddie Mannix at MGM's publicity department, knowing that he could reveal all the vital data on him.

She had never seen one of his Tarzan movies before, although she'd had a brief fling with Johnny Weissmuller, the most famous of all the screen Tarzans.

Mannix informed Lana that Barker wasn't all muscles, but the well-educated son of a rich Canadian building contractor, and a direct descendant of Rogers Williams, the founder of Rhode Island.

After his graduation from Phillips Exeter Academy, where he had played football, he attended Princeton. But in time, he dropped out to join a theatrical stock company, much to the objection of his stern father.

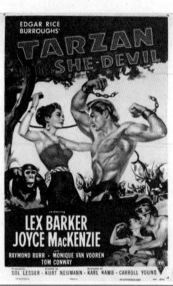

He was disowned by his family for pursuing an acting career, and worked for a time in a steel mill, studying engineering at night. He launched his fledging acting career in bit parts on Broadway, but entered World War II, enlisting in the U.S. Army, where he rose to the rank of Major. In Sicily, he'd been wounded in both the leg and head. He recovered in an Arkansas military hospital.

While still in the Army, in 1942, he'd married Constance Rhodes Thurlow, but divorced her eight years later. She was the daughter of a wealthy metal manufacturer. In 1943, Barker became the father of a daughter, Lynn Thurlow Barker, and in 1947, a son, Alexander ("Zan") Crichlow Barker III.

Barker gravitated to Hollywood. Even though married, he attracted the eye of many a lustful actress and a number of homosexuals lured to his physique.

In *The Farmer's Daughter* (1947), he had appeared as one of Loretta Young's Swedish brothers. He also had a small role in *Mr. Blandings Builds His Dream House* (1948) with Cary Grant. It was rumored that Grant invited Barker on several occasions to his dressing room, where he performed fellatio

Of all the movie posters depicting all the many actors who played Tarzan, this 1953 poster was viewed as the winner of the "high camp" prize.

Tarzan and the She-Devil was Barker's final film as Tarzan. When it was finished, he put his loincloth in mothballs and went on to make other movies, many of them in German.

But despite his many subsequent films over the course of a 25-year career, he is best remembered as the tenth actor to portray Tarzan in the movies.

on him. "At least I did it standing up and didn't have to lie on any casting couch," Barker later said, jokingly, to the director, H.C. Potter.

Barker's national fame came late in 1948, when producer Sol Lesser signed him to be the new screen Tarzan in the 1949 release of *Tarzan's Magic Fountain*. Brenda Joyce, cast as Jane, had recently made *Tarzan and the Mermaids* with Johnny Weissmuller. But by 1948, Lesser deemed the Austrian athlete as "too paunchy" to play the screen's Apeman again.

Since Lana had never seen Barker in a Tarzan movie, Mannix arranged screenings for her of his features in the jungle. Lana was tremendously impressed with his physique in action when she sat through *Tarzan and the Slave Girl* (1950), in which Vanessa Brown co-starred as Jane. Lana had signaled her interest in meeting Barker back when Brown had a small role in *The Bad and the Beautiful*.

When Barker had gone on to star in *Tarzan's Peril* (1951), his striking looks attracted the eye of a new Jane, Virginia Huston. During the shooting of that movie, Tarzan did not mind crossing the color line when he seduced the African American actress, Dorothy Dandridge, cast as Queen Melmendi.

Lana's objection to this film was based on how Huston had kissed Barker "a little too passionately" when he rescues her at the end of the film.

Lana also saw *Tarzan's Savage Fury* (1952), with a new Jane, Dorothy Hart, who had made her film debut in the light-hearted musical fantasy, *Down to Earth* (1947), starring Rita Hayworth.

Barker's last appearance on screen as Tarzan was in the 1953 *Tarzan and the She-Devil*. Its villain was Raymond Burr, who specialized in the portrayal of dark, menacing heavies as he would soon again in Alfred Hitchcock's *Rear Window* (1954), starring James Stewart and Grace Kelly. In that movie, Burr was cast as Vargo, a greedy ivory hunter who wanted to slay elephants and harvest their ivory tusks.

Lyra, the "She-Devil" of the movie, was portrayed by the beautiful, sexy, Monique Van Vooren (not to be confused with Mamie Van Doren). She plays a cold-blooded profiteer willing to slaughter elephants and to enslave men.

In his final Tarzan picture, Barker faced a new Jane, Joyce MacKenzie, the eleventh actress to shoulder the role. During World War II, she had worked as a carpenter's helper in the shipyards of San Francisco.

At the end of the picture, Barker told Lesser that throughout the production, Burr had been making homosexual advances toward him. After a sweaty scene on the set, he retreated to his shower. Burr entered the room and pulled open the shower curtain.

"I just had to see it, even though you won't let me service it," Burr said.

"Get the hell out of here!" Barker snapped.

After the last film, although Lesser told Barker that he could go on for many more years playing the screen Tarzan, Barker wanted out, hoping to become a leading man in a higher caliber of films, playing both adventure and dramatic roles.

His career, as happens so often life, didn't work out exactly as he desired.

***

Barker's first dinner date with Lana was a disaster. Over dinner, the talk was elegant, even intelligent, as he appeared well bred. At the same time, he vibrated with sex appeal. In a town loaded with handsome men, his good looks and imposing physique were fast becoming legendary. "Even our waiter went gushy over Lex," Lana later revealed.

During their drive back to her house, she decided to extend the evening by inviting him inside for a night cap, perhaps thinking it might lead to a seduction. He'd had only one glass of wine over dinner.

Settling into her living room, he requested a brandy and appeared delighted that she had stocked a favorite of his, Rémy Martin. Unknown to her, a doctor had prescribed some medication that afternoon with a warning, "Don't drink any alcohol."

The gossip heated up when Arlene Dahl, freshly divorced from Barker, began dating Fernando Lamas, who had freshly broken up with Lana. The duo of intertwined romances was referred to with headlines that included "Change Partners and Dance."

Unlike Lana, Dahl went on to marry Lamas in 1954, a union lasting until 1960. In 1958, she gave birth to his son, Lorenzo Lamas, who became an actor.

She poured brandy for each of them into a pair of pony glasses. To her surprise, as she revealed in her memoirs, he downed his in a single gulp. Not only that, but he requested another glass, which he swallowed just as fast. Then a third, even a fourth, and finally, a fifth. By now, she was filling the glass only half-full, as she feared he might be an alcoholic like Bob Topping, the husband she'd just divorced.

When Barker tried to stand up, he collapsed, fell over, and fainted. She checked to confirm that he was still alive, and prayed that he had not suffered a heart attack. He seemed to be breathing satisfactorily.

Fearing negative publicity, and not knowing what to do, she phoned her former agent, Henry Willson. Even though he no longer represented her, their friendship had endured. Considering his background he must have known what to do with a drunken sailor, marine, lumberjack, movie actor, or studio grip.

When he heard that Barker had passed out on her floor, Willson, as she later told her friends, "arrived almost panting." In her memoir, she didn't identify Willson directly, referring to him instead as "Bob."

Within half an hour, Willson was at her home, examining the unconscious body on her floor, perhaps a little too intimately for her tastes. He agreed to remove Barker from her premises. She knew that he lived in a little house off Olympic Boulevard. Willson searched his pockets, again probing rather deeply, until he found his set of keys.

It took great effort on Willson's part, but he finally carried the heavy dead weight of the very muscular Tarzan and transferred him into the back seat of his car. Lana drove ahead in her car.

With Barker's limp body, Willson drove to the actor's home. Its entrance was accessible via a steep flight of steps. Willson finally managed to haul the body to the door of what Lana defined as "a little doll's house."

In her memoirs, she described Barker as "inanimate as a chest of drawers, and twice as bulky." Willson finally got the hunk onto his bed and then turned to Lana. "Shall I undress him?"

Her advice: "Let's get the hell out of here."

In fact, however, Willson did the opposite, deciding to stay and "guard" Barker though the night, beginning with stripping him nude after she left.

What he did to the body that night remains unrecorded. Only one tantalizing detail has surfaced.

The following afternoon, Barker met with Lesser, the producer of the Tarzan movies, telling him that his decision to leave the role remained solid.

Over a late lunch, he also revealed that he had passed out at Lana's house the night before. "I was overly medicated. When I woke up the next morning, I found my limp dick buried down Henry Willson's overworked throat."

***

After his lunch with Lesser, Barker phoned Lana with profuse apologies for having passed out the night before, explaining that he had been medicated and should not have drunk her brandy. Before his call, he'd sent her two dozen red, long-stemmed roses.

She finally agreed to go out with him again, with the provision that there were "no repeat performances like last night." He didn't mention catching Henry Willson in bed with him when he'd awakened the following morning.

On their second date, another night of dinner and dancing, he was at his most charming, seductive best, and only drank mineral water. She invited him for a sleepover, the details of which became known when she phoned Virginia Grey in the morning to deliver a full report.

"Lex is hung with a 'Capital H,' Lana announced. "On the Hollywood Walk of Fame, his penis should be immortalized in cement. His directors in those Tarzan movies made him wear a heavy-duty jockstrap so it wouldn't flop out. It's said that Victor Mature, for whom I can personally vouch, and John Ireland have the biggest cocks in Hollywood. I'd like Lex to enter the contest. Perhaps you and I can summon the trio to gather together for a measuring contest."

"I think not, my dear," Grey said. "Don't you think you're getting carried away?"

"He's a great lover," she said. "Passionate yet tender. Hits all the hot spots. He is demanding yet fulfilling. Both of our needs were fulfilled in every way."

"Stop! You're getting me hot, and it's been a long time since any man has warmed my bed. As you know, Clark wouldn't marry me and has found another wife." Her reference, of course, was to Clark Gable.

After his sleepover, Barker came by nightly for extended visits. As she confessed in writing, "He began occupying all my free time. I fell in love again, slowly at first, but surely."

In the ensuing weeks, entire forests were felled in Canada for the paper needed to print the news of Lana's latest romance.

Lana and Barker flew to Aspen for a vacation. She later defined it as "the most romantic days of my entire life. At last, I've found the man who can make me forget Ty Power. I might have been closer to Ty as a spiritual soulmate, but when it came to raw sex, Lex is my man. No man has ever equaled Lex in my bed."

***

Ava Gardner dropped in at Lana's house, excited to be flying to Africa for the filming of *Mogambo* alongside Clark Gable, her former co-star and lover, and Grace Kelly. Gardner had been cast as "Honey Bear," a vivacious American showgirl trying to forget.

The movie was actually a remake of Gable's 1932 *Red Dust*, in which he had co-starred with Jean Harlow and Mary Astor.

[What Lana didn't tell Gardner was that she had previously been offered the role of Honey Bear, weeks before it was eventually assigned to Gardner. Benny Thau at MGM had offered Lana her choice of two roles: Mogambo *in Africa or* Flame and the Flesh, *to be shot in Italy.]*

Lana's doctor warned her against going to Africa, claiming that if she got sick with an infection, her Rh blood factor might kick in, to her detriment.

That night, Barker arrived with the news that he was going to Italy to make two pictures back-to-back: *Tiger of Malaya* and a costume drama, *The Temple of Kali*. In the latter, he would wear a turban and balloon-like pantaloons. "At least you'd be dressed unlike you were in those Tarzan movies," she said.

Barker made up her mind for her. So that she could be with him, she chose *The Flame and the Flesh* because of its set locale in Rome. She later regretted her decision to turn down *Mocambo*.

On many a night, Barker pitched the idea to Lana that she should co-star with him. "We'd be the hottest team on the screen, especially if we appear in scenes wearing as few clothes as possible."

One script that came to their attention was entitled, *The Great Fall*, a romantic melodrama with a strong woman's role. She loves a former U.S. Army officer back from World War II. Because of the trauma he suffered, he has a hard time adjusting to civilian life.

He is hired by Murder, Inc. Lana liked the script because it evoked memories of playing opposite Robert Taylor, cast as a murdering gangster in one of her first big hits, *Johnny Eager*.

To take advantage of income tax laws, many stars were working abroad, making films in European settings: If a star stayed out of the United States for a total of eighteen months, he or she could avail themselves of that privilege. Errol Flynn, Clark Gable, and Gene Kelly were among the first to take advantage of this loophole. Actresses who included Gene Tierney and others were flying to Europe, and Lana began her "exile" with *Flame and the Flesh*. She would send for Cheryl and

Mildred later.

As she began to consider scripts with European settings, she decided she needed a continental address and rented ("at an outrageous cost") an elegant penthouse in the 16th arrondissement of Paris.

It was understood that Mildred and her daughter would come for a visit when Cheryl's school term ended in the spring of 1953.

Barker was very ambitious, and he confided to close friends that he hoped Lana would do wonders for his career. He began to present her with other scripts, each set in Europe, that she might consider as vehicles for co-starring with him.

They were particularly intrigued with concepts then circulating for a film eventually released in 1956, *The Ambassador's Daughter.*

During a phone call to Hedda Hopper, Lana told her she wanted MGM to lend her out for the role "with a possible romantic lead going to Lex."

Its producer Norman Krasna seemed eager for her to take the role, and with the understanding that she'd be living in her new apartment throughout the course of its filming in Paris, she looked forward to making the film.

In the end, to her distress, MGM refused to "lease her out," and Krasna cast Olivia de Havilland instead. Then, in lieu of Barker, he assigned the male lead to John Forsythe, one of Lana's future co-stars.

Both Lana and Barker were deeply disappointed, but continued their search for the right script for their joint film together.

***

Flame and the Flesh, eventually released in 1954, would be Lana's first film shot in Europe. It represented the beginning of her "exile" from the United States, a means of benefitting from the Internal Revenue's new tax loophole that many members of the Hollywood movie colony were using. She still owed the IRS thousands of dollars, so any reduction in her tax burden would be welcomed.

After all her heavy dating of Lex Barker, there was a lot of press speculation that "Hollywood's most beautiful couple" were on the verge of finally getting married.

After the failure of her love affair with Tyrone Power, and her four failed marriages (that is, if the double marriage to Stephen Crane is to be counted twice), she was not eager to rush into another union. She had another reason which she shared with only her most trusted confidantes. She feared that Barker might be using her for his career advancement.

Before flying out of Los Angeles, she spoke to the

press. "I have reached that point in my life where I'm filled with skepticism about getting married again. At this moment, there is no possibility of a marriage to Mr. Barker. He's wonderful, but we're just friends. I want to concentrate on my future and my career. I'll be away from Hollywood for almost two years, and I need to adjust to a whole new way of life. Making films abroad will be my panacea."

Arriving in Italy, Lana shocked photographers, who didn't recognize her at first. *Paparazzi* lined up to photograph the blonde goddess of Hollywood, but as a brunette, Lana got off the plane and walked past most of them.

The director, Richard Brooks, asked her to dye her hair. As a brunette, Lana found that she could go shopping, navigating her way through streets in the heart of Rome, without being recognized.

MGM went to work publicizing her new look, even before the picture was shot. Publicity sent out pictures of her (revised) image, and some of them

new look at
LANA TURNER

how TONY
and JANET saved
their love

a warning
to JERRY LEWIS

In *Flame and the Flesh*, Lana presented a new image to her fans—that of a brunette. She was told to style her hair like Gina Lollabrigida.

There was another reason: Lex Barker told her he preferred brunettes like Hedy Lamarr as opposed to blondes like Marilyn Monroe.

subsequently appeared on magazines which included *Modern Screen*.

Posters were designed with the headline: THE BAD AND THE BEAUTIFUL GIRL IS A BAD AND BEAUTIFUL BRUNETTE NOW!

Barker was waiting for her in Rome. "Our first night was so romantic," she recalled. "He took me on a carriage ride through the heart of Rome at night, past the Colosseum. We rode by the Roman Forum lit at night and even visited St. Peter's Square."

After the Pantheon, they went for drinks at Harry's Bar on the Via Veneto before heading for the Piazza Navona for nightcaps.

Then it was back at their suite at the Excelsior Hotel for a night of "love-making, Tarzan style." When Mervyn LeRoy called from the U.S. the next day, he told her he was working on the final cut of *Latin Lovers*. She told him, "Lex and I made love until a pinky dawn came over the skyline of the Eternal City."

"Did you read that line in a guidebook?" he asked.

The next night, Lana and Lex dined at the chic Taverna Flavia, where she was surprised to encounter Frank Sinatra and members of the "Hollywood on the Tiber" crowd. She wasn't alone in being an American movie star making movies abroad.

Marcello Mastroianni called and invited her to a party, where he introduced her to the film elite of Rome, including director Luchino Visconti, who raved about her beauty.

She also met another director, the very *avant-garde* Federico Fellini, who told her he was envisioning a future film that would call for a blonde movie star, in case she ever wanted to dye her hair blonde again. She told him she'd be thrilled to work with him one day.

Ultimately, Fellini's "movie with a blonde," *La Dolce Vita,* was released in 1961 and became his most famous work. The blonde actress he selected was the busty Swedish star, Anita Ekberg. When she sensuously wanders into the splashing waters of the Trevi Fountain, she entered film immortality.

Before Lana read the script of *Flame and the Flesh,* its producer, Joe Pasternak, had arranged a screening for her, with Barker, of a 1937 French version of the same film. Based on a novel by Auguste Bailly, the theme had actually reached the screen in 1925 as a silent movie. The 1937 French-language version had been entitled *Naples au Baiser de Feu,* but the title was changed to *The Kiss of Fire* for its release in the United States.

***

Lana had read and memorized most of her lines before her first meeting with Brooks.

In *Flame and the Flesh,* she played Madeleine Douvane, a Neapolitan tramp, a pleasure-loving woman of the night who uses and abuses men with her seductive powers.

Near the beginning of the film, her landlady throws her out of her room for failure to pay back rent. Out on the streets, she's befriended by a kind musician, Ciccio (Bonar Collenao), who invites her to live with him. She's introduced to his roommate, Nino (Carlos Thompson), a handsome heartbreaker who is also a singer. He's engaged to a sweet Italian girl, Lisa (Pier Angeli). As could be predicted, Nino is lured away from "nice girl" Lisa and runs off with trampy Madeleine. Their affair seemed doomed from the beginning.

Before the end of the film, Nino finally tells his simmering siren, "Faithfulness is

FLESH, NEAPOLITAN STYLE

In the slums of Naples, a street urchin (a term that translates into the local dialect as a "scugnizzo") generated laughter from photographers and from members of the cast, thanks to her irreverent (and to some degree successful) imitation of Lana's sexy walk.

not one of your great virtues," and returns to the safety net of Lisa.

At the fade-out, Lana, in high heels, is seen walking into the foggy night toward an uncertain future.

Over lunch with Richard Brooks, he told her that he wanted their film to recreate one of those earthy, post-war, Neo-Realist Italian films. He even showed Lana an artist's rendering of an early version of a poster for the film. It featured an image of her standing, provocatively, under a lamppost at night.

"A real tramp," she said.

"You've got that right, even though I know it's hard for a real lady like you to play a slut."

Brooks, a talented descendant of Russian Jewish immigrants, would become one of the major players in Hollywood. He was also a screenwriter, and an occasional producer. In his near future, he would helm such classics a *Blackboard Jungle* (1955), *Cat on a Hot Tin Roof* (1958), and *Elmer Gantry* (1960).

At their first meeting, he was highly critical of the Production Code, which he felt placed too many restrictions on movie-makers. He claimed that it greatly hampered directors such as himself in both subject matter and expression.

During their upcoming work together, she found Brooks difficult and demanding, and he would often explode at her. But she always forgave him, because she knew he was trying to make her look good. Many actresses objected to his harsh style of directing, but she later said, "Brooks is tough as nails, but the finished product is worth the suffering."

Their first week was devoted to rehearsals, as Lana got acquainted with her leading man, Carlos Thompson.

On the set, she also met Pier Angeli. Born in Sardinia, Angeli was frail, tiny, and undeniably lovely, a rather innocent-appearing Italian waif and *gamine*.

But, as Lana relayed to Brooks, "I don't think she's as innocent as she looks."

Angeli was supposed to be sustaining both an affair and an engagement with Kirk Douglas. Prior to that, she had been famously linked, romantically, to James Dean.

"The only thing angelic about her is her last name," Lana said. To Brooks, Lana boasted "I had both Kirk and Jimmy before 'Miss Angelic' arrived on the scene."

During the first day of rehearsals, Lana couldn't help notice that Angeli was flirting quite openly and consistently with Thompson. During Lana's second day on the set, Lana saw Thompson disappearing with Angeli into her dressing room. At rehearsals that followed, she'd be holding Thompson's hand.

"I think Lana was jealous of her," Brooks said. "For me, that was perfect for the role. After all, in the film, Lana steals Carlos from Pier. I'm sure Lana knew that she was a decade older than Pier."

During this period, even though Lana claimed to be madly in love with Lex Barker, they were often in different parts of the Continent.

On the set in Rome, Brooks noticed that she seemed very attracted to Thompson, the third of that era's famous Latin lovers. The first was Ricardo Montalban, with whom Lana had struck out. The second was Fernando Lamas, with whom she'd had a turbulent affair.

Thompson was actually of Swiss and German descent. Before Hollywood discovered him, he had been highly visible in Buenos Aires, based on his leading roles on stage and in Spanish-language films. Like Lana's current lover, Lex Barker, Thompson would eventually migrate, postwar, to Germany and appear in a number of films there.

She found him tall, dark, handsome, and stalwart, a man who moved and spoke with manly grace. Hollywood had already decided that he was convincing on screen as a European womanizer.

Noël Coward had had an affair with him in London, and spread the rumor along the Hollywood grapevine that the matinee idol was bisexual. Lana learned later that after *Flame and the Flesh,* he'd made *Valley of the Kings* (1954), in which, as it was rumored, both Robert Taylor, a fellow bisexual, and Eleanor Parker had made plays for him.

Lana with Pier Angeli, rivals in love on and off the screen.

In the end, Thompson married Lilli Palmer, the German actress and international beauty, after her divorce from Rex Harrison in 1957.

Leaving their respective lovers (Barker and Angeli) behind, Lana and Thompson were flown to Naples for filming of *Flame and the Flesh's* exterior scenes. Each of them lodged at the Hotel Excelsior, directly on the waterfront (via Partenope), with its views over the harbor and faraway Mount Vesuvius.

Their suites had interconnecting doors. After their first night there, Lana phoned his suite and invited him over for breakfast. He gladly accepted Her excuse for wanting to see him was: "If we're going to play lovers in the film, we might as well get to know each other."

A morning newspaper had been delivered to her suite. On the frontpage was a picture of Clark Gable and Angeli strolling hand in hand along the Via Veneto.

"Your girlfriend didn't waste much time," she said. "Clark and I are going to make another picture together in Holland."

"My dating of Pier was just a harmless flirtation. She's free to do what she wants, date whom she wants."

"I guess that goes for you, too," she said.

"Is that an invitation?" he asked provocatively.

"We'll see."

During the next few days, when not filming, they set out together to explore Naples and its environs, even going to see the ruins of Pompeii. He tipped the guards to show them the private erotic frescoes.

At night, they frequented Gran Caffè Gambrinus, Naples' oldest café, dating from 1860. They sought out little *trattorie* along the waterfront, overlooking the Bay of Naples.

One Sunday, they explored the little resort town of Positano, a hillside village along the Amalfi Drive, with its legendary Sirenuse Island featured in Homer's *Odyssey*. In Positano, they learned that this was one of Tennessee Williams' favorite hideaways. Exterior scenes of the film they were making would eventually be shot there.

At the café, he kept looking over his shoulder, and she asked him why. He told her it was an old habit from his days in Buenos Aires, where he had incurred the disfavor of both Juan and Eva Perón. "I really want to be a writer, not an actor. I wrote three novels, the first of which won a prize. The other two were forbidden by both the state and the Perón government. My political views were too outspoken for Eva. It was time to get out of Argentina, after I was released from jail."

In Naples, he'd ordered the hotel to open the connecting doors between their suites. It wasn't until she got to London that Lana gave her usual report on a man's technique in bed. Thompson got an A, or so she claimed to Ava Gardner. "It was the most tender lovemaking of any man I've ever known. He searches a woman's body for her most sensitive nerve endings, which he then proceeds to tantalize. His darting tongue knows how to dance the rumba. He has a beautiful physique. God was kind to him in all the right places."

Lana and Thompson's eventual migration back to Rome signaled the end of their affair, in ways that reflected the plotline of *Flame and the Flesh*. In Rome, whereas she was reunited with Barker, Thompson did not return to Angeli.

In reference to herself and Thompson, "Both of us moved on to other lovers," Lana said.

***

Lex Barker remained in Italy, as Lana flew alone to London for interior shooting on *Flame and the Flesh* at the Estree Studios.

During her first week in London, she heard rumors that Barker had been spotted, out in public, with the Swedish bombshell, Anita Ekberg. Ironically, Barker would later be cast as her *fiancé* in Fellini's *La Dolce Vita* (1960).

Lana was not alone for very long. Her two friends, Ava Gardner and Clark Gable, had flown back from Africa after stopovers in Rome. They had completed *Mogambo*, a project that Lana had previously rejected.

Gardner was in Rome at the time, aborting Frank Sinatra's baby.

In London, Lana met with many other friends from Hollywood, who were working in Europe to take advantage of the current loopholes in the U.S. Income Tax regulations.

Director Tay Garnett and his wife invited her to dinner. He and Lana had been friends ever since he directed her in *The Postman Always Rings Twice*.

She met with another director, John Huston, who also had flown in from Africa, where he'd directed *Mogambo*. He had tantalizing tales to tell, claiming that Gable had spent more nights with Grace Kelly than he had with Gardner.

In London, he escorted Lana to party hosted by Gardner, who prepared "Tarheel fried chicken." Its guest list mostly included U.S. expatriates." The hostess claimed she had no taste for English cooking, "especially that steak-and-kidney pie with overboiled Brussels sprouts."

Gardner had rounded up a party of American exiles that included not only Gable, but Alan Ladd, Errol Flynn, and Robert Taylor. "My God," Lana said to Huston. "What is Ava trying to do? Round up a posse of my old lovers?"

"Well, I know one you've not done," Huston said. "Bogie told me he never had the privilege."

"Truer words were never spoken," she said.

While registered in London in a suite at the Dorchester, Lana did get some phone calls for dates, notably from Douglas Fairbanks, Jr., Richard Burton, and Peter Finch, but she turned them down.

Even without a lot of heavy romancing, "Lana & Ava" appeared in the London tabloids as "two funtime glamour pusses exiled from Hollywood."

The Duke of Manchester invited them to a party. The next day, reporter Harrison Carroll wrote: "These two Hollywood glamour queens caused the biggest talk in London since Margaret Rose's famous can-can. Ava and Lana harmonized 'Take Me Out to the Ball Game,' and then went into their terpsichorean routine that sent more famous names than you can shake a stick at into hysterics."

Lana appeared in *Flame and the Flesh* with Carlos Thompson, billed as "the Argentine Heartthrob."

As she confessed to the director, "I've already seduced the first Argentine heartthrob, Fernando Lamas. Now I'm falling for the second export from a country known for its beef."

Lana missed Barker desperately and talked to him on the phone nightly. She was eager to rush back to his arms.

While in London, she reportedly remained chaste, even though Errol Flynn visited her suite one night and didn't leave until the next day.

As she reported to Gardner, "For the first time ever, Errol didn't seduce me. Time seems to have passed our 'in-like-Flynn' boy bye-bye. This is not 1942. He tried to perform, but was so drunk he passed out."

[After leading a life of dissipation, the legendary actor, his days as the dashing Robin Hood on the screen only a distant memory, died of a heart attack on October 14, 1959. In spite of predictions to the contrary, Flynn had, indeed, lived to be fifty.]

***

Before the release of *Flame and the Flesh* in the U.S., Pier Angeli flew to New York to promote it. Lana learned that the designer, Oleg Cassini, was spending nights in her hotel suite. That made Lana doubly surprised when just weeks later, Angeli married the singer, Vic Damone.

When *Flame and the Flesh* opened in limited distribution, it did not, in general, receive good reviews. Many critics noted that the bylaws of the American Production Code limited Brooks from crafting the neo-realism Italian film he might have desired, a film in which Lana and Thompson might have been "unleashed" in their lovemaking.

One reviewer in Rome wrote that "Brooks could not ignite the flame in *Flame and the Flesh*. Actually, the role of the Neapolitan tramp just screams for Sophia Loren."

Newsweek stated that *Flame and the Flesh* "was only for unreconstructed and patient Turnerphiles. Helen Deutsch's script is chiefly an opportunity for Miss Turner to ogle the boys. There are many fine views of Vesuvius, but the star herself does most of the smoking."

Writing in the *New York Herald Tribune*, Otis L. Guernsey, Jr. said, "Lana Turner has done the chic thing—she has made a movie in Italy, and she plays a loose woman in it. Director Brooks concentrates on making Miss Turner look sexy in all kinds of settings from cabarets to stuffy bedrooms."

The New York Times labeled the film "a potpourri of passion, *Weltschmertz*, and true confessions, displaying some flesh but no flame. There is more talk than action, more play-acting than emotion. In the movie, Miss Turner is not allergic to men—any man."

Ruth Waterbury of the *Los Angeles Examiner* was the only critic who gushed: "Sex, sacred and profane, *Flame and the Flesh* was filmed with honesty and realism and imbued with compassion and tenderness. It's a tale of a beautiful strumpet, who pinches the fiancé of a sweet girl-next-door. In the end, the girl gets her man back from the clutches of this scarlet woman. The film is a combination of sin and sacrifice against a realistic background of Neapolitan slums, rubbish in the streets, bare bedrooms, and streetwalkers."

***

[Years after wrapping Flame and the Flesh, Lana referred to "those two doomed lovers," a reference to Carlos Thompson and Pier Angeli.

In September of 1971, Angeli was found dead in a Beverly Hills home, the victim of a barbiturate overdose. She was only 39.

In October of 1990, in Buenos Aires, Thompson's body was discovered at his apartment. A gun was found beside his body, a bullet in his head. He had committed suicide at the age of 67.]

***

Positano, on the Amalfi Coast, had also been used for some exterior shots during the filming of *Flame and the Flesh*. Lana rented a vacation villa to slip away whenever possible, to be alone with Barker. Each of them could sunbathe in the nude. The former Tarzan told her, "I don't like tan lines."

435

On at least four different occasions, he proposed marriage, but she kept turning him down. Actually, his divorce from Arlene Dahl had not come through. His two children from his first marriage were staying with their mother, and Cheryl was looked after by Mildred.

One afternoon, Kirk Douglas phoned, inviting Barker and Lana to the Cannes Film Festival for the European premiere of *The Bad and the Beautiful.* Longing for more glamour in her life, she accepted. Barker was also eager for the exposure, hoping to meet Continental film directors and producers there.

On the Côte d'Azur, "the world's most glamorous couple," as the press dubbed them, flew in. The paparazzi went wild in photographing them, and their pictures were splashed across front pages in Europe and America. They were labeled as "Hollywood's Blonde Goddess and Tarzan."

It was hardly a secret that they were living and traveling together as part of a relationship "not sanctified with marriage." Many in the press condemned their "immorality." In her memoirs, she speculated that she might not have married Barker were it not for the moral climate of the 1950s that virtually compelled her to do it.

As the pressure that urged her to marry him mounted, she finally agreed to a wedding. After the French Riviera, they retreated to a villa he had rented fifteen miles from Turin, the capital city of the Piedmont, in northern Italy. Their luxurious villa stood on a hillside overlooking the River Po and its fertile, enveloping valley.

The Villa Primo Sole ("First Daylight") became the setting for the first meeting of Cheryl with her new half sister and brother, Lynn, age 10, and Alexander, 6. In the beginning, Lynne and Cheryl were a bit leary of each other. The children had a hard time adjusting at first to this new family that seemed to have been created artificially overnight.

The wedding day arrived on September 8, 1953, and although Barker and Lana tried to keep it a secret from the press, the *paparazzi* swarmed the city. He had to fight to clear a pathway to get Lana into Turin's 16th Century Town Hall for a civil ceremony.

Their honeymoon night was spent back at the villa with the children down the hall. She wanted at least a two-week honeymoon, but MGM notified her that she was overdue in London for wardrobe fittings for her upcoming picture, *Betrayed.* *[Eventually released in 1954, it was, at the time, still entitled* The True and the Brave.*]*

Quietly, without alerting MGM as to her whereabouts, she abandoned the Villa Primo Sole for the island of Capri, where a rented villa awaited her and her new husband.

Meanwhile, MGM became frantic as Gable waited impatiently at the Dorchester Hotel in London.

Eventually, it was Ava Gardner who succeeded at reaching her on the phone, alerting her about what was going on: "Dore Schary is frantic. No one knows where you are. Honey chile, you'd better get that beautiful ass of yours to London…and *pronto!* MGM is talking right now about replacing you in the role with me. If not me, then Jennifer Jones."

There had been casting changes during pre-production: Gregory Peck had originally been offered Gable's role. When he was not available, Kirk Douglas was slated. Victor Mature's role was to have gone to Richard Widmark.

Saying goodbye to Barker, and what Lana called "His power weapon of love," she journeyed from Capri to Rome and took the next plane to London.

The next day she showed up at Balmain's for wardrobe fittings. There was a problem. The role called for a blonde. She was still a brunette. Permission came from the director, Gottfried Reinhardt, allowing her to keep her hair dark.

Gottfried was the son of the fabled Austrian theater director, Max Reinhardt. The son had gone to Hollywood, where he became an assistant to director Ernst Lubitsch. He later directed Greta Garbo's last movie, *Two-Faced Woman*, in 1941. During the war, he joined the U.S. Army, and later, he worked on the previous Gable/Turner film, *Homecoming* (1948).

It was fully understood that after inaugural conferences and rehearsals in London, shooting for *Betrayed* would begin in Holland, based on a script by Ronald Millar and George Froeschel. Each of the supporting players had at last been signed, with the noteworthy inclusion of Lana's friend, Louis Calhern, cast as General Ten Eyck.

Betrayed was a cloak-and-dagger story set in Nazi-occupied Holland in 1943, with Lana and Gable back in combat suits and steel helmets. It required fewer love clinches than their other pictures.

She was shocked at Gable's appearance. He had grown paunchier and looked older than his age of fifty-three.

There was not a lot of romance on the screen, and absolutely none off the screen, either. Gable was in poor health, and at times, she saw him shaking. He was more worried about his career and his private life than he was in seducing Lana.

Betrayed (1954) would be the last of MGM's Turner/Gable vehicles, which up until then had included *Honky Tonk* (1941), *Somewhere I'll Find You* (1942), and *Homecoming* (1948).

After twenty-three years at MGM, it would be Gable's last picture for the studio that had made him "The King of Hollywood."

Mature, her former lover from the early 1940s, had found this blonde-haired Dutch secretary, age 22, to spend nights in his bed, and was thus otherwise occupied.

Gable was cast as a Dutch intelligence officer, Pieter Deventer, who manages to escape the Nazis, with the aid of "The Scarf" (Mature), who is leading the Resistance in Holland.

Lana's role of Carla Von Oven was somewhat mysterious. Carla had collaborated with the Nazis and was anxious to live down her reputation. Deventer is ordered to recruit her as a British spy, but he wonders if she can be trusted. He has his doubts, even though falling in love with her.

In contrast, she wonders if "The Scarf" can be relied on, or else is he working for the Nazis? Nearly all of the resistance movement's raids have been ambushed, apparently based on advance tipoffs to the Nazis. Who, within the Dutch Resistance, is the traitor who's collaborating with the Nazis?

[In case you missed the movie, the collaborator, as it turns out, was indeed "The Scarf," as portrayed by Mature. Before he can be hauled away, he jumps from a window, committing suicide as atonement for his evil deeds.]

When *Betrayed* was released, critical reaction was bad. The film was viewed as the weakest of the Gable/Turner movies. *Newsweek* called it "a clumsy over-slow piece of wartime adventure. Lana Turner and Victor Mature go about their spying and resistance leading to no great conviction. The story seems artificial."

The Hollywood Reporter critiqued Gable and Turner as "a bit sexless this time around in their espionage puzzle. Seeing Gable without sex is a good deal like seeing *Ben-Hur* without the horses."

One critic wrote, "Clark Gable kisses Lana Turner like a husband with a hangover."

Many reviewers found that Mature stole the picture,

Victor Mature, cast as "The Scarf," expresses love for Lana (top photo). But when things go wrong in the espionage game, his violence toward her comes out (see below).

438

cutting a dashing figure with a silk scarf around his neck, as he goes about killing Nazi soldiers, dynamiting Holland's bridges, and having a ball as the villainous traitor. One of his lines articulated his sense of cavalier bitterness: "I'm in this strictly for the laughs."

Jeanine Basinger encapsulated the utter lack of chemistry between Gable and Turner: "They look at each other with dull eyes, their former secret twinkles and sense of mutual fun depleted. He's no longer the tomcat on the prowl, and she's not the cute kid with kittenish qualities. Alas, they don't even seem to be Clark Gable and Lana Turner. They look like two people who just want to get it over with, put their feet up, and have a cup of coffee."

Lana expected her usual attack from Bosley Crowther in *The New York Times,* and indeed, with a style that fulfilled the worst of her fears, the acerbic critic wrote: "By the time the picture gets around to figuring out whether the betrayer is Miss Turner or Mr. Mature, it has taken the audience through such a lengthy and tedious amount of detail that it has not only frayed all possible tension, but it has aggravated patience as well. Miss Turner and Mr. Gable have many long-winded talks; Mr. Mature has thumped his chest like Tarzan and bellowed his boasts a score of times. An excess of espionage maneuvering has been laid out on the screen. The beauties of the Netherlands have been looked at until they pall."

Holding a revolver, Lana, as Carla Van Oven, looks uncertain, lacking the authority that Barbara Stanwyck displayed with a gun in her hand in *film noir.*

***

Before the requisite eighteen months of expatriation had passed, Lana and Barker decided to return to California, the timing of which would prevent them from what was needed to reduce their Federal income taxes.

Then the duo decided to remarry, since their Italian marriage had technically violated clauses in that country's matrimony laws. *[The requisite delay between Barker's divorce from Arlene Dahl and his subsequent marriage to Lana had been shorter than that mandated by the Italian courts.]*

Consequently, life resumed at Holmby Hills for their "reconstituted" family, *i.e.,* Lana, Lex, Cheryl, and his son and daughter. Although he had signed a contract with Universal, they had no movie role slated for him right away.

One afternoon, he found himself alone in the house with Cheryl. That afternoon would forever be embedded in her memory. He came into her bedroom at-

439

tired only in a rather formal red Sulka dressing gown which Lana had given him.

Cheryl would record in her memoirs what happened next: "Tarzan's hair fell forward to hood his face. I could see that his lips were set in a grisly smile. He reached inside my nightie to fondle my breasts. He was stroking my legs. I stifled an urge to scream. Suddenly, I felt a frightening jab. I sprang up, arms thrashing. The nightie was pulled away, my knees yanked wide, and with a bolt of pain, he heaved his 200 pounds into the core of my loins. The pain was more than I have ever known."

She wrote with such conviction that her account rang true. However, many of Barker's loyal fans discounted his violation of her virginity. His former wife, Arlene Dahl, interviewed on national TV, also disputed the claim. "Lex's package was just too big. He would have split open a young girl."

After the rape, Barker threatened

At first glance, this could have been a scene of domestic harmony with Cheryl (left), Lana, and Lex Barker. The former Tarzan was Cheryl's new stepfather and Lana's latest husband.

her, claiming that if she told anyone, especially Lana, she'd be sent to a prison for young girls, fed a diet of bread and water, and locked away for the rest of her life, never to see Lana or Mildred again.

One week later, Lana was due in New York to promote MGM, and she flew there alone. Barker stayed behind.

Once again, he forced himself onto Cheryl, and the assaults were said to have continued, often, for three years. As she wrote, "I did not even own my insides. My stepfather did."

***

In 1955, Lana became pregnant again, and wanted to have Barker's child. But after seven months of pregnancy, the child was stillborn. This was the third time she'd suffered the loss of an unborn baby.

She didn't want to press to know it, but she suffered from endometriosis *[a painful disorder in which tissue—the endometrium—that normally lines the inside of a woman's uterus—migrates and grows in locations outside its confines. The syndrome usually encompasses abnormalities associated with the ovaries, fallopian tubes and the tissue lining the pelvis.]*

Lana's predisposition to the syndrome required her to submit to a hysterectomy late in 1956. After that surgical procedure, she knew, finally, that she would never give birth again.

***

MGM announced plans for a Biblical epic, *The Prodigal* (released in 1955), a saga about a young Hebrew who abandons his *fiancée* and family *[albeit clinging to the battered remnants of his Jewish identity]* for a rowdy set of adventures and carnal pleasures among the pagans. In the city of the infidels (worshippers of Baal and other gods), he is corrupted by Samarra, the high priestess of Astarte, the pagan goddess of love, sex, and reproduction.

After many near-death encounters and "wallowing in sin," Micah the Prodigal Son returns home to his loved ones.

The picture was originally envisioned as a star vehicle for Edmund Purdom, Ava Gardner, and Vittorio Gassman. Although Gassman and Gardner later dropped out, Purdom steadfastly remained to play the Prodigal Son. *[His character was inspired by the saga of betrayal, loyalty, and redemption that's outlined in the New Testament book of Luke, Chapter 15:11-32.]*

MGM's studio chief Dore Schary later admitted that he "hustled" Lana into accepting the role because she needed the money. According to Schary, "The truth is that I liked the script by Maurice Zimm, based on a scenario by Joseph Breen, Jr., and Samuel James Larsen, set in old Damascus in 700 BC. Lana had presented me with various scripts sent to her, and she wanted to work with Ava Gardner or Lex Barker as her co-stars.

As high priestess, Samarra presides over human sacrifices.

In one of the most dramatic scenes, a strikingly handsome male Adonis, scantily clad George Robothan, is brought before her. In her capacity as the love goddess, Lana plants a kiss on his forehead before he's plunged to his death into a pit of fire.

I turned down every one of them, wanting to make this Biblical spectacle to lure the yokels from their god damn TV sets and back into movie houses."

"I thought it would draw a big audience," Schary continued. "What I overlooked was that Cecil B. DeMille had exclusive rights to the Bible, or so it seemed. Poor Lana swayed her way through the film, but it was a hopeless task. Onscreen, the script came off as lifeless."

As inspiration for Lana's role as the pagan temptress, the scriptwriters were later accused of borrowing liberally from the silent film, *The Wanderer* (1926), which had co-starred William Collier, Jr. and Greta Nissen.

For her performance, Lana dyed her hair blonde again, which was the way most of her fans preferred her. No film role before or after required her to appear so scantily clad. As Samarra, in her first appearance in CinemaScope and Metrocolor, she displayed ample expanses of flesh.

Theater critic for *The Miami Herald*, George Bourke, wrote: "The role is the

Lana claimed, "Lex was physically the best lover I ever had. Not simply because he was well hung, which, my darling, he was, but because he was incredible at oral sex. I often prefer the oral route to conventional sex because I was always too tight."

most form-fitting Lana Turner has had since she first sashayed before the movie camera in a memorable sweater in *They Won't Forget.*"

Though tame, perhaps, by today's standards, Lana's skimpy costumes, designed by Herschel McCoy, created a scandal in the uptight 1950s. She was even denounced on Sundays by priests and pastors from their pulpits, who attacked Hollywood as "a viper pit of degenerates and shameless Jezebels."

McCoy had already designed the costumes for such "sword and sandal" epics as *Quo Vadis?* (1951), starring Robert Taylor. As Lana said when she saw that movie, "I even know what Bob looks like without the armor."

On the set of *The Prodigal*, she got along well with producer Charles Schnee, still grateful for him for having written the script of *The Bad and the Beautiful.*

Before Micah (Purdom) can win her love, he has to squander his inheritance to buy her the world's most valuable pearl. When it is stolen from him and he cannot pay for it, he is thrown into slavery.

In another dramatic scene, he is stripped and flogged in public. In the book, *Lash! The Hundred Great Scenes of Men Being Whipped*, the Purdom episode ranks as No. 66.

The director, Kansas-born Richard Thorpe, had a long career at MGM. He helmed his first silent film in 1923 and went on from there to direct some 180 movies. He'd dealt with pagan themes before, directing *Last of the Pagans* (1935) starring Ray Mala.

Despite his many successes, he is remembered today more for his failures than for his triumphs, especially for episodes associated with his role as the first director of Judy Garland's *The Wizard of Oz*. In the early stages of the film's development, he had put a blonde wig on her and ordered makeup men to give her a cutsey baby doll look, not the innocent thirteen-year-old Kansas farm girl later portrayed. Thorpe was fired after only two weeks.

Thorpe had worked with Purdom before in *Athena* (1954), starring Jane Powell, and again in *The Student Prince* (also 1954) after Mario Lanza had been fired.

Thorpe sometimes directed Lana's former lover, Robert Taylor, in such movies as *Ivanhoe* (1952), with Elizabeth Taylor, and he'd go on to helm two Elvis Presley movies, *Jailhouse Rock* (1957), and *Fun in Acapulco* (1963).

Lana's leading man, Purdom was English. In London's West End, he had played in Shakespeare plays, most notably, *Romeo and Juliet*. On Broadway, he was part of the company formed by

When Lana signed to do the film, Gardner phoned her with a dire warning: "It'll be a flop, honey chile. Don't go there. My advice? Go on being your pagan love goddess off screen—not on."

"But you got to be a goddess," Lana said. "Why not me?"

[She was referring to Gardner's role in One Touch of Venus *(1948). Hollywood's other love goddess, Rita Hayworth, had played Terpsichore in* Down to Earth *(1947).]*

Laurence Olivier and Vivien Leigh. When Lana heard this, she quipped: "I bet both Viv and Larry seduced Purdom."

Lana didn't detest Purdom as much as she had Ezio Pinza in *Mr. Imperium*, although she labeled both of them "Mr. Garlic Breath."

"Purdom had a high opinion of himself. His pomposity was hard to bear. My lines were so stupid I hated to go to work with him in the morning."

"When Purdom stripped down for his flogging scene, I found his body disappointing, but then, I was used to the world's most perfect physique, Lex Barker. In spite of Purdom's unimpressive chest, he was very good looking."

During the making of *The Prodigal*, Lana discovered a secret about his sex life. In a way, she was delighted to hear this bit of gossip. He was having an affair with Mrs. Tyrone Power (aka, Linda Christian), the Mexican actress who had captured

Power's heart, leading him to dump Lana.

After learning that, Lana became much friendlier with Purdom, because she wanted to know more details about his affair with Christian. "It's really not that much of a secret from Power," he told her. "In fact, she confessed our affair to him."

"How did he take it?" she asked.

"He took it very calmly and even delivered a bombshell of his own. He said he'd fallen in love with a young girl in New York, and was also having an affair with her. Linda's affair with me was okay by him, as long as it made her happy."

[Linda Christian divorced Tyrone Power in 1956, but waited until 1960 to marry Edmund Purdom. Her second marriage lasted only a few months. After divorcing Christian, Purdom waited thirty-seven years before remarrying.]

Lana's truce with Purdom didn't last long. In the movie, she tells him, "I can never belong to one man. I belong to all men."

After he'd filmed that scene with her, he asked her: "Are you delivering a line from the movie—or one from your own life?"

In a call to Ava Gardner, Lana said, "I'm a walking goddess adorned with baubles, bangles, and beads, really, I mean, an astonishment of beads and jeweled G-strings. I even wear a *brassiere* of faux snakes. Men, while devouring my flesh with their lusty eyes, should bring their overcoats to movie theaters so they can jerk off."

She turned her back on him and walked away.

The most dramatic scene in her entire career came at the end of *The Prodigal*. When her once-devoted worshippers turn on her, throwing stones and rotten tomatoes at her, she stands on her tower near images of Astarte and Baal. Realizing that she may be stoned to death, she jumps from the tower to a horrendous death in a flaming pit, or cauldron, the site where she had sent so many sacrificial victims before.

Two weeks into the filming of *The Prodigal*, Schary asked to see the rushes. After he'd watched them, he turned to Thorpe. "I think the studio has become mired down in quicksand. I'm going to ask production how much it'll cost us if I shut down the film."

That afternoon, he learned that MGM would suffer a considerable hit. Already $200,000 had been spent, lavish sets had been constructed or were under construction, expensive costumes designed, and contracts with stars had been negotiated and finalized.

"Our loss would have been $1.2 million, perhaps a hell of a lot more. I ordered that the picture be completed and speeded up. I told Thorpe to cut costs wherever possible. As it turned out, *The Prodigal* was the biggest and most embarrassing failure, the worst movie I ever supported."

Throughout the troubled shoot, Lana found comfort, reuniting with old friends and meeting new stars. Her longtime friend, Louis Calhern, had the third lead, playng Nahreeb, the sinister high priest of Baal, who conspires to destroy Micah because of the impertinence of his sexual interest in Samarra. Critics would later compare his costume to an "overly decorated Victorian lampshade."

Lana had two lunches with her jovial friend, Cecil Kellaway, cast as the Governor. He rushed to greet Lana, and she embraced him. "You

Edmund Purdom's role in *The Prodigal* somewhat mirrored his leading role in *The Egyptian* (1954). He had been assigned that part in the dreary Biblical epic after Marlon Brando wisely turned it down. Purdom starred in that ponderous, often unintentionally funny, Biblical soaper, tangling with another *femme fatale*, Bella Darvi.

Now he was with Lana, playing the besotted suitor to her *persona* as a lascivious pagan sex queen.

seem very much alive. I thought John Garfield and I finished you off in *The Postman Always Rings Twice.*"

Other than Lana herself, the scene stealer of the picture was Francis L. Sullivan, cast as Bosra, the wily and unscrupulous moneylender. The English film and stage actor was a heavyset man with a striking double chin and a deep voice. He'd filmed works by every author from Shakespeare to Charles Dickens and George Bernard Shaw, working with such stars as Hedy Lamarr, Ingrid Bergman, Robert Donat, and even Bob Hope. In failing health, he would die the year after *The Prodigal*'s release.

At the beginning of the film, Micah deserts his beautiful Jewish *fiancée*, Ruth, with the intention of traveling to Damascus to pursue the pagan love goddess. Born in Ireland, Audrey Dalton was cast as Ruth, perhaps hoping for bigtime stardom.

The Prodigal garnered some of the worst reviews of Lana's career. Douglas Lemza, a film historian, claimed, "*The Prodigal* is something not even Carol Burnett could parody. This sort of nonsense requires Cecil B. DeMille." Another critic wrote, "Lana Turner gives the film all her glamour but none of her talent as an actress."

Bosley Crowther, writing in *The New York Times*, continued as Lana's main critic. "*The Prodigal* is pompous, ostentatious, vulgar, and a ridiculous charade. Miss Lana Turner conducts the rituals as though she was 'Little Egypt' at the old Chicago World's Fair."

Variety claimed, "Metro has filled the movie so full of scene and spectacle that Richard Thorpe's direction is hard put to give it any semblance of movement or to get life and warmth into the characters and incidents."

One critic pounded away at the weakness of this epic, but had praise for the stunning Metrocolor beauty of Lana. *Newsweek* called the movie "a Biblical pot-boiler, a combination of an old Ziegfeld Follies and a traveling carnival."

Columnist Sidney Skolsky, who had remained Lana's friend, wrote: "The long walk Lana takes through the Temple of Love is the best reason for seeing the picture...pure poetry in motion."

Playboy labeled Lana as "the Pinup Queen of Hollywood—move over Marilyn!"

In the *Cleveland Plain Dealer,* W. Ward Marsh wrote: "Lana Turner, glorifying the flesh, also exhibits plenty of her own glorification. I have never seen her walk better in her life, as she parades around, sometimes with a candle in her hand, as the Goddess of Samarra."

Since its initial release, *The Prodigal* has gained a cult following in the wake of several television screenings.

When Lana was last asked about it, she quipped, "It should have played Disneyland."

***

Warner Brothers tapped John Farrow to direct *The Sea Chase (1955),* a World War II drama about the German sea captain of a fugitive freighter with a strange cargo that included a beautiful blonde-haired Nazi female spay. The studio paid $10,000 to acquire the rights to this thriller by novelist Andres Geer. The film was to be a vehicle for John Wayne as the anti-Nazi sea captain, but who would play the Mata Hari type spy?

Farrow couldn't seem to make up his mind, offering the role first to Grace Kelly and then to Joan Crawford. Both of them were less than thrilled to play "second fiddle" to Wayne.

Speculation in Hollywood grew about who might best execute the role. For a while, attention focused on Deborah Kerr, although she would be about the last actress that audiences at the time might even remotely associate with a Nazi spy.

Later, it was Susan Hayward, who might have been more believable, but not really. What about the Irish lassie, Maureen O'Hara? No, she was out. Gene Tierney and Arlene Dahl were also considered.

Finally, Hedda Hopper, in one of her columns during September of 1954, announced that the role had been assigned to Lana Turner and that she'd be a most unlikely choice as a Nazi spy, and that such bizarre casting would be a bit of a stretch for her.

At the time, Lana was one of the few bigtime stars still under contract

to MGM. Dore Schary decided he wanted to get the most out of her before her contract expired, as he didn't plan to renew it. He was paying her $5,000 a week, but could make more money on her by "leasing her out" to other studios.

Finally, for her collaboration in their newest movie, *The Sea Chase*, Warners agreed to pay MGM $300,000 for her services.

Audience acceptance required a leap of imagination about the "odd couple" casting of Wayne with Lana before settling back into their seats to enjoy the latest Wayne adventure story. With his distinctive voice and much-imitated walk, Wayne, often cast in Westerns as a misogynistic, *machismo*-soaked cowboy, would not even try to imitate a German accent. Nor would Lana.

Roughly based on a true event, *The Sea Chase* is the story of the German-born Captain Karl Ehrlich, who despises the Nazis, who have taken over his Fatherland. When Germany invades Poland in September of 1939, England declares war. Fearing that his vessel will be confiscated by the Australians, who are allied with the British, he

By the mid-1950s, both John Wayne and Lana had evolved into living legends, although Wayne had an advantage based on the number of tickets his name tended to sell at any box office.

They certainly were not equal in height. Even when she wore what were known at the time as "Joan Crawford fuck-me high heels," she rose only to a height of the Duke's shoulders.

hastily embarks on a mission to move his rusty, 5,000-ton freighter, the *Ergenstrasse* from Sydney to Valparaiso, in Chile.

His mink-clad passenger, Lana, playing Elsa Keller, comes aboard as a passenger. She, too, must escape from Australia before she is arrested and jailed as a Nazi collaborator and spy.

Off they sail, with a British man-of-war, the *Rockhampton*, in hot pursuit. Ironically, as part of a subplot that could only happen in Hollywood, Elsa is engaged to Jeffrey Napier (David Farrar), commander of the pursuing *Rockhampton*.

As the film unrolls, Wayne is as American as cowboy boots. Maybe Marlon Brando in his future movie in 1958, *The Young Lions*, could get by masquerading as a German, but Wayne is the same man he was in *Red River* (1948) directing a cattle drive.

As might be predicted during their race across the ocean, the captain falls in love with the lovely, immaculately groomed spy. Lana used her own wardrobe and chest of jewelry during her characterization of the role.

She would later say, "Most of my part was that of a fashion mannequin standing around wondering where all the sharks went." She also appeared with a revised hair color, called "coralescent blonde," invented by Myrkl Stoltz, whose choice was "inspired by a coral reef shimmering in the phosphorescent sea." For the first time, Lana applied coral-colored lipstick, abandoning her usual "Victory Red" lipstick used as part of her look in the films she'd made during wartime.

For *The Sea Chase*, Lana was returning to the studio, Warners, which had first discovered her in 1937, featuring her in *They Won't Forget* with that by now immortal walk that earned for her the label "The Sweater Girl."

John Farrow seemed to have been the ideal director. He had only recently directed Wayne in the successful *Hondo* (1953), in which the star had been cast as a tough, wily cavalry officer who must deal with a pending Apache uprising.

Farrow was firmly established in Hollywood as a director-producer and screenwriter. In 1942, he'd been nominated for an Oscar for his direction of *Wake Island*, starring Brian Donlevy and Robert Preston. In his immediate future, he would also be nominated for an Oscar for best screenplay for writing the 1957 *Around the World in Eighty*

Even aboard a rusty, dilapidated freighter, Lana—thanks to an army of hairdressers and a wardrobe that would NEVER fit into a cabin—had to appear glam.

Days for producer Mike Todd, then married to Elizabeth Taylor.

Ironically, Farrow had been born in Sydney, where *The Sea Chase* opens. Not only that, but as a young man, he had run away to sea aboard an American barquentine, "sailing all over the Pacific and fighting in revolts in Nicaragua and Mexico." During World War II, he joined the Royal Canadian Navy, working aboard anti-submarine patrols until he contracted typhus.

When Lana met Farrow, he was married to the actress Maureen O'Sullivan, with whom he would have seven children, including a future famous actress, Mia Farrow.

Lana was known for seducing her leading men on many a film. But she had never viewed Wayne as a sex object. He had famously said, "Women scare the hell out of me. I've always been afraid of them."

Director William Wellman told her at a Hollywood party, "Wayne walks like a fairy. He's the only screen hero in the world who can get away with that." At another party, Joan Crawford, on the rare occasion she spoke of Lana, claimed, "Get

Wayne out of the saddle and you've got nothing."

Wayne had proclaimed that Marlene Dietrich, his co-star in *Pittsburgh* (1942), "was the best lay I ever had."

When Dietrich heard that, she lit a cigarette and said, "How very strange. All I did was give him a bit of fellatio."

Besides, Wayne was already in love with the Peruvian starlet, Pilar Palette Weldy, and planned to take her as his third wife at the conclusion of shooting *The Sea Chase*.

Nevertheless, rumors of Lana sustaining an affair with Wayne made several of the gossip columns.

Before filming began, Ava Gardner sent Lana a good luck note: "I'm going to stay here in Europe, *honey chile*," she wrote. "I can't find any men in Hollywood who can go all night. Where is Gary Cooper or Jimmy Stewart? Of course, they're getting long in the tooth and can't quite cut the mustard like they used to."

Lana boarded a plane for Hawaii, with Del Armstrong, her makeup man, and Moss Mabry, her costume designer. Leaving from San Francisco, they flew to Honolulu, where they took a smaller plane to the Kona region of the Big Island of Hawaii, where the cast and crew had already assembled.

Warners had booked accommodations for Lana in a two-room suite at the Kona Inn. She wanted the second bedroom to be assigned to Armstrong, her makeup expert, who would therefore be readily accessible for those early makeup calls.

To her distress, she discovered that the other bedroom, directly accessible through a connecting door, had been assigned, at his request, to Farrow.

His reputation as a womanizer was already familiar to her. Even before he'd met her, based entirely on her own reputation, he'd described her as "a man-hungry vixen hot to trot." As he'd described to Wayne, "She'll be easy pickings. I don't plan to ever lock that connecting door between our bedrooms."

Lana threatened to fly back to the U.S. mainland if she had to have Farrow as her "roommate." He was soon replaced with Armstrong, as she had originally intended. He came into her suite every morning at 4:30AM to apply her makeup. What Lana had really wanted was a private villa like the one Wayne occupied with Pilar.

In the film, Lana is supposed to be engaged to Commander Napier (as portrayed by the English actor, David Farrar). After meeting the Englishman—voted the ninth most popular star in Britain—she told him, "You have Elizabeth Taylor eyes." She was referring to their violet color.

He'd broken into films the same year she had. "I find him dashing," she told Del Armstrong. "If I didn't have Lex, I might make a play for him." She was informed that he was still living with the wife he'd married in 1929.

One actor who relentlessly pursued Lana during the shoot was Lyle Bettger. She had recently seen him in the Oscar-winning film, *The Greatest Show on Earth* (1952). He was good looking and imbued with a strong masculine appeal, but she spurned all his sexual overtures, even though he told her, "I'm dynamite between the sheets."

In the film, he played Chief Officer Kirchner, the villain of the piece. During a refueling stop, this pro-Nazi murdered three marooned seamen. He doesn't tell his captain, who is later blamed by the British for the brutal deaths. Napier vows to bring Wayne to justice as a war criminal.

Lana spent time off the set with Richard Davalos, cast as Naval Cadet Walter Stemme, a handsome, sensitive young man of Finnish and Spanish descent. The same year he appeared with Lana, he was cast in the role that makes him famous today, that of the older brother of James Dean in *East of Eden* (1955).

The Hollywood gossipy grapevine stretched all the way to the Hawaiian islands. Lana was enraged at the news she received. Rumors reached her that during her absence, Barker was dating other women, including a weekend spent in Palm Springs with Jayne Mansfield, the chief rival of Marilyn Monroe. Had word reached her that her husband was also seducing ten-year-old Cheryl, Lana would have flown back to the mainland at once.

Fuming and alone on Hawaii, she was determined to instigate what she called a "revenge fuck." As a means of creating it, she turned not to Bettger, Davalos, or Farrow, but to one of Wayne's best friends. James Arness had been cast as Schlieter.

"When I flirted with Jim Arness, I wondered how we'd fit together in bed," Lana said to Grey. "I'm so short and he's so tall. But we worked out an accommodation and what a thrill he was. Who said all actors are sissies? Incidentally, all his length wasn't confined to his height, if you get my drift."

The brother of fellow actor, Peter Graves, Arness was soon to become a household word, thanks to his performance as Marshal Matt Dillon in *Gunsmoke,* the hit TV series that ran from 1955 to 1975.

Lana's conclusion about Arness. "In Minnesota, they grow some big boys, rearing them on corn-fed beef."

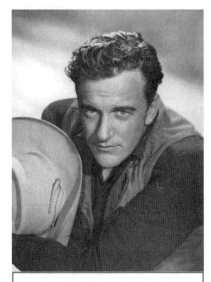

As Lana would later confess to Virginia Grey, "In those long, lonely nights away from that philandering husband of mine, I turned to James Arness, all six feet, seven inches of him. He'd wanted to be a pilot during the war, but was too tall."

That was true. Arness instead served as a rifleman in the U.S. 3rd Infantry until he was severely wounded on the Italian beaches of Anzio. Of Norwegian and German ancestry, Arness was married, although that never stopped Lana.

***

Wayne had arrived on location some time in advance of the shoot, and during the interim, he had gone snorkeling. It resulted in a serious ear infection that caused him constant pain. He was taking codeine to kill the ache, especially when his ear became so swollen that Farrow had to shoot him from one side. Often, he was in such pain, he could not remember his lines. At times, his eyes looked glazed. Off screen, Lana could be seen putting ice packs on his ear.

Tab Hunter, cast as Cadet Wesser, had many chances to observe Lana and Wayne. Toward the end of the decade, this handsome, blonde-haired actor became big box office for Warners.

In a memoir, he wrote, "Sparks often fly between a leading man and a leading lady. Not so with John and Lana. I felt a layer of cool between them on screen. Wayne wasn't like Bob Mitchum, who had that twinkle about him and was a devil with women. Wayne was more like Gary Cooper who was always very professional."

Wayne's biographers, Randy Roberts and James S. Olson, wrote that during filming, "Lana Turner was a deeply troubled woman whose recent years had been pock-marked by soured love affairs, migraine headaches, divorces, miscarriages, and a suicide attempt, plus problems with the IRS. She found solace by drinking herself into oblivion every night. Nursing disabling hangovers, she arrived late on the set not knowing her lines."

When she didn't show up for five morning calls, Farrow, the director, fired her. "Get Lauren Bacall on the phone and see if she'll fly to Honolulu. She had wanted to do the film."

Tab Hunter had a dread of John Wayne, who was known for calling homosexuals "fairies." But he liked the way Hunter was handling his role, even suggesting that he might buy out his contract with Warners and assign him to his own production company, Wayne-Fellows.

"I found Wayne a straight shooter both on and off the screen," Hunter said. "However, he had little regard "for football jocks" and deplored "macho bullshit."

When Wayne heard that Lana had been fired, he went to Farrow and finally persuaded him to give her a second chance.

After being humiliated by her firing, she showed up on time the following morning and for subsequent morning calls too, even though she continued to drink heavily at night. Her main concern seemed to be Barker. As she told Del Armstrong, "I wonder who he's fucking tonight," not realizing, of course, that it might be her underaged daughter.

Several writers had tried to fashion a script, none of which Wayne really liked. He told Lana, "Farrow took a great story and made a dime novel out of it. My role is that of an unromantic bore, just a cold, commercial guy."

Behind the backs of Lana and Wayne, Farrow complained about them after watching the first rushes. "There is just no chemistry between them. The Duke is doped up on codeine, and Lana is drunk most of the time."

Tab Hunter was a great fan of Lana Turner movies, and he'd later record his impression of her in a memoir: "She arrived on the floating set. She broke the ice by hunkering down in the tight space with all the rank-and-file actors. She was tiny, but every inch the radiant movie star. I was awed, just like John Garfield when he first sees her in *The Postman Always Rings Twice,* wearing those little white shorts and that white turban."

"I said the stupidest thing a twenty-three-year-old could say: 'I've been a fan of yours since I was a kid.' She shocked hell out of me by reclining langorously across my lap, looking up at me with a teasing smile. I must have turned ten shades of red. I didn't know what to do with my hands."

That night, at a dinner party for cast and crew at the inn where they were staying, he found himself lured into dancing the hukilau, winning a coconut frond hat. "Impulsively, he placed a plumeria *[a tropical flower akin to a frangipani]* around Lana's neck. "Her laugh was like champagne. She was sweet and funny and down to earth, and I couldn't wait to work with her."

Two days later, Farrow informed Hunter that his big scene with Lana had been cut. "As for Lana, I got so tongue-tied working with her that I flubbed a line, saying, "Thanks for *looing* my *daundry.*"

As shooting progressed, Hunter grew increasingly disenchanted with Farrow. "He made a big show of his conversion to Catholicism. But in spite of his marriage, he was a garden-variety lecher. He real interest during production was doting lasciviously on Lana. Farrow was creepy, with beady eyes like a pair of piss holes in the snow. I couldn't work up any respect for him."

Hunter went on to say that Farrow had a "lecherous quality. There was something seedy about him."

Cameraman William Clothier claimed that Farrow "spent much of his time chasing after Lana."

Paul Fix was a close friend of the Duke's and observed what was going on. He said, "Lana Turner, hangover or not, was stunning. But she seemed insecure about her talent and the script. She compensated by becoming obsessed with her looks. I mean, talk about vanity in her love scenes with Duke. She said to him, 'Don't touch my hair,' or 'Don't smudge my makeup.'"

Later, Duke complained to Fix: "How am I supposed to make love to a woman who won't let me touch her?"

Fix claimed, "He had to make sure that when he held her, his hands didn't go near her hair, and when he kissed her, he couldn't make it too passionate out of fear of ruining her makeup. That's why the love scenes in the film looked so false."

During the final scenes of *The Sea Chase*, Wayne's freighter pulls into the port at Chile, where he is welcomed as a hero by the German colony. But he learns that he is still being pursued by the *Rockhampton* for his alleged killing of those fishermen at that island outpost, although it was his chief officer who had committed the atrocities.

The *Ergenstrasse* sets said for Europe, where Wayne, as captain, devises some unrealistic plan to join anti-Nazi forces to defeat Hitler. By this time in the movie, Lana's character of Elsa has fallen madly in love with him, and she sails from Chile back into the European war theater with a reformed Nazi at her side.

Eventually, Farrer, as Napier, catches up with the freighter and sinks it with British shells.

The film does not make it clear whether Wayne and Lana escape a watery grave. At the end, Farrar, as the narrator throughout, says, "We searched for survivors, but all that we found was a riddle of the sea. Had the ocean taken them, or had they reached a nearby shore, where the fjords of Norway could hide a secret? Who can say? There are only two people who can answer that, wherever they are. But knowing Karl Ehrlich as I did, I have an opinion."

FADE OUT

***

During the filming of *The Sea Chase*, Wayne didn't spend too much time fretting about Lana, as most of his thoughts were either on Pilar or on his ear infection. At the end of the shoot, on November 1, 1954, he would wed Pilar, his third wife, in the Hawaiian town of Kailua.

Lana was invited to the ceremony, but an hour after the shoot had finished, she left the set "in a huff," boarding the next plane to California.

***

The Sea Chase opened to bad reviews, but was saved by the pairing of Lana and Wayne. In fact, it was among the top ten grossing films of 1955, where it was up against such competition as *Oklahoma!* and *Mister Roberts*.

The New Yorker wrote, "The novel by Andrew Geer was an exciting, straightforward bit of work. You'd never know that from this cinematic interpretation."

A critic found the pairing of Lana with Wayne "the strangest casting of the year. John Wayne, that All-American hunk of man, is a German sea captain, and Lana Turner, that All-American hunk of woman, is a Nazi secret agent."

Lee Rogow, writing in *The Saturday Review*, said, "Miss Turner boarded the *Ergenstrasse* with a cruise wardrobe that would have all lady spies in town asking their governments for more charge accounts."

Bosley Crowther in *The New York Times* called *The Sea Chase* "a conventionally heroic and ideologically silly sea romance. Wayne plays it like he's herding a herd of cattle up the old Chisholm Trail. Farrow and his writers have turned the Mata

Hari of Geer's yarn into a stiff-necked, mink-clad female spoil sport whose singular presence among all the men is about as exciting as would be that of an albatross. As played by Lana Turner, she is a gaudy but very dull bird. To see Miss Turner in oilskins—that's the end of the rope."

***

After her completion of *The Sea Chase*, Lana, with Lex Barker, flew to Acapulco, their favorite retreat in Mexico. For years, she'd rented a small cottage on the grounds of Villa Vera, owned by the former bandleader, Teddy Stauffer. His former wife, Hedy Lamarr, had long gone. The villa had been the scene for some of Lana's trysts with Howard Hughes.

Barker, too, had developed a fondness for the resort, enough so that he and Lana decided to buy a strip of land that opened onto the water and a good, sandy beach.

She was overly committed financially, with bills piling up and thousands still owed to the IRS. To pay for the land, she asked her jeweler in Beverly Hills to sell the marquise diamond that Bob Topping had dropped into her martini in a Manhattan nightclub when he'd proposed to her. The sale of the ring was enough to purchase the beautiful strip of land where they planned to erect a "love cottage."

During his time at the resort, Barker also purchased an adorable little German Shepherd puppy which he named "Pulco." Lana didn't really want to return home with this dog, but Barker insisted. "It was love at first sight between Pulco and Lex," she said.

Back at the villa, Barker always paraded around in the nude, evoking the lifestyle (and exhibitionism) of Fernando Lamas. She found this disconcerting, because she was certain that the two Mexican houseboys hired by Stauffer were gay. "They seemed to devour Lex with their eyes," she said. "I came to realize that Lex was an exhibitionist."

One afternoon, when Barker went on a fishing trip with Stauffer, she stayed behind. Her friend and former agent, Henry Willson, had arrived in Mexico with one of his latest beefcake discoveries. Lana invited him over "for a girl-to-girl talk."

Since Willson had already undressed Barker on that long-ago night of her first date with him, she felt that she could talk candidly with him. She shared her concerns about Barker, suggesting that if Sol Lesser had asked him to, Barker would have cheerfully appeared in those Tarzan films without the loincloth.

Willson had seen the two Mexican houseboys, and, using his gay radar, he told her that both of them were definitely homosexual.

"Lex lies nude around the pool, and the boys always find some reason to cluster around him. As you know, he's very well hung, but he seems to fluff himself up around these boys, much to their delight. Actually, I think those kids are in love with Lex. They'd be his slave if asked."

She also revealed that Barker was very oral, and he wanted her to reciprocate "in ways that I'm not prepared to do."

"In other words, a tongue on his rosebud," Willson said.

"Is that what you gay guys call it? I think that's repulsive."

"Actually, it's quite enjoyable," Willson responded. "I demand it from my stable of actors."

Then, she shared her suspicions that whenever she was away from the villa, Barker got the boys to service him—"doing things I won't do."

"Well, dear one," Willson said. "Men from Rock Hudson to Guy Madison will be men. You can't trust them out of your sight."

"What should I do?" she lamented.

"Nothing. If someone has to do the dirty deed for Lex, just be grateful it's not you. Let's face it: You just don't know what a great sexual thrill that is for some people, even certain women."

"You mean, whores?" she asked.

"You'd be surprised how many ladies become whores in bed, or so I've heard."

"You were seen around town with Margaret Truman some time back. Was that a torrid affair?"

"Oh, please!" I just took her out. Perhaps she was in love with me, I don't know. The point is, I'm not in love with her...or with any woman, except you, my love. I positively adore you, but from a safe distance, of course."

***

[In her memoirs, Lana recalled Pulco growing up, turning from an adorable little puppy into a ferocious, 75-pound dog who seemed to want to charge anyone who came onto the property. After he attacked the postman, he sued for damages.

"Pulco is starry-eyed whenever Lex pulls into the driveway," Lana told Mildred. "He runs to his car and collapses in his arms. Let anyone else come around, and Pulco becomes vicious. He will attack if not restrained."

The dog was allowed to roam the property, which was encircled with stone walls and chain-link fences. Their neighbors at the time were Judy Garland and Sid Luft, living in their house with Liza Minnelli, Judy's daughter.

Cheryl and Liza became playmates. But one afternoon, young Liza crawled over the stone wall that separated the two properties.

The young girl fell a few feet onto Lana's grounds. Pulco, with fangs bared, darted toward her, tearing into the flesh of her right leg.

In her kitchen, Lana heard the screams and rushed out the door to keep Pulco from devouring Liza.

Garland, in her bedroom upstairs, with the windows opened, had heard her daughter scream. She made her way downstairs and through the gate adjoining the two properties.

To Lana, she appeared drugged when she tried to attend to her daughter. Fortunately, her maid summoned an ambulance, which rushed Liza to a hospital. There, she had to submit to twenty-one stitches to her leg before she was allowed to go home.

That night, when Sid Luft returned home, he wanted to file a lawsuit against Lana until Garland talked him out of it.

Lana urged Barker to get rid of Pulco, but he adamantly refused, reminding her that she'd been receiving a lot of threats, and that it was necessary to have an attack dog on the premises in case some prowler crawled over the walls or fences at night.

She relented, and let Pulco stay in her house. However, within a few months, she'd evict the dog and Barker, too.]

***

When Dore Schary informed the English actor, Roger Moore, that he been given the third lead in Lana Turner's latest picture, *Diane* (1956), he was delighted.

Later, in the MGM commissary, he met up with his friend and fellow Englishman, Edmund Purdom, who had recently made *The Prodigal* with Lana. Moore shared his good news with his friend, who didn't seem all that delighted. Purdom frowned, saying, "I guess that's all right if you don't mind a lot of booze and sex in Turner's dressing room."

[Moore thought that was an ungracious response to his big break until he learned that Schary had first assigned the male lead in Diane *to Purdom, who then lost the part after Lana announced to Schary that she refused to make another movie with him.]*

Around the same time, Schary summoned Lana to his office to inform her that she'd been cast in another picture, a 16th Century saga titled *Diane,* based on Diane de Poitiers

She protested, "Not another costume picture after we bombed with *The Prodigal.* And who is this Diane?"

He gave her a fast lesson in Renaissance French history, explaining that Diane de Poitiers (1499-1566) was a French noblewoman and the courtesan of Henri II, King of France. Her bitter rival was Catherine de Medici, the jealous and temperamental wife of the king. He went on to explain that Diane was "the most cultivated woman of the French Renaissance," though sometimes evaluated as "a silken, 16th Century tramp."

"Naturally, I get another tramp role," she said. "By the way, who is my leading man?"

"Roger Moore,"

"I know of him only because I saw him in *Interrupted Melody* with Eleanor Parker and Glenn Ford, a role originally intended for me. I don't know much about this Moore fellow."

Schary explained that he'd been a model known for posing in sweaters, and he'd become known as "The Big Knit."

"He also appears in some toothpaste ads," he said.

"Oh, goodie, goodie. At least, unlike Purdom and Ezio Pinza, with their garlic breath, he sounds kissable."

456

"Better lay off," Schary warned her. He just recently got married to some Welsh singer."

"I'll try to restrain myself," she promised. "I don't understand why you won't let me play a modern woman. I want to star in contemporary dramas about today's woman."

Schary explained that Diane de Poitiers was actually a forerunner of the modern woman. "She was Europe's first outdoor girl, a health fan, an advocate of the cold bath, and a devoted horse rider. She wasn't afraid to use her head, but was never caught with her brains showing."

Lana learned later from the producer, Edwin H. Knopf, that Metro had originally acquired the property for Greta Garbo, hoping to lure her out of retirement. Then, later, Schary had offered the script to Greer Garson. This staunch Englishwoman had little interest in playing "the whore of a French king."

When Moore was told who his fellow players were, he was at least mildly surprised. "I am an Englishman playing a French prince, Henri II. My father, King Francis I, was to be played by a Mexican, Pedro Armendáriz. Lana, of course, was an American cast as a French courtesan. My wife, Catherine de Medici, I thought was going to be played by Nicole Maury, the splendid French actress, but David Miller, our director, rejected her because she had a French accent. Instead, the role went to Marisa Pavan, the twin sister of Pier Angeli, who is Italian. Hollywood… You figure."

Before shooting began, Lana met with both Miller and also the producer, Edwin H. Knopf. He had launched the 1953 hit musical, *Lili*, starring Leslie Caron, Mel Ferrer, Zsa Zsa Gabor, and Jean-Pierre Aumont, Lana's former lover. Knopf also worked with many big stars, including Gary Cooper, Gregory Peck, Robert Taylor, and Greer Garson.

As a film director, Miller had had a varied career, having helmed pictures that included John Wayne in *Flying Tigers* (1943), and the Marx Brothers in *Love Happy* (1949), featuring a young Marilyn Monroe.

In *Diane*, Lana's actual husband was Count de Brézé (Torin Thatcher), although she becomes the mistress of Prince Henri (Moore). After the death of his father, the king, Henri inherits the throne. But his affair with Diane continues even after his politically motivated marriage to Catherine de Medici.

She is antagonistic to Diane, and her scheming eventually results in the death of Henri. Ruling as regent, she banishes

Diane de Poitiers (1499-1566), the French noblewoman portrayed by Lana, became—through diplomatic skill, charm, beauty, good advice, and perhaps witchcraft—the "favorite" of one of the most powerful kings of the French Renaissance, Henri II.

Diane from the court, but spares her life.

In a memoir, Moore, the screen's future James Bond, said he could be grateful to Lana for teaching him to "screen kiss." He claimed that at the age of twenty-eight, already into his second marriage and several girlfriends, he had always thought of himself as a good kisser. On hearing of the death of Francis I, and his upcoming ascension to the throne of France, he turns to Lana. "You made me a prince. Now make me a king."

"Our lips met, and I gave her the kiss of all kisses," he said.

Lana, as a grand diva, pushed him away and coughed. "Cut! CUT!" she called to Miller, before turning to Moore: "Honey, you're a great kisser. But I'm over thirty-five, and I've got to be careful of my neckline. So, could you kiss with the same passion, but without the pressure?"

Her leading man, not her screen lover, was actually Armendáriz. Along with Maria Félix and Dolores del Rio, he was among the best-known Latin American screen stars of the 1940s and '50s.

Lana (as Diane) met her screen rival, Marisa Pavan (playing Catherine de Medici) and spoke about having worked with her twin sister, Pier Angeli in *Flame and the Flesh* in Italy. Pavan was dating Jean-Pierre Aumont and would marry him the following year. "He's great in bed," Lana told Pavan.

Her remark was not appreciated.

In one particularly difficult scene in *Diane*, a CinemaScope epic, Moore, now ascended to the throne, was slated for the filming of an episode on horseback. Astride the horse as it headed at a fast pace toward a wall, his feet became separated from the saddle's stirrups, and he hit the ground really hard. Members of the crew rushed to his side, where they removed his armor to see if any bones had been broken.

Rushing to the scene, Lana called out in a loud voice, "Is his cock all right?"

Moore recorded her question in his memoirs. Her query suggested that Moore might have been servicing her throughout the shoot, but that doesn't appear to be the case.

"Thankfully, nothing was broken, not even my cock, but I was badly bruised. So was my ego."

During filming, Lana was being serviced by another cock, which had been injured, but which was back performing again.

Noted for the opulence of its Renaissance-era costumes, Lana, as Diane de Poitiers, was lavishly outfitted in costumes that included this awe-inspiring confection of velvet, ermine, and gold braid.

458

The notorious Freddy, frequented the set almost every day. On each occasion, he visited Lana's dressing room.

As Moore wrote, "Freddy was terribly well endowed. On crowd days at MGM, he would get it out to show it around for fifty cents per person. On days when 1,000 people showed up, you can see how profitable an exercise it was for him."

Errol Flynn used Freddy for a gag he'd play at the dinner parties he hosted. Once, Flynn dressed him up as a butler in white tie and tails and placed his massive appendage on a silver tray filled with shrimp. Guests were asked to serve themselves from the tray until one of them screamed at the discovery, buried amid the shrimp and lettuce, of his large penis.

Shelley Winters was on to Flynn's trick, and she deliberately stuck her fork sharply into Freddy's penis, causing him to scream out in pain.

The future James Bond, Roger Moore, claimed that Lana taught him the art of the "screen kiss—that is, passion without pressure. Don't ruin the hair or a woman's makeup."

Fortunately, by the time Lana filmed *Diane*, his "money-maker" was back in operation. He charged a man or a woman fifty dollars for a private session.

Lana had confided to Miller that she found Moore very attractive and planned to seduce him. At the wrap party signaling the end of shooting for *Diane*, cast and crew gathered in a nightclub setting, which was used for the film, *Love Me or Leave Me* (1955), starring Doris Day and James Cagney.

Moore sat on the steps of the mock dance floor with a drink in hand. Lana approached from behind and began a slow, sensual massage of his shoulders. He was just getting into enjoying the massage, when he heard a strong, masculine voice ring out: "Hi, honey!"

He turned to star into the face of a giant of a man, Tarzan himself, Lex Barker, A jealous husband had come for his wife.

"I got the message quick," Moore said.

Two days later, when Lana visited the studio for some publicity stills, Christopher Isherwood, the famous author of *The Berlin Stories*, invited her to lunch. He had written the screenplay for *Diane* based on a story by John Erskine.

Over lunch, he told her fascinating stories about Diane de Poitiers that hadn't been included in the film. She had retained her good looks well into her 50s, her appearance immortalized in sculpture and in paintings. Rumor had it that she maintained her beauty through witchcraft. She was also known for drinking gold, pulverized into powder and flakes and mixed with wine. *[Indeed, she did. In 2009, when French experts dug up her remains, they found high levels of gold in her hair.]*

Over coffee, Isherwood spoke of the difficulty he was having with the censors at the Breen Office. "They claim I condone adultery. Frankly, if they had their way, I think those blue noses would punish adultery by stoning homosexuals and burning them alive."

At a screening of *Diana*, Isherwood invited one of his best friends, Tennessee Williams, who had once tried to write a screenplay for Lana himself.

At the end of the screening, Isherwood asked the playwright for his opinion. "I think Lana never looked lovelier."

Isherwood claimed that the script would have been better if Lana had not interfered so frequently with the director.

In this tender scene, Lana as Diane offers comfort to Prince Henri (later, King Henri II), as played by Roger Moore.

"I could have offered him even more comfort off screen," she said. "But, alas, it was not meant to be."

In advance of its release, MGM launched an aggressive publicity campaign: LANA TURNER DARES THE DEVIL IN DIANE.

Privately, she complained, "I hope this is the last time I'll have to appear in those costume stinkers."

Most of the reviews were bad. Arthur Weiler of *The New York Times* found *Diane* "more stately than exciting, more pageant than play." However, critic Frank Quinn called Diane "a brilliant Renaissance film."

As Moore lamented, "*Diane* was a huge flop and I was fired."

Lana herself would, indeed, be fired, but not until she completed one more loan-out from her home studio. *Diane* would be the last movie she ever made on the MGM lot.

***

After the filming of *Diane*, Lana, with Lex Barker, returned to their rented villa in Acapulco for a holiday. As she later wrote, "I nearly didn't come back."

On their first day in Mexico, he invited her to the beach for a swim. He did not go into the water himself, but lay on the sands for a while, reading a novel that some author had sent him, hoping he would star in a movie adaptation, cast as a serial seducer. He soon fell asleep on the beach.

Enjoying the warm waters offshore, she at first found the ocean, the sun, and the cool breezes refreshing. In desperate need of a rest, she'd been wrestling with three major problems: A lack of money, a deteriorating marriage, and a movie career drifting into limbo.

Suddenly, without warning, a mammoth wave swept toward the shore, trapping her in its undertow. "I was drowning. The wave sucked me down as the water swirled around me. I was spinning like a top. I thrashed about like a wildcat trying to break the watery grip of this riptide. I just knew I was going to die."

"Suddenly, Tarzan must have awakened from his slumber. He didn't see my head in the water, and he jumped up, later telling me, 'I have never swimmed so fast in my life.' I felt him grab my ankle and yank me out of my watery grave. Tarzan to the rescue. He was the man to save me. After all, he'd fought with ferocious, man-eating alligators in the rivers of Africa. He brought me ashore and gently put me down on the sands. I was gasping for breath itself while coughing up water from my lungs."

"But that was not the end of my troubles on that fateful day."

Back at the villa, she wanted to take a long shower, not only to remove the sand from her body, but hoping it would steady her shattered nerves. Her near-death experience had left her badly shaken.

Barker, too, was upset, but one of the gay Mexican houseboys agreed to take him to the bedroom for an "in-depth massage."

She stayed under the refreshing water for nearly ten minutes, although she wondered why she wouldn't be afraid of water for the rest of her life. After the shower, she cut off the water, and stepped out of the pink marble bathtub. Missing her footing, she fell back, hitting her head on the far side of the tub. The blow was so hard it knocked her out.

When she awakened, a doctor, along with Barker, was standing over her. The doctor reported she had suffered a concussion and should be examined more thoroughly at the local hospital.

She spent two days there, feeling despair, almost abandonment. The doctor told her that he feared she would suffer dizzy spells and migraine headaches during the months ahead.

His diagnosis was correct. Throughout the remainder of the autumn of 1954, and into the winter and spring of the following year, these ailments persisted in causing her pain and suffering.

Barker showed up only once during her hospital stay, claiming that he had met a producer from Universal, who was going to try to cast him in "a meaty drama," in which he'd have the lead, perhaps opposite Piper Laurie.

She got into a fierce argument with him. At the end of their abortive "holiday," both of them flew back to Los Angeles in relative silence.

She later learned from her host, Ted Stauffer, in Acapulco, that Barker spent time within the villa of Merle Oberon, the porcelain-skinned film star and nymphomaniac, who had seduced many of Lana's former lovers: Turhan Bey, Gary Cooper, Clark Gable, and Rex Harrison, plus countless others, including Prince Philip of England.

When Lana learned about her husband's adultery in Mexico, she said, "Now I have a new female on my hate list."

***

Lana's final film for MGM was a loan-out to Fox for *The Rains of Ranchipur* (1955), which she'd made after *Diane*. But its remake of the 1939 *The Rains Came* would be in the movie houses before MGM released the ill-fated *Diane*.

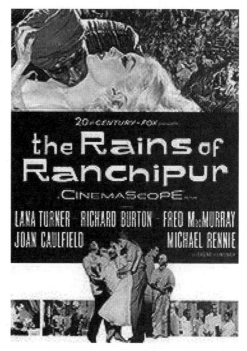

Shooting began only two days after her return from Mexico. Dore Schary could get another $300,000 by lending her services out to Fox. Darryl F. Zanuck had always wanted her to work for Fox, or so he had said. She claimed, "He's more interested in seducing me than starring me in any movie."

In spite of her protests, Schary insisted that she fulfill her contract. Her scenes would be filmed in Hollywood, so she would not have to travel abroad.

Producer Frank Ross visited her home, and she warned him of her splitting migraines and occasional dizziness, but he promised he'd film his way around them.

During his talk with Lana, Barker, clad in a very brief bikini, emerged dripping wet from the swimming pool.

Lana later said, "Perhaps he thought Ross was a homosexual, which he was not."

Barker had read the script of *The Rains of Ranchipur*, and he pitched himself for either the role of Lana's husband in the movie, an English lord, or else for the part of Tom Ransome, a semi-alcoholic, disillusioned American engineer.

Ross told him he'd already cast Michael Rennie as the lord, and Fred MacMurray as the engineer.

"Tarzan sulked for the rest of the day," Lana claimed.

***

Lana was to report to Fox the following Monday morning. On the set, she'd meet her co-star, Richard Burton.

Barker had warned Ross, "The reputation of that horndog has already preceded him. If he makes a move toward Lana, you'll have to get someone to dub his voice, because I'll turn him into a soprano."

***

There was a certain irony in casting Lana in *The Rains of Ranchipur*. Back in 1939, when she was new to Hollywood, she came very close to getting cast in the original version of this drama, a film entitled *The Rains Came*, based on a novel by Louis Bromfield. Its plot involved the effect that a devastating earthquake has on a widely mixed group of "saints and sinners" in British colonial India.

Its director, Clarence Brown, had originally offered Lana the *ingénue* role of Fern Simon, but MGM refused to lend her to Fox. Instead, Louis B. Mayer assigned her to three other pictures that year—*Calling Dr. Kildare*, *These Glamour Girls*, and *Dancing Co-Ed*. Consequently, she had not been available for *The Rains Came*. She was very disappointed, because it would be her only chance to co-star with her all-time heartthrob and future lover, Tyrone Power.

In Lana's place, starlet Brenda Joyce was cast in the Fern Simon role. There was another irony here, too, since a decade later, Joyce would play Jane to Lex Barker's Tarzan in *Tarzan's Magic Fountain* (1949). As Lana jokingly said, "Brenda got to swing on Barker's vine before I did."

Without Lana, Brown rounded out the '39 cast with Myrna Loy as Lady Edwina Esketh, supported by George Brent, Nigel Bruce, and the formidable Russian actress, Marie Ouspenskaya, playing the regal Maharini.

Sixteen years later, for the '55 remake, Lana was too old to play the *ingénue*. This time around, producer Ross cast his wife, Joan Caulfield, in the role of the younger woman. A model during World War II, Caulfield had established a reputation for playing roles that were "wholesome, pretty, and blonde."

Instead, Lana, now a more mature woman, was given the role of Lady Edwina Esketh, the character previously portrayed by Myrna Loy. Merle Miller, the gay novelist and biographer, rewrote the character, transforming Lady Edwina into a wealthy American heiress married to a weak man she loathed, Lord Esketh (played by the British actor, Michael Rennie).

The original *Rain* was in black and white. For the 1955 remake, 20th Century Fox lavishly (and expensively) filmed it in CinemaScope and DeLuxe color.

Before filming began, its director, Jean Negulesco announced to the press that there were only three women in Hollywood capable of playing Lady Esketh: Lana

Lana, as Edwina Esketh, treats her husband, Lord Esketh (Michael Rennie) as a servant. She'd wed a title, and he'd married her for her money.

463

Turner, Ava Gardner, or Rita Hayworth. This would be Lana's first film for Fox.

She would headline a cast that included Richard Burton, playing the Hindu Dr. Safti (the role originally handled by Power). Fred MacMurray would portray Tom Ransome (the role originally assigned to George Brent. And whereas Nigel Bruce had played the heroine's husband in the original 1939 version, Rennie was assigned the role in the 1955 remake. The Maharani would be played by the Russian stage actress, Eugenie Leontovich, that country's answer to Sarah Bernhardt or Italy's Eleonore Duse.

Is an earthquake on the way? Lana, in the arms of Richard Burton, cast as a Hindi doctor, fears disaster, as does the alcoholic, Tom Ransome (Fred MacMurray).

Lana plays a bored, blatant man hunter, although her stated purpose of being in India was to purchase race horses. [*Actually, the exterior shots were filmed in Pakistan.*] Her marriage to Rennie is loveless. She is introduced to the Hindu doctor (Burton was miscast). Although he resists her at first, he eventually falls under her seductive powers.

MacMurray is the hard-drinking Tom, who eventually wins back his self-respect and the love of Simon (Caulfield).

Ross, the producer, had previously made *The Robe* (1953) with Burton. He had once been married to screen legend, Jean Arthur, another blonde. Ross was anxious to work with Burton again. At the time, Burton was only a minor actor in Hollywood, years away from playing Marc Antony opposite Elizabeth Taylor in *Cleopatra* (1963).

The Romania-born director, Negulesco, was very experienced, having previously helmed Jane Wyman in her Oscar-winning performance in *Johnny Belinda* (1948) and Marilyn Monroe in *How to Marry a Millionaire* (1953). He'd also directed such divas as Barbara Stanwyck and Joan Crawford before making his most recent hit, *Three Coins in the Fountain* (1954).

Even though she was the producer's wife, Lana made no special attempt to ingratiate herself with Caulfield. She did remind her that she had originally been slated to play her role in *The Rains Came*.

"Oh, that was so long ago," Caulfield said. "I also heard that you had been set to star in *The Petty Girl* (1950), but, of course, the part went to me."

After that remark, Lana got a little catty with this former cover girl and Broadway *ingénue*. "Your career may be in danger with the arrival of Grace Kelly," Lana told Caulfield. "She has your cultivated manner, but does it better." Lana was right, as she was around to watch Caulfield's screen career fizzle.

Michael Rennie, cast as Lana's husband, generated no excitement from her on or off the screen. She had recently seen him in *The King of the Khyber Rifles* the year before, but only because Tyrone Power was the star.

During Rennie's talks with Lana, he said, "I suppose women find me attractive because I am polite, charming, courteous, and a gentleman. My romantic reputation is an exaggeration. The realities are a bit different."

"I can believe that," she said. She noted that the English actor bonded more naturally with Burton than with her, as he'd recently made *The Robe* with the Welshman.

***

When Lana saw the rushes, she told the director that she'd never been photographed so beautifully. She thanked Fox's Milton Krasner.

Helen Rose, one of her alltime favorite designers, had worked with her on such films as *The Bad and the Beautiful*, and she came through for her once again. Lana looked like a high fashion model.

The special effects would bring an Oscar nomination to Ray Kellogg. He simulated an earthquake which destroys a bridge and a huge dam, bringing floods, death, and destruction to the little town in India. Unlike the original version, in the remake, Lana was allowed to survive.

In the plot, writer Miller has Rennie denounce his wife as "selfish, greedy, corrupt, and decadent." She is a true *femme fatale*.

Her best line, delivered near the end of the movie, is uttered during a face-off with Leonotovich. "I don't give a damn," Lana says. The word damn did not cause the outrage it did when Clark Gable as Rhett Butler, in the closing scene of *Gone With the Wind*, tells Scarlett: "Frankly, my dear, I don't give a damn."

But this was 1955, not 1939.

The Rains of Ranchipur was Fox's feature film for the Christmas season of 1955, opening in theaters across the country.

Reviews were mixed. But whereas purists preferred the original Loy/Power film from 1939, *Redbook* selected the '55 version as "Picture of the Month," and the *New York Daily News* awarded it the top rating of four stars.

The movie was not a hit at the box office, garnering far fewer viewers than anticipated. At some showings, it half filled an auditorium, if that. Fox tried hard, with provocative advertising of sexy Lana and sexy Burton. One ad had Burton sneering at her: "I wonder what the word for you is in Hindi. In English, it's only one syllable."

***

Although Lana, in her memoirs, promised to tell "The Truth," she gave a very incomplete rendition of her love/hate relationship with Richard Burton during the making of *The Rains of Ranchipur*, which was shot in Hollywood, not on location in

India.

No doubt, she was restrained in her recollections because at the time that she worked with him, he was still married to actress Sybil Williams. As a potential lover, Lana wasn't robbing the cradle, as he was only four years younger than she was.

She wrote that it was hard for her to simulate any sexual chemistry with Burton in their love scenes, with her as a predatory American heiress and he as a noble Hindu doctor. At first, she was put off by his attitude, attacking his "bloated self-image." Behind his back, sometimes in the company of Rennie and MacMurray, she mocked and denounced him.

Burton constantly argued with the director, Negulesco, who accused him of not being very convincing as a Hindu.

"I'm a proud Welshman," he shot back. "Not a god damn raghead Indian."

Lana noted that Burton spent his time off-camera in his dressing room "seducing our dusky little extras, for whom he developed a great fondness."

What Lana left out of her memoirs was that after only three weeks, she, too, succumbed to the sexual magnetism of Burton and his Welsh charm, especially his speaking voice, which was the most alluring she'd ever heard.

He could be very candid about his sex life, even admitting, "Perhaps most actors are latent homosexuals, and we cover it up with drink. I was once a homosexual, but it didn't take."

[No doubt, he was referring to his time in the 1940s when, as a young actor, he was trying to break into the theater. He was seduced by some of its VIP notables, namely Emlyn Williams, Laurence Olivier, and John Gielgud.

Burton later seduced not only actresses, such as Sophia Loren, Raquel Welch, Barbra Streisand, Rachel Roberts, Tammy Grimes, Ava Gardner, Zsa Zsa Gabor, Geneviève Bujold, and especially Claire Bloom, but Elizabeth, Princess of Yugoslavia, and even a toothless middle-aged Jamaican maid "when I woke up with a big hard-on as she came in to clean my bedroom."]

The story of Burton's seduction of Lana was finally revealed in Michael Munn's biography, *Prince of Players*, published in 2008. Skyhorse Publishing advertised it as "Burton's darkest thoughts and secrets, revealing hell-raising stories that Hollywood quashed in order to save Burton's early film career—including affairs with Marilyn Monroe and Lana Turner, being caught in a brothel with Errol Flynn, and a fistfight with Frank Sinatra."

Munn was a friend of both Burton and Ava Gardner, who at the time was a rival goddess at MGM, vying with Lana, sometimes for the same film roles. Amazingly, they remained close friends, although later, their amity would get frayed, especially after Gardner, when drunk, would make derogatory remarks about Lana.

Gardner once told Munn, in reference to Lana, "That tramp fucked everyone. She fucked Burton. I bet it was one time he didn't have to chase. She would have gone after him."

"I suggest it takes two to tango, baby, and she saw Rich as a bit of a trophy. She felt she could have anyone she wanted. She wanted him because he had a reputation for fucking every one of his leading ladies."

When Lana heard about Gardner's gossipy evaluation of the situation, she quipped, "How can a pot call a kettle black?"

Munn told Burton what Gardner had said. Burton replied, "I was ever so happy being Lana's trophy during the filming of that *Ranchipur* movie. The film bored me to death, although I did my best with it. I liked to joke, 'It never rains but what it Ranchipurs.' Between takes, there was only one thing to do to make the time pass more agreeably. Lana and I passed the time together. She set out to get me, and I allowed myself to be caught. Why not? Who knows who else she was bedding? I didn't care, and I didn't ask."

A few years later, right before Burton headed for Rome to make *Cleopatra* (1963) with Elizabeth Taylor, Lana encountered him at a Hollywood party. He had been drinking heavily. She congratulated him on winning the role of Marc Antony, although he didn't seem to be looking forward to it.

"Whether she knows it or not, Miss Taylor is going to make me a star," he vowed. "I going to use that no-talent Hollywood nothing."

***

In 1970, Burton recorded in his diaries: "Elizabeth watched me in an old film last night, *The Rains of Ranchipur*, which I made with Lana Turner way back when. Elizabeth said I was very handsome and sexy-looking, and the film was nothing like as bad as I had said it was. Perhaps it's mellowed with age."

***

After wrapping *The Rains of Ranchipur* for Fox, Lana paid a final visit to MGM to pick up her clothing and other possessions. She got out of her car for a farewell look at the studio where she'd once reigned as queen in the 1940s.

MGM had notified her on February of 1956 that her contract had not been renewed. "It is not our intention to make any more Lana Turner pictures," a lawyer for MGM had written.

Packing up her things in her dressing room, she wondered what new and younger star would be occupying it.

She checked her face in the mirror, relieved that at thirty-six, a fatal age for most Hollywood actresses, she still looked beautiful, except for a minor telltale sign of age here and there. She called this period in her life a time of emotional trauma. Lex Barker still offered sex with a powerful weapon, but he was having a hard time finding suitable vehicles for himself in his post-Tarzan years.

In her time, she'd earned millions for MGM, but that was in the days of Louis B. Mayer. The former mogul had been booted out in June of 1951. He defiantly issued a statement to the press which Lana read: "I am going to be more active than at any time during the last fifteen years. It will be at a studio and under conditions where I shall have the right to make the right kind of pictures—decent, wholesome pictures for Americans and for people throughout the world who want and need this type of entertainment."

It was an idle boast, as Lana sensed it would be, although he called her twice with picture ideas, for which he never arranged financing. At least he continued to think of her as a bankable star.

Mayer died in 1957, and with his passing went Lana's glory days at MGM.

During her last hour at MGM, no one came forward to tell her goodbye, except the two old guards at the gate. Some unknown grip called out to her, "Are you finished, Miss Turner?"

Too choked up to answer, she drew a finger across her throat to signal "Cut!"

The guards told her goodbye. She paused before driving through the gate. Nostalgia was telling her to look back for a final gaze at the studio that had made her an international legend.

"What the hell!" she said. "Fuck nostalgia!"

Without looking back, she headed down the street in her car.

That glory that was MGM and the glory that was Lana Turner were over. She recalled, "A movie MGM made said it all: *Gone With the Wind.*"

The Hindu doctor, Richard Burton, nibbles at the neck of Lady Esketh (Lana herself). He boasted, "It's not really a triumph to be a success with these Hollywood ladies, because they have so little opportunity with real men. If there's a dame on the set, I can't screw, my name is not Richard Burton. And I'm including that very stuck-up Lana Turner in that. The more stuck-up they appear, the more likely you are to encounter them at the bottom of the orgy pile."

Tarzan Is Revealed as a Child Rapist

Lana in Her First Mother Role

On April 15, 1957, Hollywood learned that that Lana had changed her mind. In a column headlined LUSCIOUS LANA TO PLAY MOTHER ROLE, Louella Parsons revealed that Lana had at last accepted the starring role, that of Constance, in "the salacious *Peyton Place*...This will be the first time that Lana has stepped out of her glamour roles, but this is going to be such a picture she'd be foolish not to accept it, *pronto.*"

Fans bombarded Fox with letters, most of them urging glamorous *femme fatale* Lana not to switch to maternal parts. For Lana, however, her agreement to play Connie would be a forerunner for many equivalent roles in her future, notably *Imitation of Life*.

Throughout the course of 1956, Hollywood reporters were still fascinated by the life and loves of Lana Turner, still viewing her as hot copy, even though she'd been fired by MGM.

A reporter, Joe Hyams, visited her at her home, where she came out to greet him in a black sweater, black slacks, and gold sandals. "She looked as beautiful as ever—still very fuckable, a living wet dream."

She welcomed him warmly, offering him a drink. "I think she'd had a few belts before I got there."

She settled onto her sofa in her most seductive pose, telling him, "I've been sprung from jail. I'm still walking around in a daze, as if I can't believe it. For all of my adult life, I've been in bondage to MGM except for that brief stint at Warners in the 1930s when I screwed Ronald Reagan. Don't print that last remark. He's settled down with Nancy now, as you know."

"I had become a fixture at Metro, like the Thalberg Building. If Louis B. Mayer or Dore Schary had a rotten picture to make, they'd say, 'Give it to Lana. Maybe she can save it.' If I absolutely refused to do it, they'd threaten to suspend me or else give it to Ava Gardner."

"She wasn't turned on by most of the emerging pretty boys that came along in the 1950s," said Del Armstrong, her makeup man and confidant.

"She'd already had James Dean, but told me she found him a bit creepy. Montgomery Clift was a film star, but he was gay and a bit weird. Marlon Brando was too much of a brute for her. The one emerging new actor who really turned her on was Robert Wagner. Press agent George Nichols told me that he saw Wagner disappearing into her dressing room during her last weeks at MGM."

"Time and again on bended nylon, I pleased with the front office to give me better scripts. Joan Crawford at MGM did that before they dumped her. The last time I begged, I was cast in *The Prodigal*. Thanks a lot, guys!"

"I'm thinking about forming my own production company, Lanturn. Lex Barker wants us to team up like Spencer Tracy and Katharine Hepburn did, except I don't think the two of us on screen would be typical family fare. Our love scenes wouldn't be for the Disney people."

Later, after Hyams left, she said she hoped that she'd concealed her fragility. In many ways, her world seemed to be crumbling.

She'd been forced to sell her mansion in Holmby Hills for payment of back income taxes.

When she told her neighbor goodbye, Judy Garland wasn't all that encouraging. "Oh, Lana dear, it'll be our fate: We'll both end up, deserted by men, two old alcoholic hags with dreams of yesterday. I'll be singing 'Over the Rainbow' in some seedy tavern filled with whores and their pimps."

***

Despite her bravado, Lana faced one turbulent conflict after another. Chief among them was her deteriorating marriage to Barker. Ironically, the studio that hired her as a freelancer was Universal-International, the same studio that had Barker under contract, starring in a string of low-budget "B" pictures. Lana had seen them, privately, saying, "B is too high a rating for that garbage Lex is turning out."

Barker was in Rome making another of his cheapie pictures for an Italian film company. As Fellini said, "Rome is becoming the stockyard for Hollywood movie stars past their prime."

On the lot at Universal, during her filming of *The Lady Takes a Flyer* (1958), Lana began hearing reports that her adulterous husband was "sleeping his way" through the starlets, one by one, evocative of how Clark Gable had seduced MGM's leading ladies in the 1930s.

Del Armstrong was often at Lana's side, listening to her marital woes and, on occasion, doing her make-up. "Lex is getting home later and later every night," she told him. "On some nights, he doesn't show up at all. He never tells me where he's been, and I never ask. Perhaps I don't want to hear."

Often, when he did come home, she fought with him about money. Her salary at MGM had been larger than his, but now her paychecks were no longer delivered by the postman, who didn't even ring once.

"I knew my star status threatened him. He left the Tarzan pictures to become the leading male star of the 1950s. Now Rock Hudson seemed to be taking over. There was also an array of pretty boys who were ascending: Jeffrey Hunter, Robert Wagner, Tony Curtis, Tab Hunter, Tony Perkins, Troy Donahue, Paul Newman, and John Derek. Warren Beatty would be lurking around the corner in the near future. Lex didn't seem to fit in with these male beauties. He had been born in 1919, and these guys were hatched yesterday."

One affair of Barker's particularly infuriated Lana when she heard the gossip coming from the set of *The Girl From the Kremlin* (1957). In this picture, the star was her old rival, Zsa Zsa Gabor.

"If God did create Adam, as rumor has it, and a director wanted to make a film about the guy, Lex Barker would be my top choice for the role," gushed Zsa Zsa. "He is living proof that all men were not created equal. He is the greatest physical specimen. Coming from me, *dahlink*, that's quite a compliment, since I'm the best judge of male flesh."

She was cast in a dual role in the movie, her most improbable character that of Greta Grisenko, the nurse of Josef Stalin. Her less malevolent twin, Lili, hires an O.S.S. agent (Barker) to locate her sister in Moscow.

"During the shoot, Lex was a man after my own heart," Gabor said. "I was expecting to meet some Tarzan beefcake, but I encountered a cultured, refined man

471

who came from a society background and had gone to Princeton."

A cinematic quickie, *The Girl From the Kremlin* was shot in just ten days during February of 1957 on a budget of $300,000. In movie annals, it's listed as one of the worst films ever made, standing alongside *They Saved Hitler's Brain* (1963).

It flopped at the box office and was lambasted by critics, at least by those who had nothing else to review the day it opened. The *San Francisco Chronicle* defined it as "the most absurd motion picture of the year. *Variety* headlined its review: IF JOE STALIN DIDN'T DIE, THE GIRL IN THE KREMLIN SHOULD.

Later in life, gossipy Zsa Zsa said, "Lana Turner and I sometimes had the same men as Eva (her sister) and I did. To name a few: Richard Burton, Sean Connery, Conrad Hilton, Clark Gable, Howard Hughes, John F. Kennedy, Peter Lawford, Dean Martin, Tyrone Power, Frank Sinatra, Robert Taylor, and even that doomed gangster, Johnny Stompanato. I was especially fond of Lex's 'third leg' as Marilyn Monroe dubbed it."

***

As early as the autumn of 1956, rumors appeared in the press about the rift Lana and Barker were facing in their marriage.

Bob Thomas of the Associated Press confronted Barker about this. He wrote: "Lex Barker is perplexed by rumor mongers. Recently, he was absent from Lana Turner, his wife, for five weeks, mostly on location, and partly to visit his stricken father in the East. While he was gone, the rumors flew."

James Bacon reported that Lana was cavorting with a bullfighter in Tijuana. Another columnist claimed that she would remarry her second husband, Stephen Crane, after she divorces Barker.

"Lana likes bullfighters," Barker said. "While I was away, she went to see the fights in Mexico, visiting with some of her friends. A bullfighter happened to be in the party—and that was all there was to that. As for the Crane remarriage, he is the father of my stepdaughter, Cheryl, and he visits the house to see her. His many entanglements do not include Lana."

***

The last Christmas that Lana, Lex Barker, and Cheryl spent together had been in Acapulco in 1956. At her favorite retreat, Villa Vera, she learned that her quarters had been renamed "The Lana Turner Suite."

It was not a happy time, with a lot of bitter accusations of infidelity exchanged between the "Battling Barkers," as Del Armstrong labeled them. "I think Barker just wanted to pick a fight so he would have a chance to storm out of the villa for one of his off-the-record adventures with that great Mexican beauty, Dolores Del Rio, whose beautiful face looked like it had been dipped in porcelain. Not that I blame him. She was a kind of timeless wonder."

Lana recalled it as "a miserable Christmas. I knew I couldn't go on with Lex much longer. The only thing I liked about him is his sheer physical beauty and sexual prowess. As for his personality, he's a son of a bitch—selfish, egotistical, exasperating, devious, and thoroughly rotten."

She revealed that, "There was a lot more going on that I didn't know about. Some sort of secret life. A friend told me that he was seen dining one night at Chasens with Cary Grant. Why didn't he mention that to me? Cary Grant, for God's sake. Perhaps he was afraid to name drop."

"He was always receiving expensive presents. When we returned from Acapulco, some of those presents had been delivered to my house. But he didn't open them there, and refused to tell me who was supplying such lavish gifts. Was it a woman? Or a man? Perhaps women? Perhaps men like Grant. I know that Clifton Webb, when he didn't have his tongue out panting for Robert Wagner, gave Lex one of the most expensive watches I'd ever seen."

"I didn't find out until after our divorce that he kept a secret apartment in West Hollywood for his assignations," she said.

Back home again, the unhappy trio—Lana, Barker, and Cheryl—continued with their dreary lives. One afternoon, Lana left her house for a meeting with Greg Bautzer about legal steps needed to set up her own film production company in the future.

A lot of stars, including Burt Lancaster and Humphrey Bogart, were doing that, and she wanted to get in on it, hoping to retain most of the money from films she'd independently produce, if she could find the financing. During her absence, as she later learned, "Lex seized the day…or, put another way, seized poor Cheryl."

That day, Cheryl, as she later confessed in her memoirs, was violently assaulted by Barker

He wanted sexual gratification. When Cheryl resisted his advances, he smashed into her face with his muscular forearm, which had been so amply on display in his Tarzan films. He held her down, and, as she claimed, tightened his powerful grip on her delicate throat. As he raped her, he denounced her, calling her, "You little bitch!"

At times, as she'd later write, she felt he was killing her, that she was choking her to death. The question peppering her brain was, "How long could she continue to endure these unbearably painful assaults from her stepfather?" At the end of his assault, she claimed, "His orgasm brought an ecstatic hiss of rage that died off in waves."

These repeated attacks shattered her, both emotionally and physically. He was such a big brute of a man, and she was such a vulnerable teenager with a body still undeveloped for his raging desires. He would leave her bed as she lay crying in pain, feeling that her insides had been ripped apart.

In the meantime, Lana continued to remain unaware of all of this.

Bowing to Barker's threats, Cheryl believed him a first, that if she didn't keep silent, she would be sent away to some reform school. But in only a few short months, she began to realize that she would not be the one sent away. It would be Barker himself who'd be sentenced to jail, where he might be the one held down and gang raped.

One aspect never explained was why Barker turned to the young girl for sex in the first place. He was bombarded daily with fan letters from love-starved women and gay men whose wildest sexual fantasies were to be seduced by Tarzan. Why he didn't take advantage of these countless offers is not known. Why then would he turn to an underaged girl whose body had not fully matured?

Lana may have provided the answer later on, telling Virginia Grey, "One night, Lex and I, after intercourse, were just lying awake in the moonlight talking about our sexual fantasies. I was surprised to learn that nearly all of his fantasies were about deflowering young girls. At no point, fool that I was, did I make that link to Cheryl, realizing that she fit the description of one of his fantasies."

As this dark and murky drama was unfolding within the Turner/Barker residence, Louella Parsons, not always the most reliable source, printed an item about them in her column. "Lex Barker is good for Lana Turner. They have a happy home life that she has never had in any of her former marriages, beginning with bandleader Artie Shaw, then going on to Stephen Crane (now a successful restaurant owner), and ending with Bob Topping, the tin plate heir from back East."

***

During the final months of their marriage, the fights between Barker and Lana grew more hostile, each partner accusing the other of infidelity. He seemed to suspect that every man she was seen with was her lover, even though most of them were business associates. Actually, he was accusing her of what he was secretly guilty of as a serial seducer.

Gradually, Lana, as she relayed to Del Armstrong, "began to wise up to what he was accusing me of."

He was gone for long periods of time, making such movies as *The Deerslayer* (1957), or *The Girl in the Black Stockings* (also 1957).

George Nichols, a press agent at MGM, said, "I think both Lana and Barker were playing around. He was on location most of the time, and I know for a fact that Lana, who never wanted to be left alone, was doing the night club scene, like she did in the early 1940s. I don't think at that point in her life, she could get along without a man...any man, it seemed. She went a bit wild."

Armstrong often escorted her to the Trocadero or the Mocambo. "She had an eye out for any hot guy, and Hollywood had more per square foot of them than any other place on the planet. They arrived daily from Kansas, from the Panhandle of Florida, from the shores of Maine, all with the same goal: To become a movie star."

"She'd even go for a waiter or a bartender if he were good-looking and muscular," Armstrong said. "She never made the pitch herself as far as I know. She had me do it for her. She almost never got turned down unless a guy was gay. Even some of the gay guys fucked her because she was THE Lana Turner. All these guys hoped she would use her influence to get them cast in movies. In all cases, they were disappointed. Lana was having enough trouble relaunching her own career."

"Lana thought she had a chance with young Robert Wagner, because she'd heard that he'd been living with Barbara Stanwyck, certainly an older woman." Armstrong said. "He'd been in her movie, *Titanic* (1953), which had also starred Clifton Webb, who wanted Wagner for himself. Lana's former agent, Henry Willson, represented Wagner for a time, having met him when he was only nineteen. He may have been the one who brought Wagner and Lana together. I don't know."

Wagner was getting a great press. Willson loved his charms at the studio. He raved about his clean-cut, All-American look. The gay agent proclaimed, "The face of boyish Robert Wagner can mirror every thought and word. He's got a bright personality that really comes across on the screen. He has that casual, relaxed quality that girls go for. I don't think he'll miss."

Lana went on to tell Armstrong that Wagner had seduced her. "Perhaps it was the other way around. All I know is, she gave him a rave review without going into a blow-by-blow description. She told me, 'The boy has everything I had dreamed about…and more! He'll go far in this town.'"

***

Late one afternoon, Lana was sitting alone in her living room chain smoking. She heard the phone ring in the hallway. Was it a film offer? A man calling for a date?

She lifted the receiver to hear the smooth screen voice of Gregory Peck, with whom she'd already chatted several times. Was he calling for a date? She'd first met him when he was having an affair with Ingrid Bergman during their filming together of the memorable *Spellbound* in 1945. In 1952, he'd been scandalously exposed in *Confidential* for having an affair with the hot-to-trot blonde, Barbara Payton, his co-star in *Only the Valiant* (1952).

She was aware that Peck's first marriage to Finnish-born Greta Konen had ended in divorce in 1953. But she'd also read that he had married a Paris news reporter, Veronique Passani. He'd met her on his way to Rome to film *Roman Holiday* (1953) with Audrey Hepburn, with whom he also had had an affair.

The "date" she envisioned was not exactly what Peck had in mind. She agreed to go with him to Summit Ridge Drive in Brentwood, to see a house for sale there for $95,000. During the course of her marriage to Artie Shaw, Lana had lived there, and now it was on the market.

He told her he wanted to visit the house with her before buying it. "You don't really know a house until you live in it. I thought you might tell me any drawbacks to it that I've overlooked."

"Its main drawback is that Lana Turner no longer lives here," she said, flirtatiously.

She stood with him in the carpeted living room, in front of the fireplace, perhaps hoping he might make a pass at her. "Greg

Lana had long wanted to seduce Gregory Peck, whom she put at the top of her list of desirable males in Hollywood.

"His deep, modulated voice could cause a woman to have an orgasm on the spot," she said. "Oh, yes, and he was impossibly handsome."

475

was the perfect gentleman," she told Armstrong. "I flirted. He was polite. What was a girl to do? I know that Barbara Payton, that whore, was the aggressor. I decided to follow in her footsteps."

"I've always wanted to ask you something," she said, "but never had the courage to bring it up."

"What's that?" he asked. "To star in a picture together?"

"That, too, but for the present time, it's something else I had in mind. Something of a more personal nature."

"You want me to fuck you?" he asked.

As she'd later reveal to Virginia Grey, "I was startled at his directness."

"I've always wanted to get it on with you," Peck told her. "After all, you're the most beautiful woman in Hollywood, and I'm a mere mortal. But I considered Tarzan a tough act to follow. I haven't had much training in jungle tactics."

"None needed," she said. "Artie and I used to get it on right here on this very carpet in front of the fireplace. Why not you?"

"I'm unbuckling my belt this very moment," he said.

When she told Grey about this, she invariably asked the question, "What was it like?"

She discussed her adoration for Peck, whom she considered "about the handsomest man ever to set foot in Hollywood. He has a quiet, unassuming sex appeal."

"Let me put it this way," Lana told her. "Without going into too much clinical detail, I will tell you this. Greg had me nibbling on his big ear before the deed was done. One ear is bigger than the other, and I took the big ear."

Grey asked her if she planned any repeats. "That's up to him. I know he is happily married. I also know that even the most happily married men, at least in Hollywood, like to get something on the side."

"He told me that in the future, I had a choice. Either a 'milkman's matinee' [*i.e., a morning session in his dressing room*], or a 'sneak away' for love in the afternoon at the Château Marmont."

"I told him a milkman's matinee suited me just fine, providing he brought the cream."

"Oh, Lana, my dear, since marrying Lex Barker, you've become such a vulgar lady."

"You finally noticed," she quipped.

***

Without warning, having decided she could endure no further assaults from Lex Barker, Cheryl made a choice to reveal everything, not to Lana, but to her grandmother, Mildred, whom she still affectionately called "Gran."

In February of 1957, in the wake of that awful Christmas in Mexico , she sat with Mildred and told her the whole story. She first had a look of disbelief, then of horror. Mildred's face would be a memory that would not fade.

In her apartment, convinced that her granddaughter was telling the truth— the story was just too vivid with details—Mildred went to the phone to summon Lana. She picked up the receiver to hear her mother's command: "Get over here at once. It's Cheryl. I don't want to tell you over the phone. And don't bring Lex Barker! Come alone. You've got to hear this."

Alarmed, from inside her house, Lana did not press for any further details. Barker had already retired upstairs, a bit drunk. Both of them had just attended a party at the home of Jack Benny. On the way back in the car, he'd confessed to Lana that when he asked Benny where the bathroom was, the comedian had accompanied him. "The fucker came on to me," he claimed. "I know he plays gay in those comedy skits, but he's not just play-acting. All he got to see was me haul it out to take a horse piss—nothing else."

Slipping out of her house without alerting Barker, Lana drove to Mildred's apartment, where she found the two of them sitting on the sofa, Mildred's arms wrapped around Cheryl, who was sobbing.

Within the next few minutes, Lana heard the entire story of the assaults on her daughter. Her mother and daughter each witnessed Lana's face stiffen, at first in stunned disbelief, before fading into an acceptance of a reality that had escaped her, "even though it's been going on right under my nose."

At first she wanted to chastise her daughter for not revealing these assaults much sooner. At this point, she had not decided how she was going to confront Barker. The only move she knew she was going to make, even though it was a Sunday, involved taking Cheryl to her doctor later that morning. "He'll open the office for me."

It was decided that Cheryl would spend the night with Mildred. "I don't want her to have to face that man ever again."

Back in her Cadillac, she drove home alone, not certain about what steps to take. She came into the house and ascended the steps to her bedroom. The light was on, the TV set on "snow," with no programs being broadcast.

Barker lay on their bed, asleep, his powerful genitals looking more menacing than ever. As she'd confided to Del Armstrong later that morning, "Flashing on his using such a powerful weapon on such a tender young girl was unbearable. For a moment, I was crazed."

Ever since she'd received death threats and calls that Cheryl would be kidnapped, she'd gone to Greg Bautzer, who had arranged for her to purchase a revolver. The gun made her extremely nervous, and she could never imagine herself using the weapon to kill anyone. She had placed it in her chest of drawers, concealed amid her lingerie.

As she later told Armstrong, "I went insane, at least temporarily. I went to that drawer, took out the revolver, and approached Lex, who was still sound asleep. I pointed the gun at his head. I wanted that perverted brain of his to explode in the blast of the bullet's impact."

"My whole life flashed in front of me as I stood there with that revolver pointed at the magnificent head of Lex Barker," she told Armstrong. "Suddenly, very gradually, sanity returned. I still had the rage, but not the desire to kill."

"I didn't want to destroy my career and spend the rest of my life in prison, fighting off lesbians."

She later said she'd been horrified when she'd seen the lurid *film noir, Caged* (1950), starring Eleanor Parker, a brutal story of women imprisoned.

She also realized that if she killed Barker, all the tawdry stories about his repeated rapes of her daughter would eventually be exposed. As she told Virginia Grey, "Cheryl's life would be ruined forever. Barker's arrest and imprisonment would be one of the biggest Hollywood scandals in years."

"I knew then that I was not going to kill him." She returned to the living room, and there she sat, smoking until dawn. The TV set had been left on, its "snow" finally reverting to the morning news. At least stories about her weren't leading off the dawn roundup of news. She could just imagine the lurid headlines: LANA TURNER ARRESTED FOR THE MURDER OF TARZAN.

Finally, Barker woke up and headed downstairs, where he confronted her. "What in hell is going on?" he demanded. "Why didn't you come to bed?"

Then, as if sensing what had happened, he asked, "Has that Cheryl been telling you lies? You can't believe a word out of her mouth."

"I'm giving you twenty minutes to get out of my house!" she demanded. "And take Pulco with you. If you're not out, I'm phoning the police to arrest you."

Without arguing, he seemed to accept the fact that their marriage had just ended. He rushed upstairs, got dressed, and was out the door with his dog. He'd later send someone to retrieve his clothing and other possessions, including his gym equipment.

***

After her sleepless night, Lana climbed grimly into her Cadillac and drove over to Mildred's, where she encountered her nervous, distraught daughter. Putting her into the car, she headed in silence to the medical office of Dr. R.H. Fagin.

In a voice that was barely a whisper, she explained how her husband had sexually assaulted her daughter. He said very little until after he'd given Cheryl her first pelvic examination. She looked so very young and so very frightened.

From inside the examination room, both Cheryl and Dr. Fagin could hear Lana, out in the waiting room, sobbing. Later, she was called in to hear the doctor's report.

"There are signs of a violent penetration," he said. "She had been so stretched, she should have had stitches. There's no doubt that she's been raped, perhaps repeatedly. The girl is telling the truth. You must believe her and protect her from any future assault. She might need psychiatric help."

During the drive back home, Lana told her that she was going to report what had happened to Stephen Crane. He was in St. John's Hospital at the time, recovering from brain surgery. After that car crash in Paris, he had had a steel plate inserted and screwed into his skull by French doctors. During the months after that, he had suffered occasional fainting spells and migraines that lasted for days.

At the hospital, he was coherent. When Lana told him what had happened to his daughter, he flew into a rage, threatening to kill Barker. But finally, after she assured him that Cheryl would never have to confront Barker again, he settled down. Both of them agreed that for the sake of Cheryl, scandal must be avoided.

Through no fault of her own, Lana wasn't able to keep her promise about Cheryl never having to see Barker again. The following Monday, she had driven her daughter to a dental appointment in Westwood. When it was over, she returned to her Cadillac. Her daughter was seated in the passenger seat beside her.

Suddenly, through the open front window on the driver's side, a strong, muscular hand and arm reached in to clutch her own delicate hand as it rested on the steering wheel.

That hand and arm belonged to Lex Barker.

In one of those terrible coincidences, he was on his way to an appointment in the same medical building as Cheryl's dentist, and had just emerged from his own car, now parked in the same lot. He had spotted her.

"Lana, let's talk!" he shouted. "Your daughter over there is a liar. A god damn liar! I never touched her!"

Cheryl immediately panicked, and Lana screamed, "Let go of my arm!"

"You're a liar!" he shouted, in a rage, at Cheryl. "Tell your mother it never happened. I've warned you!"

"I want you to take me back," he pleaded with Lana. "We'll fight this thing together."

"Get the hell away from us," she yelled at him. "And stay away. I never want to see you again. I'm throwing all your stuff out on the front yard. I'll have a security guard stationed at the front door."

Then she started the ignition, shifting the gears into reverse, with the intention of backing up and driving out of the parking lot. "I'm getting out of here!" she called out.

"LIES! LIES! LIES!" he kept shouting.

"Let GO!" she threatened, "or I'll run over you"

Then, after backing out of her parking spot, she stepped on the accelerator, even though he was still holding onto the door of her car. She dragged him along for about ten feet before he lost his grip on the door and collapsed onto the asphalt.

Out on the street, she accelerated, looking back one final time. That was the last time she'd ever see Lex Barker.

***

After he and Lana broke up, newspapers carried the story of their impending divorce. "Our careers pulled us in different directions," Lana told the press. "We went our separate ways. I wish him well in his future career and life choices."

Her petition for a divorce was granted in 1958. She told the judge, "He has an uncontrollable temper, which he showed to me many times. Once at the breakfast table, he slapped my face. He used profane language to me."

"During my marriage to Mr. Barker, I was very upset and agitated. It was very hard for me to be his wife and fulfill my professional obligations."

Outside the courthouse, she had a different, more emphatic ring to her voice when she told a reporter, "Apeman belongs back in the jungle, hiding out in trees."

Barker discussed his marital breakup with a reporter in Rome. "Our marriage would have worked out were it not for her daughter telling lies about me. Cheryl Crane is responsible for our splitting up."

[Whatever became of Lex Barker? Many of his fans wanted to know.

He gained worldwide exposure when he appeared in a short but compelling role as Anita Ekberg's fiancé in Federico Fellini's La dolce vita (1960). While filming, he resumed his affair with that Swedish star.

When demand for his services dried up in Hollywood, Barker moved to Germany to make films there, and also to make recordings. His two most popular singles became "Ich bin morgen auf dem Weg zu dir" ("I'll be on the Way to You Tomorrow") and "Mädchen in Samt un Seide" ("The Girl in Silk and Velvet").

He made thirteen movies in German, a language he spoke fluently, based on the novels of the German author, Karl May (1842-1912).

He would marry two more times, the first to Irene Labhart, a Swiss actress with whom he had a son. She died of leukemia in 1962.

He then married María del Carmen ("Tita") Rosario Soledad Cervera y Fernández de la Guerra (her first marriage) in 1965. She'd been voted Miss Spain of 1962. She filed for divorce in 1972 and later married the billionaire art collector, Baron Hans Heinrich Thyssen-Bornemisza, influencing to some degree his choice to donate many of the priceless paintings in his legendary art collection to museums in Spain.

At the time of Barker's death in 1973, he was living with his fiancée, the talented actress Karen Kondazian. On Fifth Avenue in Manhattan, he collapsed on the sidewalk on the way to meet her and died instantly. He was cremated at the age of 54.

When Lana was told of his death, she asked "Why did it take him so long to die?"]

Lana not only ended a marriage in 1958, but lost "the love of my life," Tyrone Power, too. She was vacationing in Acapulco in November of that year when the owner of the Villa Vera, her friend, Teddy Stauffer, phoned with bad news: "Ty Power is dead. A heart attack."

She remembered "going numb." Even though it had been a decade since they had parted, "I wasn't prepared to hear something so final. I didn't cry: My tears had been shed years before when he closed the door on me. Now it was truly closed forever. More men were to come in my tomorrows, but none like Ty. He was special, he was the beautiful, sensitive man who broke my heart."

Stauffer listened to her lament of a long-lost love. At the time of his death, Power was married to Deborah Ann Minardos. In Spain, he'd been filming *Solomon and Sheba* with Gina Lollobrigida. He was stricken by a massive heart attack while filming a dueling scene with his frequent co-star and sometimes lover, the bisexual George Sanders, who had once been married to Zsa Zsa Gabor.

Like so many men Lana knew, either lovers or fellow actors, Power died young at the age of 44.

On hearing news of his death, Henry Fonda said, "His heart attack was probably caused by his fellow bisexual, George Sanders, wearing him out in the sack as well as on the set."

Sanders was enraged when he heard that, and delivered blistering comments about Fonda's own gay past, especially with his best friend and former roommate, James Stewart.

***

For a 1958 release from Universal-International, Lana signed on as a freelance actress to star in *The Lady Takes a Flyer*. Her leading man would be the handsome, masculine, Jeff Chandler, with Jack Arnold directing and William Alland producing.

The combination of players seemed a good match, the tall, virile, iron-jawed Chandler, the epitome of 1950s screen vitality, in love with the petite, delicate, short, and ultra-feminine blonde goddess.

Universal executives thought they had paired a winning team, capable of sexual chemistry on the screen. They toyed with the idea of a series of Turner/Chandler movies with "sparring of the sexes" plots. A hope was expressed that these movies might be Universal's answer to those 1940 hit films starring Lana with Clark Gable.

From its inception, its title was fluid, beginning with *Pilots for Hire.* That was later altered to *Lion in the Sky*, followed two weeks later by *Wild and Wonderful.* Universal finally decided *The Lady Takes a Flyer* might accurately describe the plot. Shooting began in April of 1957.

In the film, Chandler starred as a daredevil pilot, Mike Dandridge, who establishes a passenger and freight-hauling business with Al Reynolds (Richard Denning), his pal from his flight school days. Mike meets Maggie Colby (Lana, cast as the lady flyer), an unusual occupation for women in the early 1950s.

Mike and Maggie become attracted to each other during a long intercontinental flight to Japan, and eventually they fall in love. At their wedding, Al is best man before he leaves the company to join the U.S. Air Force.

When Maggie becomes pregnant, she settled down to home and hearth to rear her child and to be Mike's housewife during his infrequent moments between flights. She begins to suspect that he's romantically involved with Nikki Taylor (Andra Martin), a flirtatious colleague and pilot.

Eventually, Maggie opts to resume her career as a pilot, leaving Mike to tend to their baby. Complications invariably follow before a "period of adjustment" concludes, amicably, between the male and female pilots.

Lana worked smoothly with her director, Jack Arnold, a New Englander known for his science fiction movies. He had only recently released *It Came From Outer Space* (1953).

Arnold's main collaborator at Universal was the producer of *The Lady Takes a Flyer*, William Alland. He had just produced *Revenge of the Creature* (1953), which marked Clint Eastwood's film debut.

Lana asked to see the first rushes of her newest film, but seemed disappointed. She told Arnold, "I'm not Amelia Earhart, not even Rosalind Russell impersonating Earhart in *Flight for Freedom* (1943).

During the shoot, Lana, since having evicted Barker from her life, was a free agent again, not only as an actress booted out of MGM, but as a woman on the prowl. She began to lead a promiscuous life evocative of her early Hollywood days in the '40s. *The Lady Takes a Flyer* offered many possibilities for seduction, not just with Chandler, but with actors Chuck Connors and Richard Denning, too. She decided to make a play for Connors first.

***

Cast as Frank Henshaw, Alan Hale, Jr., was privy to Lana's off-screen flirtation. The son of character actor Alan Hale, Sr., he had worked with Lana before in such pictures as *The Sea Chase* with John Wayne.

"All the gals—and half the guys, at least the gay ones—were after Chuck. He stood 6'6", and was Lana's tallest conquest, or so she said."

A former basketball and baseball star, he had been one of America's best athletes before becoming an actor.

Hale said, "Chuck was a handsome, blonde-haired stud, a great guy, a prankster with a real sense of humor, a lot of fun to hang out with, and a dude who liked all sorts of people. He was captivated by Lana's beauty and told me he'd never seen such a gorgeous woman in his life."

"Once, when we were washing in a communal shower, I saw that Chuck was 'bigger than life' if you know what I mean. Now I know why he drove the gals crazy."

Connors had first appeared on the screen in a gay porn film which was later shown at a New York Times Square Theater along with several other porn scenes populated with actors who later became famous. In *Hollywood Blue*, Connors as a sailor sodomizes a young man.

He made his "official" film debut in *Pat and Mike* (1952), co-starring Spencer Tracy and Katharine Hepburn. The bisexual Tracy fell for him, and George Cukor "directed" him to his casting couch every afternoon.

"Chuck might have let the gays have their fun as a means of breaking into the movies, but he sure knows his way around a woman's body," Lana said. "What

Lana getting high on love with Jeff Chandler.

a man!"

Connors would become famous across America when he starred as a widowed homesteader in the hit TV series, *The Rifleman* (1958-63).

***

In contrast to Connors, Richard Denning, like his producer and director, became known for science fiction films in the 1950s. Right before meeting and seducing Lana, he had starred in *Creature from the Black Lagoon* (1954) and *Day the World Ended* (1955). In time, he would become even better-known for appearing in the hit CBS-TV crime drama, *Hawaii-Five-O* (1968-1980).

Del Armstrong, Lana's makeup man and companion, was often on the set. She told him, "Richard is a real gentleman. He's tall, he's blonde, and he has a good body, but he doesn't take acting too seriously. He told me he views it just as a way to take home a paycheck. As a lover, he's the kind of man you marry, take home to introduce to dear ol' dad, and then settle down with into a happy family life with some kids."

She confessed, "He's a real decent guy, and seems uncomfortable having an affair with me. Richard can return home to his wife and watch *The Wolf Man* and *Son of Dracula.*"

Her reference was to Evelyn Ankers, whom he'd married in 1942, when she was known as "The Horror Film Queen."

***

Brooklyn-born Jeff Chandler was one of Universal's most popular stars of the 1950s. At an early age, his hair had turned gray, and he never dyed it. Before working with Lana, he had been seduced by Joan Crawford on the set of *Female on the Beach* (1955).

"Once again, that bitch got him before I did," Lana complained to Armstrong. "Thank God she didn't damage any of his vital parts. Everything is still in working order. She likes it rough, you know. Actually, Jeff was a schoolmate of my dear friend, Susan Hayward, and may have been the one who took her teenage cherry."

"I didn't know he was Jewish until he took me to bed, and I found a bit of skin missing. I hear he's a switch hitter. He does women, but wanders down detours with the likes of Rock Hudson and Tony Curtis. That bit of data came from Henry Willson, my expert on all things gay."

Less glam but eternally perky—Lana as a lady aviator.

483

***

In her memoir, *The Million Dollar Mermaid*, Esther Williams admitted, "I was drifting dangerously close to the kind of lifestyle at which I had cast a jaundiced eye in my early years in Hollywood, critical of the carrying on of both Lana Turner and Marlene Dietrich, among others."

In that same book, Williams also wrote about the end of her affair with Jeff Chandler. She was in the kitchen of his house, cooking chicken cacciatore for his dinner, and went upstairs to his bedroom when he didn't answer her call.

"At the bedroom door, I froze and started screaming," she wrote. "I couldn't trust myself. It was a high-pitched scream that a woman makes when she sees a mouse. It's a scream that has no logic—sheer, uncontrolled panic."

She found Chandler standing in the middle of the floor with a red wig,

Regardless of what distractions were happening in their personal lives, Lana and Jeff Chandler made convincing lovers in *The Lady Takes a Flyer*.

He was hoping he'd work with her again in *Return to Peyton Place*, but she rejected the role.

wearing a chiffon dress and expensive high-heeled shoes, plus lots of makeup.

"He was my lover—a strong, manly figure standing there in high heels and a dress. This was no joke He enjoyed this kind of thing. He was a cross-dresser."

He left early the next morning to report to the studio. During his absence, she discovered a secret closet and opened it to find lots of dresses, hats, *négligées*, and high-heeled shoes. When he returned home that night, he tried to explain his preference for drag: "I like to envision myself as a beautiful woman making love to another beautiful woman."

She admitted to having discovered and entered his secret closet. "I saw blouses with polka dots, dresses with polka dots, even hats with big polka dot bows. "Jeff, you're too big for polka dots."

That was the last she ever saw of him.

[Lana was dead when Esther Williams published her memoirs in 1999. She could have warned her about Chandler. At the end of the filming of The Lady Takes a Flyer, *when he was sleeping over at her house, she had come home early and had gone upstairs to her bedroom. She found him trying to fit into her lingerie. He stood before her in a black négligée. He had applied a coating of lipstick.*

"Are you getting dressed for a night with Rock?" she asked. "I'm breaking our date for tonight. I've got a bigger offer from Chuck Connors."

She never saw Chandler again.]

On screen, Chandler and Lana made a convincing pair of lovers, especially in a scene where he perches on the side of her bathtub, and in which she is indeed a bathing beauty.

The New York Times defined *The Lady Takes a Flyer* as "surprisingly ingratiating," though suggesting that the stars could have used a better script.

In the *New York Daily News*, Wanda Hale found the movie "a pleasing, honest comedy. Lana Turner moves and expresses herself just right as the woman torn between being a practical mother and a sweetheart to her husband."

***

In 1955, Broadway audiences were stunned when the controversial play, *Cat on a Hot Tin Roof*, by Tennessee Williams, opened. Its stars included Ben Gazzara in the role of a repressed homosexual, Brick, playing opposite his young wife, Barbara Bel Geddes, cast as the sexually frustrated Maggie the Cat trying to maneuver and lure her husband into bed.

Word traveled quickly to Hollywood that Williams' play would adapt into a dynamic film, with the condition that censors weren't so homophobic that they'd forbid any mention of "that perverted love" on the screen.

Many actors and actresses wanted to play Brick or Maggie after MGM acquired the play's film rights. Gazarra hoped to repeat his Broadway triumph, but he was curtly informed that an actor of more potent box office appeal was needed, instead. Bel Geddes received the same bad news.

The moguls at MGM felt that Grace Kelly would be ideal for the female lead. But she had another idea and ran off with Prince Rainier to Monaco.

Elizabeth Taylor's husband, producer Mike Todd, took her to see the play on Broadway, and her eyes lit up. "I'd give my left nipple to sink my claws into Maggie the Cat."

At first, George Cukor was set to direct the film version. After he devised a proposal to cast Vivien Leigh as the female lead, Williams vehemently objected, claiming, "I just adored Viv in *A Streetcar Named Desire*, but she's a bit long in the tooth for Maggie."

Cukor's proposal for the male lead was Montgomery Clift, in reference to which he told Williams, "What could be more perfect? A closeted homosexual playing a closeted homosexual."

When presented with the role, Clift rejected it as "too close to home."

Within two weeks, Cukor was ousted as the film's director, the position going to Richard Brooks. He had recently helmed Lana in *Flame and the Flesh* in Italy, and thought she might be ideal as Maggie. During a phone conversation with her, he learned that she and Lex Barker had seen the play on Broadway months before their divorce. "I'd be perfect as Maggie the Cat," Lana said, "and Lex claims he'd be the perfect Brick. He thinks as Brick in his underwear, and me in my petticoat will generate long lines at the box office."

"File this under Believe It or Not," Brooks said. "Elvis Presley went to see the play and then phoned me. HE wants to play Brick, so that he can prove to the world that he can act—and not just in the shit his manager, Col. Tom Parker, has cast him in."

"Can you imagine a marquee with Lana Turner and Elvis Presley starring in a Tennessee Williams play?" Lana asked. "It would be the biggest hit of the year."

"Perhaps," Brooks said. "But we'd have to adjust the billing. It would have to read: 'Elvis Presley and Lana Turner.'"

Later that same day, Brooks learned that Marilyn Monroe had also seen the play, and she wanted to play Maggie, too. Brooks alerted MGM that both "Marilyn and Elvis want to do it. If they can, it will become the biggest hit of the 1950s."

But Monroe didn't follow through, and Col. Parker called Brooks, telling him, "There's no way in hell I'm gonna let Elvis appear in that faggot writer's crappy play. His fans would storm the movie houses in protest. Elvis as a fag? No way!"

The next time Brooks phoned Lana, telling her that MGM planned to cast Paul Newman as Brick. "Why don't you let me set up a rendezvous with you guys? I'll check out the sexual chemistry between the two of you."

"I can't wait," Lana responded.

The next day, over lunch with Newman, Lana expressed a fear that she might be too old to play Maggie. "Of course, makeup and lighting can do wonders."

"You're still beautiful and always will be," Newman assured her. "You are a very sexy woman, perhaps the sexiest ever to grace the screen, you and Ava. What a pair!"

She leaned over the table and kissed him lightly on the lips. "Ever since I saw you in *The Silver Chalice* (1954), I've wanted to play opposite you. I think we'd make a great screen team. I've always regarded you as the heir apparent to those matinee idols—Tyrone Power, Errol Flynn, Clark Gable, and Robert Taylor. Of course, you're different from them, more modern, a star of tomorrow. I predict that before the end of the 1960s, your reputation will be equal to those guys."

"Talk like that will make me fall in love with you," Newman responded.

"If you like blondes so much, I wish you'd married me instead of Joanne Woodward."

"But if I'd done that, I could never be myself, ever again. I'd be forever known as Mr. Lana Turner."

She dismissed such an idea. "You're joking, of course. The world will be talking about Paul Newman long after Lana Turner is a forgotten memory, kept alive only by the soldiers who won World War II."

"I doubt that. You're unforgettable."

"Of all the actors in Hollywood, you're the one I most would want as a leading man."

"I'm flattered," he said. "You were always my dream girl."

"And dreams do come true," she said. "At least sometimes."

After lunch, driving his own car, he followed her Cadillac to a private villa that he later learned was owned by Howard Hughes. She planned to spend the weekend there and invited him for an afternoon swim, adding, "or whatever…"

He didn't know how the preliminaries would go, but, as he later told Brooks, "We got down to business right away. As soon as we were inside the door, she was in my arms."

"I think she's desperate," Newman said. "At one point, when we were in bed, I held her. She was trembling like a leaf. In a very plaintive voice, she said, 'Please, don't ever leave me.'"

Within two weeks, Brooks phoned Lana with the devastating news that MGM had decided to cast Elizabeth Taylor instead of her as Maggie the Cat.

***

Months later, Elizabeth Taylor was busy filming *Cat on a Hot Tin Roof* and was unable to accompany her husband, Mike Todd, on a hastily scheduled flight from California to New York. He departed from Burbank on March 2, 1958, and she would never see him again.

His aircraft, the badly named "Lucky Liz," crashed during a storm over New Mexico.

Taylor was distraught. She was so hysterically upset that there was speculation that she might commit suicide.

When Lana learned through the gossip mill that Taylor might not complete the picture, she phoned Brooks: "I'm your Maggie the Cat."

"Not so soon," he cautioned her. "I think Elizabeth will pull herself together and report back to work at some point. The girl is a real trouper."

"Perhaps," she said. "But remember, darling, I'm only a phone call away."

Brooks was right. Taylor recovered and finished the movie, which became one of her all-time most memorable performances.

Even though she'd lost the lead role in *Cat*, Lana had not abandoned her desire to play a Tennessee Williams heroine. In her future, a role far better suited to her age and talent emerged after she popped into a Broadway theater one night for a performance of *Sweet Bird of Youth*.

***

Lex Barker was gone from her life, and, as a divorced woman, Lana was determined to resume a role that was both comfortable and familiar to her: playing the field. As the 1950s moved to its conclusion, Marilyn

Paul Newman, cast as a repressed homosexual, and Elizabeth Taylor in Tennessee Williams' *Cat on a Hot Tin Roof.*

Lana always regretted that she didn't "get to sink my claws into the role of Maggie the Cat. At least I got Paul Newman before Taylor seduced him."

487

Monroe had become the most talked-about blonde in Hollywood.

Lana's old rival, Betty Grable, was well on her way to being a forgotten face—and set of legs—of World War II.

Carole Landis was dead, and Veronica Lake, that Peek-a-Boo Blonde, was a has-been.

Grace Kelly had flown off to Monaco to live unhappily ever after with the prince of a principality that Katharine Hepburn had defined as "a pimple on the face of France."

Jayne Mansfield and Mamie Van Doren were trying unsuccessfully to move in on Monroe's territory, terrain which she had previously "confiscated" from Lana.

Lana was well aware of "what time it is," as she said to Virginia Grey. "After a few summers, I'll be forty, retirement time for most Hollywood Cinderellas."

She felt that men had an unfair advantage. Lex Barker, according to reports, was one of the most desirable men in Europe, sought out by starlets across the Continent. Stephen Crane, having recovered from brain surgery, was seen about town, either with Mamie Van Doren or with Terry Moore, who was alleged to have married Howard Hughes, Lana's former lover.

A fear of growing old and not being alluring to the new generation of handsome young men may have been the reason Lana was lured into the arms of a handsome young actor, Michael Dante. He was all of twenty-two when she launched their affair. In case her seductive powers weren't enough to entice him, Lana promised Dante that she'd use her influence to get him movie roles.

As director Richard Brooks said, "Lana was using a reversal of the old casting couch approach that Hollywood biggies had used for years with young women—Darryl F. Zanuck at Fox and Harry Cohn at Columbia were the best examples of that. 'Sleep with me, baby, and I'll get you in the movies.'"

"Lana's worst fear in dating Dante was that some waiter or hotel desk clerk would mistake him for her son," said Virginia Grey.

Hollywood biographer Edward Z. Epstein summed it up: "Handsome hangers-on have always been part of the Hollywood scene. Many clever young men, with no visible talents, travel in Hollywood's highest circles, entertaining the lonely, vain, bored women who find excitement and diversion in them as they would with a new toy. So few of these men succeed. Most of them fade quietly into oblivion and are forgotten, as they are replaced by a newer, younger breed."

In spite of how it might look to some of her harshest critics, Del Armstrong claimed, "Even though she was much older than Michael Dante, Lana liked to be seen out on his arm, arriving at night clubs with him. It was like she was signaling the world, 'I'm still young myself, still alluring, still able to capture a fresh hunk of male flesh new to the scene. After all, Joan Crawford had been pulling that stunt for years.'"

In March of 1957, Lana invited her daughter, Cheryl, who was enrolled at Flintridge Sacred Heart Academy near Pasadena, for a weekend in Palm Desert at the Shadow Mountain Club. Other guests included Cheryl's friend, Maggie Douglas, daughter of character actor Paul Douglas and Virginia Fields, an English star of "B movies." Fields was the owner of the club, and it was understood that Lana's guests, after transiting from other points across L.A., would assemble there.

Lana showed up for the weekend with her latest boyfriend, whom Cheryl had not yet met, and as such, she was introduced to Dante. (His name had, until recently, been Ralph Vitti.)

A strapping athlete as well as a bit part actor, he played shortstop for the Hollywood Stars baseball team.

After the horror of the Barker scandal, still not known to the public, Cheryl wanted space between Lana and herself. As she wrote, "Newly divorced, nearly broke, her career in a slump, she was short-tempered and proud, not much fun to be with."

Perhaps jealous of her daughter's youth and beauty, Lana, on the second day of what was supposed to be a recuperative weekend, confronted Cheryl. She was filled with accusations, charging the young girl with flirting with Dante, "Smiling *that* way, wiggling your butt, your arm slung possessively around his broad shoulders."

Lana was not just angry, but furious. In the most outrageous accusation she'd ever made against Cheryl, she said, "You've done this *before*, and you know just what I'm talking about."

It was all too clear to Cheryl. She was being accused of flirting with Barker, leading him on, suggesting that in some way, she was responsible for his repeated rapes of her. To Cheryl, it seemed hopeless to deny any of these absurd accusations or implications. "You're a boy-crazy slut!" her mother charged.

As time would reveal, Cheryl was not boy crazy at all. That would become clear, based on her eventual declarations about gender attractions.

During their angry drive home, Dante and Lana were in the front seat, Cheryl in the back seat with her school chum Maggie.

At Union Station in downtown L.A., Lana let the two girls off, with the understanding that from there, they'd board a bus for the twenty-minute continuation of their trip to their school in Pasadena.

But after her mother's departure with Dante, with a sense of independence and rebelliousness, Cheryl told Maggie she wanted to remain in the city,

When Cheryl ran away from home, it made headlines across the nation. When she was rescued, photographers were waiting at Lana's home to capture her return.

Looking ever so glum are (left to right) Lana, Cheryl, and her father, Stephen Crane.

489

and that she should continue by bus to Pasadena without her. She had never before ventured into the seedy downtown neighborhood of Los Angeles, filled with hustlers, bums, beggars, perverts, and winos, who co-existed, densely among a coterie of respectable citizens going about their business.

As Cheryl later revealed in her memoirs, she began to explore the area, carrying only an alligator case and $12 in her pocketbook. She had adopted Veronica Lake's peek-a-boo hairdo. Along the way, she attracted unwanted attention. Three menacing young men followed her, perhaps for a gang rape in one of the many back alleys littered with garbage.

She fled, but soon encountered a Chicano in his 30s who wore blue jeans and a windbreaker. He introduced himself as "Manuel" and asked if he could help her.

To Manuel's surprise, she got into his car, believing his promise that he'd drive her to a cheap hotel. Once inside the car, he didn't seem to want to go anywhere, but just talked and joked with her, perhaps getting her to trust him.

Then, instead of taking her to a fleabag hotel, he delivered her to Skid Row's Hollenbeck Police Station. He escorted her inside the station, where she encountered other police officers who nailed her as a runaway.

Finally, under pressure, she correctly identified herself as Cheryl Crane.

"My god, you're Lana Turner's kid!"

Unknown to Cheryl, Lana had been notified by a nun at Sacred Heart that Cheryl had not returned to the school with Maggie, and that she'd last been seen in the most dangerous part of Los Angeles.

Based on the fear that she'd been kidnapped, bulletins had been broadcast across the city with her physical description, and instructions had been issued to the police to find and retrieve her.

Within the hour, fighting their way through a mob of reporters and photographers, Lana, with Stephen Crane at her side, showed up at the station house to retrieve their daughter.

The next day, a headline read: LANA TURNER'S RUNAWAY DAUGHTER CAUGHT.

In her column, Louella Parsons publicly chastised Cheryl, praising Lana for being "a wonderful mother and strict with Cheryl." Back at Lana's house, Dante was waiting at the front door with a drink for her. Cheryl was ordered to her bedroom.

But instead of going to her room, she entered Lana's bedroom and opened a drawer in which she discovered a revolver and a bottle of Nembutal. She considered suicide as an option, preferring the sleeping pills to a violent end with a gun.

But she finally decided against killing herself and fell asleep.

***

In the mid-1950s, a young ex-Marine from Indiana arrived in New York wanting to become an actor. Like his rival, James Dean, he would morph into a major movie star, "the King of Cool," Steve McQueen.

[Details about McQueen's rise to prominence and his tumultuous private life are best explored in the tell-all biography, Steve McQueen, King of Cool—Tales of a Lurid Life.

Authored by Darwin Porter, it was published by Blood Moon Productions in 2009.]

In 1956, McQueen would replace Ben Gazarra in *Hatful of Rain* on Broadway. But money was hard to come by, and the cash he brought in as an actor didn't manage to pay his bills and expenses at the time.

His chaotic finances and his turbulent path to stardom led to his meeting and getting hired as a male escort by Floyd Wilson, a pimp who had tried but failed to succeed as an actor himself. "Handsome, intelligent, with oodles of charm" (Wilson's own appraisal), he established a high-priced escort agency that provided attractive men as escorts to rich, lonely women in and around Manhattan. His agency's patrons included visiting Hollywood divas, who often arrived in town without a proper date. Wilson's "Gentlemen for Rent" service flourished.

McQueen made himself available as a player in this scenario, acquiring his first tuxedo as a necessary accessory for his act.

After McQueen proved he was a hit with women, Wilson arranged for him to go out on "your date of dates." In need of an escort, Marlene Dietrich had arrived in Manhattan with the intention of attending an event at the Plaza Hotel.

At a gathering there, in 1955, McQueen met Joseph and Rose Kennedy and Senator John F. Kennedy and his wife, Jacqueline Bouvier Kennedy.

Before the evening ended, McQueen got to chat with the future president of the United States.

[A few years later, in 1963, McQueen, by then a bigtime movie star, wanted to portray Kennedy as a World War II naval hero in the film adaptation of Robert Donovan's 1961 overview of JFK's wartime exploits, PT-109. His friend and rival, Paul Newman, also wanted the Kennedy role, but was rejected by the President "as looking too Jewish." The part was eventually assigned to Cliff Robertson.]

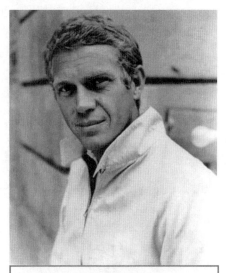

Because McQueen's date with the great Dietrich had gone so well, she phoned Wilson, giving him an A-plus.

That led, a few weeks later, to another escort job with another legendary Hollywood blonde, Lana Turner. McQueen, as a paid escort, agreed to pick her up at her suite at the Plaza Hotel and escort her downstairs to a "Rat Pack" party hosted by Frank Sinatra for a few choice friends.

In a form-fitting white satin gown and a ruby necklace, Lana looked to him as good as when he saw her on the screen in *The Postman Always Rings Twice*. Either she was incredibly skilled

As a rule, Lana did not want to go out and be photographed with dates who had blonde hair. "I want to be the only blonde in the picture," she told Steve Mc-Queen, who—a struggling actor at the time—was working as an escort for an agency in New York.

He was surprised by what unfolded on his one night with Lana.

at makeup, or age had been kind to her.

"So you're a blonde," she said, appraising him after he was ushered into the living room of her hotel suite. "Usually, I don't date blondes. The agent, Henry Willson, always told me I should date men with raven black hair to offset my own blondeness. That's why he fixed me up with Rory Calhoun."

"If I'd known, I would have kept my hair black," McQueen said. "That's what I did when I appeared in the play, *A Hatful of Rain*. I was playing an Italian, and I thought black hair would make me look the part."

Actually, I like blonde-haired men," Lana continued. "You're adorable looking in an offbeat kind of way. Of all my movies, which of them did you like the best?"

"*The Merry Widow,*" he answered. "As for Fernando Lamas, he can stick a dildo up his ass."

Arriving at Sinatra's party, Lana, with Steve, made a grand entrance. Sinatra's guests included Sammy Davis, Jr., Dean Martin, Peter Lawford, Marilyn Maxwell, and Judy Garland.

At the time, it seemed beyond McQueen's wildest dreams that one day soon, he would be co-starring with Sinatra in a movie, *Never So Few* (1958).

McQueen was intrigued by Sammy Davis, Jr. It was the beginning of a beautiful friendship.

At his party, Sinatra sang for his pals, and on the dance floor, McQueen danced with Lana until Garland, claiming a privilege usually reserved for men, cut in.

At the end of the party, McQueen's biggest surprise came when Davis grabbed him and lip-locked him with a sloppy wet kiss. He did the same to Lana, too. McQueen discovered Davis' fondness for French kissing without discrimination for gender.

On their way out, McQueen turned to Lana. "I hope Sammy doesn't think I'm a fucking faggot."

"Oh, darling, don't be so judgmental," Lana said. "Without so-called faggots, there would BE no Hollywood."

McQueen fully expected her to invite him back to her suite, where he hoped to spend the night. Instead, she asked for her sable and headed outside, where the doorman hailed them a taxi.

"Come with me," she said. "I have an errand for you. We're going to the Carlyle."

Once inside that swanky nearby hotel, she directed him to the bar. "I have to meet a special friend upstairs: He never takes very long, so I'll be back down here within the hour. I want you to wait for me."

About thirty minutes later, a waiter tapped him on the shoulder. "You're wanted on the house

At the Carlyle Hotel, Steve McQueen was shocked when Senator John F. Kennedy opened the door in his underwear. Lana was in the next room putting back on her clothing.

phone." It was Lana calling from a suite upstairs.

"He says he knows you," she said. "He met you one night with Dietrich. Come on up."

When McQueen arrived at the suite whose number Lana had indicated, Senator John F. Kennedy opened the door clad in his underwear. Presumably, Lana was inside, repairing her makeup after the sexual encounter they'd just concluded.

Kennedy invited him in, and suggested that during his next visit to Hollywood, each of them should join in a race, as to which man could bed the most movie stars. "I must say, you're dating from the top of the A-list. Lana Turner and Marlene Dietrich. My dad had Dietrich before I got my chance on the French Riviera."

McQueen and Kennedy indulged in what men used to call "locker room talk" before Lana emerged from one of the suite's other rooms. She did not look like she'd been ravished at all. McQueen's duties as an escort weren't over yet. It was back to the Plaza, where that long-awaited invitation to Lana's suite did eventually emerge.

As he told his friend and fellow actor, Rod Steiger, the next day, "Guess what? I woke up this morning in the bed of Lana Turner."

"Cut the bullshit, McQueen," Steiger said, obviously not believing him. "I've got an even better tale to tell. Queen Elizabeth is my mistress." Then he put down the phone.

***

During a consultation in the office of producer Jerry Wald, Lana was defiant. "There is no way in hell I'm going to play the mother of a grown-up teenager. Forget it!" Then she stormed out of the office.

Wald had reminded her that she only recently co-starred in a "string of clunkers in your dying days at MGM. You need a big box office attraction to put you on top again."

He also reminded her that in 1945, he'd convinced Joan Crawford to play the title role in *Mildred Pierce*, as the mother of an ungrateful daughter (Ann Blyth). Based on her portrayal of a mother, it had brought Crawford her first and only Oscar, and radically revitalized her career.

The role being offered to Lana was that of Constance MacKenzie, the romantic lead in a script based on the 1956 novel, *Peyton Place*, by Grace

Metalious, a bawdy, rebellious housewife in New Hampshire. At the age of
thirty, she was described as "broke,
smelly, thirsty, exhausted, and desperate," feeding her three children an ongoing diet of lettuce-and-tomato
sandwiches.

The studio associated with the
production, 20th-Century Fox, had
originally recommended Rita Hayworth as Constance. Susan Hayward
was also a strong contender, and in
many ways, the part seemed tailor-
made for her.

As part of a prolonged casting
drama, Fox had already sent Wald a
number of actresses that its executives
deemed suitable—Barbara Stanwyck,
Irene Dunne, Joan Fontaine, Ann Sheridan, Dorothy McGuire, Audrey Meadows, Deborah Kerr, Virginia Mayo,
even Betty Hutton. None had survived
the scrutiny.

It took some doing, but Lee Philips,
Lana's leading man, finally melted the
secretive character she was playing, "the
ice queen of Peyton Place."

The plot of the novel—denounced as "literary sewage"—had outraged critics,
The New York Times calling it a "small town peep show." It had nonetheless swept
the nation, many readers devouring it in secret, not wanting their neighbors, who
were also reading it, to catch them "in the act."

Despite these howling protests, the novel remained on the bestseller list for
fifty-nine weeks, selling 60,000 copies in just ten days in 1956, when most novels
sold 3,000 copies or less. When it became clear that the book was a runaway bestseller, Wald paid Metalious $250,000 for the film rights.

Unusually forthright for a film during the Eisenhower years, its plot involved
rape, incest, murder, abortion, and multiple seductions. Fox feared that it would
run into censorship issues with the Production Code.

Most of Lana's friends warned her not to take the role, reminding her that at
the age of thirty-six, she was "as glamorous as ever." It was also noted that her rival
love goddesses of the 1940s, including Betty Grable and Rita Hayworth, had not
yet been reduced to portraying mothers.

In the end, it was money—not the role—that persuaded Lana to play Connie.
Wald offered her a contract for $125,000. She desperately needed it, as she was
nearly broke.

In an interview with the press, Lana asserted that the mother of a teenage
daughter did not have to look matronly. Reporters noted sardonically that Lana
would be portraying, as Metalious' novel had revealed, an inhibited and sexually
frustrated woman.

"Sexually frustrated?" said columnist James Bacon. "Lana Turner! You've got to be kidding. She's going to have to do a lot of acting to pull that one off."

The novel centered on the moral hypocrisy of a small, seemingly tranquil community, a fictional mill town in New England, in the years just before World War II.

Lana did not in any way resemble a drab housewife, not in wardrobe designer Charles LeMaire's dresses and gowns. The script had established her as the owner of the best dress shop in town, a device that allowed her character to appear in chic apparel throughout the run of the film. Her platinum blonde hair was darkened to a honey blonde. Makeup was by Ben Nye and hair styles by Helen Turpin. In CinemaScope and color by DeLuxe, Lana was prepped, primped, and coiffed, ready and set to appear on camera, looking much younger than her years.

Lana played Constance as a widow with a dark secret: She was hiding the true origins of her daughter's father. Allison had been born out of wedlock to a married man.

Allison's best friend is Selene Cross, who lives on the wrong side of the tracks with an abusive stepfather, Lucas Cross, who rapes and impregnates her.

The town doctor, Matthew Swain, forces the rapist to leave town after he signs a confession. Based on the circumstances of Selene's pregnancy, the doctor performs an illegal abortion.

When Selene's stepfather returns from the war effort many months later, he assaults her again. This time, she kills him and buries his body in a deserted sheep pen.

Lloyd Nolan as high-integrity Dr. Swain, "morally forced to perform an abortion."

Lorne Green interrogates Lana: Art imitating life?

As the film's prosecuting attorney, the Canada-born actor would go on to become a household name when he starred as the patriarchal Ben Cartwright in the long-running TV series, *Bonanza* (1959-73).

In the background are lots of tangled romances and lesser dramas. Selena's secret is eventually discovered, and she stands trial for murder.

At the trial, Lana is summoned as a witness, performing her most dramatic scene in the movie. *[Ironically, in real life, in the months ahead, she would be summoned as a witness in the investigation of the murder, within her home, of her gangster lover, Johnny Stompanato.]*

When *Peyton Place* was released, moviegoers drew parallels between the on-screen Lana on Peyton Place's witness stand and their favorite star testifying in a real life courthouse in Beverly Hills. Both of them were testifying about a murder.

At the beginning of the film, Lana, as Connie, is a frigid ice queen, shunning the possibility of any romantic involvement. That changes when the handsome new principal of the local high school arrives in town. Michael Rossi (Lee Philips) slowly begins to thaw her out.

***

The goal of scriptwriter John Michael Hayes was to tone down the more blatant sexual scenes in the Metalious novel. He was better known for "doctoring" scripts for director Alfred Hitchcock, including *Rear Window* (1934). He also showed that he had a talent for big budget melodramas such as *Torch Song* (1953) with Joan Crawford, or *BUtterfield 8* (1960), a role for which Elizabeth Taylor won the Oscar.

[Hayes would later incur Lana's animosity when he wrote the screenplay for Where Love Has Gone *(1964), starring Susan Hayward and Bette Davis. The plot was clearly based on the Johnny Stompanato murder and her involvement in it.]*

Lana worked smoothly with Mark Robson, her Canada-born director, who had earned a reputation as a brilliant film editor. He'd previously helmed, or would eventually helm, such films as *The Bridges at Toko-Ri* (1955), starring William Holden and Grace Kelly, and Ingrid Bergman in *The Inn of the Sixth Happiness* (1958).

When it came to casting, Lana, as always, wanted to know who her leading man would be.

For a while, Errol Flynn was the choice, before it was decided that the role would be better performed by Robert Mitchum, with whom Lana had also had a fling.

When an involvement by Mitchum didn't work out, it was decided that Richard Burton, Lana's co-star from *The Rains of Ranchipur,* should be offered the role.

But when that fell through, Gregory Peck was accepted as an ideal candidate

Russ Tamblyn was viewed as an odd choice to play the role of Norman Page, who eventually captures the heart of Allison (Diane Varsi).

He was mostly known as a dancer, having performed brilliantly, even acrobatically, in the incredible dance number in *Seven Brides for Seven Brothers* (1954). After *Peyton Place*, his next job involved designing the choreography for Elvis Presley's *Jailhouse Rock* (1957).

for her leading man. Lana, perhaps remembering her secret sexual tryst with him, agreed, until that didn't work out, either.

When James Stewart's name was suggested, Lana asked Robson, "What in hell are you doing? Rounding up all my lovers from yesterday?"

Far down on the list was Van Heflin, another of Lana's former co-stars. "I just can't see him as a leading man. I never could."

Then Robert Ryan was suggested. "I saw something there when he made *Clash by Night* (1952) with Barbara Stanwyck, but he just doesn't ring my bell," Lana said.

Four of Lana's future co-stars were also considered, any of whom, in Lana's words, "could send me ring-a-dinging."

They included Sean Connery, who would be cast as her co-star in her upcoming *Another Time, Another Place.* Another suggestion was John Gavin, her future co-star in *Imitation of Life.* "He's just too beautiful for words," Lana said. Efrem Zimbalist, Jr., her future co-star in *By Love Possessed,* and Cliff Robertson, a future co-star in *Love Has Many Faces,* were—at least temporarily—also considered, fruitlessly, as Lana's onscreen lover and co-star.

After each of those big-name actors, Lana was rather disappointed to learn that the role of her lover, Michael Rossi, had been assigned to Lee Philips. Although he'd started out on Broadway, this handsome but relatively unknown New York-born actor was not familiar to movie audiences.

Cast as a rape victim, Selene Cross (Hope Lange) lives on the wrong side of the tracks with her abusive stepfather, Lucas Cross (Arthur Kennedy), who impregnates her.

"He's handsome enough," Lana said, "although he seems to lack the charisma needed for a matinee idol. Fortunately, our love scenes are sort of vanilla, so no great sexual chemistry is required from me. It just wouldn't be there."

When Robson introduced Lana to Lee Philips, he later asked her opinion of him. "Nice guy. But a movie star? No way!"

Maybe she was right. By the 1960s, Philips had shifted mostly to directing.

Lana played the mother of newcomer Diane Varsi, who starred as her daughter Allison. Lana is a concerned and chic matron with a scandalous past she hopes to conceal from her daughter.

Ironically, when *Peyton Place* was adapted into a TV series, Philips was named as its director.

He was one leading man who Lana didn't seduce. Within the year, he would be married to Barbara Shrader.

When Lana sat through the film's final cut, she said, "My love scenes with Philips were those performed by respectable middle-class American couples."

One of the film's most pivotal roles was that of the much-victimized Selena Cross. At first, Debbie Reynolds, who'd had a minor role with her in *Mr. Imperium*, was suggested until it was determined that "she is just too sweet."

Then, briefly, ice blonde Carroll Baker was considered. Robson had been impressed with her role in *Giant* (1956), with Rock Hudson and Elizabeth Taylor.

Finally, Robson decided to hire newcomer Hope Lange, who had recently made her film debut in William Inge's *Bus Stop* (1956), starring Marilyn Monroe and Don Murray. In the movie, although Marilyn made off with Murray, in real life, Lange married him.

The role of Lana's daughter, Allison MacKenzie, was debated as a vehicle for Joanne Woodward. Lana objected vehemently, claiming that Woodward was far too old for the part, having been born in 1930.

Other possibilities that were under discussion for the daughter role included Elizabeth Montgomery, Julie Harris, Susan Strasberg, Eva Marie Saint, and Natalie Wood. The part eventually went to the relatively unknown Diane Varsi.

Making her film debut in *Peyton Place*, Varsi, born near San Francisco, was considered "an oddball" even in high school. She'd dropped out of

Cast as Nellie Cross, the downtrodden wife of the man who raped her daughter, was Betty Field (right).

As the drab, bitter, plain-Jane housekeeper for Constance, she had a colorless, depressive role. During the course of the film, she commits suicide by hanging herself in a closet.

Barry Coe, in the role of Rodney Harrington, was the best-looking man in the cast. He'd appeared with Elvis Presley in *Love Me Tender* (1956). Lana thought he might have a chance to join the ranks of the pretty boys on movie screens of the 50s, but that didn't happen.

In *Peyton Place*, he conducts a torrid romance with the town slut, Betty Anderson (as played by Terry Moore). Moore had had a far better role in *Come Back, Little Sheba* (1952), opposite Burt Lancaster. She'd been nominated that year as Best Supporting Actress.

Moore was the longtime partner, on and off again, of Howard Hughes, and may indeed have married him.

school at the age of fifteen, suffering from boredom. Shortly thereafter, she married an 18-year old, but the union was annulled.

She'd wanted to be a ballet dancer before switching her ambition to that of a folk singer.

Soon after hitchhiking to Los Angeles, she was discovered by producer Buddy Adler, who put her under contract to Fox, who decided to showcase her in *Peyton Place*.

After working with Lana, Varsi was involved in only a handful of other film roles, including *Compulsion* (1959), before suffering a nervous breakdown. By the spring of 1959, she'd bolted from Hollywood, claiming, "I'm running away from destruction."

During filming, she told Lana, "Unlike you, I'd rather meet Aldous Huxley, not Clark Gable."

"I know Gable very well," Lana answered. "But who is this Huxley actor?"

The key role of Dr. Matthew Swain was played by veteran actor Lloyd Nolan. He was mostly a B-movie star, though he did appear with such actresses as Dorothy McGuire, even Mae West. He was always steady, always reliable.

The role of the rapist and town sleazeball, Lucas, went to Arthur Kennedy, always brilliant on both the stage and screen. On Broadway, he'd been part of the original cast of Arthur Miller's *The Death of a Salesman*.

Rodney's romance with Terry Moore is forbidden by his stern father, Leslie Harrington (played by Leon Ames). The owner of the local woolen mill, he is the town's biggest employer.

Cast in the sympathetic role of Miss Thornton, veteran actress Mildred Dunnock gave her usual stellar performance. On Broadway, she'd been the first Mrs. Loman in *Death of a Salesman*.

Before joining the cast of *Peyton Place*, she had delivered a stunning performance in the 1956 film version of Tennessee Williams' *Baby Doll*.

Selena's boyfriend, Ted Carter, was played by David Nelson, the son of Ozzie and Harriet Nelson, whose younger brother was the famous singer, Ricky Nelson.

David would go on to become a producer and director, too.

Lana shared a reunion with Ames, who had played the district attorney hot on her trail in *The Postman Always Rings Twice*.

As one reviewer of *Peyton Place* noted, "It may be a long, long time before Hollywood gets another supporting cast of such talent and magnitude. Virtually every actor, based either on past performances or possible future roles, has star potential, even the character actors."

In 1957, *Peyton Place* became the second highest-grossing film of the year, earning $26 million in the United States alone. When it first opened, box office receipts were somewhat average, but after the Lana Turner/Johnny Stompanato murder flared into headlines, long lines assembled at box offices around the country.

Ironically, although Lana feared that the murder of her gangster lover would destroy her standing as a movie star, it produced the opposite effect: It revitalized her career.

Grace Metalious saw the movie and phoned director Mark Robson. "I hated the fucking thing. You've botched up all my characters."

Months later, he told her that even though she despised *Peyton Place*, the film, he hoped that she would accept a $400,000 check for royalties.

Critical reaction was mixed, the *Chicago Times* hailing it as "one of the best films ever made." A critic in Baltimore wrote, "Lana Turner was nominated for an Oscar, although she resembles a department store mannequin that has somehow wandered away from the window."

Variety claimed that "in leaning backward not to offend, scriptwriter John Michael Hayes has gone acrobatic. He underplays the dirty sex secrets of the little town depicted in the Metalious novel. In the film, these characters are not the gossipy, spiteful, immoral people she portrayed. There are hints of their hypocrisy, but only hints."

Even Lana's harshest critic, Bosley Crowther of *The New York Times*, wrote, "Lana Turner did the role remarkably well." In *The Saturday Review*, Stanley Kauffman said, "Lana Turner, given a role of some depth, proves that she can be as persuasive as some of the Method-dedicated girls flocking into the movies these days."

The *National Board of Review* cited *Peyton Place* as "an example of a fine motion picture that can be made out of a cheap and dirty book."

Wanda Bale in the *New York Daily News* claimed, "Putting *Peyton Place* on the screen was a gigantic undertaking. And from it, Fox has made a picture that is better than the book. It is less shocking, although it is as candid as a French drama, as unreserved as Italian neo-realism. Grace Metalious couldn't ask for a better cast to bring her characters to life."

When Lana saw this publicity still, she quipped: "Lee Philips got no more intimate with me than this when we shot *Peyton Place*."

Chapter Sixteen

Who Killed Johnny Stompanato?

Lana Turner Fears Reprisals from the Mob: Acid Thrown in Her Face, or a Bullet.

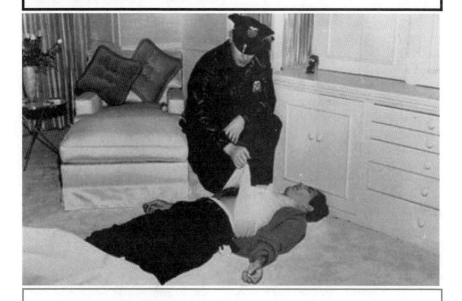

The shocking murder of Johnny Stompanato made frontpage news across the nation, with bulletins issued frequently on radio. In Hollywood, the rumor mill began grinding out an alternate claim to the official version, and that was that Lana had plunged the knife into Johnny's stomach and allowed her daughter to take the fall.

Lana obviously knew that if she were exposed as the guilty party, it would mean not only the end of her movie career, but perhaps a lifetime in prison.

Cheryl, or so Lana's attorney, Jerry Giesler, had told her, would get off with only a few months in reform school, if that. Again, he pressed the case that a judge and jury would probably rule it as "justifiable homicide."

As Lana wrote, in her memoirs, about the most notorious event in her life, "It all started with flowers and an innocent invitation for a drink, and it was to end in screaming headlines, in tragedy, and in death."

In April of 1957, Lana, newly released from MGM, was working at Universal International. She was starring in *The Lady Takes a Flyer* with Jeff Chandler, with whom she was having a fling.

At the studio, she began to receive phone calls from a stranger, who identified himself as "John Steele." At first, she ignored the calls, refusing to come to the phone. She wrote him off as "another god damn stalker—I've had plenty of them, but this one is more persistent than most."

The calls came in frequently to her dressing room, whose number he had obviously obtained from someone. Flowers, enough for a funeral, arrived daily, along with his card and private phone number.

He appeared to know someone familiar with her, as he sent yellow roses, her favorite, not red ones. He also sent the

Lana confessed, "Johnny's consuming passion for me was strangely exciting. Call it forbidden fruit. My attraction to him was very deep—maybe it was something sick within me."

Months later, when columnist Lee Mortimer learned about Stompanato's break-in of Lana's apartment, he called it "asphyxiation sex."

"Lana was hot for the bastard," Frank Sinatra said. "I hated the shithead. He was selling his dick to the highest bidder, male or female."

most expensive boxes of chocolates in Beverly Hills, which she fed to the crew working on her picture, since she did not want to gain weight. As the calls increased, and as the flowers became annoying and overwhelming, more costly gifts arrived, beginning with a diamond bracelet.

Even sets of records were delivered. He knew that Tony Martin and Frank Sinatra, both of them former beaux, were her favorite singers.

Finally, she decided to come to the phone and speak to him. She liked the sound of his strong, virile voice. As a way of introduction, he told her that he was a friend of Ava Gardner, who often spoke lovingly of her. Gardner was in London at the time, and Lana made no attempt to confirm his connection with her.

"I've also dated Janet Leigh," he claimed. "She told me that you and she became friends at MGM."

That, of course, was true.

He invited her for dinner, but she turned down the offer, claiming, "I'm too busy."

Actually, in the wake of her divorce from Lex Barker, she was experiencing many lonely nights. There was no one man in all of Hollywood that she wanted to date. "Most of my lovers are getting gray at the temples and have found other mates," she complained.

One night, when Lana worked late at the studio, she got into her "Baby Whale," the nickname for her steel-gray Cadillac. She drove to the apartment house, where she was living temporarily. During that unsettling period of her life, she seemed to be constantly changing addresses.

There was space in front of her apartment house, and she parked Baby Whale there. She could not help but notice a black Lincoln Continental parked across the street. A red glow of a cigarette signaled to her that the driver was behind the wheel, perhaps that of her stalker, John Steele. She didn't know for sure, but at least his name flashed in her mind.

She hurried into the elevator and quickly got off on her floor and went inside, where her Mexican maid, Armida, was waiting, telling her that her dinner was in the oven and ready.

Fifteen minutes later, Armida announced that a Mr. Steele was standing outside her door, wanting to see her.

Out of curiosity, perhaps with the thrill of danger, she told Armida to let him enter her living room.

She didn't know what to expect coming face-to-face with this man of mystery, who seemed rather rich, to judge by that diamond bracelet, the endless flowers, and the lavish gifts, including the most expensive of French perfumes.

Before entering her living room to greet him, she spent at least ten minutes before her vanity mirror, working on her makeup, which had faded by this hour in the early evening. She also put on a beautiful champagne-colored cocktail dress and high heels before emerging. What greeted her dazzled her a bit. She later described him as "very handsome, very masculine, sexy as hell. He treated me like he was in the presence of the Queen of England. This Mr. Steele was oozing with masculinity, and wore a tailored gray suit with a red silk shirt unbuttoned all the way to the silver buckle of his belt."

He had obviously learned

While working as a bouncer in one of gangster Mickey Cohen's bars, Johnny Stompanato (left) met the mobster himself. The two men almost immediately struck up a friendship, a very unusual move on Johnny's part.

He was subsequently hired as one of Cohen's bodyguards at $300 a week, although Cohen later admitted that his job was more akin to that of a pimp. "He could attract the babes, and I needed plenty of gorgeous gals in my enterprise to entertain my clients."

how to dress from watching George Raft movies, and was most often described as "cunning and cocksure," with an emphasis on *cock*.

Not wanting to appear overly awed by his striking presence, she chastised him: "You should have called first."

"I *have* called," he protested. "Day after day, spending my nights alone, dreaming of you. You're the first person I think of when I go to bed at night, hoping you will visit me in my dreams, which you always do. But a man can't spend his life dreaming. Will you go to dinner with me tonight?"

She turned him down, claiming that she had an early call. "Perhaps lunch in my apartment Saturday at one? Now, Mr. Steele, good night."

As he walked to the door, he leaned in as if he wanted to kiss her, but she backed away. "Until Saturday, I said."

"I'll bring the food."

Arriving exactly at one o'clock, he brought one of her favorite dishes: Vermicelli in white clam sauce from Mario's, an Italian restaurant she sometimes frequented. How did he know to do that?

Two hours before he showed up, a diamond bracelet had been delivered. It was fashioned from miniature gold leaves surrounding the sparking stones.

She greeted him, and after the maid had served him a drink, she protested. "I can't accept such an expensive gift! You must take it back!"

"I can't. I've had it engraved."

She checked the engraving. "To my beloved Lanita." She put it on her wrist. "Do you own a money tree?"

"Just the leaves," he answered.

"Never in my life have I had lunch with a man of such charm. He was flirtatious, courtly, treating me like a goddess, hanging on my every word like it was divinely inspired. When I dismissed him at three that afternoon, I promised I'd go out dining and dancing with him."

She later confessed to Virginia Grey, "His first sexual come-on was a winner. Since he knew so much about me, he'd found out that I have thing for well-endowed men. He told me he and Oscar shared something in common."

"What might that be?" Grey asked. Both of them knew what he was implying.

Oscar is a foot long. She assumed he was exaggerating, as so many men do. "Every man with six inches often claims it's at least nine," Lana said.

That night, Johnny slept in Lana's bed.

During a phone call to Grey, Lana confessed, "John Steele did not exaggerate. He could penetrate as far as Oscar. It was unbelievable. He can satisfy a woman's deepest desires. I really don't know much about him, but a man who can thrill a woman like John could be Jack the Ripper, and still a woman would invite him into her boudoir. He's a walking streak of sex."

Word of his endowment had already become legendary. Columnist James Bacon defined him as "The John C. Holmes of his day," referring to the most famous male porn star in history.

Despite his flair as a great lover, Lana did not immediately make him her boyfriend. In fact, during the summer of 1957, she seemed to tantalize him, going out with other men, usually former beaux who were between marriages.

In early September, he told her, "I want to totally possess my little Lanita."

She still wasn't ready to commit, and for the next few days, claimed that she was always too busy to see him. He accused her of "dangling me like a puppet, knowing how much I love you."

One night, after she'd turned him down ten times in a row, he climbed up the fire escape of her apartment house and broke into her living room window. She was in bed at the time. A noise must have awakened her, and she rose, seeing this shadowy figure moving toward her.

Before she could scream, he was on top of her. "With a jump, he was on the bed shoving a pillow over my face. Holding my arms pinned to my side, he straddled me and held my legs tight." *[She wrote that in her memoirs.]*

What she didn't put in her memoirs was that he raped her. At least it was rape in the beginning, but, as she told Grey, "before a minute or two, my fingernails were digging into his back."

***

Who was this mysterious John Steele? She didn't really know.

He told her that he was forty-two years old, as compared to her thirty-six. She was sensitive about being seen as an older woman dating a younger man. Hollywood was filled with sex-for-pay couplings like that.

Over the years, the identity of John Steele has been revealed after massive research into his background and the testimony of various people who knew him, many with revelations appearing here for the first time.

John Steele was a pseudonym. His real name was John ("Johnny") Stompanato, born into an Italian-American family in Woodstock, Illinois, on October 10, 1925. His father, John Sr., owned a barbershop, and his mother, Carmela, was a seamstress. Both parents were immigrants, but they had met in Brooklyn, fell in love, and married.

In 1961, they went to Illinois, seeking a better life. It was there that Carmela gave birth to four children, Grace and Teresa and a boy, Carmine. Her final child was John Jr., the youngest. He never knew his mother, who died of peritonitis six days after his birth. A few months later, Johnny had a new stepmother, Verena Freitag.

During his freshman year at Woodstock High School, Johnny got into trouble. "It was time to get out of Dodge," as the local police chief said of the boy. He had impregnated two teenaged girls, causing a local scandal.

His father shipped him off to Kemper Military School for boys in Booneville, Missouri. Ironically, his roommate there was the future movie and TV star, Hugh O'Brian, born Hugh Charles Krampe the same year as Johnny.

In the 1950s, O'Brian became a household word starring in the hit TV series, *The Life and Legend of Wyatt Earp*, which ran on ABC from 1955 to 1961. In 1965, O'Brian would co-star with Lana, playing a gigolo in *Love Has Many Faces*. During that time the two co-stars sustained a torrid affair in Mexico.

"Johnny was an amazing guy," O'Brian recalled. "Unfortunately, not all of it was put to use in the right direction. In the gym after playing football, we headed

505

for the communal shower, a dozen showerheads in a row of naked boy ass. Usually, we walked to the showers with a towel around our waists, hanging them up at the door. But Johnny stripped bare-assed naked in the locker room, and he didn't just walk to the shower, he paraded, shaking that monster dick. We had three or four gay guys in our gym class, and they always followed him with their tongues hanging, taking the showerheads on each side of Johnny. He was the 'big' attraction."

"He was also the prize stud of school. All the gals were after him. At one point, he seduced the much older school nurse. Older women never turned him off. Maybe because he lost his mother, I don't know. A lot of girls were attracted to me, too, but John was clearly the chief rooster of the henhouse."

After his graduation from military school in 1942, at the age of seventeen, Johnny joined the U.S. Marines the following year. He served in the South Pacific theater, engaging in some of the most horrific warfare as American troops invaded island by island with an aim to attack the Japanese mainland. He saw some of the most horrendous battles in Okinawa.

He was on the island when U.S. forces captured it from the Japanese. An Army nurse, Betty Nulle, remembered him. "Johnny, as a Marine, was always getting into trouble. He attracted women to him like flies to a raw steak left out in the sun. He'd even borrowed the uniform of this gay lieutenant, who was in love with him, and he would wear it into the officers' mess which served better food that the grub offered enlisted men."

"That was the kind of guy he was. Nobody, not even a general, could tell that cocky bastard what to do. He was a great lover…the best. None of my future four husbands ever measured up to Johnny."

Although World War II ended in September of 1945 after two atomic bombs were dropped on Japan, Johnny wasn't discharged from the Marines until March of 1946. At the time of his discharge, he was stationed in Tianjin, China.

Instead of returning to America, he decided to stay on for a while, opening a seedy little nightclub, where he hired underaged Chinese girls. His clientele consisted mostly of expatriates living in China and figuring out how to flourish (or at least how to survive) as foreigners in a post-colonial society ripped apart by war and the tides of history.

Barry Edwards, one of the American Marines who opted to remain in China for several months, said, "Johnny's sleazy bar became a great hangout, especially for pickups. Right after the war, a five-dollar bill would have bought anything. Of course, Johnny 'auditioned' every gal before hiring her. Some were gorgeous. He knew how to pick 'em."

Johnny's life changed when he walked into a dress shop in Tianjin where he was immediately attracted to a Turkish woman, Sarah Utish. "I just had to have her, even if it meant converting to Islam, which she demanded. Religion means nothing to me, so what did it matter? She was just so fucking petite and pretty." He made this confession to Edwards.

He didn't know her age when he married her. He was only twenty-one, and she was five years older.

Both Johnny and his new wife ran into some kind of trouble in China, Johnny no doubt with the police. He took her back to Woodstock, where he got a job driving a bread truck, later in an auto parts factory. In time, John Stompanato III arrived.

Sarah worked at night in a sewing factory, freeing Johnny to "sample the most gorgeous bitches of Woodstock," he later claimed.

Sarah modestly said, "Johnny had a good heart, but he was the boy who never grew up."

Eventually, he deserted his wife and son in Woodstock, and headed for Chicago.

There, in the bar of a hotel, he met Sir Charles Hubbard, a British aristocrat and heir to a fortune and a country estate in England.

Hubbard seemed much impressed with this handsome, sexy young man, and Johnny became his live-in companion. It was Hubbard who flew Johnny to Los Angeles, where he settled and, in Lana's house, eventually died.

Johnny came under an audit from the IRS for failing to pay income tax. An agent discovered that he had not reported $85,000 in cash that Hubbard had given him. In his defense, Johnny claimed it was a loan. The IRS didn't think so, interpreting it as a fee for services rendered, perhaps in blackmailing Hubbard.

This experience launched Johnny on his new profession, that of a hustler and blackmailer.

While working for Mickey Cohen, Johnny answered to a number of nicknames. One was Johnny Valentine, inspired by Rudolph Valentino, the legendary silent screen star who died young. He was also called "Handsome Harry" and "Johnny Stomp."

Marilyn Maxwell nicknamed him "Oscar," claiming that he had something in common with the size of the Academy Award statuette. She also boasted "He's got more than Sinatra."

In her memoir, Cheryl used the term "Academy Award size phallus," in reference to Johnny's outsized penis.

At night, he frequented Lana's favorite night clubs, the Trocadero, Mocambo, and Ciro's, hoping to meet rich women.

During the afternoon, he could always be seen by the swimming pool at the Beverly Hills Hotel. Merv Griffith, the homosexual TV host, spotted him there. Charmed and deeply impressed, he spread the word to his gay friends, including Liberace.

"Johnny wore a collection of almost sheer male bikinis," Griffin said. "As he emerged from the water, the fabric became almost transparent. It was at least eight inches long, soft, and very thick." Griffin picked Johnny up the first afternoon he met him and became a regular customer.

Liberace turned out to be the biggest tipper, at one point rewarding Johnny with a thousand-dollar bill.

During his first year in Hollywood, Stompanato met and married Helen Gilbert, a 33-year-old actress. The marriage lasted much less than a year.

Gilbert, who was eight years his senior, had appeared in Mickey Rooney's *Andy Hardy* series. In filing for divorce, Gilbert told the judge, "During our short marriage, Stompanato had no visible means of support. I did what I could for him."

In 1953, he married another actress, Helene Stanley. She had starred in several

B pictures, and was much older than he was. His marriage to this former Fox contract player lasted two years, but he was gone most of the time.

At her divorce hearing, she told the judge, "Stompanato has an awful temper. He once tried to choke my mother when she mislaid his handkerchiefs."

Even during his marriages, Johnny went out with other men and women. He had an affair with a very young Janet Leigh and engaged in a torrid romance with Ava Gardner. Sinatra found out about this and protested to Mickey Cohen.

He pleaded with Cohen to force Johnny to break off from Gardner. At the time, Cohen was under 24-hour surveillance by the police. "I couldn't believe that Frankie wanted me to risk the cops looking me over in a case of his 'hot nuts.'"

Cohen told Sinatra, "I don't mix with my guys and their broads. Frankie, why don't you go back home to Nancy where you belong and quit running after this Tarheel slut?"

Stompanato's real money came from various scams, notably blackmailing Hollywood stars, male and female, by secretly photographing them in compromising situations. He went through a vast fortune at the time, mainly to pay off his gambling debts. He always lost money gambling, but was drawn to it like an addict to heroin.

Certainly not all of his dates were with movie stars, of course. It was discovered that the wife of a doctor, Rosemary Trimble, claimed she made two payments to Johnny—one for $2,500, another for

Helen Gilbert became Johnny Stompanato's second wife. She was a beautiful woman—at least Mickey Rooney thought so when she appeared in his Andy Hardy series.

"In her looks and blonde hair, she reminded me of Lana Turner," the pint-sized actor claimed.

Helene Stanley, Stompanato's third wife, was pretty and perky. She arrived in Hollywood hoping to make it as a star. She did get cast in some low-budget pictures, but major stardom eluded her.

Johnny also eluded her much of the time, occupying the beds of other "lucky broads" (his words).

$25,000.

These payoffs were first revealed in the Dell book, *Lana: The Public and Private Lives of Lana Turner.* In a separate, unrelated incident, a widow, Doris Jean Cornell told police she gave him $8,150 so that he could open a pet shop.

***

One Saturday afternoon, Lana's old friend, Mickey Rooney, dropped in. He'd heard rumors that Lana was dating Johnny Stompanato, and he wanted to warn her about the dangers involved.

She was very candid with her lover of long ago. In reference to Stompanato, "I think I've fallen in love with him, even though he broke into my apartment and raped me one night."

"He's bad news," Rooney claimed. "I mean *really* bad news. You referred to him as John Steele. That's not his god damn name. He's the notorious Johnny Stompanato, the henchman of Mickey Cohen. His name has been in the papers."

Before leaving that afternoon, Rooney gave her a copy of *U.S. Confidential*, a book-length exposé written in 1951 by Lee Mortimer and Jack Lait. He'd marked a passage for her to read.

"One of the minor tough guys is handsome Johnny Stompanato, who is the general stooge for Mickey Cohen. Johnny is the introducer of gals to visiting mobsters, and the dancing escort to stars and would-be's." Passages in the book also claimed, accurately, that Stompanato had a record of arrests by the Los Angeles police.

That night, Lana confronted Johnny with Rooney's revelations. He admitted that they were

During the early 1950s, police records in Los Angeles reveal that Stompanato was arrested eight times, based on charges ranging from suspicion of robbery to vagrancy.

Cohen later mocked the vagrancy arrest. "When the cops took him in, Johnny had $5,000 in his wallet, all in one-hundred dollar bills."

As a front, he opened the Myrtlewood Gift Shop in Westwood, selling wood carvings as fine art and crude pottery.

true. "If I'd revealed who I really was, you would not have had anything to do with me. I was planning to tell you, but only after you'd fallen in love with me and could not leave me. Now that I have you, I'll never let you go."

She recalled that the sound of his voice was ominous. Was this not a veiled threat? If so, it would be the first of many to come in the months ahead.

Almost from the beginning, money was a constant source of friction between Lana and Johnny. She paid his living expenses, but objected to having to settle his gambling debts. The first that he presented to her was for $3,500. "If I don't pay up," he warned, "I'm likely to meet up with a stray bullet one night."

"I know that Lana was giving Johnny sums of money at least every other day," Virginia Grey said. "Not huge sums, but at least hundreds of dollars. She told me

509

that every time they had sex, he seemed to bill her. Of course, she was exaggerating, but there was some truth in that. I never confronted Lana with this—she was too much in love—but all of her friends, and especially her enemies, knew that he was nothing but a gigolo."

By now, Lana knew not only that Johnny was a gangster, but that he had a violent streak in him. In spite of that, she introduced him to Cheryl and even allowed them to spend afternoons alone together.

"Johnny and the kid were real close," Cohen said. "She was crazy about him. He told me that himself."

Cheryl even described her first impression of him. "B-picture good looks, thick set. Powerfully built and soft spoken. He talked in short sentences to cover a poor grasp of grammar and had a deep baritone voice. With friends, he seldom smiled or laughed out loud, but always seemed coiled, holding himself in."

"His watchful, hooded eyes took in more than he wanted anyone to notice. His wardrobe on a daily basis consisted of roomy, draped slacks, a silver buckled leather belt, and lizard shoes. By this time, he was also wearing a heavy, gold-link bracelet on his wrist with 'Lanita' inscribed inside."

Cheryl later said that the two of them went horseback riding together or else swimming, during which Johnny liked to show off his manly physique. Their closeness sparked rumors that he might be seducing Cheryl, evoking memories of her repeated rapes by Lex Barker. But there is no evidence that Johnny ever forced himself on the girl.

As a surprise gift, which delighted her, he purchased a red Arabian mare with a flaxen tail and mane. This was the same horse that Lana had ridden in her historical costume drama, *Diane* (1956). Cohen later said that he gave Johnny $900 to purchase the mare.

Johnny and Cheryl often went riding in the Hollywood Hills, overlooking the flatlands where the original silent screen version of *Ben-Hur* had been shot. It had starred Ramon Novarro, who, like Johnny, would meet a violent death.

At the stable, where the horses were kept, an associate of Stephen Crane later reported back to him: "That Stompanato guy seems to be putting his hands all over your daughter."

When Crane confronted Lana with this nasty bit of gossip, she denied that Johnny had ever come on to Cheryl.

***

Although Lana was still entranced with Johnny's lovemaking, she decided not to fly him with her to England, where she had signed to make her next picture, *Another Time, Another Place* (1958). It was to be the first venture of Lanturn, her independent film company.

510

Paramount had agreed to distribute it.

Before she left, she and Johnny had some severe arguments after he learned that he was not going to accompany her. She still found him very attractive sexually, but had ruled him out as marriage material—in fact, she'd abandoned any illusion about a long-term relationship with him.

She told a few friends, "Johnny is what is known as an interlude." Privately, she was hoping that with thousands of miles between herself and his sexual magnetism, she would be in a better position for a clean break, perhaps after sending him a "Dear John" letter.

Two weeks before her departure for England, he'd been in her bed every night. As she confessed to Virginia Grey, one session with him that began late one Saturday night lasted until dawn Sunday morning. "He has the stamina of a bull," she claimed. "He can't seem to get enough. A little rest and he's on fire again."

She decided to fly to London with her makeup man and confidant, Del Armstrong. Because of strict union laws in Britain, he could not practice his profession there, so she arranged to have him listed as an associate producer.

She met with her director, Lewis Allen, to discuss the production of the film. Although born in England, he had worked mainly in the United States, turning out eighteen movies from 1944 to 1959. He was also a film actor. After shooting war propaganda movies for Britain, he made his film debut as a (non-military) director in 1944 when he helmed *The Uninvited,* an atmospheric ghost story starring Ray Milland.

The screenplay for *Another Time, Another Place* was by Stanley Mann, a Canadian, who had penned a TV adaptation of *Death of a Salesman* in 1957. Lana's soapy film was based on *Weep No More,* a novel by Leonore Coffee. [*Coffee had also written for the screen, winning an Oscar nomination for* Four Daughters *back in 1938.*]

She had told Lana, "Hollywood picks your brain, breaks your heart, ruins your digestion—what do you get for it? Nothing but a lousy fortune."

Lana ordered Mann to come up with a new title. After lots of debate, it emerged as *Another Time, Another Place.* Although as a title, it was weak and somewhat nonspecific, Lana liked it.

From the beginning, she announced that it would be a woman's picture. Set in England during the closing months of World War II, it's the story of the wife of an English soldier killed in battle, in conflict with his grieving mistress. Whereas his kind and unpretentious wife lived in a small Cornish village, his emotionally bereaved mistress, Sara Scott (as played by Lana), had been stationed in London as a chic, mink-clad, impeccably groomed American newspaperwoman.

During her character's work-obsessed wartime sojourn in London, she had met Mark Trevor, finding him handsome and charming, a news commentator for the BBC. She begins to see a lot of him, as they start to date. By the time he confesses to her that he has a wife and son living in Cornwall, she has fallen desperately and irretrievably in love with him.

During the final weeks of the war, Mark is sent on a mission to France. His plane crashes, and he is killed instantly.

The sends Sara into shock and generates a kind of grieving obsession for her lost lover. Impulsively, she decides to visit the Cornish village where he'd lived and where his wife, and young son, also grieving, are living. The picturesque Cornish village of Polperro, in the southwest of England, was selected for the exterior shots. The interior shots were to be filmed at Elstree Studios outside London.

Jack Hildyard, who had won an Oscar for his high-caliber camera work on *The Bridge on the River Kwai* in 1959, would brilliantly recapture the English countryside, and photograph Lana looking as lovely as she did in the early 1950s.

Seeking emotional closure, in defiance of the strident advice of her friends, Sara leaves London, traveling to Polperro to see where her lost lover had lived. Overcome with emotion, she falls ill there, and, by coincidence, is invited to recuperate within the home of Mark's wife, Kay, and his young son, Brian.

As would be inevitable, Sara's true identity as "the other woman" (Mark's grieving mistress) is revealed to Kay before the end of the film.

To complicate matters, Sara (i.e., Lana) has been conducting a subdued romance with her *fiancé*, Carter Reynolds, her publisher, and he's longing to marry her.

That role went to Barry Sullivan, who had worked with Lana before in, among others, *The Bad and the Beautiful*. When they'd met for drinks in Hollywood, he told her, "I've pursued you for years. But this time, I've thrown in the towel, deciding you're unobtainable. At least out of my league."

Glynis Johns was assigned the role of Mark's cheerful, long-suffering British wife, Kay. Noted for her husky trademark voice, she had begun acting and dancing as a child. She'd made her film debut in 1938, the same year Lana did. Over time, she had co-starred with Douglas Fairbanks, Jr., Alec Guinness, David Niven, James Stewart, and Danny Kaye.

During filming, Lana was often frustrated and in a nervous state, based on her ongoing difficulties with Stompanato and in her capacity as the producer of the film as well as its star. The actual producer—the one in charge of arranging and organizing its business affairs—was Joseph Kaufman.

In her anxiety, Lana nervously lashed out at Johns, at one point calling this talented and engaging actress, "the bitch of the world."

Two other actors had key supporting roles: Raymond Burr as Walt Radak, and the English actor, Terrence Longdom, as Alan Thompson.

***

Although her star power had waned since she'd been fired from MGM, Lana still retained the right to select her leading man. Twenty actors

While her character decides who she's in love with, her boss, Barry Sullivan, waits patiently on tenderhooks.

512

were considered before she settled on a newcomer to films, Sean Connery.

A Scotsman, the son of a cleaning woman and a factory worker, he'd been a milkman, truck driver, day laborer, coffin polisher (that's right), and bodybuilder. He'd also been a nude model. A student artist, Arlene Hector, later said, "Young Sean was magnificent in the nude and lacked nothing 'down there.' In fact, it was the biggest I'd ever seen. It made me drop my charcoal pencil."

Prior to his gig with Lana in *Another Time, Another Place,* Connery's film work was so insignificant that Lana decided to bill his appearance as "introducing Sean Connery."

Her hunch about his sex appeal proved Lana right. He would go on to become the movie's first "Bond...James Bond" in the highly successful *Dr. No* (1962). Not only that, he would become one of the biggest screen sex symbols in the world, accessorized by guns and a bevy of glamorous women lusting after him.

During the making of the film, Connery and Lana were seen everywhere together. She even rode on the back seat of his motorcycle. Rumors of an affair reached Hollywood, especially the ears of Johnny Stompanato, who became enraged. Even at this early stage of his career, Connery had a reputation as a superb lover.

Cheryl wrote that "people working on the picture were persuaded that mother and Sean were really having a secret fling. They had a certain familiarity with each other."

"Lana was Sean's type," said journalist Peter Noble. "How far did it go? With all that red-hot chemistry, one would imagine all the way. He certainly entertained Lana at his flat, and he accompanied her on a number of outings."

There was a ten-year difference in their ages, but Connery didn't see that as an obstacle. At one point, a London reporter asked him, "How does it feel to make love on the screen to an old woman?"

He later said, "I should have punched the bloke."

Years later, in 1992, all that Connery would say was, "Who can forget Lana Turner? She was a lovely lady. I adored her."

He didn't confess to an affair, but Lana did. "I've had them all," she told Virginia Grey, "and Sean ranks up there near the top."

Her name now appears on Connery's

In spite of (or perhaps in part because of) his bushy, caterpillar eyebrows—in contrast to Lana, who had none—she viewed Sean Connery as "very handsome, sexy, and virile." She was drawn to that glint in his eye and admired his rugged charm and physicality.

list of actress lovers, alongside Ursula Andress, co-star in *Dr. No* (1962); Claudine Auger, co-star in *Thunderball* (1965); Brigitte Bardot, co-star in *Shalako* (1968); Jill St. John, co-star of *Diamonds Are Forever* (1971); and Kim Basinger, co-star of *Never Say Never Again* (1983).

Others of Connery's seductions included Zsa Zsa Gabor (who had sustained intimacies with both Johnny Stompanato and Lex Barker); Shelley Winters; Lana Wood (sister of Natalie Wood); British actress Sue Lloyd; another British actress, Carol Sopen; Polish actress Magda Knopka, English photographer Julie Hamilton; and singer Lyndsey de Paul.

As he confessed, "There was never any trouble getting girls, but it's big trouble getting rid of them."

***

Although Lana claimed that her original intention involved staying in England alone as a means of dumping Johnny, her love letters to him (which were later published) indicate otherwise. From London, a typical one read: "Sweetheart, please keep well because I need you so—and so you will always be strong and able to caress me, hold me, tenderly at first, and crush me into your very own being."

In another letter to him, in which she addressed him as "My

Biographer Michael Feeny Callan, wrote: "Friends of Sean Connery broadly hinted that the friendship between the Scot and Lana eventually bloomed into an impassioned affair.

'Big Tam' (his nickname) had Hollywood Incarnate in his arms, and he did with it what he did most effortlessly—he made love."

Lana with her nemesis, the very charming Glynis Johns. Lana was "the other woman."

Beloved Love," she wrote: "Every line of your precious, exciting letter warms me and makes me miss you each tiny moment—and it's true—it's beautiful, yet terrible. But, so is deep love. Hold me, dear lover. I'm your woman and I need you, my man! To love and be loved—don't ever doubt or forget that!"

She often received transatlantic phone calls from him, and he, too, wrote her, declaring his undying love.

However, while all this was going on, he had rented a $125-a-month motel room at the Malibu Sands Motel on the Pacific Coast Highway, where he became a resident for one month. Outside his door, he'd park two ostentatiously expensive cars: a white 1957 Thunderbird and a late model black Lincoln Continental.

Jeffrey Woods, the night manager there, spoke to the tabloid press after Johnny's murder.

"I may have missed a few, but I counted at least eighteen men—never a woman—who came and went from his apartment during the night hours when I was on duty. Some of them stopped and asked me the number of his motel room. I was convinced he was a male prostitute, since these guys were out of shape. No self-respecting homosexual would take them on unless they were paid."

Johnny continued to implore Lana to invite him to London, and she finally acquiesced. Many sources claim that Mickey Cohen supplied him with the airfare, but the mobster denied it. "He asked me for it, but I told him to make her send him a ticket. And she did. A one-way ticket."

He joined her at her rented house in Hampstead Heath.

In the beginning, "He was the most loving and kind I'd ever seen him," she said. "He couldn't get enough love making. But after a week or two, things changed."

He was angry that she refused to let him accompany her every day to the studio. He was growing increasingly bored, wandering around Central London, mostly near Piccadilly Circus. In Del Armstrong's view, "I think Johnny turned a trick or two there, since it was a gathering place for homosexuals in the Underground's men's toilets."

Sean Connery at the debut of his career, as a contestant in a Mr. Universe bodybuilding competition.

The arguments began when he accused her of having an affair with Connery. She denied it, telling him, "We're just good friends."

Once again, he revived his long-standing ambition to become an actor. He wanted her to produce and star in two screenplays he had read but not optioned, since he didn't have the money.

A homosexual friend of his, Philip Coburn, had written a script entitled *By Love Betrayed*. Ironically, the title evoked a former movie of Lana's, *Betrayed*, and a future one, *By Love Possessed*.

By Love Betrayed was about two A-list movie stars—one blonde, the other brunette—who not only vied for an Oscar, but for the same man, a world-famous aviator (i.e., Howard Hughes). The plot seemed to dip into the biography of those sisters and stars, Joan Fontaine and Olivia de Havilland. Johnny wanted Lana and Ava Gardner as the two stars, with himself cast as the aviator.

He showed Lana another script, *The Bartered Bride*, available for option for $1,000. The story by Robert Carson had already been publicized in Louella Parsons' column. She wrote that it might be a starring vehicle for Lana and Frank Sinatra. Johnny wanted to produce it, with the understanding that financing would be provided by Lanturn.

Lana rejected any involvement with the script, and refused to indulge the acting ambitions of the wannabe star (Stompanato), even if some producer could be found with the money. Every night when she arrived home, tired and exhausted from the strain of production, he increased his pressure and his demands.

One night, she could take it no more, and she screamed at him, "Get out of my house. Pack you god damn bags and get the fuck out of England. Go back to your gangsters!"

Defiantly, he refused to leave the house, but retreated instead to the living room, where he sulked until around 2AM. At that point, he barged into her bedroom. She was asleep, but he woke her up, shouting, "Like hell I'm going to leave!"

Although she feared a scandal, she threatened to call the police. "They'll kick you out of the country, especially when I tell them you're traveling under a fake passport with the name of John Steele."

Finally, he could no longer control his temper. She later wrote: "After he choked me and threw me on the floor, he then barged into the bathroom and came back with a razor. He came over to me and grabbed my head, all the time screeching violent things at me. Then he claimed that he was going to use the razor to make only a small incision at first, but soon, he would carve bigger scars. He said he'd scar my face for all time. I pleaded and pleaded with him to let me alone. I said I'd do whatever he wanted if he wouldn't destroy my face."

"If you claim you love me, why can you hurt me?" she asked. "PLEASE DON'T!"

She desperately reached for her phone. As she did, he lurched toward her, ripping the phone from her hands. Then his strong fingers tightened around her delicate throat. She screamed for help before he cut off her vocal chords.

Her maid, Annie, was asleep in a small room upstairs, and she heard the commotion. In her night gown, she came galloping down the steps and into the bedroom. A strong, bulky woman, she headed straight for Johnny.

She managed to yank him off Lana. For a while, they wrestled together on the floor. He could have overpowered her, even killed her, but sanity prevailed, and he did not use his full force upon her.

Jumping up from the floor, Annie covered Lana with her own bulk. "Get out of this room, or I'll kill you!" she shouted at him.

At that, he seemed to bring his rage under control, storming out of the bedroom and out of the house. He slammed the front door behind him.

Annie spent the rest of the night with Lana, promising to protect her should he return.

Johnny stayed away from the house for several days. It was not known at the time where he went. Years later, Diana Dors, Britain's sex symbol of the 1950s, revealed that he had stayed with her. She had been called "Britain's answer to Lana Turner" and later, "Britain's answer to Marilyn Monroe."

It is not known how Johnny met Dors. However, this highly sexed star was known for staging orgies, and no doubt, he managed to come by an invitation to one of these sex parties, where he intrigued Dors with his sexual prowess.

Lana woke up that Monday morning with laryngitis, and Annie called Del Armstrong to alert the studio that she was too sick to report that day to work.

She'd lost her speaking voice. She had been flirting with a cold all weekend, and Dr. Stanwood Williams, who had once treated Laurence Olivier, was summoned. After examining her, he told her that her cold had developed into influenza.

She had to remain in bed for a week, shutting down production on the film and even threatening the existence of Lanturn, which was severely underfinanced.

Finally, Johnny returned to Lana's home, and she was too weak to indulge in any more fights with him. He apologized for attacking her, claiming, "It's because I love you so much."

She demanded that he exit at once, but he made his most serious threat again. "If you kick me out, I'll see that one of Cohen's henchmen takes care of Mildred and Cheryl."

That week, Lana returned to the set, but still could not speak in a normal voice. It would be another three weeks before "I sounded like myself. Otherwise, my voice recorded like a victim choking on a tough piece of steak."

The director shot scenes where she had no dialogue, including shots of her walking, sometimes unsteadily, on high heels and in mink, across the uneven cobblestones of Polperro.

Alone again at Hampstead Heath during the day, Johnny grew bored and impatient. Rumors still persisted about the affair that Connery was having with Lana, Finally, one afternoon, Johnny bribed Lana's driver to take him to the studio where they were filming. He wore a suit which contained a revolver in his breast pocket.

If necessary, he planned not to kill Connery, but to use the gun to threaten him.

He arrived just in time to stand in the background and watch Connery and Lana perform a love scene on camera. He whispered to a grip, "Those two obviously had a lot of practice off screen."

Connery came off the set with an arm around Lana. Suddenly, Johnny shouted at him. "You keep away from her!" As he did, she let out a little scream.

Johnny took out his revolver and pointed it at Connery's chest. As if in rehearsal for a future scene from a James Bond movie, the actor sprang into action before Johnny could pull the trigger. He twisted Johnny's wrist until he dropped the gun, then he delivered a right hook to Johnny's nose, causing him to bleed all over his tasteless lime-green suit.

Stunned by the blow, he did not rise at once. He reached for his handkerchief to cover his bleeding nose. By the time he rose to his feet, security guards had been summoned, and they forcibly escorted him out of the studio.

"You'll get yours, you mother fucker!" he shouted back at Connery, as Lana stood looking on in stunned and horrified disbelief.

Raging and swearing, Johnny was deposited into the back seat of Lana's chauffeur-driven limousine and driven back to her rented home.

Del Armstrong rushed to the scene and urged her to call Scotland Yard, explaining that he had a contact there who would hustle Johnny out of the country, based on, among other factors, his previous entry into Britain using a fake passport.

Two detectives from Scotland Yard agreed to go to Lana's home to force Johnny to pack his luggage before escorting him to the airport for the next plane leaving for Los Angeles. Each of the detectives promised Lana that they would not leave the airport until his plane was airborne.

Days later, Lana awoke with the fear that Johnny might carry through with his threat to harm Cheryl and Mildred. "I decided to test the waters."

Although she had vowed never to speak to him again, she wrote him two conciliatory letters, each of which she later described as "too sentimental."

Perhaps they were, because what she wrote in them was so loving that it convinced him that he still had a chance with her, in spite of his previous violence.

***

After Johnny was murdered, Paramount advanced the release date of *Another Time, Another Place* by three months to take advantage of all the notorious publicity Lana was getting. Even so, that didn't help the box office for this film. *[It did, however, greatly beef up the audiences for* Peyton Place, *a movie she had made previously, which was currently playing in theaters across America.]*

Nearly all the major reviews of *Another Time, Another Place* were unfavorable. The film historian, Leslie Halliwell, wrote: "Drippy romance unsympathetically played and artificially set in a Cornish village. Lana Turner unsympathetically played an American newspaperwoman who has an affair with a British war correspondent, unsympathetically played by Sean Connery."

The New York Times ripped into the picture. *"Another Place, Another Time* is a long way from making any contact with any interests that might serve to entertain. This one was made in England, evidently as part of the current 'Go Home, Yank' plan."

The New York Post noted that Connery was being introduced to American movie audiences. "The BBC commentator is played by a newcomer, Sean Connery, who will not, I guess, grow old in the industry."

How wrong could one critic be?

Mary Astor

June Allyson

Fred Astaire

Lucille Ball

Jack Benny

George Cukor

Marion Davies

Sammy Davis, Jr.

Yvonne De Carlo

Anita Ekburg	Errol Flynn	Zsa Zsa Gabor
Ava Gardner	Cary Grant	Merv Griffin
Rock Hudson	Alan Ladd	Janet Leigh

Liberace

Marilyn Maxwell

Marilyn Monroe

Barbara Payton

Cole Porter

George Raft

Spencer Tracy

Clifton Webb

Lovely Lana Turner

Lana decided, after her ordeal in London, that she desperately needed a vacation at her favorite retreat in Acapulco. She'd go there even before returning to Los Angeles.

In those days, there was no direct air link to the resort in Mexico except from Copenhagen. She remembered it as a gray, rainy day when she left England, telling Connery goodbye.

"I don't like English weather. You should move to California where it is always bright and sunny."

En route to Denmark, she recalled that she was overcome with an ominous feeling that her life was about to come apart.

After the plane landed in Copenhagen, she remained aboard until the other passengers had disembarked. Then, a young male flight attendant approached her: "Miss Turner, there is a gentleman waiting for you at the end of the ramp."

Startled as to who that might be, she followed him off the plane. From her position at the top of the ramp, she noted a tall man in a trench coat standing at its bottom. Slowly she descended until she came face to face with him. She would later remember his smile. "It was more of a smirk. It was Johnny Stompanato."

"Now I've got you," he said.

She didn't even speak to him, as he took her arm and directed her into the terminal. There, she found a bevy of photographers and reporters waiting to interview her.

She felt awkward and nervous throughout the conference, as she was peppered with the usual questions, such as, "What's your next picture?" She bluffed that, as she didn't know what her agent, Paul Kohner, might come up with. Throughout the press conference, Johnny hawkeyed her.

Finally, they left and she was alone with him. "It's time to board our plane. I'm going to Acapulco with you."

"The hell you are!" Those were her first words to him since arriving in Denmark.

He took her arm again, and almost blindly, she followed along with him. "I'll never let you go." It turned out that he had a ticket on her plane. Not only that, but he had the seat next to hers. She was amazed by how much information he'd gathered about her.

It isn't known what she said or did *en route* to Mexico. When they arrived at Teddy Stauffer's Villa Vera, Stauffer immediately noticed how chilly Lana was toward Johnny.

He was at the height of his season, but he had reserved for her a one-bedroom suite overlooking the bay, with a private swimming pool for nude sunbathing. When she saw the double bed, she turned to him. "Johnny here needs to be booked in separate quarters. I must keep up appearances, you know."

But almost every accommodation was booked. As he protested, Johnny was led to what looked like a broom closet with a cot. It had a sink but no toilet.

"I'll take it, but I plan to spend my nights in bed with Lana," he told Stauffer.

Somehow, word reached Louella Parsons back in Hollywood. On February 22,

1958, she wrote in her column: "I sincerely hope it isn't true that Lana Turner, who is now in Acapulco, is not going to marry Johnny Stampanat (sic)."

During their second day in Acapulco, Johnny, with her money, rented a small yacht captained by Juan García, a salty old skipper who had been born in Galicia in northwestern Spain and spoke passable English. He owned the *Rosa Maria,* which he claimed he'd won by gambling in Venezuela. He later told a reporter, "Lana Turner and that Italian guy spent 20 of their 49 days in Mexico on my boat."

García said, "I couldn't understand why a movie queen would have to keep chasing after this man, no matter what he was doing on board. She was always at his side, even following him into the shower. He would be sitting nude in a deck chair, and she would come over and plop down on him, causing a natural reaction as she wiggled her shapely butt across his genitals. Then he'd pick her up, his raging hard-on at full staff, and carry her below to their cabin. To judge from her squeals, he was a treat for any woman. She didn't bother to muffle her screams of delight."

***

From Hollywood, film producer Jerry Wald placed some urgent phone calls to Lana's suite in Acapulco. He was casting William Faulkner's *The Sound and the Fury* for a 1959 release. The script followed the lives and passions of the Compsons, a degenerate once-proud Southern family now just scraping by.

The leads had already been cast with Yul Brynner and Joanne Woodward. Lana was offered the role of Caddy Compson, a fading Southern belle.

Critics had hailed the Faulkner novel as one of the hundred greatest of the 20th Century.

Wald outlined her role as the third lead. She turned him down, even though she needed the money. "There's no way I'm going to play a fading Southern belle. I've not reached the point in my career where I'm reduced to that."

Having failed to convince her, Wald cast Margaret Leighton the next day.

***

It wasn't all love-making in Mexico. Stauffer had room service deliver bottle after bottle of vodka to Lana's suite. Johnny wanted her to go with him to fancy restaurants and night clubs; he wanted her to back film projects with him as the star, and he wanted to marry her. She rejected every proposal.

When she'd heard too much from him, she shouted "You're not the kind of man a woman marries, Johnny boy, especially to a world class movie star."

He struck her, and she fell on the floor, where he kicked her before storming out. During their "vacation," she got knocked around a lot. Once, he pointed a revolver at her head when she refused to have sex with him.

In her own memoirs, Lana contradicted the report of the skipper. "I had no intimacies with Johnny in Mexico until he forced his lovemaking on me at gunpoint."

One night when she refused his invitation to go to a nightclub with him, he plowed his fist into her stomach, knocking her down. "I hate you!" she sobbed. Finally, he won her over, and she began to appear again in public with him.

One Friday afternoon, when she was sailing aboard the *Rosa Maria* with him, her agent, Paul Kohner, placed several urgent calls to her suite from Hollywood.

She had tried a number of agents before settling on this Austrian-American who managed top stars, at one point directing the careers of Greta Garbo and Maurice Chevalier. He signed big names, both movie stars and directors, including Marlene Dietrich, Billy Wilder, John Huston, even Ingmar Bergman.

Among other prestigious clients that Kohner had gathered were Liv Ullman, Henry Fonda, David Niven, Dolores Del Rio, and Erich von Stroheim. Many of his clients had fled from Nazi-occupied Europe for relocation in Hollywood.

Kohner was married to the Mexican actress, Lupita Tovar, who had starred in the Spanish-language version of *Dracula* (1931). He was also the brother of screenwriter Frederick Kohner. Paul's daughter was Susan Kohner, who would be Lana's co-star in the upcoming *Imitation of Life*.

The phone was ringing when a sunburned Lana returned with Johnny from yet another day trip aboard the *Rosa Maria*.

"Lana! Lana! Kohner shouted into the phone. You've been nominated for a Best Actress Oscar for your performance in *Peyton Place!*"

She couldn't believe the news. She'd always felt she'd deserved Oscars for *The Postman Always Rings Twice* and *The Bad and the Beautiful*. But *Peyton Place!*

"But Paul, I didn't have all that much to do in that film."

"Obviously, the Academy disagreed with you. Aren't you delighted?"

"Of course I am," she said. "But can I win? Who are the other bitches I'm up against?"

He informed her, beginning with Joanne Woodward in *Three Faces of Eve*.

"Oh shit," Lana said. "Newman's bitch has got it."

"We'll see. She's got to beat out, first, Lana Turner. Then Deborah Kerr in *Heaven Knows, Mr. Alison;* Anna Magnani in *Wild Is the Wind;* and Elizabeth Taylor in *Raintree County*."

***

On her last night of her holiday in Mexico, Lana woke from a deep, vodka-induced sleep. It took a long moment for her to come to, until she realized that Johnny was sitting in an armchair near the foot of her bed, his features outlined in the moonlight streaming in. She became aware that he was pointing a gun at her head.

She sat up in bed and screamed.

"Shut the fuck up!" he yelled at her. "This gun is just a reminder that you're mine. I'm not going anywhere. You're going to let me escort you to Oscar night, including the ball to follow."

"And if I don't? she asked.

"Then I'll shoot you, even if I have to go to the chair for it. Better yet, after shooting you, I'll fall down on top of you and put a bullet to my own head."

"You'd take your own life just for me?" She was astonished. The suspicion that he might be insane swept over her.

"You see, Miss Turner, if I don't have you, I have nothing. You make me somebody."

The picture of Cheryl greeting Lana and Johnny on the occasion of their return from Acapulco was carried in dozens of newspapers, often on the frontpage. One of the headlines read: LANA TURNER RETURNS WITH MOB FIGURE.

On her home turf, Lana was filled with excitement about attending the 1958 Academy Awards presentation. Even Johnny behaved himself, thinking that he was going to be her escort to Hollywood's biggest night of the year.

Back in California, Johnny was on his best behavior for a while, and she even took him out in public. They were seen dancing together at the Mocambo, dining at Chasens.

Her rented home was not yet available, so she'd checked into a suite at the Bel Air Hotel. For appearances, Johnny stayed at his apartment on Wilshire Boulevard, although he was at Lana's every night. "He remained glued to me," she said.

Finally summoning her courage, she told him he wasn't going to be her escort. Instead, she'd invited Cheryl and Mildred to attend the Oscar presentations with her.

For once, he controlled his fury. Instead of becoming violent, he acted like a little boy who had been deeply wounded. He sulked around her hotel suite with his hurt feelings on display. Once, in anger, he said, "I'm good enough to fuck you, to make love to you, to hold you in my arms all night, but I'm not good enough to be photographed with you walking the red carpet."

"It's your own fault," she said. "If you hadn't been publicly linked to Mickey Cohen, it would be different."

On the afternoon of the premiere, she began working on her makeup and her outfit. Her designer had created a gown for her "to evoke the image of a mermaid." It was a clinging, strapless, white lace sheath. At the knees, it flared into three tiers of lace stiffened with tulle. She also wore dazzling diamonds: Rings on her fingers, a necklace around her shapely neck, a diamond bracelet, and diamond earrings like big raindrops.

The big event was staged at the Art Deco Pantages Theater, the last time the ceremony would be presented there.

She dazzled the waving, cheering fans as she walked along the red carpet. Everyone commented on her appearance and her deep Mexican suntan.

She had been selected to present the Best Supporting Actor Award, the

Lana made several attempts to dump Johnny Stompanato because of his increasing violence toward her. At one point, he threatened to shoot her.

But in public, they concealed what was going on behind the scenes.

Oscar going to Red Buttons for his role in *Sayonara* (1957). He impulsively gave her a big kiss. Some observers noted that she seemed nervous and jittery. After all, this was the first time she had appeared before a live audience of fifty million people without a script.

There was entertainment, highlighted by Burt Lancaster and Kirk Douglas singing, "It's Great Not to Be Nominated" followed by that show stopping number "Baby, It's Cold Outside," sung by "the odd couple," Rock Hudson and Mae West.

As she'd predicted, the Best Actress Oscar went to a Georgia-born blonde, Joanne Woodward, who had once been dubbed "Plain Jane." In addition to her Oscar, she also had another Hollywood prize: Paul Newman.

Peyton Place was nominated for Best Picture of the year, Mark Robson for Best Director. The movie received several other nominations, too, all of which the stars or the production crew would lose. A Best Screenplay nomination from an adapted work went to John Michael Hayes.

In a surprise twist, both Arthur Kennedy and Russ Tamblyn were nominated for Best Supporting Actor, and both Hope Lange and Diane Varsi competed for Best Supporting Actress.

William Mellor was nominated for Best Cinematography for his brilliant depiction of a New England rural setting, at autumn, when the leaves turn.

After the ceremony, Lana attended a ball at the Beverly Hilton, where Sean Connery, flown in from England, sat at her table and later danced with her, holding her intimately, causing some gossip.

Before the night ended, she also danced with men with whom she'd had flings: James Stewart, Gregory Peck, and Clark Gable, even Cary Grant, whom she'd never seduced.

When Lana returned to her suite at the Bel Air, she put Cheryl to bed in the adjoining room. Mildred had left for her own apartment. Shutting the door to her daughter's room, Lana walked into her darkened living room where she saw that the only light came from the glow of a cigarette being inhaled.

She switched on the light to discover Johnny sitting in an armchair. Apparently, he'd bribed someone on the staff to admit him. He seemed anxious to have a fight with her for not taking him as her escort to the Oscar presentations.

Biographer Jane Ellen Wayne described what happened next. "He slapped her so hard, she hit the floor. He picked her up and hit her in the face. As she was still wearing those diamond earrings, the stones cut into her cheeks. He punched her body, knocked her to the floor, picked her up, and socked her once more. He threw her on the bed as she pleaded with him to stop."

"I want you to promise not to go anywhere without me again."

"In the bathroom, she rinsed her mouth, which was full of blood. Her cheeks were bruised, and her jaw was turning purple," Wayne wrote.

After a sleepless night, she rose from her bed, battered and bruised. He'd left her suite after the beating, but she expected him to pop in on her at any minute. She knew of no way she could get rid of him without inviting a scandal. By now, she was convinced that he was insane, as visions of herself being beaten and mutilated crossed her mind. She also feared attacks on Cheryl and Mildred, as he had threatened.

***

April 4, 1958 would live in infamy in the annals of Hollywood murders. In the case of Lana Turner, there would be sensational stories of sex, mystery, suspense, shocking revelations, and courtroom drama.

It all began on Good Friday. The setting was 730 North Bedford Drive on Beverly Hills in a large, fully furnished, colonial-style house that had been occupied by Lana and Cheryl for only four days. It had been built by Laura Hope Crews with money she'd earned as Aunt Pittypat in *Gone With the Wind*.

The afternoon had begun innocently enough when Lana invited her friend, Del Armstrong, over for a drink. He arrived with a newly minted friend, Bill Brooks, whom he and Lana met on the set of *The Sea Chase* with John Wayne.

Their trio sat amicably together in the living room, talking. Then Johnny entered through the front door with some purchases he'd made. At the sight of Brooks, he hastily retreated into the kitchen before Lana could introduce him.

After he was out of hearing, Brooks turned to Lana. "Who is that man? I think I know him. We went to military school together."

"Johnny Stompanato," she said.

"That's the guy!" Brooks said. "At Kemper Military School, we were in the class of '43."

"I think Johnny would have been too old to be in that class, that year. He's forty-three."

"I was two years ahead of him, and I'm thirty-five. That would make him thirty-two."

She was shocked, as it was suddenly obvious to her that Johnny had lied about his age.

The subject was dropped, and she spent another half-hour talking and drinking with her friends. As a parting gesture, Brooks said, "Give my regards to John. I sorry we didn't have a chance to catch

Dripping in diamonds, a suntanned Lana made a dazzling appearance in her "Mermaid Dress" at the 1958 Academy Awards ceremony, where she'd been nominated for a Best Actress Oscar.

She not only lost the award, but faced a severe beating when she returned to her hotel suite.

Her gangster lover, Johnny Stompanato, unleashed his fury on her for not letting him escort her to the presentations. She feared he was going to disfigure her, perhaps even kill her.

up."

By now, Johnny had retreated to the upstairs bedroom. When he heard the two men leave, he came downstairs, where Lana was alone with a stiff drink of vodka. She immediately turned to him, accusing him of lying to her about his age.

He tried to defend himself. "I heard you say you never wanted to be seen going out with a younger man like a lot of dames in Hollywood. You once told me you didn't want to be Norma Desmond supporting a gigolo, Joe Gillis." *[He was referring to the 1950 movie,* Sunset Blvd.*, in which Gloria Swanson, as a brittle, aging, egomaniacal, and ultimately demented silent screen vamp, supports her lover, William Holden.]*

From that point on, the events of the approaching night went downhill. He was in one of his darkest moods, seemingly ready to pick a fight. He needed $4,000, but she refused to write him a check. He stormed out of the house in anger.

But he called at around 8PM, announcing that he was coming over to take her to see Tennessee Williams' *Baby Doll* (1957), a film that Lana had missed because she was out of the country.

She told him that she had a lot of unpacking to do, and refused the invitation. He arrived within the hour and, as she remembered it, he seemed to be "itching for a fight." One argument led to another. She told him that she planned to dine the following night with Armstrong and Brooks. That set him off in a rage, as he obviously feared what Brooks would tell her about his days in military school.

"You were going to go off with those guys without me?" he accused her. At this point, he was shouting, and she asked him to keep his voice down. Cheryl was in her bedroom upstairs, watching television.

She headed upstairs to her own bedroom, and he followed close behind her, still haranguing her. Her own rage had been building for months, and now she was on the verge of exploding. Any love or a longing for intimacy with him had faded.

When he announced that in the future, she was to make no more plans without him, she, too, was ready for a fight. He was still shouting, even demanding, that she drop Armstrong, never to see him again.

Finally, she could take him no more. Nor could she tolerate his demands.

"You've become a god damn lush!" he shouted. "You do nothing but break promises to me!"

Lana and Stompanato on holiday in Acapulco.

Upon their return, the *Los Angeles Times* wrote: "Tanned of face and bleached of hair, Lana Turner flew in from Acapulco, her favorite vacation retreat. She'd been to England and Mexico with Johnny Stompanato, one-time bodyguard to gangster Mickey Cohen."

Her face was contorted as he'd never seen it before, as she turned all her fury onto him. "I want you right this minute to get the fuck out of my house—never come back! I don't want to ever see you again as long as I live."

At first, she'd been so distracted that she didn't hear a tinkling sound at her door. She recognized it as Cheryl's gold charm bracelet. She called out, "Cheryl, get away from the god damn door! Go back to your bedroom."

"Are you okay, Mother?"

"Just go and let us alone," she ordered her daughter.

When she had ascertained that Cheryl had gone, she turned once again to face Johnny, whose own rage seemed near to exploding. "Tonight, Mister, I'm giving you your walking papers. I'm through with you. It's over! You wouldn't be the first man I've kicked out on his ass."

"I'm sure the tally runs into the hundreds," he charged. "You're the ultimate user. You use people, suck them dry, and them kick them out, moving on to your next conquest. Lovers and husbands alike. When Miss Turner wants a new dick, it's bye-bye!"

"I could have a thousand and one guys like you any day, any time I want. All I have to do is cock my little finger, and they'll come running to my side."

"Don't fuck with me," he said, "or you'll live to regret it. That is, *maybe* you'll live. Maybe not. After I've taken care of you, I'll go after Cheryl and Mildred. I'll mutilate all three of you bitches!"

According to testimony, Cheryl had returned to her bedroom when she heard Johnny threatening to mutilate her mother and maybe go after her, too, as well as her beloved "Gran" (Mildred).

Impulsively, Cheryl opened her bedroom door and, in her pink mule slippers, ran down the stairs and into the kitchen, where she picked up a knife with a nine-inch blade and darted back up the steps.

[Other sources claimed it was an eight-inch blade.]

Once again, Lana heard the tinkling of her daughter's charm bracelet. Armed with the knife, Cheryl stood at the open door. "Mother, Mother, are you okay? What's wrong?"

Lana didn't answer.

What happened next has caused a debate in Hollywood that has continued for decades. Although there were slight discrepancies, the version of both Cheryl and Lana more or less paralleled each other. Their accounts became known as "the official version." There would be many other versions to challenge their testimony.

In the account that was made public, the events of that fateful night unfolded more or less like this:

Cheryl pounded on the door but did not open it or enter. "Let's talk. Stop fighting!"

Thinking that he and Lana might go out that night, Johnny that afternoon had brought over a white shirt and a jacket, which he'd hung in one of her closets on large wooden hangers. She later said that when she saw him going to her closet to retrieve his clothing, she was overcome with relief, thinking that he was going to leave without any more fights or arguments.

Before that, he had been "running around the room looking like an enraged bobcat," in her view.

With his clothing thrown across his right shoulder, he confronted her. "You'll never get away with this, you stinking cunt!"

Then his voice grew louder: "I'll cut you up. I'll carve up your ugly, wretched face. You'll never work in this town again. You may not even be alive when I've finished with you!"

"You're a psycho!" she screeched. "Get out! never come across my doorstep ever again."

Suddenly, Cheryl threw open the door and saw that his arm was upraised. Lana was heading out the door, and he was in hot pursuit right behind her. From Cheryl's perspective, it appeared that he had a weapon that he was going to use against Lana's head. She did not know that it was wooden hangers slung across his back.

As Cheryl testified, "I took a step forward, and he ran into the knife."

Looking stunned, he said, "My god, Cheryl, what have you done?" Those were the last words he'd ever utter.

The kitchen knife she'd plunged into his abdomen had sliced one of his kidneys, struck a vertebra, and punctured his aorta.

Lana later claimed she did not see the knife in her daughter's hand. "It looked to me like she'd punched him in the stomach. John took little circling steps in slow motion. Instead of clutching his stomach, he fell backward onto the floor, landing on his back. The sound coming from his throat was a weird gasping."

As she bent over him, she looked up to see Cheryl holding a bloody carving knife. At that point, she dropped the knife and retreated to her bedroom, consumed with hysterical sobbing.

Lana didn't see the wound until she lifted Johnny's sweater. There, she viewed the puncture, but little blood, since the great injuries were internal, where he was bleeding profusely.

She picked up the murder weapon and ran with it into the bathroom, where she dropped it into the sink before reaching for a towel.

When she came back into the room, she must have realized how a towel would be of no help whatsoever. She dropped it and rushed to her phone to call Mildred, since she'd been away so long, she'd forgotten the number of her doctor.

As Mildred picked up her phone, she heard the hysterical voice of her daughter. "Mother, John is dead. Get Dr. John McDonald over here at once. There is no time to explain."

Within twenty minutes, Mildred was on the scene, rushing at once to confirm that Cheryl was all right before heading for Lana's bedroom. There, she took in the horrid scene, as she gazed upon a sobbing Lana and on Johnny's body lying on the floor with his stomach wound bleeding. She bent over and tried to detect a heartbeat. Moving to his head, she began to give him mouth-to-mouth resuscitation.

As Lana later wrote, "I didn't want her mouth on his."

Dr. McDonald was the next to arrive on the scene. He put a stethoscope to Johnny's chest, hoping to detect a heartbeat. There was none. From his bag, he removed a needle. It contained adrenaline, which he plunged into Johnny's heart. It was of no use. "He's dead," he told a sobbing Lana. "I can't help him now."

She might have phoned the police, but instead, she placed an urgent call to the attorney, Jerry Giesler.

He was a tough, battle-hardened lawyer, a veteran of many a court trial, having defended Errol Flynn on statutory rape charges, Charlie Chaplin in a paternity case, and Bugsy Siegel on a murder rap.

A short, plump man with a nasal voice, Giesler soon arrived and took immediate charge. What happened next differed remarkably from the official version.

One of his main tasks was to make sure that Cheryl and Lana did not contradict each other during their interrogations. Those would most likely be conducted with each of them in separate rooms.

Jerry Giesler, the attorney you called when you'd committed murder.

It was later alleged that he did not find Johnny's body on the floor, but on Lana's bed. Giesler called Fred Otash, who later revealed "what really happened" (his words).

Otash presented a rather limited and highly censored overview of his life in *Investigation Hollywood: Memoirs of Hollywood's Top Private Detective*. Author James Ellroy used a fictionalized version of Otash in two of the novels from his *Underworld U.S.A.* trilogy.

In Roman Polanski's 1974 movie, *Chinatown*, Jack Nicholson's character was based on Otash. At the time of his death, Otash was writing a memoir to "blow the lid off Hollywood's greatest scandals." It included an overview of his secret involvement in the Stompanato murder. That manuscript was stolen and has never resurfaced.

Privately, Otash gave his own account of what he discovered in Lana's murder house.

Giesler often worked on cases with Otash, who claimed that on the night of Stompanato's murder, he received desperate call for assistance from Giesler.

"It was right in the middle of knocking off a choice piece of ass. When I picked up the phone, Giesler told me what had happened. 'Get your ass right over here. Stompanato's on Lana's bed, which looks like a hog was butchered.'"

When he got to Lana's house, Otash was ordered to remove the bloody sheets and replace them with clean ones at once. He stashed the bloody linens in the trunk of his car and burned them later. That would explain why there was no blood found around the body when the police looked it over later.

Otash later told fellow detective Milo Speriglio that by the time he'd arrived, Johnny's body had been moved from the bed to the carpeted floor.

"From what I gathered, Lana had walked in on Johnny in bed with Cheryl," Otash said. "Both of them were in a post-coital sleep. At least that's what I was told."

531

Otash also said, "Lana confessed to Giesler that she'd bought the kitchen knife the day before to protect herself against Johnny, who was threatening her. When she'd assumed he'd seduced her daughter, she went for the knife in a drawer in her nightstand, and plunged it into his stomach."

James Bacon, the famous columnist, heard the report of the murder late on the night it happened and drove at once to Lana's house, telling a policeman stationed at the door that he was from the coroner's office. A reliable reporter, Bacon later claimed that he saw Otash on the scene. He knew him well over the years.

Lana was also alleged to have placed a call to Frank Sinatra, perhaps hoping he might intervene with members of the mob, especially if Mickey Cohen wanted to take revenge on her. Sinatra's role in the events of that night has mostly been overlooked.

Lana reportedly confessed her version of what happened directly to him. "I can't bear to tell it," she told Sinatra in the presence of Giesler and Otash. "I discovered Cheryl and Johnny in bed together. They were both sleeping, but it was obvious what he'd done to her. I went berserk. I took the butcher knife I kept beside my bed in the drawer of my nightstand. I don't know what overcame me. I grabbed the knife

Fred Otash had been a police officer at one time, and a private investigator, and he was also the chief sleuth for the scandal magazine *Confidential*.

After his involvement in the Stompanato murder case, he would evolve, four years later, in 1962, into a key figure in the mysterious death of Marilyn Monroe, having been hired by Peter Lawford.

and plunged it into Johnny's stomach. He was on his back, resting up having done the dirty deed. I really wanted to castrate him, not to kill him. Cheryl woke up screaming. It's all a sort of blur now."

Sinatra gave her some vague reassurances and then slipped out of the murder house before the police arrived.

At the scene of the murder, Giesler warned Lana that a jury would "throw the book at you. Let Cheryl take the fall. She'll get off easily, maybe a little detention—that's it. I'll try to get it ruled as justifiable homicide. She was protecting you. If you confess, it'll destroy your life for all time."

By the time the police were summoned, those who had gathered within the murder house seemed to be fairly well-rehearsed in their testimonies to come... well, almost.

Two police officers were on the scene before Clinton B. Anderson, police chief of Beverly Hills, barged through the door. He was all too familiar with the career of Johnny Stompanato, as he'd long predicted that the gangster would come to some violent end. He ordered that Lana and Cheryl be placed in separate rooms during their respective interrogations.

He was directed first to Lana's bedroom, furnished with pink carpeting, pink curtains, pink bed linen, and even a vase of pink roses resting on one of the tables. One of the officers knelt over the body and pulled up Johnny's sweater, revealing the stab wound in his stomach.

After grilling Lana, he was led into her bathroom, where he saw the bloody murder weapon in the sink. He ordered that it be carefully removed, preserving whatever fingerprints that might be on it.

Two days later, the report from the police laboratory stated that no identification of fingerprints could be concluded because the handle of the knife had been "smudged."

In another room, Anderson was introduced to Cheryl, who was crying. "I stabbed him! I didn't mean to kill him. I just meant to scare him!"

After a preliminary grilling of both Lana and Cheryl, Anderson later said, "Their stories were a perfect match…perhaps too perfect. Had they been given a script?"

Cheryl later admitted that Anderson had been rankled that Giesler had beaten him to the scene of the murder. He wanted both Lana and her daughter to be taken to the police station for more questioning.

In the hall, Lana confronted him. "Can I take the blame for Cheryl?" she asked. "I'll say I did it."

Almost immediately, he was suspicious of such a spontaneous confession. Was this so-called confession part of the cover-up?"

Later, when Cheryl read reports of what had happened that night, she said, "The reading public must have imagined me to be a young Lizzie Borden."

Clinton Anderson, Beverly Hills Police Chief.

From the beginning, he was suspicious that a fourteen-year-old girl could attack a hardened street fighter and survive, unscathed.

Stompanato, a tough ex-Marine and street gang leader, had successfully defended himself in knife fights since he was a kid.

***

Stephen Crane was working late at his restaurant when the desperate call from Cheryl came in. "Daddy, Daddy," she cried out to him. "Something terrible has happened!"

"What's the matter?" he demanded to know.

"Don't ask questions," the teenager said. "Daddy, hurry. Please come!"

Arriving shortly thereafter, after outrunning a motorcycle cop, Crane came running through the front door of the murder house. Almost immediately, Cheryl raced into his arms. "I did it, Daddy! I killed John Stompanato! I did it! He was threatening mother. I didn't mean to, Daddy. Please help me. Don't let them take me."

Like the loyal father he was, Crane stood by Cheryl through all the horrendous events that were soon to befall her.

The murder caused great tension between Lana and him. Up to now, they had enjoyed a rather peaceful relationship, having put their long-ago divorce far behind them.

"I'll never forgive Lana for making our daughter take the blame for the murder," Crane later told Jerry Giesler one night in his restaurant. "What was she thinking? Moving a gangster into her house? She was just inviting trouble."

***

Sydney Guilaroff had been Lana's favorite hairdresser during her glory days at MGM, and their friendship had lasted. In his memoir, *Crowning Glory,* he revealed that just before the Stompanato murder, he had gone to a drugstore in Beverly Hills to pick up some medication. As he was coming out, he spotted Lana emerging from the nearby Pioneer Hardware Store.

"So this is where you go to buy your expensive perfume?" he joked.

"I needed a kitchen knife," she said.

After some small talk, he suggested they have dinner some night, and she agreed. After kissing him on both cheeks, she got into her car and drove away.

He thought no more about the knife until the next day, when he heard over radio that Johnny had been stabbed to death at Lana's home. Perhaps it was the same knife he'd seen after she'd purchased it the day before.

After hearing the news, Guilaroff wrote, "I got into my car and flew to Lana's house. When I arrived, none of the servants were on duty, and she opened the door herself. "Oh, Sydney, I'm so glad you came." She sobbed, falling into his arms. "She wept for a long time."

Apparently, this scene took place the morning after she had returned from further interrogations at the police station.

"Did you ever dream that this would happen?" she asked. "And with that very knife I bought yesterday?"

In her own memoir, Lana contradicted her hairdresser's account, claiming that Johnny had gone with her to the hardware store to purchase not one knife,

Sydney Guilaroff with Ava Gardner. Other than Lana Turner, she was his most favored client. "Whenever possible, each of them demanded I do their hair."

"but several kitchen knives." She claimed that she let him select the knives "because he was an expert on knives, having indulged in many a knife fight in his life."

When Mickey Cohen got a call that Johnny had been stabbed to death, he, too, drove to Lana's house. Giesler was still there, although Lana and Cheryl were at the police station.

"If Lana comes back and sees you," Giesler said, "she's gonna fall apart. John's dead. The body has been sent to the morgue. Go there! You're the only person around who can make the funeral arrangements. I'll get the address for you."

***

Even though Lana was no longer a client of MGM, both Howard Strickling and Eddie Mannix went to work to plant sympathetic news articles about her. What followed was a steady stream of news depicting her as the "victim of Johnny Stompanato's insane rages and violent attacks on both her and Cheryl."

Otash later disputed the story that Lana had volunteered to the police to take the blame for the murder. "I was there," Otash told fellow detective Milo Speriglio. "She did no such thing. That was a lie about her volunteering to claim she murdered Johnny. It was a crock of the smelly stuff. What I saw was Lana running around hysterically. She didn't seem concerned about who murdered Johnny. She was screaming hysterically, 'My career! What's going to happen to my career? This will ruin me!'"

"I was the one who wiped the fingerprints off the knife in Lana's bathroom sink," Otash told Speriglio. "I was a naughty boy doing what I'm not supposed to do. But I never did what I was supposed to do. Rules were made to be broken, not followed in my book."

Otash later claimed, "Some fucker ratted me out about the cover-up at Lana's house. I was called into Anderson's office two days later, and he threatened to charge me as an accessory based on what he'd heard that I did with Giesler. He told me that Giesler stood to lose his license, even though he was the most powerful lawyer in Hollywood."

"I can't go into details," Otash continued, "but I told Anderson that a number of people held very damaging stuff on him that would also ruin his own god damn career. He was a smart fox. He never brought any charge against me or against Giesler."

Years later, Otash wrote: "Giesler summoned me to the hospital, where he was dying."

"Don't ever tell the story of what happened that night at Lana Turner's home," the dying man pleaded.

"I promised I would not," Otash said. "But who has to follow a promise to a dying man once he's dead?"

***

The coroner's inquest began at 9AM on Friday, April 11, 1958, in the spacious but sweltering Hall of Records on the 8th Floor of the Courthouse in Beverly Hills. The temperature soared to 88°F at noon. Crowds of onlookers had formed as early as 5:30AM. Of the 160 seats, some 120 of them were occupied by the overheated press corps.

Authorities had ruled that Cheryl did not have to appear in court, but Lana did. At the entrance to the hall, she had to battle her way through a crowd of reporters, photographers, cameramen, and just the idle curious, plus many of her loyal fans. She looked distraught but glamourous in a gray coat and gray silk, tweed-type dress.

She took the stand in the crowded courtroom. As one reporter described it, "A hush fell over the crowd as the famous actress sat down and filled her lungs with a deep, steady intake of air. Photographers, desperate for a better shot, stood up on their seats and even on the large window sills. Almost everyone was standing on their seats."

Another journalist wrote: "The audience soon grew frozen, the stillness broken only by the click and clatter of the desperately laboring cameramen."

Lana's voice came out identifying herself, as if she needed it, in a throaty, halting tone.

She dramatically removed one glove, revealing she'd polished her nails silver instead of her usual blood red. Her hand went up to her forehead, as she was visibly trembling. At times, she looked as if she were going to faint in the almost unbearable heat. She recited testimony—nothing new—that had already appeared in newspapers around the globe.

A skilled prosecutor at a trial might have pointed out a lot of inconsistencies in eyewitness accounts of what had happened on the night of the murder, but that didn't happen.

It was brought out, however, that if Johnny had been stabbed in the stomach, chances were that he would have fallen forward, not onto his back. Lana tried to explain that by the "dance" she alleged that he did before his collapse onto his back.

Finally, since Lana had nothing new to add, she was dismissed after sixty-two minutes on the stand.

Mickey Cohen appeared in court, dressed like a gangster in one of those movies from Warner Brothers in the 1930s. He was chewing gum as he sat down for his questioning. He was asked if he had identified the body in the morgue. He then uttered a shocking statement: "I refuse to identify the body

A week after the death of Johnny Stompanato, Lana was grilled on the witness stand.

Some members of the press claimed that she gave "the greatest Oscar-worthy performance of her career."

on the grounds that I may be accused of murder." He was then dismissed.

The autopsy report showed that Johnny had died only minutes after the stabbing. Attempts to revive him had been in vain, and it was made clear that even if an attempt had been made to rush him to any of the hospitals in the neighborhood, he would have arrived DOA.

A tantalizing detail emerged from the autopsy report, which claimed that even if Johnny had not been murdered, he would have died within a few months, as he suffered from an incurable liver ailment.

As Lana's defender, Jerry Giesler appeared before judge and jury, claiming, "This case is justifiable homicide. There is no justification for a trial."

When Johnny's stepmother, Verena Freitag Stompanato, heard that, she later claimed, "There is no such thing as justifiable homicide."

The jury of ten men and two women took just twenty-five minutes to deliver a verdict of justifiable homicide. Then Judge Allen T. Lynch ruled that the case was closed.

As he did, an unidentified spectator rose from the rear of the courtroom, shouting "*Lies! Lies! Lies!* This mother and daughter were in love with Stompanato. He was better than the both of them. All you people in Hollywood are no good." He was seized and led out of the hall by two security guards. On his way out, the spectator shouted back at the judge. "Johnny Stompanato was a real gentleman."

Cohen had nothing but contempt for the inquest. He told the press, "It's the strangest case I ever saw. The first time in history where the murdered corpse has been found guilty of his own murder."

Sitting through the entire inquest was District Attorney William R. McKenson, who had objected to Cheryl going free on bail. Although he had the legal right to prosecute the girl in a separate trial, he chose not to.

The judge also ordered that the teenager undergo psychiatric consultation. He announced there would be a separate hearing in Juvenile Court to determine the fate of the girl. Until that happened, she would be locked away in Juvenile Hall.

Without actually saying so, McKenson left the suggestion that Cheryl might be sent to live with her grandmother, Mildred, or perhaps placed in a decent foster home where she might be reared properly. Looming over those arrangements was the nagging fear that she might be sent to reform school.

A tense Stephen Crane and Lana, parents of Cheryl, appeared in court after the inquest. Up for a ruling: Who would gain custody of their daughter?

***

By the time Lana returned home from the police station, her press agent, Glenn Rose, was handling the traffic and the reporters. "Lana that night was climbing the wall," he said.

"Why can't they let me take my baby home?" she asked.

Lana met with Del Armstrong. He realized at once that a strong glass of vodka would not solve the problem. She seemed on the verge of a nervous breakdown, so he once again summoned Dr. McDonald to give her a sedative.

Mildred and her hovering presence was also there, sometimes sobbing out her grief, which did little to help ease Lana's anxiety.

Author Dominick Dunne lived nearby, and he rushed to the scene. He said, "It was a damn circus. Cars were arriving on the scene, disgorging entire families. People were hanging out of the trees like monkeys with binoculars trained on the house. The traffic jam in front of Lana's house went on for a month or two. Apparently, the public couldn't get enough of the gory details."

That night, Sinatra reappeared to offer whatever comfort he could and to express his condolences. Cheryl later praised the singer for lending his support to her mother during her time of crisis, when many members of the film colony were predicting the end of her career.

Too many horrible memories haunted Lana in her rented house on Bedford Drive.   Not only that, but crowds of onlookers formed outside to watch anybody coming and going.

Armstrong suggested she move into another furnished house, and he found one that was suitable on Canon Drive, about six blocks away. That address would be kept secret.

As for Cheryl, she said, "At least I missed the gas chamber."

***

For the most part, the press pillorried Lana, citing her as an unfit mother. But in his column, Walter Winchell defended her. "It seems sadistic to me to subject Lana Turner to any more torment. No punishment that could be imagined could hurt her more that the memory of this nightmarish event. And she is condemned to live with this memory to the end of her days."

Winchell, however, also ran a comment he'd received from the silent screen vamp Gloria Swanson: "I think it is disgusting that you're trying to whitewash Lana Turner. She is not even an actress...only a trollop."

Ava Gardner in London was more charitable. She'd had a fling with Johnny long before Lana. She told the press, "When it comes to men, my friend Lana and I are the world's lousiest pickers."

Time magazine was one of Lana's harshest critics, labeling her as "a wanton woman."

The *Los Angeles Times* reported, "Lana Turner has always found the way to heal yesterday's hurts with tomorrow's diversions. In the turnover of husbands, wives, lovers, and mistresses, the Cheryls of Hollywood are the misplaced baggage, lost and found and lost again. In the Turner case, Cheryl isn't the juvenile delinquent. Lana is!"

The *Los Angeles Times* ruled Cheryl as blameless: "Lana Turner is a hedonist whose narrative showed the lack of almost any reference to moral sensitivity in the presence of a child. Cheryl isn't the juvenile delinquent: Lana is!"

Columnist Dorothy Kilgallen was one of many reporters who questioned the claim as to how Johnny got stabbed—that is, just by running into a knife. "The evidence shows that the knife was done with the skill of a trained commando."

James Robert Parrish, the prolific Hollywood biographer, wrote: "To this day, there are people who insist that on that long-ago evening, it was actually Lana Turner who ended the life of her combative lover."

***

Johnny Meyer, the right-hand man (read that "pimp") of Howard Hughes, phoned his boss to report that Johnny Stompanato had been stabbed to death at the home of Lana Turner, and that the blame had been placed on her daughter, Cheryl.

Then, Meyer went on to tell his boss, who was staying in a bungalow on the grounds of the Beverly Hills Hotel, that it had, in reality, been Lana who had murdered Johnny, and that Cheryl had been configured as the fall girl because she'd get a light sentence.

Lana herself phoned Hughes the next day, allegedly confessing that she had stabbed Johnny. In a state of panic, she told him she'd received death threats from the mob and that she needed protection. One caller had threatened to throw sulfuric acid in her face.

Hughes had always liked Lana when they were having an affair, and had even considered marrying her. He agreed to divert some of his security guards to protect her from any mob attack. Meyer later claimed that Hughes spent $50,000 on her security protection.

"I will always be grateful to Howard for coming to my rescue," Lana said. "For eight months, I lived in fear of reprisal from the mob. He sent his men to fend off any possible attack on me or Cheryl."

When Hughes learned that Jerry Giesler had suddenly become reluctant to represent Lana because of his pre-existing links to Mickey Cohen, the aviator reminded him that he, Hughes, was a far more valuable client of his than Cohen. "Protect Lana. That's an order, Giesler. If you don't, I'll take my business elsewhere. Need I remind you, you've made millions off me."

***

In the beginning, Cohen didn't believe the ruling of the court in the Stompanato murder case.

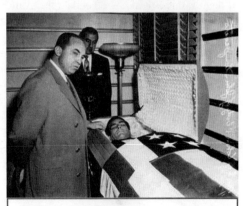

Mickey Cohen mourning and/or raging beside the corpse of Johnny Stompanato.

"I have no proof," he later wrote in his autobiography, "but I don't believe that Cheryl killed Johnny Stompanato. You know, Johnny was an athlete. He wasn't a guy that would go and slug somebody, nothing like that, but if somebody came to challenge him, he could stand up for himself pretty well."

"They say he was stabbed while he was standing," Cohen continued. "But I can't believe that anybody could. I think he was in bed by himself sleeping. Someone must have broke in and stabbed him. I don't believe it was Cheryl or Lana."

Regardless of what his ghost writers put into his memoirs, Cohen put the blame on Lana. His longtime mistress was the voluptuous,

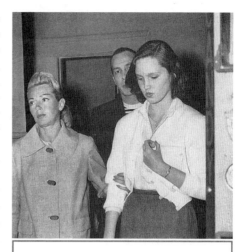

Cheryl is seen with her grief-stricken parents, Lana and Stephen Crane. Her fate was to be decided by a judge.

blonde-haired, and very outspoken actress, Liz Renay, who once won a Marilyn Monroe lookalike contest.

According to Renay, "Mickey told me one night that it was Lana Turner herself—not her daughter—who plunged the knife into Johnny. He was seriously considering having one of his boys toss acid into her beautiful face."

Furious that "Hollywood likes to protect its own—in this case, Lana Turner—Cohen vowed, "I'll get even with her. She needs to be humiliated for killing Johnny, unless I decide to have my boys do something more dangerous."

He also expressed resentment that he'd been stuck with Johnny's funeral bills. A famous photograph of Cohen viewing Johnny's corpse in its casket was flashed around the world.

Cohen had an apartment in the same building as Johnny's. He had been given a key. When he first heard that his henchman had been stabbed to death, he went upstairs and entered the apartment.

What he was looking for was a wooden box that contained pictures of movie stars in compromising positions, always sexual. These photographs were being used for blackmail.

To his horror, he discovered that someone had

Liz Renay was the sometimes mistress of Mickey Cohen, and she even went to jail for him for refusing to testify against him.

The Beverly Hills police, in their review of evidence left behind by Johnny Stompanato, revealed that she had been a participant in a blackmail scheme against Lana.

already broken into the apartment by cutting the screen in Johnny's bathroom window and climbing in. When he saw that the glass window pane wasn't broken, he surmised that Johnny must have left the window open.

There was no wooden box with the blackmail photographs. Obviously, the box and its contents had been removed shortly after Johnny's death and before the police arrived to search the apartment.

Before exiting, almost as a keepsake, Cohen removed an alligator leather shaving kit he'd presented as a birthday present to Johnny.

It was only later, back in his own apartment, that he discovered that the shaving kit contained "mushy" love letters from Lana to Johnny. The thief had obviously overlooked this stash. He decided to have them published in the newspapers as a means of humiliating Lana.

He did admit that Johnny, on occasion, might have had to get rough with Lana. "My god, the bitch was deballing him, and what would Johnny be without his grapefruit-sized nuts?"

Lana suffered her most acute embarrassment when her gushy love letters to Johnny were reproduced word for word in the *Los Angeles Herald Examiner,* and then picked up by other media outlets too. "The letters were a stark reminder of how foolish I was," she said. "I sound like a lovesick schoolgirl with a crush on the high school football captain."

"I released the letters because Lana had been intimating that she was fleeing from Johnny's unwanted advances," Cohen said. "But the letters show that they were deeply in love."

The mobster's biographer, John H. Davis, wrote: "One of Mickey Cohen's rackets was sexually compromising Hollywood stars for the purpose of blackmail. He had engineered the torrid affair between his accomplice and Lana Turner in the hope of getting pictures of the two of them in bed together."

Davis also claimed, "Others have reported that Cohen was successful in recording a sexual tryst between Stompanato and Turner. Copies of the videotape sold at fifty bucks a pop, and played to the delight of horny Friars Club members on both coasts."

In the wake of the murder of Bugsy Siegel, Cohen had become Mobster No. 1. There are records of him presenting Johnny with bundles of cash, once $4,000 in twenty-dollar bills, based on their lucrative scheme of blackmailing movie stars, both male and female, who had

A grieving Cheryl Crane said, "At least I missed the gas chamber!"

541

been secretly photographed having sex with Johnny.

He had once bragged, "My penis has been the most photographed in the history of the world."

"Well, it's damn photogenic," Cohen told him.

Columnist Lee Mortimer had exposed the mob's blackmail ring. Although it officially operated out of Chicago, it was mostly centered in Los Angeles and New York. Cohen handled the illegal operation in Los Angeles.

The Mob's blackmailers also went after political figures in Washington. Some congressmen had been paying off blackmailers for years.

Mortimer revealed that "The ring employed gigolos of the Johnny Stompanato type, luscious babes, and homos who entrapped gay celebrities."

Police chief Anderson said he knew that Johnny, for several years, lived off funds generated from blackmail victims.

Brad Lewis, another Cohen biographer, wrote, "One of Stompanato's pimping chores was to keep a constant stable of women on hand for Mickey's out-of-town guests. His supply chain stretched all the way to Las Vegas, where demands for a steady flow of hot flesh ran high at the hotels."

Lewis also revealed that Johnny, on occasion, was seen in the company of wealthy homosexuals in the film colony. One informant stated that Johnny went with both men or women.

Mickey Cohen's so-called autobiography was not the most truthful of books. In it, he absolved Lana of the murder.

But privately, he told his associates, "Lana did it. She stabbed Johnny. He was having an affair with Cheryl, and Lana was jealous to see her lover attracted to a young girl—and not to her. It was a plot out of *Mildred Pierce*."

He was referring to Joan Crawford's Oscar-winning performace in which her on-screen daughter, Ann Blyth, steals her husband, Zachory Scott.

***

Two days before Cheryl's hearing in Juvenile Court, Carmine Stompanato, Johnny's older brother, filed a lawsuit against both Lana and Stephen Crane, seeking $752,250 in damages for alleged parental negligence.

Johnny's brother flew from Illinois to Los Angeles, where on the first day in California, he obtained a trial lawyer and also contacted police chief Anderson. The 45-year-old barber was an elder in the Presbyterian Church in Woodstock, Illinois.

Johnny's stepmother, Verena Freitag Stompanato, charged that "a cold-blooded murder should be more thoroughly investigated."

Carmine told the press, "Lana Turner is a liar. She's trying to save herself, her career, and her daughter. I demand that she take a lie detector test."

He also told reporters, "Turner phoned her mother, her ex-husband, her press agent, and her lawyer before calling a doctor and the police. Johnny lay dying while all this cover-up was plotted. The police might have arrived with an ambulance, and Johnny's life could have been saved."

After Carmine presented his credentials to the police, Chief Anderson allowed him to go to Johnny's apartment house with two policemen and break in. Pulling up at the Del Capri, police also learned that this was one of the residences of Mickey Cohen.

Once they entered the apartment, the cops and Carmine found that the apartment had already been broken into and looted. There was nothing of value left. However, they did discover a key to a locker at Union Station in downtown Los Angeles.

The key was given to Anderson, who received a court order that the contents of that locker should be turned over to the police.

Carmine had to leave town, but Anderson told him he would forward the contents of that locker to him after a thorough investigation of its contents.

In 1961, the suit against Lana was settled out of court, some $20,000 going directly to Johnny Stompanato's son, who lived in Hammond, Indiana, with his mother.

***

In the locker at Union Station, Johnny had stored a wooden box, which was retrieved and brought back to Anderson's headquarters. A ticket inside led to four cardboard boxes stashed in a warehouse in West Hollywood. Their contents—discarded clothing, kitchenware, cowboy boots, and a lot of documents—were also sent to Anderson. Included in the documents were statements for a bank account maintained jointly by Stompanato and the wife of a prominent Los Angeles attorney, and several unpaid promissory notes to women for heavy debts he would never repay.

Police also found an unregistered .32 caliber revolver, eight cheap wedding rings, and some token gifts from "Lanita."

But even more than the documents, what intrigued Anderson the most was the large wooden box. It was stuffed with photos and some undeveloped negatives. Anderson examined each photo carefully. Many of the men and women depicted in compromising positions were well-known; others were not. Anderson was particularly interested in whatever photos, compromising or not, there might have been of Lana and/or Cheryl, but found none. Then he ordered his henchmen at the police lab to process the negatives.

In his own memoirs, Anderson did not reveal the names of the movie stars who were "clients" of Johnny's. However, he did cite them to his editors, and word leaked out. His publisher was reluctant to publish the identities of Johnny's conquests based on fear of libel.

It was later revealed that the women in these sexually compromising photos included Barbara Payton, Mary Astor, Lucille Ball, Marion Davies, Yvonne De Carlo, and Ava Gardner. Among the male stars were photos of Cary Grant, Rock Hudson, Fred Astaire (a surprise to Anderson), Jack Benny, Sammy Davis, Jr., Errol Flynn, Spencer Tracy, Cole Porter, Liberace, George Cukor, and Alan Ladd.

Most of these men were already known to Anderson as gay or bisexual. The appearance of George Raft among the photos provided another surprise, even though his former lover, Betty Grable, had once said, "George is probably a latent homosexual." Perhaps he wasn't that latent.

In her own memoirs, Lana wrote that Johnny's black book left within her house after his body was hauled off contained "dozens of phone numbers of Hollywood women—Anita Ekberg, Zsa Zsa Gabor, and June Allyson, among them—and some prominent male personalities as well."

When the negatives were processed, Anderson discovered several nudes taken of Lana when she was sleeping on top of the covers of her bed.

Two days later, his assistant, Louis Blau, arrived—after setting up a meeting— at Lana's newly rented house on Canon Drive. She described this private meeting in her memoirs, asserting that Blau had arrived with "a pool of exposed film."

She was horrified at the nude pictures of herself. As she recalled, Johnny once gave her a glass of vodka after she'd announced that she wanted to get some rest. "I must have passed out for six or seven hours. The drink was probably drugged. That's when he took those pictures."

She wrote, "Another sequence showed a blonde woman I didn't recognize performing fellatio on John."

The police later ascertained that the blonde was actually the part-time actress and prostitute, Liz Renay, Mickey Cohen's sometimes mistress who may have been hired as a participant in a set-up.

Blau speculated that Johnny might have been planning to do some trick photography, wherein the original image of the other woman's body might be retained, with the understanding that Lana's face might be substituted for the blonde's, giving the impression that it was Lana who had been performing the fellatio.

"He was always threatening to ruin my career," she said, "and this was how he might have plotted to do it."

She claimed that "the negatives were cut into tiny pieces and burned." She didn't mention the photographs which had been printed in the police lab. Blau assured her that each of the prints of her nudes would be destroyed.

Throughout the rest of her life, she wondered if someone had made copies for a private collection.

***

Days after her appearance in court, the Associated Press received a call from an informant within the Beverly Hills Police Department. At least he identified himself as such. Reporters were accustomed to receiving tips from informants who did not want to be identified out of fear of losing their jobs.

The AP was told that two policemen had been summoned to Lana's new address on Canon Drive where they found Lana's nude body sprawled out on her bathroom floor with an empty bottle of sleeping pills nearby.

The reporter who'd received the call immediately alerted his editor. Within minutes, alarm bells—each of them a warning to hold the press for a fast-developing story—were ringing in newsrooms across the country.

Unexpectedly, within ten minutes, the AP sent out an urgent message to newspaper editors that the report was unconfirmed. That was followed, two minutes later, by another urgent message. "Police find Lana Turner alive at her home."

It had become obvious, by now, that whomever had reported the incident had intended it as a hoax.

Constantly surrounded with security guards, Lana continued to receive death threats at regular intervals for a period of at least three months. The anonymous callers always managed to procure her frequently changing unlisted phone numbers. "Johnny had a lot of friends who were loyal to him—and not just Mickey Cohen," she said. "They wanted revenge and held me responsible for his death. I had become a target. At times, I was afraid to leave the house. Thanks to Howard Hughes, I had security. Otherwise, I would have been afraid to go to bed at night, thinking some mob members might break in and kill me."

The next time Frank Sinatra phoned Lana to find out how she was holding up, he found her a bit delusional, as he later reported to Sammy Davis, Jr. and to Peter Lawford.

She believed in reincarnation and seemed convinced that in an ancient life, she was Cleopatra herself, Queen of Egypt. To escape from the post-murder trauma, she seemed to wander into some remote past that had never existed for her.

She'd been drinking heavily," Sinatra said, "and this made her think that she was Cleopatra incarnate, and that her long-lost lover, Tyrone Power, was alive and well playing the part of Marc Antony." At one point, Sinatra asked her, "So who am I in this drama on the Nile? Julius Caesar?"

On looking back on those horrible weeks, Lana said, "I shake my head every now and then, puzzling over how things had gone so wrong. I can never forget what happened that night, or even why it happened. I was weak, I'll admit, lonely and vulnerable when Johnny came along. He moved in and seized the advantage, trying to get the upper hand. I never meant to harm anyone—God is my witness to the truth of that."

As 1958 came to an end, Lana defined it as, "The worst year of my life. What's past is past. I can't let it destroy me. I must go on."

Years later, on looking back, she said, "When two human beings go through tremendous emotional experiences, as Cheryl and I did, it either cracks them apart or brings them closer together. Cheryl and I became closer."

***

Years later at a dinner party hosted by TV talk show host, Merv Griffin and his co-hostess, Eva Gabor, Eva's sister Zsa Zsa entertained their guests with her witty conversation. At one point Zsa Zsa discussed Lana and Cheryl.

Zsa Zsa had long suspected Lana of having conducted an affair with her former husband, Conrad Hilton, and a separate affair with his son, Nicky.

According to Zsa Zsa, "I got involved with Johnny Stompanato when he was shopping around for a wealthy woman in Beverly Hills to live with. He'd already had affairs with Elizabeth Taylor (*who hasn't, dah-link*), Ava Gardner, Janet Leigh, and Marilyn Monroe."

"He asked me if I thought he should continue with Lana because she was increasingly difficult and really didn't have a lot of money for a movie queen," Zsa Zsa said.

"I gave him the wrong advice and told him to stay with Lana, who might put him in charge of her new film company, Lanturn. My reasoning was that he couldn't last forever as Hollywood's young stallion—and he'd need some other profession. I also told him, 'of course, if you turn her down, I'd understand. Frankly, I can take Lana Turner or leave her.'"

The Budapest bombshell also claimed that she was one of the few women who'd had affairs with both Johnny Stompanato and Lex Barker.

"As everybody knows, *dah-link*, all the international studs such as Porfirio Rubirosa have passed in and out of my boudoir. If it's true that both Lex and Johnny raped young Cheryl, it must have caused her great pain because of their huge size. Those two men would be a challenge for the most experienced prostitute. I'm not surprised that getting assaulted by darling Lex and darling Johnny would turn her off men for life."

***

In his book, *The Bad and the Beautiful—Hollywood in the Fifties,* Sam Kushneer wrote: "Like many other celebrity children, Cheryl Crane rarely saw her mother. The girl would reach out to hug and kiss her flawlessly styled mother, and Turner would gently push her away, 'Sweetheart, the hair,' she'd say."

"Cheryl would lie in bed at night looking up at the phosphorescent stars stuck to the ceiling. On a shelf stood a three-foot-high, life-sized Lana Turner doll a fan had sent her, but the real Lana Turner almost never made an appearance to tuck her daughter in."

"Mother and daughter," Kushner continued, "would soon find themselves forever bonded by one horrific moment, and forever at the heart of one of Hollywood's most enduring scandals."

***

In her later years, Lana lived with Eric Root, one of the leading hairdressers of Hollywood, familiar with the "crowning glory" of Rita Hayworth, Greta Garbo, Bette Davis, Veronica Lake, and—lest we forget—Richard Burton and Frank Sinatra.

Root also developed a deep-rooted friendship with Karen Kondazian, an award-winning actress who was Lex Barker's last lover—in fact, the former Tarzan

546

was walking along Fifth Avenue in Manhattan, on his way to meet her, when he collapsed and died of a heart attack.

Kondazian had become known for her skill at portraying characters from the plays of Tennessee Williams—*The Rose Tattoo, Sweet Bird of Youth, Vieux Carré, Baby Doll, The Night of the Iguana,* and *The Milk Train Doesn't Stop Here Anymore.*

She told Root that Barker had spoken to Lana just days after the Stompanato murder. "She admitted to Lex that in the panic and hysteria to save her career, she allowed Cheryl to take the blame for her own misdeed."

Then, Kondazian disputed Cheryl's claim that Barker had repeatedly raped her during the course of his marriage to Lana. "Lex was the perfect gentleman. He was kind and gentle in every aspect of our relationship."

"Never did he force or insinuate himself in any improper way, although there was nearly a thirty-year difference in our ages."

Based on what Barker had told her, Kondazian believed that "Cheryl was very jealous of her mother. Lex said she flaunted her body in front of him. He always predicted that the girl would cause Lana a lot of trouble. She sure did!"

Lana also addressed the rape issue directly with Root, telling him, "When Cheryl made allegations against Lex, I had no choice but to believe her. I couldn't take a chance. Had it been true, and the world found out, my career would have been finished for allowing her to stay under the same roof with him. I've always had my doubts about her accusations against Lex."

In 1996, a year after Lana's death, Root published his memoirs, *The Private Life of Lana.* In it, he recalled the night both of them were living in a suite at the Plaza Hotel in Manhattan. "We were watching TV and a documentary came on about Hollywood scandals. When pictures were flashed about the Johnny Stompanato murder case, I asked her, 'Do you want me to turn it off?'"

She insisted he keep the television on, as she sat through all the lurid scenes. Finally, when it was over, she said, "Turn the damn thing off!"

Then, after reaching for a cigarette, she confessed: "I killed the son of a bitch, and I'd do it again."

She also told Root that after she was dead, she wanted the world to know the truth. "You should not let my Baby take the rap all of her life for my mistake. Someday, when I'm gone, tell it all. *I was the one.*"

In an interview with reporter Diesmond Lee, Root claimed, "When my book was published, I was called a liar and even threatened with death. If convicted, Lana would probably have been given the death penalty. Faced

Eric Root, hairdresser, companion, friend, and confidant to Lana, claimed that she confessed to him that she stabbed Johnny Stompanato.

with that, it was obvious that the only real recourse would be to let Cheryl take the fall. There was also speculation that Stompanato was frequently having sex with Cheryl."

Biographer Patricia Bosworth, in a feature story for *Vanity Fair* published in 1999, asked Cheryl about Root's claim that Lana murdered Stompanato.

Cheryl answered, "The idea that Root had in his book is far-fetched. You know, everybody has something to sell. I guess it was the only way he could get his book published."

Yet Cheryl herself at one point backed up her mother's confession. In her own memoir, *Detour,* she told her new lover, Joyce (Josh) LeRoy, "You know, I didn't do it. I love you so much more than anyone before in my life, Josh, that I don't want you to think I could do a terrible thing like that."

Josh responded, "I think it was a very brave and noble thing to go to your mother's defense. You have to live with that the rest of your life. Now you have someone to share it with."

As Cheryl wrote, "In that moment, while sitting in a candlelit booth in a Sunset Strip restaurant, my life changed."

***

In Root's memoir, he also claimed that Lana was devastated when Cheryl published her own memoirs, *Detour,* in 1988.

"Who in the fuck does she think she is?" Lana asked. "How could she do this to me?"

He may have exaggerated, but Root claimed that after the publica-

After her tumultuous childhood, which had included rape and murder, Cheryl bonded with her mother in later life.

"We became closer, having shared so many tragedies together, Lana said.

Joyce ("Josh") LeRoy, pictured on the left, became Cheryl's lifelong companion.

She offered love, understanding, and stability after Cheryl's survival as Lana Turner's daughter.

tion of *Detour,* Lana took to her bed for six months. She was horrified by the revelations, especially Cheryl's charges of rape by Lex Barker.

However, when Lana appeared in public and was asked about the book, she said, "I think it took guts for Cheryl to write it."

***

In 2007, it was announced that a new film, entitled *Stompanato,* was in pre-production. The script, according to a press release, would retell the scandalous murder of "the thug and wannabe actor," the notorious hustler, Johnny Stompanato.

Lana would be played by Catherine Zeta-Jones, the wife of Michael Douglas. The role of Johnny Stompanato would be cast with Keanu Reeves. Adrian Lyne, a respected director known for such movies as *Jacob's Ladder* (1990) with Tim Robbins, and *Indecent Proposal* (1993) with Robert Redford, was set to direct.

The screenwriters, so it was reported, were going to nail Lana, not Cheryl, as the culprit.

Writing about the proposed film, Mark Umbach said: "Rumors have surrounded the death, including that Crane and Stompanato had been lovers, and that Lana Turner actually killed Stompanato and her 14-year-old daughter took the rap."

The actress who'd portray Cheryl was never announced, but the script called for love scenes between the underaged teenager and the hardened hustler. It was recommended that an 18-year-old be used, an actress could at least give the illusion that she was 14.

One scene called for the character playing Lana to walk in on Stompanato and Cheryl making passionate love on her own pink satin sheets in her own bedroom.

Zeta-Jones told the press that her father-in-law, Kirk Douglas, the rumored lover of Lana during the making of *The Bad and the Beautiful,* would be her "research engine" on the blonde love goddess.

"It's a great role for me," she said. "I have always wanted to play Lana Turner, but I'm nervous about it."

News of the casting provoked outrage across the internet. One fan protested the casting choice for Johnny. "Reeves just doesn't cut it as the handsome, macho stud, Johnny Stompanato."

One fan lodged yet another complaint. "Zeta-Jones is totally wrong for the part of Lana. There is no way this actress can duplicate the star, who was stunningly beautiful, one of the most desirable women in the world at the time."

The person who was the most disappointed about the casting was Sharon Stone, who, for years, had wanted to bring Lana to the screen. Reporters asked, "Is Sharon Stone getting the ice pick?"

That was a reference, of course, to Stone's role as the vagina-flashing ice-pick murderer in *Basic Instinct* (1992).

Stone claimed, "I met with Lana herself, and she told me I was the only actress in Hollywood who could bring her image to the screen."

The film was never made, as Cheryl refused to give her permission for her image to be depicted on screen.

Actually, in 2001, there had been another, earlier attempt, *The Goddess and the Gangster*, to adapt a movie from the Stompanato murder case. A news item claimed that Antonio Banderas had been tapped to play Johnny, with Sharon Stone as Lana. This film, too, was never made.

Over the years, many producers considered filming their own versions of the murder. A number of actors were considered for the role of Johnny Stompanato, including Richard Gere, Benjamin Brett, and Paul Hipp, known for playing rocker Buddy Holly in *Buddy* (1990) and for a role in *Midnight in the Garden of Good and Evil* (1997).

A gay casting director said, "There is only one actor who can play Johnny Stompanato, and that's Hugh Jackman. He's sure sexy enough. Just imagine how he'll look imitating Johnny, with his silk shirt unbuttoned to that tantalizing navel Jackman has on that magnificent Aussie body."

[A NOTE FROM THE PUBLISHER: There is only one person, now alive, who knows exactly who murdered Johnny Stompanato on that long-ago night back in April of 1958. That is Cheryl Crane, the daughter of Lana Turner.

Compiled over many years, the information in this chapter, with all its conflicting opinions, is similar to what might have been presented at a murder trial.

Lana with baby Cheryl. Having survived death-defying medical problems at birth, both mother and daughter went on to face an array of other tragedies in life.

Cheryl later recalled her unhappy life growing up as "the baby of a star" in the glamourous Hollywood era of the 1940s and 50s.

Since that never happened, it is up to you, the reader, to form your own opinion. Was it the mother or the 14-year-old daughter who plunged the kitchen knife deep into the bowels of the ill-fated gambler, hustler, and blackmailer?

Chances are good that a definite answer will never be known unless Cheryl, perhaps on her death bed, revises previous statements.]

Chapter Seventeen

The Twilight of a Film Career

THE DECLINE OF LANA TURNER'S FILM ROLES:

No Longer Cast as a Glamourous Millionaire Buying Hustlers, She Now Portrays a Broken-Down Old Whore

In *Madame X,* the public saw Lana Turner as she'd never been depicted on screen before. She cried when she first gazed at her aged and defeated image in the mirror.

In this scene, she appears with her hair brushed severely back and with dark circles under her eyes. The embittered, violently betrayed character she's portraying is, in fact, facing death.

She lamented to her friends, "My appearance in this remake of an old, old theme is going to destroy what career I have left."

"For mother, life was a movie," said Cheryl Crane.

Her friend, Virginia Grey, put it another way: "If the movies had not existed, they would have to be invented just for Lana Turner. She could have been nothing less but a movie star."

In the weeks that followed the Johnny Stompanato verdict, Lana felt she was sinking into quicksand. Almost daily, some figure in Hollywood announced that her film career was over. Some producers sidestepped the issue. David O. Selznick claimed, "I would hire her in a minute, but I don't have any suitable property right now."

"Of course, I'd cast her," Jerry Wald said. "Before all this shit came down, I tried to get her to co-star in *The Sound and the Fury*. Should another role arise, I'd be the first to go knocking on her door."

"After all this publicity, Lana will come back bigger than ever at the box office," predicted producer Byron Foy. "Audience surveys have shown that most of the public is sympathetic to her."

It was Lana herself who almost daily told someone, "I fear even my most loyal fans have now turned against me."

Money was one of her biggest problems. She needed work, because she still owed MGM a lot of money for covering her debt to the IRS. Her legal bills had become colossal, and she also had to support not only herself, but Mildred and Cheryl.

On April 24, 1958, Cheryl had been made a ward of the court, the judge ruling that she should go and live with her grandmother, Mildred.

After the court hearing, as she exited from the courthouse, Lana flashed a smile. As she said, "It was called putting up a brave front."

"I'm pleased with the decision of the judge," she assured reporters, perhaps masking her true feelings.

By December, the arrangement of Cheryl living with Mildred was extended by the judge with no definite cutoff date. His ruling did not bring any objection either from Lana or from Stephen Crane.

She gave up her rented house on Canon Drive, turning it over to Cheryl and Mildred, while she went to live at her mother's former apartment. She was not happy with the accommodation, and soon moved into a small house at 515 North Roxbury Drive.

Del Armstrong had remained her trusted friend and confidant. She told him,

"I'm not going to look back, but go forward into my uncertain future. I've got to push myself. That means facing up to my personal problems. Any future love affairs will have to be put on hold. I've got to find film work. What else is there for me to do? Work behind a sales counter in a department store? I saw Bette Davis attempt that in her movie, *The Star* (1952). It didn't work out for Bette in that film, and it wouldn't work out for me, either."

Letters addressed to her still poured in at MGM, although she was no longer under contract. The mail department faithfully delivered all correspondence from both fans and enemies, perhaps censoring some of the most vicious ones. A telephone operator from Cleveland wrote, "There's hardly a woman alive who at one time or another hasn't loved an unworthy man. Only Lana got caught."

On looking back at her life at the time, she dredged up a *cliché*, "For me, it was darkest before the dawn."

***

That "dawn" arrived in the form of producer Ross Hunter, who since 1956 had wanted to remake the 1934 movie, *Imitation of Life,* starring Claudette Colbert as "The Pancake Queen" and Louise Beaver as her faithful black maid. The plot was based on a novel by the best-selling author, Fannie Hurst.

Originally, his intention was to turn the soapy melodrama into a musical, starring Shirley Booth and Mahalia Jackson. Hunter had become known for employing actresses "beyond their expiration date," as in the case of Ann Sheridan and Joan Bennett.

When he changed his mind and decided to make *Imitation* into a melodrama, his phone started ringing. Three of the most honored and distinguished "drama queens" in the history of Hollywood called, each wanting to star in the remake. They were Katharine Hepburn, Bette Davis, and Joan Crawford. But he wanted Lana Turner.

In the 1934 film, Colbert launched an empire based on a pancake recipe from her maid, as portrayed by Louise Brooks. Colbert's daughter was played by Rochelle Hudson. The maid, Delilah Johnson, in the script, has a daughter, Peola (Fredi Washington) whose fair complexion allowed her to pass as white, even though she was of mixed-race ancestry.

From the day it was published in 1933, the Hurst novel had generated controversy. Until the 1967 Supreme Court

Although Juanita Moore is employed as Lana's housekeeper, she is more like a comforting, surrogate mother.

553

ruling (*Loving v. Virginia*), Southern states required that persons of any known African American ancestry had to be officially classified in records as "black."

When Hunter announced he was remaking the movie, the censors at the Production Code sent an advance warning, "You're just asking for trouble."

The day Hunter drove over to see Lana, he was at the peak of his success. He'd scored a big hit with Rock Hudson and Jane Wyman in *Magnificent Obsession* (1954). In the same year as *Imitation of Life* (1959) he'd also launched *Pillow Talk* with Rock Hudson and Doris Day, one of the most successful comedies of the 1950s, ranking up there with Marilyn Monroe's *Some Like It Hot* (1959).

Even though the critics attacked Hunter's films, the public flocked to them, especially women. "In my pictures, I give women the chance to live vicariously, to see beautiful women in jewels and gorgeous clothes, with plenty of melodrama going on in their love lives."

Here's John Gavin, later a U.S. ambassador to Mexico, who NEVER tried to build a wall—at least not between Lana and himself.

Over a drink at Lana's house, Hunter pitched the rewritten starring role to her. As a girl, Lana had been taken to see the Claudette Colbert version of *Imitation of Life*.

She listened patiently as Hunter outlined the character to her. When he'd finished, she said, "What? Another mother role?" She was referencing *Peyton Place*.

He quickly pointed out, "You did god damn well with that one."

One aspect of the plot particularly disturbed her. "In the movie, my daughter and I are in love with the same man. Don't you think that will revive rumors that Cheryl was in love with Johnny Stompanato?"

"So what?" Hunter asked. "You'll have to face life at some point, dear. It's a great role—potentially your greatest—and I think your fans will admire you all the more for the courage and bravery of your doing it."

"I need work, but this script is just too close to home," she protested.

"Take the role, or you'll regret it. Your friend, Susan Hayward, thinks it'll be an Oscar winner. Why don't you win that Oscar instead of Susan? To be nominated for *Peyton Place* is one thing. How about actually taking home the Oscar for a change?"

It took another three hours and a half bottle of vodka before she agreed to do the role. "Announce it to the press. Lana Turner is coming back!"

***

554

During their long session at her home, Lana had been impressed with Hunter's brutal honesty, especially when it came to himself. At one point, he admitted, "I'm in love with Rock Hudson. He's got a big one that he lets me sample two or three times a week. I don't kid myself. He's not in love with me, but that doesn't mean he won't have sex with me."

"That's the story of my life, too," she said, sympathetically.

The next week, one of her hopes was dashed, as she'd been wishing that Hunter would give her perhaps $150,000, maybe more, for her appearance. But over dinner with him, he told her the bad news.

Universal didn't have a lot of faith in the remake and would allow him only a budget of $1.2 million. The studio was willing to settle for another deal, paying her a salary of only $2,500 a week. But as an amazing concession, she would be given fifty percent of the profits. However, if the movie failed at the box office, she would have worked for far less than what she was accustomed to.

Finally, after listening to all of his reassurances, she agreed to sign the contract. As she recalled months later, "That was the best financial decision I ever made. I made at least a million dollars for the role long before Elizabeth Taylor became famously paid a million dollars for appearing in *Cleopatra* (1963)."

Before filming began, Hunter assured her she'd have a spectacular wardrobe that Jean Louis would design for her. "That, plus you'll be seen in at least a million dollars worth of jewelry. Just because I'm a gay man and not turned on by female flesh doesn't mean I can't make you look like a goddess."

Author Sam Staggs wrote, "Like *Myra Breckinridge* (a novel by Gore Vidal), Lana in the film embodies both heterosexual and homosexual camp while remaining oddly sexless."

To many other critics, Lana in the character of Lora Meredith was playing herself.

Hunter hired a German-Danish film director, Douglas Sirk, who had in the early years of the Nazi regime worked for Josef Goebbels at the UFA Studios in Berlin. He left Hitler's Germany in 1937 because he was married to a Jew, Hilde Jary.

Before her, he'd been married to Lydia Brinken, a member of the Nazi Party who had arranged for their son, Claus Detlef Sierck, to join the *Hitler Jugend*. In time, he became the leading child star of Nazi cinema. The last Sirk heard of his son was to learn of his death at the age of nine on the Russian front.

Sirk told Lana that he'd never been a Nazi, and he offered to arrange a screening of his first Hollywood picture for her, *Hitler's Madman* (1942).

Within days, Hunter and Sirk had arranged Lana's supporting cast. No longer a "pancake queen," like Claudette Colbert, Lana's Lora Meredith was a stunningly beautiful stage actress on Broadway. Her daughter, Susie, age 16, would be played by Sandra Dee.

Instead of the more racially charged part of the black maid, the Louise Beavers role would be essayed by Juanita Moore, cast as Annie Johnson, Lana's "housekeeper and companion."

Before deciding to cast Moore, Hunter had considered both Pearl Bailey and

Marian Anderson.

Her mulatto daughter, Sarah Jane, would be played by Susan Kohner, the daughter of Paul Kohner, Lana's agent.

As a freelance photographer, Steve Archer, the leading man role would go to John Gavin.

Dan O'Herlihy was cast in the part of the playwright scripting those hit shows for Lana's character.

Troy Donahue would play Frankie, Sarah Jane's boyfriend until he learns she's a mulatto. Actor Robert Alda was cast as Lana's agent, Allen Loomis, in the film.

Growing up in the backwoods of segregated Mississippi, Moore and her family had gravitated to California in hopes of a better life. She made her film debut in *Pinky* (1949), with Jeanne Crain and Ethel Barrymore. This was Hollywood's other pioneer racial drama of a black girl passing for white.

During filming, Lana and Moore had many sympathetic talks. Hunter claimed, "Juanita became a sort of mother figure to Lana, even though she was born in 1914. And, as such, was only a few years older than Lana."

Lana was quite blunt with Moore. "When I signed for this picture, I was on my ass."

"*Honey chile*, you can't get much lower than that," Moore replied.

The former Merle Johnson, Jr., Troy Donahue was one of Henry Willson's boys, having been worked over on the casting couch.

He was a handsome, rather bland, blonde-haired, blue-eyed sensation, one of the fabled "pretty boys" of the Eisenhower 1950s. Its ranks included such competitors as Tab Hunter and Rock Hudson.

Even though she didn't get one of the leads, Mahalia Jackson, the African American singer, hailed as "The Queen of Gospel," appeared at the end of the movie, singing a brilliantly moving rendition of "Trouble of the World" at the funeral of the character played by Moore.

In her memoirs, Lana wrote about this "heartbreaking spiritual. When I heard the first strains of the song in rehearsal, I simply broke down. Images of my own life, by own dark fears flooded my mind, and I dissolved in tears. I fled to my dressing room."

The dashing John Gavin was a "dreamboat leading man" (as defined by both Lana and his gay agent, Henry Willson), who seemed to have a crush on Gavin. Willson had been the first to alert her to Gavin's manly charms and male beauty.

"As you know, my boy Rock Hudson is the biggest money maker in pictures today," Willson said. "I'm calling Gavin 'Rock Junior.' He is tall, dark, and gorgeously handsome. You'll cream in your jeans when he takes you in his arms for a love scene. Some critics call him wooden. But with those looks, that body, who needs to act?"

"Is he one of your boys?" she asked.

"Don't take me for a total pansy," he said. "I know who to put on the casting couch, and I also know where not to trespass. When it comes to John, I can only dream of those mighty inches. He doesn't put out to get a role."

Hunter arranged a screening for Lana of Gavin's latest picture. *A Time to Love and a Time to Die* (1958), based on Erich Maria Remarque's anti-war novel, the story of a young German soldier who wakes up to both the horror and futility of war.

"I'm awed by Gavin's screen presence," she told Hunter. "So strong, so virile, so yummy."

Once again, as in *Peyton Place*, Lana played a stylish mature woman involved in a mother-daughter conflict, this time with Sandra Dee.

"During filming, I never got to seduce John," she confessed to Virginia Grey. "If he had raised only a little pinkie and beckoned to me, I would have come running. No woman in her right mind would turn down a guy like this. He could even change a lesbian's sexual preference."

"If anything, I found him a bit square," she said. "After work, he goes home to his wife, Cecily Evans. They have a small apartment in Beverly Hills, and they're expecting a baby."

Lana later became friends with Gavin and his second wife, Constance Towers, whom he'd married almost a decade after his divorce from Cecily came through.

Look magazine labeled Gavin a "non-neurotic newcomer," and Alfred Hitchcock cast him as Janet Leigh's boyfriend in *Psycho* (1960).

[Although Lana lobbied to play opposite Gavin in *Back Street* (1961), based on another Fannie Hurst novel, she was rejected. The role went instead to Susan Hayward.]

Susan Kohner played Sarah Jane, 18, the daughter of the black housekeeper who grows up "to pass." She performed brilliantly, her role winning her an Oscar nomination as Best Supporting Actress.

The year Lana met her, she had appeared opposite Sal Mineo in *The Gene Krupa Story*. The fabled drummer had been one of Lana's earliest beaus. She told Kohner, "I liked the original title of your movie better. If it was the story of Gene, it should have been called *Drum Crazy*."

From the depths of Bayonne, New Jersey, Sandra Dee, born in 1942, launched her career as a beautiful, blue-eyed, blonde-haired child model. Her parents divorced in 1950, and her new stepfather reportedly molested her.

Ross Hunter discovered Sandra on Park Avenue in Manhattan, and by 1957, she was lured to Hollywood to make her film debut in *Until They Sail*, co-starring Paul Newman, Joan Fontaine, and Piper Laurie.

When Hunter cast her in *Imitation of Life* as Lana's daughter, she became a teenage sensation. Her position was firmly established that same year when she co-starred with Troy Donahue in *A Summer Place*, a "soaper" of adultery and teenage love.

Also in 1959, she released her titular role of *Gidget*, a teenage comedy. In 1960, she married singer Bobby Darin and would go on to fill in the role of Tammy created by Debbie Reynolds in two sequels for Universal.

Cast against type in *Imitation*, Troy Donahue played a thug who beats

INTERRACIAL IRONIES *(IMITATION OF LIFE)*

Psychic sisters, one white (Sandra Dee, left), another (Susan Kohner), "passing as white."

up Susan Kohner when he learns she is a mulatto. In a pivotal scene, Donahue once struck her so hard, she ended up in the hospital. Hunter sent her flowers with a note: "Yellow roses for blue bruises."

In private life, Donahue was known to beat up on women, which, in one case at least, led to threatened legal action that was later settled out of court.

To Lana, Donahue didn't strike her as a sex symbol, even though he was called "The Blonde Cobra of Sex." The move magazines cited him as being the most worshipped young male star in pictures. Girls screamed hysterically whenever he appeared in public.

"I assumed he is bisexual," Lana said to Hunter.

"He certainly is," the producer said. "Right now, both of us are competing for Rock Hudson."

Donahue also became known for orgies staged at his open house. "One night he invited me, but I turned him down," Lana said. "First, I thought I'd be the oldest person there. Second, I feared his notorious parties would be raided by the police. All I needed was to end up on the frontpage in another scandal."

Robert Alda was cast as Lana's agent, with Dan O'Herlihy as her playwright.

The son of an Italian barber, Alda became the father of two actors, Alan (famous for his involvement in, among others, the TV serial M.A.S.H.), and Antony. Before becoming a Broadway star, Robert worked in vaudeville and burlesque, appearing with such stars as Bud Abbott and Lou Costello, as well as Phil Silvers. He won a Tony Award for starring in *Guys and Dolls* (1950).

O'Herlihy was no great admirer of Lana. "She was very much the star," he said. "Playing a love scene with her was hell. She was always worried about her makeup. I was afraid to touch her. Goddesses are only to be admired from a distance, not mauled. 'Don't smear my lipstick. Don't mess my hair.' Sirk had made an anti-Nazi film, but I think he learned directing from Josef Goebbels himself. He was always barking orders at me that sounded like a Hitler rant, throwing me off my mark."

An Irishman, O'Herlihy appeared as Macduff in Orson Welles' *Macbeth* in 1948, his first American film. In 1954, in Luis Buñuel's *Adventures of Robinson Crusoe*, he'd won an Oscar nomination for Best Actor. He would later co-star with Lana in *The Big Cube* (1967), playing her husband.

Her fabulous wardrobe in *Imitation* was designed by the Parisian, Jean Louis, who had also created Rita Hayworth's famous black satin strapless gown in *Gilda* (1946) and Marlene Dietrich's celebrated beaded *soufflé* stagewear for her cabaret world tours. He'd also designed clothes for Ginger Rogers, Vivien Leigh, Joan Crawford, Julie Andrews, Katharine Hepburn, and Judy Garland. In time, he'd be nominated for thirteen Oscars for costume design. In 1993, he married an aging Loretta Young, who was long hailed as the best dressed actress in Hollywood.

When Lana sat through the final cut with Hunter, she turned to him. "It's a four-handkerchief tear-jerker." She also told columnist James Bacon, "This is how old Louis B. (Mayer) used to make movies before MGM kicked him out on his fat ass."

Bosley Crowther in *The New York Times* echoed Lana's point of view, labeling it "the most shameless tear-jerker in years."

Time magazine called the remake "still a potent onion."

Struggling financially, Universal was rescued by its release of *Imitation of Life*, which became its alltime biggest grosser at the box office.

***

Two blondes from different generations—Lana Turner and Sandra Dee—made two movies together, *Imitation of Life* followed by *Portrait in Black*.

They were completely different personalities, and had little in common. Ross Hunter, their producer, believed that Lana was jealous of Sandra's bubbling youth and beauty. Her star was rising on the Hollywood sky as Lana's sun was setting.

There was one factor in both of their lives that each of the stars had in common: celebrity psychic John Cohan.

At various times and through different periods, both actresses found comfort, support, and good advice from this kind, loving man.

Over the years, his other clients read like

John Cohan has been a celebrity psychic to the stars for more than three decades. He was a soulmate to both Lana Turner and Sandra Dee during turbulent times in their roller-coaster lives.

a *Who's Who* in the entertainment world, including Elvis Presley, Elizabeth Taylor, Joan Crawford, Rock Hudson, La Toya Jackson, Lucille Ball, and Julia Roberts, among many others.

Cohan was introduced to Lana through a family friend, actor Ray Danton. Her former agent, Henry Willson, once suggested that he thought Danton and Lana would make the ideal screen team. "His raven-black hair and your blondness would make a vanilla and chocolate image on screen."

Danton was known not only for his hair, but for his intense good looks with a distinctive cleft chin evocative of Kirk Douglas.

Willson helped launch the career of Rory Calhoun by sending the dark-haired actor on dates with the blonde goddess, having warned her not to date men as blonde as she was.

Danton and Lana, in spite of Willson's wish, never made a picture together. However, she was impressed with his virile image when she'd seen two of his pictures: *The Rise and Fall of Legs Diamond* (1960), and *The George Raft Story* (1960). As arranged by Willson, the movie gangster had been one of her first lovers when Lana arrived at Warner Brothers in 1937.

Cohan was particularly helpful to Lana during her decline in the 1980s. As she admitted herself, "I was on a serious downhill slide, in terrible health, and suffering a weight loss to the point of emaciation." She wasn't eating properly, but drinking too much and chain smoking, too. When she appeared in New Orleans in the early 1980s in *Murder Among Friends,* she often could not go onstage and had to send out her understudy as a replacement.

Sometimes, she and Cohan talked about her previous lovers. As she claimed, "All of them were unfaithful. My heart was broken into so many pieces I never thought I could put it back together again."

He tried to arouse her survival-sharpened instincts and instill in her a love and respect of self, giving her the will to go on. Or, as she put it, "to face the final curtain. I know that's a *cliché.* But, like most *clichés,* it's true."

Over the course of his relationship with Lana, he had a brief fling with her. "She was desperate for love," he recalled. But that fleeting romance turned into a deep friendship which led to her calling him "my soulmate."

Cohan also brought comfort and love to Sandra Dee after her film career started to flicker and die in the late 1960s. Universal didn't renew her contract. Her divorce from Bobby Darin came through in 1967.

Cohan was there for her during the years she suffered from poor health and lived as a virtual recluse. For many years, she battled depression, *anorexia nervosa,* and alcoholism, and also had to cope with a drug problem.

He acknowledged that Sandra "was the love of my life" on the dedication page of his revelation-laden memoirs, *Catch a Falling Star,* published in 2008.

In that book, he described how, on five or six different occasions, Sandra had urged him to marry her, but that did not come about.

He spoke to her on the phone in January of 2005, a month before she died. As he had so many times before, he talked about her health and heating habits. She revealed her desire to make a comeback, perhaps as a host on NBC's *The Today Show.*

He promised he'd be in California by the spring of that year, but by then, it would be too late. Sandra was gone.

As he remembered it in her desperation, she shared a dream with him that Darin had reached out his hand from above, beckoning her to come and join him, as a kind of "See you in Heaven," offer.

"I told her that Bobby wants you to stay here and live life to the fullest," Cohan said. "But she was ready to go. I loved and adored her. She will be missed."

***

With lines forming around the block for *Imitation of Life*, more film offers poured in for Lana. For various reasons, many of them fell through. Projects were either completely abandoned, or else she rejected roles which were then assigned to another actress.

Ever since he had cast *Forever Amber*, the tyrannical director, Otto Preminger, had wanted to star Lana in a picture. But the studio had insisted on Linda Darnell. Even before that, Lana had wanted to star in the director's *Laura*, but that role had gone to Gene Tierney.

Preminger had already cast James Stewart in *Anatomy of a Murder* when he approached Lana and asked her to take the female lead. She read the script and liked the role, since it evoked memories of her starring role as Cora in *The Postman Always Rings Twice*.

She was concerned that the title of the movie, *Anatomy of a Murder*, would revive recent memories of the fatal stabbing of Johnny Stompanato at her home. She told a reporter, "I wish I could have learned these things another way, but what's past is past. I can't let it destroy me, and I want to move on. It's a terrific role, and I want to do it."

The problem arose over wardrobe and her appearance. Preminger took her to be fitted for the wigs she'd wear in the film. "She objected to everything," he told his staff. "This woman, I fear, is going to drive me crazy. I'm having second thoughts about casting her. To begin with, I think she's too old for the part. I should have gone with a younger actress."

Hope Bryce, the costume coordinator, made an appointment to meet Lana at a western shop on Rodeo Drive, then waited two hours for her to show up. The plan involved purchasing off-the-rack clothing for her, perhaps slacks, Capri pants, or Western pants *à la* Dale Evans.

Lana signed a contract to co-star in *Anatomy of a Murder*, a taut suspense thriller directed by the ferociously undiplomatic Otto Preminger, who's depicted above.

A bare-knuckled dispute over Lana 's wardrobe demands ("couture, and only by Jean Louis!") led to screaming arguments and a bitter parting of their ways.

Since she didn't show up, Bryce bought some outfits in her size and drove to her home for fittings.

But when Lana saw the selection, she refused to even try them on. "I want the clothes I wear in the film to be designed by Jean Louis!"

When Bryce informed Preminger of her rejection, he exploded: "I, and nobody else, determine what my actors are to wear. Her character is a junior officer's wife living in a trailer. How in hell can she afford Jean Louis? It's ridiculous to dress her up and turn her into a glamour puss. This is not *Imitation of Life."*

He ordered Bryce to assemble "some cheap, sleazy clothes that a slut in a trailer camp would wear. Even some plastic shoes."

When Bryce presented Lana with this apparel, it was her time to explode. She immediately called her agent, Paul Kohner, and ordered him to present her costume demands to Preminger.

Kohner called Preminger with Lana's demands and objections.

"Fine," the director said. "Send me a letter stating that she wants to cancel the contract she signed with me unless her clothes are designed by Jean Louis. Once I get the letter, I'll release her at once."

That night he'd been drinking heavily, fuming about Lana. He phoned her and, in his thick Viennese accent, began to denounce her. In her memoirs, Lana referred to the vile expletives hurled at her, without mentioning the actual words.

In his final screech, he shouted "CUNT! CUNT! CUNT!" into the phone right before she put down the receiver never to speak to him again.

"I can't possibly work with this beast," she told Kohner. "I hope my family is never so hungry that I would have to be in a picture he directed. Too bad, though, as I would love to have co-starred with Jimmy Stewart again."

***

Portrait in Black, Lana's only film release for 1960, was once again produced by Ross Hunter from a script that had gone dusty on the shelves at Universal International for thirteen years.

Hunter told his director, Michael Gordon, "Lana turned down scripts for *Luanne Royal* and for *The Chalk Garden,* but at last she's found something she can sink those painted claws of hers into. A murderess."

Gordon answered, "It's type casting, Ross old pal, A murderess playing a murderess."

"Don't let her hear you say that," Hunter cautioned.

The play by Ivan Goff and Ben Roberts had opened on Broadway in 1947, running at the Booth Theatre for sixty-one performances, starring Clair Luce, Sidney Blackmer, and Donald Cook.

After seeing the play, produc-

ers Jack Skirball and Bruce Manning acquired the screen rights. Sir Carol Reed, famous for his 1949 *The Third Man,* was set to direct, with Joan Crawford in the star role. The project didn't get off the ground, and the rights were sold to Universal but the studio let it languish until 1960.

As a follow-up to *Imitation of Life,* Hunter wanted an all-star cast and crew. Gordon had just directed *Pillow Talk* (1959), one of Hunter's most successful movies, starring Rock Hudson and Doris Day.

In the early 1950s, during the McCarthy era, Gordon had been blacklisted and was *persona non grata* in Hollywood. Ironically, in 1950, he'd just directed Jose Ferrer in his Oscar-winning performance in *Cyrano de Bergerac.*

Lana insisted the Jean Louis once again be tapped to design her fabulous wardrobe. Music would be by Frank Skinner. The original playwrights, Goff and Roberts, had revised their script. Russell Metty, who had photographed Lana so beautifully in *Imitation of Life,* was

Portrait of a cinematic murderess, Lana Turner, starring in *Portrait in Black.*

Her role, and the publicity it generated, traumatized Lana with comparisons to the recent, spectacularly controversial, death of Johnny Stompanato.

also hired for *Portrait in Black.* Richard Ried had won an Oscar for his art direction of *Pillow Talk,* and he was hired. Photography would be in EastmanColor.

Portrait in Black would be a murder/blackmail mystery filled with some gaping holes that Hunter would try to conceal with a glamourous décor and offbeat casting, including Anthony Quinn as her leading man. When the role was first presented to him, he told Hunter, "You've got to be kidding."

He would be cast as David Rivera, a doctor who falls in love with mink-clad, diamond-laden Sheila Cabot (Lana). He's treating her ailing husband, shipping magnate Matthew Cabot (Lloyd Nolan). The couple have a stepdaughter, Catherine Cabot, played by Sandra Dee, who had been Lana's daughter in *Imitation of Life.* Unable to get a divorce, Lana plots with the doctor to murder her husband by injecting an air bubble into his veins.

Once again, she was plotting with a lover to murder her husband, evoking *The Postman Always Rings Twice.*

"This will be my first role as a drawing room menace," Quinn told Kirk Douglas, who had recently co-starred with him in *Last Train from Gun Hill* (1959). Knowing that he was miscast, Quinn signed on anyway, telling Douglas, "It's the money, comrade, money, money, money."

As it turned out, Quinn was right: The role was wrong for him. As *Time* magazine noted, "His speech was oddly strangled, and his general acting was that of a beaten prizefighter who routinely protests a decision he knows to have been fair."

Before he had established himself as a Hollywood star, Quinn had played an Indian, a Mafia don, a Hawaiian chief, a Filipino freedom fighter, a Chinese guerilla, and an Arab sheik, among other varied roles.

[Quinn was born in Chihuahua, Mexico, to a Mexican mother with Indian blood and an immigrant father from Ireland. The family later came to the U.S., where as a young boy, Quinn picked walnuts in El Paso, harvested tomatoes in San Jose, and, as a "Chicano," ran with gangs in the Mexican slums of Los Angeles. For a time, he played the saxophone at the street corner rallies of Aimee Semple McPherson, the most famous evangelist of her era.

In just a few years, he'd be in Hollywood, hanging out with John Barrymore and "fucking Mae West" (his words). She'd cast him as a Latin gigolo in her play, Clean Beds.*]*

When he got to know Lana, he told her, "Back then, I wanted to be Napoléon, Michelangelo, Shakespeare, Picasso, Martin Luther, and Jack Dempsey—all rolled into one body."

By 1937, he'd married Katherine DeMille, the adopted daughter of Cecil B. DeMille. Regrettably, their little son, Christopher Anthony, drowned in the swimming pool of W.C. Fields.

When Lana began emoting on camera with Quinn, and as he nuzzled her neck, she was well aware of his reputation in Hollywood as a master seducer of movie stars, ranging from Carole Lombard to Shelley Winters. While making *Blood and Sand* with Rita Hayworth in 1941, he'd seduced her, too, and also agreed to lie on the casting couch of the gay director, George Cukor, who later boasted about the size of Quinn's penis.

Lovers colluding and trapped in the murder of her inconvenient husband.

Above, Lana, as an *haute* diva ("I am a movie star!") draped in mink, with Anthony Quinn, spruced up as a society doctor who kills.

As Evelyn Keyes, "Scarlett's O'Hara's Younger Sister," said, "There was simply too much of Tony—yes, down there, too."

Quinn's manly charms did not fail to attract the attention of Lana. Ross Hunter said, "Before the first week of filming, Quinn was making visits to Lana's dressing room. I even asked her if Quinn had exaggerated his sexual prowess, as so many men do. I should know! She assured me he's hot as a firecracker."

On the set, Quinn introduced Lana to Anna May Wong, who had emerged from retirement after eleven years to play her mysterious maid, "Tani," in *Portrait in Black*.

Lana asked her why she'd been absent from the screen for so long.

"My father told me not to be photographed too much or else I'd lose my soul." After a long and distinguished career, *Portrait* would be her last film role, as she died the following year (1961).

Wong and Quinn were old friends, having worked together before, co-starring in such movies as *Daughter of Shanghai* (1937) and *Dangerous to Know* (1938).

Although born in Los Angeles, Wong became the first Asian American actress to gain international renown and was labeled as "the first Chinese American movie star."

Lana still had enough star power to make demands, and she successfully urged Hunter to cast her dear friend, Virginia Grey. He gave her the small part of "Miss Lee," and the actress made the most of her role as a secretary.

Lloyd Nolan was cast as Lana's husband, Matthew Cabot, a dying shipping magnate lying in a hospital bed stroking his Siamese cat. He's still trying to hold onto his shipping empire with the help of Howard Mason (Richard Basehart), his lawyer.

Sandra Dee had played Lana's daughter in *Imitation of Life*, but in *Portrait,* she was her stepdaughter, Catherine Cabot. Behind Dee's back, Lana told Grey, "She's the new blonde on the block. Hollywood's getting a new crop. As strange as it seems, Marilyn Monroe in a few years is going to be forty."

Over lunch, Dee told Lana, "The last man I'm going to marry is a man in show business. They're selfish, unreliable, and make lousy husbands. A Hollywood type marriage is not for me."

The next time Lana heard of Dee's marital status was when she read in the newspaper that she'd married singer Bobby Darin, who definitely was in show business. The press dubbed Darin and Dee as "the dream lovers"—that is, until reality set in.

When Lana met Richard Basehart, he was just ending his marriage to the Italian actress, Valentina Cortese. She found his

In 1960, just minutes before the explosion of "flower power" and the hippie movement, Sandra Dee—portrayed above in *Portrait in Black*—was critiqued for dressing like a young nubile twenty-something who never evolved from the tastes and fashion aesthetics of her cinematic mother and the Eisenhower era.

deep, distinctive voice and good looks appealing, but, according to Grey, she made no attempt to go after him. "Actually, I was the one who went after Richard, but he turned me down."

An Italian American born in Brooklyn, John Saxon was cast as Blake Richards, a tugboat owner who is the fiancé of Lana's stepdaughter.

Henry Willson had seen a picture of the handsome Saxon on a magazine cover and had contacted him with a familiar line, "Do you want to be in pictures?"

Willson went after him, promising him to get him a movie role. Meeting him for the first time, the agent said, "He looks like a male Sophia Loren, age twelve." Saxon was seventeen at the time.

Portrait in Black was filmed against the dramatic backdrop of San Francisco. As usual, Lana made a glamorous screen presence, especially in one scene where she is shown wearing a big white orchid on her black sequined gown and adorned with her favorite diamonds.

In the film, in the aftermath of Nolan's murder, the homicidal lovers, Lana and Quinn, think that they've gotten away with it. Then, anonymous letters arrive, nailing them as the murderers.

Suspicion falls on Nolan's daughter (Dee); his lawyer (Basehart); and the Chinese housekeeper (Wong). Lana and Quinn finally decide that Basehart is sending the threatening letters and that he will also have to be eliminated. Basehart is murdered, this time the suspicion centering on Saxon.

Even with Basehart out of the way, the letters keep coming. Near the end of the film, Quinn manages to make Lana confess that she is the one sending those letters. She believes that she can hold onto him based on their shared guilt and their murderous dark secret.

Dee eavesdrops on their dialogue wherein their collaboration in the murder of both her father and his lawyer is expressed, and Quinn goes after her. She eludes him, and he falls to his death from a window ledge. That leaves Lana to face the grim reality of a lifetime in prison, or possibly the electric chair.

***

Before the release of *Portrait in Black*, Hunter sent most of its cast, including Lana, on a publicity tour through key cities which included New York and Chicago. It became a box office success, although critics, for the most part, blasted it.

Variety attacked it as "a contrived murder melodrama with psychological character interplay that is more psycho than logical." *Cue* magazine pronounced it "Highly polished and generally incredible. The high-class killings are done amid the lushest settings and the most expensive costumes."

An unusual appraisal came from a critic on London, where *Portrait in Black* had once served as a stage vehicle for Diana Wynyard, a famous actress in the West End.

Susan Mann, writing in *Women's Mirror*, said: "There she is in *Portrait in Black*, Lana Turner, as ravishing and wildly improbable as ever. The moment she slipped her mink coat carelessly around her shoulders and rushed out to meet a secret lover, leaving her bedridden husband behind, I breathed a sigh of luxurious relief. To me, she's the *grande dame* of tormented heroines. She used to turn up in film after film; so did Bette Davis and Joan Crawford. Neither Joan or Bette have been filming lately. So Lana Turner has taken over as the top representative of my favorite species of celluloid Queen Bee."

***

Lana had lost out on playing the role of Maggie the Cat in Tennessee Williams' *Cat on a Hot Tin Roof.* That part had gone to her friend, Elizabeth Taylor. In competing for the role, she'd had a brief fling with the film's co-star, Paul Newman.

Once again, she made a final stab at appearing as a Tennessee Williams heroine in *Sweet Bird of Youth.* There weren't that many good roles for an actress of a certain age, and she wanted to see why the play was generating such excitement on Broadway.

The play had opened on March 10, 1959 at the Martin Beck Theatre in Manhattan, with Geraldine Page starring as Alexandra del Lago and Paul Newman as the hustler, Chance Wayne.

Lana came back into Newman's life when she became one of the many actresses who flocked to see Tennessee's new play.

She phoned the playwright and agreed to meet him for a drink at Sardi's before the curtain went up. They laughed about his long-ago attempt *[described in Chapter Ten of this book]* to write "a celluloid brassiere" for her, a reference to her movie *Marriage Is a Private Affair.]*

He spoke about his dismissal, and she chimed in, "MGM and I parted ways, too. There was no one to show me to the gate. But if they buy the screen rights for *Sweet Bird,* maybe I'll return to the studio."

That night at the performance, Tennessee noted that Lana studied Page's every movement and expression "like a hawk. She was already rehearsing for the movie version."

After watching the play, Lana suggested that it might have to be "cleaned up for the screen."

She was all charm and grace when Tennessee escorted her backstage for a reunion with Newman. Right in front of the playwright, she kissed Newman. It was a long and lingering, open-mouthed kiss that forced her to repair her makeup in the mirror of his dressing room.

"I'm all alone in New York," she told him in front of Tennessee. "I'm so dependent on a man. But aren't most women

Geraldine Page, an aging actress, pays for the sexual services of a younger man, Paul Newman, in the film version of Tennessee Williams' *Sweet Bird of Youth.*

One can only wonder how Lana, as an older actress, might have fared in her place?

like me?"

"I can definitely assure you that most women aren't like Lana Turner," he said.

It was agreed that Tennessee would take both of them to dinner at Sardi's before he had to go elsewhere. Lana wanted to go dancing later, and Newman agreed to escort her.

Later at Sardi's, all heads turned as the famous trio made their entrance. Newman seemed indifferent to all the attention, but Lana and Tennessee basked in the glow.

Over dinner, Tennessee appeared drunk or drugged, and he made a startling revelation: He was going to Cuba.

"You'd better stay out of there," Newman warned him. "You could be kidnapped and held for ransom."

"If that's what it takes to come together with Fidel Castro, I'll take that risk," he assured them. "I dream at night of getting raped by him. I'm willing to take the risk."

Lana told him that she found a rape by Castro a ghoulish idea, and she feared for his safety. "We need you to write dramas for Paul and me in our future."

After dinner, Tennessee told them farewell, and tottered off into the night. "I have a date with a hustler," he confessed. "The most expensive in New York. Five-hundred dollars a night instead of the usual twenty-five."

At a nightclub uptown, a hush fell over the patrons when "the most beautiful couple in Manhattan" entered. She looked gorgeous sheathed in a body-clinging white gown that was slit high up one side and low down the front. Her blonde hair was cropped short.

Dancing in Newman's arms, she told him, "Everybody is looking at us. We'd make a fabulous pair on the screen."

"Everybody is looking at YOU," he corrected her. "To attract attention, I'll have to take off my jacket, shirt, and undershirt."

"Later, darling," she whispered to him.

He never shared the details of what happened to them later that night. But he took her back to her suite and didn't leave until the following morning.

He did admit to Tennessee two nights later, "I found her clinging and desperate. The next morning, as I was heading out, she delivered a shocker."

"You may not know it now, but one day in the not-so-distant future, you are going to be my next husband."

Of course, that never happened. Neither did her chance to play Alexandra del Lago in *Sweet Bird of Youth*. Both Newman and Geraldine Page repeated their stage roles on screen.

***

Lana was excited to learn that she was being offered the lead role in *By Love Possessed* (1961), whose script would be adapted from the best-selling novel by James Gould Cozzens. It had won the William Dean Howells Award "as the most distinguished work of fiction published during the last five years," although *Time* magazine labeled it "the worst good novel of the past decade."

Lana was paid $300,000 to star in the movie, plus a percentage of the profits. As always, she wanted to know who her leading man would be, and was told that Robert Taylor had been offered the role of her lover. She anticipated working with him again. It had been a long time since the two of them had made love on and off the screen in *Johnny Eager.*

She was also told that the scenario had been written by Charles Schnee, the Oscar-winning writer of one of her three most famous films, *The Bad and the Beautiful.*

He'd been given the awesome task of dramatizing Cozzens' 575-page novel, which was mostly filled with "twenty-five years of soul-searching among its characters. Much of the novel had been revealed

through flashbacks and introspections, not ideal material for film-making.

The final script spun around rape, suicide, embezzlement, and sexual unfulfillment, the movie drawing comparisons to *Peyton Place.*

Lana invited the director, John Sturges, and the producer, Walter Mirisch, to her home to discuss the upcoming film. It was to be a joint venture of Mirisch Pictures and Seven Arts, with distribution by United Artists.

Director Sturges had just completed *The Magnificent Seven* (1960), starring Yul Brynner and Steve McQueen. In time, it would become a film classic. He'd also directed Spencer Tracy in *Bad Day at Black Rock* (1955), for which he received a Best Director Oscar nomination.

Born to a Jewish family in New York, Mirisch had founded Mirisch Productions, an independent film company that would win three Best Picture Academy Awards—*The Apartment* (1960), *West Side Story* (1961), and *In the Heat of the Night* (1967). His film version of the mammoth James Michener novel, *Hawaii* (1966), was nominated for seven Oscars.

The good news was followed by some bad news. Sturges called to tell Lana that Robert Taylor had dropped out because of other commitments. She tried to conceal her disappointment when he told her that he had been replaced by Efrem Zimbalist, Jr. He was hardly a name she knew, or a career with which she was familiar. She set out to learn what she could about him.

Born to Russian Jewish parents in New York, the handsome young actor had gone to Yale, later serving in the U.S. Army during the war for five years, during which time he'd won the Purple Heart.

He'd made his Broadway debut in *The Rugged Path,* starring with Spencer Tracy. By 1956, he'd landed at the gates to Warner Brothers, where he signed a contract. After that, he'd made both feature films and performed in TV roles, starring with James Garner in the hit series, *Maverick.*

Lana had already sized up "the sexual potential" of her leading man. But in spite of his good looks and seductive appeal, Zimbalist seemed off limits to her predatory eyes. She was told that he was "quite spiritual," having converted to Christianity.

Even before rehearsals began, Lana was informed that Sturges had not liked the scenario written by Schnee and had employed three "script doctors"—William Roberts, Isobel Lennart, and Ketti Frings. When Schnee read what this trio had done to his scenario, he threat-

Lana "possessed" by then-newcomer Efrem Zimbalist Jr.

ened to sue to have his name removed from the credits. A compromise was reached: Upon the film's release, he was identified as "John Dennis."

In a quiet New England town, there are three partners in the local law firm: Zimbalist as Arthur Winner; Jason Robards as Julius Penrose; and Thomas Mitchell playing Noah Tuttle, the aging senior partner.

Winner is a solid citizen married to Barbara Bel Geddes (Clarissa) until he develops a passionate affair with Lana in her role as Marjorie Penrose, the wife of his law partner, Julius.

He is impotent because of a car accident, but he won't give his wife a divorce. He tells her, "Go find what you want somewhere else. Just don't tell me about it."

It all works out in the end, as the errant spouses return to their respective mates. However, the film never answers the question: What is a hot-to-trot love-hungry female like Lana going to do for sex?

During the first week of rehearsals, Lana met her strong supporting cast, headed by the third male lead, veteran actor Jason Robards, Jr. He had recently married Lauren Bacall, the widow of Humphrey Bogart.

Cast as the wife of Zimbalist in the film, Bel Geddes was reduced to a very minor role. In her heyday, she'd starred as Maggie the Cat on Broadway in *Cat on a Hot Tin Roof*. Two of her greatest films had been *I Remember Mama* (1948) and Alfred Hitchcock's *Vertigo* (1958).

Once again, Lana was cast with Susan Kohner, the daughter of her agent, having recently completed *Imitation of Life*. Lana praised her for her talent and predicted a great future for her in film.

That did not happen. In 1964, she married John Weitz, the writer and menswear designer, and retired from the screen.

Thomas Mitchell had played Scarlett O'Hara's father in *Gone With the Wind* (1939), and had won a Best Supporting Actor Oscar, cast as the drunken Doc Boone in *Stagecoach* (1939) with John Wayne. He had become the first actor to win a triple crown: Academy Award, Tony, and Emmy.

In the film, he played a fading, aging lawyer, Noah Tuttle, who is guilty of having embezzled funds from the firm to repay "a debt of honor."

A native of Tennessee, the perpetually suntanned George Hamilton was growing tired of hearing reporters claim that he resembled Warren Beatty. When he met Lana, he had starred in the romantic comedy, *Where the Boys Are* (1960). Before that, he'd starred in a more serious film, *Crime and Punishment U.S.A.* (1959), a re-imagining of the Fyodor Dostoyevsky novel, his performance winning him a Golden Globe.

Hamilton was assigned the role of Warren Winner, Zimbalist's son, a Harvard Law School graduate forced to enter his father's law firm. He becomes sexually involved with Kohner's character, Helen Detweiler.

In his memoir, *Don't Mind If I Do,* he described her character as a "virgin orphan heiress client." After he deflowers her, she commits suicide by drinking a can of cleaning fluid.

In that same memoir, Hamilton recorded his impression of working with Lana. "She was the most notorious woman in America right then, coming off the murder of gangster Johnny Stompanato. All the rumors were that Lana had stabbed him to death and gotten her teenage daughter to take the fall."

"But those rumors were never spoken anywhere near the Great One," Hamilton wrote. "Not that Lana and I hung out. Instead, she hung me out, forcing me to do at least thirty takes of a scene in which all I had to do was help her on with her mink coat. The idea was to slide the mink to her neck, then let it drop away. Having learned from the master of the game, I thus became adept at putting an endangered species on an endangered species. I had a future in cloakrooms if all else failed."

By Love Possessed opened in Manhattan in July of 1961. It also made another debut, becoming the first movie ever shown on the regularly scheduled first-class flights of Trans World Airlines.

Reviews for the most part were poor, critic Brandon Gill writing in *The New Yorker,* "*By Love Possessed* contains few traces of filmable material. It's a very talky affair."

Robert Freund, in a review in Fort Lauderdale, cited Lana "for playing her usual role—and doing it well, the dame with surface elegance glossing a wanton brassiness."

***

Since the 1950s, Lana and Bob Hope had been friends, and had worked together on television, but never in a feature film. She was surprised when he phoned her and asked her if she would co-star with him in the romantic comedy, *Bachelor in Paradise,* to be released in 1961, which would mark her second picture that year, following in the wake of *By Love Possessed.*

"What's the problem?" she asked. "Lucille Ball not available?"

Talking it over with Hope, she decided to accept the role of Rosemary Howard, a single woman living among married couples in suburbia.

There was another reason she wanted to do the film, and that was for business purposes. It would mark her return to MGM, a studio that had not renewed her contract back in 1956.

However, before leaving the studio, she had arrived at a rather loose agreement that for the next five years, she'd make one picture a year for the studio at a relatively modest salary.

Although she did not follow through with that agreement, based on her agreement to film this final movie for MGM, she'd be allowed to collect $92,000 from MGM's pension fund.

Bachelor in Paradise cast Hope as Adam J. Niles, a writer who has penned books on the sex lives of every nationality from the Greeks to the Swedes. After months of "research" overseas, he returns to America to face a daunting problem. Because of his crooked business manager, he owes a million dollars in back taxes to the IRS. His publisher wants him to write a book, *How the Americans Live*, about the sex lives of the "happy couples" living in postwar suburbia.

To facilitate that, the publisher had arranged for Hope to move into a rented home in Paradise Village, a modern suburban housing development awash with such innovations as big supermarkets, gadgets like a garbage disposal, babysitters, the hazards of the new freeways, and bored housewives waiting claustrophobically at home as their husbands labor frantically at white-collar jobs.

Hope moves in, causing speculation, since he's a bachelor.

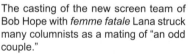

The casting of the new screen team of Bob Hope with *femme fatale* Lana struck many columnists as a mating of "an odd couple."

One headline read: LANA TURNER TO PLAY STRAIGHT MAN TO BOB HOPE.

Of course, the assumption of any sexual chemistry between Hope and Lana would not be palatable to most viewers today, but, after all, it was only a movie. It might have been the type of comedy Doris Day would make with either Cary Grant or James Garner. As anticipated, Hope was ready to deliver his one-liners and his by now familiar facial expressions.

Lana confessed to Grey, "I think sometime, years ago, that Bob made a pass at me. I didn't catch it. I was afraid that if he took me to bed, I'd end up laughing hysterically. I'm told that men don't like that."

"I wonder why," Grey answered.

At the age of forty-one, Lana appeared perfectly coiffed with makeup by her friend, Del Armstrong, wearing dresses and gowns by Helen Rose. She was photographed in CinemaScope and MetroColor by Joe Ruttenberg, who made her look years younger.

Hope had warned her, "This *Bachelor* is not Oscar material." In fact, however, Henry Mancini, who wrote the title song, would be nominated for an Academy Award for his music.

Some viewers thought that Lana looked like a stylishly dressed "robot," but she does break loose in one scene. After downing one too many Polynesian cocktails, she takes to the dance floor to perform a hip-swinging hula, her fun moment on screen.

The best review for *Bachelor in Paradise* derived from Bob Considine, who claimed that it was "Bob Hope's funniest movie ever." Of course, that was gross exaggeration. Hope himself told friends, "I'm not proud of this one. Of course, Lana, as always, looked luscious."

***

Finished forever with MGM, Lana received an unexpected offer for a Paramount release, *Who's Got the Action?* It would be the only film she'd make in 1962 before disappearing from the screen for three years.

As with Bob Hope, *Who's Got the Action?* would be another "odd couple" pairing, this time with singer-actor Dean Martin, the "King of Cool." He was the No. 2 rodent in the "Rat Pack" led by Frank Sinatra.

The script about betting on horse races was by the film's director, Jack Rose, who based it on the novel, *Four Horse Players Are Missing,* by Alexander Rose (no relation).

This wacky racetrack yarn would be promoted not based on what happened on the track, but in the boudoir.

Rose picked Daniel Mann to direct, which came as a surprise to Lana. *Who's Got the Action?* seemed like a lightweight comedy farce for a respected director whose reputation had been built on such distinguished films as William Inge's *Come Back, Little Sheba* (1952) with Burt Lancaster and Shirley Booth; Tennessee Williams' *The Rose Tattoo* (1955) with Lancaster and Anna Magnani; *I'll Cry Tomorrow* (1955) with Susan Hayward in the saga of the alcoholic singer, Lillian Roth; and *BUtterfield 8* (1960), an Oscar winner for Elizabeth Taylor.

The plot has Lana playing Melanie Flood, a dizzy but engaging socialite and wannabe author, married to happy-go-

IT'S THE MOST RIOTOUS BEDTIME STORY EVER

DEAN MARTIN ! LANA TURNER
the movable object   the irresistible force

WHO'S GOT THE ACTION?
TECHNICOLOR
...EDDIE ALBERT·WALTER MATTHAU·PAUL FORD with TALBOT

lucky Steve Flood, as charmingly depicted by Dean Martin. At first, she
thinks his obsession is with other
women, but soon learns that it involves gambling on horses.

She comes up with a far-fetched
scheme that plot-wise doesn't make a
lot of sense. Martin is losing a lot of
their money at the tracks.

She turns to his law partner, Clint
Morgan (Eddie Albert), to help her in
her scheme to secretly become her
husband's "bookie."

That way, his losses would be
paid to her.

Her plot backfires when, unexpectedly, Steve starts to score big wins
on his bets, and as his (clandestine)
bookie, she has to raise the money to
pay him off.

Her financial position becomes
more hazardous when he involves two

In *Who's Got the Action?*, Lana got to appear in a bathtub scene for the fourth time
in a movie.

Before that, she'd been bubble-bathed in
Ziegfeld Girl, *The Merry Widow*, and *The
Lady Takes a Flyer*. She told Mann, "Why
not call me Bubbles?"

horse-playing, gambling-addicted judges, portrayed by Paul Ford and John Mc-
Giver. One reviewer called Ford "hilarious as a bird-brained, spaniel-eyed llama-
lipped pony player."

To raise the money she needs to keep "the action" going, Lana, as the secret
bookie, is forced to sell her jewelry and their furniture.

Lana's role in this gambling network attracts the attention of syndicate boss
Tony Gagoots (Walter Matthau), who is furious about losing bets. He decides his
boys will have to eliminate the competition, in this case Melania (Lana herself).

Matthau's role—as was much of the picture—was inspired by Damon Runyon.
Matthau delivers such lines as *"Give disgenulman eighteen tousan' dolluhs frum petty
cash."*

As it so happens, Gagoot's girlfriend, "Saturday Knight" (the very charming
and funny Nita Talbot, who stole most of the scenes she appeared in) lives next
door to Lana and buys many of her possessions. A New Yorker, Talbot, a sort of
latter-day Eve Arden, usually played "slick chicks" and sharp-witted career girls.

Since it's a movie, everything works out happily in the end. Lana weans Martin
from the horses and even is able to reclaim her furniture.

Even though she had passed the big 4-0, a burial ground for most Hollywood
female stars, Lana managed to look gorgeous throughout the movie in gowns and
costumes designed by Edith Head, who had previously dressed virtually every
major star in Hollywood.

Both Eddie Albert and his wife Margo, were cast in the film, with Margo playing Rosa, Melania's wacky Hispanic maid. Both Albert and Margo had had some
rough rides in their careers, ever since they landed on the Red Channels list in the

1950s.

The movie did not get good reviews. *The New York Morning Telegraph* wrote, "Dean Martin, Eddie Albert, and Lana Turner go through their paces with great good will. None of the film can be taken seriously, a good deal of it is as ridiculous as it is preposterous." *Time* magazine wrote, "The syndicate has the last laugh in this yak derby, but the customers get most of the others. The film is not the merriest 'oatsmobile' that ever came down the track, but Dean and Lana make a surprisingly smooth entry."

Most critics panned the movie for not getting out of the starting gate.

***

Nicknamed the "King of Cool," Dean Martin was one of the most popular singers and actors in America when he teamed up with Lana to make *Who's Got the Action?*

Ashe first met him in Los Angeles early in his career when he was teamed with comedian Jerry Lewis. She was seen in the audience at a club called Slapsy Maxie's, which was a popular spot, attracting many stars such as Doris Day and Danny Kaye.

At the time, Martin was married to his second wife, Jeanne Biegger, a model and former Orange Bowl Queen from Coral Gables, Florida.

But that didn't stop his womanizing, something he shared in common with another of Lana's beaux, Frank Sinatra.

"The most beautiful broads were crazy for Dean," Lewis said. "In truth, I fucked more than he did, but it was always like they wanted to burp me."

Ann Sheridan, one of his early movie star conquests, said, "Dean was a love 'em, leave 'em kind of guy. He was a bastard, all wine and candlelight at night. For your efforts in the boudoir, you got a pat on the ass in the morning, right before he headed out the door."

Sinatra is credited as the man who fixed Lana up with Dean in encounters that included a long weekend in Palm Springs. He joked to Martin and some of his other "Rat Packers," like Peter Lawford, "As is well known, Lana seems to like Italian pepperoni, the bigger the better."

Martin's biographer, William Schoell, wrote: "Lana had the hots for Dean and wasn't afraid to let him—or

A strong supporting cast zestfully poured themselves into their roles as eccentrics indulging Lana in her (adorable) whims.

Above, Nita Talbot, playing a gun moll, and Eddie Albert.

575

anyone else in the room—know how she felt."

Years before she co-starred with him in a film, Lana showed up with Martin at such clubs as Herman Hover's Ciro's, later going to a late night party at Hover's home after the club closed. After a wild night of heavy drinking, Lana with Martin would slip out the door at around 2AM in the morning and disappear into the night.

***

One afternoon, Lana encountered Marilyn Monroe on the set, heading to Dean's bungalow. The two blondes had not seen each other since the days when Monroe was trying to get her career launched in Hollywood, using Lana as one of her inspirations.

"Lana, you look gorgeous," Monroe said. "*Still.* As you remember, I once used you as a role model before I created my own screen persona. And now I'm a bigger star than you are—that's Hollywood for you!"

"The fires of September" had cooled to a burning ember when Dean Martin and Lana reunited on the set of her latest movie.

He told Peter Lawford, "Lana is still beautiful, even a bit sexy, but she's become a bit matronly for me. As you know, I like 'em young and fresh. I hope she doesn't demand that I fuck her regularly, like we used to do in the good ol' days."

"All stars flicker out," Lana said. "You'll find that out one day."

"I don't want to think about that," Monroe said.

Then Marilyn reported that she was going to be the star of a new movie with Martin as her leading man. "It's called *Something's Got to Give.*" She explained that it was a remake of *My Favorite Wife,* the 1940 film that had starred Cary Grant and Irene Dunne.

"Which role do you play? Lana asked with a smirk.

"The Irene Dunne part, silly," Monroe said. "Gotta go." Then she tottered off on high heels.

That afternoon, Lana told her makeup man, Del Armstrong, "Dean might make it through the picture, but I don't think Marilyn will. She's coming unglued."

She was right. Marilyn was murdered in August of 1962 after the picture had been shut down, her death still a mystery.

***

Lana's next movie, *Love Has Many Faces,* set by Columbia for a 1965 release, evoked those women's pictures of the 1940s.

The plot by Marguerite Roberts focuses mainly on Kit, who is married to a former beach boy and hustler, Pete Jordan (Cliff Robertson). Kit is pursued by Hank Walker (Hugh O'Brien), another sexy hustler who preys on older women, often blackmailing them.

One line in the movie was drawn from Lana's own life. "She was meant to have seven husbands, and I'm next." It was uttered by Hank.

To complicate matters, yet another "beach boy" has washed up on the sands dead. Lt. Riccardo Andrade (Enrique Lucero) sets out to investigate his death. It is discovered that he was a former paid lover of Kit, who had given him a bracelet engraved LOVE IS THIN ICE.

The dead American's deserted girlfriend, Carol Lambert (Stefanie Powers), flew in from Detroit to learn what she can about her former boyfriend's death. As a subplot, she falls in love with Pete, Kit's husband.

There is another subplot, as Hank and his friend pursue two American women on vacation—Margot Eliot (Ruth Roman) and Irene Talbot (Virginia Grey). Lana had insisted that her friend, Grey, be cast as one of the aging women with an eye for young beach boys on the make.

Roman, known as the "Ice Beauty" in many films of the 1950s, was at the nadir of her career after a successful run of A-list pictures in the past decade. Those included her most memorable, Alfred Hitchcock's *Strangers on a Train* (1951), co-starring Farley Granger and Robert Walker.

Near the climax of the film, Kit and her hus-

Still looking gorgeous in a bathing suit, Lana was cast as one of the richest women in the world, buying male flesh in Acapulco.

Here she has a tense scene with Cliff Robertson, whom she'd "purchased" and married.

This time, Lana's competition was a brunette, Stefanie Powers. It was speculated that Lana was jealous of the screen beauty, a star of tomorrow, all fresh-faced and beautiful, as Lana herself was drifting into middle age.

band go to a Mexican ranch where bulls are trained. Here, she meets Manuel Perez, an actual bullfighter played by Jaime Bravo. Carlos Montalban, the older brother of Ricardo Montalban, was cast as Don Julain. Lana talked with him about working with his brother on *Latin Lovers*.

Kit has seen a relationship developing between Pete and Carol. Exasperated, she rides off on a horse but falls from it and is gored in the stomach by a rampaging bull. This near-fatal accident seems to rekindle Pete's love for his wife, and he rushes to her side to see her through recovery. A wiser Carol returns to Detroit.

A large selling point of the movie, views of which were included in the advertising, was the fabulous wardrobe created for Lana by Edith Head, who had designed her wardrobe for *Who's Got the Action?*

Producer Jerry Brasler had ads released with headlines that screamed LANA TURNER IN A MILLION DOLLAR EDITH HEAD WARDROBE.

During its filming in Mexico, Lana may have taken the role of Kit Jordan too literally, as noted by press agent George Nichols.

Del Armstrong, her makeup man and confidant, claimed, "Lana was happy working again in such a glamorous role. As a fringe benefit, she had two of the handsomest leading men in Hollywood to enjoy after dark, each of them very sexy, and very available, each unattached at the time they worked with Lana—not that that would have stopped her."

Depicted above, Lana with Cliff Robertson.

"Acapulco reminded Lana of some of the good times in her life, as well as a nightmare or two, especially when she spent time here with Johnny Stompanato. It was difficult for me to believe that Lana drank during working hours, but she did. She also had romantic flings, as she was very lonely, a frightened child. Alcohol gave her the confidence to face life every day."

The entire cast, especially Grey, became aware of Lana's flings with both Cliff Robertson and Hugh O'Brian, as well as the charismatic bullfighter, Jaime Bravo.

Hugh O'Brian had fascinated Lana ever since she'd watched an episode of his hit NBC-TV series, *The Life and Legend of Wyatt Earp* (1955-61). She learned that he'd been the roommate of Stompanato when they'd attended military school together.

In *Love Has Many Faces*, O'Brien appears in a tight-fitting bathing suit "that made things—or rather his thing—rather obvious," Lana said to Grey.

Lana knew that O'Brien had never married, although he'd had certain affairs, including one with singer Margaret Whiting.

As regards his inspiration for how he interpreted the character he played, O'Brien admitted to the director, "I'm basing my character on everything I've heard about Stompanato."

She was even more intrigued by Robertson, who had appeared as Lt. John F.

Kennedy in the 1963 PT 109. After his rather thankless role in *Love Has Many Faces,* he would go on to win a Best Actor Oscar for his 1968 role in the movie *Charly.*

Her affair with Robertson occurred right before he married the elegant and rich Dina Merrill, actress and Post Cereals heiress.

He was a skilled pilot and one weekend, when they were free, he rented a private plane and flew her along the western coast of Mexico. They landed at a cactus-studded outpost, a modest inn, where he first seduced her.

Back in Acapulco, Lana had a somewhat chilly relationship with Stefanie Powers. She had just appeared in the 1966 film, *Die! Die! My Darling* (released in Britain as *Fanatic)* starring Tallulah Bankhead.

Born in Hollywood, Powers was 21 years younger than Lana. And both seemed to have an eye for Jaime Bravo, a well-known matador of his era, known for his skill as a bullfighter and his many widely publicized celebrity affairs.

Lana was a devotee of bullfights, and an "aficionado" of Bravo. He'd received rave reviews from her friend, Ava Gardner, who had seduced the handsome young man in 1957.

The first time he took Lana to bed, she reported to Grey, "Jaime shares something in common with the bull. When he appears in that bullfighter costume, he doesn't need padding like some matadors."

Shooting *Love Has Many Faces* wasn't all about lovemaking. For a week, Lana came down with some mysterious virus and was unable to report to work. At one point, her temperature hovered at 104 degrees. Even after she returned to work, she had a relapse and had to go to bed again.

Another Dubious Day in Paradise

Depicted above are Hugh O'Brian (left) and Ron Husmann, cast as two omnisexual and amoral beach boys who peddle their flesh to older women.

Love Has Many Faces was a precursor of such later novels as *Midnight Cowboy* and *Butterflies in Heat* about young men who hustle and their dynamic with women (or men) they service in sex-for-cash deals.

Her career fading, Ruth Roman was cast as an aging American heiress who goes to Acapulco for a vacation and hooks up with the beach boy and hustler, Hugh O'Brian, who really has his eye trained on bigger and richer game–Lana herself.

Reacting to that, Bresler began secret negotiations with both Joan Crawford and Susan Hayward as replacements for Lana. But she recovered in time.

In spite of Lana's highly advertised million dollar wardrobe, *Love Has Many Faces* was not a success at the box office. However, one critic found it, "the perfect antidote for bored housewives who thrive at the sight of beautiful clothes and emotional turmoil in opulent surroundings."

One of the leading film critics of her era, Judith Crist, wrote, "It's a soapy melodrama, the kind of film that over the years has given the term 'a woman's picture' all the opprobrium it bears."

Another critic dismissed it as "a lushly wrapped dime novel escapade on a Mexican beach and a luxurious villa." Yet another reviewer found it "a sordid romantic tale of the beach boy set."

After the movie failed at the box office, Lana knew she had to have a good strong role, as well as a hit movie, if she were to continue with her film career.

***

As the 1960s marched forward, Hollywood was a radically different town from what it had been in 1937, when a plucky little starlet arrived at the gates of Warner Brothers. The Golden Age had ended, and each year brought more and more deaths of her friends and lovers of long ago.

She was desperate for the right role. Her brand of movies, called "a woman's picture," just weren't being made any more in this era of Dustin Hoffman, Steve McQueen, Joan Collins, Jane Fonda, and Faye Dunaway.

She had rechristened her company Eltee Productions, and in the mid-1960s, she searched for the right script.

Lana had had such great success working with Ross Hunter, she turned once again to him to revive a tired old property of yesterday.

A four-handkerchief "soaper," *Madame X* was first presented on stage in 1908 by the French playwright, Alexandre Bisson. It was one of the prototypes for the many "fallen woman" plots that followed. The role was cited as one of the best known examples of the literary tradition of portraying the mother figure as "being excessively punished for a slight deviation from her maternal role."

In 1916, Pathé filmed it with Dorothy Donnelly in the lead role. Four years later, Samuel Goldwyn put his stamp on it, casting Pauline Frederick— a celebrated star of the silent screen—in

WHEN IN SOUTHERN CALIFORNIA VISIT UNIVERSAL CITY STUDIO

THERE WAS ALWAYS A MAN...NEVER A NAME!

LANA TURNER as *Madame X*

A ROSS HUNTER production / co-starring
JOHN FORSYTHE · RICARDO MONTALBAN
BURGESS MEREDITH · CONSTANCE BENNETT
and KEIR DULLEA / Technicolor®
Screenplay by JEAN HOLLOWAY · Directed by DAVID LOWELL RICH
Produced by ROSS HUNTER · A Ross Hunter-Eltee Universal Picture

580

the role.

More versions were to follow.

In 1929, Lionel Barrymore had directed Ruth Chatterton, one of the reigning stars of early talkies, in the first sound version of *Madame X.*

The only version screened for Lana was a sanitized 1937 remake of the pre-Code version, directed by Samuel Wood and starring Gladys George, with Warren William. The film was released by MGM and did well at the box office.

Lana knew that there was only one producer who could get financing for another remake and that was Ross Hunter. They'd had such success in the past. She met with him, and they agreed to do a remake as a Ross Hunter-Eltee production with Universal releasing it and also financing it.

Hunter went to Douglas Sirk to ask him if he'd direct Lana again, but found him in such ill health it was not possible.

Hunter assigned a former radio actor, Jean Holloway, to pen the script, but after several versions, neither Lana nor Hunter were satisfied. The movie was delayed for three years before shooting began in April of 1965.

When Sirk turned down the job, David Lowell Rich, whose resumé included many television dramas, was signed as director.

This New Yorker helmed 100 films and TV episodes between 1950 and 1987. When Lana met him, he'd just shot *See How They Run* (1964). She considered him "very commercial—just grind them out and under budget." She was shocked when he told the cast and crew that they would have only eight weeks to bring "this soaper in on time."

Whereas she was allowed to look glamorous in the beginning, especially in gowns by Jean Louis, she'd have to age twenty-four years during the course of the film.

Although by now, 1966, most housewives were getting their soap opera fix on TV dramas in the afternoon, Lana and Hunter hoped that the targeted audience, women of Lana's age, would drag their husbands to see *Madame X* in an actual movie house.

The plot of this tired old tear-jerker was familiar to old-time Hollywood people.

In a nutshell, it was the story of a lower class woman, Holly Parker (Lana), who marries into the wealthy Anderson family. Her husband, Clayton Anderson (John Forsythe), has political ambitions and is always away, neglecting her to pursue his career in the diplomatic corps.

A well-known playboy, Phil Benton (Ricardo Montalban), lures her into a tryst. He and Lana had been good friends since they made *Latin Lovers* together.

During one of their encounters, he is killed in an accident. Her venomous mother-in-law (Constance Bennett) becomes aware of it and seizes upon the playboy's death to break up Holly's marriage. She had always detested her daughter-in-law anyway. She convinces her to abandon her family as a means of saving her husband's career and to avoid disgracing her young son.

Holly (Lana) runs away to Europe, and, when her money runs out, sinks into a pit of despair, turning to absinthe and prostitution.

Hunter had lured Constance Bennett out of a twelve-year retirement. The sister of Joan Bennett, she had been a bigtime star in the 1920s and '30s. In the early 1930s, she was the highest-paid actress in Hollywood. Before appearing with Lana, she had starred with some of the biggest names in Hollywood: Cary Grant, Clark Gable, even Greta Garbo.

It seemed inevitable that the blonde goddess of the 1930s, and the blonde goddess of the 1940s and 50s, would be envious of each other when they came together on the set. They did not engage in open warfare, but there was tension between them.

Lana had managed to get Virginia Grey cast in the role of "Mimsy," and as such, she had a front row seat to watch the simmering rivalries between Lana and Bennett.

There was no love lost between Lana and Constance Bennett (right) when they made *Madame X*. But producer Ross Hunter got them to agree to appear with him at the film's premiere.

Madame X would be Bennett's last screen appearance. Shortly after this picture was taken, she collapsed and died from a cerebral hemorrhage at the age of sixty.

"Each actress wanted to be better dressed and better made up than the other," Grey said. "In the movie, they were supposed to dislike each other intensely. Believe me, those two weren't just acting."

Columnist Sheilah Graham didn't endear herself to Lana. She visited the set one afternoon and wrote that Bennett, in her late 50s, looked younger than Lana, even though at that stage of the filming, Lana was beautifully made up and attired.

As a rejoinder to the comments she'd made, Lana called Graham: "Regardless of what you wrote, I'm still here, still going strong. You can't say that for Hedy Lamarr or Rita Hayworth, can you?"

"Lana and Bennett were very competitive in their scenes together," Grey said. "Each actress wanted to be better dressed and better made up than the other. In the movie, they also disliked each other. They weren't acting: They meant it."

As the plot unfolds, Lana's descent into degradation and despair deepens. By now, the plot has moved her into a seedy hotel in Mexico, where she gets involved with Dan Sullivan (Burgess Meredith), a con artist and blackmailer. When he learns of her identity, he concocts a plot where he plans to contact her diplomat husband and reveal her identity to her young son, who has become a lawyer on the rise.

Lana hadn't seen Meredith in years, not since he was married to her friend, Paulette Goddard, and had made a pass at her.

Learning of his scheme, she fatally shoots him and goes on trial for murder, where she is identified as "Madame X."

In one of the ironies so often found in films, the court appoints Clayton Anderson, Jr. (Keir Dullea) as her attorney to defend her on a charge of murder. He doesn't know he's fighting for his mother's life.

Before a verdict comes in, Lana collapses and dies.

She found Dullea, playing her son, quite handsome. "If only I had been fifteen years younger." He was on the dawn of his greatest success: astronaut David Bowman, whom he portrayed in the 1968 film *2001: A Space Odyssey.*

The year he met Lana, he had co-starred with Laurence Olivier, Carol Lynley, and Noël Coward in *Bunny Lake Is Missing (1965).* Lana found Coward's assessment of Dullea a bit cruel: "Keir Dullea, gone tomorrow."

Unlike *Love Has Many Faces,* Lana was not in a seductive mood with any of her leading men. John Forsythe was cast as her husband. She found him good looking but dull. "He was a good family man," she said.

The actor from New Jersey, who signed a contract with Warner Brothers when he was 25, would be married to the same woman, Julie Warren, for fifty-one years. When Lana met him, he was best known for his TV sitcoms, *Bachelor Father.*

Makeup was by her trusted friend, Del Armstrong. Their friendship was tested during the filming of *Madame X* when he had to apply makeup to add some quarter of a century of hard living to her face.

He would not let her look in a mirror when he aged her. When he turned her around and allowed her to evaluate the changes he'd wrought, she screamed in horror. "When my fans see me looking this old, they'll desert me in droves."

Because of the intense production schedule, she and Hunter frequently conflicted, often engaging in bitter arguments where the word "fuck" would pop up.

But at the end of production, she made up with him and even sent him an "epergne" *[a tiered decorative centerpiece]* of lemons. "For some reason, Ross was queer for lemons," she told Grey.

***

Hunter and Lana, hoping for the box office bonanza of *Imitation of Life,* were disappointed by the box office receipts of *Madame X.* Many of the reviews were bad.

Writer René Jordan wrote: "Even the carefully resurrected dream world of the Ross Hunter-Lana Turner Rhinestone melodramas became *passé* in the 'serious' Sixties. Fakery had permeated the real life of the public beyond the saturation point. Blatantly glamourous movies were being rejected with a wave of the hand."

In the *Chicago Tribune,* Clifford Terry claimed, "When Lana Turner takes the stand in the final courtyard scene, her face resembles a Dust Bowl victory garden."

The most devastating review came from Pauline Kael: "Lana Turner is not *Madame X.* She's Brand X. She's not an actress. She's a commodity."

One critic made another bitchy comment: "If you haven't seen a movie since 1930, you may think Lana Turner's *Madame X* is just great."

In the *Los Angeles Times,* Charles Champlin championed Lana's acting in her courtroom scene and in her death-bed performance. "The unsparing, guileless honesty of her performance is very touching."

The Chicago critic, Ann Marsters, claimed, "Corny, perhaps, and mawkish, too, but it plays with a kind of dramatic splendor. I haven't cried so much in years."

In the *Hollywood Reporter,* James Powers wrote, "Only producer Ross Hunter would dare to do a remake of *Madame X,* and it has turned out to be an electrifyingly right decision. A superb cast of players, headed by Lana Turner, takes this rather shabby old piece and gives it immediacy, vigor, and credibility."

In one of her most dramatic scenes in *Madame X,* the young actor, Keir Dullea, cast as Clay Anderson, Jr., is an attorney defending her in court on a murder charge. He doesn't know that *Madame X* is his mother. He develops a compassion for her and fights valiantly to save her from the electric chair.

Fans of Lana have defined poignant moments like this as "four-hanky weepers."

The *London Evening Standard* wrote: "We should be grateful that Hollywood still has the face to make an unabashed weepie with the sluices open."

London critic David Quinland wrote: "One can never remember a more affecting performance by Lana Turner, especially in the latter half of the movie, when she is so much more impressive than one could ever imagine. She is almost entirely captive to a portrayal in which she is utterly deglamourized and says so much with brown eyes that seem old and fathomless.

Film reviewers in Italy told moviegoers to "get out your handkerchiefs." In fact, the picture proved quite popular in Italy. Even though the Academy ignored her, Lana won the David Donatello Award as "Best Foreign Actress" in Rome. Theater owners of Italy presented her with La Perle Verde, the Green Pearl Award, for her fine performance.

***

Near the end of her life, Lana told her friends, "*Madame X* should have won an Oscar. Regrettably, I was lured into making four more feature films, and I even agreed to appear in that hit TV series, *Falcon Crest* (1982-3). I had to appear with that bitch, Jane Wyman, who resented me."

"When I appeared, it became the most highly rated show in the history of nighttime soapers. Wyman was furious and tried to sabotage me. Perhaps she resented that I had fucked Ronald Reagan before she did. I told her she should have hung in with Reagan and she'd be First Lady now, a figure for the history books. As it was, I told her, 'Now you'll be only a footnote in Hollywood history.' For some reason, she didn't like that."

***

In an attempt to hook into the youth culture that had emerged in the turbulent 1960s, Lana agreed to star in *The Big Cube* (1969), the title a reference to sugar cubes spiked with LSD, then all the rage.

The movie threw her into a world of drug parties, psychedelic episodes, rock music, and more nudity than any picture she'd ever made.

It was set for a release through Warner Brothers and Seven Arts, with Tito Davison directing and Lindsley Parsons producing.

It was a low-budget picture shot in

Jane Wyman had long resented Lana.

Tensions flared when producers of Wyman's hit TV series, *Falcon Crest*, hired Lana as its co-star for an appearance as Jacqueline Perrault, earning the highest ratings for the series.

Ferociously territorial, Wyman ordered the producers to "kill off Miss Turner," suggesting that her rival be buried in a coffin in the season's final segment.

Mexico, employing some high-class talent, including Gabriel Figueroa, the foremost cinematographer in Mexico, and the famous "Travilla," who had been the costume designer at 20th Century Fox, dressing many of Tinseltown's biggest stars before beautifully attiring Lana.

She was cast as Adriana Roman, a major star on Broadway, who is retiring to marry Charles Winthrop (Dan O'Herlihy), a business tycoon. Previously, she had starred with him in *Imitation of Life,* and both of them agreed that *The Big Cube* was a comedown for them.

One part of the plot cast Lana in a familiar theme of stepmother vs. stepdaughter. Winthrop's daughter Lisa (Karin Mossberg) resents Lana from the moment she gets emotionally involved with her (somewhat clueless) father. An actress from Sweden, she had not lost her native accent, and spoke with such a thick Swedish accent that her voice had to be dubbed.

ALMOST KILLING LANA: Campy cliffside struggle, fueled by clandestine ingestions of acid, with evil stepdaughter and her hustling boyfriend.

Winthrop is killed in a boating accident, leaving Lana as his heir with the ability to disinherit Lisa if she marries her sleazy boyfriend (George Chakiris). In the 1961 film version of *West Side Story,* he'd played the leader of "The Sharks," a performance that won him a Best Supporting Actor Oscar.

In *The Big Cube,* his role is pure evil, a womanizing medical student who sells LSD cubes for profit. He convinces Lisa that her father was murdered by Lana. They conspire to lace her prescribed sedatives with enough LSD to drive her in-

HOW did Lana's character get herself into this druggy-hippie LSD-fired mess? Like many of the characters she played, SHE DID IT FOR LOVE.

Here, Lana's character cuddles while cruising with her new husband, mega-rich but clueless Dan O'Herlihy, whose untimely drowning sets off the chain of events that redefine her as a drug-tolerant flower child who trips.

sane. Johnny intends to drive her, in a state of utter terror, to suicide.

At the last minute, however, Lisa saves her. Johnny is revealed to be the homicidal hustler he is, and stepmother and stepdaughter reconcile.

As one of the male leads, Richard Egan has the sympathetic role of Frederick Lansdale, a playwright friend of Lana's who is secretly in love with her. He is mostly known today for starring as Elvis Presley's older brother in the 1956 *Love Me Tender*.

Maurice Forley in *Motion Picture Daily Review* called the film "*Peyton Place* with generous doses of LSD." Since it had been filmed in Mexico, it did better business South of the Border than it did in the United States. It was entitled in Spanish *El Terron de Azucar*.

The Big Cube was one of the least distributed of all Lana Turner movies. Kinney Services, Inc., an American conglomerate, took over Warner Brothers from 1966 to 1972.

In the confusion of that acquisition, several films slated for release in the U.S. more or less ended up on the junk heap. *The Big Cube*, if it was released at all, played in second-tier movie houses or in drive-ins, always as the less important half of a double feature.

Lisa Marie Bowman wrote: "In 1969 mainstream Hollywood, filmmakers were still struggling to figure out how to deal with the counter-culture. In *The Big Cube*, old school movie stars like Lana Turner were menaced by long-haired men and amoral girls in miniskirts. Not only do you get to watch some of the most evil hippies in history, but you get a once-in-a-lifetime experience of seeing Lana Turner on acid!"

Critic Jeanine Basinger wrote: "*The Big Cube* is one of the worst films ever made. After thirty-two years in the business, Lana looks less than gorgeous on film for the first time. She wears an expensive wardrobe, but is undermined by a series of gorgonlike wigs, knee-high boots that belong on a teenager, and armloads of jewelry. She is an imitation of Lana Turner. Or, worse, an imitation of Mae West."

Lana's primal scream, as recorded as part of the plot line of *The Big Cube*.

Were equivalent screams being expressed by Lana, secretly, and at home, during this period of her wildly traumatized life?

Swedish actress Karin Mossberg was cast as Lana's vengeful stepdaughter, plotting with George Chakris, an LSD-peddling male hustler who wants to drive Lana to suicide.

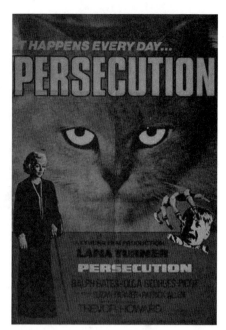

Throughout most of the 1960s, Lana had resisted the temptation of appearing in horror films, as had Barbara Stanwyck, Joan Crawford, and Bette Davis before her.

Yet finally, her former lover from World War II, Robert Hutton, called her and asked her if she'd read a script he'd co-written with Rosemary Wootten. She agreed to read it, but warned: "I will not wear a fright wig, and I won't wield an ax."

"That's not called for," he said. "The role calls for you to be felinely wicked. You'll still get to look glamorous as Carrie."

"Send it over, darling," she said, "and I'll read it this afternoon. And, Bob, dear, we had some good times, didn't we? Even though there was a war on."

"It was the pinnacle of my life," he assured her.

"In a fit of madness, I agreed to star in the film even though it was to be shot in London with that horrible weather," she said. "I don't know how the locals endure it. Now, if only they'd agree on a title."

The film was generally called *Persecution* when it was released in 1974. Since much of the plot centered on a series of ominous Persian cats, each named Sheba, other titles included *PURRsecution, Sheba, The Seven Lives of Sheba,* and even *I Hate You, Cat.* She detested the last title. For a VHS release in the 1980s, the title was changed to *The Graveyard.*

Persecution was an obvious attempt to create a British version of *What Ever Happened to Baby Jane?* (1962).

Arriving in London, Lana told the press, "I'm sure I'll get a lot of hate mail playing a very wicked mother who torments her poor son. It's unlike any role I've ever played before."

At Pinewood Studios, she met with Kevin Francis, the film'sproducer. He was the son of Freddie Francis, a noted cinematographer and horror film director.

He introduced Lana to her talented English director, Dan Chaffey, who was also a writer, producer, and even an art director.

He had been tapped for *Persecution* because of his involvement in a number of Anglo-horror movies.

She would be appearing with co-stars, Trevor Howard, Ralph Bates, Olga Georges-Picot, and Suzan Farmer. Only Howard was a familiar name to her.

Lana's character, Carrie Masters, was a mother from hell, with an obsession with a series of cats, each of them known as Sheba. "In this psychological horror tale I play a matriarchal monster," she told her friends. "There's a hint of the supernatural, me with my creepy Persians."

Early in the film, a child actor, Marks Weavers, played her ten-year-old son, David. An American *émigré* to England, Carrie has been crippled in her leg, and she blames her boy for her state and sets out to wreak vengeance on the poor lad, with the aid of her wicked Sheba.

Frightened almost out of his mind, David retaliates by drowning the cat in its milk, claiming that his mother loves it more than she loves him.

Time goes by, and David (played by Bates) is now twenty-four. He arrives at his mother's house with his wife, Janie (Farmer) and their newborn baby.

Carrie (Lana) is opposed to her son's marriage and wants to break it up. It's as if she is toying with him, in a style copied from the way her Sheba might play with a mouse before devouring it. Her latest cat, another Sheba, malevolently suffocates the tender little infant under a pillow.

After the death of her child, Janie suffers a nervous breakdown. In a diabolical scheme, Carrie hires a sexy, sultry French nurse, ostensibly to look after her daughter-in-law. Actually, Carrie wants her son to be seduced by Monique Kalfon (played by Olga Georges-Picot).

Monique manages to seduce David. At that point, Janie enters their bedroom, catching her young husband in intercourse with the so-called "nurse" (who's really a prostitute). Janie rushes from the room, but stumbles, falling down the stairs to her death.

At this point, David "flips out." He not only kills the prostitute, but goes into the garden to dig up the graves of the past Shebas. In doing so, he discovers the bones of Carrie's former husband, Robert Masters.

As it turns out, he was not David's father. Carrie murdered her husband years ago. Her son's actual father is Paul Bellamy (Trevor Howard). It was Bellamy who crippled Carrie.

All of these revelations are too much for poor David. At the conclusion, he drowns his mother in the cat's milk.

What Becomes a Movie Legend Most? HORROR!

Like Lana, near the end of their careers, movie queens of yesteryear also "descended" into roles conveying psychoses, mental illness, and decay.

Top to botton: Joan Crawford in *Strait Jacket* (1964); Bette Davis in *Hush...Hush, Sweet Charlotte* (1964); and Lana in *Persecution* (1974), carrying the corpse of her beloved Sheba in a mini-coffin.

Lana said she was honored to be working with Howard, who arguably was described as "the greatest British actor of his generation."

"I'm semi-retired," he told her. "But I wanted to work so I took on this thankless role. Blame it on my poor state of mind."

***

Persecution, with later title changes, received very limited distribution in the United States and became known as one of Lana's worst failures. She infuriated the producer when she told the press, "It's a bomb!"

In promoting the film, the following taglines were used: THE HORROR OF A TWISTED MIND! A WARNING: THIS FILM IS NOT FOR THE SQUEAMISH. NOW IT'S DAVID'S TURN TO GET EVEN—AND HE HAS A VERY SPECIAL TREAT FOR HIS MOTHER.

Thus goes the way of all flesh:

Lana, former sex goddess of MGM, plays a vengefully geriatric lunatic with a penchant for pampered, homicidal cats.

In the *London Daily Mirror,* Margaret Hinxman said: "Silly as it seems, here is the spectacular Lana Turner playing a crippled, cat-loving mother dominating the life of her unfortunate son (Ralph Bates, who deserves a better fate). Given a more astute script, I imagine that able director, Don Chaffey, would have done justice to his star. As it is, the film is surprisingly stodgy, barely a gasp of surprise in it."

Richard Schleib in the *Science Fiction, Horror, and Fantasy Movie Review* wrote: "Turner hams it up, and she and Ralph Bates have fun playing games with one another."

Geoff Brown, in *BFI Monthly Film Bulletin,* called *Persecution* "a tawdry and tedious psycho-drama, and as repulsive as most movies exploiting Hollywood's leading ladies. One can only admire Lana Turner's fortitude. She strives to exhibit the same dignity of *Portrait in Black* and *Madame X.* Aside from her, there is little of interest in this strike-out."

In *Variety,* the critic called the movie "an old-fashioned meller riddled with ho-hum and sometimes laughably trite scripting. Also, it's very tame in the shock-horror department. But under the circumstances, Turner's performance as the perverted dame of the English manor has reasonable poise."

It came as a total surprise to Lana, after all the bad reviews, but in October of 1975 at Sitges, on the Mediterranean coast of Spain, she won the Silver Carnation Award at the annual festival of horror films, walking off with the Best Actress prize.

After making the film, she flew back to California to settle into her condo at Century Park East on Santa Monica Boulevard in Century City. Often she stood there at night, looking at the city lights and thinking about yesterday. After a somewhat nomadic existence, moving from one place to another, this would be her last and final home.

***

Jac Fields, Lana's agent for the 1970s, persuaded her to star in the melodrama, *Bittersweet Love,* set for a 1976 distribution from Avoc Embassy Pictures. A Zappala-Slott Production, it was written by Adrian Morrall and D.A. Kellogg. Lana would head a talented cast that included Robert Lansing, Celeste Holm, Scott Hylands, and Meredith Baxter-Birney.

Lana as a rich, lonely widow confronting an incest issue in *Bittersweet Love*, seems, in her later years, to cling more desperately than ever to her expensive accoutrements.

In it, as a rich, lonely widow, Lana confronted an incest issue. To make herself more glamourous, she clung to her fur coats and diamonds, but the film bombed. She said, "I'm semi-retired. But I wanted to work, so I took on this thankless role. I'll never return to the screen," she vowed.

But she did.

***

For a 1980 release, *Witches' Brew,* Lana made her last big screen appearance playing a witch. Once again, she was allowed to wear her diamonds and furs as a rich society lady indulging in the black arts.

On seeing the final cut, she said, "I didn't know whether to laugh at myself or cry. What a sad *adieu* to a film career!"

Why Lana, among the best-preserved of the Golden Age stars, wanted to appear in an *adieu* to feature films as a witch would require a probe of her psyche.

Witches' Brew was actually shot in 1978 by first-time writer and director Richard Shorr, but few were pleased with the editing and final result. Another director, Herbert L. Strock, came in months later and reshot several scenes, hoping to salvage the project. Plagued with lawsuits that broke out among the principals, *Witches Brew* never had a theatrical release. However, in 1985, it had a TV premiere and was also made available on home video.

When a reporter asked Teri Garr—who was later famous for her Oscar-nominated role as Best Supporting Actress in *Tootsie* (1982)—about working with Lana, she said: "I don't think either Miss Turner or myself will be remembered for *Witches' Brew*. The film will not be mentioned in our obits."

On looking back at her career, Lana said, "I shouldn't have made those last four films after *Madame X*. I also, in the 1960s, should not have married my last three husbands. But I did."

Chapter Eighteen

Where Love Has Gone

Three Failed Marriages
To Much Younger Husbands

Sporting a buzzcut that Lana the Barber had given him, rancher Fred May, Husband #5, escorted Lana to the Bal Montmartre in 1959, where she was photographed as the epitome of oldtime Hollywood glamour.

"He loved me for myself and, unlike all my other husbands, before and since, he didn't fall for a celluloid image, but for me as a woman. Our breakup was silly, all my fault. Blame it on my cheating heart, I guess."

"I accused him of being the Gestapo. He was so punctual, so well organized, but he loved me and I loved him. If only I'd been a faithful wife, we might still be married. Fred was the kind of man a gal could grow old with. He was also good looking and a wonderful lover. How stupid of me to leave him."

In the weeks following the murder of Johnny Stompanato, Lana became a recluse, not wanting to go out "to be observed like some sort of freak murderess by the public."

However, that summer, she accepted an invitation from an actor friend, Kem Dibbs, to go to a beach party in Malibu, where she would eventually move. The host was film executive Robert Whittaker, whom she knew only casually.

Other than the host, she didn't know anybody at the party, and the much younger guests paid no attention to her, intent as they were on having fun at the beach.

Sitting all alone, she noticed the arrival of a handsome young man.

As she remembered him, he was "dressed all in brown—everything about him was brown, especially his tanned face and sandy hair. Even his dark glasses were brown."

"Something about him grabbed me," she said. "Maybe it was his resemblance to Tyrone Power."

Dibbs brought him over to introduce him to Lana. He was Fred May, a 34-year-old real estate agent and horsebreeder. She was forty-four at the time, with her greatest movies in her past.

He reminded her that he'd been introduced to her in 1939 when he was an extra on her picture, *Dancing Co-Ed.* "Back then, you had eyes only for Artie Shaw."

"Don't remind me," she said.

As they talked, he told her that he owned a ranch where he raised thoroughbreds for racing. She flirted with him, suggesting that she'd like to visit it sometime. He asked for her telephone number, and she gave it to him, noting that he didn't write it down. She never expected to hear from him after that, especially when she saw him talking to an attractive, much younger woman later on.

He must have had a good memory because he phoned her two days later, suggesting she visit him for barbecued steaks at an apartment he had in Hollywood. He'd recommended that venue because she had told him that she did not go to restaurants in the wake of the death of Johnny Stompanato because she didn't like to be stared at.

After their dinner, she left his apartment with the understanding

Unlike most of her husbands or lovers, Fred May was said to have fallen in love with "the real Lana, not the celluloid Venus up there on the screen."

that she would go with him the next day to his ranch, the Circle M, at Chino, California, about an hour's drive from Los Angeles.

When she got there, as she was putting away some casual clothing she'd brought along, she noticed a large stack of newspapers in the closet. All of them focused on coverage of the murder of Johnny Stompanato.

Over dinner, she asked him about the collection.

"From afar, I think I had fallen in love with you. But I wanted to know everything about you, even all the bad stuff people unfairly wrote attacking you. I read through all that, finding it to be crap. If anything, it made me more sympathetic to you than ever. I wanted to love and protect you from the bastards exploiting you."

She accepted that and trusted him enough to move in with him. Throughout most periods of her past life, she went out in public only if she were "glamourized." At the ranch, however, she was often seen wearing sweat shirts and blue jeans.

When Virginia Grey arrived, Lana told her, "I get up with Fred at 6AM, and, after breakfast, I'm out there shoveling shit out of the stables."

Grey said, "I liked Fred. He seemed to be bringing her back to life after the tragedy she'd suffered."

At around this time, Cheryl had violated her probation. On two separate occasions, she had escaped from El Retiro Reform School, but was apprehended each time.

Lana's first months with May seemed idyllic, a new lifestyle for her. They attended horse races, went marlin fishing off the coast of Baja, California, and enjoyed trout dinners in Pomona. She was surprised that she was rarely recognized in her drab garb, and with little or no makeup except for her painted eyebrows.

On another occasion, when Grey arrived to spend the weekend, she found Lana out mowing the sheep meadow.

"I had Fred chase away the snakes first," Lana told her.

As a real estate agent, May arranged for her to acquire a home in Malibu Colony, an exclusive enclave of mostly film people. These were a series of beach homes with glass walls opening onto sundecks with views of the Pacific. She redecorated the house and installed a swimming pool. This became her home for the next seven years.

Lana later told Grey, "As you know, the first thing I notice about a man is whether he's handsome or not." More important than that, I want to know what he's concealing in his pants. But with Fred, it's different. I've learned to look past those surface things. I'm attracted to his mind, his heart, and the feeling of stability he gives me."

He also played a role in her business affairs, taking care of details and advising her about what he thought she should do with the remainder of her career.

Both of them were intrigued when Frank Sinatra came to visit. *Variety* published a story the next day, stating that Lana might hook up with Frank Sinatra's Essex Productions, turning out starring roles for them as a team. The stars had never made a movie with each other before, and May agreed that as a duet, they might become strong contenders at the box office.

But the deal fell through.

As the autumn arrived, Lana became aware that certain tensions had arisen because of their differing habits and lifestyle priorities. Grey called May "the cruise director." Whereas he was incredibly punctual, and always on time, she liked to delay a public appearance for hours, working on her hair, makeup, and wardrobe. "I fear I tested his nerves."

One day, while driving to the race track at Del Mar, both of them agreed to stop at the courthouse in Santa Ana and apply for a marriage license. A county clerk leaked word to the press, and the morning papers carried the headline— LANA TURNER TO MARRY AGAIN.

Six months would pass before they finally wed. It was on the day before the license expired.

Lana placed a phone call to Virginia Grey, asking her to serve as her matron of honor. May selected as his best man, George Mann, a well-known comedian. The wedding took place on November 27, 1960, at the Miramar Hotel in Santa Monica, with a Methodist minister officiating at the ceremony.

The public had already been made aware of the couple, based on photos of them at the Hollywood premiere, on June 29, of *Portrait in Black*. Both Cheryl and Mildred attended.

After Lana and May were married, Cheryl was allowed by a judge, beginning in January of 1961, to come and live with them. Unlike her previous stepfathers, especially Lex Barker, the young girl and May got along very well. She later referred to him as "a warm, huggy-bear of a man."

As time went by, Lana seemed to grow bored with staid married life. After all, she'd been known as the party girl of the 20th Century. There were reports that her "roving eye" had returned, even rumors that she was holding "auditions" in her dressing room, seducing well-built young men who worked on the crew of the pictures she was making. She began to return home to May later and later in the evening.

In an unusual statement, *Time* opined: "Lana Turner has never been compatible with a man one day longer than the moment she grows bored with him in bed."

While Lana was filming *Who's Got the Action?* with Dean Martin, May suspected her of having an affair with the womanizing singer-actor. Actually, she wasn't. She'd had an affair with Martin more than a decade before.

One night, when Lana didn't return home until around ten o'clock, and had not called, she and May got into an argument. Although she'd been drinking, she fled back to her Cadillac and took off into the night.

Both of them were staying at her house in Malibu at the time. After two hours had passed, without a call from her, and worried for her safety since she was driving drunk, he drove along the Pacific Coast Highway in an attempt to find her.

In the meantime, she'd pulled up at a bar called "The Cottage." After more drinks there, she'd been attracted to "a dreamy man," a very handsome blonde-haired, blue-eyed 22-year-old. Cody Ryan was a former cowpuncher from her native state of Idaho. She was turned on by his imposing physique, and agreed to wait around for him until he got off work at 1AM.

They left the bar together, and in her Cadillac, she followed his battered Ford to his modest apartment up the coast.

She braked in front of his apartment house, encountering the manager in the hallway and engaging in a dialogue. He even asked Lana for her autograph.

Meanwhile, driving along the coastal highway, frantically searching from Lana's car from the vantage point of his own car, May spotted Lana's convertible parked in front of the cowpuncher's apartment building. He went inside the apartment house and knocked on the manager's door. With no sense of discretion at all, the manager told May that Lana and Ryan were in the building's rear apartment.

Pounding on their door, May heard rumblings inside. Lana, in bed with Ryan, hastily grabbed only her dark glasses and wrapped her mink coat around her otherwise nude body, fleeing through his rear kitchen door to the back of the building where she made her escape.

In one of those strange coincidences, Mildred, too, was driving by *en route* to Lana's Malibu house, and she spotted Lana driving off in her highly visible Cadillac. May later told his mother-in-law what Lana had done.

In the days that followed, the would-be actor, Cody Ryan, peddled the story of his encounter with Lana to *Confidential* magazine. Since Lana had left her undergarments behind in his apartment, including a pair of pink silk panties, he sold them to "a Lana Turner fetishist."

In the aftermath of all this, May did not return to Malibu, but drove to his ranch instead. He phoned Lana and asked her to come for the weekend. It was a rather tense reunion that ended with him asking her for a $5,000 loan, which he agreed to pay back with interest. She them gave him a check for that amount.

Two days later, when they were driving together to Del Mar, he stopped in front of a Cadillac dealership. She didn't want to enter the store, but May insisted. Once inside, a salesman directed her to a white Cadillac with a large red ribbon tied around it. "It's a gift from me to you," May told her.

She exploded, sensing that's why he had wanted the loan. "I already have a god damn Cadillac, and I don't need another one," she shouted.

That night exploded again. She later admitted, "In the middle of a Battle Royal, we broke up our marriage. I felt used. I felt cheated. I felt stupid. Maybe I was wrong to have erupted like that."

In September of 1962, a reporter discovered May living at a hotel in Santa Monica, although he claimed he visited Lana two or three times a week. Within weeks, Lana was on her way to Juarez, Mexico, for a quickie divorce. She was a free woman again, and was soon on the prowl, although later, she regretted divorcing May.

For most of her life, she remained his friend, and they often talked on the phone. Eventually, he became the mayor of Malibu.

He met an artist named Julie, and the couple settled into a seeming happy marriage that lasted until his death in 1994.

In the wake of his divorce, May said, "Real life can't be lived as if it were a movie script. And husbands and wives can't exist happily every moment of the day as though a movie camera were turned on them."

Lana responded, "Yes people do learn from their mistakes. But their characters never essentially change."

***

597

"I started fucking when I was eleven years old. All I know is I get violent headaches if I don't fuck every day."

—Robert Eaton

Long before Lana met him, Robert P. Eaton was known around Malibu as "The Stud." Like Fred May, he was a decade younger than Lana.

He was a close friend of a handsome, rising young star, Clint Eastwood. It was Eastwood who introduced Eaton to Lana, and they chatted for about an hour on the sundeck at a cocktail party in Malibu.

It was around this time that he had to get rid of his competition, a young man dating Lana who had been identified with different names. Currently, he was using "Carl David."

At Malibu, while Lana was waiting around for a good script, David had moved in on her during one of her "extended vacations," spending her long days sunning, swimming, and entertaining an assortment of people she didn't really know.

According to Lana, "After only a week or so, Carl was running my life. He began inviting his friends for drinks every afternoon at five, and the partying often lasted past midnight."

As she told Virginia Grey, "He wasn't very much in the romance department."

After he'd known her for a while, he asked her for a loan of $6,000 so that he could invest in a business in New York City.

David was known to Eaton, who had learned that he was a hustler, working the bored, rich women of Beverly Hills and Malibu and also making himself available to wealthy homosexuals.

As Eaton talked to Lana, he let her know that David was not in New York, but in Palm Springs, driving around in a shiny pink Cadillac, which he claimed that Lana had bought for him.

When David returned to Lana at Malibu, she confronted him with Eaton's revelation. Finally, he admitted it was true. In the bedroom, he packed his clothing. At the front door, he turned and looked back at her. "You're a pathetic old woman. Out with Lana Turner, in with Alfredo de la Vega. Thanks for the Cadillac."

He slammed the door and disappeared from her life forever.

***

Lana had met De La Vega, a wealthy Mexican real estate tycoon, at a party at the home of Nancy and Ronald Reagan. He was known as a serial seducer of handsome young men, and in the 1980s, would become the frequent escort of First Lady Nancy Reagan when "my Ronnie is too busy."

Lana felt grateful to Eaton for alerting her to what David was up to. She came together with Eaton at a New Year's Eve party to bring in 1965.

Actually, she did more than that. As Eaton later confessed, "She took me to her home, and I didn't leave her bedroom for the next two weeks."

He suggested, but didn't actually say so, that she was so turned on by his love-making that she didn't want to let him go.

As she told Grey, "We made love time and time again, day after day, night after night. What stamina! At least I've found a man who can keep up with me in bed!"

She also informed Grey that "Bob is definitely marriage material."

Her actress friend cautioned her not to enter into another marriage, "but Lana was in love. She didn't know much about this guy, other than he was handsome and extremely well endowed. If he had any imperfection, she told me, it was one bad eye. But he'd soon have it replaced with a glass eye, which she paid for. She didn't really know what he did to support himself, some vague thing about being in "film production."

As winter gave way to spring, which blossomed into summer, Lana journeyed with Eaton to Arlington, Virginia. There, on June 22, 1965, she married her sixth husband in the home of his father, a retired U.S. Navy captain who had seen action in World War II. The service was performed by a magistrate whose Southern accent, as she remembered it, "was so thick I thought he was spitting cotton."

Her dress was described as "peach-colored Italian lace over China silk." Peach-colored carnations were laced into her honey blonde hair, and she was glittering in diamonds—earrings, a necklace, and a bracelet. Eaton placed a wedding band of Florentine gold on her hand.

She told the first reporter she met in Virginia that, "Age to me is what I feel inside. I have no fear of growing old."

That statement was perhaps the second-biggest fib she ever told. The first was her declaration that, "Sex doesn't mean that much to me," and that from a siren who had devoted much of her time in Hollywood to the pursuit of sexual conquests, even dwarfing the affairs of Marilyn Monroe, Marlene Dietrich, and Joan Crawford.

In distinct contrast to his very famous

It was sex, not love, that drove Lana into the arms of Robert Eaton, who at the time, was known as "The Stud of Malibu."

Robert Eaton and Lana snapped as they are about to enter a restaurant.

Although he was great in bed, he squandered her money and staged orgies at her home when she was absent.

wife, Eaton was unknown to the press, and when she was asked about what he did, she said, "Bob is going to head my film production company."

After marrying him, she began to hear stories about her roving playboy, who was known to Clark Gable, Gene Kelly, and even to her former lover, Greg Bautzer. It was rumored that Bautzer had been the one who previously introduced Eaton to Ginger Rogers.

Like Lana, this aging, legendary star had fallen for Eaton's good looks and his sex appeal, and had invited him to come to live with her, where she paid all the bills. When she caught him dating other women, she had kicked him out.

Eaton was frequently seen on the Beverly Hills Tennis Courts, where he was sometimes mistaken for Robert Wagner. Eaton announced that this was his first marriage.

A snooping reporter for *Time* magazine turned up a different story. He discovered that Eaton had no record in film production. Not only that, he'd been married once before, on August 11, 1956, in Las Vegas to a 26-year-old actress, Gloria Pall, who stood six feet tall. She divorced him the following year. In court, she testified that during their short marriage, she was his sole means of support.

Perhaps "sole" was not the right word. She also claimed that "another woman purchased a Thunderbird for him." That other woman was later identified as the sultry French actress, Denise Darcel, who in 1949 had co-starred with Van Johnson in MGM's *Battleground.*

For their honeymoon, Lana flew Eaton to Acapulco, her favorite vacation retreat, where she'd had trysts with Tyrone Power, Howard Hughes, Fernando Lamas, Lex Barker, and where Johnny Stompanato had beaten her.

But there was evidence that she was tiring of the Mexican resort. At the airport, she was spotted by a reporter. She told him, "I didn't enjoy Acapulco as much this time. The party crowd down here is even wilder than the jet set."

After her honeymoon with Eaton, they returned to Hollywood, where she knew she'd have to support him. But she was convinced that he'd succeed as a film producer.

In the meantime, she wanted to improve his wardrobe. She was seen taking him to exclusive men's stores in Beverly Hills, where he was measured for tailor-made suits. The scene evoked the famous episode in *Sunset Blvd.*, where Gloria Swanson gets a gigolo, as portrayed by William Holden, outfitted with a new wardrobe.

Lana was a millionaire now, and she could afford

Robert Eaton (left) dines out with Lana and his best friend, the emerging young actor, Clint Eastwood.

"After meeting Clint, I wondered if I had married the wrong man," Lana confessed.

it, thanks to her work with Ross Hunter. "Thank God for gay men," she said.

She even had Eaton's bad teeth fixed, as well as that previously mentioned glass eye, and she bought a car for him as well.

Lana and Eaton flew to New York *en route* to Miami Beach for the premiere of *Madame X*. In Manhattan, she spoke to Howard Thompson of *The New York Times*. An outwardly adoring Eaton was at her side. "Love is the only security there is," she told the reporter. "Don't let anyone tell you different. You know something? I've got real roots now." Then she leaned over to plant a kiss on Eaton's lips.

In Florida at the premiere, with Eaton, she made a dazzling appearance in a floor-length white mink and a gown provocatively slit up one side, where you could see "all the way to Honolulu."

At a post-premiere party thrown by the TV talk show host, Ed Sullivan, Lana showed up drunk.

Madame X was a big hit on Miami Beach, no doubt because of Lana's appearance. But when it played across America, audiences diminished. A columnist, George Bourke, claimed, "The fabled career of 'The Sweater Girl' is now all but over. All that remains is for the corpse to be buried."

However, she flew with Eaton to Italy to accept the David di Donatello Award as Best Actress in a Foreign Film for her dramatic performance in *Madame X*.

In Rome, Eaton and Lana dined with his good friend, Clint Eastwood. There was talk of forming a production company, in which Eastwood and Lana would co-star.

She also met with producer Carlo Ponti, who suggested she should co-star in an Italian movie he was producing, with Marcello Mastroianni as her leading man. That never happened. The role went to his wife, Sophia Loren.

Back in Hollywood, recovering from a mysterious virus, she was mentioned in *Variety*. It was announced that she and Gregory Peck would co-star in *The Stalking Moon* (1969), but the role was eventually assigned to another blonde, Eva Marie Saint.

By January of 1966, she financed the opening of a lavish new office for Eaton in the 9000 Sunset Building on Sunset Strip, the same building where her former agent, Henry Willson, had an office.

To call attention to her new production company, she called in the press, sitting on a desk and showing off her still shapely legs for photographers. As she'd once told Grey, "The legs are the last to go."

Lana told *Variety*, "I'm hoping to audition new talent."

Gossips ridiculed her remark: "Lana Turner has been auditioning 'new talent' ever since she got off the bus from Idaho."

During her marriage to Eaton, Lana would make only one film, *The Big Cube*.

Bored with life in Hollywood, "where nothing seems to be happening, at least for me," Lana agreed in the autumn of 1967, to go on a good will tour of Vietnam, entertaining the homesick soldiers, many fighting a war in which they didn't believe. She had a mishap there, seriously spraining her ankle. As she put it, "I did that by jumping from trench to trench."

After her return to California, after three days in Malibu, while Eaton was at the office on Sunset Strip, Mildred came to her in tears. "While you were gone,

Eaton turned your home into a madhouse. Nonstop parties day and night. They began the moment you boarded the plane."

She called the maid, who had saved the bedsheets as evidence. Lana was aghast at the sight of lipstick smears and semen stains on her linens. Within the hour, she phoned Eaton, demanding that he leave his office and return to Malibu at once. After confronting him with the evidence, she ordered him to leave her house.

Eastwood's biographer, Patrick McGilligan, wrote: "Clint and Robert Eaton, Lana Turner's husband, were running-around pals, and when she was off on location, her house was open range."

As members of their "tight-knit" group, he named actors Brian Keith, Jim Arness, and Chill Wills.

But after a few days in exile, Eaton, turning on all his charm, came back into her life with great apologies for his behavior.

When Grey asked her why she'd taken him back, she said, "The sex is that good."

Her reconciliation with Eaton didn't last. There were rumors that the marriage was deteriorating when Eaton flew alone to Rome.

When asked about that, Lana told a reporter, "Bob is going over to talk about a co-production deal with Clint Eastwood. Maybe hooking up with an Italian film company."

Back in California, Eaton announced that he had formed his own company, Forum Films, and that his first picture would co-star Lana Turner and Clint Eastwood.

Although he purchased a thoroughbred for her for Christmas, the Associated Press carried the headline—LANA'S SIXTH HUSBAND MOVES OUT.

Columnist Sheilah Graham wrote: "Lana Turner insists there is no hope for a reconciliation with her sixth husband, Robert Eaton.

However, by February of 1967, it was reported "Lana Turner and Robert Eaton, or so it seems, are back together again. But how long will it last this time?"

She spoke to the press: "Bob and I are still looking for a woman's picture, which no one seems to be making anymore. It's a man's world: Steve McQueen, Paul Newman. Young actresses today think that making a movie is all about showing your bosom. As for me, I look twelve years younger than my actual age. People think I'm fifty because I've been around for so long. I arrived in Hollywood when I was in diapers. Doris Day and I are about the same age, and she's still playing virgins being pursued by Rock Hudson or Cary Grant."

***

Harold Robbins was one of the best-selling novelists of all time, writing more than two dozen best-sellers, including the mega-hit *The Carpetbaggers* (1961), selling more than 750 copies in 32 languages. He was called "as much a part of the sexual and social revolution as The Pill, *Playboy,* and pot."

He often based his characters on actual people. The main character in *The Carpetbaggers* was a loose composite of Howard Hughes, Harry Cohn, and Louis B.

Mayer.

In the wake of the 1958 murder of Johnny Stompanato in Lana's home, he wrote a 1962 novel entitled *Where Love Has Gone*.

Lana was horrified when she read it. She later wrote, "He had turned the worst tragedy of my life into a cheap, mean, best-selling novel based on cruel fabrications."

Her hatred of Robbins grew more intense when a movie, also entitled *Where Love Has Gone* (1964), revived the Stompanato scandal once again. Amazingly, perhaps as an "enhancement" for this dark and provocative film, its director, Edward Dmytryk, and its producer, Joseph E. Levine, even offered Lana its lead role. "We've disguised your identity. Instead of an actress, we'll make you a sculptor," Levine told her.

"Harold Robbins was an oversexed, overpaid, hack of a novelist, and I hated him for libeling me in his novel and film, *Where Love Has Gone*," Lana said.

"Now, I'm appearing in a TV series he's conceived. You figure."

Without hesitation, she rejected the role, which went instead to Susan Hayward, which caused a rift in their long-standing friendship. Bette Davis was cast in a role based on Mildred, with Joey Heatherton tackling the role inspired by Cheryl Crane.

While Lana was in Mexico shooting *The Big Cube*, Eaton, back in Hollywood, was negotiating with Robbins about a TV series. He offered to get Eaton hired as part of the production staff if he could convince his wife to play the lead in the series, that of a troubled married woman in the habit of going from bed to bed.

The first Sunday after her return from Mexico to Malibu, Eaton invited Lana to the Bel Air Country Club, where he introduced her to Robbins. She had extended her hand, but snatched it back at once when she heard his name. "It was as if I'd touched a snake."

Ironically, Robbins had moved into the office she'd originally rented for Eaton in the 6000 Sunset Building. Eaton, in contrast, had been moved into a small cubbyhole.

Lana and Eaton had a violent argument that night. "How could you do that to me?" she asked Eaton. "You know what pain Robbins has caused Cheryl and me?"

Days later, her new agent, Sam Kamens at William Morris, approached her about appearing in a television series. With the scarcity of movie roles, she had seriously considered a move to TV for some time. But when Kamens told her Robbins was the writer behind the series, she was furious.

Nonetheless, Kamens finally convinced her to consider the role, which would be filmed on the French Riviera, among other locales, as part of twenty-six teleplays running for an hour each.

"Lana, in Hollywood, you've got to let bygones be bygones," Kamen told her.

603

"You, of all people, known that everybody betrays everybody out here."

Both her agent and Eaton finally convinced her to sign for the role, which would be entitled *The Survivors*. "A survivor, that's what I am, all right!"

To launch the series, Robbins himself hosted a lavish bash at The Bistro in Hollywood. Although Lana would always detest him, she was friendly to the novelist on the surface.

Invitations had been extended to columnists and other members of the Hollywood elite. They read, "If you're interested in booze, broads, and the better things of life, why not join Lana Turner and George Hamilton, stars of our new ABC-Universal television show, *The Survivors*, in an old-fashioned drink-up upstairs at The Bistro?"

Lana dazzled by appearing in a black strapless chiffon, her bosom covered with black ostrich feathers on which she'd pinned eight diamond brooches and pins. Her blonde hair was page-boy style.

Although Robbins was highly paid for his scenario, his plot was never used by Universal, which dismissed it as "too blatantly sexual." In one scene of his proposed scenario, Lana's lover is depicted positioning himself down under the sheets to perform cunnilingus on her, the camera concentrating on her impassioned facial expression as she enjoys a powerful orgasm.

As it turned out, Robbins would not write that series. He was too busy working on another exploitative novel with the intention of co-opting it into a new and unrelated series, tentatively entitled *For the Survivors*. He'd written only a nine-page synopsis, for which he'd been paid one million dollars, a historic first for a television series.

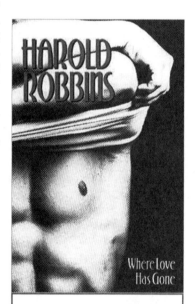

***

For her contribution to *The Survivors*, ABC-Universal agreed to pay Lana $12, 500 a week. Along with Eaton, she was flown to Nice on the French Riviera. From there, they were driven in a limousine to Cannes. The next day, she was introduced to her director, William Frye, who had produced *General Electric Theater*, a weekly half-hour anthology TV series hosted by Ronald Reagan.

Frye introduced her to her fellow cast members. She needed no introduction to her co-star, George Hamilton, since they had previously appeared together in the movie, *By*

When the British edition of *Where Love Has Gone* came out, its publishers fully realized that its authorship by Harold Robbins was more important than the book's title.

Its publishers also understood that cover art depicting a hot male stripping down could sell as many books—perhaps more— than a traditional depiction of a woman on the cover.

Love Possessed.

Lana would play Tracy Carlisle Hastings, the daughter of a banking tycoon, as portrayed by veteran actor Ralph Bellamy. She would be the mother of Jan-Michael Vincent, and Hamilton would be her half-brother. Rosanno Brazzi played the father of her illegitimate son. Her estranged husband was acted by Kevin McCarthy, with Louis Hayward cast as her uncle.

Ultimately, the family gets involved with South American revolutionaries.

Beginning the first week, the filming was a disaster. Lana exploded when she learned that Hamilton was not only getting paid $17,500 a week, but would get star billing over her. Frye explained that he was more of a name than she was because of all the publicity he'd received while dating the daughter of President Lyndon B. Johnson.

Hamilton claimed that Lana on two different occasions threatened suicide "because I was getting more money than she was. Every day, she tried to banter my self-esteem. She picked on me mercilessly, typically accusing me of trying to upstage her by wearing a brightly colored coral tie, which had been given to me by the costume designer."

At one point, Robbins, with the almost universal understanding that his lavish yacht was conspicuously docked in the harbor, showed up. According to Hamilton, "I found him looking more like a bookie than a best-selling author. He wore a flowered hat, big collars, and more chains than a sommelier."

Lana complained constantly to Frye. New writers came and went, each of them tinkering, adding to, or tearing apart the scripts. Some days, at the end of filming, she was assigned ten pages to frantically memorize. The next morning, she'd be handed an entirely different script.

Totally fed up, Frye became tired of her complaining and called her a bitch in front of the cast and crew. She slapped his face, and he slapped her back. In a rage, she took the afternoon off, secluding herself in her dressing room and applying an ice pack to her face.

The next day, she went to the Cannes Yacht Club for lunch. There, she discovered Frye. She walked over to his table to continue their argument. Tensions escalated, and she became so angered this time that she punched him in the face. He rose to his feet and punched her right back, knocking her down onto the floor.

Back in her dressing room, she called executives at Universal, demanding that

Lana with her two leading men, George Hamilton (standing) and Kevin McCarthy, in the ill-fated TV series, *The Survivors.*

"It was a question of which actor I disliked the most," Lana said.

Frye be fired for attacking her.

He was immediately dismissed, and Grant Tinker—the husband of Mary Tyler Moore and, from 1981 to 1986, the Chairman of NBC—was flown to the Riviera to assume temporary command. After two days on location, he surmised that *The Survivors* was a "turkey."

The studio rescued him by sending in director Walter Doniger, who had piloted the TV series based on *Peyton Place*.

In the meantime, Eaton claimed, "I was squeezed out of all decisions." With nothing to do, he began to disappear during the course of workdays. Lana claimed, "He was whooping it up with his new French female chums."

She said, "In the beginning of the shoot, the cast hated each other. We ended up merely disliking each other."

Lana feuded with the noted fashion designer, Luis Estevez, claiming that his wardrobe made her look "too matronly." She succeeded in getting him fired, too. He told columnist Joyce Haber, "I was kind to

Lana is depicted here with her on-screen son, Jan-Michael Vincent.

"I think the series would have been a hit if the writers had made him my young lover instead of my son. It would have been hotter."

Miss Turner. I should have been awarded the *Croix de Guerre.*"

She also feuded with Kevin McCarthy, cast as her husband. She told him, "I've worked with the great leading men of Hollywood. You are not one of them." She ordered the director to curtail her scenes with him, suggesting "We should get a divorce so he won't be in any more of the series."

She and Eaton occupied the same two-bedroom hotel suite, but they came and went at different hours. On the plane back to Los Angeles, they sat in different seats, each of them in First Class, but far away from the other.

Lana had already announced, "My marriage to Eaton is over."

As it turned out, most of the episodes shot on the Riviera ended up on the junk heap.

Shooting resumed in Hollywood on fifteen episodes. The series would never be completed.

In August, one month before *The Survivors* had its debut on ABC-TV, an anonymous ad appeared in *Daily Variety*. It read: "Congratulations to ABC-TV for coming up with the new series, *The Survivors,* starring $8 million and no sense."

As predicted, the series was viciously panned by critics, Lana receiving some of her worst reviews. She called it, "The revenge of Harold Robbins on me."

William Greeley, writing for *Variety*, said, "This meller about the jet set turned into an old-fashioned soap opera about a banking family. There was the taint of a novel in the Machiavellian twists of character and plot, but it finally boils down to suds with the gambits of daytime drama working overtime. The old debbil pregnancy, etc."

A midnight call came in for Lana from Stan Kamen, her agent, letting her know she'd been fired.

Because of clauses within his contract, Hamilton, however, was retained in a downsized TV production that was renamed *Paris 7000*. It tried for ratings using stars past their prime, such as Anne Baxter.

As Hamilton said, "That series, like *The Survivors*, went nowhere."

***

Back in Hollywood, Lana announced to the press that she was divorcing Robert Eaton. At her divorce hearing on April 1, 1969, she testified, "I found myself living under almost unbearable anxiety and nervous tension, which was beginning to tell on me, as reflected in the strained look on my face and in my actions. All this was seriously damaging my work as an actress."

The judge listened to her testimony and granted her a default decree. At last, she was freed of Husband No. 6.

She appeared on *The Today Show* and was interviewed by Bryant Gumbel. "Eaton was charming, handsome, and he adored me, carrying me around on a satin pillow. He wooed me, really introduced me to beautiful physical love that I had never known before." She'd never been so candid on TV.

To Virginia Grey, she confessed, "It was the best sex I ever had, and, as you know, darling, I've had the best of 'em."

After the divorce, she continued to live in Malibu until one day a real estate developer knocked on her door and offered her $350,000 for the property. Even though she was given only thirty days to vacate, she accepted. Hurriedly, she moved into a rented home on Coldwater Canyon in Beverly Hills.

She vowed, "I will never make another movie. I will never appear in another television series. And I will never marry again."

As the weeks quickly passed, she broke all three of those vows.

***

In the meantime, the divorced Eaton was pounding out a sensationalized *roman-à-clef,* entitled *The Body Brokers,* based on his marriage to Lana.

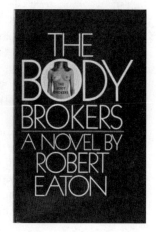

Its publisher announced that it was a complete work of fiction, not based on the life of any living person. Readers, however, knew differently.

Marla Jordan, the leading character in the novel, was a fading movie actress, who had been discovered at a soda fountain in Hollywood when she was seventeen. In her movie debut, she showed off her bouncing breasts in a tight sweater.

As Eaton rather artlessly phrased it in his novel,

607

Marla used her "tits and cunt" to advance herself as a movie queen. She also had a teenage daughter and took a young lover. At one point, she demanded that he seduce both of them—mother and daughter—at the same time. When he refuses, she pushes him off a steep cliff.

Marla was also depicted as a boozer, who had to work for hours before she could appear in public. Not only that, but she was depicted as a "switch hitter," who had once been caught by a popular male vocalist in a sexually compromising position with another Hollywood beauty queen.

Readers quickly identified those veiled references as Frank Sinatra and Ava Gardner.

In promoting his novel to columnist Sheilah Graham, Eaton told her, "I truly believe there's not a man in the world who can handle marriage to a movie star—the old-time film star. The mere fact of all the divorces proves my point."

He seemed aware that Lana had a large gay cult following, and he called *The Advocate,* the nation's most widely circulated GLBT magazine, to set up an interview.

The writer described the encounter. "The super stud knew how to dress for the part. He appeared in tight white pants, and it was obvious he wore no jockey shorts. He slid back in his chair, making his mighty bulge even more obvious. There was meat there for the poor."

"Every other word that came out of his mouth was 'fucking. Fuck Harold Robbins. Fuck this one, fuck that one.' He claimed he attended his first orgy at the age of twelve, where he was the prime attraction. He said he'd been broken into sex by his babysitter, who demanded he wear a sailor hat."

The writer from *The Advocate* concluded, "Even now, close to forty, Robert Eaton could command a very good price. Maybe a Rolls-Royce, if he were being kept. Perhaps a Caddy, or an Impala for sure."

***

In Hollywood, The Candy Store was a popular, sexually liberated disco that was packed every night, luring dancers into its darkened premises with its strobe lighting and loud music. To Lana, it seemed that all Hollywood had "gone hippie," especially along the Sunset Strip. Although she wasn't ready to live the rest of her life as a recluse, she felt isolated from "the scene,".

One night, she ventured alone into The Candy Store. From her position within the roiling crowd, she focused her eyes on the bar, where, to her dismay, she saw her divorced husband, Robert Eaton, talking to a seductive brunette who looked like Elaine Stewart, the starlet who had stolen Kirk Douglas from her in *The Bad and the Beautiful.*

Suddenly, a handsome man in a white suit emerged from the crowd and asked her to dance. He had come to her rescue. About the last thing she wanted was for Eaton to discover her wandering dateless at The Candy Store.

In the smoke-filled disco, the stranger took her into his arms and held her close to his body. With little room to maneuver, they were encircled by gyrating dancers. Rescuing her again at one point, he guided her over to a distant table. There, he introduced himself as Ronald Dante. Then he asked, "And who might my dance partner be?"

Surprised that he did not know who she was, she answered, "I'm Lana Topping," giving the surname of her third husband.

As they talked, she learned that he was a hypnotist who performed his act in night clubs. She said she was a heavy smoker, and that he might hypnotize her so she could break the habit. Then she suggested that he might visit her sometime, and she gave him her phone number.

He telephoned her two days later, and asked if he could come by. "It was unlike any date I'd ever had. "I thought Marlon Brando in *The Wild One* had arrived on my doorstep. He had a persuasive voice and strange, compelling eyes."

As the venue for their first date, he rode into her driveway on a motorcycle wearing a leather jacket. He invited her to get on, holding onto his back as he roared off, speeding through the hills above Malibu. That led to moonlit walks along the beach. He even taught her how to fly a kite.

A new Lana emerged, not accessorized with ostrich feathers and satin gowns, but an updated version wearing cowgirl boots, fringed leather jackets, and designer blue jeans.

Only weeks before, she'd told syndicated columnist Shirley Eder, "There is no new romance in my life, and I suspect there will never be again. Six husbands are enough for anyone, except Zsa Zsa Gabor. She once told me, 'A woman can't have too many husbands.' I want to be free as a bird."

Dante soon learned who Lana Turner was, although he had never seen one of her movies. One afternoon, she invited him to watch *Madame X*. As he remembered it, "She cried through most of the picture."

She phoned Virginia Grey: "I'm in love again. A young man named Ronald Dante, a hypnotist who appears in night clubs. Maybe he's put me in a hypnotic trance, I don't know. I know I'm in love when he holds me in his arms at night. When I wake up, he's still there, sleeping peacefully by my side. It's 5AM, and I have to rush to Universal to be made up."

"I can't warn you enough," Grey answered. "He sounds like trouble. Don't get too involved. It's safer to use this new male escort service that's opened. Very professional. Handsome, well-hung young men, some of whom look like Tyrone Power, Clark Gable, or Robert Taylor. Why don't you call them when you get the urge? A hundred dollars and

"I was ripe for it when Ronald Dante came into my life," Lana said. "I also fell for a good snow job and then later got kicked in the teeth. He seemed to be my salvation. It turned out worse than the Inferno. He would have charmed a bird out of a tree. So would a snake."

they're out the door when you finish with them."

"Dear, that's not for me. I know for many women it is. But I want romance with a capital R."

"Believe it or not, on the doorstep of the big 5-0, I'm still a romantic. Insecure, lonely, looking for love. I'm ripe for one final chance at happiness when the right man comes into my life. Even though I had vowed never to remarry, perhaps I was wrong."

Dante left her for several days as he had a night club act to perform in Phoenix. He deliberately opted not to phone her during that interim, hoping that "absence would make the heart grow fonder." The ploy worked. She eagerly welcomed him back to Beverly Hills into her warm embrace and hot bed.

Two nights later, he proposed that they elope to Las Vegas. "I'm game," she said, although she didn't really want to marry him.

When she'd first met Dante, she was living at the Sheraton-Universal Hotel on the Universal lot. But by the time they started seriously dating, she had moved into a large rented home in Beverly Hills—"One that befits a movie star" (her words).

Universal urged her to start granting interviews to help promote *The Survivors*, as the TV series "needed a blood transfusion."

A reporter and photographer from *Life* arrived to interview her. Her picture with Dante was taken beside her swimming pool. His arms are around her, and her own arms are outstretched to the sun.

When Lana was asked about Cheryl, she responded that her daughter was now working for Stephen Crane, her father, and doing well in the restaurant business. "She's a very successful business woman," Lana said.

On another occasion, another writer showed up and found Lana dressed in "flower power" garb, an aging hippie. She told the woman reporter, "My boyfriend, Ronald Dante, has thrown out all my Jean Louis designed gowns in favor of what I'm wearing now. My dress cost twelve dollars."

Yet another reporter, Terry Watson, showed up on her doorstep and found her intoxicated. "I tried to interview her, but she seemed in some far and distant place. I talked to her about her leading men. She remembered Clark Gable and Spencer Tracy, but didn't seem to know who Van Heflin and John Hodiak were."

He decided not to publish his interview because it would be too unflattering, too contrary to the Lana Turner image. Watson said, "Lana was turned down for the role of Alexandra Del Lago in Tennessee Williams' *Sweet Bird of Youth*. Now, she is living the part. Ronald Dante is her Chance Wayne."

***

Just who was this strange new man who had become her seventh and final husband?

She knew little about him, only what he'd told her. He said he had been born in Singapore and that he had a doctorate in psychology. He also claimed that he'd been a lieutenant colonel in the U.S. Marines, and that he was thirty-nine years old.

He did not have a doctorate; he had not served in the military. Nor was he born in Singapore. The city of his birth was Chicago, in 1930.

To anyone who asked, Lana referred to her new husband as "Dr. Dante," asserting that he was writing a book on hypnotherapy. In the days that followed, Lana, with Dante, was often seen dining in one of Stephen Crane's restaurants, where her former husband never presented her with a bill.

She was still a faithful reader of *The Hollywood Reporter*, whose publisher had discovered her decades before at a soda fountain. In a gossip column appeared an item that shocked her. "Is Lana Turner's seventh husband, Ronald Dante, the same hypnotist—real name Robert Peller—who had such a messy annulment suit against him in Florida in 1963?"

As it turned out, her new husband was indeed Ronald Peller. In Hollywood, Florida, he had married Clair Kisie, who a few weeks later asserted in court that he had hypnotized her and taken her $20,000 in savings.

Her request for an annulment was granted, and the judge ordered him to return the money, or whatever was left of it.

During the first weeks of Lana's marriage, further embarrassments emerged for Dante. He called the police and claimed that he'd been shot at six times in a parking lot by an unidentified assailant wearing an "Aussie bush hat." He went on to assert that he'd fallen on the ground, and the bullets had shattered his windshield. The police diagnosed him with cuts and bruises, but without any serious injuries.

The item made the news. When it was broadcast, a policeman was listening and wondered if this were the same Ronald Dante for whom a grand theft felony warrant had been issued the previous year in Santa Ana.

Despite his marriage to Lana, Dante still maintained a private apartment. By a strange coincidence, Cheryl worked at one of her father's restaurants across the street. She had been drawn to the window to see the arrival of squad cars, as four policemen, two with their guns drawn, entered his building. Within twenty minutes, Dante, handcuffed, was escorted out and hauled off for questioning. Cheryl called her mother and reported what she'd witnessed.

As it turned out, the owner of a boat company had accused Dante of breaking into his lot at night and hauling off $18,000 worth of boats in a rented truck. He was arrested, but allowed to post $12,500 in bail. He later jumped bail and never showed up for his court date.

To get him out of jail this time, Lana phoned Greg Bautzer, asking him to handle Dante's case, and even posted bail for him on this second charge. Somehow, Bautzer managed to have the charges against Dante dismissed.

***

In August of 1969, Taylor Pero entered her life as her secretary / personal manager. He would remain for a decade.

Lana had been invited to appear at a fundraising benefit for children in San Francisco at the Presbyterian Hospital Auxiliary. She flew north, with a publicist for Universal, Phil Sinclair, who had organized the event. Pero and Dante went with them.

The highlight of the evening occurred when she was to be auctioned to the highest bidder, who would be awarded with a date with her.

At the time, it would have been impossible for her to imagine that this was the last time she'd ever see Dante.

Herb Caen, a columnist for the *San Francisco Chronicle,* reported on her check-in at the Mark Hopkins Hotel, where she was mobbed by autograph seekers. Some of her most loyal fans turned out for the event. Because she was running late for the scheduled event, she was soon back on the sidewalk in front of the hotel, getting once again into a limousine.

She was wearing a Nolan Miller original. *[He had designed her wardrobe for* The Survivors.*]* For her appearance, he'd created a red jumpsuit over which she wore a magnificent floor-length lace vest made of the most expensive Spanish lace.

It was estimated that she was adorned with $250,000 worth of diamonds. She told a reporter, "I sleep with my diamonds. That way, if a thief breaks in to steal them, he'll have to steal me, too."

Caen would later write: "Lana Turner may look her 49 or 50 years under close scrutiny, but she's still every inch (or every other inch) the kind of movie goddess they don't make any more. By turn regal and petulant, demanding and generous, temperamental and cuddly."

At the charity event, which included a fund-raising auction, in front of an adoring public, a richly dressed young man, who looked no more than nineteen, entered the winning bid for a date with her. After the auction, she was seen "smothering him in motherly kisses."

Before leaving, she arranged details of their upcoming date, with the understanding that it would occur two nights later, in San Francisco.

Then Lana, with her tuxedo-clad husband, along with Pero and Sinclair, went to Finocchio's, the most famous female impersonator club in San Francisco. It was here that Howard Hughes had once fallen in love with a drag queen but demanded that he submit to a sex-change operation, in Mexico, before bedding her.

As the evening wore on, Lana was surrounded by her fans and by many of the drag queens who jealously evaluated her designer outfit, her jewelry, and her furs.

After the show, Lana wanted to continue to party, inviting her guests to a flamenco club, Casa Madrid. At one point, she put a flower in her teeth and danced a drunken flamenco in the center of the floor.

Back at the Mark Hopkins, Sinclair agreed to go out to retrieve some submarine sandwiches. For some reason, Dante wanted to accompany him. Both men set off together in the studio limousine, whose driver had not yet been dismissed for the night.

It grew later and later. Finally, Sinclair returned from his errand and seemed reluctant to tell her what had happened. He reported, "Dante told the driver to stop, telling him, 'I want to get out.' Those were his last words. I saw him hail a taxi and disappear into the night, or whatever was left of the night."

Lana tried to make up excuses for him, expecting him to call. By mid-morning, when he still hadn't called, she left the suite and toured San Francisco on Pero's arm. She phoned the hotel repeatedly during her absence, but there was no news of Dante.

Eventually, she and Pero flew back to Los Angeles. Arriving at her home, they each noticed that Dante's expensive, Italian motorcycle was missing from the driveway. Inside her house, they entered the bedroom, ascertaining that all his clothing had been removed from his closet. Only empty hangars remained. In her bathroom, he'd pasted a note, written on her personal blue stationery.

It read: "It's obvious that you have your thing to do, and I have mine, and I have to keep on doing it."

It was signed "Muggs," her nickname for him.

Pero reminded her that she'd transferred funds to him worth $35,000 for the launch of a real estate development he'd defined as "a stack sack." Conceived as the lowest-cost housing in the area, it was to have been constructed with walls of cement bags.

She phoned her business manager and learned to her dismay that he'd fraudulently written checks against this deposit to fictitious people for all but $1,000 of her original deposit. Fortunately, she was able to stop payment on most of these checks, all except for one, which had been made out to "Harry Firestone" for cash.

As Pero observed, Lana then entered one of her worst periods. She'd lost her young husband, and her fading career was battered by the dismal ratings of *The Survivors*.

Her nerves shattered, she asked Pero to accompany her to Palm Springs, where her interior decorator, Vincent Patere, had made his home available to her.

***

In Palm Springs, at 3AM, Pero and Lana were asleep when he was awakened by the persistent ringing of the phone. He answered to learn that it was Dante calling, insisting that he urgently needed to speak to Lana.

Pero aroused her from her bed, and she went to the phone.

"I was thinking about you," came his familiar voice. "I just had to hear the sound of your voice."

"At three o'clock in the morning?" she asked.

He did not explain his sudden disappearance. He went on to tell her how much he loved her and how he wanted to come back into her life. She agreed to think it over later that morning.

Before ringing off, he asked her, "How long do you plan to be in Palm Springs?"

She told him, "three or four nights."

The next morning, she told Pero and Pastere, "There was something fishy about that call."

She learned just how fishy when she returned three nights later to her home. Pero went into the house first. Nothing seemed out of place until they entered the bedroom.

It had been ransacked, her locked chest of drawers forced open. One drawer had contained a box with $100,000 worth of jewelry. A thief had made off with it.

Fearing a scandal, she never phoned the police, although both of them knew it had been Dante. That explained his phone call to her in Palm Springs. He had planned to loot her jewelry while she was away.

In December of 1970, she was in the divorce court once again, charging Dante with embezzlement of the $35,000. She did not mention the $100,000 in stolen jewelry.

Her attorney presented her with a document containing her signature. The document stated that she had agreed to give Dante $200,000 in case of a divorce. She felt he had tricked her into signing this document through some subterfuge.

The judge seemed to agree with her, and dismissed the document as fake. He went on to accuse Dante of "malice, oppression, and fraud." He was ordered to pay her $25,000, plus another $10,000 in compensatory damages. Yet she obviously had no intention of pursuing him, fearing additional scandal.

After her divorce from Dante was granted, Lana told a reporter, "Each one has its own individual hurt. I'm not bitter. You know to love and be loved are two different things. I always believed I was being loved for myself—and not just for the image of Lana Turner. But time and time again, I have been so god damn gullible. I'm sick and tired of being gullible."

She told friends, "Please do not speak of my marriage No. 6 or my marriage No. 7 ever again."

***

Whatever happened to the mysterious Ronald Dante? Four years after his divorce from Lana, on November 9, 1974, the Associated Press moved a story about him across its wires.

> *"Ronald Dante, the nightclub hypnotist, was found guilty in Tucson, Arizona, yesterday of attempting to contract for the murder in San Diego of the widely known hypnotist and entertainer, Michael Dean, his chief rival. In the Pima County Superior Court, a jury found Dante, 53, former husband of Lana Turner, guilty of second degree attempted murder."*

He was sentenced to five years in prison, but served only three and a half before his release. In the 1990s, he was also tried and convicted for what was called "the greatest diploma-mill scam in U.S. history." He was granting doctorates from Columbia State University, which did not exist. This time, he served eighteen months.

The last that was heard of him was in the summer of 2006, when J. Henry Jones, a staff writer for the San Diego *Union Tribune,* found Dante living in a modest mobile home in Pauma Valley, California. At the age of 86, although he claimed that $20 million had been stolen from him, he was surviving on a Social Security check of $450 a month.

He was making extra cash by creating artificial flowers from napkins and toilet paper. "I'm suffering from cancer," he told Jones. "Do you know I was the last husband of Lana Turner?"

***

In 1982, Taylor Pero wrote a book, *Always Lana,* about his decade of service to her. In it, he said, "Dante had come into her life when she was at an emotional nadir. She could have been perfectly content to let him come home and spend the night and then dismissed him. But he proved too magnetic than that. He must have charmed the pants off her, for at first she acknowledged she felt very safe and loved by Dante."

Without any good reason, Lana dismissed Pero after his loyal and faithful service to her. His book reflected his bitterness. "Lana Turner is the ultimate user and manipulator of people. Accordingly, she discards people, friends, and husbands alike, when she has no further use for them."

EPILOGUE

A heavy smoker for decades, Lana was diagnosed with throat cancer in May of 1992. "I'm going to fight this," she vowed and bravely carried on. She never smoked another cigarette. In February of 1993, she announced, "I'm cancer free."

But by July of 1994, the cancer had returned to her throat and also to her jaw and lungs. It was now hopeless for her, and she knew she had only months to live. Not able to speak, she communicated by writing notes.

Cheryl now stood to lose her mother. In February of 1985, Stephen Crane had died of cirrhosis. He'd made millions with his restaurants, but in the last months of his life, he sank into despair and alcoholism.

On June 29, 1995, a bulletin went out across the wire services that the legendary Lana Turner, reigning screen goddess of the 1940s, was dead of throat cancer. She was to be cremated, her ashes turned over to Cheryl. She requested that there be no funeral.

Tributes poured in from around the world from her beloved fans, many of them aging, although she'd discovered a new fan base, based on the television revival of many of her films.

One headline read: THE LOVE GODDESS IS DEAD.

Comments varied, one critic defining her as "a beautiful lie."

Another claimed, "Born a star, dies a star."

Yet another stated, "She downloaded her fabulousness onto us."

Months before she died, she was asked how she wanted to be remembered before the memory of Old Hollywood itself grew dim for future generations.

"I want to be known as the dame who put *tinsel* into Tinseltown."

With Respect and Admiration and Affection to the Queen of MGM

Lana Turner

American Movie Star
(1921-1995)

One reporter described her as "The timeless beauty for the ages, a woman who brought passion to the screen and lived a turbulent life to the fullest, surviving countless love affairs, broken marriages, a murder, endless tragedies, suicide attempts, abortions, a failing career, and the first telltale signs of aging."

"She survived all the disasters until the final curtain. She must have said, 'God, enough is enough!'"

LANA TURNER
Hearts & Diamonds Take All
Its Authors:

DARWIN PORTER

As an intense nine-year-old, **Darwin Porter** began meeting movie stars, TV personalities, politicians, and singers through his vivacious and attractive mother, Hazel, an eccentric but charismatic Southern girl who had lost her husband in World War II. Migrating from the Depression-ravaged valleys of western North Carolina to Miami Beach during its most ebullient heyday, Hazel became a stylist, wardrobe mistress, and personal assistant to the vaudeville *comedienne* **Sophie Tucker**, the bawdy and irrepressible "Last of the Red Hot Mamas."

Virtually every show-biz celebrity who visited Miami Beach paid a call on "Miss Sophie," and Darwin as a pre-teen loosely and indulgently supervised by his mother, was regularly dazzled by the likes of **Judy Garland, Dinah Shore,** and **Frank Sinatra.**

It was at Miss Sophie's that he met his first political figure, who was actually an actor at the time. Between marriages, **Ronald Reagan** came to call on Ms. Sophie, who was his favorite singer. He was accompanied by a young blonde starlet, **Marilyn Monroe.**

At the University of Miami, Darwin edited the school newspaper.

He first met and interviewed **Eleanor Roosevelt** at the Fontainebleau Hotel on Miami Beach and invited her to spend a day at the university. She accepted, much to his delight.

After graduation, he became the Bureau Chief of *The Miami Herald* in Key West, Florida, where he got to take early morning walks with the former U.S. president **Harry S Truman**, discussing his presidency and the events that had shaped it.

Through Truman, Darwin was introduced and later joined the staff of **Senator George Smathers** of Florida. His best friend was a young senator, **John F. Kennedy.** Through "Gorgeous George," as Smathers was known in the Senate, Darwin got to meet Jack and Jacqueline in Palm Beach. He later wrote two books about them—*The Kennedys, All the Gossip Unfit to Print,* and one of his all-time bestsellers, *Jacqueline Kennedy Onassis—A Life Beyond Her Wildest Dreams.*

For about a decade in New York, Darwin worked in television journalism and advertising with his long-time partner, the journalist, art director, and distinguished arts-industry socialite **Stanley Mills Haggart.**

Stanley (as an art director) and Darwin (as a writer and assistant), worked as freelance agents in television. Jointly, they helped produce TV commercials that included testimonials from **Joan Crawford** (then feverishly promoting Pepsi-Cola); **Ronald Reagan** (General Electric); and **Debbie Reynolds** (Singer sewing machines). Other personalities appearing and delivering televised sales pitches included **Louis Armstrong, Lena Horne,** and **Arlene Dahl,** each of them hawking a commercial product.

Beginning in the early 1960s, Darwin joined forces with the then-fledgling **Arthur Frommer** organization, playing a key role in researching and writing more than 50 titles and defining the style and values that later emerged as the world's leading travel guidebooks, *The Frommer Guides,* with particular emphasis on Europe, California, New England, and the Caribbean. Between the creation and updating of hundreds of editions of detailed travel guides to England, France, Italy, Spain, Portugal, Austria, Hungary, Germany, Switzerland, the Caribbean, and California, he continued to interview and discuss the triumphs, feuds, and frustrations of celebrities, many by then reclusive, whom he either sought out or encountered randomly as part of his extensive travels. **Ava Gardner** and **Lana Turner** were particularly insightful.

It was while living in New York that Darwin became fascinated by the career of a rising real estate mogul changing the skyline of Manhattan. He later, of course, became the "gambling czar" of Atlantic City and a star of reality TV.

Darwin began collecting an astonishing amount of data on Donald Trump, squirreling it away in boxes, hoping one day to write a biography of this charismatic, controversial figure.

Before doing that, he penned more than thirty uncensored, unvarnished, and unauthorized biographies on subjects that included **Peter O'Toole, James Dean, Marlon Brando, Merv Griffin, Katharine Hepburn, Howard Hughes, Humphrey Bogart, Michael Jackson, Paul Newman, Steve McQueen, Marilyn Monroe, Elizabeth Taylor, Frank Sinatra, Vivien Leigh, Laurence Olivier, the notorious porn star Linda Lovelace, Zsa Zsa Gabor and her sisters, Tennessee Williams, Gore Vidal,** and **Truman Capote.**

Darwin is also the author of *Love Triangle,* devoted to the Hollywood careers of **Ronald Reagan** and his two actress wives, **Jane Wyman** and **Nancy Davis.**

As a departure from his usual repertoire, Darwin also wrote the controversial *J. Edgar Hoover & Clyde Tolson: Investigating the Sexual Secrets of America's Most Famous Men and Women,* a book about celebrity, voyeurism, political and sexual repression, and blackmail within the highest circles of the U.S. government.

In time for the 2016 race for the White House, and in addition to the Donald Trump book *(The Man Who Would be King)*, Darwin also wrote *Bill & Hillary—So This Is That Thing Called Love.*

Porter's biographies, over the years, have won twenty first prize or "runner-up to first prize" awards at literary festivals in cities or states which include Boston, New York, Los Angeles, Hollywood, San Francisco, Florida, and Paris.

Darwin can be heard at regular intervals as a radio and television commentator, "dishing" celebrities, pop culture, politics, and scandal.

A resident of New York City, Darwin is currently at work on history's first comprehensive biography of Rock Hudson, *Erotic Fire.*

DANFORTH PRINCE

The co-author of this book, **Danforth Prince** is president and founder of Blood Moon Productions, a firm devoted to salvaging, compiling, and marketing the oral histories of America's entertainment industry.

Prince launched his career in journalism in the 1970s at the Paris Bureau of *The New York Times.* In the early '80s, he joined Darwin Porter in developing first editions of many of the titles within *The Frommer Guides.* Together, they reviewed and articulated the travel scenes of more than 50 nations, most of them within Europe and The Caribbean. Authoritative and comprehensive, they became best-selling "travel bibles" for millions of readers.

Prince, in collaboration with Porter, is also the co-author of several award-winning celebrity biographies, each configured as a title within Blood Moon's Babylon series. These have included *Hollywood Babylon—It's Back!; Hollywood Babylon Strikes Again; The Kennedys: All the Gossip Unfit to Print; Frank Sinatra, The Boudoir Singer, Elizabeth Taylor: There Is Nothing Like a Dame; Pink Triangle: The Feuds and Private Lives of Tennessee Williams, Gore Vidal, Truman Capote, and Members of their Entourages;* and *Jacqueline Kennedy Onassis: A Life Beyond Her Wildest Dreams.* More recent efforts include *Peter O'Toole—Hellraiser, Sexual Outlaw, Irish Rebel; Bill & Hillary—So This Is That Thing Called Love;* and *James Dean, Tomorrow Never Comes.*

One of his recent projects, co-authored with Darwin Porter, is *Donald*

Trump, The Man Who Would Be King. Configured for release directly into the frenzy of the 2016 presidential elections, and winner of at least three literary awards, it's a celebrity overview of the decades of pre-presidential scandals—personal, political, and dynastic—associated with The Donald during the rambunctious decades when no one ever thought he'd actually get elected.

Prince is also the co-author of four books on film criticism, three of which won honors at regional bookfests in Los Angeles and San Francisco.

Prince, a graduate of Hamilton College and a native of Easton and Bethlehem, Pennsylvania, is the president and founder of the Georgia Literary Association (1996), and of the Porter and Prince Corporation (1983) which has produced dozens of titles for Simon & Schuster, Prentice Hall, and John Wiley & Sons. In 2011, he was named "Publisher of the Year" by a consortium of literary critics and marketers spearheaded by the J.M. Northern Media Group.

Publishing in collaboration with the National Book Network *(www.NBN-Books.com)*, he has electronically documented some of the controversies associated with his stewardship of Blood Moon in at least 50 documentaries, book trailers, public speeches, and TV or radio interviews. Most of these are available on **YouTube.com** and **Facebook** *(keywords: "Danforth Prince" or "Blood Moon Productions")*; on **Twitter** *(#BloodyandLunar)*; or by clicking on **BloodMoonProductions.com**.

He is currently at work writing and researching two upcoming biographies, one that focuses on Rock Hudson, the other on the mother-daughter saga of Carrie Fisher and Debbie Reynolds.

Available in September, 2017, from Blood Moon Productions

Rock Hudson Erotic Fire

By Darwin Porter & Danforth Prince

In the interim since Rock Hudson's tragic death as one of the early (and perhaps the most shocking, based on his celebrity) victims of AIDS, his legend has evolved into a nationwide cult. Yet despite his post-mortem fame, his salaciously poignant story has never been fully told. Until now.

Loaded with details never set into print before, this unvarnished, uncensored overview of Rock Hudson's scandal-soaked rise to fame and subsequent fall from grace, in commemoration of the 30th anniversary of his death, is the most comprehensive ever published.

Compiled in the aftermath of 50 years of research, this provocative, scandal-soaked overview of the most macho sex symbol of his era presents an empathetic look at the ironies, hypocrisies, and compromises of a Great American movie star.

A Shocking and Salacious Softcover with Information about Rock You've Never Read Before.
600 pages, with dozens of photos. New from America's Hottest Celebrity Biographers.
ISBN 978-1-936003-55-6

LOVE TRIANGLE

Ronald Reagan, Jane Wyman, & Nancy Davis

Unique in the history of publishing, this scandalous triple biography focuses on the Hollywood indiscretions of former U.S. president Ronald Reagan and his two wives. A proud and Presidential addition to Blood Moon's Babylon series, it digs deep into what these three young and attractive movie stars were doing decades before two of them took over the Free World.

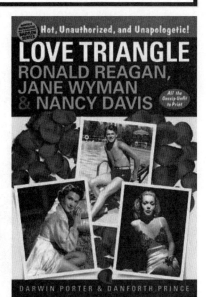

***

As reviewed by Diane Donovan, Senior Reviewer at the California Bookwatch section of the Midwest Book Review: *"Love Triangle: Ronald Reagan, Jane Wyman & Nancy Davis may find its way onto many a Republican Reagan fan's reading shelf; but those who expect another Reagan celebration will be surprised: this is lurid Hollywood exposé writing at its best, and outlines the truths surrounding one of the most provocative industry scandals in the world.*

"There are already so many biographies of the Reagans on the market that one might expect similar mile-markers from this: be prepared for shock and awe; because Love Triangle doesn't take your ordinary approach to biography and describes a love triangle that eventually bumped a major Hollywood movie star from the possibility of being First Lady and replaced her with a lesser-known Grade B actress (Nancy Davis).

"From politics and betrayal to romance, infidelity, and sordid affairs, Love Triangle is a steamy, eye-opening story that blows the lid off of the Reagan illusion to raise eyebrows on both sides of the big screen.

"Black and white photos liberally pepper an account of the careers of all three and the lasting shock of their stormy relationships in a delightful pursuit especially recommended for any who relish Hollywood gossip."

In 2015, LOVE TRIANGLE, Blood Moon Productions' overview of the early dramas associated with Ronald Reagan's scandal-soaked career in Hollywood, was designated by the Awards Committee of the **HOLLYWOOD BOOK FESTIVAL** as Runner-Up to Best Biography of the Year.

LOVE TRIANGLE: Ronald Reagan, Jane Wyman, & Nancy Davis
Darwin Porter & Danforth Prince
Hot, scandalous, and loaded with information about their Hollywood careers that the Reagans never wanted you to know.
Softcover, 6" x 9", with hundreds of photos.   ISBN 978-1-936003-41-9

THE KENNEDYS

ALL THE GOSSIP UNFIT TO PRINT

A Staggering Compendium of Indiscretions Associated With Seven Key
Players in the Kennedy Clan; A Cornucopia of Relatively Unknown but
Carefully Documented Scandals from the Golden Age of Camelot

Darwin Porter & Danforth Prince

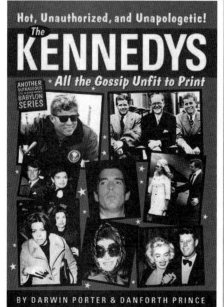

Hot, Unauthorized, and Unapologetic!

The KENNEDYS

ANOTHER OUTRAGEOUS BABYLON SERIES

All the Gossip Unfit to Print

BY DARWIN PORTER & DANFORTH PRINCE

*The great enemy of truth is very often not
the lie—deliberate, contrived, and dishon-
est, but the myth—persistent, persuasive,
and unrealistic."*

—John F. Kennedy

*"Pick this book up, and you'll be hard-
pressed to put it down"*
—Richard Labonté, Q-Syndicate

The Kennedys were the first true movie stars to occupy the White House.
They were also Washington's horniest political tribe, and although America loved
their humor, their style, and their panache, we took delight in this tabloid-style
documentation of their hundreds of staggering indiscretions.

Keepers of the dying embers of Camelot won't like it, but Kennedy historians
and aficionados will interpret it as required reading.

Hardcover, with hundreds of photos and 450 meticulously researched, highly
detailed, and very gossipy pages with more outrageous scandal than 90% of
American voters during the heyday of Camelot could possibly have imagined.

ISBN 978-1-936003-17-4.
Temporarily sold out of hard copies, but available for e-readers.

BLOOD MOON
Productions, Ltd.

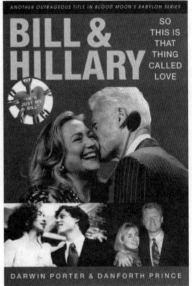

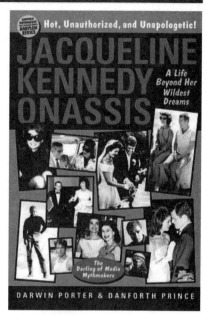

After floods of analysis and commentary in tabloid and mainstream newspapers worldwide, this has emerged as the world's most comprehensive testimonial to the flimsier side of Camelot, the most comprehensive compendium of gossip ever published about America's unofficial, uncrowned queen, **Jacqueline Kennedy Onassis**. Its publication coincided with the 20-year anniversary of the death of one of the most famous, revered, and talked-about women who ever lived.

During her tumultuous life, Mrs. Onassis zealously guarded her privacy and her secrets. But in the wake of her death, more and more revelations have emerged about her frustrations, her rage, her passions, her towering strengths, and her delicate fragility, which she hid from the glare of the world behind oversized sunglasses. Within this posthumous biography, a three-dimensional woman emerges through the compilation of some 1,000 eyewitness testimonials from men and women who knew her over a period of decades.

An overview of the life of Mrs. Onassis is a natural fit for Blood Moon, a publishing enterprise that's increasingly known, worldwide, as one of the most provocative and scandalous in the history of publishing.

"References to this American icon appear with almost rhythmic regularity to anyone researching the cultural landscape of America during the last half of The American Century," said Danforth Prince. "Based on what we'd uncovered about Jackie during the research of many of our earlier titles, we're positioning ourselves as a more or less solitary outpost of irreverence within a landscape that's otherwise flooded with fawning, over-reverential testimonials. Therein lies this book's appeal—albeit with a constant respect and affection for a woman we admired and adored."

Based on decades of research by writers who define themselves as "voraciously attentive Kennedyphiles," it supplements the half-dozen other titles within Blood Moon's Babylon series.

J. Edgar Hoover & Clyde Tolson

Investigating the Sexual Secrets
of America's Most Famous Men & Women
Darwin Porter

This epic saga of power and corruption has a revelation on every page—cross dressing, gay parties, sexual indiscretions, hustlers for sale, alliances with the Mafia, and criminal activity by the nation's chief law enforcer.

It's all here, with chilling details about the abuse of power on the dark side of the American saga. But mostly it's the decades-long love story of America's two most powerful men who could tell presidents "how to skip rope." (Hoover's words.)

"Everyone's dredging up J. Edgar Hoover. Leonardo DiCaprio just immortalized him, and now comes Darwin Porter's paperback, *J. Edgar Hoover & Clyde Tolson: Investigating the Sexual Secrets of America's Most Famous Men and Women*. It shovels Hoover's darkest secrets dragged kicking and screaming from the closet. It's filth on every VIP who's safely dead and some who are still above ground."

—Cindy Adams, The New York Post

"This book is important, because it destroys what's left of Hoover's reputation. Did you know he had intel on the bombing of Pearl Harbor, but he sat on it, making him more or less responsible for thousands of deaths? Or that he had almost nothing to do with the arrests or killings of any of the 1930s gangsters that he took credit for catching?

"A lot of people are angry with its author, Darwin Porter. They say that his outing of celebrities is just cheap gossip about dead people who can't defend themselves. I suppose it's because Porter is destroying carefully constructed myths that are comforting to most people. As gay men, we benefit the most from Porter's work, because we know that except for AIDS, the closet was the most terrible thing about the 20th century. If the closet never existed, neither would Hoover. The fact that he got away with such duplicity under eight presidents makes you think that every one of them was a complete fool for tolerating it."

—Paul Bellini, FAB Magazine (Toronto)

Winner of Literary Awards from the Los Angeles & the Hollywood Book Festivals
Temporarily sold out of hard copies, but available for E-Readers.   ISBN 978-1-936003-25-9

PINK TRIANGLE: The Feuds and Private Lives of Tennessee Williams,

Gore Vidal, Truman Capote, and Famous Members of their Entourages
Darwin Porter & Danforth Prince

This book, the only one of its kind, reveals the backlot intrigues associated with the literary and script-writing *enfants terribles* of America's entertainment community during the mid-20th century.

It exposes their bitchfests, their slugfests, and their relationships with the *glitterati*—Marilyn Monroe, Brando, the Oliviers, the Paleys, U.S. Presidents, a gaggle of other movie stars, millionaires, and international *débauchés*.

This is for anyone who's interested in the formerly concealed scandals of Hollywood and Broadway, and the values and pretentions of both the literary community and the entertainment industry.

"A banquet... If PINK TRIANGLE had not been written for us, we would have had to research and type it all up for ourselves…Pink Triangle is nearly seven hundred pages of the most entertaining histrionics ever sliced, spiced, heated, and serviced up to the reading public. Everything that Blood Moon has done before pales in comparison.
Given the fact that the subjects of the book themselves were nearly delusional on the subject of themselves (to say nothing of each other) it is hard to find fault. Add to this the intertwined jungle that was the relationship among Williams, Capote, and Vidal, of the times they vied for things they loved most—especially attention—and the times they enthralled each other and the world, [Pink Triangle is] the perfect antidote to the Polar Vortex."
—Vinton McCabe in the NY JOURNAL OF BOOKS

"Full disclosure: I have been a friend and follower of Blood Moon Productions' tomes for years, and always marveled at the amount of information in their books—it's staggering. The index alone to Pink Triangle runs to 21 pages—and the scale of names in it runs like a Who's Who of American social, cultural and political life through much of the 20th century."
—Perry Brass in THE HUFFINGTON POST

"We Brits are not spared the Porter/Prince silken lash either. PINK TRIANGLE's research is, quite frankly, breathtaking. PINK TRIANGLE will fascinate you for many weeks to come. Once you have made the initial titillating dip, the day will seem dull without it."
—Jeffery Tayor in THE SUNDAY EXPRESS (UK)

PINK TRIANGLE—The Feuds and Private Lives of Tennessee Williams, Gore Vidal, Truman Capote, and Famous Members of their Entourages
Darwin Porter & Danforth Prince
Softcover, 700 pages, with photos   ISBN 978-1-936003-37-2   Also Available for E-Readers

THOSE GLAMOROUS GABORS

Bombshells from Budapest, by Darwin Porter

Zsa Zsa, Eva, and Magda Gabor transferred their glittery dreams and gold-digging ambitions from the twilight of the Austro-Hungarian Empire to Hollywood. There, more effectively than any army, these Bombshells from Budapest broke hearts, amassed fortunes, lovers, and A-list husbands, and amused millions of *voyeurs* through the medium of television, movies, and the social registers. In this astonishing "triple-play" biography, designated "Best Biography of the Year" by the Hollywood Book Festival, Blood Moon lifts the "mink-and-diamond" curtain on this amazing trio of blood-related sisters, whose complicated intrigues have never been fully explored before.

"**You will never be Ga-bored...this book gives new meaning to the term compelling.** Be warned, *Those Glamorous Gabors* is both an epic and a pip. Not since *Gone With the Wind* have so many characters on the printed page been forced to run for their lives for one reason or another. And Scarlett making a dress out of the curtains is nothing compared to what a Gabor will do when she needs to scrap together an outfit for a movie premiere or late-night outing.

"For those not up to speed, Jolie Tilleman came from a family of jewelers and therefore came by her love for the shiny stones honestly, perhaps genetically. She married Vilmos Gabor somewhere around World War 1 (exact dates, especially birth dates, are always somewhat vague in order to establish plausible deniability later on) and they were soon blessed with three daughters: **Magda**, the oldest, whose hair, sadly, was naturally brown, although it would turn quite red in America; **Zsa Zsa** (born 'Sari') a natural blond who at a very young age exhibited the desire for fame with none of the talents usually associated with achievement, excepting beauty and a natural wit; and **Eva**, the youngest and blondest of the girls, who after seeing Grace Moore perform at the National Theater, decided that she wanted to be an actress and that she would one day move to Hollywood to become a star.

"Given that the Gabor family at that time lived in Budapest, Hungary, at the period of time between the World Wars, that Hollywood dream seemed a distant one indeed. The story—the riches to rags to riches to rags to riches again myth of survival against all odds as the four women, because of their Jewish heritage, flee Europe with only the minks on their backs and what jewels they could smuggle along with them in their *decolletage*, only to have to battle afresh for their places in the vicious Hollywood pecking order—gives new meaning to the term 'compelling.' The reader, as if he were witnessing a particularly goredrenched traffic accident, is incapable of looking away."

—New York Review of Books

Those Glamorous Gabors, Bombshells from Budapest, by Darwin Porter.
Softcover, 730 pages, with hundreds of photos   ISBN 978-1-936003-35-8

PETER O'TOOLE
Hellraiser, Sexual Outlaw, Irish Rebel

At the time of its publication early in 2015, this book was widely publicized in the *Daily Mail,* the *New York Daily News,* the *New York Post,* the *Midwest Book Review, The Express (London), The Globe,* the *National Enquirer,* and in equivalent publications worldwide

One of the world's most admired (and brilliant) actors, Peter O'Toole wined and wenched his way through a labyrinth of sexual and interpersonal betrayals, sometimes with disastrous results. Away from the stage and screen, where such films as *Becket* and *Lawrence of Arabia*, made film history, his life was filled with drunken, debauched nights and edgy sexual experimentations, most of which were never openly examined in the press. A hellraiser, he shared wild times with his "best blokes" Richard Burton and Richard Harris. Peter Finch, also his close friend, once invited him to join him in sharing the pleasures of his mistress, Vivien Leigh.

"My father, a bookie, moved us to the Mick community of Leeds," O'Toole once told a reporter. "We were very poor, but I was born an Irishman, which accounts for my gift of gab, my unruly behavior, my passionate devotion to women and the bottle, and my loathing of any authority figure."

Author Robert Sellers described O'Toole's boyhood neighborhood. "Three of his playmates went on to be hanged for murder; one strangled a girl in a lovers' quarrel; one killed a man during a robbery; another cut up a warden in South Africa with a pair of shears. It was a heavy bunch."

Peter O'Toole's hell-raising life story has never been told, until now. Hot and uncensored, from a writing team which, even prior to O'Toole's death in 2013, had been collecting under-the-radar info about him for years, this book has everything you ever wanted to know about how THE LION navigated his way through the boudoirs of the Entertainment Industry IN WINTER, Spring, Summer, and a dissipated Autumn as well.

Blood Moon has ripped away the imperial robe, scepter, and crown usually associated with this quixotic problem child of the British Midlands. Provocatively uncensored, this illusion-shattering overview of Peter O'Toole's hellraising (or at least very naughty) and demented life is unique in the history of publishing.

PETER O'TOOLE: *Hellraiser, Sexual Outlaw, Irish Rebel*
Softcover, with photos. ISBN 978-1-936003-45-7.
Also available for e-readers

This book illustrates why *Gentlemen Prefer Blondes*, and why Marilyn Monroe was too dangerous to be allowed to go on living.

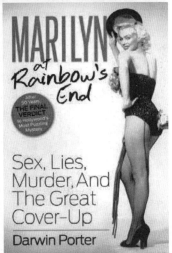

Less than an hour after the discovery of Marilyn Monroe's corpse in Brentwood, a flood of theories, tainted evidence, and conflicting testimonies began pouring out into the public landscape.

Filled with rage, hysteria, and depression, "and fed up with Jack's lies, Bobby's lies," Marilyn sought revenge and mass vindication. Her revelations at an imminent press conference could have toppled political dynasties and destroyed criminal empires. Marilyn had to be stopped…

Into this steamy cauldron of deceit, Marilyn herself emerges as a most unreliable witness during the weeks leading up to her murder. Her own deceptions, vanities, and self-delusion poured toxic accelerants on an already raging fire.

MARILYN AT RAINBOW'S END

SEX, LIES, MURDER, AND THE GREAT COVER-UP, BY DARWIN PORTER
ISBN 978-1-936003-29-7
Temporarily sold out of hard copies, but available for E-Readers

"Darwin Porter is fearless, honest and a great read. He minces no words. If the truth makes you wince and honesty offends your sensibility, stay away. It's been said that he deals in muck because he can't libel the dead. Well, it's about time someone started telling the truth about the dead and being honest about just what happened to get us in the mess in which we're in. If libel is lying, then Porter is so completely innocent as to deserve an award. In all of his works he speaks only to the truth, and although he is a hard teacher and task master, he's one we ignore at our peril. To quote Gore Vidal, power is not a toy we give to someone for being good. If we all don't begin to investigate where power and money really are in the here and now, we deserve what we get. Yes, Porter names names. The reader will come away from the book knowing just who killed Monroe. Porter rather brilliantly points to a number of motives, but leaves it to the reader to surmise exactly what happened at the rainbow's end, just why Marilyn was killed. And, of course, why we should be careful of getting exactly what we want. It's a very long tumble from the top."

—**ALAN PETRUCELLI, Examiner.com, May 13, 2012**

Elizabeth Taylor, *There is Nothing Like a Dame*

All the Gossip Unfit to Print from the Glory Days of Hollywood

For more than 60 years, Elizabeth Taylor dazzled generations of movie-goers with her glamor and her all-consuming passion for life. She was the last of the great stars of Golden Age Hollywood, coming to a sad end at the age of 79 in 2011.

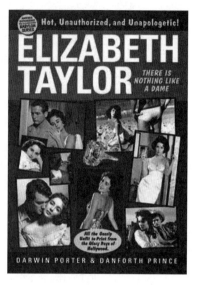

But before she died, appearing on the Larry King show, she claimed that her biographers had revealed "only half of my story, but I can't tell the other half in a memoir because I'd get sued."

Now, Blood Moon presents for the first time a comprehensive compilation of most of the secrets from the mercurial Dame Elizabeth, whose hedonism helped define the jet set of the tumultuous 60s and beyond.

Throughout the many decades of her life, she consistently generated hysteria among her fans. Here, her story is told with brutal honesty in rich, juicy detail and illustrated, with a new revelation on every page.

It's all here, and a lot more, in an exposé that's both sympathetic and shocking, with a candor and attention to detail that brings the *femme fatale* of the 20th century back to life.

"What has never been denied about Elizabeth Taylor is that the young actress, though small for her age, was mature beyond her years, deeply ambitious, and sexually precocious...Insiders agreed she always had a strong rebellious streak. Could the studio system's vice-like grip on publicity have stopped scandals about their most valuable child star from leaking out?

"A recent biography of Taylor claims that as a teenager, she lost her virginity at 15 to British actor Peter Lawford, had flings with Ronald Reagan and Errol Flynn, was roughly seduced by Orson Welles, and even enjoyed a threesome involving John F. Kennedy.

The authors—Darwin Porter and Danforth Prince—also allege Taylor was just 11 when she was taught by her close friend, the gay British actor, Roddy McDowall, the star of Lassie Come Home, *how to satisfy men without sleeping with them."*

Tom Leonard in THE DAILY MAIL, October 19, 2015

"Before they wither, Elizabeth Taylor's breasts will topple empires."

—Richard Burton

Softcover, 460 pages, with photos ISBN 978-1-936003-31-0.
Temporarily sold out of hard copies, but available as an E-book.

James Dean, *Tomorrow Never Comes*

Honoring the 60th anniversary of his violent and early death

America's most enduring and legendary symbol of young, enraged rebellion, James Dean continues into the 21st Century to capture the imagination of the world.

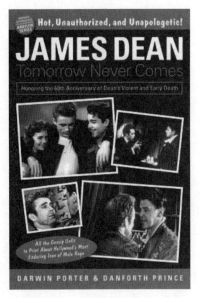

After one of his many flirtations with Death, which caught up with him when he was a celebrity-soaked 24-year-old, he said, "If a man can live after he dies, then maybe he's a great man." Today, bars from Nigeria to Patagonia are named in honor of this international, spectacularly self-destructive movie star icon.

Migrating from the dusty backroads of Indiana to center stage in the most formidable boudoirs of Hollywood, his saga is electrifying.

A strikingly handsome heart-throb, Dean is a study in contrasts: Tough but tender, brutal but remarkably sensitive; he was a reckless hellraiser badass who could revert to a little boy in bed.

A rampant bisexual, he claimed that he didn't want to go through life "with one hand tied behind my back." He demonstrated that during bedroom trysts with Marilyn Monroe, Rock Hudson, Elizabeth Taylor, Paul Newman, Natalie Wood, Shelley Winters, Marlon Brando, Steve McQueen, Ursula Andress, Montgomery Clift, Pier Angeli, Tennessee Williams, Susan Strasberg, Tallulah Bankhead, and FBI director J. Edgar Hoover.

Woolworth heiress Barbara Hutton, one of the richest and most dissipated women of her era, wanted to make him her toy boy.

Tomorrow Never Comes is the most penetrating look at James Dean to have   emerged from the wreckage of his Porsche Spyder in 1955.

Before setting out on his last ride, he said, "I feel life too intensely to bear living it."

Tomorrow Never Comes presents a damaged but beautiful soul.

JAMES DEAN—TOMORROW NEVER COMES
DARWIN PORTER & DANFORTH PRINCE
Softcover, with photos. ISBN 978-1-936003-49-5

INSIDE LINDA LOVELACE'S DEEP THROAT

DEGRADATION, PORNO CHIC, AND THE RISE OF FEMINISM

DARWIN PORTER

An insider's view of the unlikely heroine who changed the world's perceptions about pornography, censorship, and sexual behavior patterns

The Most Comprehensive Biography Ever Written of an
Adult Entertainment Star
and Her Relationship with the Underbelly of Hollywood

Darwin Porter, author of some twenty critically acclaimed celebrity exposés of behind-the-scenes intrigue in the entertainment industry, was deeply involved in the Linda Lovelace saga as it unfolded in the 70s, interviewing many of the players, and raising money for the legal defense of the film's co-star, Harry Reems. In this book, emphasizing her role as a celebrity interacting with other celebrities, he brings inside information and a never-before-published revelation to almost every page.

The Beach Book Festival's Grand Prize Winner: "Best Summer Reading of 2013"

Runner-Up to "Best Biography of 2013" *The Los Angeles Book Festival*

Winner of a Sybarite Award from HedoOnline.com

"This book drew me in..How could it not?" Coco Papy, *Bookslut.*

The Award-Winning overview of a story that changed America and the Entertainment Industry forever:

Another hot and insightful commentary about major and sometimes violently controversial conflicts of the American Century by

Darwin Porter

Softcover, 640 pages, 6"x9" with photos.
ISBN 978-1-936003-33-4

Paul Newman, The Man Behind the Baby Blues

His Secret Life Exposed

Darwin Porter

Drawn from firsthand interviews with insiders who knew Paul Newman intimately, and compiled over a period of nearly a half-century, this is the world's most honest and most revelatory biography about Hollywood's pre-eminent male sex symbol.

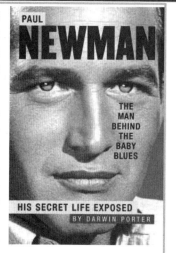

This is a respectful but candid cornucopia of once-concealed information about the sexual and emotional adventures of an affable, impossibly good-looking workaday actor, a former sailor from Shaker Heights, Ohio, who parlayed his ambisexual charm and extraordinary good looks into one of the most successful careers in Hollywood.

Whereas the situations it exposes were widely known within Hollywood's inner circles, they've never before been revealed to the general public.

But now, the full story has been published—the giddy heights and agonizing crashes of a great American star, with revelations and insights never before published in any other biography.

"Paul Newman had just as many on-location affairs as the rest of us, and he was just as bisexual as I was. But whereas I was always getting caught with my pants down, he managed to do it in the dark with not a paparazzo in sight. He might have bedded Marilyn Monroe or Elizabeth Taylor the night before, but he always managed to show up for breakfast with Joanne Woodward, with those baby blues, looking as innocent as a Botticelli angel. He never fooled me. It takes an alleycat to know another one. Did I ever tell you what really happened between Newman and me? If that doesn't grab you, what about what went on between James Dean and Newman? Let me tell you about this co-called model husband if you want to look behind those famous peepers."

—**Marlon Brando**

Merv Griffin, A Life in the Closet

by Darwin Porter

HOT, CONTROVERSIAL, AND RIGOROUSLY RESEARCHED,

HERE'S MERV!

Merv Griffin began his career as a Big Band singer, moved on to a failed career as a romantic hero in the movies, and eventually rewrote the rules of everything associated with the broadcasting industry. Along the way, he met and befriended virtually everyone who mattered, including Nancy Reagan, and made billions operating casinos and developing jingles, contests, and word games. All of this while maintaining a male harem and a secret life as America's most famously closeted homosexual.

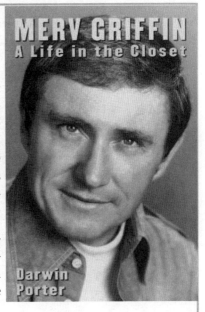

In this comprehensive and richly ironic biography, Darwin Porter reveals the amazing details behind the richest, most successful, and in some ways, the most notorious mogul in the history of America's entertainment industry.

***

"Darwin Porter told me why he tore the door off Merv's closet.......*Heeeere's Merv!* is 560 pages, 100 photos, a truckload of gossip, and a bedful of unauthorized dish."

Cindy Adams, The New York Post

"Darwin Porter tears the door off Merv Griffin's closet with gusto in this sizzling, superlatively researched biography...It brims with insider gossip that's about Hollywood legends, writ large, smart, and with great style."

Richard LaBonté, BOOKMARKS

Merv Griffin, a Life in the Closet, by Darwin Porter.
Hardcover, with photos. ISBN 978-0-9786465-0-9. Also available for E-Readers.

FRANK SINATRA, The Boudoir Singer

All the Gossip Unfit to Print from the Glory Days of Ol' Blue Eyes

Darwin Porter & Danforth Prince

"Every time I sing a song, I'm actually making love on stage. Call me 'The Boudoir Singer.'" —Frank Sinatra

"When Sinatra dies, they'll donate his zipper to the Smithsonian." —Dean Martin

"F-R-A-N-K-I-E-E-EE! Take my virginity!" screamed a bobby-soxer in midtown Manhattan in 1943

"Our problems were never in bed," said Ava Gardner, his greatest love. "We were always great in bed. Ten pounds of Frank, 110 pounds of cock."

Even If You Thought You'd Heard It All Already, You'll Be Amazed At How Much This Book Contains That Never Got Published Before.

Vendettas and high-octane indiscretions, fast and furious women, deep sensitivities and sporadic psychoses, Presidential pimping, FBI coverups, Mobster mambos, and a pantload of hushed-up scandals about **FABULOUS FRANK AND HIS MIND-BLOWING COHORTS**

"Womanizer Sinatra's Shocking Secret Sins are revealed in a blockbuster new book, including his raunchy romps with Liz Taylor, Marilyn Monroe, Jackie-O, and Nancy Reagan. Every time the leader of the Free World would join him in Palm Springs, the place was a sun-kissed brothel, with Kennedy as the main customer."

— THE GLOBE

Frank Sinatra, The Boudoir Singer
Hardcover, 465 pages with hundreds of photos
ISBN 978-1-936003-19-8 Also available for E-readers

Finally—A COOL biography that was too HOT to be published during the lifetime of its subject.

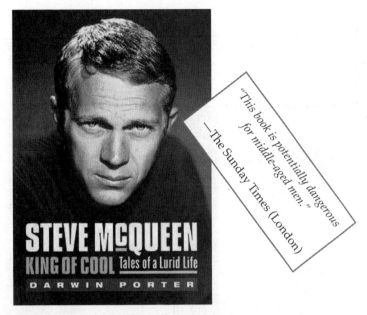

"This book is potentially dangerous for middle-aged men."
—The Sunday Times (London)

The drama of Steve McQueen's personal life far exceeded any role he ever played on screen. Born to a prostitute, he was brutally molested by some of his mother's "johns," and endured gang rape in reform school. His drift into prostitution began when he was hired as a towel boy in the most notorious bordello in the Dominican Republic, where he starred in a string of cheap porno films. Returning to New York before migrating to Hollywood, he hustled men on Times Square and, as a "gentleman escort" in a borrowed tux, rich older women.

And then, sudden stardom as he became the world's top box office attraction. The abused became the abuser. "I live for myself, and I answer to nobody," he proclaimed. "The last thing I want to do is fall in love with a broad."

Thus began a string of seductions that included hundreds of overnight pickups--both male and female. Topping his A-list conquests were James Dean, Paul Newman, Marilyn Monroe, and Barbra Streisand. Finally, this pioneering biography explores the mysterious death of Steve McQueen. Were those salacious rumors really true?

Steve McQueen
King of Cool
Tales of a Lurid Life
Darwin Porter

A carefully researched, 466-page hardcover with dozens of photos
Temporarily sold out of hard copies, but available now for e-readers

ISBN 978-1-936003-05-1

Humphrey Bogart, *The Making of a Legend*

Darwin Porter

A "CRADLE-TO-GRAVE" HARDCOVER ABOUT THE RISE TO FAME OF AN
OBSCURE, UNLIKELY, AND FREQUENTLY UNEMPLOYED BROADWAY ACTOR.

Whereas **Humphrey Bogart** is always at the top of any list of the Entertainment Industry's most famous actors, very little is known about how he clawed his way from Broadway to Hollywood during Prohibition and the Jazz Age.

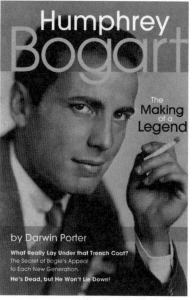

This pioneering biography begins with Bogart's origins as the child of wealthy (morphine-addicted) parents in New York City, then examines the love affairs, scandals, failures, and breakthroughs that launched him as an American icon.

It includes details about behind-the-scenes dramas associated with three mysterious marriages, and films such as *The Petrified Forest, The Maltese Falcon, High Sierra,* and *Casablanca.* Read all about the debut and formative years of the actor who influenced many generations of filmgoers, laying Bogie's life bare in a style you've come to expect from Darwin Porter. Exposed with all their juicy details is what Bogie never told his fourth wife, Lauren Bacall, herself a screen legend.

Drawn from original interviews with friends and foes who knew a lot about what lay beneath his trenchcoat, this exposé covers Bogart's remarkable life as it helped define movie-making, Hollywood's portrayal of macho, and America's evolving concept of Entertainment itself.

This revelatory book is based on dusty unpublished memoirs, letters, diaries, and often personal interviews from the women—and the men—who adored him.

There are also shocking allegations from colleagues, former friends, and jilted lovers who wanted the screen icon to burn in hell.

All this and more, much more, in Darwin Porter's *exposé* of Bogie's startling secret life.

WITH STARTLING NEW INFORMATION YOU'VE NEVER SEEN BEFORE
ABOUT BOGART, THE MOVIES, AND GOLDEN AGE HOLLYWOOD

542 PAGES, WITH HUNDREDS OF PHOTOS   **ISBN**   978-1-936003-14-3
ALSO AVAILABLE FOR E-READERS

Katharine the Great

HEPBURN, A LIFETIME OF SECRETS REVEALED

BY DARWIN PORTER

Katharine Hepburn was the world's greatest screen diva--the most famous actress in American history. But until the appearance of this biography, no one had ever published the intimate details of her complicated and ferociously secretive private life.

Thanks to the "deferential and obsequious whitewashes" which followed in the wake of her death, readers probably know WHAT KATE REMEMBERED. Here, however, is an unvarnished account of what Katharine Hepburn desperately wanted to forget.

"Darwin Porter's biography of Hepburn cannot be lightly dismissed or ignored. Connoisseurs of Hepburn's life would do well to seek it out as a forbidden supplement."
The Sunday Times (London)

"Behind the scenes of her movies, Katharine Hepburn played the temptress to as many women as she did men, ranted and raved with her co-stars and directors, and broke into her neighbors' homes for fun. And somehow, she managed to keep all of it out of the press. As they say, Katharine the Great is hard to put down."
The Dallas Voice

"The door to Hepburn's closet has finally been opened. This is the most honest and least apologetic biography of Hollywood's most ferociously private actress ever written."
Senior Life Magazine, Miami

The First Book of Its Kind, A Fiercely Unapologetic Exposé of the Most Obsessively Secretive Actress in Hollywood

Softcover, 569 pages, with photos

ISBN 978-0-9748118-0-2
Also Available for E-Readers

BANDO UNZIPPED

An Uncensored *Exposé* of America's Most Visible
Method Actor and Sexual Outlaw

by Darwin Porter

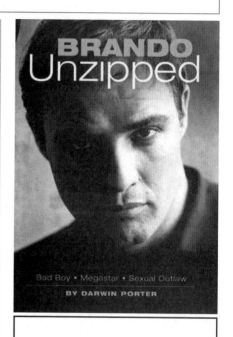

Jacko, His Rise and Fall

The Social and Sexual History of Michael Jackson

Darwin Porter

He rewrote the rules of America's entertainment industry, and he led a life of notoriety. Even his death was the occasion for scandals which continue to this day.

This is the world's most comprehensive historical overview of a pop star's rise, fall, and to some extent, rebirth as an American Icon. Read it for the real story of the circumstances and players who created the icon which the world will forever remember as "the gloved one," Michael Jackson.

"This is the story of Peter Pan gone rotten. Don't stop till you get enough. Darwin Porter's biography of Michael Jackson is dangerously addictive."
—*The Sunday Observer* (London)

"In this compelling glimpse of Jackson's life, Porter provides what many journalists have failed to produce in their writings about the pop star: A real person behind the headlines."
— *Foreword Magazine*

"I'd have thought that there wasn't one single gossippy rock yet to be overturned in the microscopically scrutinized life of Michael Jackson, but Darwin Porter has proven me wrong. Definitely a page-turner. But don't turn the pages too quickly. Almost every one holds a fascinating revelation."
—*Books to Watch Out For*

This book, a winner of literary awards from both *Foreword Magazine* and the Hollywood Book Festival, was originally published during the lifetime of Michael Jackson. This, the revised, post-mortem edition, with extra analysis and commentary, was released after his death.

Hardcover 600 indexed pages with about a hundred photos

ISBN 978-0-936003-10-5   Also available for E-readers

Out of the Celluloid Closet, a Half-Century Review of
HOMOSEXUALITY IN THE MOVIES
A Book of Record, Reference Source, and Gossip Guide to 50 Years of Queer Cinema

Out, outrageous, provocative, and proud, this comprehensive anthology and library resource reviews 500 of the best of Hollywood's output of gay, bisexual, lesbian, transgendered, and queer questioning films, with a special emphasis on how gays changed the movies we know and love.

Conceived as a working guide to what viewers should stock within their DVD queues, it reviews everything from blockbusters to indie sleepers, with about a dozen special features discussing the ironies, betrayals, subterfuge, and gossip of who, what, and how it happened when the film world's closet doors slowly creaked open beginning in 1960.

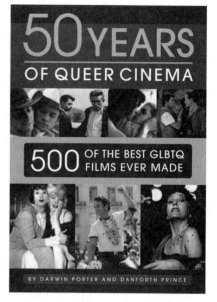

***

"In the Internet age, where every movie, queer or otherwise, is blogged about somewhere, a hefty print compendium of film facts and pointed opinion might seem anachronistic. But flipping through well-reasoned pages of commentary is so satisfying. Add to that physical thrill the charm of analysis that is sometimes sassy and always smart, and this filtered survey of short reviews is a must for queer-film fans.

"Essays on Derek Jarman, Tennessee Williams, Andy Warhol, Jack Wrangler, Joe Gage and others—and on how The Front Runner *never got made—round out this indispensable survey of gay-interest cinema."*

RICHARD LABONTÉ
BOOK MARKS/QSYNDICATE

Winner of the New England Book Festival's
Best GLBT Title of 2010

50 YEARS OF QUEER CINEMA
500 of the Best GLBT Films Ever Made

Softcover, 400 pages, with photos. ISBN 978-1-936003-09-9

HOLLYWOOD BABYLON
· STRIKES AGAIN!

THE PROFOUNDLY OUTRAGEOUS VOLUME TWO OF
BLOOD MOON'S BABYLON SERIES

Hot, Unauthorized, and Unapologetic!

HOLLYWOOD BABYLON
Strikes Again!

Volume #2
of the Babylon Series

All Those Celebrities!

All That Nudity!

All Those Scandals!

...and All That Sin!

BY DARWIN PORTER & DANFORTH PRINCE

Winner of the Los Angeles Book Festival's Best Non-fiction Title of 2010, and the New England Book Festival's Best Anthology for 2010.

"Monumentally exhaustive...The Ultimate Guilty Pleasure"
Shelf Awareness

Volume Two of Blood Moon's overview of exhibitionism, sexuality, and sin as filtered through 85 years of Hollywood indiscretion.

"If you love smutty celebrity dirt as much as I do, *then have I got a book for you!*"
The Hollywood Offender

"These books will set the graves of Hollywood's cemeteries spinning."   Daily Express

Hollywood Babylon Strikes Again!

Darwin Porter and Danforth Prince
Hardcover, 380 outrageous pages, with hundreds of photos

ISBN 978-1-936003-12-9

This is What Happens When A Demented Billionaire Hits Hollywood

HOWARD HUGHES
HELL'S ANGEL
BY DARWIN PORTER

From his reckless pursuit of love as a rich teenager to his final days as a demented fossil, Howard Hughes tasted the best and worst of the century he occupied. Along the way, he changed the worlds of aviation and entertainment forever.

This biography reveals inside details about his destructive and usually scandalous associations with other Hollywood players.

"The Aviator flew both ways. Porter's biography presents new allegations about Hughes' shady dealings with some of the biggest numes of the 20th century"
—**New York Daily News**

"Darwin Porter's access to film industry insiders and other Hughes confidants supplied him with the resources he needed to create a portrait of Hughes that both corroborates what other Hughes biographies have divulged, and go them one better."
—**Foreword Magazine**

"Thanks to this bio of Howard Hughes, we'll never be able to look at the old pinups in quite the same way again."
—**The Times (London)**

Winner of a respected literary award from the Los Angeles Book Festival, this book gives an insider's perspective about what money can buy —and what it can't.

814 pages, with photos. Also available for E-Readers

ISBN 978-1-936003-13-6